SOCIALISM IN AMERICA

From the Shakers to the Third International

SOCIALISM IN AMERICA

From the Shakers to the Third International

A DOCUMENTARY HISTORY BY

ALBERT FRIED

Columbia University Press
New York

Columbia University Press Morningside Edition
Columbia University Press
New York   Oxford
Morningside Edition with new preface
Copyright © 1992 Columbia University Press
Copyright © 1970 Albert Fried
All rights reserved

Library of Congress Cataloging-in-Publication Data

Socialism in America from the Shakers to the Third International :
a documentary history / [compiled] by Albert Fried.
p.   cm.
Originally published: New York : Doubleday, 1970.
Includes bibliographical references (p.   ) and index.
ISBN 0-231-08140-5 (cloth)
ISBN 0-231-08141-3 (paper)
1. Socialism—United States—History.
I. Fried, Albert.
HX86.S643   1992
335'.00973—dc20
92-32772
CIP

Casebound editions of Columbia University Press books are
Smyth-sewn and printed on permanent and durable acid-free paper.

Printed in the United States of America
c 10 9 8 7 6 5 4 3 2 1
p 10 9 8 7 6 5 4 3 2 1

To Bernard G. Richards

Who Remembers . . .

CONTENTS

PREFACE TO THE MORNINGSIDE EDITION

Twenty-three years have passed since this anthology was first published. During that time, the literature on American Socialism has burgeoned, but what I wrote in the original preface still holds true: this is still the only available anthology on the subject. And so, I am very pleased that it is being reprinted in such a handsome format by such a fine press to be read, I hope, by an audience wishing to be acquainted with America's rich Socialist literature.

The thesis of this book is that Socialism, contrary to popular opinion, was organic to American life. Not only did Socialism champion the egalitarian and cooperative principle of the social contract on which America was founded but the various Socialist sects, movements, and parties justified themselves as avatars of that principle and as the legitimate alternative to possessive individualism, a form of liberty based on cupidity and exploitation. The thesis implicitly assumes, furthermore, that these Socialisms emerged during times of reform when forces advocating radical change such as the redistribution of wealth were also flourishing, when groups which were once deemed extremist and confined to the margins were drawn closer to and even permeated the center of American politics because the majority, usually content with the status quo, had become disaffected by an unjust social order. Thus, reform meant that the majority came to accept obscure or unpopular minority positions and, in the process, moved to the outer limits of what was permissible by generating a new political dynamic—a new ideological equation. This was the liberal or progressive tradition in America which kept a valued place for the Socialist ideal. Today, I would modify this thesis by emphasizing its historical matrix, that is the conditions under which America's Socialisms took shape and had their effect on society.

The century and a half covered by this book can be defined by America's neutrality in world affairs, the absence of external danger, and an acute anxiety induced by fear. Physical security allowed America to march across the continent in seven league boots and by ruthlessly brushing aside every human and natural obstacle from its path become almost overnight both the colossus of the hemisphere and the premier industrial nation in the world. This astonishing feat was accomplished with a minuscule army and navy and no permanent officer corps to speak of. America fought its share of wars—six major ones between 1775 and 1918 and numerous minor ones against Native Americans—but after each one it returned to its familiar non-military or anti-military status. Although the correlation could not have been accidental, the extent to which this long reign of external well-being, which precluded the establishment of an internal national security system, contributed to the health of American democracy is impossible to measure. However, had such a system been developed from the time of Washington and Hamilton, both exponents of a standing army, it would have exerted a significant effect on the character of American democracy. America might have been a different country.

It is instructive to review the three occasions when, in the time of this book, national security concerns did exert an effect. Each instance provides us with some insight into what America's fate might have been:

1. In the 1790s, America struggled to stay out of the war with Britain and revolutionary France. Eventually, the Federalist administration of John Adams tilted toward Britain, and France retaliated. The result was the Alien and Sedition Acts which were directed against the pro-French Americans. Fearing greater French reprisals and also being pro-French, Vice-President Jefferson and his Republican followers supported the Kentucky and Virginia Resolutions which held that the federal government had no right to exercise powers not specifically delegated to it by the Constitution. When Jefferson became President, the Alien and Sedition Acts were allowed to lapse.

2. During the Civil War, Lincoln suspended habeas corpus, the bedrock guarantee of due process. Disregarding Supreme Court rulings to the contrary, the federal government jailed or exiled leading Copperheads. As soon as the crisis abated, the repression was ended.

3. The *sturm und drang* that began when the United States officially entered World War I in April 1917 lasted three years—a year and half longer than the war. Immediately after the war, the fierce hatred for Germany gave way to a fear that the Reds or Bolsheviks—by then, catchwords for radical dissenters in general—would seize power in America as they had in Russia. The repression started with the sweeping provisions of the Espionage Act and culminated in the post World War I Red Scare, a period when authorities picked up thousand of "radicals" in lightning raids and either imprisoned or deported them without the benefit of trial. Once again, the repression died when the fear subsided. However, this time a few repressive institutions managed to continue on:

the so-called "red squads" at the state and local level and the Federal Bureau of Investigation under the egregious J. Edgar Hoover endured.

Thus, as long as America remained strictly neutral, a national security system could never firmly take root. Even after Pearl Harbor, America persisted in believing that the status quo ante could be restored and that no large standing army and navy, no security system or the like would be necessary after the war. To be sure, the imperative of internationalism now replaced the historical faith in neutrality and isolationism. Only now, it would be an internationalism, so America believed, that would provide the same guarantee of physical security.

This time, however, there was no restoring the status quo ante. Hard upon the euphoric end of World War II came the deadly global conflict with the Soviet Union and Communism that dragged on decade after decade with one tense encounter after another and with each side brandishing more and more sophisticated weapons of mass annihilation. In fighting the interminable Cold War, Americans acceded to a tremendous growth of state power in the form of the national security system. Psychologically, morally, politically, as well as militarily, we armed ourselves against both internal and external enemies. The result was an environment virulently hostile to Socialism and every other radical ideology. McCarthyism is the word that has come to symbolize that environment. By McCarthyism, I am not referring to the antics, now reviled but at one time cheered, of the man—the Wisconsin Senator who in his short career as the paladin of anti-Communism (1950–1954) acted out the prevailing psychosis. I am referring to the repression in general and its extensive manifestations that began in the early days of the Truman administration and continued past McCarthy's scarcely noticed death in 1957 until practically the present. A vast armamentarium of intelligence organizations came into being. The CIA, NSA, and the DIA which were heavily funded and bursting with high-tech equipment joined the older ones—the FBI, Army, Navy, State Department, and local police, each of which had also been beefed up to serve the various legislative and executive bodies at both the state and federal level—in order to drive from political life Socialists and other assorted recreants, naysayers, and "untrustworthy" citizens of every stripe. At a minimum, these intelligence organizations compiled names and dossiers to be stored for the government's use should the need arise. If the repression abated, it was because it had achieved its purpose. Radical dissentient movements had ceased to be viable. In that sense, McCarthyism proved triumphant.

This is not to say that radical dissenters were no longer heard or that they disappeared from view. Even in the darkest days of the witch-hunts, blacklists, harassments, humiliations, defamations, and jail sentences, they could speak and write and associate freely. It was simply that they found themselves on the fringes of politics, suffered to live in peace and often enjoy the blessings of American affluence as long as they did not participate in, still less lead, any movement of political consequence.

The marginalization of the radical left during the Cold War period, not surprisingly, had its counter-effects on society as a whole, specifically on the reform impulse. Without radical "extremists" to goad and provoke it, reform is impoverished and society drifts toward the safe and conservative middle or is pushed further right by extremists on that side of the divide. The two great 20th century reform movements abundantly illustrate this point. Progressivism, which cut such a wide path across the American landscape before World War I, can not be separated from either the enormous Socialist upsurge of the times or the still more radical tendencies exemplified by the Industrial Workers of the World and their Anarcho-Syndicalist soulmates. And, inseparable from the New Deal was the hodgepodge of radical groups which ranged from undifferentiated populists to revolutionary Marxists. They appealed to America's insulted and injured organized workers, the unemployed, the ethnic underclass, sharecroppers, and poor farmers, and compelled timid governments to respond with programs of their own. Chief among these radical groups, it must be acknowledged, were the Communists— their allegiance to the Soviet Union notwithstanding. The point need not be labored. The impoverishment of reform since the 1940s can largely be attributed to the demise of the radical left. And, the demise of the radical left can largely be attributed to the reach and magnitude of the national security system that arose with the Cold War. So averse to reform had America become that in the 1988 presidential election the more conservative candidate accused his opponent of being a liberal. With excellent results, he invoked what was by then the dreaded "L-word."

The reader may ask how I can square this thesis with the extraordinary outburst of radicalism in the 1960s that energized so many racial, cultural, social, political, and judicial reforms. How could these reforms have occurred under the watchful eye of the national security system and especially its intelligence organizations? I would be the first to praise the accomplishments that came out of the tumultuous 60s—the mass protests that brought down Jim Crow and helped end the monstrous

Vietnam War, and the insistent demands for sexual rights, gender equality, environmental protection, privacy rights, consumer safeguards, protection for the physically challenged, and unrestricted freedom in the arts. Significant, however, is what these robust progeny of rebellion did not accomplish.

The national security system survived unscathed and went on to prosper for many a season. Indeed, during the Reagan era, it prospered as it had never done before in peacetime. The chasm between the rich and the rest of America widened in the 1970s and 80s to pre-New Deal proportions. Meanwhile, trade union membership as a percentage of the total work force fell to its lowest level since the 1930s. The ranks of the poor and those who had succumbed to utter destitution rose drastically. In truth, the changes wrought by the 1960s failed to address what has always been fundamental to Socialism, that is the question of how to best break up the concentrations of wealth and power and distribute them to the majority, including the poorest and most dispossessed, and the question of how to replace an ethic of predatory individualism with one that elevates cooperation and the collective good to the summit of its values and treats each person as an end, not a means. Because Socialism addressed itself to these questions, I would argue that it represents a species of radicalism which the propertied and national security elites anathematized as a mortal threat to their liberties and in that spirit fought against it.

Nothing in modern times is more amazing than the disintegration of the Soviet Union and its vast empire. Between 1989 and 1991, America won total victory in the Cold War. It follows, then, that if the thesis presented here is correct, the Socialist cause may eventually resume a place in America. This is possible for two reasons. First, the once dominant national security system and its repressive institutions can be expected to play a reduced role and have less and less influence. Second, Socialists will no longer need to distinguish themselves from or apologize for the satanic evil that went by their name. They can now take their case to a public as receptive and open-minded as it was before World War II. A recrudescence of American Socialism in the near or not too distant future would bring the country in line with the rest of the industrialized world. What is more, movements for economic and political reform which have been starved and defensive would enjoy a recrudescence of their own. America may even begin to resemble its sister democracy, Canada, where Socialism has come to be a mighty presence.

The years since *Socialism in America* was published have seen a proliferation of books on the subject. As radical movements declined during the Cold War period, many young radicals found sanctuary in academe just when it was undergoing an unprecedented expansion. There, as scholars, they were able to pursue subjects of particular interest to them and incidentally advance their professional careers. A highly productive industry specializing in labor and radical studies has developed over the past three decades. How productive is evident to anyone who examines university press catalogs and dissertation abstracts.

This phenomenon has brought forth a fury of criticisms of the academic left. The critics, chief among them Paul Hollander (*Anti-Americanism* [New York: Oxford University Press, 1992]), Roger Kimball (*Tenured Radicals* [New York: Harper & Row, 1990]), Dinish D'Souza (*Illiberal Education* [New York: Free Press, 1990]), and Martin Anderson (*Imposters in the Temple* [New York: Simon & Schuster, 1992]) argue that because professors are caught up in their scholarly game of attempting to impose their politically correct views on defiant colleagues and innocent students, they no longer teach enough nor teach adequately nor teach objectively. This is the burden of the right-wing assault on the last, beleaguered outpost of the American left. It is an effort to isolate and marginalize the offending professors. Worth mentioning too is Russell Jacoby's opposite critique of the same phenomenon, *The Last Intellectuals: American Culture in the Age of Academe* (New York: Basic Books, 1987). He maintains that intellectuals have, in opting for an academic refuge, lost some of their independence, their spirit of freewheeling dissent, and their creativity. They have ceased to be intellectuals in the true sense of the word—better Greenwich Village than the Ivies! Jacoby may be right as far as he goes but he has the sequence wrong. Is the intellectual environment dying because intellectuals are succumbing to the temptation of ease and security provided by academe? Or, is a dying intellectual environment driving them to academe?

Since the time the bibliography was compiled for the original edition, many important works have been published. Especially worthy of note are the reference works that have been published in the last several years, each with suggested readings. Indispensable are Mari Jo Buhle, Paul Buhle, and Dan Georgakas, editors, *Encyclopedia of the American Left* (New York: Garland Publishers, 1990), Gary M. Fink, editor, *Labor Unions* (Westport: Greenwood Press, 1984) and Ronald L. Filippelli and Carol Reilly, editors, *Labor Conflicts in the United States* (New York: Garland Press, 1990). Two interesting works on communitarianism are Gairdner B. Moment and Otto F. Kraushaar, editors, *Utopias: The*

American Experience (Metuchen: Scare Crow Press, 1980) and Robert S. Fogarty, *Dictionary of American Utopian and Communal History* (Westport: Greenwood Press, 1980).

If possible, I would make one major addition to this collection. I would include excerpts on and preferably by women Socialists from Margaret Fuller to Kate O'Hare and Margaret Sanger. Fortunately, several excellent studies on Socialism and women have been written: Mari Jo Buhle, *Women and the American Left: A Guide to the Sources* (Boston: G. K. Hall, 1983), Meredith Tax, *The Rise of the Women* (New York: Monthly Review Press, 1980), and Mari Jo Buhle, *Women and American Socialism, 1870–1920* (Urbana: University of Illinois Press, 1981). Important also is Philip S. Foner and Sally W. Miller, *Kate Richards O'Hare: Selected Writings and Speeches* (Baton Rouge: Louisiana State University Press, 1982). Biographies of Emma Goldman and Margaret Sanger are worthy of notice not only because of what they tell us about their personal lives but for what they reveal of their involvement in the radicalisms of their day: Candace Falk, *Love, Anarchy and Emma Goldman* (New York: Holt, Rinehart, and Winston, 1984), Alice Wexler, *Emma Goldman: An Intimate Life* (New York: Pantheon Books, 1984) and Ellen Chesler, *Woman of Valor* (New York: Simon & Schuster, 1992), the last word on Margaret Sanger.

The interested reader may want to consult Paul Avrich, *The Haymarket Tragedy* (Princeton: Princeton University Press, 1984) for the best account of this signal event in American radical history. A thorough but unflattering portrait of Bellamy and the Nationalist Movement can be found in Arthur Lipow, *Authoritarian Socialism in America* (Berkeley: University of California Press, 1982). In *Three American Radicals* (Boulder: Westview Press, 1991), Sender Garlin pays a warm tribute to three prominent Socialists of a bygone era: John Swainton, William Dean Howells, and Charles P. Steinmetz. Further insight into the life and times of Steinmetz can be gained from Ronald R. Kline, *Steinmetz: Engineer and Socialist* (Baltimore: Johns Hopkins University Press, 1992). Nick Salvatore, *Eugene V. Debs: Citizen and Socialist* (Urbana: University of Illinois Press, 1982) is the most scholarly biography of this icon of American Socialism. A superior study of another outstanding individual is Glen L. Sereton, *Daniel DeLeon: The Odyssey of an American Marxist* (Cambridge: Harvard University Press, 1979). In *Morris Hillquit: A Political History of an American Jewish Socialist* (Westport: Greenwood Press, 1979) and *Victor Berger and the Promise of Constructive Socialism* (Westport: Greenwood Press, 1978), Norma Fain Pratt and Sally W.

Miller, respectively, have given us serviceable biographies of these leading, but now little remembered, figures in the movement during its
heyday. And, for a trenchant and eloquent criticism of the movement
from a onetime devotee of the left, Aileen S. Kraditor, *Radical Persuasion, 1890–1917* (Baton Rouge: Louisiana State University Press, 1981)
should be carefully read.

Albert Fried

August 10, 1992

PREFACE

There is no anthology of this kind now available, and most of the documents appear here for the first time since their original publication. I should emphasize that the book contains only a sampling of a great body of material, most of it known to scholars in the field. The purpose of *Socialism in America* will have been achieved if it arouses the reader to pursue the subject further, make his own discoveries, and arrive at his own conclusions.

I wish, first of all, to thank Columbia University for allowing me to use its superb libraries and other facilities. My deepest gratitude goes to my friends for taking so much of their time to help me: to Irwin Shapiro for advising me a long time ago on how an anthology on American Socialism might be organized; to my editors at Anchor Books, Kay Scheuer and Anne Freedgood, for generously applying their talents beyond the call of professional duty; to Judith Bloch, for patiently listening to me read each of the drafts and then delivering trenchant comments on them; to B. J. Widick, for his valuable insights and numerous favors; to Ralph della Cava for questioning me on many points of interpretation and detail; and to Richard M. Elman, for carefully reading the manuscript and criticizing it in depth.

My wife, Edith Firoozi Fried, collaborated every step of the way, from the inception of the book to its completion. To her I owe more than I can express in words.

SOCIALISM IN AMERICA

From the Shakers to the Third International

CHAPTER I

THE COURSE OF AMERICAN SOCIALISM:

A SYNOPTIC VIEW

> In the suburb, in the town,
> On the railway, in the square,
> Came a beam of goodness down
> Doubling daylight everywhere:
> Peace now each for malice taken,
> Beauty for his sinful weeds,
> For the Angel hope aye makes
> Him an angel whom she leads.
>
> RALPH WALDO EMERSON,
> *"New England Reformers"*

Six years ago Ronald Sanders and I brought out an anthology of writings in the history of European Socialist thought.* The controlling assumption of our book was that modern Socialism, despite its failure everywhere to measure up to its orginal ideals, has been one of the most successful movements of all time. The story need not be re-told here. It is sufficient to note that only a hundred years ago Socialism was an abstract ideal held by a handful of revolutionaries and intellectuals and workers. Today Socialist parties hold power, alone or with other parties, or constitute the main body of opposition, in every country of Western Europe. And as for Eastern Europe, whatever one thinks of the Communist regimes there, however profound one's aversion to the brutalities and despotism and subservience to Moscow that have characterized the histories of most of them, they too descend from, or lay claim to, the Western Socialist tradition. Our aim was to trace the development of that tradition through documents.

In doing so we deliberately omitted American Socialism, which we regarded as a minor by-product of European Socialism, and, as such, not worth including in a work that attempted to cover so much

* *Socialist Thought* (Anchor Books, New York, 1964).

in so little space. We knew that a fairly significant Socialist movement had grown up in America before World War I, that it had
produced an outstanding public figure in Eugene V. Debs, and
that it had attracted the support of such world-famous writers as
Jack London, John Reed, and Upton Sinclair. But the movement
had suddenly collapsed, and by the time we published our book
practically nothing was left of it, only a congeries of sects, all quite
small and ineffectual. It was without apologies, therefore, that
Sanders and I restricted *Socialist Thought* to Europe.

Yet my ignorance of American Socialism whetted my curiosity
about it. I was already aware of the reasons for its "failure;" these
had been spelled out in every study of the subject. Socialism could
gain no foothold in a country where a feudal heritage, hence a
sense of class consciousness, was missing, where political freedom
and social mobility were taken for granted, where the two-party,
single-member district system placed insuperable handicaps on third
parties. But I was also aware that the Socialist tradition was deeply
embedded in American life and kept cropping up throughout its
history. In due course, I discovered a rich vein of native Socialist
literature (much of it disintegrating on library shelves), deposited
by men (Brisbane, Noyes, Channing, Herron, Spargo, Walling, and
others) whom I had heard of or briefly encountered but had never
read at length. It became obvious to me that an important part of
the American past was being neglected by everyone but the specialist,
and I decided to write an extended survey of American Socialism,
one that would include a representative sampling of its literature.

It became obvious to me, too, as I read more deeply that Socialism was not an alien but an integral part of the American past.
Here, in fact, lay the root of its "failure," of its inability to develop
into an independent and sturdy movement. In Europe, Socialism,
with its radically egalitarian ethic, stood in militant opposition to,
or at war with, established authority. Not until the early twentieth
century, when liberalism had at last triumphed in Western Europe,
did Socialism acquire legitimacy and take its place as simply another
ideology. But the ideals of American Socialism were embodied,
implicitly at least, in the creation of America itself. America's dominant conception of justice, its ethical norm, was forged in rebellion
and insurgency. The principle of the contract (or covenant) assumed
that all members of civil society (or the congregation) were
equal in rights and duties and were responsible for the authority

they would obey. But once agreed to, how was the contract to be applied? Who, in fact, did authority represent? How rigorously was the standard of equality to be observed? What were the permissible limits of inequality? And if impermissible, how was the change to be effected? These questions arose at every stage in the development of the country, before and after the Revolution. Socialism represented itself as the authentic expression of the American egalitarian norm, as the true legatee of the original contract.

It would be more accurate to say that America, in the course of its history, called forth a variety of Socialisms: communitarian, both religious and secular, Marxist, Anarcho-Communist, Christian, etc. What animated these Socialisms, what underlay their enormous differences—and why it is proper to bring them under the same rubric—was their conviction that each person's obligation to society as a whole was the absolute condition of his equality, that society was a brotherhood, not a collection of strangers drawn together by interest (the usual interpretation of the contract), that the individual derived his highest fulfillment from his solidarity with others, not from the pursuit of advantage and power. Whatever their persuasion, all Socialists regarded the opposition of self and society as a false one, reflecting the prevailing ethic of greed and domination. All envisioned an end, really a return to the beginning, in the form either of the perfect community, or the Kingdom of Heaven on earth, or the cooperative commonwealth, each the realization of the promise of America.

Each of the Socialisms had its counterpart in a more broadly based contemporary social movement. The religious communities that sprang up in the first half of the nineteenth century reflected, in their extreme way, the felt disquietude of the times. The periodic eruptions of revivalism and millenarianism—the fear that the world was about to terminate in a fiery holocaust—were typical responses to the changes that were rapidly breaking down accepted values in the customary church-centered community. As the great westward migration got under way in the 1780s and 90s and gained momentum in the decades that followed, the religious hegemony of the country burst asunder. New revivalist churches proliferated everywhere, especially in the outlying settlements. Their mission, simply stated, was to re-establish the congregation of saints that seemed to be disappearing in the hurly-burly of economic gain and expansion.

But however far ·they departed from orthodoxy, however antinomian their rituals and organizations, these churches were careful to stay within the Christian fold. They continued, that is, to acknowledge the separation between this world and the next, to profess the doctrine of original sin, and so to assert the mere possibility of election.

Inevitably, some religious zealots demanded the unqualified assurance of election. They insisted on going beyond a churchly compromise which *symbolically* united men to each other and to God. A church, after all, was an invisible congregation of saints. How was it to become a visible one? For those determined at any cost to live free of sin, the answer lay in turning the congregation into a community—in surrendering body and soul to a Kingdom of God on earth, perfect in itself, with its own laws, economy, dogma, and mode of worship, above all its own prophet of deliverance.

From the 1790s through the 1850s thousands of Americans made the leap to religious communitarianism, joining the Shaker or Perfectionist orders, the two main indigenous sects in the country. (There were a host of German colonies—themselves products of the revivalism in the Lutheran world—that were planted in the wilderness during the same period, but they shut themselves up completely and sought no American converts.) The Shakers were much the larger of the two native sects. By the 1850s there were 18 Shaker colonies, each containing a minimum of 150 members, and some as many as 600. The one sizable Perfectionist community, at Oneida, New York, never accommodated more than a few hundred votaries.

In theology and in social behavior the Shakers and Perfectionists could not have been more dissimilar. The Shakers, who followed the precepts of the prophetess Mother Ann, believed that celibacy restored to man the state of grace he had lost when Adam and Eve learned to lust for each other's bodies. A tightly drawn hierarchy and an elaborate set of rules sustained the Shaker system of celibate communism. The Perfectionists lived in strict conformity to the teachings of John Humphrey Noyes, who interpreted the Fall as the consequence of selfish and exclusive desire. To redeem sin, he invented the institution of "complex marriage," i.e., the sexual union (under group supervision) of all adult males and females. But whatever their dissimilarities, Shakers and Perfectionists (and the foreign sects, too, for that matter) were distinguished by what they held in common. Being millenarians they lived in a state of suspended time. They had appropriated the future, merging it with the present. In preparation for the day of reckoning they had united their separate selves into the communal family, led by the prophet-founder. They had discovered the only real security against the ravages of change and disorder that afflicted the world at large.

An ancient drama was thus re-enacted in America. Only it was a drama void of the violence and the tragic effects of the past. Millenarianism had been a cardinal heresy throughout the history of Western Christendom, and had been stamped out with fire and sword by the orthodox churches (Protestant as well as Catholic) whenever it appeared. America, however, left the communitarian sects alone.* In a society without established churches, divided into a multiplicity of denominations, they lived in tranquillity.

But the industrialization of the country and the creation of an all-enveloping market economy after the Civil War inevitably doomed the small-scale, communal-size unit of production. Moreover, as society grew more secular so fewer people took religion seriously enough to seek salvation through communitarianism. Slowly, peaceably, the sects died out one by one, some of them enduring well into the twentieth century. The tradition of Western millenarianism died with them.

Most Americans, even in an age of religious enthusiasm, were content to take salvation as it came, as a gratuitous gift of God. Their abiding concern was how to achieve happiness in this world. The pursuit of happiness, not salvation, was their birthright, ratified by war and revolution and inscribed in their charter of national independence. Yet as the nineteenth century wore on it became clear that the ideal of happiness contained serious ambiguities, even contradictions. The Declaration of Independence affirmed that the unalienable rights of men rested on their natural equality. Successive generations of Americans went on to define these rights in terms of property and self-interest, with the result that class divisions and injustices—in short the inequalities between men—grew increasingly pronounced. Liberty, it seemed, was being exercised at the expense of equality, to the advantage of the few and against the well-being of the majority. But the majority responded by demanding the

---

* The Shakers, it is true, were persecuted in the early 1780s (Mother Ann herself was beaten up), but not so much for religious reasons as political. Some of the communities in which they proselytized took them to be pro-British.

extension of liberty so that they might be enabled to participate, with a fair chance of succeeding, in the great quest for property. The pursuit of happiness meant equality of opportunity.

From the 1820s on, some Americans challenged this conventional view of happiness. By and large they were intellectuals and professionals living in the larger cities of the East who were offended, perhaps threatened, by the changes and the conflicts they witnessed first hand. At any rate, they pointed out the cruel paradox inherent in the ethic of individualism, according to which the maximum degree of individualism led to the maximum degree of social harmony and rationality, relations between men resembling a smoothly functioning machine. But the evidence already demonstrated that America was farther from harmony and rationality than ever. It was divided into sharply contending political factions, it sanctioned the suffering of the poor and the indulgences of the rich, and it accepted one economic crisis after another, the alternations of boom and bust, as acts of God. Opposition to the morality of the system prompted these critics to take the next step. They established their own secular communities of cooperation—communities where economic concerns would be relegated to their properly subordinate place; where life would no longer be left to the uncertainties of the open market but would be rationally planned; where the invidious distinctions of class and status would be effaced once and for all; where every activity and function, industrial, agricultural, artistic, intellectual, etc., would be organically united; and where individuals would cease to be predators and become members of the same family. The community, in a word, would be precisely what existing society was not, a center of education, virtue, and happiness.

Secular communitarianism embraced two movements. The first in point of time consisted of the followers of Robert Owen, the famous British philanthropist and manufacturer. Owen had come to espouse the cause of "villages of cooperation" on concluding, from his own experiences as a reformer, that mankind could not be educated in a capitalist, or selfishly individualist society. The seeds of the Owenite faith had been planted years before Owen himself, in 1825, set up the New Harmony, Indiana, community. Within months after it had been opened, New Harmony was filled beyond its capacity, and numerous other communities, from Ohio to New York, suddenly sprouted at the same time. These secular communitarians believed that the rest of America would soon be converted by the self-evident truths they were promulgating in word and deed; that their moral idealism would lay the groundwork on which to build the society of the future. But the habits of the past, the habits of individualism, were not to be shaken off so easily. And none of the Owenite communities were as fortunate as New Harmony, which at least had abundant reserves of capital. Yet all of them, New Harmony included, were short-lived. By 1830 none of them survived.

When the secular communitarian movement re-emerged in the 1840s it was only one of a great number of reform movements that swept the North. The cultured middle class of the cities and towns, threatened more than ever by the accelerated pace of economic change, took up such causes as anti-slavery, the rights of women, public schools, temperance, world peace, etc. One of its causes was Associationism, a term adopted by the disciples of the late Charles Fourier. Fourier claimed to have discovered the principle uniting all things in the universe, from inanimate matter to complex relations between men. This was the principle of "attraction," an elaborated, extended, and refined version of Newton's law of gravitation. Civilization, Fourier maintained, had failed because it had supressed the passions, the force of attraction native to man. To liberate the passions he invented the Phalanx, or Association, a community roughly the same size as Owen's ideal village of cooperation, where perfect harmony would prevail within each man (thus reconciling mind and body, thought and action), between man and man, and between man and nature. Associationism caught on quickly, especially among old line Unitarians and Transcendentalists for whom the principle of attraction, culminating in the organization of the Phalanx, furnished the hope of a new epiphany.

But the Associationists, even more than the Owenites, were unfitted for the harsh labors and dull routine of communal life. Also, the price of land, labor, and capital was much more expensive than it had been twenty years before. And so Fourierists suffered the same fate as their Owenite predecessors. Scores of Phalanxes arose in the 1840s; all but one had disappeared within a decade. The demise of Associationism marked the end of secular communitarianism in America.

Marx was justified, then, in applying the epithet "utopian" to the various communitarianisms of the early nineteenth century. It was true that they sought to resist the advance of industrialism, that the doctrines put forward by their founders were arbitrary and ahistorical, that their abstract moral injunctions seemed to bear no relation to the reality they proposed to change. Yet the fact remained that the communitarians upheld the ideals of social solidarity and individual good to which Americans in general paid homage. It was in the country at large, after all, that the gap between ethical norms and the imperatives of practical life had been widening; the gap, that is, between the old-fashioned ideal of the integrated community and the increasingly atomized, fragmented, and mobile nature of American society.

In the thirty years or so following the Civil War the United States was suddenly transformed from an agricultural country to the mightiest industrial nation on earth. Yet these were years of political stability if not quietude. By way of contrast, the same process of change in Europe called forth a vigorous Socialist movement, one that rested on the support of the working class and looked forward to the acquisition of state power, peacefully, if possible, violently if necessary. Why did a comparable movement fail to take root in America? For one thing America was open and free and profoundly averse to class consciousness and class politics. For another, its labor force, being largely foreign born, lacked a sense of social and cultural solidarity. Perhaps most important, America was still traumatized by the Civil War. It had had enough of conflicts and crusades. It wanted nothing more than to lose itself in work and in the relentless accumulation of wealth. Americans welcomed industrialism as a sort of therapy, and the sudden appearance of an enormous capitalist oligarchy disturbed them less than the prospect of disorder.

Such Socialism as did exist was confined to a tiny group of German immigrants, most of them professionals and intellectuals. They brought their radical critique of modern society with them to the New World, where they settled in the larger cities of the Northeast and Midwest. One can easily dismiss them (as writers on American Socialism usually do) as incorrigible doctrinaires who were bound to fail, since America was hardly in the mood for a heavy dose of reform, much less Socialism, least of all one administered by foreigners. But it should be pointed out that these German

Socialists were under no illusion about the difficulty of their task. They expected no imminent mass conversions. What they did expect was that sooner or later the structure of industrial capitalism would crash down of its own weight, and that the working class, by then the majority of the people, would pick up the pieces and build a wholly new society: the cooperative commonwealth (a phrase that came into vogue in the 1870s). Let it be said further in their defense that the Germans tried to make their ideas palatable to the public, especially after they formed the Socialist Labor Party in 1877. They campaigned in elections, offered their own candidates for office, and whenever feasible joined labor and reformist groups. America, however, offered them no chance of discovering a middle ground between political assimilation and sectarianism.

One reason Americans turned a deaf ear to German Socialism was that it seemed to lack a moral dimension. Americans had once been attracted to communitarianism because it had presented a vision of equality, harmony, and virtue that was pure and trans-cendent; it had withdrawn from the world in order to save it. The German Socialists, too, postulated an ideal of equality, harmony, and virtue; only they proposed to reach it by apparently paradoxical means. To end class warfare, they argued, one must intensify it (by siding with the oppressed workers). To end the monopoliza-tion of industry one must favor the monopolists (who were inad-vertently preparing the way for the nationalization of the means of production and distribution). To end political domination one must advocate the extension of government authority (which, on falling to the proletariat, would be used to usher in the cooperative commonwealth). Americans did not grasp this kind of dialectical reasoning according to which conditions must worsen before they can be improved. And certainly reform-minded Americans rejected the Socialist argument out of hand. They were reformers precisely because they believed in individualism and laissez-faire and property rights. Their complaint was that such rights were inequitably dis-tributed, and they regarded Socialism as the substitution of one kind of monopoly for another.

Nonetheless, some Americans came to see the world as the Ger-man Socialists did. The country was in fact being split into classes. The conflicts between workers and capitalists were growing in-creasingly acute. The trustification of society was continuing uninterruptedly. It was harder and harder to sustain the pretense that the government was impartial in administering the laws and responsive to the popular will in passing them. Under the circumstances, a new Socialist literature appeared in America in the late 1880s and early 1890s, best exemplified by the popular writings of Laurence Gronlund, Edward Bellamy, and William Dean Howells. Their detailed descriptions of the cooperative commonwealth to come bore witness to the influence that German Socialism, seeping up through subterranean channels, was beginning to exert on the American mind. (Gronlund, whose *Cooperative Commonwealth* laid the intellectual foundations for Bellamy's *Looking Backward* and Howells' *A Traveler from Altruria*, was a long-time member of the Marxist Socialist Labor Party.) They adopted the German Socialist view that capitalism must be understood objectively, dispassionately, scientifically; that it was expanding and evolving in obedience to the laws of historical inevitability; and that it must, accordingly, metamorphose into the cooperative commonwealth, the highest stage of civilization.

But Gronlund, Bellamy, and Howells diverged sharply from German Socialism in their motives for wanting the cooperative commonwealth established and therefore in the means they advocated for its realization. The prospect of class conflict appalled them. If the proletariat won their sympathy it was not as heroes but as victims. On principle they abhorred an ethic that exalted class interest as much as one that exalted individual interest. They looked to the disinterested idealists of America—the educated, the professionals, the men of conscience and hope, in short, the enlightened middle class—to be the agents of transition and the leaders of the new order. The America they envisioned was to embody a fundamental shift in values, away from property, conflict, selfishness, and domination, and toward the organic solidarity of man and man, man and society, man and work, toward the unchallenged supremacy of art and science and leisure over economics. It is clear what these apostles of the cooperative commonwealth had accomplished. They had fused German (or scientific) Socialism and native communitarianism. They had given Socialism a distinctively American cast.

Their ideas were caught up in the great turbulence of the 1890s. The decade opened with the spectacular rise of the Bellamyite, or Nationalist, movement. Thousands of morally troubled middle class Americans joined Nationalist clubs and discussion groups in hopes of bringing the new society into existence well before the year 2000. Closely akin to the Bellamyites were the Christian Socialists, who had officially begun their career in 1889, after breaking away from one of the Nationalist clubs. Apart from resting their arguments on the authority of Christ, the Christian Socialists differed not at all from the apostles of the cooperative commonwealth. They prophesied that the Kingdom of Heaven was about to descend, that Christ would re-appear with the dissolution of capitalism. The Christian Socialists were important far beyond their numbers, for they represented the logical culmination of the whole Social Gospel movement that was attempting to liberalize the Protestant churches. For a while it seemed that a significant Socialist clergy would emerge in America.

These essentially urban, middle class, and rather genteel desires for reform accompanied more active expressions of discontent. The number of working men enrolled in trade unions rose perceptibly, and the threat of labor insurgency grew more ominous than ever. Meanwhile the farmers of the South and West rebelled against the plutocrats and the politicians who served them. In the early 1890s a series of rather fruitful ad hoc alliances sprang up between the Nationalists, the Christian Socialists, the Populists, and the trade unions. These proved ephemeral. The Nationalist clubs suddenly melted away and the Populist and Christian Socialist crusades lost their momentum. The Depression of 1893, which provoked random acts of protests and several important strikes—all of them put down without difficulty—destroyed whatever possibility there once might have been for an enduring radical coalition. The conservative mood of the country was reflected in the overwhelming victory of William McKinley and the Republican Party.

The left by 1897 was reduced to two main components. One consisted of the liberal and moderate reformers who had sided with William Jennings Bryan in the recent election. The other consisted of the Socialist Labor Party, headed by Daniel DeLeon, an orthodox Marxist who symbolized the changes that had lately come over the Socialist movement. It was no longer a predominantly German movement. It now contained a large number of native Americans (again, mostly urban and middle class) along with Russian Jews and other newly arrived immigrant groups. As further evidence of its Americanization, the SLP was regularly offering candidates in elections and was receiving more and more votes. At the same time, however, the Party was disintegrating, thanks to DeLeon's purist ideology and personal authoritarianism. Most galling to the SLP's rank and file was his policy of establishing unions to compete with the non-Socialist ones, in particular the American Federation of Labor. As a result, one faction of the Party after another broke away from DeLeon and gravitated toward a reformist brand of Socialism.

Those segments of the American left dissatisfied with liberalism and DeLeonism eventually came together and formed the Socialist Party of America. Specifically, it was the product of a merger in 1901 between Eugene V. Debs (the immensely popular labor leader) and his followers and a sizable contingent of SLP dissidents. The character of the Socialist Party was defined at the start of its career. It was an amalgam of workers, intellectuals, farmers, professionals, ethnic minorities, and radicals of every stripe. And though it spoke the language of Marx and class struggle and revolutionary change, it was essentially moderate and constructive. It represented itself as merely another political party seeking to democratize American life. It tended to be idealistic in the manner of the Christian Socialists and the Nationalist clubs; it was a party consecrated to the materialization of the cooperative commonwealth. It was an American party in style and in substance, espousing a cause rooted in the American tradition and made up mostly of American-born members and leaders.

Just as the communitarian movement was a part of the liberalism characteristic of the pre-Civil War era, so the Socialist movement was inseparable from the progressivism characteristic of the first decade and a half of the twentieth century. The popular impulse for reform provided the nutriment for the spectacular growth of the Socialist Party. The extraordinary rise in the number of votes cast for Debs, its regular Presidential candidate, the rise in the number of offices it won in local and state elections, of newspapers and magazines it published, of people who signed up as members—these indexes of success gave the Socialists reason to believe that the Party would take power in the near future. This being so, prudence dictated that it play down the theme of class struggle. Why should the Party run the risk of antagonizing its primary sources of support, the middle class, unionized labor, and small farmers, when it stood so close to achieving a breakthrough? At every turn, it rejected, or cast out from its midst, those who veered too far to the left. That was why it resolutely refused to support the militant Industrial Workers of the World, and why it purged itself of Syndicalists. The Socialist Party, in sum, was at once pragmatic in its quest for power in an imperfect world and intensely idealistic in its hope for a thoroughgoing transformation of American values. But that transformation lay in the future and waited upon circumstances—the collapse of the system, the discontent of the masses—beyond its control.

But the future did not come. The circumstances that confronted the Socialist Party of America were not those it anticipated or was prepared to deal with. The system endured. It was the Party and the movement that collapsed.

America's entry into World War I confronted the Socialist Party with a dangerous choice; whether to follow the example of the other Socialist parties in the belligerent countries (Italy's Socialist Party was the lone exception) and support the war; or, by opposing it, court the displeasure of the masses whom it was trying to win over. It chose, by an overwhelming vote of its membership, to oppose the war. It immediately lost a high proportion of its intellectuals, its native American members, and its trade union backing. Many of these former Socialists went on to accuse the Party publicly of treason and to call for its punishment. This was precisely the opinion of the Wilson administration, which, armed with plenary authority, imprisoned Party leaders, terrorized its members, and shut down its publications. In effect, the Party went underground for the duration. Yet it might have recovered even after the war. Conditions were ripe for a large-scale insurgent movement. The country was disillusioned; many liberals who felt betrayed by Wilson had nowhere to go; and workers and farmers were more discontented than at any time since the 1890s.

It turned out, however, that the Socialist Party was incapable of taking advantage of the mass unrest. It suffered from a deep-seated, ultimately fatal, malaise, the cause of which could be traced to the Russian Revolution of November 1917. The Party had no quarrel with the aims of the Bolsheviks; after all, it too favored ending the war, and it was not averse to a general rising of the European (or American) proletariat. But hardly had the Soviet regime attained a modicum of stability than it pursued a two-front war of its own: against the capitalists and against the "renegade" Socialists of the

Second International, including, of course, the Socialist Party of America. The Soviets encouraged the Party's "Left Wing," hitherto a small minority, but now bolstered by a great influx of Eastern European foreign-language groups, to overthrow its long-established leadership and policies. Following the Bolshevik example, the Left Wing proclaimed revolution and the dictatorship of the proletariat as its immediate goals. It also followed the Bolshevik example in forming an elite, vanguard party of activists—the spiritual embodiment of all history, as it were—to lead the masses in revolt. The differences between the two factions in the Party were insuperable, and in the summer of 1919 the American Socialist movement broke into pieces.

It was all downhill after that. The Socialist Party became an exceedingly minor political entity, a bare simulacrum of its former self. The Communists (who for a time were themselves divided into rival parties), though they claimed a larger membership—one, moreover, that was young, idealistic, and talented—were even less relevant than the Socialists. The Communists identified themselves not only with the cause of Marxism-Leninism, but with its homeland, the Soviet Union. Increasingly, they took their orders from the Soviet Union, or, what was the same thing, the Third International. The decline of American Socialism, arrested briefly in the 1930s—when the Depression struck and Fascism appeared on the horizon—was inexorable. Hardly anything was left of it after World War II, the period of the Cold War and the McCarthy persecutions. Today (circa 1970) there is a melange of very tiny Socialist sects—Communist, Trotskyite, Socialist Labor, and others—that endure on the outermost margins of American life.

The "New Left," which emerged in the 1960s on the strength of the civil rights movement, the protests against the Vietnam war, and the increasingly experimental character in personal styles and habits, is too amorphous and syncretistic to define with any assurance. Its hallmark, in fact, lies in its indefinability, its looseness and deliquescence. It appeals mainly to disaffected youth, most of them from middle class homes, who find little in America worth redeeming. It is indifferent to the issues (reform vs. revolution, the nature of the Soviet Union, the viability of capitalism, the organization of the working class, etc.) that meant so much to previous generations of radicals. These issues it regards as so many "hang-ups" calculated to destroy spontaneity and authenticity. The New Left seems to favor forms of Socialism that are at once extremely libertarian and extremely authoritarian. Its heroes are a mixed bag of native black militants—e.g., Malcolm X and Eldridge Cleaver—and exotic Latin American and Far Eastern revolutionaries, such as Fidel Castro, Che Guevara, Mao Tse-tung, and Ho Chi Minh. Despite the interest it has called forth, the New Left is still only a mood, and moods are notoriously fugacious.

It will be understood, then, why I have ended the book with the collapse of the Socialist Party and the creation of the Third International in 1919. These events sounded the knell of defeat for Socialism in America, at least down to the present. That there have been interesting struggles between Socialist and Communist groups over the years, that both have on occasion played an important part in American life—for example, the formation of the largest industrial unions (steel, autos, electrical, etc.) in the 1930s—goes without saying. But a pall has settled over the American Socialist movement for the last half century, a pall that has grown heavier with time and now appears to be a permanent feature of the landscape.

CHAPTER II

RELIGIOUS COMMUNITARIANS

Be faithful to keep the Gospel; be neat and industrious.
Put your hands to work and your hearts to God.

ANN LEE

The marriage of the flesh is a covenant with death and
an agreement with hell.

ANN LEE

> We love to dance, we love to sing,
> We love to taste the living spring,
> We love to feel our union flow,
> Which round, and round, and round we go.
>
> (Shaker) *Millenial Praises*

We are not "Free Lovers" in any sense that makes love
less binding or responsible than it is in marriage.

Oneida Handbook

We can now see our way to victory over death. Reconciliation with God opens the way for the reconciliation with the sexes. Reconciliation of the sexes emancipates women, and opens the way for vital society. Vital society increases strength, diminishes work and
makes labor attractive, thus removing the antecedents
of death. First we abolish sin; then shame; then the
curse on women of exhausting child bearing; then the
curse on man of exhausting labor; and so we arrive
regularly at the tree of life.

JOHN HUMPHREY NOYES,
Bible Communism

One day in June 1779, a group of men and women in the village of New Lebanon (situated in the New York Berkshires, just over the Massachusetts boundary) set up a provisional church in a local barn. Their regular Congregational and Presbyterian churches had left them dissatisfied; the possibility of salvation had grown too remote and too dependent on reasoning and learning. Now, in the sanctuary of a barn, they could bear witness to Christ's presence without the impediments of tradition and ceremony, symbol and rite. Possessed by the Holy Ghost, transported by the ecstasy of redemption, they moaned and shrieked and trembled before collapsing to the ground as though they were "wounded in battle." The revival of Christ went on this way night after night throughout the summer and fall of 1779.

Meetings like the one at New Lebanon were not unusual. They had been taking place in the interior of the country since the 1730s and '40s, the time of "Great Awakening." It was common for poorer frontier communities to break away from their increasingly formal and hieratic parent churches and to establish new denominations based on the Baptist, or Anabaptist, principle of direct communion with God—a communion requiring no intermediaries, no external authorities, no theology. But the Great Awakening, for all the passion it generated, was itself no revolutionary departure; it continued a tradition that had begun with the Puritan fathers. Schism, after all, was built into the Calvinist doctrine, which in its most radical form asserted that nothing may stand between the individual congregation and God. Successful heresy, however, had a way of hardening into orthodoxy. After the dionysian phase of revivalism passed, the ad hoc churches tended to become permanent ones in their turn. At New Lebanon, too, the revival quickly exhausted itself, and the people who had met each night in the barn soon met only on the Sabbath, in their newly formed Baptist church.

But some of these radical or "New Light" Baptists were as profoundly convinced as ever that the Second Coming was at hand. They had had a vision of the Kingdom of Heaven; nothing could now stop them from entering it. They had heard that a tiny English group, "The United Society of Believers," who lived near Albany in a place called Niskeyuna (now Watervliet), claimed to be the true millennial church. They decided to investigate the matter further. On May 10, 1780, three of the New Lebanon Baptists, led by one Joseph Meacham, were welcomed at Niskeyuna by the whole body of Believers, thirteen members in all, including their prophetess, "Mother" Ann Lee. The visitors were impressed by the appearance, the manners, and the comportment of the Believers, by the comfortable, well-wrought cabins, by the large tracts of cleared land and the stores of food and fuel. The visitors were impressed still more by the responses to their questions. At one point Meacham asked the Believers, "Are you perfect? Do *you* live without sin?" The answer was yes. "The Power of God, revealed in this day, does enable souls to cease from sin; and we have received that power; we have actually left off committing sin, and we live in daily obedience to the will of God."

The high-point of the day was the worship period. Meacham and his companions had looked forward to this moment. How their hosts prayed would tell them, as no words or conscious acts could, what they wanted to know. They observed a scene very much like the following one, which was reported by another visitor a few weeks later. The Believers, he wrote,

begin [their worship] by sitting down, and shaking their heads, in a violent manner, turning their heads half round, so that their face looks over each shoulder, their eyes being shut; while they are thus shaking, one will begin to sing some odd tune, without words or rule; after a while another will strike in; and then another; and after a while they all fall in, and make a strange charm. . . . The Mother, so called, minds to strike such notes as make a concord, and so form the charm. When they leave off singing, they drop off, one by one, as oddly as they come on. . . .

In the best part of their worship everyone acts for himself, and almost everyone different from the other: one will stand with his arms extended, acting over odd postures, which they call signs; another will be dancing, and some times hopping on one leg about the floor; another will fall to turning round, so swift, that if it be a woman, her clothes will be so filled with the wind, as though they were kept out by a hoop; another will be prostrate on the floor; another will be talking with somebody; and some sitting by, smoking their pipes; some groaning most dismally; some trembling extremely; others acting as though all their nerves were convulsed; others swinging their arms, with all vigor, as though they were turning a wheel, etc. Then all break off, and have a spell of smoking, and some times great fits of laughter. . . .

The reason the Believers came to be called Shakers (a name to which they had no objection) is obvious from this description. To outsiders they often seemed quite mad or, like Don Quixote, an incomprehensible mixture of madness and sobriety. To anyone familiar with the revivalist tradition, however, the Shakers' way of worship was distinguished only by the intensity and frequency of their raptures.

But as Meacham was quick to recognize, the Shakers were different from run-of-the-mill revivalists. Their religious experience was more than an occasional upsurge of feeling, more than a spontaneous ebullition; it was integral to their whole way of life. It was inseparable from their daily habits, from everything they thought and did. In a conventional revival, one might in a privileged moment gain a glimpse of salvation. The Shakers lived in the conviction that every moment was privileged. So it appeared to Meacham and his companions, who joined the United Society of Believers on the spot. They returned to New Lebanon to spread the good news that the messiah had come.

By messiah they meant Ann Lee. They had become Shakers because they believed in her divinity. To them she was "Ann the Word," the chosen instrument of God. She had been born in 1736, the second of eight children of a Manchester blacksmith. Unremitting poverty, toil, and misfortune was her lot in early life and in marriage. All of her four children died at birth or in infancy. She belonged to a group of religious dissidents, simple working-class people like herself, who bore witness to Christ by shaking, groaning, writhing, collapsing, and the like. They were caught up in the English version of the Great Awakening—the Wesleyan, or Methodist, movement that stirred the passions of the country's poor in the mid-eighteenth century. Shortly after the death of her last child Ann Lee gave evidence of possessing special thaumaturgic powers. Her prophetic illuminations convinced the members of her sect that Christ had chosen her to complete His mission. "It is not I who speak," she declared, "it is Christ who dwells in me." Christ was her "lover," her "husband," her "lord." He "embraced" her and took her as his. "I feel the blood of Christ running through my soul and body, washing me."

These sexual images were not fortuitous. The message that Ann Lee brought from God was that sex must be banished totally and irrevocably from the lives of the elect; she had already banished it from hers. She identified "concupiscence" as the source of the evil and suffering and folly that have afflicted man since the Fall. Renunciation of lust would, she said, lead to the renunciation of desire as such, and therefore to the triumph of the spiritual over the material self. And so Ann Lee—now Mother Ann—revived the venerable Christian heresy of millenarianism: the belief that the millennium had arrived and that men must prepare themselves, by faith and works, for the day of judgment. In her quiet unobtrusive way she was following in the footsteps of such notorious medieval movements as the Cathari, the Albigensians, and the Waldensians, as well as the various Anabaptist sects of the Reformation and the English Civil War. She too bore the consequences of her extreme dissidence. She was subjected to continuous persecution by her neighbors and by civil and religious authorities. Conditions in England having grown intolerable, Mother Ann and her little flock decided to go to America, where they could live openly and freely as a family. They sailed in 1774. Two years later they were securely settled at Niskeyuna.

Ann Lee died in 1784. Leadership of the Shakers shortly after fell to Joseph Meacham, their first American convert, whom she had once described as her "first Bishop," the keeper of "the keys of the kingdom." With his accession, New Lebanon became the center of the Millenial Church. The Shakers ceased to be an English sect and emerged as an American one. Since Meacham's first visit to Niskeyuna the sect had grown rapidly, nearly all of its recruits being native born. The critical problem that faced him was how the Church could continue to expand yet avoid succumbing to the temptations of the world. Under Mother Ann this problem had been less compelling, first because of her holy presence, and second, because the nucleus of the sect had consisted of the original band of apostles. It had not been necessary, therefore, to ban every form of "selfishness" at Niskeyuna, such as the ownership of private property and the maintenance of separate families.

Meacham's solution was to convert the Shaker religion into a communitarian theocracy. He ordered the Believers to yield up their possessions to the Church and to move inside the New Lebanon compound. There they were to live and work as members of a single collective family. They pledged to give "themselves and their services with all their temporal interest, for the mutual support and benefit of each other, and for the charitable uses, according to the light and revelation of God which they have received." And so the last remnant of concupiscence was removed. The Shakers now belonged to an autonomous, tightly knit communist society; the purity of their faith was assured. But the price of this assurance was withdrawal from the world, from Christendom at large. Even the most extreme of the New Light Baptists subscribed to Augustinian-Calvinist tenets and continued to believe in original sin, the Trinity, the "gift" of salvation—a gift to which men could lay no claim whatever. The Shakers announced that they had received the gift; they had overcome sin, and they had achieved unity with God.

The economic system that arose at New Lebanon—and at every other Shaker settlement—flowed directly from their ethical and religious absolutes. The desires of each member were ruthlessly simple. Superfluities were forbidden, and the merest display of extravagance, in taste as in behavior, was an abomination. The Shakers labored neither to accumulate nor to consume, but to live perfect lives in the sight of God. Everything about them reflected the sacramental nature of their calling. Their dress, furniture, and buildings were austere and durable, models of elegant utility. And the goods they produced—e.g., baskets, cloth, chairs, blankets, bonnets, brooms—were so well made they instantly found a market in the outside world. Before long they attained complete self-sufficiency.

But the Shakers could not afford to take their spiritual fellowship for granted. They constituted a minuscule island in an ocean of sin and depravity. To maintain the community's distance from the world, to foreclose the possibility of personal backsliding, Meacham laid down a vast and complicated set of rules. Celibacy, the foundation of the commonwealth, was scrupulously observed. The brethren and sisters were kept as far apart from each other as the business of community life permitted. They could not pass each other on the stairs, visit or write or in any way communicate with each other except under supervision. When the brethren and sisters met the sexual taboos were extreme. The men had to stay at least five feet from the women, who were not allowed to whisper, wink, or cross their legs. Shakers hardly ever broke these rules, but they often confessed to evil intentions or to weaknesses of the flesh. They were afflicted by more, not less, guilt than the fallen and unredeemed. They had discovered the way to perfection; their problem was to avoid straying from it.

Equality of the sexes was a fundamental article of the Shaker creed, and the brethren and sisters jointly presided over the government—an uncompromising, rigidly hierarchical theocracy. At the summit of the hierarchy stood "the Holy Anointed" (Father Meacham and his help mate, Mother Lucy Wright), who, as "the leading Ministry" of New Lebanon, could pass, alter, or repeal any regulation at any of the Shaker vineyards. Immediately below the leading Ministry were the Elders and Eldresses, who ruled over "families" of from thirty to one hundred members each, two or more families comprising a "bishopric," or colony. The Elders and Eldresses were required to hear confessions and to know "everything owned and possessed by everyone under their charge." Acting as intermediaries between the members and the hierarchs were the Deacons and Deaconesses and the Trustees. They took care of the family's business transactions, its relations with other families, and its trade with "the great and wicked cities" of the world. It might appear, then, that the Shakers led insufferably circumscribed lives, the more so since they had nothing to say in choosing their superiors or their laws. But if their society was a despotism, it was one to which they submitted voluntarily and only for so long as they liked. They regarded the freedom of the world as frivolous, illusory, ephemeral at most. True freedom for them lay exclusively in the Holy Kingdom.

Meacham also worked out a Shaker theodicy, culminating, of course, in the person of Mother Ann. Adam and Eve sinned when they yielded to sexual desire. This was the knowledge of good and evil that God wished to conceal from them. Four illuminating moments in history, or dispensations of grace, followed the Fall: the patriarchate of Abraham, Isaac, and Jacob; the covenant between God and Moses; the advent of Christ, who was the promise of redemption; and the appearance of Mother Ann, who fulfilled the promise by restoring the pre-lapsarian virginity of soul and body. The conversion of mankind to the Millenial Church was prophesied by Ezekiel and Daniel. The Shakers acknowledged that it might take a long time for the glorious day to come. They were patient; they had transcended the limits of mortality.

By the time Joseph Meacham died in 1797 the Shakers had demonstrated that they could not only survive, they could prosper and increase. No fewer then nine Shaker Bishoprics had sprung up on the New England frontier (four in western Massachusetts, two each in New Hampshire and Maine, and one in Connecticut), each of them containing two or more families and housing from 200 to 800 members. Never had the country witnessed anything like this successful experiment in native religious communitarianism. There had been religious communitarian sects before the Shakers, but all save one had either disappeared after a few years in the wilderness, or, like the Moravian Brethren and the Hutterites, had jettisoned their experiment in communism. The lone exception was the Ephrata Cloister of Lancaster, Pennsylvania, which had been founded in 1732. By the end of the century it had lost much of its vitality.

After 1805 the Shakers entered another period of expansion, this time mainly into Kentucky, Indiana, and Ohio. And once again they drew their adherents—thousands of them—from the extreme left-wing of a new revivalist movement, the so-called Second Awakening, that swept the frontier with powerful animus in the first two decades of the nineteenth century. As the Shaker kingdom grew, so its character imperceptibly changed. Its rituals became more formalized and decorous. The individual paroxysms of Mother Ann's day were replaced by collective dancing and singing. The hermeneutics laid down by Meacham were enlarged and embellished by succeeding generations of Believers. Meanwhile, a Shaker publication industry had emerged. Partly to satisfy an increasingly interested public, and partly to answer their "apostates," some of whom wrote sensational accounts of their sexual behavior, the Shakers brought out an immense number of tracts explaining their history, theology, and way of life in general. Their decline could be measured by the intensity of their preoccupation with the past and by the number of apologies they were constrained to write.

In addition, there were the reports by visitors to Shaker communities. One could compile a volume of articles or brief descriptions on the Shakers by such men as Emerson, Cooper, Greeley, Hawthorne, and Whitman. It was *de rigeur* for foreign authors, to drop in on the Shakers, who were unfailingly cordial to their guests. Nearly every one of these visitors, American and foreign both, admired the well-ordered little communities they saw, where crime and poverty and the distempers of every day life were absent, and where the fundamental Christian vitues were honored more in the observance than in the breach. Dickens, however, found all the virtue tiresome and dull. "We walked into a grim room," he wrote in his *American Notes*, "where several grim hats were hanging on grim pegs, and the time was told by a grim clock which uttered every tick with a kind of struggle, as if it broke the grim silence reluctantly, and under protest."

While the Shakers were expanding into the West, a second chapter in the history of American religious communitarianism opened with the appearance of the foreign sects. In 1805 Father George Rapp and his flock of German farmers and mechanics planted a colony in Pennsylvania and called it Harmony. In 1817, another German community, the Separatists, settled in Zoar, Ohio. In the 1840s two more German millennial communities arose: The True Inspirationists formed theirs at Ebenezer (near Buffalo), New York in 1843; and the followers of William Keil formed theirs in Bethel, Missouri a year later. Finally, in 1856, Eric Janson and his Swedish brethren established a colony in Bishop Hill, Illinois. These were the most prominent of the foreign communities. They had nothing in common with the Shakers, or, with a single exception (some of the Bethelites had once lived under Father Rapp), with each other. The fact that they were all millenarian sects, each convinced by infallible signs of its election, precluded cross-fertilization or continuity of experience and thought. Each was a completely self-enclosed unit.

What they did have in common with each other, and with the Shakers too, was the same process of development, the same formal cause, as it were. They all started out as dissenters from established churches during a period of general religious disquietude. Just as Mother Ann had been a member of a group that had broken with the Anglican Church, so Rapp and Keil and Janson and the other prophets were swept up by the strong pietist current in the Lutheran Church that began in the late eighteenth century and continued through the 1820s and '30s. As in America so in these parts of Europe the religious rebels tended to be poor and simple folk who no longer felt at home with a ministry that served the rich or the urban middle class, that spoke the language of the schools, and that rested on a self-perpetuating, increasingly remote ecclesiastical oligarchy.

Their motive for coming to America was also similar: to maintain the integrity of the group, more precisely, to transform it into a family headed by the founding messiah. Once established as a community, the family received its laws—really a series of improvisations grounded in the redeemer's teachings. In every instance private property was anathematized, and everyone labored for the community, which is to say, for God. But each sect varied in its rules governing sex and family life. As a general principle they regarded marriage and cohabitation as a threat to the collectivity. Father Rapp strictly forbad sex (though he could not always prevent it: children were continually being born at Harmony).* The other colonies, though disapproving of sex, were more or less lax in exorcizing it. Their aversion to sex and marriage may have been justified. For a rough correlation can be drawn between asceticism and prosperity in the religious communities: those that succeeded best, namely the Shakers and the Rappites, were the most emphatic in renouncing conventional marriage.† The individual family unit turned out to be a far more divisive force than private property.

In trying to hold on to their integrity, the foreign communities had more to worry about than did the Shakers, who at least knew how to deal with their fellow countrymen. They knew, that is, how much of the world they could bear, and how deeply to withdraw into themselves the moment they felt their faith threatened. This knowledge enabled the Shakers to flourish inside the belly of Leviathan, near the crowded cities and well-settled countryside. The foreign sects, however, needed to preserve a *physical* distance from their neighbors—neighbors, moreover, who tended to be tolerant, even friendly. Toleration, which brought the sect into closer touch with the world, sometimes led to a weakening of the faith, then to a questioning of sanctified authority, then to disobedience, finally apostacy. In response, the foreign prophets sometimes found it necessary to take drastic measures—to give up everything, the fruits of

---

* Lord Byron was amused by Father Rapp. He wrote the following lines in Canto XV of *Don Juan:*

> When Rapp the Harmonist embargo'd Marriage
>   In his harmonious settlement which flourishes
> Strangely enough as yet without miscarriage,
>   Because it breeds no more mouths than it nourishes,
> Without those sad expenses which disparage what
>   Nature most encourages—
> Why call'd he 'Harmony' a state *sans* wedlock?
> Now here I've got the preacher at a deadlock,
>
> Because he either meant to sneer at Harmony
>   Or Marriage, by divorcing them thus oddly.
> But whether reverend Rapp learn'd this in Germany
>   Or not, 'tis said his sect is rich and godly,
> Pious and pure, beyond what I can term any
>   Of ours. . . .

† As we shall see, the Oneida Perfectionists, who were militantly anti-celibate, did quite well too. But they did have this in common with the Shakers and Rappites: they abolished the family unit.

years of toil, and return to the wilderness in the hope of re-enacting the original thaumaturgic experience.

Twice Father Rapp and his charges pulled up stakes and abandoned their thriving, well-managed little communities. In 1814 they left Harmony, Pennsylvania, to found Harmony, Indiana. Ten years later they sold the second Harmony to Robert Owen and settled, this time for good, in western Pennsylvania. The True Inspirationists, twelve years after building up Ebenezer, moved to central Iowa, where, once again they made a trackless waste flower with abundance. The most unusual expedition was undertaken by William Keil. After its establishment in 1844 his community of Bethel prospered; by the mid-1850s it contained more than a thousand inhabitants. It was then that he decided to go to the Oregon Territory, which had recently opened up, at the head of several hundred Bethelites. While preparing for the trip his son and heir apparant died of malaria. Keil had promised the boy before his death that he would take him to Oregon, come what may. Keeping his promise, he placed the coffin in the lead wagon. For weeks a great funeral cortege of wagons slowly made the trek northward across the silent, unexplored regions of the country. En route, the faithful sang a dirge that Keil had composed in memory of his son, *"Das Grab is tief und still."* Within months after their arrival in Oregon the Bethelites had wrested a community from the forests, and they named it Aurora to herald the coming of the new day. Keil remained in Aurora and governed far-off Bethel through his assistants.

Both the Shakers and the foreign sects came out of revivalist movements. So did the Oneida Perfectionist Society, the last and probably most famous of the millenarian groups to plant a colony in America. The history of Perfectionism concides with the biography of its founder, John Humphrey Noyes; he conceived it, built it, ran it, and oversaw its dissolution. Noyes was born in Putney, Vermont, in 1811, one of many children of a prominent New England family on both sides. At the age of twenty, just after graduating from Dartmouth, he was "converted" by the revivalist, John Finney. A social as well as religious crusade, the Finney revival fueled some of the radical causes—notably, anti-Masonism, "Barnburner" Democracy, and abolitionism—that flared up in western New England and central New York. Finney himself was an abolitionist, and so for a while was Noyes.

Noyes studied divinity at Andover and Yale, but he found himself deviating further and further from established Calvinist doctrines. When he publicly denied original sin and the need for visible churches, recognizing only "purity of heart and the answer of a good conscience toward God," his superiors withdrew his teaching license. For a decade or so he traveled extensively, read widely, and reflected at length on how man can attain spiritual and material perfection— meaning how man can return to the Garden of Eden. At a time of gravely unsettling economic conditions and mounting social discontent, he was determined to find a way of replacing "the Sin System, the Marriage System, the Work System, and the Death System." In due course, he came to the conclusion that mankind progressed through four "grades" of experience, corresponding to four historical epochs: "the natural state," or the age of pre-lapsarian freedom; "the legal state," or the age of Jewish Covenant; "the spiritual state," or the age of Christ's brief sojourn among men; and last, "the glorified state," or the age of Christ's return, this time forever—an age marked by the abolition of pain and death and of all the principalities of the world. To Noyes was revealed the means of bringing about "the glorified state."

At Putney, he gathered together a small number of acolytes, recruited mainly from his own and his wife's families. Having established the nucleus of a new religion, Noyes in 1846 proceeded to put his Perfectionist theories into effect; in other words, to organize a community. He and his followers surrendered their wealth to a central fund, and, as far as feasible (since some of them still had obligations in the world), worked in concert according to a rational division of labor. They simultaneously submitted to the practice of "complex marriage." For years Noyes had been objecting to conventional marriage and family life. Like Mother Ann and other millenarians he felt that marriage, the consequence of original sin, gave rise to divisiveness, jealousy, and the sexual and economic domination of men over women.

But Noyes prescribed the opposite of celibacy. Complex marriage meant the sexual love of every adult male for every adult female in the community. It was to be consummated through a love-making technique that Noyes invented, which he called "male continence." This technique taught men to hold back their seed during coitus, enabling them to engage in "amative" love indefinitely. Amative love, according to Noyes's reading of Scripture was "the first and noblest of the social affections," because it was the love of Adam and Eve before their Fall. Afterwards, it became subordinate to "the propogative function"—love-making for the sake of conceiving children. Complex marriage, then, would restore the original order of these two forms of sexuality. Conceiving would be secondary to amative love, the proof of man's freedom from sin, the mark of his habitation in the glorified state.

It was not long before the people of Putney learned of the outrageous experiments being carried out by the little group of Perfectionists. Noyes was accused of promoting wild orgies in his house, of indulging in free love and promiscuity and even incest. What the good people of Putney did not realize—how could they? —was that free love in the commonly accepted meaning of the term, namely spontaneous, uninhibited, completely natural sexuality, void of consequences and obligations, was furthest from the minds of the Perfectionsts. The choice of partners, the purpose of love-making (amative or procreative), these and other considerations had to be worked out collectively. At least on the part of the male, continence demanded the renunciation of pleasure. Love among the Perfectionists was hardly "free."

In 1848 Noyes and his followers moved from inhospitable Putney to Oneida, in central New York, where a few of his converts lived. Within a year of their settlement they had laid the foundation of a "Bible Communist" society at Oneida. They had put up a four story building to house themselves and their children—fifty residents in all—and had cleared the ground for cultivation. There was as yet no definite division of labor, and the women took their places alongside the men, often performing the same work. In doing so, the women assumed simple, unaffected modes of dress and appearance. The outside world would have been as scandalized by their functional clothes (they wore bloomers and slacks) and short hair as by their sexual practices. Though the Perfectionists worked long hours and cut their expenses to the bone, Oneida in its first few years kept losing money. The reason was obvious to Noyes: the community was too dependent on agriculture; to survive it would have to turn to manufacturing. In fact, Oneida's fortunes did change for the better when it began to produce steel traps of excellent quality. The success of this venture persuaded Noyes to establish other profitable enterprises—e.g., sewing silk, preserved fruit, and above all silver cutlery. Though Oneida's population had increased five-fold by 1855 there was more than enough work for everyone. By then Oneida had taken on the aspect of a prosperous, exceedingly well-managed capitalist corporation.

It was not a capitalist corporation, however, because its purpose was to transcend worldly goods, not accumulate them, to liberate men from the tortures of original sin, not reinforce them. The Perfectionists worked short hours (by mid-nineteeth century standards) and spent the bulk of their time in communal activities: playing, reading, conversing, confessing (of which more later), worshipping, and love-making. They avoided specialization—the bane of the communitarian ethic—and rotated from job to job and (since they had to be administrators too) from office to office. Oneida's educational system pointed up the extent of its difference from the outside world. It regarded children not as creatures, refractory and disobedient by nature, who had to be broken before they could be taught, but as sinless and potentially perfect. Corporal punishment played no part in Oneida pedagogy. Children over three were brought up by the community and were encouraged to discover and pursue their own desires.

Oneida, then, was far less austere than the other religious sects. It felt less menaced, less beleaguered. Not only did it trade extensively with the outside, it hired workers from the outside to do some of the menial chores, and it sent some members, mostly students, to outside trade schools. Compared to the other religious communities Oneida was open and free in its relations with the world at large.

Noyes and his co-adjutors had their devices for holding the society together. A fearful method of confessions known as "mutual criticism" kept incipient backsliders to the mark. When a member was charged with wrong-doing, or fell under suspicion, a committee interrogated him until it was satisfied that his guilt had been laid bare and expiated. In serious cases the whole community would assemble, and Noyes himself would lead the session. How effective mutual criticism was can be gauged by this description of a newcomer's first encounter with it:

> Every trait of my character that I took any pride or comfort in seemed to be cruelly discounted; and after, as it were, being turned inside out and thoroughly inspected, I was, metaphorically, stood upon my head, and allowed to drain till all the self-righteousness had dripped out of me. . . . For days and

weeks after I found myself recalling various passages of my criticism and reviewing them in a new light; the more I pondered, the more convinced I became of the justice of what at first my spirit had so violently rebelled against. . . . *Today I feel that I would give many years of my life if I could have just one more criticism from John H. Noyes.*

With the rise of the Oneida community in the late 1850s American religious communism reached its apogee. By then there were about forty-five sectarian colonies, including 18 Shaker and two Perfectionist (the other was at Wallingford, Connecticut), scattered across the country from the Berkshires to the Pacific, and embracing almost nine thousand people. By this time, too, the colonies were no longer considered perverse and strange; they had in fact gained a large measure of respectability. Society in general—at least the well-informed portion of it—had become familiar with their works and in some instances with their doctrines.

But the high-point of millenarian communism was also the beginning of its demise. In an age of advancing industrialism and secularism, self-sufficient religious sects were increasingly anachronistic. The great revival movements that had periodically stoked the fires of millenarianism here and abroad died out in the course of the nineteenth century. And such revivalisms as did take place appealed to individuals rather than to whole communities; they sought to rescue souls rather than bring about the Kingdom of Heaven on earth.

And so the sects atrophied as the older members died. Except for the Shakers the death of their prophet-founders left them moribund, though often it was some time before the communities gave up the ghost. George Rapp died in 1847; the few survivors in Economy dissolved their ancient ties in 1905. The Zoar community came to an end in 1898, nearly a half century after the death of its leader. The True Inspirationists of Amana, Iowa, held out until the 1920s. The Shakers held out longer, and at the moment this is being written several of them, all quite old, still live. The other sects scarcely survived their leaders. The Jansonites broke up in 1857, seven years after Eric Janson was slain. And Bethel and Aurora quietly expired less than five years after William Keil died. John Humphrey Noyes, who died in 1886, lived long enough to see his Perfectionist experiment turn into a joint stock company.

THE SHAKERS

CALVIN GREEN AND SETH Y. WELLS,
A Summary View of the Millenial Church or United Society of Believers*
1848

This classic account of the Shaker religion, written by two elders of the New Lebanon church, was first published in 1808. It went through many editions.

INTRODUCTORY REMARKS:

COMPRISING A SHORT REVIEW OF THE FORMATION OF ASSOCIATIONS AND COMMUNITIES.

1. The present age of the world is an age of wonders. The most extraordinary changes, revolutions and remarkable events are rapidly rolling on, through the physical, moral and religious world, that were ever known on earth. These premises, we believe, will generally be admitted. It appears to be the prevailing sentiment and expectation among nearly all ranks and orders of people, that something wonderful is about to take place; that there will be such a revolution of public sentiment, and such a reformation will be effected in the various branches of human economy as never has been exhibited in the world since the creation of man.

2. These expectations are evidently effected by the operations of Divine Providence upon the hearts of the people, and are manifestly the precursors and signals of coming events. These events can be truly understood in no other light than as allusions to the period of Christ's second coming. The general expectations of the near approach of a Divine Ruler and Teacher called the Messiah, which prevailed among the Jews, and more or less among other nations, about the time that Jesus Christ came into the world, were also

* Pp. 1–3, 58–60, 68, 90–93, 260–266.

the effects of the same overruling Providence. These two events are the most important to mankind of any that have ever taken place on earth, and will yet appear so to all people, whether they believe it or not.

3. The events relating to Christ's second appearance, of which we are more particularly to treat in this volume, are rapidly progressing towards their accomplishment, in many and various ways. But among all the hopeful expectations, labors and desires of mankind, in the present age, none appear more evident than those which lead to the formation of associations in which all the members can enjoy equal rights and privileges, physical and moral, both of a spiritual and temporal nature, in a united capacity. Many have become fully convinced that this is the ultimate destiny of mankind, and that they never can enjoy that happiness for which their Creator designed them, in any other way than in such united capacity. This is true; but this united capacity must be built on the true foundation, which is nothing less than divine revelation, or it cannot stand.

4. Some of the greatest pursuits of the age appear to be directed to these communities. They have their combined associations for almost every kind of improvement, whether of a religious, moral or physical nature. Yet to attain this desirable object, and support it in its true order, they have not the power; in this they are greatly deficient. The great inequality of rights and privileges which prevails so extensively throughout the world is a striking evidence of the importance of a reformation of some kind. Who can view the unequal state of human society, the overgrown wealth of the few, and the abject poverty of the many, and not be convinced of this? Surely it is too obvious to escape the notice of any rational mind.

5. To see the luxurious state of the pampered rich, the oppression and destitution of the poor, who are perishing by thousands, yea, hundreds of thousands, for the want of the necessaries of life; and the consequent bitter animosities and increasing collisions between the rich and the poor, must suggest to every benevolent mind the indispensable necessity of some system of operation among men, that will confer a much greater equality of rights and privileges, both in person and property, than any which now prevails, in order to prevent mankind from rushing on to utter ruin.

6. Multitudes of people have been so firmly persuaded of the utility and practicability of such a system, that they have attempted to form communities upon the plan of equal rights and privileges, with a unity of interest in all things, believing that it is the design of the benevolent Creator that man should be a social and benevolent being; that their joys and sorrows, as fellow beings, may be shared together. These sentiments are evidently the impressions of *Divine Goodness*, and clearly show his benevolent designs for his creature man, who is his intelligent representative in this lower world. This was prefigured under the law, when Divine Providence fed the people of Israel with manna. Of this they all shared equally, according to their necessities.[1]

7. During the present century, many attempts have been made to form associations upon the plan of a community of interest, in various parts of Europe and in the United States of America. Many societies have been formed in part or wholly upon this plan. But it is well known that with all their wisdom, skill, benevolent designs, unity of intention, convenience of location and confidence of success, they have soon failed in their expectations, and been scattered as before. This signal and general failure has more or less disappointed the votaries of this system, and set many to devising some other plan to accomplish their object. Many, of course, scoff at the idea of such communities, while others, after having tried the system, have given up the object as unattainable.

8. But notwithstanding these general failures, we are prepared to show that there is a sure system, founded upon the principles of a unity of interest in all things, which has stood the test a sufficient length of time, to prove that it can be attained and supported. This system has been established and maintained for many years, in seven different states in this Union, and in many locations in these states.

9. The United Society of Believers (called Shakers) was founded upon the principles of equal rights and privileges, with a united interest in all things, both spiritual and temporal, and has been maintained and supported in this Society, at New-Lebanon, about sixty years, without the least appearance of any failure. Is not this proof sufficient in favor of such a system?

10. We believe it will generally be granted that no institution,

[1] Exod. xvi. 4 to 18.

either social or religious, ever founded on earth, has, in any age of the world, stood half a century without a manifest declension in the general virtue of its principles, and the integrity of its members, however extensive and durable may have been its name and popularity of character.

11. But this United Society, though formed of characters, views and dispositions of all kinds that can be named, of various nations, of rich and poor, bond and free, male and female, has maintained its primitive institution and the integrity of its first principles, with a continued increase of the same to this day. And although it has founded and established branches in various states of the Union, where the laws and customs of the people vary, it has not failed in its ability to maintain its institutions and the purity of its religious principles in a single instance.[2] . . .

PART II.

THE ESTABLISHED ORDER AND RELIGIOUS PRACTICE OF THE UNITED SOCIETY.

CHAPTER I

Formation of the Society into a united Body, possessing a consecrated Interest.

1. As the manner of God's work, both in the natural and spiritual creation, has always been progressive, increasing from one degree of order to another until it arrives to perfection; so the order which has been established in the church of Christ on earth, was necessarily progressive, being effected by the progressive operations of his Divine Spirit in the hearts of the faithful. While the believers, as a people, remained in their respective natural families, scattered about in different places, possessing respectively the temporal interest inherited by natural heirship, or acquired by their own labors in their respective callings, there could not be much order among

---

[2] If individuals who have belonged to these societies have violated their religious faith and principles, and refused to reform, they have been obliged to depart; because no violation of virtuous principles can be tolerated among us.

them, excepting the common order of nature. But all who had honestly confessed and forsaken their sins, and faithfully continued to take up their crosses, according to the manifestation of the gift of God which they had received, who had paid all their just debts, and freed themselves from all outward embarrassments, and by their faithfulness and obedience, had gained a sufficient degree of mortification to the fallen nature of the flesh, were thereby prepared for a further increase of gospel order. To gain this increase, it was necessary that they should be brought into a nearer connection together, and thereby be enabled to serve God in a more united capacity, as members of the body of Christ in a church relation.

2. To constitute a true church of Christ, there must necessarily be a union of faith, of motives and of interest, in all the members who compose it. There must be "one body and one bread:"[3] and nothing short of this union in all things, both spiritual and temporal, can constitute a true church, which is the body of Christ. And wherever that united body exists, it will bring into operation every individual talent for the general good of the whole body. And herein is the prayer of Jesus answered; "That they may be one, even as we are one."[4] In this united capacity, the strength of the whole body becomes the strength of each member; and being united in the one Spirit of Christ, they have a greater privilege to serve God than they possibly could have in a separate capacity, and are better able to be mutual helps to each other; and they also find a greater degree of protection from the snares of a selfish and worldly nature.

3. The way having been gradually prepared for the attainment of this important object, particularly by the ministration of Father James, it now began to take place under the ministration of Father Joseph and Mother Lucy. The first step was to gather the believers into a body, where they could enjoy all things in common, both of a spiritual and temporal kind, and in which their temporal interest could be united together, and be consecrated to religious purposes. This proceeding, being dictated by Divine Wisdom, was a matter of free choice to every individual: for no one was compelled to give up his interest contrary to his own faith and inward feelings. But all who had faithfully kept pace with the work of God, in its increase thus far, and had been able to settle their

[3] 1 Cor x. 17.
[4] John xvii. 22.

temporal concerns, were prepared for it, and esteemed it a special privilege to be admitted into that united body, and be numbered with the most faithful. But the permanent establishment of order was necessarily a progressive work, and could not be suddenly accomplished.

4. The gathering of the society began at New-Lebanon, in the month of September, 1787, and continued to progress as fast as circumstances and the nature of the work would admit. Elders and deacons were appointed to lead and direct in matters of spiritual and temporal concern; suitable buildings were erected for the accommodation of the members; and order and regularity were, by degrees, established in the society: so that in the year 1792, the church was considered as established in the principles of her present order and spirit of government. Those who were thus gathered into a united body, were denominated *The Church*; being a collective body of Christians separated from the world, and enjoying in their united capacity, one common interest. In this situation they were enabled to gain a greater degree of victory over the nature of selfishness, and thus to subdue more effectually, the evil propensities of a carnal nature. By this means they found a greater degree of mortification and death to the nature of sin, and experienced a gradual growth in love and union, peace and harmony, and all those heavenly graces which adorn the man of God, and render him perfect in every good word and work. . . .

11. In every society, elders are appointed and established in each large family, consisting, generally, of two persons of each sex. These are considered as the head of the family. They are required to be persons of blameless character, well approved for faithfulness, integrity and stability of soul, and gifted in wisdom and spiritual administration. As faithful watchmen upon the walls of Zion, it becomes their duty to watch over their respective families, to teach, exhort and lead in spiritual concerns.

12. The management of temporal concerns, in such families, is intrusted to the deacons and deaconesses, as trustees of the temporal property of the society or family to which they belong. To these pertain the duties of providing for the support and convenience of their respective families, of regulating the various branches of business in which the members are employed, and of transacting business with those without. All the members are equally holden, ac-

cording to their several abilities, to maintain one united interest; and therefore all labor with their hands, in some useful occupation, for the mutual comfort and benefit of themselves and each other, and for the general good of the society or family to which they belong. Ministers, elders and deacons, all without exception, are industriously employed in some manual occupation, except in the time taken up in the necessary duties of their respective callings.

13. Thus all are faithful, cheerful and happy in the conscientious performance of their respective duties; and such is the spirit of industry that pervades the whole Society, that an idle, lazy person will not long abide in it. And this is effected by no other coercive power than the force of conscience, and the spirit which prevails throughout the Society: for none are required to labor beyond their strength and abilities, and each one must act conscientiously in this, as in all other duties. If reproof or admonition is at any time found necessary, it must be applied through the medium of the conscience: for the law of Christ admits of no external compulsion. But none can be allowed to remain in the Society, who maintain disobedience to its established faith and principles.

14. No selfish or party feelings can have any sway in the Church of Christ: for the whole power of government being founded in the law of Christ, and supported by the union of the members, any power, authority or influence, which has any tendency to produce disunion, contrary to that law, is necessarily excluded from any participation in the government. In short, the whole government of the Church is effected, and all its important concerns are regulated and maintained, by the spontaneous union and subjection of all the faithful to the law of Christ, established in the Church. . . .

22. "Therefore they shall come and sing in the height of Zion, and shall flow together to the goodness of the Lord:—Then shall the virgin rejoice in the dance, both young men and old together: for I will turn their mourning into joy, and will comfort them, and make them rejoice from their sorrow. And I will satiate the soul of the priests with fatness, and my people shall be satisfied with my goodness, saith the Lord."

23. What can be more plain and clear to the point than these declarations, of the prophet? What words could describe with more certainty, not only the fullness of joy, comfort and satisfaction of those who should come into this plain and perfect way, but also

the divine exercises, and very manner of worship in which they would be engaged? The term *virgin*, signifies purity; and this prediction of the prophet was evidently intended to imply, that those who should be called to this glorious work, and enjoy these blessed privileges, must be a pure people. Hence, "both young men and old," being characterized by the title *virgin*, must possess purity of heart, and live a virgin life.[5]

24. We are aware that a strong prejudice prevails against the exercise of dancing, as an act of divine worship, in consequence of its having been, for many ages, perverted to the service of the wicked. Hence, it is considered by many as, at best, but a vain recreation, much more calculated to gratify the levity of giddy, thoughtless mortals, and to divert the mind from sober reflections, than to enliven the devotional feelings of the heart, and promote the solid enjoyments of the Christian. Therefore they judge it altogether unreasonable and inconsistent to suppose it can be acceptable to God as an act of divine worship. But we would seriously ask whether the same objections will not operate, still more forcibly, against singing, as an act of divine worship?

25. It is a well known fact, that every created talent, pertaining to fallen man, which was designed for the service of God, has been perverted and abused to vain, foolish and wicked purposes; and perhaps none more generally so than that of singing. Music, unconnected with dancing, is doubtless much more generally used, as an amusement of the wicked: besides, as it is the very life of dancing, it must, at least, be equally reprehensible in that view alone. But this is not all. The talents of poetry and music, exclusive of their connection with dancing, are still far more abused by being devoted to base purposes.

26. Is there a single base passion or evil propensity, in human nature, which has not been more or less excited, indulged and gratified by means of poetical and musical compositions? How often have the angry passions been roused by war songs, and urged mankind to mutual butchery, blood and slaughter? How often have the

[5] It is the prevailing opinion that this prophecy alluded to the return of the Jews from Babylon; but admitting that the prophecy had a literal allusion to that event; yet their return was but a figure of the restoration of the true church: and as the character of the Jews was by no means answerable to the title of *the virgin*; therefore the true spirit of that prophecy could not be fulfilled in them; its real accomplishment must be in *the virgin church of Christ*.

lascivious passions been excited and indulged by obscene songs! How often is morality set at naught, and piety and religion abused, yea, and the name of God and all sacred things blasphemed by the wicked, in their profane songs! How often has vice been exalted, and virtue depressed—yea, how often has the virtuous mind been robbed of its innocence, and villany emboldened in crimes, by songs calculated and used for those very purposes! Do not the revels of drunkards and profane swearers often owe their excesses to their bacchanalian songs, as well as to their bottles?

27. In short, have not thefts, robberies and murders, and indeed every species of villany, been much more excited and encouraged by music than by dancing? And yet music has been encouraged and practiced, as a part of divine worship, by nearly all denominations, while dancing has been condemned and excluded. But upon what principle? Why truly upon this; that dancing cannot be an acceptable mode of worship, because it is practiced in the carnal recreations of the wicked! Thus man assumes the right of deciding in what manner God shall be worshiped! But will God acknowledge such a decision as this? And must the followers of Christ, in compliance with this decision, bury a portion of their talents in the earth, which were given for the service of God, because the wicked have profanely abused such like talents, in the service of the Devil? Does such a decision appear honorable to the wisdom of man, even upon the supposition that he has a right to decide in what manner God shall be worshiped? Is it not rather a glaring evidence of the total insufficiency of human sagacity to regulate those things which belong to Divine Wisdom?

28. God has created man an active, intelligent being, possessing important powers and faculties, capable of serving himself according to his needs and circumstances; and he is required to devote these powers and faculties to the service of God. To devote only a part to the service of God is to render an imperfect service, which God never will accept. Man is required to love God with all his heart, soul, mind and strength. Every faculty must therefore be devoted to the love of God; but it is in vain to talk of loving God with all the faculties, without serving him with all the faculties: for no man who truly loves God with all his faculties, can refrain from devoting all to his service; and he who is unwilling to devote all to the service of God, can never devote all to his love. . . .

PART VI

CHAPTER IV

The Manifestation of Christ in the Female.

7. The many instances recorded in the sacred writings prove beyond dispute, that in past ages, God did condescend to reveal his mind and will to females, who were then commissioned, by Divine Authority, to bear testimony thereof to man. And the two signal instances of deliverance effected through the instrumentality of Deborah and Esther are sufficient to show that God did, on each of these extraordinary occasions, raise up and empower a female to accomplish an extraordinary deliverance, which was beyond the power of man to effect without their assistance.

8. If then, God has, in these last days, raised up a female to reveal the true testimony and Spirit of Christ, and endowed her with power to effect the deliverance of lost man from the bondage of sin, and to usher in the latter day of glory, shall man reject the work on that account? Is it too debasing to the pride and haughtiness of fallen man? If so, let it be remembered that, "The Lord of hosts hath purposed it, to stain the pride of all glory, and to bring into contempt all the honorable of the earth. And the loftiness of man shall be bowed down, and the haughtiness of men shall be made low: and the Lord alone shall be exalted in that day."[6]

9. It is well known that when souls come to be awakened to a feeling sense of their need of salvation, their general cry is, "What shall we do to be saved?—Lord, send by whom thou wilt send—Work by means of thy own choosing; only show us thy will—bring us salvation from the bondage of sin." It is on these conditions we are willing to receive Christ, tho' revealed in a manner contrary to every feeling of a fallen nature. We are determined to exalt the Lord alone—to know none but Christ, wherever manifested and in whomsoever found, and to bear the cross, tho' it crucify us to the world, and the world to us.

10. Altho' it was necessary that the spirit of Christ should be

[6] Isa. ii. 17, and xxiii. 9.

manifested in both male and female; yet no man nor woman that ever appeared on earth, could ever be a proper object of divine worship. "God is Spirit; and they that worship him, must worship in spirit and in truth."[7] God is therefore the only proper object of divine worship; and no one can ever worship in the spiritual work of God, unless called and directed by the Spirit of Christ: for according to his own testimony, "No man cometh unto the Father but by me."[8] Therefore no man can worship God, but through Christ; and the only true worship that we can render to God, is to honor and glorify him by yielding obedience to his will. And tho' a portion of the Spirit of Christ must be in every soul, in order to unite them to his body; yet the manifestation of the will of God for the guide and direction of souls, in his true spiritual work, must be revealed in the order of God's appointment, through those witnesses whom he sends for that purpose.

11. As the divine Spirit and Will of God, in these last days, has been manifested in Christ,[9] through the two first messengers of salvation: so the same spirit continues to manifest his will, through the same line and order, in the Church of Christ, and will ever continue so to do, as long as Christ shall continue to have a true church on earth. Therefore, as the ancients worshiped the God of their fathers; so worship we that God who has been revealed to us by our spiritual parents in the gospel, whom God hath raised up and sent to open the way of salvation to us. We worship neither man nor woman; but we honor and obey the Spirit of Christ, whether revealed in man, woman or child.

12. The natural creation, and the things therein contained, are figurative representations of the spiritual creation which is to supercede it, as we have already shown. The first parents of the natural world were created male and female. The man was first in his creation, and the woman was afterwards taken from his substance, and placed in her proper order to be the second in the government and dominion of the natural world; and the order of man's creation was not complete till this was done. For it must be acknowledged by all, that without male and female, the perfection of man, in his

---

[7] John iv. 24.
[8] John xiv. 6.
[9] See 1 John vi. 6: also 1 John i. 1 and 2. The term here translated *Word*, properly signifies, in the original, Divine Intelligence, or mind of Power and Wisdom. For in this *mind*, which is true Christ, God is revealed to us. See 1 Cor. ii. 16.

natural creation, must have been less complete than that of the inferior part of the creation, which was evidently created male and female. Hence it must appear obvious, that in the spiritual creation, man and woman, when raised from a natural to a spiritual state, must still be male and female: for the spiritual state of man, which is substantial and eternal, cannot be less perfect in its order, than his natural state, which is but temporal, and figurative of the spiritual.

13. As the true Church of Christ, which is his body, is composed of male and female, as its members; and as there must be a correspondent spiritual union between the male and female, to render the Church complete, as a spiritual body; so it is essentially necessary that such a spiritual union should exist in the head of that body, which is Christ; otherwise there could be no source from which such a correspondent, spiritual union could flow to the body. It must be admitted by every reasonable person, that the order of man cannot be complete without the woman. If so, then the Church cannot exist, in its proper order, without male and female members: for "neither is the man without the woman, nor the woman without the man, in the Lord."[10] And it would be very unreasonable to suppose that the body of Christ should be more complete and perfect in its order, than the head. This would give the body a superiority over the head.

14. This spiritual union between the male and female, in the body and in the head of the Church, is that which the apostle calls *a great mystery*.[11] And indeed it is a great mystery to the lost children of men, who seem to have no conception of any other union between the male and female, than that which is natural, according to the order of the flesh. Nor do they seem to know any other design in the creation of the female, nor any other essential use for her than that of carnal enjoyment in a sexual union, and the production of offspring through that medium. But the work of Christ, being a spiritual work, the union must therefore be spiritual; and it is impossible for souls to come into this work, and enjoy this union, unless the Spirit of Christ becomes their life.

15. Since, then, Christ must appear in every female, as well as in every male, before they can be saved; and since that Divine Spirit has appeared in one man, whom God hath chosen as the Captain

10 1 Cor. xi. 11.
11 Eph. v. 32.

of our salvation, and an example of righteousness to all men; is it not reasonable and consistent that the same anointing Power (which is Christ) should also appear in a woman, and distinguish her as a leader, and an example of righteousness to all women?

16. It may be asked, How can Christ appear in a woman? With the same propriety we might ask, How can Christ appear in a man? Christ is a Spirit: "The Lord is that Spirit."[12] In that Spirit is contained the only power of salvation. If Christ could not appear in a man, then no man could be saved; so also, if Christ could not appear in a woman, then no woman could be saved. Christ first appeared in Jesus of Nazareth, as the Bridegroom, by which he was constituted the head and Father of the new and spiritual creation of God. The Spirit of Christ was in the primitive Church; and the Spirit of Christ is also in every one of his true and faithful followers. The Spirit of Christ is the same, in substance, whether revealed in man, woman or child, but in different orders.

17. It may perhaps be urged, by way of objection, that if a female was to be raised up, to stand in a correspondent connection with the first-born Son of God, in order to usher in the latter day of glory, and bring about the regeneration of a lost world, it would appear reasonable that she also, as well as he, should have been brought forth by a miraculous birth. But a little reflection will show the impropriety of this. Such a birth would not have corresponded with the figure given in the creation of the first man and woman. Adam was called "the figure of him that was to come."[13] He had a miraculous creation, being formed out of the dust of the earth, and was the son of God in the natural and figurative creation. (See Luke iii. 38.) Jesus had also a miraculous birth, being born of a virgin, without the co-operation of man, and being the agent of the Divine Intelligence, became the son of God in the Divine order. (See John i. 14.) But this virgin, being a natural woman, a daughter of Adam, her body was of the earth; and in this sense, she was as the dust of the earth, tho' in its highest state of natural perfection under the fall, as was needful it should be, when designed for such an extraordinary purpose.

18. Eve, who was "the figure of *her* that was to come," was not created out of the dust of the earth, as Adam was, but was formed of his substance, and taken from his body; therefore she was de-

[12] 2 Cor. iii. 17.
[13] Rom. v. 14.

pendent on him, and it was her duty to be subject to him as her head and lord. Had the woman been created in the same manner that the man was, there would have been two separate heads of the creation; and as neither of them could have had the pre-eminence, as to the origin of their creation; so neither of them could thereby have been placed in a state of subordination to the other. So also, agreeable to this figure, the second Eve was not brought forth in the same manner that the second Adam was; but, as to her person, she came into the world as all women do. But as the substance of the first woman was taken from the body of the first man, so that Divine Spirit with which the second woman was endowed, and which constituted her the second Eve, and the Mother of the new creation, was taken from the Divine Spirit of the second Adam, the Lord Jesus Christ; therefore she was necessarily dependent on him, was subject to him, and always acknowledged him as her head and lord.

19. It was absolutely necessary that the human tabernacle, soul and body, of Jesus Christ, should not only be created in a supernatural manner, by the Divine agency of the Eternal FATHER and MOTHER; but also in a state superior to that of the first Adam; otherwise he could never have had the pre-eminence, as to the superiority of his origin. As no stream can rise higher than its fountain, so no being could proceed by natural generation, from the loins of Adam, with a life superior to that which he possessed; for he was formed of the elements of temporal life, and not of the elements of eternal life.[14] Therefore, had Jesus been begotten of the seed of Adam, his life could not have been superior to the life of Adam; nor could he have been the medium of superior power; hence he could not have been the first to possess eternal life; and therefore the source of eternal life could not have been in him; consequently it could not have been brought to light by him.

20. But Jesus being created in an order superior to that of the first Adam, he was the first who received the elements of eternal

[14] Had Adam been formed of the elements of eternal life, he could not have died: for that which is eternal can never die. But when God spake to Adam concerning the tree of the knowledge of good and evil, he said, "In the day thou eatest thereof thou shalt surely die." This was fulfilled. This shows the absurdity of the idea, that Jesus Christ came into the world for no higher purpose than to raise man to the state from whence Adam fell. His work was to overcome the death of the fall, and rise out of the life and order of nature, into eternal life, and heavenly order; and his Spirit will effect the same in his followers, or children. See Heb. ii. 13, 14.

life from his *Eternal Parents*. His divine creation and superior order was announced by the message of the angel to Mary: "The Holy Ghost shall come upon thee, and the power of the Highest shall overshadow thee."[15] Here was plainly manifested the operation of the ETERNAL TWO, the HIGHEST and the HOLY SPIRIT, by whom the Holy Child Jesus was created, in whom the Son of God was revealed, and eternal life was brought to light.[16] He was doubtless the superior production of human nature, and possessed the greatest natural powers. How else could he have been the head of the human race? This is evident from his temptations on the mount, for the temptation could not have been disproportioned to the capacities of his creation. It is further evidenced by his own words: "Behold a greater than Solomon is here." He was created in a manner and order which showed that in *him* the works and order of natural generation ceased, and a new and spiritual creation, not "according to the will of the *flesh*, nor the will of man," should begin.

21. Let it be here understood that Christ is a Divine Spirit, and the man Jesus was not constituted the Christ, or the real Messiah, until anointed of God, and put in full possession of that Spirit which, at his baptism, descended upon and abode with him, in form of a *Dove*. This heavenly Dove was the real Christ, the Son of God.[17] And as the human race, in their fallen and lost state, are composed of male and female; so it is necessary that the Spirit of Christ, in which is the only power of salvation, should be manifested in both male and female, in order to complete the work of regeneration and salvation. . . .

[15] Luke i. 35.
[16] It is proper to remark here, that in all languages, the term Holy Ghost is the same as Holy Spirit, and is generally expressed by a substantive in the neuter gender, which, of itself, implies neither male nor female. The application of masculine or feminine terms to the Holy Spirit, must depend on its relative manifestations, and its operation in the line of male or female.
[17] See John i. 33, 34.

"Four Months Among the Shakers"
1842–1843

We do not know who wrote this account. It found its way into the manuscript of one A. J. Macdonald, who was compiling an enormous study of American communities. Macdonald left his manuscript with John Humphrey Noyes, who included portions of it in his *History of American Socialisms.**

Circumstances that need not be rehearsed, induced me to visit the Shaker Society at Watervliet, in the winter of 1842–3. Soon after my arrival, I was conducted to the Elder whose business it was to deal with inquirers. He was a good-looking old man, with a fine open countenance, and a well-formed head, as I could see from its being bald. I found him very intelligent, and soon made known to him my business, which was to learn something about the Shakers and their conditions of receiving members. On my observing that I had seen favorable accounts of their society in the writings of Mr. Owen, Miss Martineau, and other travelers in the United States, he replied, that "those who wished to know the Shakers, must live with them;" and this remark proved to be true. He propounded to me at considerable length their faith, "the daily cross" they were obliged to take up against the devil and the flesh, and the supreme virtue of a life of celibacy. When he had concluded I asked if those who wished to join the society were expected to acknowledge a belief in all the articles of their faith? To which he replied, "that they were not, for many persons came there to join them, who had never heard their gospel preached; but they were always received, and an opportunity given them of accepting or rejecting it." He then informed me of the conditions under which they received candidates: "All new comers have one week's trial, to see how they like; and after that, if they wish to continue they must take up the daily cross, and commence the work of regeneration and salvation, following in the footsteps of Jesus

* Pp. 597–601, 603–606, 610–612.

Christ and Mother Ann." My first cross, he informed me, would be to confess all the wicked acts I had ever committed. I asked him if he gave absolution like a Catholic priest. He replied, "that God forgave sins and not they; but it was necessary in beginning the work of salvation, to unburden the mind of all its past sins." I thought this confession (demanded of strangers) was a piece of good policy on their part; for it enabled the Elder who received the confession to form a tolerable opinion of the individual to be admitted. I agreed however before confession to make a week's trial of the place, and was accordingly invited to supper; after which I was shown to the sleeping room specially set apart for new members. I was not left here more than an hour when a small bell rang, and one of the brothers entered the room and invited me to go to the family meeting; where I saw for the first time their mode of worshiping God in the dance. I thought it was an exciting exercise, and I should have been more pleased if they had had instrumental, instead of vocal music.

At first my meals were brought to me in my room, but after a few days I was invited to commence the work of regeneration and prepare for confession, that I might associate with the rest of the brothers. On making known my readiness to confess, I was taken to the private confession-room, and there recounted a brief history of my past life. This appeared rather to please the Elder, and he observed that I "had not been very wicked." I replied, "No, I had not abounded in acts of crime and debauchery." But the old man, to make sure I was not deceiving him, tried to frighten me, by telling me of individuals who had not made a full confession of their wickedness, and who could find no peace or pleasure until they came back and revealed all. He assured me moreover that no wicked person could continue there long without being found out. I was curious to know how such persons would be detected; so he took me to the window and pointed out the places where "Mother Ann" had stationed four angels to watch over her children; and "these angels," he said, "always communicated any wickedness done there, or the presence of any wicked person among them." "But," he continued, "you can not understand these things; neither can you believe them, for you have not yet got faith enough." I replied: "I can not see the angels!" "No," said he, "I can not see them with the eye of sense; but I can see them with the eye of faith. You must labor for faith: and when any thing troubles you that you can not understand or believe, come to me, and do not express doubts to any of the brethren." The Elder then put on my eyes a pair of spiritual golden spectacles, to make me see spiritual things. I instinctively put up my hands to feel them, which made the old gentleman half laugh, and he said, "Oh, you can not feel them; they will not incommode you, but will help you to see spiritual things."

After this I was permitted to eat with the family and invited to attend their love-meetings. I was informed that I had perfect liberty to leave the village whenever I chose to do so; but that I was to receive no pay for my services if I were to leave; I should be provided for, the same as if I were one of the oldest members, with food, clothing and lodgings, according to their rules.

DAILY ROUTINE

The hours of rising were five o'clock in the summer, and half-past five in the winter. The family all rose at the toll of the bell, and in less than ten minutes vacated the bed-rooms. The sisters then distributed themselves throughout the rooms, and made up all the beds, putting everything in the most perfect order before breakfast. The brothers proceeded to their various employments, and made a commencement for the day. The cows were milked, and the horses were fed. At seven o'clock the bell rang for breakfast, but it was ten minutes after when we went to the tables. The brothers and sisters assembled each by themselves, in rooms appointed for the purpose; and at the sound of a small bell the doors of these rooms opened, and a procession of the family was formed in the hall, each individual being in his or her proper place, as they would be at table. The brothers came first, followed by the sisters, and the whole marched in solemn silence to the dining-room. The brothers and sisters took separate tables, on opposite sides of the room. All stood up until each one had arrived at his or her proper place, and then at a signal from the Elder at the head of the table, they all knelt down for about two minutes, and at another signal they all arose and commenced eating their breakfast. Each individual helped himself; which was easily done, as the tables were so arranged that between every four persons there was a supply of every article intended for the meal. At the conclusion they all arose and marched away from the tables in the same manner as they marched to them; and during the time of marching, eating, and re-marching, not one word was spoken, but the most perfect silence was preserved.

After breakfast all proceeded immediately to their respective employments, and continued industriously occupied until ten minutes to twelve o'clock, when the bell announced dinner. Farmers then left the field and mechanics their shops, all washed their hands, and formed procession again, and marched to dinner in the same way as to breakfast. Immediately after dinner they went to work again, (having no hour for resting), and continued steady at it until the bell announced supper. At supper the same routine was gone through as at the other meals, and all except the farmers went to work again. The farmers were supposed to be doing what were called "chores," which appeared to mean any little odd jobs in and about the stables and barns. At eight o'clock all work was ended for the day, and the family went to what they called a "union meeting." This meeting generally continued one hour, and then, at about nine o'clock, all retired to bed. . . .

THE DANCING MEETINGS

At half-past seven P.M. on the dancing days, all the members retired to their separate rooms, where they sat in solemn silence, just gazing at the stove, until the silver tones of a small tea-bell gave the signal for them to assemble in the large hall. Thither they proceeded in perfect order and solemn silence. Each had on thin dancing-shoes; and on entering the door of the hall they walked on tip-toe, and took up their positions as follows: the brothers formed a rank on the right, and the sisters on the left, facing each other, about five feet apart. After all were in their proper places the chief Elder stepped into the center of the space, and gave an exhortation for about five minutes, concluding with an invitation to them all to "go forth, old men, young men and maidens, and worship God with all their might in the dance." Accordingly they "went forth," the men stripping off their coats and remaining in their shirtsleeves. First they formed a procession and marched around the room at double-quick time, while four brothers and four sisters stood in the center singing for them. After marching in this manner until they got a little warm, they commenced dancing, and continued it until they were all pretty well tired. During the dance the sisters kept on one side, and the brothers on the other, and not a word was spoken by any of them. After they appeared to have had enough of this exercise, the Elder gave the signal to stop, when immediately each one took his or her place in an oblong circle formed around the room, and all waited to see if any one had received a "gift," that is, an inspiration to do something odd. Then two of the sisters would commence whirling round like a top, with their eyes shut; and continued this motion for about fifteen minutes; when they suddenly stopped and resumed their places, as steady as if they had never stirred. During the "whirl" the members stood round like statues, looking on in solemn silence.

A MESSAGE FROM MOTHER ANN

On some occasions when a sister had stopped her whirling, she would say, "I have a communication to make;" when the head Eldress would step to her side and receive the communication, and then make known the nature of it to the company. The first message I heard was as follows: "Mother Ann has sent two angels to inform us that a tribe of Indians has been round here two days, and want the brothers and sisters to take them in. They are outside the building there, looking in at the windows." I shall never forget how I looked round at the windows, expecting to see the yellow faces, when this announcement was made; but I believe some of the old folks who eyed me, bit their lips and smiled. It caused no alarm to the rest, but the first Elder exhorted the brothers "to take in the poor spirits and assist them to get salvation." He afterward repeated more of what the angels had said, viz., "that the Indians were a savage tribe who had all died before Columbus discovered America, and had been wandering about ever since. Mother Ann wanted them to be received into the meeting to-morrow night." After this we dispersed to our separate bed-rooms, with the hope of having a future entertainment from the Indians.

INDIAN ORGIES

The next dancing night we again assembled in the same manner as before, and went through the marching and dancing as usual; after which the hall doors were opened, and the Elder invited the Indians to come in. The doors were soon shut again, and one of the sisters (the same who received the original communication) informed us that she saw Indians all around and among the brothers and sisters. The Elder then urged upon the members the duty of "taking them in." Whereupon eight or nine sisters became possessed of the spirits of Indian squaws, and about six of the brethren became Indians. Then ensued a regular pow-wow, with whooping and yelling and strange antics, such as would require a Dickens to describe. The sisters and brothers squatted down on the floor together, Indian fashion, and the Elders and Eldresses endeavored to keep them asunder, telling the men they must be separated from the squaws, and otherwise instructing them in the rules of Shakerism. Some of the Indians then wanted some "succotash," which was soon brought them from the kitchen in two wooden dishes, and placed on the floor; when they commenced eating it with their fingers. These performances continued till about ten o'clock; then the chief Elder requested the Indians to go away, telling them they would find some one waiting to conduct them to the Shakers in the heavenly world. At this announcement the possessed men and women became themselves again, and all retired to rest.

The above was the first exhibition of the kind that I witnessed, but it was a very trifling affair to what I afterward saw. To enable you to understand these scenes, I must give you, as near as I can, the ideas the Shakers have of the other world. As I gathered from conversations with the Elder, and from his teaching and preaching at the meetings, it is as follows: Heaven is a Shaker Community on a very large scale. Every thing in it is spiritual. Jesus Christ is the head Elder, and Mother Ann the head Eldress. The buildings are large and splendid, being all of white marble. There are large orchards with all kinds of fruit. These are also very large gardens laid out in splendid style, with beautiful rivers flowing through them; but all is spiritual. Outside of this heaven the spirits of the departed wander about on the surface of the earth (which is the Shaker hell), till they are converted to Shakerism. Spirits are sent out from the aforesaid heaven on missionary tours, to preach to the wandering ones until they profess the faith, and then they are admitted into the heavenly Community. . . .

A DAY OF SWEEPING AND SCRUBBING

An order was received from Mother Ann that a day should be set apart for purification. I had no information of this great solemnity until the previous evening, when the Elder announced that to-morrow would be observed as a day for general purification. "The brothers must clean their respective work-shops, by sweeping the walls, and removing every cobweb from the corners and under their work-benches, and wash the floors clean by scrubbing them with sand. By doing this they would remove all the devils and wicked spirits that might be lodging in the different buildings; for where cobwebs and dust were permitted to accumulate, there the evil spirits hide themselves. Mother had sent a message that there were evil spirits lodging about; and she wished them to be removed; and also that those members who had committed any wickedness, should confess it, and thus make both outside and inside clean."

At early dawn next mornng, the work commenced, and clean work was made in every building and room, from the grand hall down to the cow-house. At ten o'clock eight of the brothers, with the Elders at their head, commenced their journey of inspection through every field, garden, house, work-shop and pig-pen, chanting the following rhyme as they passed along:

> Awake from your slumbers, for the Lord of Hosts
>   is going through the land!
> He will sweep, He will clean his Holy Sanctuary!
> Search ye your lamps! read and understand!
> For the Lord of Hosts holds the lamp in his hand!

A REVIVAL IN HADES

During my whole stay with the Shakers a revival was going on among the spirits in the invisible world. Information of it was first received by one of the families in Ohio, through a heavenly messenger. The news of the revival soon spread from Ohio to the families in New York and New England. It was caused as follows: George Washington and most of the Revolutionary fathers had, by some means, got converted, and were sent out on a mission to preach the gospel to the spirits who were wandering in darkness. Many of the wild Indian tribes were sent by them to the different Shaker Communities, to receive instruction in the gospel. One of the tribes came to Watervliet and was "taken in," as I have described.

At one of the Sunday meetings, when the several families were met for worship, one of the brothers declared himself possessed of the spirit of George Washington; and made a speech informing us that Napoleon and all his Generals were present at our meeting, together with many of his own officers, who fought with him in the Revolution. These, as well as many more distinguished personages, were all Shakers in the other world, and had been sent to give information relative to the revival now going on. In a few minutes each of the persons present at the meeting fell to representing some of the great personages alluded to.

This revival commenced when I first went there; and during the four months I remained, much of the members' time was spent in such performances. It appeared to me, that whenever any of the brethren or sisters wanted to have some fun, they got possessed of spirits, and would go to cutting up capers; all of which were tolerated even during the hours of labor, because whatever they chose to do was attributed to the spirits. When they became affected they were conveyed to the Elder's room; and sometimes he would have six or seven of them at once. The sisters who gave vent to their frolicsome feelings were of course attended to by the Eldress. I might occupy great space if I were to go into the details of these spiritual performances; but there was so much similarity in them, that I must ask the reader to let the above suffice.

THE PERFECTIONISTS

JOHN HUMPHREY NOYES
Bible Communism
1848

Noyes incorporated parts of *Bible Communism*, his authoritative work on the Perfectionist faith, in his *History of American Socialisms*.*

CHAPTER I.—*Showing what is properly to be anticipated concerning the coming of the Kingdom of Heaven and its institutions on earth.*

PROPOSITION 1.—The Bible predicts the coming of the Kingdom of Heaven on earth. Dan. 2:44. Isa. 25:6–9.

2.—The administration of the will of God in his kingdom on earth will be the same as the administration of his will in heaven. Matt. 6:10. Eph. 1:10.

3.—In heaven God reigns over body, soul, and estate, without interference from human governments. Dan. 2:44. 1 Cor. 15:24, 25. Isa. 26:13, 14, and 33:22.

4.—The institutions of the Kingdom of Heaven are of such a nature, that the general disclosure of them in the apostolic age would have been inconsistent with the continuance of the institutions of the world through the times of the Gentiles. They were not, therefore, brought out in detail on the surface of the Bible, but were disclosed verbally by Paul and others, to the interior part of the church. 1 Cor. 2:6. 2 Cor. 12:4. John 16:12, 13. Heb. 9:5.

CHAPTER II.—*Showing that Marriage is not an institution of the Kingdom of Heaven, and must give place to Communism.*

PROPOSITION 5.—In the Kingdom of Heaven, the institution of marriage, which assigns the exclusive possession of one woman to one man, does not exist. Matt. 22:23–30.

* Pp. 623–636.

6.—In the Kingdom of Heaven the intimate union of life and interest, which in the world is limited to pairs, extends through the whole body of believers; i.e. complex marriage takes the place of simple. John 17:21. Christ prayed that all believers might be one, even as he and the Father are one. His unity with the Father is defined in the words, "All mine are thine, and all thine are mine." Ver. 10. This perfect community of interests, then, will be the condition of all, when his prayer is answered. The universal unity of the members of Christ is described in the same terms that are used to describe marriage unity. Compare 1 Cor. 12:12–27, with Gen. 2:24. See also 1 Cor. 6:15–17, and Eph. 5:30–32.

7.—The effects of the effusion of the Holy Spirit on the day of Pentecost present a practical commentary on Christ's prayer for the unity of believers, and a sample of the tendency of heavenly influences, which fully confirm the foregoing proposition. "All that believed were together and had all things common; and sold their possessions and goods, and parted them to all, as every man had need." "The multitude of them that believed were of one heart and of one soul; neither said any of them that aught of the things which he possessed was his own; but they had all things common." Acts 2:44, 45, and 4:32. Here is unity like that of the Father and the Son: "All mine thine, and all thine mine."

8.—Admitting that the Community principle of the day of Pentecost, in its actual operation at that time, extended only to material goods, yet we affirm that there is no intrinsic difference between property in persons and property in things; and that the same spirit which abolished exclusiveness in regard to money, would abolish, if circumstances allowed full scope to it, exclusiveness in regard to women and children. Paul expressly places property in women and property in goods in the same category, and speaks of them together, as ready to be abolished by the advent of the Kingdom of Heaven. "The time," says he, "is short; it remaineth that they that have wives be as though they had none; and they that buy as though they possessed not; for the fashion of this world passeth away." 1 Cor. 7:29–31.

9.—The abolishment of appropriation is involved in the very nature of a true relation to Christ in the gospel. This we prove thus: The possessive feeling which expresses itself by the possessive pronoun *mine*, is the same in essence when it relates to persons, as when it relates to money or any other property. Amativeness and acquisitiveness are only different channels of one stream. They converge as we trace them to their source. Grammar will help us to ascertain their common center; for the possessive pronoun *mine* is derived from the personal pronoun *I*; and so the possessive feeling, whether amative or acquisitive, flows from the personal feeling, that is, it is a branch of egotism. Now egotism is abolished by the gospel relation to Christ. The grand mystery of the gospel is vital union with Christ; the merging of self in his life; the extinguishment of the pronoun *I* at the spiritual center. Thus Paul says, "I live, yet not I, but Christ liveth in me." The grand distinction between the Christian and the unbeliever, between heaven and the world, is, that in one reigns the We-spirit, and in the other the I-spirit. From *I* comes *mine*, and from the I-spirit comes exclusive appropriation of money, women, etc. From *we* comes *ours*, and from the We-spirit comes universal community of interests.

10.—The abolishment of exclusiveness is involved in the love-relation required between all believers by the express injunction of Christ and the apostles, and by the whole tenor of the New Testament. "The new commandment is, that we love one another," and that, not by pairs, as in the world, but *en masse*. We are required to love one another fervently. The fashion of the world forbids a man and woman who are otherwise appropriated, to love one another fervently. But if they obey Christ they must do this; and whoever would allow them to do this, and yet would forbid them (on any other ground than that of present expediency), to express their unity, would "strain at a gnat and swallow a camel;" for unity of hearts is as much more important than any external expression of it, as a camel is larger than a gnat.

11.—The abolishment of social restrictions is involved in the antilegality of the gospel. It is incompatible with the state of perfected freedom toward which Paul's gospel of "grace without law" leads, that man should be allowed and required to love in all directions, and yet be forbidden to express love except in one direction. In fact Paul says, with direct reference to sexual intercourse—"All things are lawful for me, but all things are not expedient; all things are lawful for me, but I will not be brought under the power of any;" (1 Cor. 6:12) thus placing the restrictions which were necessary in the transition period on the basis, not of law, but of expediency and the demands of spiritual freedom, and leaving it fairly to be inferred that in the final state, when hostile surroundings and powers of bondage cease, all restrictions also will cease.

12.—The abolishment of the marriage system is involved in Paul's doctrine of the end of ordinances. Marriage is one of the "ordinances of the worldly sanctuary." This is proved by the fact that it has no place in the resurrection. Paul expressly limits it to life in the flesh. Rom. 7:2, 3. The assumption, therefore, that believers are dead to the world by the death of Christ (which authorized the abolishment of Jewish ordinances), legitimately makes an end of marriage. Col. 2:20.

13.—The law of marriage is the same in kind with the Jewish law concerning meats and drinks and holy days, of which Paul said that they were "contrary to us, and were taken out of the way, being nailed to the cross." Col. 2:14. The plea in favor of the worldly social system, that it is not arbitrary, but founded in nature, will not bear investigation. All experience testifies (the theory of the novels to the contrary notwithstanding), that sexual love is not naturally restricted to pairs. Second marriages are contrary to the one-love theory, and yet are often the happiest marriages. Men and women find universally (however the fact may be concealed), that their susceptibility to love is not burnt out by one honey-moon, or satisfied by one lover. On the contrary, the secret history of the human heart will bear out the assertion that it is capable of loving any number of times and any number of persons, and that the more it loves the more it can love. This is the law of nature, thrust out of sight and condemned by common consent, and yet secretly known to all.

14.—The law of marriage "worketh wrath." 1. It provokes to secret adultery, actual or of the heart. 2. It ties together unmatched natures. 3. It sunders matched natures. 4. It gives to sexual appetite only a scanty and monotonous allowance, and so produces the natural vices of poverty, contraction of taste and stinginess or jealousy. 5. It makes no provision for the sexual appetite at the very time when that appetite is the strongest. By the custom of the world, marriage, in the average of cases, takes place at about the age of twenty-four; whereas puberty commences at the age of fourteen. For ten years, therefore, and that in the very flush of life, the sexual appetite is starved. This law of society bears hardest on females, because they have less opportunity of choosing their time of marriage than men. This discrepancy between the marriage system and nature, is one of the principal sources of the peculiar diseases of women, of prostitution, masturbation, and licentiousness in general.

CHAPTER III.—*Showing that death is to be abolished, and that, to this end, there must be a restoration of true relations between the Sexes.*

PROPOSITION 15.—The Kingdom of Heaven is destined to abolish death in this world. Rom. 8:19–25. 1 Cor. 15:24–26. Isa. 25:8.

16.—The abolition of death is to be the last triumph of the Kingdom of Heaven; and the subjection of all other powers to Christ must go before it. 1 Cor. 15:24–26. Isa. 33:22–24.

17.—The restoration of true relations between the sexes is a matter second in importance only to the reconciliation of man to God. The distinction of male and female is that which makes man the image of God, i.e. the image of the Father and the Son. Gen. 1:27. The relation of male and female was the first social relation. Gen. 2:22. It is therefore the root of all other social relations. The derangement of this relation was the first result of the original breach with God. Gen. 3:7; comp. 2:25. Adam and Eve were, at the beginning, in open, fearless, spiritual fellowship, first with God, and secondly, with each other. Their transgression produced two corresponding alienations, viz., first, an alienation from God, indicated by their fear of meeting him and their hiding themselves among the trees of the garden; and secondly, an alienation from each other, indicated by their shame at their nakedness and their hiding themselves from each other by clothing. These were the two great manifestations of original sin—the only manifestations presented to notice in the record of the apostasy. The first thing then to be done, in an attempt to redeem man and reorganize society, is to bring about reconciliation with God; and the second thing is to bring about a true union of the sexes. In other words, religion is the first subject of interest, and sexual morality the second, in the great enterprise of establishing the Kingdom of Heaven on earth. . . .

19.—From what precedes, it is evident that any attempt to revolutionize sexual morality before settlement with God, is out of order. Holiness must go before free love. Bible Communists are not responsible for the proceedings of those who meddle with the sexual question, before they have laid the foundation of true faith and union with God.

20.—Dividing the sexual relation into two branches, the amative and propagative, the amative or love-relation is first in importance, as it is in the order of nature. God made woman because "he saw it was not good for man to be alone;" (Gen. 2:18); i.e., for social, not primarily for propagative, purposes. Eve was called Adam's "help-meet." In the whole of the specific account of the creation of woman, she is regarded as his companion, and her maternal office is not brought into view. Gen. 2:18–25. Amativeness was necessarily the first social affection developed in the garden of Eden. The second commandment of the eternal law of love, "Thou shalt love thy neighbor as thyself," had amativeness for its first channel; for Eve was at first Adam's only neighbor. Propagation and the affections connected with it, did not commence their operation during the period of innocence. After the fall God said to the woman, "I will greatly multiply thy sorrow and thy conception;" from which it is to be inferred that in the original state, conception would have been comparatively infrequent.

21.—The amative part of the sexual relation, separate from the propagative, is eminently favorable to life. It is not a source of life (as some would make it), but it is the first and best distributive of life. Adam and Eve, in their original state, derived their life from God. Gen. 2:7. As God is a dual being, the Father and the Son, and man was made in his image, a dual life passed from God to man. Adam was the channel specially of the life of the Father, and Eve of the life of the Son. Amativeness was the natural agency of the distribution and mutual action of these two forms of life. In this primitive position of the sexes (which is their normal position in Christ), each reflects upon the other the love of God; each excites and develops the divine action in the other.

22.—The propagative part of the sexual relation is in its nature the expensive department. 1. While amativeness keeps the capital stock of life circulating between two, propagation introduces a third partner. 2. The propagative act is a drain on the life of man, and when habitual, produces disease. 3. The infirmities and vital expenses of woman during the long period of pregnancy, waste her constitution. 4. The awful agonies of child-birth heavily tax the life of woman. 5. The cares of the nursing period bear heavily on woman. 6. The cares of both parents, through the period of the childhood of their offspring, are many and burdensome. 7. The labor of man is greatly increased by the necessity of providing for children. A portion of these expenses would undoubtedly have been curtailed, if human nature had remained in its original integrity, and will be, when it is restored. But it is still self-evident that the birth of children, viewed either as a vital or mechanical operation, is in its nature expensive; and the fact that multiplied conception was imposed as a curse, indicates that it was so regarded by the Creator.

CHAPTER IV.—*Showing how the Sexual Function is to be redeemed, and true relations between the sexes restored.*

PROPOSITION 23.—The amative and propagative functions are distinct from each other, and may be separated practically. They are confounded in the world, both in the theories of physiologists and in universal practice. The amative function is regarded merely as a bait to the propagative, and is merged in it. But if amativeness is, as we have seen, the first and noblest of the social affections, and if the propagative part of the sexual relation was originally secondary, and became paramount by the subversion of order in the fall, we are bound to raise the amative office of the sexual organs into a distinct and paramount function. [Here follows a full exposition of the doctrine of self-control or Male Continence, which is an essential part of the Oneida theory, but may properly be omitted in this history.]

CHAPTER V.—*Showing that Shame, instead of being one of the prime virtues, is a part of original Sin and belongs to the Apostasy.*

PROPOSITION 24.—Sexual shame was the consequence of the fall, and is factitious and irrational. Gen. 2:25; compare 3:7. Adam and Eve, while innocent, had no shame; little children have none; other animals have none.

CHAPTER VI.—*Showing the bearings of the preceding views on Socialism, Political Economy, Manners and Customs, etc.*

PROPOSITION 25.—The foregoing principles concerning the sexual relation open the way for Association. 1. They furnish motives. They apply to larger partnerships the same attractions that draw and bind together pairs in the worldly partnership of marriage. A Community home in which each is married to all, and where love is honored and cultivated, will be as much more attractive than an ordinary home, as the Community out-numbers a pair. 2. These principles remove the principal obstructions in the way of Association. There is plenty of tendency to crossing love and adultery, even in the system of isolated households. Association increases this tendency. Amalgamation of interests, frequency of interview, and companionship in labor, inevitably give activity and intensity to the social attractions in which amativeness is the strongest element. The tendency to extra-matrimonial love will be proportioned to the condensation of interests produced by any given form of Association; that is, if the ordinary principles of exclusiveness are preserved, Association will be a worse school of temptation to unlawful love than the world is, in proportion to its social advantages. Love, in the exclusive form, has jealousy for its complement; and jealousy brings on strife and division. Association, therefore, if it retains one-love exclusiveness, contains the seeds of dissolution; and those seeds will be hastened to their harvest by the warmth of associate life. An Association of States with custom-house lines around each is sure to be quarrelsome. The further States in that situation are apart, and the more their interests are isolated, the better. The only way to prevent smuggling and strife in a confederation of contiguous States, is to abolish custom-house lines from the interior, and declare free-trade and free transit, collecting revenues and fostering home products by one custom-house line around the whole. This is the policy of the heavenly system—"that they *all* [not two and two] may be one."

26.—In vital society, strength will be increased and the necessity of labor diminished, till work will become sport, as it would have been in the original Eden state. Gen. 2:15; compare 3:17–19. Labor is sport or drudgery according to the proportion between strength and the work to be done. Work that overtasks a child, is easy to a man. The amount of work remaining the same, if man's strength were doubled, the result would be the same as if the amount of work were diminished one-half. To make labor sport, therefore, we must seek, first, increase of strength, and secondly, diminution of work: or (as in the former problem relating to the curse on woman), first, enlargement of income, and secondly, diminution of expenses. Vital society secures both of these objects. It increases strength, by placing the individual in a vital organization, which is in communication with the source of life, and which distributes and circulates life with the highest activity; and at the same time, by its compound economies, it reduces the work to be done to a minimum.

27.—In vital society labor will become attractive. Loving companionship in labor, and especially the mingling of the sexes, makes labor attractive. The present division of labor between the sexes separates them entirely. The woman keeps house, and the man labors abroad. Instead of this, in vital society men and women will mingle in both of their peculiar departments of work. It will be economically as well as spiritually profitable, to marry them in-doors and out, by day as well as by night. When the partition between the sexes is taken away, and man ceases to make woman a propagative drudge, when love takes the place of shame, and fashion follows nature in dress and business, men and women will be able to mingle in all their employments, as boys and girls mingle in their sports; and then labor will be attractive.

28.—We can now see our way to victory over death. Reconciliation with God opens the way for the reconciliation of the sexes. Reconciliation of the sexes emancipates woman, and opens the way for vital society. Vital society increases strength, diminishes work, and makes labor attractive, thus removing the antecedents of death. First we abolish sin; then shame; then the curse on woman of exhausting child-bearing; then the curse on man of exhausting labor; and so we arrive regularly at the tree of life.

CHAPTER III

THE SECULAR COMMUNITARIANS

Any character, from the best to the worst, from the most ignorant to the most enlightened, may be given to any community, even to the world at large.

ROBERT OWEN,
Essay First, A *New View of Society*, 1813

And here we now are, as near perhaps as we can be in the center of the United States, even, as it were, like the little grain of mustard seed! But with these *Great Truths* before us, with the practices of the social system, as soon as it shall be well understood among us, our principles will, I trust, spread from Community to Community, from State to State, from Continent to Continent, until this system and these *truths* shall overshadow the whole earth, shedding fragrance and abundance, intelligence and happiness, upon all the sons of man.

ROBERT OWEN,
Speech at New Harmony, July 4, 1826

Far away in the distant future I saw a globe resplendent, cultivated and embellished, transformed into the grandest and most beautiful work of art by the combined effort of humanity. I saw upon it a race developed, perfected by the continued influence, generation after generation, of true social institutions; a humanity worthy of that Cosmic Soul of which I instinctively felt it to be a part.

ALBERT BRISBANE,
REDELIA BRISBANE,
Albert Brisbane: A Mental Biography, 1893

Alons en Icarie!

ÉTIENNE CABET, 1847

In 1819 the United States experienced the first economic slump in its history. Industrial production and the price of goods dropped sharply, unemployment rose in the large cities, banks failed by the score, and farmers and businessmen found themselves more deeply in debt than ever. The depression, which had descended very suddenly, provoked a lively debate between long-standing antagonists. On the one hand the Hamiltonian-oriented conservatives argued that to preserve order and prosperity the government must collaborate more closely with the large commercial and banking interests; it must impose higher tariffs, augment the authority of the Bank of the United States, and stimulate native industries. On the other hand the agrarian radicals attributed America's difficulties to the monied aristocracy and to monopolies in general, and favored government policies beneficial to small farmers, small businessmen, and mechanics. Whatever their differences, both the conservatives and the radicals took the rights of property for granted—rights that, they assumed, derived from natural law and preceded society itself. Their essential disagreement turned on the question of how and for whom the property should be distributed.

There was also a third position, which had not been heard before because it lay outside the traditional limits of controversy in America. In 1820 a New York City physician named Cornelius C. Blatchly published an *Essay on Common Wealth*, a brief tract that offered a novel analysis of the prevailing injustice in the country, along with a novel plan to abolish it. The injustice, Blatchly maintained, resulted not from the way property was parcelled out, but from the existence of private property as such. To justify property as a natural right was a fallacy. It was a "gift" conferred by society upon privileged individuals. It could, therefore, be withdrawn at any time to serve the collectivity. This withdrawal, the assertion of society's preeminence over the individual, would, in fact, restore to man the equality he once had had when he roamed the forests and fields in his "unassociated" state of nature. "If men lived in pure and perfect communities, where all things were as they should be," Blatchly wrote, "man's social rights would not *destroy*, as they now do, the natural *rights* he possessed in his wild and unassociated state. . . . And, as men claimed a right in their *natural* and *unassociated* state to *everything around them*; so they should claim, in a pure community, a right to *all around them*."

Blatchly, then, was proposing the establishment of "pure communities," where the good of the collectivity would replace the selfishness and individualism on which property rights rested. To advance that proposal he founded, in 1820, The New York Society for Propagating Communities, for which the *Essay on Common Wealth* was to serve as preface and justification.

Blatchly hoped that "the pious of all denominations," "every religious congregation," would somehow institute "a system of social, equal, and inclusive rights, interests, liberties, and privileges to all real and personal property." Yet he was no religious communitarian. Conversion of "the pious" was to be only the first step toward a universal, trans-denominational reform of man. He conceived "the pure community" as the instrument of moral virtue, not salvation; of material happiness, not spiritual beatitude. How to live the rational life was Blatchly's credo, as it was the credo of every secular communitarian of the nineteenth century.

There were a surprisingly large number of people in America who thought as Blatchly did—surprising because standard histories of the period have ignored them. Some of them were attracted to his Society for Promoting Communities. A few zealots actually sought to create little commonwealths, but nothing came of their efforts. By and large the advocates of secular communities in America were, like Blatchly, intellectuals who lived in cities, mainly New York and Philadelphia. They included a high proportion of European emigrés who had fled the despotism and unreason of the Old World. There were, for example, William Maclure, a pioneer geologist; Charles A. Luesuer, a naturalist; Thomas Say, a zoologist; and three active disciples of Pestalozzi: Marie Frategeot, Phiquepol d'Arusmont, and Joseph Neef. Pestalozzi was the famous Swiss educator whose experimental schools eschewed class distinctions and taught children to learn by doing and to value manual work as highly as abstract knowledge. Educational reform along Pestalozzian lines was the integument that united this heterodox group of foreign-born communitarians. They envisioned pure communities as places where the pursuit of science and learning would replace the pursuit of self-interest, where harmony would replace coercion, where each would obey himself in the act of obeying all.

In his *Essay*, Blatchly omitted to say in his own words just what kind of pure communities he had in mind or how they were to be organized. Instead, he included long excerpts from Robert Owen's *New View of Society*, which had recently come to his attention. It was in Owen's writings that Blatchly found a program of the future most akin to his own. In effect, he and the other communitarians were "Owenites," the first such group to emerge outside of Owen's own little circle in Britain. Though they did not know it at the time, Owen himself would presently come to America to build a pure community.

The force of Owen's ideas could be ascribed in part to his great fame as a man of action and as a reformer. His life was already a legend. In 1781, at the age of ten, he left his home in Wales and began to make his way in the world. It did not take him long to prove that he was a managerial genius. At twenty he was running a huge cotton mill in Manchester. Nine years later he became the director and part-owner of the New Lanark (Scotland) cotton mills, one of the largest factory complexes in the world. As he rose in wealth and position, his passion for reform deepened. Early in his youth he had concluded that religion was the bane of mankind and had come to embrace (as he later described it) "the spirit of universal charity—not for a sect or a party, or for a country or a colour—but for the human race, and with a real and ardent desire to do them good."

The particular object of Owen's charity was the working class poor, whose condition had been deteriorating under industrialism. He was one of the first to be struck by the paradox of "progress": as wealth grew, thanks to the introduction of labor-saving machinery, the lot of labor worsened. At New Lanark, he was in a position to help the working class, or that segment of it that he employed. Turning his managerial genius to humanitarian ends, he transformed a demoralized, run-down, debauched company town into a model community, admired by philanthropic-minded visitors from all over the world. Owen saw to it that the workers enjoyed full employment; health, housing, and sanitary conditions were exemplary; and the children received at least a rudimentary education.

But he was not interested in mere good deeds. He regarded New Lanark as a laboratory for testing his social theories. Adopting the views of the most audacious of the French *philosophes* (e.g., Condillac, LaMettrie, Helvetius, Condorcet), and the English agrarians, best typified by William Godwin, Owen assumed that man's character was shaped by his physical and social environment. If the environment could be mastered, so could one's character, and so therefore could the conditions of one's happiness. How was the environment—and one's self—to be mastered? By science and rationality; in other words, by overcoming religious superstition, caprice, sectarianism, and selfishness. But the discipline of science and rationality had to be inculcated in one's youth; the older generation was after all the product of *its* environment. And so for Owen the logic of reform was incontrovertible: education alone unlocked the door to happiness and self-mastery. The task was to create an environment congenial to such a system of education.*

Owen arrived at the communitarian position slowly under the stress of events. The great depression and civic disorders that swept Britain (amounting almost to a civil war) after 1816 persuaded him that the conventional methods of dealing with poverty and unemployment—namely, the poor laws—were inadequate, viciously punitive, and ultimately self-defeating. He concluded that only the total reformation of society was equal to the enormity of the problem. Accordingly, in 1817 he brought out his plan for the establishment of "Villages of Cooperation," to be financed by the state and by rich philanthropists. He spent thousands of pounds subsidizing publication of his plan in leading newspapers, and before long the entire country was aware of his *New View of Society*.

Owen was typical of the social theorists of the day in his propensity for drawing up very detailed blueprints and charts. His plan left nothing to chance or spontaneity. Each cooperative village was to contain between five hundred and fifteen hundred people. It was to be a mixture—or rather an organic unity—of agriculture and industry, country and city life, private and communal functions. The buildings were to be arranged in the form of a "parallelogram." Each family was to possess its own apartment, though the children over three were to be brought up by the community. The school, the library, the children's quarters, the kitchen and dining hall, the reading room, and the place of worship were to occupy a cluster of buildings in the center of the parallelogram. Work was to be done in another part of the village. The establishment of the first such village, Owen was certain, would announce the era of emancipated humanity. The transition from the old order to the new would be rapid and peaceful. "The only real practical difficulty,"

---

* The logical contradiction here is obvious and goes to the heart of the whole Enlightenment conception of life. If the environment determines character, how is it possible to *begin* the process of reform? How could the chain of environmental cause and characterological effect ever be broken?

he wrote, "will be to restrain men from rushing too precipitately from one to the other." Who would not prefer to live a life of virtue, harmony, freedom, and abundance?

At the same time Owen hastened to emphasize that the purpose of village cooperatives was to produce happy and healthy Englishmen, not outlaws and rebels. He had no intention, that is, of encouraging class conflict. In fact, his plan carefully observed the proprieties of class and status. It called for the creation of four types of villages, each inhabited by a different social stratum: paupers, workers, moderately rich, and extremely rich. And to insure that the distinctions of the outside world were maintained (for a while at least) the prospective villagers were to be classified according to their particular religious and political affiliations. Owen came up with no less than 140 possible combinations, so that, to take an extreme example, a man who was a High Church Anglican and a Tory could not be thrown together with a Dissenter and a liberal Whig. Owen made these concessions to the spirit of privilege, sect, and faction because he felt he had no choice. How else would he receive financial support?

But he failed to win over men of substance, and the government dismissed his scheme. Owen was regarded as a worthy and talented man who had gone eccentric. Apart from a few reformers—Jeremy Bentham and several other philosophical radicals—no one shared his optimism about human nature and the possibilities of education. Many were alienated by his profound and openly expressed opposition to religion. On this matter he offered no concessions. Yet if there was one conviction held by the upper classes of Britain and the rest of Europe (Owen solicited support on the Continent too) it was that religion, as defined by established churches, was the bulwark of social order. They were not about to subscribe to a plan, however humanitarian and well-intentioned, that might undermine their authority. The French Revolution was still fresh in their minds.

When it became clear to him that he was getting nowhere Owen decided to leave "the Old Immoral World" and set up a cooperative colony in the United States, where the people were free, open-minded, and idealistic, where he could begin afresh, with a pure environment, as it were. He had previously shown no apparent interest in the country or its people; his proselyting efforts had been concentrated exclusively in "the Old Immoral World." Thus his decision was not the result of careful research and reflection, but a sudden response to a fortuitous event. In the summer of 1824 he learned that Father George Rapp was offering to sell Harmony, Indiana, with its 20,000 acres of cultivated land, its well-laid streets, its factories, mills, shops, and houses. Here was an opportunity that Owen could not let go by. He saw Harmony as the first of countless village cooperatives in America. In August he provisionally agreed to buy the property for $135,000, and two months later he sailed for the United States.

He arrived in New York City in November and proceeded slowly and circuitously to Indiana. Wherever he stopped en route he received a triumphant welcome, not only from his followers, who looked forward to joining him later on, but from a host of prominent Americans. After signing the contract with Father Rapp, he went on a second tour, which was an even greater triumph. He was now a public celebrity, a subject of constant interest in the press. The crowning moment came in Washington, on February 25, 1825. In the Hall of Representatives, before the chief dignitaries of the country—outgoing President James Monroe, President-elect John Quincy Adams, House Speaker Henry Clay, and numerous Representatives, Senators, Supreme Court Justices, and Cabinet members—Owen spoke at length of his plans for the future and for America. His audience seemed to find nothing odd or reprehensible in his ideas. His principle of communal living did not offend them. They might even have approved of it, for they returned ten days later to hear him a second time.

Owen was not surprised by his reception in America. The people, he assumed, were applauding not him but the ideas he embodied and would soon put into operation. He expected "the New System" to carry everything before it. "The United States," he wrote with customary euphoria,

but particularly the States west of the Alleghany Mountains have been prepared in the most remarkable manner for the New System. The principle of union and cooperation for the promotion of all the virtues and for the creation of wealth is now universally admitted to be superior to the individual selfish system and all seem prepared or are rapidly preparing to give up the latter and adopt the former. In fact the whole of this country is ready to commence a new empire upon the principle of public property and to discard private property and the uncharitable notion that man can form his own character on the foundation and root of all evil. For years past everything seems to have been preparing in an unaccountable and most remarkable manner for my arrival. . . .

No study has been made by scholars of the 900 or so people who crowded into the village of New Harmony (as it was now called) in the spring of 1825. But from available accounts we know that an unusually high number of them were city dwellers who had come for idealistic reasons, and that comparatively few (few, that is compared to the ratio for the country as a whole) were skilled workers and farmers. In other words, Owen admitted individuals and families indiscriminately, without careful screening, and therefore without regard for the requirements of the community. And after taking up residence in New Harmony they waited for an unconscionably long time before being assigned to a work routine. The haphazardness of the experiment in its critical first stage was all the more startling in view of Owen's obsessive theorizing and planning. The contrast between the exigencies of life and the symmetry of the drawing board could not have been more sharply drawn. Owen, however, was unperturbed. He expected difficulties during the period of transition from an individualistic to a communitarian society. That was why he called New Harmony a "half-way house," the "best," he claimed,

> I could procure for those who are going to travel this extraordinary journey with me; and although it is not intended to be our permanent residence, I hope it will be found not a bad traveller's tavern, in which we shall remain only until we can change our old garments, and fully prepare ourselves for the new state of existence into which we hope to enter.

It was while Owen was away (inexplicably, he went to Britain for a long visit just when New Harmony needed him most) that the society began to function with some coherence. It organized frequent public lectures, discussions, sports, and other forms of "amusement," permitted religious meetings of each denomination to take place, sent the children (130 of them) to well-staffed boarding schools, published a fine newspaper, the *New Harmony Gazette,* and established a primitive division of labor. But it was very far from being economically self-sufficient: most of the inhabitants subsisted on funds (about \$1.50 a week each) supplied by Owen. And no equitable standard existed for measuring one's productive capacity against one's withdrawal from the common fund. Nonetheless, Owen was as sanguine as ever when he returned in January 1826. He was impressed by New Harmony's solidarity and high spirits and was confident that the economy would soon right itself. He was especially pleased by the arrival of forty distinguished scientists and educators—freethinkers, reformers, and communitarians all—led by the wealthy geologist, William Maclure. Some of them sought to continue the work that Pestalozzi had begun in Switzerland. Others set about creating an academy of science and manual training. New Harmony was developing into the educational laboratory that Owen had always envisaged.

He was so convinced that New Harmony was successfully launched he suddenly brought the transition period to a close; it had lasted nine months instead of the minimum of two years he had originally prescribed. The people of New Harmony, he decided, no longer needed a half-way house. In its place arose a permanent structure, a "Community of Equality," in which all property was held in common and authority resided in a democratically elected council representing the various community departments (general economy, domestic economy, agriculture, manufacture, education, science, etc.). But it was just when Owen was driving New Harmony toward communism that its fragile structure came apart. Inevitably, the differences of class and status and culture that had been formed by the outside environment asserted themselves; the wonder was that they had not exploded sooner than they did. "Oh, if you could see some of the rough, uncouth creatures here," complained a lady who had come to New Harmony because she was an idealist, "I think you would find it rather hard to look upon them as brothers and sisters." Conflicts appeared between the intellectuals and the manual workers, between the freethinkers and the pious, between the English settlers (a very small minority) and the Americans, between the extreme egalitarians and those who favored a scale of wages corresponding to productivity, and, not least, between Owen and his chief collaborator, William Maclure, who finally built his own school and ran his own sub-community on the premises. With New Harmony riven by hostile factions and his fortune nearly exhausted, Owen gave up the experiment two years after starting it and allowed the settlers to buy or lease the property on generous terms. New Harmony thus became another American hamlet, but its inhabitants did not soon forget what it had once been and stood for.

After abandoning New Harmony, Owen, undaunted as ever, sought to interest the Mexican government in his village cooperative scheme. When this fell through, he shook the dust of the New World from his feet and returned to Britain, to fresh struggles for social reform, fresh triumphs and defeats.

In its brief career New Harmony provided a model of community building for Owenite groups in other parts of the country. Some well-to-do Cincinnatians organized a colony in Yellow Springs, Ohio (the present site of Antioch College), in the summer of 1825. Early the next year a Philadelphia contingent settled in Valley Forge. Meanwhile, a group of New York City free-thinkers and utopians (Cornelius Blatchly was not among them) created an Owenite society in Haverstraw, about thirty miles up the Hudson. Later, most of them emigrated further upstate to participate in another communitarian experiment in Coxsackie. Two other Owenite communities arose in 1826: in Blue Springs, Indiana (near Bloomington), and in Kendal, Ohio (now Massillon). Although all of these colonies had certain obvious advantages over New Harmony—they were quite small and homogeneous, and the settlers knew each other— few lasted more than six months; one (Kendal) held out for as long as three years. Their virtue and high-mindedness were the root of their problem. Even more than New Harmony they attracted middle class idealists, not skilled workers, who could, during good times at least, count on high wages and abundant opportunities. Workers lacked certain options; they could not afford to escape from the toils of the open market.

One Owenite colony deserves special mention—the famous Nashoba Community, in Shelby County, Tennessee. Its founder, Frances Wright, was one of the remarkable women of that era, the forerunner of a whole generation of female reformers in America, none of whom, however, proved to be as much a *femme terrible* as she.

Born in 1795 of a prosperous Scots family she was espousing radical ideas in her youth and writing treatises on morals which brought her to the attention of, among other philosophers, Bentham and the elder Mill. One of her books was an encomiastic description of America, which she wrote following a long stay in the country. LaFayette liked the book, made her acquaintance, and became a close friend—so close that he took her with him when he sailed to the United States in 1824.

Inevitably, she found her way to New Harmony, where she converted to secular communitarianism. For some time she had been thinking about solutions to the slavery problem. Now, thanks to her new-found faith, she came up with one. Briefly, her plan was to settle from 50 to 100 slaves in village cooperatives, where they could, within ten years, earn the price of their freedom by their own labor, and simultaneously acquire the habits of self-reliance. Each colony would be "a school of industry." To the Southern slaveowner she held out the promise of gradual, peaceful, and even profitable manumission. She actually received some help from them—enough, at any rate, to buy fifteen slaves and 2000 acres of land on the Wolf River, near Memphis. When a group of idealistic whites (including her sister) arrived in 1826, Frances Wright began the Nashoba experiment. On its outcome, she felt, rested the hopes of American republicanism.

Her communitarian ideas grew more and more daring. She concluded that family life should be abolished as well as private property, sexual equality guaranteed no less than economic and racial equality. She interpreted the emancipation of mankind to mean desire unleashed and fulfilled. "Let us not teach," she wrote in her "Explanatory Notes" on Nashoba, "that virtue consists in crucifying of the affections and appetites but in their judicious government! Let us not attach ideas of purity to monastic chastity, impossible to man or woman without consequences fraught with evil, nor ideas of vice to connections formed under auspices of kind feeling." To these scandalous words (the "Explanatory Notes" were printed in a Memphis newspaper) was added scandalous behavior. The world learned that the blacks and whites of Nashoba were freely cohabiting. The people of Colby County were outraged by the presence of "one great brothel" in their midst (though sexual intercourse between blacks and whites was not unknown in the slave South).

Nashoba's troubles, however, were not with the public nor with its neighbors; they were economic and self-generated. Its debt had not diminished in the course of a year. Not enough was being produced to pay for upkeep, much less to amortize the capital (i.e., the cost of the slaves). In hopes of salvaging at least some of the experiment, Wright and a group of trustees (among them Owen and LaFayette) whom she had appointed to oversee Nashoba, tried unsuccessfully to replace cooperative labor with a system of private property. The colony lingered on until 1830, when the slaves were packed off to Haiti and the land was sold to the highest bidder. One can dismiss Nashoba as an interesting but grotesquely utopian scheme. Yet it was no more utopian than any of the "realistic" plans for dealing with slavery—such as colonizing the slaves in Liberia—dreamed up by the most responsible and level-headed statesmen of the time.

While the Owenite communities disappeared, the Owenites did not. The upsurge of radical reform, which began in the mid-1820s, gave them a new lease on life. The thrust of reform came from two main directions: from debtor farmers and small entrepreneurs strapped by high interest rates imposed by large banks (in particular, the Bank of the United States); and from working men—actually, skilled craftsmen and nascent manufacturers—threatened by monopolies. Workingmen's parties sprang up first in Philadelphia, then in New York and Boston, and by 1830 in most of the urban centers of the country. "Throughout this vast republic," wrote an Albany newspaper, "the farmers, mechanics and workingmen are assembling . . . to impart to its laws and administration those principles of liberty and equality unfolded in the Declaration of Independence." Specifically, the workingmen wanted a ten hour day, elimination of imprisonment for debt, free public education for their children, and the extension of the voting franchise.

Owen's ideas struck root in this rich soil. In 1826 one Langdon Byllesby, a Philadelphia printer and inventor, wrote a short treatise, *Observations on the Sources and Effects of Unequal Wealth*, which argued for a socialist commonwealth. Like Owen, Byllesby looked forward to a society where men would work few hours and possess "an abundance of all things that the most voluptuous now enjoy." But unlike Owen he thought this state of happiness could be best accomplished if all the producers of wealth united their forces on a national scale, using the existing political system. Byllesby, little known though he was, pointed the way toward a broader, more inclusive conception of socialism based on the economic and class realities of American life.

In 1829 the most vigorous of the workingmen's parties arose in New York City where the Owenite influence was deepest. One faction of the New York Workingmen's Party was led by Thomas Skidmore, a mechanic and journalist, who preached an extreme form of egalitarianism. His long and tedious book, *The Rights of Man to Property!*, kept faith with the agrarian tradition of William Godwin and the later Tom Paine (*vide, Agrarian Justice*) in calling upon the state to expropriate superfluous wealth and re-divide it into equal lots. This peaceful revolutionary upheaval, according to Skidmore, should take place once every generation on the theory that "the earth belonged to the living." Once the wealth was re-distributed the tasks of social and individual regeneration would immediately follow.

Opposing Skidmore in the same party was a group headed by Owen's son, Robert Dale Owen, and Frances Wright. They had recently moved to New York from New Harmony, bringing with them the *New Harmony Gazette,* renamed the *Free Enquirer.* "Fanny" Wright now came into her own as a speaker and purveyor of heterodox ideas. Workers eagerly attended her lengthy exhortations against capitalists and prelates and coercive authority in general. And the more insulting the criticisms levelled at her—"whore of Babylon" and "priestess of Beelzebub" were among the better known epithets—the greater her popularity became. She and Robert Dale Owen felt that Skidmore was damaging the cause of the workingman. While they, too, believed in absolute economic equality, as ex-communitarians they had come to realize that man must be re-educated before society could be revolutionized. They proposed the establishment of state-run boarding schools, cut off from the polluted environment of adult society, where children would learn to live cooperatively, rely exclusively on reason, and prize science and the mechanical arts. In other words, they wanted to graft the New Harmony experience on the stem of a modest reform program that would prove acceptable to the electorate.

These disputes between contending factions of the New York Workingmen's Party quickly burned themselves out. Skidmore died in 1832; the same year Fanny Wright left America (only to return in 1837 and settle down to a rather sedentary married life in Cincinnati); and Robert Dale Owen went off to Indiana, where he later attained some prominence as a Democratic politician. Eventually the Workingmen's Party in New York, as elsewhere, joined the radical Democrats in a common struggle against the Bank of the United States, the creditor class, and the privileged corporations.

And so, at last, the Owenite movement ran its course, leaving only the religious sects to uphold the claims of beneficent society over predatory individualism.

It was the Panic of 1837 and the consequent depression that revived the dormant ideal of secular communitarianism. Although small farmers and unskilled workers suffered most from the breakdown of the economy, the new communitarianism drew its adherents primarily from the educated middle class. Fearful of losing their status, offended by the congenital disorders, the wastefulness, and the inequities to which unrestrained capitalism was prone, actuated by humanitarianism, and vivified by the hope of personal redemption, these concerned members of the middle class embraced the social philosophy of Charles Fourier. Discussions of Fourierism—or Associationism, the name of its American variant—filled the pages of numerous publications in the 1840s. It called forth a passionate response from intellectuals, Unitarian ministers, and idealists of every persuasion. For a season it excited the country as few of the other multitudinous reform movements of the period did.

Hardly anyone in America had heard of Fourier before 1840, the year Albert Brisbane published his *Social Destiny of Man*. This book, which contained some translations of Fourier's writings along with Brisbane's exegesis, marked the beginning of Associationism in America. Brisbane himself might be defined as the prototypical Associationist. Born in 1809 in Batavia, New York—in a district notably receptive to one or another variety of millenarianism—he received a broadly liberal, secular, and humanistic education. His tolerant, well-to-do father encouraged him to pursue the truth wherever it led him and at whatever expense. In the late 1820s, while observing the unspeakable contrast between wealth and poverty in Paris, Brisbane was struck by the fact "that a certain class in society lived on the labor of the masses." To resolve all the questions that this raised in his mind he went to Berlin to study under Hegel. But he was dissatisfied with the great philosopher's answer, as he was with all the others he subsequently encountered in his travels through Europe. One day he happened to look into Charles Fourier's *L'Association Domestique-Agricole*. The scales fell from his eyes and the truth was revealed to him. "Now for the first time," Brisbane later recalled, "I had come across an idea which I had never met before —the idea of *dignifying* and *rendering attractive* the manual labor of mankind; labor hitherto regarded as divine punishment inflicted on man." He hastened to Paris to meet Fourier and study the master's teachings first hand. In 1834 he returned to America as the apostle of a new secular millennial faith.

To Fourier, as to his followers, the quest for justice was at bottom the quest for order and harmony. Fourier's genius lay in his capacity, demonic in its thoroughness, to systematize the world. All things found their exact place in his monumental hierarchy of classification. And they fell into place because they were subject to the cosmic principle of "attraction." Fourier, who did not pretend to modesty, conceived of himself as the only authentic legatee of Newton and Copernicus; he believed that he had consummated their labors. Man, according to Fourier, obeyed the principle of attraction through his 12 "passions." These rose hierarchically on the scale of social values, from the five senses to the more universalizing passions, such as friendship, love, ambition, and paternity. The combinations of these formed an endless number of possibilities, which determined the character of each person. Unlike Owen (whose theories he derided), Fourier asserted that the passions were unalterable. The duty of man was to create a society that would liberate them and so permit human nature to follow its normal course.

His perfect society, the Phalanx or Association, attempted to reconcile apparent opposites: the most rigorous planning and the greatest degree of freedom. His blueprint was similar to Owen's in omitting no detail, in accounting for every contingency. He specified how many people the Phalanx should contain (between 1800 and 2000), how much space it should occupy, how the buildings should be arranged and whom they should house, what vocations should be taken up (agriculture being the primary one), and, most important, of course, how the young should be educated. Fourier saw these rules not as restraints but as the indispensable conditions of a free and passionate life. Only by submitting to them could the inhabitants of the Phalanx act as they pleased, choose their livelihoods—or choose none—read, play, make love—in short, do whatever they desired. Coercion would disappear; so would the parasitism of state and church; so would acquisitiveness and want.

Human nature, then, would shape the organization of the Phalanx. The free play of the passions would lead people to engage spontaneously in the common activities that best suited them. Those who were attracted to animals might form a "Group" of cattle-raisers or a Group of veterinarians each containing from seven to

35 members. Cognate Groups would form a Series (e.g., cattle-raising would be incorporated in the farming Series), the totality of which would constitute the Phalanx as a whole. Within loosely defined limits the members would be encouraged to experiment freely and improvise. The more energetic or passionate they were, the greater the number and variety of Groups and Series they would establish. Fourier hoped the Phalanx would be as diverse, as heterogeneous, as richly textured as possible. But while he abhorred competition as alien to freely felt and expressed passions he opposed common ownership of property. Under his rules of equity—which read like a carefully drafted business contract—each person would be rewarded according to his mode of activity: those who labored with their hands would receive one-twelth more than those who invested capital, and those who invested capital would receive one-twelfth more than those who contributed their talent and intellect. Fourier had no doubt that Phalanxes, once erected, would prove irresistible. He envisioned the time when they would cover the earth, some two million of them, each self-sufficient, each living in perfect concord with the rest.

It was this incandescent hope that Brisbane brought home with him in 1834. But not until 1840, when he published his work on Fourierism, did he find converts. Chief among them was Horace Greeley, the well-known writer, publisher, and defender of radical causes. Greeley went over to the Associationist faith because, like Brisbane, he had become convinced that piecemeal help for the poor resolved nothing and that only the total transformation of society could end poverty and rapacity and restore to labor the full measure of its productivity. The New York *Tribune*, which he founded in 1842, spread the Associationist gospel far and wide. Soon a host of intellectuals recruited from the Brahmin caste—Parke Godwin, John Dwight, William Henry Channing, Charles A. Dana, George Ripley, and others—had joined the movement. They were as active as early Christians and inspired by the same certainty of triumph. To work out a common creed they held a succession of councils; they planned the building of phalanxes, and brought out a plethora of magazines and pamphlets.* They had been swept up by a new revivalism as absolute as any of the grosser messianic movements of the day in promising absolution from evil.

* The titles of some of their publications will suggest the intensity of their optimism: *The Future, The Pathfinder, The Harbinger, The Spirit of the Age, The New Industrial World*, etc.

Associationism appealed to liberal-minded Americans who thirsted for religion even as they rejected established theologies and churches. Associationism forged the link between the eternal and the temporal. Under its dispensation pain and negation would be banished from human affairs. Man would be in harmony with himself, with other men, and with the universe at large. "Our moral aim is the grandest that ever elevated human thought," said Parke Godwin, the most eloquent of the Associationist preachers. "We want the love and wisdom of the Highest to make their daily abode with us; we wish to see all mankind happy and good; we desire to emancipate the human body and the human soul; we long for unity between man and man in true society, between man and nature by the cultivation of the earth, and between man and God, in universal joy and religion."

But in exalting "the Highest" the Associationists kept their distance from the tempests and ephemeralities of everyday life as experienced by common men. To be sure, Brisbane, Godwin, Greeley and the others sympathized with contemporary reform movements; they supported the abolitionists, the trade unions that plumped for a ten-hour day, the advocates of temperance and women's rights. But these worthy ends, they believed, would come about only through the establishment of a network of phalanxes. They opposed the conventional radical strategy of turning the lower classes against the upper, of inciting conflict, of using power to destroy power; they believed that power must be transcended.

In 1842 a handful of Associationists from Brooklyn bought land in the Pennsylvania Poconos, but their phalanx never came to life. A year later, near the same site, a larger and wealthier New York City group, aided by Greeley, formed the Sylvania Association. Soon phalanxes were sprouting like mushrooms across northern United States, from the East Coast to the Mississippi River. For a while the leading Associationists were convinced that their moment had arrived, that "The Social Destiny of Man" was about to be fulfilled. But their celebrations were, to say the least, short-lived. Most of the phalanxes expired in the year of their birth. Of the twenty-eight known to have been created—there were others of which no records were kept—only two lasted as long as five years. One, the North American Phalanx, near Red Bank, New Jersey, held out for twelve years. By the mid-1850s they were all gone, victims of the same malaise: too few people with the capacity for sustained and specialized work, too little capital, and too much reliance on hope, good intentions, and the prophecies of Fourier.

The most famous of the Associationist experiments, Brook Farm, was a case in point. It was founded in 1841 as a religious utopia (the West Roxbury Community), not a Fourierist one. Its mission was to provide a spiritual sanctuary for the radical Unitarians and transcendentalists of the Boston area. Led by such men as George Ripley and William Henry Channing (the nephew of the founder of Unitarianism), the West Roxbury Community grew increasingly secular and universal in its moral philosophy. In 1843 it was renamed the Brook Farm Institute of Agriculture and Education. The purpose of the Institute, said George Ripley, its guiding spirit, was to insure

> a more natural union between intellectual and manual labor than now exists; to combine the thinker and the worker, as far as possible in the same individual; to guarantee the highest mental freedom, by providing all with labor adapted to their tastes and talents, and securing to them the fruits of their industry; to do away with the necessity of menial services by opening the benefits of education and the profits of labor to all; and thus to prepare a society of liberal, intelligent, and cultivated persons, whose relation with each other would permit a more wholesome and simple life than can be led amidst the pressure of our competitive institutions.

By 1845 the Brook Farm Institute had become the Brook Farm Phalanx, and it was professing Fourierism as its official ideology. The example of Brook Farm, Channing claimed, would indoctrinate America "with the principle of associative unity." The nation, "like one man," would "organize into townships upon the basis of perfect justice."

For a time Brook Farm did quite well. Membership rose from thirty to seventy and preparations went on apace to accommodate many more. Occupational Groups and Series were formed according to Fourier's teachings. The work day was short (ten hours in the summer, eight in the winter), and the duties were varied and interesting (especially for those unaccustomed to manual work). During their leisure time the members edified and amused themselves with discussions, readings, lectures, concerts, dances, and visits by distinguished guests. Some of them worked on the *Harbinger,*

Brook Farm's official publication, which was by all accounts the best of the Fourierist journals, and, indeed, one of the best journals of its kind ever put out in America. The school, the pride of the Phalanx, introduced radical changes both in the curriculum and in the method of pedagogy. Students were taught to overcome the invidious distinctions that characterized the outside world: distinctions between class, occupation, and sex, between technical skills on the one hand and the fine arts and the humanities on the other, between thought and action, culture and life.

Even the critics of Brook Farm freely acknowledged its virtues and accomplishments. Hawthorne, who stayed there long enough to gather material for his devastating portraits in *The Blithedale Romance*, honored his youthful dream "of a noble and unselfish life" and looked back nostalgically on his socialist experience.

> Were my former associates now there [Hawthorne wrote]—were there only three or four of those true-hearted men still laboring in the sun—I sometimes fancy that I should direct my world-weary footsteps thitherward, and entreat them to receive me for old friendship's sake. More and more I feel we struck upon what ought to be a truth. Posterity may dig it up and profit by it.

And Emerson, who commented wittily on the concealed materialism of Brook Farm life, had to admit: "what accumulated culture many members owe to it; what mutual pleasures they took of each other! A close union like that in a ship's cabin, of persons in various conditions; clergymen, young collegians, merchants, mechanics, farmers' sons and daughters, with men of rare opportunities and culture."

But Brook Farm was unable to survive a serious crisis and went the way of the other phalanxes. On March 3, 1846, a fire demolished the nearly completed main building, or "phalanstery." Its hopes had rested on this "large unitary edifice" (170 feet long and three stories high) which was expected to attract scores of people and considerable amounts of capital. Further expansion was now out of the question. Demoralization quickly set in, and instead of new members entering Brook Farm the old members began leaving it. Meanwhile long-standing debts had to be paid off. Concluding that the situation was irreparable, the stockholders and creditors of the corporation quietly brought the experiment to a close in 1847.

And so for the second time the apostles of utopian socialism were defeated in their attempt to transform the world by withdrawing from it. Their defeat was implicit in the act itself, their withdrawal from the world only testifying to their dependence on it. Associationism, after all, arose largely in response to a depression. With the return of prosperity in the mid-1840s the movement collapsed. But the cause of the collapse was not economic alone. A radical shift of moral emphasis was taking place in precisely those circles most drawn to communitarian ideals. To them the creation of righteous little communities, admirable in themselves, suddenly seemed trivial when weighed against such life and death questions as the spread of slavery and the disintegration of the country.

The Owenite and Fourierist communities were American movements, though their theories originated in Europe. Icaria, the last of the major secular communities, was different: it was European, specifically French, through and through, in its personnel no less than in its theory. Icaria, then, might more accurately be classified with the religious sects than with the secular communities. It resembled the religious sects even in its longevity, lasting 46 years in the teeth of incredible hardships and suffering and intestine conflict.

The founder of the sect, Étienne Cabet, was as much a prophet as Father Rapp or William Keil. Born in Dijon in 1788, Cabet gave up a successful law practice in his home town to join the underground democrats of the Paris Carbonari Society. In 1834 Louis Philippe exiled him to England. There, after meeting and coming under the influence of Robert Owen, he decided to frame his own ideal society. He studied the writings of the great utopians—Plato, Thomas More, Campanella, Morelly, Mably, as well as Fourier and Owen— and in 1840, a year after his return to France, published his *Voyage en Icarie*, Icar being the eponymous hero of the new order. The fictive Icaria conformed to the classic utopian model: it was communist rather than socialist; property was held in common; equality governed private life as absolutely as it did public; individuals behaved with exemplary virtue, living as they did for the sake of the collectivity rather than for themselves; and censorship of ideas and news was rigorously enforced.

At a time of burgeoning discontent among all classes in France, *Voyage en Icarie* found a large and responsive audience. By the mid-1840s hundreds of thousands of Frenchmen were proclaiming themselves Icarians. In 1847 Cabet finally announced that he would establish an Icarian colony. It was a matter simply of putting an infallible scheme into effect. The response from his followers was immediate and overwhelming, and early the next year he bought a vast tract of land in Texas—enough to hold (on paper) untold thousands of settlers. The land was sold to him, however, on condition that it be occupied at once. Cabet hastily got together an advance guard of sixty-nine adepts who sailed from France on the eve of the February Revolution. They were to take possession of the property; he and the others were to follow in due course.

From the moment they arrived in New Orleans, disaster galled the Icarians every step of the way. After a harrowing 250 mile trek into the interior, they discovered that, for a variety of reasons, no communist community could be planted on the land Cabet had bought. They nonetheless built cabins and cultivated the earth. But the burdens were too onerous, and, their numbers reduced by death and defection, they returned to New Orleans. There they were met by Cabet and several hundred Icarians, a tiny fraction of the number he had expected would accompany him. Instead of claiming the land in Texas, he bought part of Nauvoo, Illinois, from the Mormons, who had recently abandoned it. In March 1849, 260 Icarians took over what once had been a thriving community. At first they throve, too, under a fairly democratic constitution that Cabet drew up (under pressure from the Illinois legislature). However, he himself was becoming more and more crotchety and authoritarian. Soon Icaria was rent into pro- and anti-Cabet factions. In 1856 a majority of his brethren ostracized him. Accompanied by a group of his faithful he left for St. Louis, determined as ever to create the true Icaria. But he died of a stroke only a few days after he arrived. His votaries carried out his wishes and built the community in a suburb of St. Louis. One schism followed another here too, and the second Icaria disintegrated in 1864.

The original Icarians, meanwhile, unable to pay their debts, had moved to the trackless plains of southwest Iowa. There they struggled for years to raise a new colony. Though they did manage to establish a viable—never a prosperous—community, they could not overcome their propensity for factional discord. In time, a split developed between the generations: between the young, who sought reforms that would put the community in closer touch with modern reality, and the old, who refused to surrender the pristine values for which they had endured so much since the 1840s. In 1884 some of the young Icarians broke away and founded a community of their own: Icaria Esperanza, in southern California; it closed down three years later. Icaria proper was now more an old age home than a utopian society. Even so, it kept alive a form of socialism that history had long before consigned to the archives. Icaria was the fragile remains of an extinct species. Its passing in 1895 went practically unnoticed, a minor item in a local Iowa newspaper.

THE OWENITES

*An Essay on Common Wealth**
1822

Hardly anything is known about Blatchly except that he went to
the New York College of Physicians and Surgeons, and that he
organized the New York Society for Propagating Communities. The
excerpts below are taken from a copy in the Columbia University
Rare Books Collection.

. . . Let the uncultivated forests and prairies of western Fredonia
be settled by Moravian, Episcopal, Methodistical, Presbyterian,
and other communities of common stock. What time will be
so suitable as the present? In a century more, these United States
may be replenished with a hundred millions of inhabitants, extending from the Atlantic to the Pacific, and from the Gulf of Mexico
to the Great Lakes. Such communities may *now* purchase the wilds,
and settle together compactly; but this will not always be so. Let
each community be founded on *justice, wisdom,* and *love.* Let
love actuate *wisdom,* and let wisdom regulate *justice* in every thing.
Love, wisdom, and justice are *human,* or *divine*; temporal, or *eternal.*
Where *human* justice is, there is *political* freedom; and where *divine* justice is in dominion, there is *religious* freedom. *Love to our
neighbours* as much as to ourselves, should attach us to *human justice:* and *love to God* with all our hearts and minds should unite us
to *divine justice.* Is it *right,* that men in a *social* state should
possess an *equality of rights, privileges,* and *property,* in an *inclusive*
way? We answer in the affirmative; and that in no systems of government can such an *equality* be produced, unless it be in a community
of wealth and interest; and *there,* only can *liberty* and *equality* exist
in perfection. For *social equality,* and *social liberty,* cannot flourish
in any society, country, or nation, where *exclusive rights* and *prop-*

* Pp. 24–26, 31–32, 35–38.

erty exist. Indeed, *how* can social equality, liberty, and love flourish, where *exclusive* property generates that *root of all evil*, selfhood, or the *spirit* of selfishness, and *"love of money"*? *Exclusive* rights to wealth is the origin of *greedy* avarice, and lustful covetousness. To obtain *exclusive wealth*, and *advantages*, men and women are daily tempted to cheat, counterfeit, swindle, extort, oppress, steal, lie, deceive, rob, and murder. By usury, rents and interest, they feed like drones on the labours of the industrious. To enjoy exclusive advantages, they have *annually* enslaved, and caused the death of about 80,000 blacks from Africa. For these *exclusive* uses, men litigate, declare war, encourage piratical privateering, pillage, massacre, and destruction.

We sincerely believe, we dare assert a paradox, that no man has *a just right*, (though the laws of all governments have granted a *legal right*) to *exclusive* property. To prove this assertion, we must consider *whence* social beings derive *all* they claim *exclusively*. That men would have remained in their *natural* state, unless *civilized* society had been instituted, is a self-evident proposition. In a *state of nature*, man would be in a *worse* condition than the *savages*; and could claim an *exclusive* title to nothing. His state would resemble the beasts of the forests. Hence the inference clearly arises, that all the property which men now possess *exclusively*, has been bestowed on them through the favour of *social laws, privileges, customs* and *advantages*. In other words, that real and personal wealth is derived from, and is the *gift* of society. Joel Barlow says, "Society is the first proprietor, and original cause, of the appropriation of wealth." The *gifts* which society bestows, belonged to her before she *gave* them; and she is religiously obligated to use and bestow her blessings and donations in the most wise, just, equal and social manner;—In other words, the productions and wealth produced by society, should not be *individual, selfish*, and *exclusive property*, but *social* and *common* benefit and wealth. We will illustrate this farther. Man in a natural, solitary and unsocial state, has no exclusive right, though a common right, to every natural thing the woods and waters afford him in his poor, weak, ignorant and timorous condition. And, as the wild beasts would claim, and *share* dominion over the forests with such men in a state of nature, we conclude that men in an unsocial state would suffer, and often perish for the necessaries of life. As soon as men become *social* beings, they acquire *wealth* and *power*, and increase in *wisdom*; so that, in the *most civilized* society, they have become very opulent, potent and erudite. If men lived in pure and perfect communities, where all things were as they should be, man's social rights would not *destroy,* as they now do, the *natural* rights he possessed in his wild and unassociated state; but would *increase, exalt* and *perfect all* his *natural* into *social* rights. And, as men claimed a right in their *natural* and *unassociated* state to *everything around them;* so they should claim, in a pure community, a right to *all around them.* No man by entering into civil government should be abridged of any equitable right of nature. Civil government should extend and enlarge every one of them. Life, liberty and advantages should be inviolate, extended and exalted. This is *true,* and paradoxical. Joel Barlow confirms these sentiments in his advice to privileged orders. ch. 4, p. 76, &c.

A *pure common wealth* would put an end to the vast riches of a *few,* and the miserable indigence of *many. All* would have what Agur prayed for, when he said, *"Give me neither poverty nor riches."* Great *wealth,* as well as *great penury, is a great evil,* and produces luxury, sensuality, dissipation, vanity, pride, cruelty, oppression, hatred, and ruin. A pure common wealth would put an end to the evils and oppressions of crafty rulers; and of lords temporal and of lords spiritual; and of all aristocrats, brokers, bankers, usurers, and knaves. It would terminate the numerous mischiefs framed into laws by crafty, ambitious and selfish men and legislatures; such as tythes, taxes, imposts, (absurdly called duties,) excise, and stamp-acts; things, which unjustly operate so as to make the poorer class of society pay the same price, for the same things, as the opulent, who are a hundred times more able to bear it. The rich and poor, agreeable to Deut. xvi. 17. ought to pay in *proportion* to their *income* and *wealth.* It would put an end to litigation, imprisonment for debt, and debtor's jails; and to pensioners, office-hunters, war and a hireling ministry. Indeed, what present *evils* of association would not cease to scourge us? *Evils,* by which men of opulence, office, learning and power now oppress the poor, weak, ignorant, servile and laborious parts of society; whose industry would, if society did them justice in her institutions and laws, produce them abundance. The monied and governing part of society have done, and still do, all they can to maintain and exalt themselves in affluence and dominion, and in indolence, luxury and grandeur. Their great instruments of effecting these objects are arms, and the exclusive rights of fealties:—interests. rents and banks; monopolies, imposts miscalled *duties*, &c. These enhance their *exclusive* opulence: by these they grind the poor to powder. . . .

We know of but two or three orders of governments among human beings. Inferior animals are governed most generally by instinct, affections, appetites, and passions; but men are associated and governed by, 1st, bestial, 2ndly, human, or 3rdly, divine influences. The government of men in an *unassociated* or *natural state*, is likely to be too similar to inferior animals; but in their *associated states*. their governments may be generally said to be *human* or *divine*. Hence the reason may be seen, why human governments are called in the Scriptures, written by divine inspiration, kingdoms of *this world*; and why the divine government of men is called the kingdom *of God* and our Lord Jesus Christ. Of human governments *despotism* is most *bestial* and *passionate*; and *republicanism* the most *enlightened* and *rational*. Of *divine* governments we have but a few national examples. One was the *theocracy* by Moses, which continued in some purity till the Israelites, preferred and hailed *Saul* as their king. A *divine* government of mortals, as far excels the *human* government of reason and philosophy, as *this* excels a government of *bestial appetites* and *passions*.

Having shown that some things are held in common in *every* state of society, and that the *more* things are possessed in common, the more just and happy the state of society is; and that a community ruled by *divine* influences, is infinitely better than any one that is administered by *human reason* and philosophy; because an infinitely holy, just, and beneficent God, is the author, governor, and preserver of it. We might here conclude this address to your consciences and understanding, by portraying the paradisiacal love, happiness, and harmony, of a truly pious community. Here, a beautiful, enchanting, sublime, and delightful theme presents itself, wherein an orator, expatiating under divine influences, might induce us to engage ardently in promoting pious communities from every religious denomination of people; and cause the forests of nature, and the wilds of society to bloom as gardens: where women would no longer be considered inferior to men, and men would love them as equals; information and learning would abound; the youth would be nursed, and bred with prudence, wisdom, and good associates; civil and religious liberty, justice, and mercy, would cause universal felicity, and God's will would be done on earth as it is in heaven. . . .

[OBJECTIONS ANSWERED]

Obj. 4. The learned, great, rich and potent characters of the world would never descend from their present superior situation and privileges, to be on a *level* with the lowest grade of mankind, to form communities where all would be in similar circumstances, as to wealth, and where they might be hindered in their pursuits of science, honour and dominion.

Ans. The spirit of *self* is too visible in this objection to be mistaken. By nature all mankind are *equal* at their birth, and would continue much on an equality through life, if all human things were what they ought to be. For social rights, privileges and immunities ought to be common, *equal* and *impartial*. If some become superior to others by nature, art, opportunities and virtue, why should they be so *selfish* as to appropriate the advantages of their superiority to their *private* aggrandizement, in preference to *public* utility? *Selfish* love should not absorb *social* love. Men and their talents, whether natural or acquired, should be devoted to the benefit of *all* the world. When men are thus devoted, they are *esteemed*; and when their superior talents are thus applied, they are *honoured*. The *selfish* man, (to wit, the miser, the sensualist, or niggard,) is neither esteemed nor respected, because he prefers *self* to *others*. We should prefer the good of the *world*, to that of our *country*; the good of our *country*, to that of our *families*, and our *family's* good to our *own* benefit. "*Non nascimur nobis ipsis*," i.e. "We were not born to be selfish," was the Roman patriot's maxim; and Jesus Christ commanded to deny self, take up the cross, and follow him: therefore, *self-denial* should be the christian's maxim. If great, potent or learned men are not *good* and *self-denying* men, they are unfit, and would be injurious to our communities. If they were truly virtuous characters, and were convinced, that a theocratical community was a natural paradise on earth, they would find it their duty and delight to descend to a just and common level of liberty and equality of rights and privileges, and assist with their talents and energies to promote peace, love, arts, science and felicity. A well regulated and rightly established community could do more to advance and diffuse useful science and erudition among its male and female members, than *other kinds* of society can now do. Lectures on chymistry, agriculture, mechanism, anatomy, surgery, botany, mineralogy, astronomy, physics, metaphysics, and other useful branches of erudition, would be attended by adults and youth of *both* sexes: females might give lectures to females, as well as men to men. They who assert that *no rich* men would join us, judge and condemn them all, as being selfish and uncharitable. Such a judgment is *illiberal.* We believe many opulent persons of both sexes are benevolent, charitable and bountiful to the poor and needy. We have *seen* their self-denial, and do fully believe them disposed to do whatever reason, revelation and conscience, convince them to be right. They would, in such cases, sell all that *self* possessed, take up the cross that crucifies self, and follow the Lamb of God. All who are *selfish,* whether they be rich men, or nobles on the earth, or very learned men, or ambitious heroes, would surely be out of their favourite element, were they to live in a disinterested community. But all who deny self, whether they be rich, noble, scientific or heroic, would delight to dwell in a self-denying community, where every one is in the habit of denying self, to increase the *good* and *happiness* of others. The learned and virtuous Lord Chief Justice Hale, says, in his discourse for employing the poor, that "They that are rich, are stewards of their wealth; and they that are wise, are stewards of their wisdom, unto that great master of the family of heaven and earth, to whom they must give an account of both; and one of the best accounts they can give of both is, to employ them in the relief and reformation of those that want both or either. 'Am I my brother's keeper?' was the answer of one of the worst of men."

Obj. 5. Communities cannot prosper, some objectors say, because they are without the stimulus of *selfish* and *exclusive* interest, profit and honour, to excite them to industry, science and enterprise. This is advanced as a *strong* objection to any community. But facts disprove their theory. The Shakers are a very ingenious, neat, frugal, almsgiving and diligent people; so are the Harmonists, &c. Moravians are a mild, patient and enterprising people. Ants, bees and beavers live in communities, and manifest unceasing diligence, art and enterprise; then surely we ought to be wise enough to perceive, "that true self-love and social, are the same." Besides this, *social* honour, social interest, and social felicity, are three as powerful motives in characters who are truly patriotic and self-denying, as *selfish* honour, interest and pleasure. Add to these considerations the motives of *piety,* and then we may perceive, that *better, more,* and *greater* excitements to labour, science and duty, exist in a community of pious people, than in any other kind of state. If men of piety did not prosper in communities, bees, ants and beavers would reprove and disgrace them. Melish, in the journal of his travels, describes the happy, pious and flourishing community of the Harmonists. In the present governments which support the principle of *selfishness*, by encouraging *exclusive* titles to honour, profit and wealth, a *few* are very rich, and *many* are very poor. For many poor and suffering persons are necessary in society, to maintain one opulent man, surfeiting himself in the pleasures of this life. "*Riches are a snare*" of Satan; and the rich, like flies, are caught by him, in this his sweetened trap. Wise was the prayer of Agur: "Give me," said he, "neither poverty nor riches: feed me with food convenient for me, lest I be full and deny *thee*, and say, *Who is the Lord*? or lest I be poor and steal, and take the name of my God *in vain*. We do not doubt that Agur would have been delighted in a pious community. Those who are rich, are *generally* the *drones* of the national *hive*. Were we like *bees*, what would become of them? Twelve millions, or three-fourths of the population of Great Britain and Ireland are censused poor and working folks. The industrious and poor part of the society are *really*, though not nominally, in municipal slavery and degradation to the honoured opulent. The poor labour too much; they are contemned; they cannot study the sciences; they mourn under their grievances; they perish under their hardships. What is their stimulus to labour? It is not for the accumulation of wealth, nor honour, nor the comforts of life. *Three-fourths* of mankind are *compelled*, by dire necessity, to drudge and slave for an uncomfortable subsistence. But in a pious and pure community, such *servitude, misery* and oppression could not exist; neither would dronish lordlings. Men and women would labour *diligently*, but not *continually*. They would do so for health, happiness, competence, and a good conscience towards God and man. Part of their daily time would be occupied in the study of useful arts, sciences and literature. Every person should alternately strengthen the *body* by labour, and the *mind* by study. But in governments of *exclusive* property, most of the rich live without healthy bodily labour; and most of the poor and needy live without literary exercise. These views concerning the stimuli to exertion, are sufficient to prove, that men in pure communities, have both *greater* and *better* excitements to be usefully employed in bodily and mental pursuits, than those who live in nations where property is held exclusively, and where the poor have only the lash of necessity to drive them. Besides these things, other stimuli or motives to good conduct might be enumerated, favourable to wise, just and pious associations with common stock. No militant and contending *interests,* for example, existing therein, as must necessarily exist in all governments, where wealth is held *exclusively* by individuals, they would enjoy in a community the loving sympathy and counsel of their brethren. How many unhappy persons, who now fail in their attempts to gain a competency, become disheartened for want of the friendly sympathy and counsel of their neighbours, whose interest, in the present state of society, is too frequently *adverse.* Again; the wise and virtuous smiles and approbation of a virtuous brotherhood of one common good, are stimuli to useful, ingenious, virtuous and noble deeds. Their approving smiles are purer, better, and superior to the *smiles* of a despot, to the *honours* of a monarchy, the *rewards* of a republic, or the *plaudits* of popular meetings. We may exultingly say of pure and pious communities—"Behold how good and how pleasant it is for brethren to dwell together in unity! how like the precious ointment upon the head, that ran down the beard of Aaron, that went down to the skirts of his garments." Ps. 133. Or, in the words of the poet,

> "How pleasant 'tis to see, kindred and friends agree,
>   Each in their proper station move;
> And each fulfill their part, with sympathizing heart,
>   In all the cares of life and love.
>
> "'Tis like the ointment shed on Aaron's sacred head,
>   Divinely rich, divinely sweet,
> The oil thro' all the room diffused a choice perfume,
>   Ran thro' his robes, and blest his feet."

We omit answering all such objections, as falsely presuppose and presume that our intended communities of interest shall be composed of the undevout and irreligious, as well as the pious and good; because their objections have no just reference to our prospects. Permit us to recommend a book called, "A New View of Society," by Robert Owen, belonging to the city library of New York. He justly reprobates the *extreme* degree of *selfishness* which the feudal and exclusive systems of conquerors and bigots have established in Europe; and which, in a high degree still exists to enslave men and minds. He advocates the common good education, character, and happiness of the community, and proves how they are the exaltation and glory of each individual. He has given a sketch of some of the errors and evils arising from the past and present state of society, with an explanation of some of the peculiar advantage to be derived from the arrangement of the unemployed working classes, into agricultural and manufacturing villages of unity and interest, and mutual co-operation.

He proves, by an example of two thousand people or more, of very immoral habits, at Lanark, in Scotland, that communities of interest may be so managed, as to moralize even the *worst* of mankind, and make them happy. His work is a great encouragement for irreligious people to engage heartily in establishing communities for their individual *health, benefit* and *happiness.* We should be greatly gratified to see an American edition of his work in the hands of every philanthropist and politician.

Where is charity's residence more evident, than in a pure common wealth? For there men are *kind,* and envy not; they vaunt not themselves; are not puffed up; do not behave unseemly; no one seeks his own, in a community, but every one promotes the general good. This is charity.

First Discourse on a New System of Society*
1825

This was the speech Owen delivered on February 25th in the Hall
of Representatives, before the President, the President-elect, heads
of departments, members of Congress, etc.

The subject which I shall now endeavor to explain is, without
exception, the most important that can be presented to the human
mind; and, if I have been enabled to take a right view of it, then are
changes at hand greater than all the changes which have hitherto
occurred in the affairs of mankind.

But if, on the contrary, I have been deceived in my ardent, and
earnest, and honest endeavors to discover truth for the benefit of my
fellow-men, then it behoves those distinguished individuals now before me and all, indeed, who are interested in the improvement of
our species, to take the most effectual means to show wherein I am
wrong.

For believing, as I do most conscientiously, that the principles
which I am about to explain are founded in fact, are in unison with
all nature, and are abundantly competent to relieve society from its
errors and evils, I must, while this conviction so remains, adopt every
measure that my faculties and experience can suggest, to enable all
men to receive the same impressions, and to act upon them.

It is, therefore, no light duty that is about to devolve on those
who are to direct the affairs of this extensive Empire. For the time
is come when they will have to decide, whether ignorance and poverty, and disunion and counteraction, and deception and imbecility,
shall continue to inflict their miseries upon its subjects; or whether
affluence and intelligence, and union and good feeling, and the
most open sincerity in all things, shall change the condition of this
population, and give continually increasing prosperity to all the
states, and secure happiness to every individual within them. And

* *New Harmony Gazette*, April 18, 25, May 2, 1827.

this is but a part, and a small part of the responsibility with which they cannot avoid being invested: for it is not merely the ten or twelve millions who are now in these states who will be injured or essentially benefited by their decisions, but their neighbors in the Canadas, in the West Indies, and over the whole continent of South America, will be almost immediately affected by the measures that shall be adopted here. Nor will their responsibility be limited within this new Western world: the influence of their proceedings will speedily operate most powerfully upon the Governments and people of the old world.

If, upon a fair and full examination of the principles which I am to present to you, they shall be found true and most beneficial for practice, those who are appointed to administer the general affairs of the Union, and of the respective states of which it is composed, will have to decide upon the adoption of measures to enable the people of this continent to enjoy the advantages which those principles and practices can secure to them and to their posterity.

And, through long experience, I am prepared to say, that the advantages to be derived from these principles and practices, will be superior to any now possessed by any people, so that, if the Governments of the old world do not gradually alter their institutions, so as to permit the subjects of their respective states to partake of similar benefits, then will the population of the old world come to the new; for, within its limits, from north to south, there is an abundance of capacity to sustain and support, in high comfort, much more than all the present population of the old world. Therefore, the ruler of these states, in coming to a decision on this subject, will have to decide upon the destinies of the human race, both in this and in future generations.

The knowledge which I possess upon this subject has been derived from reading and reflection, from practice, and from personal communication.

To make myself acquainted with the facts to be collected from the past history of our species, I read, in my early life, at least five hours each day, on an average of twenty years. This reading was in English, the only language I have acquired, and I know it but imperfectly.

To ascertain whether the principles which the reading of those facts, and the reflections thereon, produced in my mind were true, and, if true, beneficial for practice, I commenced a series of experiments, which have now continued, without intermission, for nearly thirty-five years.

To make myself quite sure that I could not be deceived in the truth of these principles, in the results of the experiments, or in the advantages to be derived from their universal application to practice, I have employed a considerable portion of each year, of the last twelve, to mix freely with all descriptions of society, and to communicate, in person, confidentially, with the leaders of the various classes, sects, and parties, to be found in my own country, and in the most civilized parts of Europe. I have also, in the same manner, communicated with many strangers, of every rank and condition, who came as visitors from different parts of the world, to examine the results of the experiments which I commenced, more than twenty-five years ago, at New Lanark, in Scotland, where they continue in daily successful progress.

Among these strangers not a few were from this country; for the experiments were made for the benefit of mankind, and they have ever been open to inspection of all my fellow-creatures, from every quarter of the world.

The result of such reading, reflection, experiments, and personal communication, has been to leave an irresistible impression on my mind, that society is in error; that the notions on which all its institutions are founded are not true; that they necessarily generate deception and vice; and that the practices which proceed from them are destructive of the happiness of human life.

The reflections which I was enabled to make upon the facts which the history of our race presented to me, led me to conclude that the great object intended to be attained, by the various institutions of every age and country, was, or ought to be, to secure happiness for the greatest number of human beings. That this object could be obtained only, first, by a proper training and education from birth, of the physical and mental powers of *each* individual; second, by arrangements to enable *each* individual to procure in the best manner at all times, a full supply of those things which are necessary and the most beneficial for human nature; and third, that *all* individuals should be so united and combined in a social system, as to give to each the greatest benefit from society.

These are, *surely*, the great objects of human existence: yet the facts conveyed to us by history, and the experience of the present,

assure us that no arrangements have been formed—that no institutions exist, even to this hour, competent to produce these results.
For, is it not a fact, that, at this moment, ignorance, poverty,
and disunion, pervade the earth? Are not these evils severely felt in
those countries esteemed the most civilized? Do they not now
abound in those nations in which the arts and sciences and general
knowledge, and wealth and political power, have made the most rapid
and extensive progress? Then, permit me to ask, why have these
plain and simple, yet most important objects, not been attained?
Why has so little progress been made in the road to substantial
happiness? My reading and reflection induced me to conclude, that
man continued degraded, and poor, and miserable, because he was
forced, by the prejudices of past time, to remain ignorant of his
own nature, and, in consequence, that he had formed institutions
not in unison, but in opposition to it—and thence proceeded the
conflict between a supposed duty and his nature.

To aid me in discovering whether this conclusion was true or false,
my attention was turned to the examination of facts calculated to
assist in forming a right judgment upon the subject. A steady and
persevering examination of these facts confirmed the early impression made by reading and reflection.

The records of history informed me that human nature had been
governed by force and fraud, and that a general conviction prevailed
that it could not be otherwise controlled with safety or benefit to
itself. Yet, from the most impartial consideration I could give to the
past transactions of mankind, I was obliged to conclude that those
principles of government proceeded from error regarding the real
constitution of human nature.

It seemed to me that a government founded on justice, kindness,
and sincerity, as soon as the world could be induced to admit of
sincerity in its transactions, would be one more suited to human
nature, and much more likely to improve the condition of any
people. To enable me to ascertain the truth or error of these sup-
positions, at the age of eighteen I commenced a series of experiments upon a limited population.

At that period circumstances occurred which placed five hundred
persons—men, women, and children—under my management; and
from that time to this, I have had from 500 to 2,500, the present
number, under my immediate direction.

Without any regard to the previous character of these people, I determined to govern them upon principles of strict justice and impartial kindness.

I wished, also, to have adopted a system of open sincerity with all of them; but the irrational state of their minds, of those around them, and of the public at large, at that period, rendered such a proceeding impracticable, and the attempt to introduce a practice so new and strange to the world, would have destroyed my usefulness.

I was therefore, by the force of circumstances, compelled to reflect much, to speak little, and to practice extensively: and these were my habits during the first twenty years of these experiments. In all that period I did not intrude one sentence upon the world; for I deemed it a duty to make myself quite sure of the truth of all the principles upon which I acted, before I recommended them for the adoption of others.

But, during that period, I had a full opportunity of proving the truth and value of the principles which had governed my conduct.

These principles enabled me to proceed, from one step of success to another, until more was accomplished than the world deemed possible to attain in practice. Many would not believe, on any testimony, that such results could be produced, until they came to examine the facts for themselves; and even then it was with difficulty they admitted the evidence of their own senses, many of them exclaiming with astonishment, "The beings before me do not appear to belong to the human nature I have been accustomed to see, or with which I have previously associated."

They saw a population that had been indolent, dirty, imbecile, and demoralized, to a lamentable extent, who had become actively industrious, cleanly, temperate, and very generally moral, in all their proceedings. They saw the children of these people trained and educated, from two years of age and upwards, without individual reward or punishment; and they had never seen children who were their equals in disposition, habits, manners, intelligence, and kind feelings, or who appeared to enjoy an equal degree of active happiness. Yet this population had been so changed by an unknown and uneducated individual, without fortune and friends, and in opposition to almost every conceivable obstacle that the prejudices derived from ages of ignorance could unite, and while, comparatively, a few only of the circumstances most favorable to their well-being and happiness could be combined for their improvement.

It may now be the wish of many to inquire, Whence this influence? Wherein does its efficacy consist? And by what unheard of means, or magic power, are these beneficial, yet strange results, now brought to pass? I reply, by means the most natural, obvious, and simple, and the knowledge of which we obtain from the facts around us; from facts, too, which have been familiar to man in every stage of his existence, and which, as they are derived from the direct evidence of our senses, no intelligent mind will now dispute. For, is it not a fact, in accordance with the direct evidence of our senses, that infants at birth are ignorant of themselves, and of all things around them? Is it not a fact, that they are unconscious how their senses were formed, or any part of their organization was generated or produced? Is it not a fact, that the senses and organization of no two infants have ever been known to be alike, although all possess the same general principles of human nature; and that no two individuals have ever been made the same, although trained and educated under apparently similar external circumstances? Is it not a fact, that all infants are most powerfully influenced by the general and particular external circumstances which exist around them at birth, and through childhood and youth, to manhood.

Is it not a fact, that these circumstances may be so varied as to give an almost infinite variety of character to any infants, on principles as fixed and certain as those on which any of the sciences are founded; and that, by such varied circumstances, any, or all infants, may be trained to become ignorant or intelligent, cruel or humane, selfish or liberal—a Cannibal or Hindoo—a miserable being—or one whose existence shall be a life of happiness? Is it not a fact, that all infants are capable of being formed by the overwhelming influence of circumstances, acting upon their original individual nature, into any of these characters, provided their physical and mental organization be not imperfect; and that, in such case, as nature has been disturbed in her process, that the beings thus injured, physically or mentally, become objects for compassion and for increased care and kindness, in proportion to their malformation? And is it not a clear and evident deduction from these facts, that those who govern society possess the power, if they knew how to use it, to combine and regulate the circumstances which ought to influence and form the character of every individual of the rising generation? And thus do they possess within themselves the sure means of creating affluence, intelligence, virtue, and happiness, throughout the whole population.

These are living facts, confirmed by the history of every nation and people; and they are in strict accordance with whatever we know from the evidence of our own senses.

And it was in consequence of acting upon the belief in the truth of these facts, that the characters of those placed under my direction were so much changed for the better, and that their condition has been so materially improved.

With a knowledge of these facts, I could not be angry or displeased with any of those placed under my guidance on account of any original personal defects; for to me it was evident they could not have had the slightest influence in producing them. Neither could I be angry or displeased with them, on account of the injuries which they might have received from being surrounded with unfavorable circumstances, over which they could have no control, but which circumstances formed their language, dispositions, habits, sentiments, religion, feelings, and conduct. If these were defective and inferior, they necessarily created in my mind compassion for their misfortunes, and my thoughts were employed in discovering the circumstances which produced these unfavorable effects, and all my efforts were directed to remove them, and to replace them by others having a beneficial tendency. Having discovered that individuals were always formed by the circumstances, whatever they might be which were allowed to exist around them, my practice was to *govern* the circumstances; and thus, by means imperceptible and unknown to the individuals, I formed them, to the extent I could control the circumstances, into what I wished them to become; and in this manner were the beneficial changes effected in the population under my care. In this process I could not be disappointed; for I did not expect any evil to disappear, until I had removed the cause or causes which produced it; nor will evil of any kind ever be excluded from society, until the cause which gives it existence shall be discovered and removed.

Here, then, have we before us the *natural* means by which, on sure grounds, society may be made virtuous, and immediately improved, to an extent that no one can limit; and, by a similar practice, the causes which generate all the inferior motives, and, consequently, actions of man, may be easily withdrawn; and, by the same means, universal charity, benevolence, and kindness, may be made to become the ruling principles in the government of mankind.

With a knowledge of the facts which I have enumerated, relative to the constitution of human nature, the error and childishness of praising and blaming each other, and of devising rewards and punishments, and of applying them, through a gross ignorance of our nature, to particular individuals, must become too obvious to admit of their longer continuance among those who have any real pretensions to rationality.

For what shall we praise or blame each other? Not, surely, for our personal qualifications, which we had no will in forming! Still less for being born within the circle in which Jewish, Christian, Mahomedan, or any other general impressions are, at an early age, forced into our minds! Or do we praise and blame each other because we have come into existence a member of any particular sect, class, or party, in any country within either of these large circles which now so effectually divide man from his fellow-man, and, in consequence, make him one of the most unjust and irrational of all beings? Or shall we praise or blame each other because we have been born of rich or poor, virtuous or vicious parents; or because the more or less favorable circumstances, existing in the place of our birth and training, made the population around us more or less wise or foolish, strong or weak? Or shall we praise or blame each other for any conceivable combination of our personal or acquired advantages or disadvantages?

In this irrational conduct, behold the real cause of almost all the evils that have ever afflicted humanity, save those extraordinary overwhelming dispensations of Providence, which seldom occur, and soon pass away.

Man, through ignorance, has been, hitherto, the tormentor of man.

He is *here*, in a nation deeming itself possessed of more privileges than all other nations, and which pretensions, in many respects, must be admitted to be true. Yet, even *here*, where the laws are the most mild, and consequently the least unjust and irrational, individuals are punished even to death, for actions which are the natural and necessary effects arising from the injurious circumstances which the government and society, to which they belong, unwisely permit to exist; while other individuals are almost as much injured by being as unjustly rewarded for performing actions for which, as soon as they shall become rational beings, they must be conscious they cannot be entitled to a particle of merit.

It is true that, from obvious causes, the great mass of the people, in all countries, have been so trained by the circumstances around them, that they have been forced, unknown to themselves, to receive notions which are opposed to the great and important truths which I have placed before you, and, in consequence, the most lamentable ignorance of human nature universally prevails, and poverty, and injustice, and vice, and misery, at this hour, everywhere superabound.

Vast numbers of men, and more particularly women, in all countries have been forced, from generation to generation, to receive in infancy, as true, various imaginary notions, long prevalent in those countries, and they have been taught that their happiness or misery depended upon their belief or disbelief in the truth of those notions. In various countries, these notions differ materially. In some they are in direct opposition to others, and, as all are trained to think that the notions taught in their own country are so true that it is impossible they can be deceived, and that those in opposition to them are so false that none but the most ignorant and weak will be made to believe in them, and that such false and wicked notions must produce vicious conduct,—every imaginable bad feeling that can be implanted in human nature, is generated and fostered. National, sectarian, and individual antipathies necessarily follow; division and counteraction of every description succeed; and the world is thus forced to become a chaotic scene of confusion, disorder, and misery.

It is so at this moment, and strange to say, it has been made to be so through those original qualities of our nature, which, whenever they shall be rightly directed, and justice shall be done to them, will produce the fullness of charity, and kindness, and sincerity, from each to all, until we shall become, in fact, and in reality, a new people, having but one common interest; and then all the benefits of the world will be freely open to every one, and in consequence, all will be gainers, to an extent that no imagination has been yet trained to be competent to conceive.

The original faculties of our nature, which have been thus abused, are the natural love of truth, and the desire to benefit our fellow-creatures to the greatest possible extent. These are the genuine feelings which *now* actuate the conscientiously religious in all the countries throughout the world. These are the sole motives which animated the *real* religious of all the past times, and which gave an inexpressible pleasure to the dying moments of martyrs of all sects, in every age and country. Why should these inestimable qualities of the human mind be longer abused, and forced to become the instruments of universal discord, confusion, and suffering? Is it wise in those that govern to allow this wretched error to continue?

Are there not men around me, even now, in the actual possession of tenfold more power and influence than are requisite to stem this torrent of error and misdirection of the finest feelings and best faculties of our nature?

I know there are, and I trust they will now manfully and promptly step forward, and place themselves in the gap between the present and the future, and from this Capitol, in their collective capacity say to the world, "Now shall the government of force, and fraud, and disunion cease, and from henceforth, truth, and sincerity, and charity, and kindness, and union, shall take their place, and superstition and prejudice shall no longer have dominion here."

This is the mighty deed that the intelligent part of the population of this country, and the enlightened men among all the nations of the earth, will expect at their hands. And can any position be conceived so important, or, at this moment, so highly to be desired, for the accomplishment of the greatest good to this country and to the world, as that to which the new administration of this empire has been just appointed?

Knowing well the favorable circumstances which, in the most extraordinary manner, have been combined, and are in full force to aid its attainment, I conjure them, on account of their own feelings and reflections, but I conjure them, most particularly in the name of those innumerable beings throughout the world, who are now afflicted with penury and want, with ignorance, and vice, and superstition, with the inferior motives which have been instilled into their minds from infancy, and the consequent misery which they suffer, that they will not allow this inestimable opportunity to escape. If the leading men of these States, forgetting every little and unworthy party and sectarian distinction, will now cordially unite, they may, with ease, break asunder the bonds of ignorance, superstition, and prejudice, and by thus acting they could not fail to dispel error, and to give and secure mental freedom and happiness to the world. To effect this change, the greatest ever yet made in human affairs, no sacrifice on their parts will be neccessary. If they possess, as I trust they do, sufficient moral courage to will this deed, and without delay to express that will openly and decisively to the world, then will mental slavery soon cease every where, and the victory over ignorance and poverty, and sin, and misery will be achieved. Here, fortunately for you and for the future destinies of the human race, no legal power sustains ignorance, error and superstition, and without such support, what chance of success can those have in opposition to the most obvious facts around us?

The Government and Congress of this new empire have only now, as I have previously stated, to will this change, and it will be at once effected; and by such act, they will give and secure liberty, affluence, and happiness, to America and to the world.

I have said, give liberty to America; but the natives of this empire have been taught to believe, that they already possess full liberty. I know it is *not* so; and in proof of this denial, permit me to ask, how many present feel they possess the power to speak their real sentiments, freely and openly, on subjects the most important to themselves and to the wellbeing of society? Until this can be done, and done without any disadvantage whatever to those who do it, liberty has not been attained, and you have yet to work out for yourselves this, the most precious and valuable part of liberty. Many must be now conscious that they are to a great extent under the despotism of weak minds, who are themselves the slaves of superstition and prejudice. Until human beings shall, without any inconvenience whatever, speak openly and frankly the genuine impression of their mind on all subjects, they must be considered to be in a state of mental bondage, and in that condition all men have ever yet been, and to a greater extent perhaps, than you suspect, you are so even now. By a hard struggle you have attained political liberty, but you have yet to acquire real mental liberty, and if you cannot possess yourselves of it, your political liberty will be precarious and of much less value. The attainment of political liberty is, however, a necessary step towards the acquirement of real mental liberty, and as you have obtained the former, I have come here to assist you to secure the latter. For without mental liberty, there can be no sincerity; and without sincerity, devoid of all deception, there can be no real virtue or happiness among mankind.

My desire now is to introduce into these States, and through them to the world at large, a new social system, formed in practice of an entire new combination of circumstances, all of them having a direct moral, intellectual, and beneficial tendency, fully adequate to effect the most important improvements throughout society. This system has been solely derived from the facts relative to our common nature, which I have previously explained.

In this new social arrangement, a much more perfect system of liberty and equality will be introduced than has yet any where existed, or been deemed attainable in practice. Within it there will be no privileged thoughts or belief; every one will be at full liberty to express the genuine impressions which the circumstances around them have made on their minds as well as their own undisguised reflections thereon, and then no motive will exist for deception or insincerity of any kind.

Every one will be instructed in the outline of all the real knowledge which experience has yet discovered. This will be effected on a plan in unison with our nature, and by which the equality of the mental faculties will be rendered more perfect, and by which all will be elevated much above what any can attain under the existing despotism of mind; and by these arrangements the general intellect of society will be enabled to make greater advances in a year, than it has been hitherto allowed to attain in a century. The innumerable and incalculable evils and absurdities which have arisen from the inequality of wealth, will be effectually overcome and avoided throughout all the future. By arrangements, as simple and desirable as they will be beneficial for every one, all will possess, at all times, a full supply of the best of every thing for human nature, as far as present experience on these matters can direct our knowledge.

The degrading and pernicious practices in which we are now trained, of buying cheap and selling dear, will be rendered wholly unnecessary: for, so long as this principle shall govern the transactions of men, nothing really great or noble can be expected from mankind.

The whole trading system is one of deception; one by which each engaged in it is necessarily trained to endeavor to obtain advantages over others, and in which the interest of all is opposed to each, and in consequence, not one can attain the advantages that, under another and a better system might be, with far less labor, and without risk, secured in perpetuity to all.

The consequence of this inferior trading system is to give a very injurious surplus of wealth and power to the few, and to inflict poverty and subjection on the many.

In the new system, union and cooperation will supersede individual interest and the universal counteraction of each other's objects; and, by the change, the powers of one man will obtain for him the advantages of many, and all will become as rich as they will desire. The very imperfect experiments of the Moravians, Shakers and Harmonites, give sure proof of the gigantic superiority of union over division, for the creation of wealth. But these associations have been hitherto subject to many disadvantages, and their progress and success have been materially counteracted by many obstacles which will not exist under a system, founded on a correct knowledge of the constitution of our nature.

We cannot fail to be alive to the superiority of combined over individual efforts, when applied to destroy. We all know the increased power acquired by a small army, united, and acting as one body, over the same number of men acting singly and alone—and if such advantages can be gained by union to destroy, why should it not be applied to our benefit for civil purposes?

The new combinations proposed, will be associations of men possessing real religious and mental liberty, with every means for obtaining great mental acquirements; and these, it is expected, will rapidly increase among all the members.

Under this system, real wealth will be too easily obtained in perpetuity and full security to be much longer valued as it now is by society, for the distinctions which it makes between the poor and rich. For, when the new arrangements shall be regularly organized and completed, a few hours daily, of healthy and desirable employment, chiefly applied to direct modern mechanical and other scientific improvements, will be amply sufficient to create a full supply, at all times, of the best of every thing for every one, and then all things will be valued according to their intrinsic worth, will be used beneficially, and nothing will be wasted or abused. I did expect, before this time, to have received from Europe models, upon a large scale, of these new combinations, and, without which, it is difficult to comprehend that which is so wholly new in principle and practice to you. I have here drawings of some of them; they are, however, upon too small a scale to be seen by the whole assembly, but I shall have pleasure in opening them after the meeting, for the inspection of any parties who may wish to examine them.

Well knowing the great extent of these advantages, my wish now is to give them, in the shortest time, to the greatest number of my fellow creatures, and that the change from the present erroneous practices should be effected, if possible, without injury to a human being.

With this view, I am prepared to commence the system on my own private responsibility, or with partners having the same principles and feelings with myself; or by joint stock companies, under an act of incorporation from the state governments of Indiana and Illinois, in which the new properties which I have purchased, with a view to these establishments, are situated—or, by a general incorporated company, formed of the leading persons in each state, who could easily form arrangements by which the benefit of the system might be obtained, with the least loss of time, by all the inhabitants within each Government, belonging to the Union. Improbable, and impracticable, as I well know it must appear to you, and to the mass of the public, I do not hesitate to state confidently from this chair, from which you have been accustomed to hear so many important truths, that the system which I am about to introduce into your states, is fully competent to form them into countries of palaces, gardens, and pleasure grounds, and, in one generation, to make the inhabitants a race of very superior beings.

When the principles on which this new system is founded, and the practices to which they will necessarily lead, shall be so investigated as to be fully understood, it will be discovered that the present system of society must almost immediately give way before it.

The principles of human nature, on which its morals are founded, will render union and cooperation, to any extent, not only easy, but delightful in practice. The pecuniary effects which will be produced by union and cooperation, will make the division and combinations of labor, in the same persons and interest, complete, and, in consequence, all individual competition must prove unavailing, and cause loss of time and capital.

I am therefore desirous that the knowledge of this change being about to commence, should be speedily known over the Union, that as little capital as possible should be lost by its application to objects which might be rendered of no value by the new measures which may be soon carried into extensive execution in all the States.

Many, who have partially considered this subject, and who are converts to the principles, and fully alive to the benefits to be derived from the practice, are, nevertheless, impressed with the belief that the system can advance but slowly, as other great changes have been effected.

This supposition is very natural; it is in unison with the experience of the past; but their minds have not yet had time to expand to the full extent of this subject, and to discover how different its character is from all former changes. These have been merely an alteration of the mode of acting, while the fundamental principles remained untouched; but, in the present case, there will be an entire change of the fundamental principles on which society has proceeded in all countries, from the earliest period of which we possess knowledge, to the present. Compared with the mighty consequences which must flow from this change, all former revolutions in human affairs scarcely deserve a name.

This is a revolution from a system in which individual reward and punishment has been the universal practice, to one, in which individual reward and punishment will be unpracticed and unknown, except as a grievous error of a past wretched system. On this account, my belief has long been, that, wherever society should be fully prepared to admit of one experiment on the new system, it could not fail to be also prepared to admit the principle from which it has been derived, and to be ready for all the practice which must emanate from the principle; and, in consequence, that the change could not be one of slow progression, but it must take place at once, and make an immediate, and almost instantaneous, revolution in the minds and manners of the society in which it shall be introduced—unless we can imagine that there are human beings who prefer sin and misery to virtue and happiness.

Let the subject be sifted and examined with the most scrutinizing care and caution, and it will prove to be as I have now stated. The truth is, that the great principle on which the new system rests, is directly opposed to that on which old society has been founded; they lead to the same opposition in practice; and there is not the slightest connection between them, nor is it possible they can long exist together. For, whenever these two principles shall be brought into fair and open competition, one or other must speedily prove to be false, and a mere notion of the imagination. The one attributes merit and demerit to belief. The other gives neither merit nor demerit to any belief, because belief has never been under the will or control of man. The one generates in man anger and irritation, because his fellow-man differs from him in sentiments, habits, and feelings. The other instructs how men are necessarily made to differ in color, in language, in habits, in sentiments, in religion, in feeling, and in conduct, and thereby implants in every one the principle of universal charity, benevolence, and kindness, and withdraws all anger from the human constitution. The one separates man from man, individualizing the human race, and thereby creating endless causes of division and opposition of interest and of feeling, and thus generates and fosters all the inferior motives and bad passions and actions which have ever pervaded society. The other forms man at once into a rational being; and, by removing every cause of dislike and jealousy, prepares the most effectual means to unite him with his fellows, and to combine them in one general system of action for their mutual benefit. In short, the one is, in reality, an imaginary notion, which has ever been impressed in infancy on the mind of the human race, in direct opposition to every known fact; a notion derived solely from the ignorance of the darkest ages, and which has so perverted the human faculties, as, with slight exceptions, to keep the whole race of men almost continually involved in war and violence, in direct opposition to the real interest of every individual. While the other is a principle derived from experience, in unison with all facts, past and present—a principle which deprecates all war and violence, and punishment of every kind; which harmonizes every feeling and faculty of the human mind, rendering it rational and humane, and uniting all in one bond of interest and affection. Therefore, between this principle, and this imaginary notion, there can be no resemblance whatever; they must abjure each other—the one being the cause of all happiness to man, the other of all misery; and the time is now come, when the principle of good is about to predominate and reign triumphant over the principle of evil; and when, in consequence, society may be most easily arranged to exist without ignorance or poverty, or vice, or crime, or misery.

It is to effect this change that I am here this night; that, if possible, a mortal blow shall be now given to the fundamental error which, till now, has governed this wretched world, and inflicted unnumbered cruelties and miseries upon its inhabitants. The time has passed, within the present hour, when this subject can be no longer smothered or hidden from the public mind of this country. It must now be open to the most free discussion, and I well know what will be the result.

At this time a match has been applied to a train, that, if I mistake not, will dispel past errors, until old things shall pass away, and all shall become new, and beautiful, and delightful, bringing unnumbered and unlimited blessings to every one. I trust this subject now appears paramount to every other; and that the necessity for a speedy examination of it, by the highest authorities, is equally evident.

Placed as it now is before the public, a day ought not to be lost in stamping it with its proper terms of truth or falsehood. The system now advocated can be of no equivocal character—it must be full of benefit or of evil to you all; I therefore beseech you, for your sakes, and for the public benefit, to ascertain its value, that the people may know whether I have brought them a vision to amuse them, or a substantial blessing. To effect this object, may I be permitted to suggest, competent persons be appointed, under the name of commissioners, or committee, or any other name, to examine the whole subject, a mere outline of which, in this discourse, has been hastily and slightly sketched. That, after such examination, the parties appointed to investigate, make a report for the satisfaction of the public, whose interests are so deeply involved in the result.

In what has been said I have endeavored to show, that the subject I have introduced, is the most important that can engage the attention of mankind; that the cause of all past and present evil in society is the notion that there can be merit or demerit in any belief whatever; that this error generates all the bad passions, keeps them in perpetual activity, produces nothing but unhappiness to the human race; and that, while it shall be allowed to irrationalize each succeeding generation, sin and misery must have dominion over the world.

I have stated, also, that by the undeviating constitution of our common nature, each individual has hitherto been formed by the circumstances which have been allowed to exist around him from birth to manhood; that these circumstances have been uniformly opposed to our constitution, and, consequently, of a very injurious character, producing only various degrees of vice and misery. I afterwards explained what appeared to me to be the real constitution of our nature and state; that, when circumstances shall be judiciously combined by those who have acquired an accurate knowledge of it, that each individual of our species, without a single exception, may be trained to become virtuous, intelligent, and happy, to a degree much exceeding what has been experienced under the old system of society in any part of the world: and thus far only time allows me to proceed on the present occasion.

That which requires yet to be explained, to enable the public to form a right judgment of the entire system now advocated, is a detail of the circumstances which, in combination, are to possess sufficient power to produce the extraordinary results which I have promised, and a development of the means by which, without injury to anyone, they can be carried without delay into national and general practice, so as to give, almost immediately, many of the benefits of the change to the whole population of the Union, by relieving them from poverty or the fear of it, and very soon, from ignorance, and all the lamentable effects which these two evils necessarily produce.

FRANCES WRIGHT

Statement on Nashoba*
1826

Frances Wright appended this statement to a deed giving control
of Nashoba to a group of trustees, among them Owen and Lafayette.

In attempting an institution in the United States, for the benefit
of the negro race, I was fully aware that much assistance would
be necessary, before any thing of importance could be effected.

To secure a title to this assistance, I have ever felt it requisite,
that some guarantee should be given to the public, not merely
for the sincerity of my intentions, but for my probable chance of
success.

The mode that most naturally present itself, on the first view of
the subject, is to place the institution, by some legal arrangement,
under the management of some public body; and to appoint
trustees subject to the control of that body. The objections to this
mode, are, I conceive, substantial. There is no public body, with
which I am acquainted, that is not, and must not of necessity
be, by the political constitutions of the country, a representative
of the feelings of a majority of the nation. In these feelings, as
regards the object I have in view, the benefit of the negro race,
no reflecting individual can or ought to repose confidence. Every
part of the United States feels, more or less, the contamination of
slavery. The negro race is every where, more or less, held, by a
great majority of the population, in contempt and suspicion. Its
very color is an object of disgust. And in the speeches and votes
of congress, we find an evidence, that the most northern sections
of the country harbour prejudices, equal in strength to those of the
extreme south.

Next to the national securities, apparently offered by the legislatures and official characters of the states, some more private
associations or bodies seem to present themselves; such as the

* *New Harmony Gazette*, February 21, 1827.

emancipation and colonization societies. In the former of these, I could alone suppose any real sympathy of feeling; as, however excellent the intentions of many members of the colonization societies, I cannot but consider the essence of the institution to be favorable to slavery; as they tend,—rather to relieve the slaveholders from some of those inconveniences which might force them to abandon their system,—than to effect a change in that system itself. The names of many of the Presidents and Directors of these societies will sufficiently bear testimony to the justice of this observation.

In the members of the emancipating societies, I acknowledge with pleasure, the real friends of the liberty of man. And my only reason for not placing this property in some way or other, under their control, is that I conceive their views, respecting the moral instruction of human beings, to differ, essentially, from my own. This moral instruction I hold to be of even greater importance, than the simple enfranchisements from bodily slavery; inasmuch as the liberty of the mind, and the just training of the thoughts and feelings, can alone constitute a free man, and a useful member of society.

My enquiries and observations have led me to believe, that the benevolence of the societies alluded to, is based on, or connected with, peculiar tenets of religion; and that the management of any individuals, who should not take these for their guide, would naturally be disapproved, and probably interrupted.

Let nothing unfriendly be found in these observations. I respect and esteem the intentions of the societies spoken of, and only differ from them in opinion. This difference of opinion, however, we both agree in considering of the first importance.

There being, thus, two objects to be attained, the giving some guarantee to the public, that the institution will not be perverted to the private interest of an individual,—and the possessing some security for myself and friends, that such guarantee will not endanger our ultimate views of moral regeneration—it has been felt necessary to have recourse to sureties of a still more private nature, which alone seem to embrace the desired objects. Let us place trust and responsibility where we will, we must still place it in men; and our security must ever principally rest on a belief in their integrity, and a knowledge of their feelings and opinions. In consequence, I have made choice of a certain number of individuals in whom, and, failing them, in others, chosen as before mentioned, the possession and management of this property, in trust for a certain object, is vested.

I am fully aware that by this expression of sentiments, different from those commonly received in the world, the institution will forfeit much assistance which it might otherwise obtain. But I hold a plain expression of opinion to be not only a right, but a duty, and that in the exercise of this duty, every individual not only best consults his own dignity, but renders the most important of all services to mankind.

Emancipation based on religion, has hitherto effected but little; and, generally speaking, has by the tone and arguments employed, tended rather to irritate than convince.

In facing the subject of slavery, it is necessary to bear in mind, the position of the master, equally with that of the slave;—bred in the prejudices of color and authority; untaught to labor, and viewing it as a degradation. We should consider, that what we view, at first sight, as a peculiar vice and injustice, is not more so, in fact, than any other vice, and injustice, stamped by education on the minds and hearts of other men. We must come to the slaveholders, therefore, not in anger, but in kindness, and when we ask him to change his whole mode of life, we must shew him the means by which he may do so, without the complete compromise of his ease and of his interests. There are comparatively few holders of slaves, who will not admit in argument the worst evils of the system, more particularly the idleness, violent passions, and profligacy, it but too generally fixes on their children. But, they will say what can we do; we are unfit for labor, and are dependent, for our very subsistence, on the labor of the negro.

Let us then, propose to them to unite their property, to pursue such occupations as their previous habits may bend to, and to continue to impose the harder tasks of labor, during their lives or necessities, upon the present generation of slaves; conferring such an education on the children of their slaves, as shall fit them for the station of a free people. Let them, at the same time, train their own children in the habits worthy of free men; rendering them independent of the labor of others, by a complete and practical education, that shall strengthen the body equally with the mind, render just and amiable the opinions and feelings, and introduce at once, in a new generation, that complete equality of habits and knowledge, alone consistent with the political institutions of the country.

In this place, the trustees will be found ready to enter into such terms with the owners of slaves, as shall forward the object above specified. It must be understood, however, that here is no invitation to the slaveholder in feeling and obstinate habit. None can be received, who do not come with the feeling of good will to all men; and who, regretting the prejudices of their own education, shall not desire, for their children, one of a completely opposite character. No difference will be made in the schools between the white children, and the children of color, whether in education or any other advantage.

What degree of assistance, this infant institution may receive, must depend on the amount of sympathy, scattered throughout the world, with the views and feelings expressed in this paper.

To those acknowledging such sympathy, the paper is addressed. Those who have money or other property will bring it; they who have only their arms or their heads will bring them.

To secure this assistance cheerfully and lastingly, it is necessary that the independence of every individual should be secured, beyond the possibility of interruption. Without such security, human exertions must be feeble, and human happiness incomplete. Perfect independence, and entire exemption from all anxiety respecting the future, both as regards the parents themselves, and their children, it is one of the objects of this deed to ensure.

Therefore it is, that so many difficulties are thrown in the way of the *admission* of members. Were a system of prevention followed instead of punishment, laws would be unnecessary. And in all the transactions of life, the only effective precautions seem to be those, which provide against the occurrence of evil, not those which attempt provisions for remedying the evil when it has occurred.

It will be seen that this establishment is founded on the principle of community of property and labor; presenting every advantage to those desirous, not of accumulating money, but of enjoying life, and rendering services to their fellow-creatures;—these fellow-creatures, that is, the blacks here admitted, requiting these services, by services equal or greater, by filling occupations, which their habits render easy, and which, to their guides and assistants, might be difficult, or unpleasing. No life of idleness, however, is proposed to the whites. Those who cannot work, must give an equivalent in property. Gardening or other cultivation of the soil, useful trades practised in the society, or taught in the school; the teaching of every branch of knowledge; tending the children; and nursing the sick—will present a choice of employments sufficiently extensive.

Labor is wealth; its reward should be enjoyment. Those, who feel and admit this truth will see that it needs not to be rich, in the now received sense of the word, to contribute towards the building up of an institution, which, however small in its infancy, may be made, with their cooperation, to open the way to a great national reform. Deeds are better than words. After all that has been said, let something be at least attempted. An experiment, that has such an end in view, is surely worth the trial.

To the friends of man, and their country; to the respecters of the institutions of this republic; to all imbibed with liberal principles; to all who wish, and believe in the possibility of the improvement of man; to all, in short, who sympathise in the sentiments expressed in this paper,—this appeal is made. Let us, then, come forward. Let us dare, to express our feelings, and to act in accordance with them. Let us view, in a spirit of kindness, the prejudices, as well as the misfortunes, of our fellow-beings; remembering that prejudice is not a crime, but an evil entailed by education, and strengthened by habit. Witness my hand and seal this 17th December, 1826.

LANGDON BYLLESBY
Observations on the Sources and
Effects of Unequal Wealth*
1827

About Byllesby all we know is that he was a self-taught printer and inventor (he had written a satire defending patents), and that he eventually became a rather successful Philadelphia businessman.

The "Sage of Monticello" has put it on record, in a shape that will not speedily be obliterated, "that mankind are most disposed to suffer, while evils are sufferable, than to right themselves by abolishing the forms to which they are accustomed." How near or how distant the verity of this dogma may place the remedy of the evils of unequal wealth which it has herein been attempted to array and expose, remains to be seen; and, perhaps, a conclusion could only be obtained by determining the point to which these evils will *continue sufferable*, and this must be one of two cases; either,

First, When the evils result in general distresses, that cannot be resisted or repaired under the existing forms; or,

Second, When the conviction becomes general that such distresses *must* ensue, unless the existing forms are abolished and replaced by better kinds.

Reform, under the first circumstances, is mostly accompanied with violence and disorder, owing to the distress coming, partially, by surprise, and the urgency for relief not being able to brook the delay necessary for digesting the plans which are abundantly suggested for obtaining it, or to overcome the interests that may be adverse to reform. In the second case, the same wisdom and foresight that perceives the approaching dilemma, deliberately provides its remedy, and avoids the worst by timely stepping out of its course into the newly prepared forms.

However, whatever amelioration in this matter takes place, there

* Pp. 97–98, 102–112, 116–119, 129.

can be no fear but that it will proceed in the latter manner; for ages of experience, and abundance in late years, demonstrate, that though violence may change the operation of oppressive circumstances, yet the very means of violence plant anew the seeds from which it must again spring up and grow with renewed vigour. But there is good reason to believe that the germ of peaceful reform has already sprouted, and will in good time shower its fruit around us. . . .

What will be the precise features of a system that shall supplant the existing systems of unequal wealth and individual privation, will probably require some experiment to disclose; yet, with the aid of the light shed on it by that distinguished philanthropist, Mr. Robert Owen, and his coadjutors, we may venture to say, the most prominent ones will certainly be,—

First, Such an arrangement as will secure to the producer the full products and control of the fruits of his labour, from the incipience to their consumption.

Second, That all exchanges of products will be based on principles of reciprocity, or equal quanties of labour for other equal quantities.

Third, That no one consume the products of labour without yielding exact compensation therefor, in some shape or other, unless incapacitated; and,

Fourth, The consequent evasion of those uses of money from which it has been customary to derive interest.

It has not yet been demonstrated, that a perfect community, or state of *measured equality,* can permanently exist, even when its objects are confined to the pursuit of the arts of life alone; but that they are not likely to when enthralled by any extraneous observances or pre-requisites has already been assumed and argued. Indeed, there seems to be something in the human disposition or temper that revolts at the idea of a *pure* community, as well as an intermixture of injustice in their practice, which it is difficult to reconcile with the common notions of the "rights of things." If it could so happen that some persons should be born with *four* eyes, and the perfect use thereof, they would have as just a right to see all that they qualified them to see, as they who are born with only *two.* So also it would seem if natural strength, acquired dexterity, or more vivid intellect, enabled one to ply his labour with such effect as to produce a greater quantity than another; he would have as fair a right to the larger as the other to the lesser quantity, provided such superiority be not used to the depression of another; and, altogether, extended capacity admits of extended enjoyments; and it has a right to such enjoyments, so far as it fabricates them for itself in conformity to the general good. But, that something approaching the nature of a community, or, more properly, an association for securing equal advantages, could be made to procure those results for every department of Productive Industry, the elucidations of the subject by the experiments and disquisitions of Mr. Owen and others already adverted to, leave no room to doubt; and, with modifications suited to each particular kind, would be easily put to practice; though it cannot be said that more than the fundamental principles have yet been laid out, and they must depend much on experience for their perfection.

Nevertheless, whatever be the power of such establishments as they have projected to effect general comfort and happiness, by equalizing interests throughout both agricultural and manufacturing affairs, and in the efficiency of which we have the most implicit belief, yet we do not perceive how the means they propose, to wit, the erection of limited and independent villages, comprising a variety of concerns, are to include the immense and important interests, with valuable uses, embraced in the composition of large cities, in which an equalization of advantages, in order to obtain the same benefits, is full as desirable as in other situations. However, we believe it practicable to come at a similar result by the most feasible means, and at the same time preserve from desolation, by turning to account, the stupendous quantity of the products of labour which are there bestowed in the variety of buildings accommodated to the present systems of inequality and deprivation, in conjunction with maintaining, and confining the precious metals to their legitimate and happy uses, in the form of a circulating representative of labour performed, or wealth actually produced; for which purposes the felicity of the contrivance seems to fall little short of divine inspiration, apart from its profanation and abuse to the devices of injustice and oppression, through the operations of unfair profits, usury, and stock institutions. We will therefore refer, for the merits of the propositions for the former purpose, to the plans themselves, introduced in an appendix to this book, under the title of Practical Illustrations, and proceed to offer some ideas towards the latter object.

The term Equality, unfortunately, from its association with other words of similar force and value in recent transactions that have left recollections of horror on men's minds, ever comes before them with suspicious aspect; and when plans for equalizing the condition of mankind are spoken of, the unreflecting, measuring things to be with things that were, accompany them with apprehensions of commotion, disorder, irreligion, rapine, and destruction; when, at the same time, they are as foreign to its establishment, as is *unequal wealth* to that of sound morality, strict honesty, and unaffected piety. The establishment of forms that shall effect a system of equal advantages, would, in their very progress, offer additional security against irruptions on any man's property, and never cost either the wealthy or needy the contribution of a single cent which they did not cheerfully give, however it might, by its peaceful operations, interfere with the revenues of a few of the former class, though the circumstances of nineteen twentieths of society would be vastly improved. But in order to obtain this result, it is proper that all distinctly first understand the origin of the insecurity and inconveniences with which they are burdened, and then unite in concert of action to cultivate the means of relief, for which there are multitudes of *imperfect* models around them. Small capitalists have discernment enough to join, in companies of greater or less numbers, to give effect to their operations; and the greater ones have sufficient ingenuity to combine their wealth for a mutual profitable investment, in the shape of stock, for the erection of some institution, as a bank, insurance office, or other establishment professing to be a public benefit, and, by their processes, contrive to forward and uphold each other in the advantages they have become possessed of, until the insecurity inseparable from the dishonesty of the present systems, may happen to prostrate them. Now, it wants nothing more than the institution of associations on almost the identical principles of any of those, to complete the object; except that instead of *money* composing the stock, it should consist of the *productive labour* of its members, properly adjusted and applied; and a short course of discreet application would demonstrate to every man that the ability to perform the manipulations and labour of any handicraft or art, in connection with the assistances that ingenuity has already devised, would be of similar value to him as the dividend on a capital of many tens of thousand dollars, under the prevailing forms.

This character and nature of such an institution would, perhaps, be best expressed by a title like this,—"Association for Securing Equal (or Mutual) Advantages, (or Interests)," preceded by the appelation of such particular kind of mechanics, or other departments of industry who adopt it; the objects and operation of which will be best illustrated by an outline of some articles proper for organizing an association of the kind contemplated, and which might, with alterations to suit circumstances, be found applicable to every branch of productive industry, and even commercial and maritime pursuits. However, to display it more familiarly, we will adapt it generally to mechanical businesses of *permanent location* as they are commonly practised in cities, by the following

EXEMPLIFICATION

We, whose names are hereunto annexed, in order and with intent to secure to ourselves the full profits and benefits of our labour and application, as also to escape the inconvenience and distress of unsteady employment, arising from the practices and arts of competition, or from the caprice of those who have obtained the management and control of the exercise of our craft; and further, with an intention to equalise the value of labour when devoted to the production of different articles of necessity or convenience, and also to avail ourselves of such devices to relieve our toil, and increase our ease, as our craft has been, or from time to time may be found susceptible, Resolve, to unite and organize ourselves into a co-operative body, under the title of "The ——'s Association of Mutual Advantages, of the city of ——;" to pursue which objects, severally and collectively,—

We do agree, To advance, in shares of —— dollars* each. the sum of —— dollars, to be appropriated to the providing of such buildings, and the purchase of such materials, as will be necessary for the prosecution and exercise of our craft, and to appoint certain

* It will readily occur to all that these shares should be of as diminutive an amount as the carrying of their views into effect will possibly admit, in order to open the prospect to the greatest number; for many artisans are so circumscribed in their means that a small amount presses them hard. In many mechanical trades, perhaps 30 or 40 dollars per member would be sufficient.

of our number, whose abilities may be competent, to apportion the work and superintend the sales of our products.

We do agree, That no other requisite shall be necessary for admission to this association, than being a reasonably good workman, and paying the amount of a share into the general stock. But, if an applicant be not a competent workman, he shall submit himself to the instruction of a member who is, on such terms as they can accommodate, until he may be so acknowledged.

We do agree, That while we freely admit to the advantages of this association all whose handicraft and wishes accord with ours, we will likewise unreservedly discard all whose conduct may tend to injure or dishonour its character and views, after due admonition and notice.

We do agree, That every member, so far as practicable, shall be supplied with that kind of work at which he is most expert, or that may be most agreeable; and to arrange compensation in such order as will best equalize the avails of equal dexterity and industry.

We do agree, So to divide what work is to be done, that all may have an equal chance to receive a fair share of the profits; provided that in no case work shall be retarded on account of the negligence or indolence of any one to whom it may be apportioned.

The foregoing, it is believed, will be found to contain the *fundamental* principles for an association that would have the power of securing to its members the products of their labour, though some variations and numerous additions would be required to suit it to every kind of manufacture, as the circumstances of each have need, particularly in the case of builders, comprising masons, carpenters, &c. But all mechanics, traffickers, mariners, and others, will have no great difficulty in perceiving by what modifications it might be made applicable to their condition and pursuits.

It will readily occur to any who consider of the project, that the amount of capital for erecting such an institution should be confined within as moderate bounds as possible, as well as being divided into shares of a very small compass, in order that the whole trade may be enabled to fall in; for, the more nearly the whole are embraced, the more decisive and certain will be its success, and the necessity for the remainder acceding, as also their ability to contend with competition from without. If an association comprise the whole of the workmen of a particular species of manufacture in a certain locality, the bone and muscle of it belongs to that association; therefore, an individual who might persist in maintaining an exclusive establishment could only supply it with his own labour; but, as the attendant burdens of rent, &c. would be proportionably greater, he would persevere to disadvantage, if not finally sink. It can likewise scarcely escape notice, that the establishment of such associations would relieve its members and their business from the oppressive charges for rents, in situations where the artificial circumstances of the existing systems have rendered the position more valuable; for any location within a convenient distance of the centre of consumption would answer equally well, there being no attraction to particular places by competitors, all being involved in this establishment. Hence, in proportion as similar institutions should be adopted by other manufacturers whose accommodation would be equally untrammelled by arbitrary location, the inequality of wealth arising from disparity in the value of houses and position, would at once fall to the ground; for while the principles of such institutions should be conformed to and persevered in, none could have any superiority over others: and the immense sums yearly extracted from the labour of mechanics, in the form of rents, would be saved them; for the high rate of the value of property in cities, or rather in particular parts of cities, arises wholly from the artificial circumstances attending the existing systems of competition and exclusion, in the production of necessaries and conveniences, and distributing them by the agency of extensive capital. But under a system of equalization they would descend to a value corresponding with the labour expended in their erection, except occasionally some little advance on account of the preferences for a city, or superior situation for domestic enjoyments or other satisfactions. . . .

What the average result would be as to the extent of the means of comfort and enjoyment which each individual would possess in the event of a general change of systems, cannot yet be distinctly determined: but there is sufficient data to warrant the assertion that each can have abundance, with ample leisure to enjoy it: and though some may, possibly, have greater affluence (if the term will apply,) than others, yet *poverty* would become an obsolete word.

THOMAS SKIDMORE
The Rights of Man to Property!*
1829

Skidmore was a leader of the radical or agrarian wing of the New
York Workingmen's Party. The full title of his book suggests the
burden of his argument: *The Rights of Man to Property! Being
a Proposition to Make it Equal Among the Adults of the Present
Generation: and to Provide its Equal Transmission to Every Individual of Each Succeeding Generation on Arriving at the Age of
Maturity.*

The principle which the first of all governments in any country,
and, indeed, every succeeding government, should adopt and prac-
tise, is this. In dividing that which is the equal and common
property of all, the apportionments should be equal; and if it is
concluded, as it will be, where men understand how best to pursue
their own happiness, that a life-lease of property is better than any
other, that will be the term preferred to every other. Then will
every one understand that he has full liberty to use the materials
of which, during his life-time, he is the master, in such a manner
as, in his judgment, shall promote his own happiness. He will
understand, too, that if the use which he shall make of them, shall
be such as to meet the approbation of those who come after him,
they will be disposed to follow his example; but if not, that still
the successor has a right to make such other use of the same, as
to him shall seem good, with the knowledge that every other person
coming after him, too, will be equally free. Society, thus organized,
gives notice to all its members, that they are to use their own industry, with a view to their own happiness; and cannot be allowed,
on any pretence whatever, whether of kindness or otherwise, to
interfere with others in the same pursuit. Under these circumstances,
then, no one would seek to acquire property for the purpose of
making it an instrument (to be placed in the hands of children),
of domination over the children of other parents; and every one

* Pp. 119–121, 124–129, 136–139, 142–144.

would be willing that all, in whatever age or generation they might appear, should have equal possession of the materials of the world, and, of course, of the means of assuring their own happiness.

If any thing can add force to these observations, it is, that as regards the prevailing ideas, as to who are and who are not successors to property, they are altogether founded in error. In a community where the soil, the equal and common property of all, should be divided equally, and the equal portions held by each member, *for one year only*, what member could say he had a successor? Is there any one on whom he could confer the right of occupying that which, by the death of his own tenure, he is compelled to vacate and abandon? Where the tenure extended to the term of *ten* years, who then would have a successor? If, indeed, there be any at all, the community itself is the successor; and there is no other. So also is the community the successor, and the sole successor, in the case where the government is so organized, that every member of it holds, property during his life. At his death, it returns to the community, and these, in duty to every member of which it is composed, yield to them, at the suitable age, *their* share of the common property, and secure to them its enjoyment during their lives. There is, therefore, no such thing, then, as successor, in the meaning in which the word is received among men at the present day. It is only a misunderstanding of our rights that could have tolerated its use or existence among us. . . .

We may go yet farther, and suppose any and every nation, at its first settlement, to have a population as great as ever it can support, and as ever will be desirous to draw support from its soil and other resources. If now, a given, and, as near as may be, an equal portion of its population, be imagined to die off, every day; and if it be further imagined also, that a portion of new individuals, so to call them, arrived at maturity, should appear, equal in number to the deceased, and take their places; this substitution of a new population, thus daily, supplying the waste of human beings produced by death; would make the nation perpetual. And in the operation of this daily substitution, the same principles would bear sway, that I have endeavored to inculcate throughout this work; that of the equal rights of man to the property of the great domain of nature. It is not here the place, to say, how beneficially such principles would act in promoting human happiness, should it be found that this substitution can easily and happily be accomplished. It is enough now, to observe, that they are *our rights*; that they belong to *every human being*; that they are not to be contravened, withheld or denied, among a people who understand them, *without incurring a terrible responsibility*; and that there is every reason to believe that a method will be devised, before the conclusion of this work, which shall assure to every individual, all that his rights and his happiness require.

CHAPTER IV

THE PROPOSITION

If I have seemed, to the reader, to understand myself; if I have taken the world as it is; and placed man, as it regards his rights to dominion over it, where he ought to be; it must be conceded that I have done much; but it is also to be conceded, that much more remains to be done, to put the rightful owners in possession. Whoever looks at the world as it now is, will see it divided into two distinct classes; proprietors, and non-proprietors; those who own the world, and those who own no part of it. If we take a closer view of these two classes, we shall find that a very great proportion even of the proprietors, are only nominally so; they possess so little, that in strict regard to truth, they ought to be classed among the non-proprietors. They may be compared, in fact, to the small prizes in a lottery, which, when they are paid, leave the holder a loser.

If such a phenomenon in the history of man, for such is the situation in which we find him in all countries and in all ages, could have possibly found an existence, under a system that should have given *each individual* as he arrived at the age of maturity, as much of the property of the world, as any contemporary of his, was allowed to possess at a similar age; I say, if under such a system, such an unhappy result should have arisen, as we now see, afflicting the human race; there would be nothing to hope. We might despair of seeing things better than they now are, and set ourselves down in quiet content, that there was no remedy. But when we see that the system which has prevailed hitherto, and prevails to this moment, is not of this description; that it acts on principles in direct opposition to it; that it gives to some single descendant of some holder of property under William Penn, possessions of the value perhaps of a million of dollars; while, it may be, an hundred thousand other inhabitants of Pennsylvania, collectively, have not half that sum; *and all this, merely because of a few beads having been given to some Indians, some two hundred years ago;* how is it possible to have had a different result? The system is one, that *begins*, by making whole nations paupers; and why should it not be expected that they would *continue so?* Indeed it would be a miracle, exceeding everything of the kind that has ever been supposed to have happened, if we had seen, from such an organization of things, anything but what we now see.

The truth is, *all* governments in the world, have begun wrong; in the *first appropriation* they have made, or suffered to be made, of the domain, over which they have exercised their power, and in the *transmission* of this domain to their posterity. Here are the two great and radical evils, that have caused all the misfortunes of man. These and these alone, have done the whole of it. I do not class among these misfortunes, the sufferings with which sickness afflicts him, because these have a natural origin; capable, however, of being nearly annihilated by good governments, but greatly aggravated by those that are bad.

If these remarks be true, there would seem, then, to be no remedy but by commencing anew. And is there any reason why we should not? That which is commenced in error and injustice, may surely be set right, when we know how to do it. There is *power* enough in the hands of the people of the State of New York, or of any other State, to rectify any and everything which requires it, when they shall see wherein the evil exists, and wherein lies the remedy. These two things it is necessary they should see, before they can possess the moral power and motive to act. I have succeeded, I think, in shewing, for that is self-evident, that man's *natural* right to an equal portion of property, is indisputable. His artificial right, or right in society, is not less so. For it is not to be said that any power has any right to make our artificial rights unequal, any more than it has to make our *natural* rights unequal. And inasmuch as a man, in a state of nature, would have a right to resist, even to the extremity of death, his fellow, or his fellows, whatever might be their number, who should undertake to give him less of the property, common to all, than they take each to themselves; so also has man now, in society, the same right to resist a similar wrong done him. Thus, today, if property had been made equal among all present, right would have taken place among them; but if tomorrow a new member appear, and provision be not made to give him a quantity substantially equal with all his fellows, injustice is done him, and if he had the power, he would have the perfect right to dispossess all those who have monopolized to themselves not only their own shares, but his also. For it is not to be allowed, even to a majority, to contravene equality, nor, of course, the right, even though it be of a single individual. And if, alone, he has not power sufficient to obtain his rights, and there be others, also, in like condition with him, they may unite their efforts, and thus accomplish it, if within their power. And, if this may be lawfully done, upon the supposition that yesterday, only, a government was made, and an equal enjoyment of property guaranteed to all, how much more proper is it when, unjust government existing, it has never been done at all. When the whole mass of people, as it were, ninety-nine out of every hundred, have never had this equal enjoyment, in any manner or shape, whatever? If still there be those who shall say that these unjust and unequal governments ought not to be destroyed, although they may not give to man, in society, the same equality of property as he would enjoy in a state of nature; then I say, that *those are the persons* who, in society, *if any body*, should be deprived of all their possessions, inasmuch as it is manifestly as proper for them to be destitute of property, as it is for any one else. If slavery and degradation are to be the result, they are the proper victims. After an equal division has been once made, there seems nothing wanting but to secure an equal transmission of property to posterity. And to this, there is no irremovable objection. For, I think I have succeeded in shewing, that the right of a testator to give, and of an heir to receive, is a mere creature of the imagination; and that these rights, as they are called, ought to be abolished, as interfering with the real rights of the succeeding generation. . . .

But, in some respects, the reasoning in which I have allowed myself to indulge, in the course of the present chapter, is of a kind calculated to compel me to blend two things together, which ought to be kept separate; that is the injustice and enormity of unequal first-possession, and the *effects* growing out of it. The reader will know what I call first-possession; it is, that which the governments of every country order to be given to him who is so fortunate as to have what is called a legator, whatever he shall have requested, out of anything which he possessed at the termination of his life. The *effects*, of which I spoke, as growing out of it, are, the additions made to it, by acquisition, thro' the operation of that state of things, where a few have all, and the many nothing. I use the word legator; but the word donor is equally applicable; since the latter gives the property, it may be, a few years sooner; the difference being only in time. It will be better, therefore, to defer combatting any further objections, which will naturally arise, to that which is yet to be proposed, until a full view can be had by all, of the features it will exhibit.

So much has been said as to what really is not, and should not be, that the reader is, no doubt, prepared to anticipate, in part, what *should* be; to foresee the modification, which it is necessary our State Government should undergo, before the rights of property, which belong to man in his natural state, can be secured to him, in the artificial state in which society finds him; and before the rights of posterity can be preserved to them, as they should have been to us, for their own exclusive use and benefit.

This modification will be accomplished by pursuing the following.

PLAN

1. Let a new State-Convention be assembled. Let it prepare a new Constitution, and let that Constitution, after having been adopted by the people, decree an abolition of all debts; both at home and abroad, between citizen and citizen; and between citizen and foreigner. Let it renounce all property belonging to our citizens, without the State. Let it claim all property within the State, both real and personal, of whatever kind it may be, with the exception of that belonging to resident aliens, and with the further exception of so much personal property, as may be in the possession of transient owners, not being citizens. Let it order an equal division of all this property among the citizens, of and over the age of maturity, in manner yet to be directed. Let it order all transfers or removals of property, except so much as may belong to transient owners, to cease, until the division is accomplished.

2. Let a census be taken, of the people; ascertaining and recording in books made for the purpose, the *name, time* when born, as near as may be, and annexing the *age*, the *place* of nativity, *parentage, sex, color, occupation, domicil or residence* and *time* of residence

since *last* resident in the State, distinguishing aliens from citizens, and ordering, with the exception of the Agents of Foreign Governments,—such as Ambassadors, &c. that all such aliens shall be considered as citizens, if they have been resident for the five years next previous to the time when the before mentioned division of property, shall have been ordered.

3. Let each citizen, association, corporation, and other persons at the same time when the census is being taken, give an inventory of all personal property, of whatever description it may be, and to whomsoever it may belong, in his, her, or their possession. Let also a similar inventory of all *real* property, within the State, be taken, whoever may be the owner of it. And from these data, let a General Inventory, be made out of all the real and personal property, within the State, which does not belong to alien residents, or transient owners. To this, let there be added all property in the possession of our tribunals of law and equity; and such State property, as can be offered up to sale without detriment to the State.

4. Let there be, next, a dividend made of this amount, among all such citizens, who shall be of and over, the age of eighteen, if this should be fixed, as I am inclined to think it should be, as the age of maturity; and let such dividend be entered in a book for the purpose, to the credit of such persons, male and female.

5. Let public sale be made, as soon after such dividend is made, as may be practicable, to the highest bidder, of all the real and personal property in the State. Care must be taken that the proper authority be required to divide all divisible property, that shall require it, into such allotments or parcels, as will be likely to cause it to bring the greatest amount, at the time of sale. . . .

13. Property belonging to persons, not citizens, but transiently resident among us, and dying here, to abide by the laws which govern the State or nation to which such person belonged, in the disposal of property in such a situation; provided such State or Nation allows the property, or the value thereof, of *our* citizens, dying *there*, and leaving property, to be sent home, to abide by the operation of our own laws.

14. Other States or Nations adopting a similar internal organization, as it regards the transmission of property to posterity, and consenting to bestow patrimonies upon minors born in this State (and who shall prefer receiving them in any such foreign State), upon their producing documents certifying the fact of their nativity, age,

&c. and that they have received no patrimony from their native State: shall have the favor reciprocated, under like circumstances: otherwise, a minor born in another State must reside the last ten years of his minority in this, before he can be considered as entitled to the patrimony of a native born citizen, and must moreover be liable to severe punishment, if, either after he has received his patrimony, he accepts aught from his native or other State by way of legacy or gift; or, before maturity, he receives such legacy or gift, and then accepts the patrimony in question.

15. All persons of full age, from abroad, Ambassadors &c. excepted, resident one year among us, are citizens, and must give up all property over an amount equal to the patrimony of the State for the year being, unless such persons were citizens of a State, acknowledging the equal rights of all men to property, in manner the same as this State is supposed to do.

16. All native born citizens from the period of their birth, to that of their maturity shall receive from the State, a sum paid by monthly or other more convenient instalments, equal to their full and decent maintenance, according to age and condition; and the parent or parents, if living and not rendered unsuitable by incapacity or vicious habits, to train up their children, shall be the persons, authorized to receive it. Otherwise, guardians must be appointed to take care of such children and receive their maintenance—allowance. They are to be educated also, at the public expense.

17. When the death happens, of either of any two married persons, the survivor retains one half of the sum of their joint property, their debts being first paid. The other half goes to the State, through the hands of the Public Administrator; this Officer taking charge of the effects of all deceased persons.

18. Punishment by imprisonment, for a term of fourteen years, should be visited upon him, who, during his life time, gives away his property to another. Hospitality is of course not interdicted, but charity is, inasmuch as ample provision will be made by the State for such persons as shall require it. The good citizen has only to inform the applicant for charity where his proper wants will be supplied.

19. All persons after receiving their patrimony, will be at full liberty to reside within the State; or to take it, or its avails to any other part of the world which may be preferred, and there to reside, as a citizen or subject of another State.

20. Property being thus continually and equally divided forever, and the receivers of such property embarking in all the various pursuits and occupations of life; these pursuits and occupations must be guaranteed against injury from foreign competition, or, otherwise, indemnity should be made by the State.

I have thus developed the principles of the modification which the Government of this State should undergo, and the means necessary to accomplish it, in order that every citizen may enjoy in a state of society, substantially, the rights which belong to him in a state of nature. I leave the reader therefore for the present to his own reflections; intending in the next chapter to offer such reasons as the subject admits, for enforcing the propriety of adopting such modification, and of the means proposed, of accomplishing it. . . .

THE ASSOCIATIONISTS

ALBERT BRISBANE

A *Concise Exposition of the
Doctrine of Associationism**
1843

In 1840 Brisbane published his seminal book, *Social Destiny of Man*. By 1843 there was an Associationist movement abroad in the land, and it was time to apply Fourier's principles to real societies. Brisbane wrote A *Concise Exposition* as a primer on how to build phalanxes. It might be noted that he disapproved of the haste and euphoria attending the rise of the phalanxes. He favored a more deliberate kind of experimentation.

Association is the Social Destiny of Man—is the true and natural system of Society, predestined for him by the Creator, and will, when established upon earth, secure to him that happiness for which he has so long sought in vain, and the elements of which exist in and around him—in the beautiful creations of material Nature, and in the noble faculties and sentiments with which God has endowed him.

This true and natural System of Society cannot be established at once; it must be a gradual work, and before it can become universal, the truth and goodness of its Principles must be demonstrated practically and upon a small scale. For that reason a commencement must be made with a single Association, which will show its immense advantages—show the happiness and prosperity which it will secure to man, and lead to a general adoption.

We shall explain the laws and mechanism of this single Association, which is the germ or primary element of the System of Society which we advocate, as the village or township is the germ or primary element of the present System of Society. A county, as we know, is composed of townships, a state of counties, and the United States

* Pp. 2–5, 15–17, 33–34, 74–75.

of states; thus, the United States is but a repetition of townships. Now, if the township be falsely organized—that is, if the families composing it, live according to a false system; if there be conflicts of interests, opposition, discord, waste and poverty among them, then the whole body politic, composed of these falsely organized townships, will contain all their defects, and discord, injustice, poverty, and the numerous evils which they engender, will exist universally. But if we can organize the townships rightly, so that unity of interests, concert of action, vast economies and general riches will be attained, then, in spreading these rightly organized townships, and rendering them general, a Social Order will be gradually established, in which peace, prosperity and happiness will be secured to all.

The great and primary object which we have in view is, consequently, *to effect the establishment of one Association,* which will exhibit practically the great economies, the riches, the order and unity of the system, and serve as a model for, and lead to the founding of others.

We shall explain the laws and mechanism of this one Association, and we will remark that in so doing, we shall explain the whole System of Society which we seek to establish, the same as in explaining the physiological laws of one Individual, we explain those of the whole Human Race.

The system of Association which we propose to the world, is not the plan or scheme of an individual; it is not the invention of mere human reason, like so many political systems which have been established, from the Republic of Lycurgus down to our modern Democracies. It is deduced from and based upon universal Principles, and is the application to the social relations of Mankind of the laws of Order and Unity, which govern the Universe.

Fourier discovered the laws of UNIVERSAL UNITY, or the laws which govern Creation in its five grand Spheres or Movements, which are: 1st, the MATERIAL MOVEMENT, or the laws which govern the movements of the heavenly bodies, or universal Matter; 2d, the AROMAL, or the laws which regulate the distribution and influences of the imponderable fluids on the kingdoms of Creation—animal, vegetable and mineral; 3d, the ORGANIC, or the laws according to which God distributes forms, properties, colors, flavors, etc. to all created things; 4th, the INSTINCTUAL, or the laws according to which God distributes instincts and passions; and lastly, the SOCIAL, or the laws which govern the succession and mechanisms of the societies of intelligent Beings throughout the Universe.

From a knowledge of these laws of Universal Unity, Fourier deduced the true and natural system of society, destined for Man, and which, when realized in practice, will produce social Order and Harmony upon the globe—a reflex of the Harmony which reigns in the Universe. Throughout his works, he declares that he gives no system or plan of his own; he claims the merit only of having discovered the system of Nature, which will secure to Mankind as many blessings as the false social Institutions, set up by human reason, have entailed upon them miseries and misfortunes. . . .

Before concluding these general remarks, let us particularly request the reader not to confound the system of Association, discovered by Fourier, with the trials made by the Shakers, Rappites and others, nor with the system devised by Mr. Owen. The views of the latter have excited in the public mind the strongest prepossessions against the magnificent problem of Association, and raised up most serious obstacles to its impartial examination. The errors of individuals, however, should be carefully separated from so grand and important a subject, and to condemn Association because Mr. Owen has advocated a community of property or attacked religion, shows a want of impartiality and discrimination which no reflecting mind, we hope, will be guilty of.

NECESSITY OF A SOCIAL REFORM

When new views and principles are put forth, they invariably meet with the opposition and condemnation of the great majority of men, no matter how good or true they may be, or how important the results which they promise to realize. Against this procedure we protest, and, in behalf of suffering Humanity, we ask that preconceived notions and prejudices as well as hasty criticism be for a time laid aside, and an impartial and conscientious investigation of the system, which we advocate, be entered into.

If we look around us, we see numerous Parties, laboring isolatedly to carry out various reforms—political, administrative, currency, abolition, temperance, moral, &c. &c.—which proves, *First*, the depth and extent of the evil that preys upon Society, and *Second*, the necessity of a fundamental Reform, which will attack that evil at its root and eradicate it effectually, instead of lopping off a few branches.

If the plan of such a reform has really been discovered, how worthy of the candid examination of every being, whose Soul burns with a desire to see poverty and misery banished from the earth, and who feels a sacred pride for the happiness and elevation of his Race!

To meet and disarm fears and suspicions which may arise in the conservative Mind, we will hasten to state that the reform we contemplate, although fundamental in its character, is not destructive, but constructive: it will not tear down, but build up; it will respect what is true and good in Society, and will change quietly and by substitution, what is false and defective; it will violate no rights, injure no class; it will not impoverish the Rich to enrich slightly the Poor; it will not change the victims of poverty and misery, but will improve and elevate the condition of all, without taking from any. It can moreover be tried on a small scale, and it will only spread, when practice has shown its superiority over the present system. Unlike political reforms, which, to effect the smallest change of policy, agitate and often convulse a whole country, and array one half of the People against the other half, it will not affect a space as large as a township and but a few hundred persons, and will not extend beyond these narrow limits unless its advantages—*practically demonstrated*—excite a strong and general approbation in its favor.

To show the necessity of a Social Reform, we will glance at the misery which exists upon earth; its extent, depth, and intensity prove that political and other partial reforms can effect but little permanent good, and that recourse must be had to new and thorough measures.

Men of talent and genius, who are devoting your energies to political, administrative and other minor Reforms, examine the grand question of a Social Reform—so much more vast, and so much more pregnant with great results! Why waste your powers upon ephemeral projects, which, if carried out, will effect but little good, and will soon be forgotten—sinking into oblivion your names and your efforts? In fifty years hence, how small will the question of a sub-treasury or national bank appear, and who will remember the men that frittered away their day and hour in discussing it? When the broad field of a Social Reform, which spreads out so far beyond the narrow field of political reform, lies open before you—when a Reorganization of Society, which is the grandest undertaking that any Age can offer, calls for your efforts, how can you consent to labor for minor and secondary reforms, which disappear for the most part with the day that brings them forth?

If a Social Reform can be effected which will dignify Industry and render it attractive—increase immensely production or real wealth—secure abundance to the Poor and permanent prosperity to the Rich—extend the refining and elevating influence of superior education to all—widen the sphere of intellectual existence, and combine the pleasures of Art and Science and social Life with the pursuits of useful Industry, how desirable would be the result, and how worthy of the persevering efforts of men of pure motives and exalted ambition!

The mind of Man has not yet elevated itself to the Idea of undertaking with intelligence and foresight a Social Reform, but the Age is sufficiently prepared for this grand Idea to warrant its being broached and discussed. The World has run through and accomplished those various minor and preliminary reforms—political, legislative, judiciary, &c.—which first occupy the attention of men, and there is nothing now to prevent them from comprehending, that it is not changes in the Government, and Administration, or on the surface of society that are required, *but a fundamental Reform in the social Organization itself.*

Let us now turn from these general considerations, and cast a glance at the condition and tendency of things in our own land.

The history of the United States proves practically and beyond the possibility of denial, that political and administrative reforms cannot secure to the People Happiness and Social Elevation. We have enjoyed a long period of peace; the best talent of the country has been devoted to Politics; various parties—Federal and Democratic—have had the ascendency; different policies—Hamiltonian and Jeffersonian—have been carried out; the labors of from thirteen to twenty-six State Legislatures, of a National Congress and an unshackled Press, have been devoted to the work of improvement, and after all, what great results have been attained? Are the People happier? are they more elevated, morally and socially? have they pleasing and encouraging prospects before them? are they moving onward toward some high Destiny which excites enthusiasm? No, far from it; real Evils, such as collective poverty and dependence, anxiety for the future, fluctuations in trade and in industry, and instability in political policy, have increased and with marked rapidity.

It is true that Commerce has been greatly developed and extended, but it has been in so incoherent and disorderly a manner that violent revulsions have every few years taken place, which have plunged the country at each period into the greatest distress, and entailed ruin upon all classes of society. Besides, Commerce prospers in proportion to the amount of profits which it draws from productive Industry—from agriculture and manufactures, so that its prosperity is a very deceptive sign of public welfare.

It is true, also, that great internal Improvements have been carried out, but how injudiciously and wastefully have they been prosecuted! A majority of them are unfinished and pay no returns, and many of the States that have undertaken them, have become bankrupt—causing the ruin of thousands of individuals, who loaned them their money.

The great achievement of the country is its progress in Industry, which has been most rapid; vast forests have been cleared, towns and cities built, immense lines of roads made, vessels and steamboats without number constructed, and the resources of the country wonderfully developed.—But this great movement is not to be ascribed to political and legislative action, but to the fact that the energies of the People, instead of being wasted in war, or repressed by military power, as has been the case in all other countries, have been directed to practical Improvements and the development of Industry.

This great industrial Progress is worthy of the highest praise and excites admiration, but while it has taken place, Social Evils, as we said, have increased and with surprising rapidity. Our anarchical commercial and financial system, together with free competition, which is exceeding in intensity and relentlessness all bounds, are engendering universal distrust, antipathy, selfishness and antagonism in society, and contaminating all the practical affairs of life with fraud, injustice and double dealing.

Competitive strife among the Laboring Classes, which arrays them in hostility against each other, and machinery in the hands of the few which works against them, are gradually reducing the price of wages and prolonging the time of toil, and these and other circumstances prognosticate for them a future of poverty and degrading dependence. Their condition has already become more precarious; the difficulty of obtaining employment is greater, and the means of living more uncertain than ever. The Mechanic and Laborer can no longer look forward as in former years with the hope of securing a home for old age, but consider themselves fortunate if they can satisfy present exigencies and obtain the means of subsistence for the day.

While this change in the Social condition of the Masses has been going on, frauds and revulsions in trade and finance have become more frequent, more sweeping and unforeseen, spreading ruin among the Rich, and rendering them extremely insecure in their possessions.

Our whole system of Commerce and industry has become a round of killing cares, harassing anxieties, disgusts, hopes blasted, and unforeseen reverses and ruin. The business world is an arena of conflicts, overreaching and fraud—a school for the most callous selfishness and duplicity; its spirit has rendered business tact, craft and petty cunning the most important of qualifications—made the practice of truth and justice impossible—degraded the higher faculties of the mind—sunk the pursuits of Art, Science and useful Industry below the mere ability of money-making—set up wealth as the standard of excellence and respectability, and rendered its acquisition a mania, to which all the higher and more noble aims of life are sacrificed.

Such are results which are growing out of the present system of Society, as it is advancing to maturity. With the spectacle of them before us, should we remain satisfied with the political, administrative and other partial reforms, which occupy public attention, or undertake a Social Reform, which will eradicate at once the numerous evils which the present false organization of Society engenders?

PRACTICAL ORGANIZATION
OF ASSOCIATION

NUMBER OF PERSONS

The proper number of persons for an Association is about Eighteen Hundred, or, if we suppose six persons on an average to a family, three hundred families. This number is not chosen arbitrarily, but is based upon the number of distinct Characters which we find in Man, and which compose the full scale of human Character. It is only in large Associations of eighteen hundred persons, that all varieties of talents and capacities, as well as the proper capital, skill and knowledge, can be combined, which are necessary to secure a perfect prosecution of Industry, and the Arts and Sciences.

If the members of an Association are of different degrees of fortune, of different characters, tastes and talents, and possess varied

theoretical and practical acquirements, the easier it will be to associate and harmonize them. Diversity in these respects will, in a true
system of Association, be a source of Concord, Union and Harmony.

For an Association on a small scale, four or five hundred persons,
or eighty to a hundred families, will be sufficient; but this is the
smallest number with which an Association can be organized, in
which the Harmonies of the system—moral, material and social—can
be sufficiently developed to show its immense superiority over the
present organization of Society,—in which Industry can be rendered
Attractive, vast Economies introduced, and the Passions usefully
employed and rightly directed.

These conditions cannot be fulfilled, and Social Harmony cannot be attained in small Associations of two or three, or even
twenty or thirty families; eighty families or about four hundred
persons, at least, are necessary.

All Harmony is based upon a variety of elements properly combined, and the science of Association teaches us that the smallest
number of individuals, or elements of Social Harmony, with which
the essential parts of the mechanism of an Association can be organized, is the number we have here given.

Small Associations of two hundred persons, or about forty families,
could be established, which would offer great advantages, as regards
economy, profit, material comfort and a judicious application of labor
and capital, over the present system of Isolated Families; but the
mechanism would be so much reduced, and so incomplete, that it
would afford but few of the charms and advantages of a large Association.

A great many persons will wish to form small and incomplete
Associations; they would do better to combine their means and form
a large establishment. To show the importance of doing so, we will
state that it is only in large Associations that the following essential
conditions can be fulfilled.

1. Dignify Industry and render it Attractive.

2. Effect great Economies, which, in large Associations, are four-
fold what they are in small ones.

3. Establish a great variety of occupations, in Art and Science
and Industry, suited to the tastes, talents and capacities of both
Sexes and of all Ages, and offer to every one congenial spheres of
activity.

4. Secure to every person congenial and pleasing social relations,

and the choice of sympathetic characters; avoid all forced contacts, and absorb any individual antipathies in collective affinities.

5. Combine Capital sufficient to prosecute Industry, and particularly Agriculture, which is the main branch of it, upon a vast and scientific scale, and to give to every thing connected with them—to the fields, gardens, workshops, tools, implements and working dresses—convenience and elegance, without which Industry cannot be rendered attractive.

6. Organize the mechanism of the Groups and Series, without which the Passions—now so discordant and rebellious—cannot be usefully and legitimately employed, and harmoniously developed.

7. Give to children a complete moral, intellectual and physical development, which is only possible in large Associations, where Industry is rendered Attractive, and the Arts and Sciences are extensively cultivated.

Let these conditions be fulfilled, and the advantages of Association will be found so immense, that the isolated Household, with its cares, waste and monotony, will be abandoned at once. . . .

CONTRAST BETWEEN ASSOCIATION AND THE PRESENT SOCIAL ORDER

If we wish to picture to ourselves in imagination an Association established and in operation, we must imagine spreading out before us a fine Domain, covering an area of three miles square, beautifully and scientifically cultivated, diversified with gardens, fields, fruit-orchards, vineyards, meadows and woodlands; in the centre a large and elegant Edifice, with spacious and commodious out-houses, combining architectural beauty with convenience and economy; fine flocks, teams and implements greeting everywhere the eye, and an intelligent and prosperous Population engaged from Attraction in the care and cultivation of the whole. The Useful and the Beautiful would be in every way united: the loveliness of Nature would be heightened by the works of Man; and the charms of Social life and the pursuits of Art and Science and useful Industry, would be in every way combined.

Would not eighteen hundred persons, united in an Association, prosecuting with order and economy all their industrial and business operations, and dividing equitably the product of their Labor and Talent—each receiving a share according to the part which he or she has taken in creating it—live much more in accordance with the dictates of wisdom, than if they were divided into three hundred families, inhabiting as many isolated little tenements, as lonely in general as they are inconvenient, with poor farms and workshops, poor flocks, tools, implements and machinery, and without the charm of varied social relations—without Art, Science and other intellectual enjoyments, which give to human existence its elevation, and constitute the true life of Man? We leave the reader to answer the question himself.

To furnish more data for forming an opinion, let us contrast more minutely the manner in which three hundred families now live, and the manner in which they would live in Association. The contrast will show us the immense superiority of Association, as regards Economy, and Unity of action and interests over the present System.

Three hundred families require at present three hundred separate houses, three hundred kitchens, three hundred kitchen fires, three hundred sets of cooking utensils, three hundred women to do the cooking—and if they are farming families—three hundred little farms, three hundred barns and sheds, three hundred teams, innumerable walls and fences, and everything else equally as complicated and uselessly wasteful.

All the cares and labor attendant upon providing for the wants of a family, such as cooking, washing, marketing and keeping up fires, must be gone through with three hundred times daily by the three hundred families, and with the same detail as for an assemblage of eighteen hundred persons, except the difference of scale.

Association will avoid this monstrous complication and waste; instead of three hundred little kitchens and three hundred fires, it will have four or five large and convenient kitchens, with as many fires, by means of which, not only the cooking can be done, but the entire Edifice warmed; instead of three hundred little fire-places and cooking-stoves, and as many sets of cooking utensils, it will have its extensive kitchen ranges, its large boilers and ovens, and machinery on the largest scale and the best that can be invented for facilitating culinary operations; instead of three hundred women to do the cooking, it will have a few experienced cooks, engaged by turns every other day; instead of three hundred poor teams, half the time idle, it will have merely the requisite number, and of the best quality; instead of the immense number of walls and fences now required, it will have a few extensive hedges; and instead of making all its sales and purchases at retail, paying in profits to traders one-half of the product of its labor, it will make them at wholesale, and in the most economical manner.

To what immense Economies would Association give rise! What a source of Riches it would be! We live in an Age, the all-absorbing desire of which is wealth. If men would but add sentiments of justice and philanthropy to their greedy strife after money, they would see, that it is only in Association that their wishes can be satisfied, and that all can attain prosperity. . . .

UNITY OF INTERESTS
RESULTING FROM THE SYSTEM OF JOINT-STOCK
PROPERTY OF ASSOCIATION

We will briefly explain the means by which Association will effect a perfect Unity or Identity of the individual with the collective Interest. Unless we can render the interest of the Individual that of the Whole, and the interest of the Whole that of the Individual—or, in other words, unless we can establish Unity in the sphere of worldly interests, we can never introduce practical Truth and Justice into the relations of men, nor attain those higher Unities in Church and State, after which more advanced minds—sick of strife, dissension and controversy—are beginning to aspire. Let us explain how this primary Unity will be attained.

The interest upon the stock of the members of an Association, will not be paid out of the product of this or that part of the domain, or out of this or that branch of manufactures, but out of the total product of the entire domain and all branches of manufactures. As a consequence, every individual owning stock, if it be but a single share, will wish that every portion of the soil should be cultivated in the best manner, and every branch of manufactures prosecuted with the greatest skill and judiciousness; the better all this is done, the larger will be the interest which each individual will receive; and as the desire of large dividends will exist in Association as at present, there will be, as a consequence, a general desire on the part of all members to render the Association in the highest degree productive and prosperous.

Not only will every individual wish that all branches of Industry should be prosecuted in the best possible manner, but he will wish that the edifices, tools, implements, flocks, fences, etc. should be carefully taken care of and preserved from injury or damage, for if any damage were done to them, the expense of repairs would have to be deducted from the general product, which would lessen the interest which he, in common with the other stockholders, would receive.

What each individual Member will wish, the entire Association will wish, and from this *Unity of Interests* will result a concert of action in prosecuting all branches of Industry, and a perfect unanimity of feeling in all temporal affairs and interests.

No one can promote his own prosperity without promoting at the same time the prosperity of all those around him, and no one can injure his neighbor without injuring himself.

It is only in joint-stock Associations, where each individual is interested in the entire capital invested, that a perfect Union of interests can be established, and Man can be made to desire truly and ardently the welfare and prosperity of his fellow-man. From this *solidarity*—this reciprocal and mutual dependence, will result a unity of feeling, which will soon extend from pecuniary affairs to political, religious, and other spheres of society. In such an order of things how easy will it be to realize practically the precept—"Do unto others as you would that others should do unto you!" In fact, the practical operation of Association will lead to it, as the present system of Society leads to a conflict of all interests and to universal antagonism and enmity.

And when a body of persons, perfectly united, are working for each other's welfare, how easy will it be also to put in operation that other precept—"Love thy neighbor as thyself!" . . .

IMPOSSIBILITY OF ANY TYRANNY
OF CAPITAL IN ASSOCIATION

It is often asked, whether one or more capitalists will not become owners of the stock of an Association, and exercise a tyrannical control and dictation over its members and its affairs. Nothing of the kind can take place; to explain this, we will suppose an extreme case—we will suppose that one individual has become the proprietor of all the stock of an Association. This monopoly will give him, as we shall see, no arbitrary control over the Association and its affairs.

The Council of Industry—the members of which will be elected by the inhabitants of the Association—will have a general supervision of the domain, workshops and manufactories, and the regulation of its industrial affairs and interests. The person who owns the stock may be elected a member of this Council, and, as such, will have a voice in the management of its affairs, but out of the Council and as a private individual, he can exercise no control; he cannot dictate, for example, the system of cultivation which shall be pursued, the crops which shall be grown, the branches of manufactures which shall be prosecuted, where the fences or hedges shall be located, how the fields and gardens shall be laid out and cultivated, or direct any similar operations. All these details must come under the direction of the Council, which, composed of the most talented and experienced members of the Association, will of course be able to exercise a far more judicious control than can a single individual.

No individual in Association will possess the absolute ownership of the soil, manufactories and other means of production as at present, "to use and abuse them as he wishes," and to prevent the rest of the members from working upon or in them, if his caprice shall so dictate; he will own the stock, which represents them—a much more desirable form of property—but the soil and manufactories will remain under the control and direction of the Association, and the Right of working in or upon them will be secured to all its members. We see this restriction upon capitalists in operation at present in stock companies: a stockholder in a railroad cannot, for example, alter the direction or tear up a part of the track equal in value to his stock, or prevent travellers from going over the road,—and this restriction is found advantageous to all.

Capitalists will possess in Association very great advantages: their money will be safely invested; they will be exempt from the frauds, revulsions and the numerous accidents of business, which ruin upon an average three fourths of them; they will be relieved from the anxiety and the trouble of constant supervision, and as the profits of Association will be large, they will receive a liberal interest on their money.

But Capitalists in Association will not wish to exercise any dictation or tyranny; they would disgust their fellow-men by such a course, who, being secured the Right of Labor or of constant employment, would be pecuniarily independent, and would not submit to any imposition: should capitalists, however, endeavor to exercise any tyranny, the members could move off in a body and leave their property unproductive;—and, besides, any arbitrary dictation on their part would derange the operations of Industry, decrease production, and lessen as a consequence their profits. The Tyranny of Capital, one of the last relics of tyranny, and the most repulsive, will be swept from the face of the earth by Association!

If it be feared by some persons that a few individuals in an Association will monopolize the stock, and exercise an absolute control, it is very confidently asserted by others that the selfishness of men, and their rapacity to acquire wealth, will be insurmountable obstacles to social Union and Concord. Let us answer this objection.

The reader will bear in mind that the interest upon the capital or shares will be paid out of the *total product* of the Association, so that no one can desire large profits for himself without desiring the same for all the other members.

Suppose then that there are some extremely avaricious persons in an Association, who are very desirous of accumulating wealth: what means will they have to employ to attain their end? They will have to see that all parts of the domain are cultivated in the best manner—all branches of manufactures prosecuted judiciously—that the edifices, implements, machinery, etc. are not injured, and that no waste takes place. This is the policy which they will have to pursue. They cannot, as a consequence, promote their own prosperity without promoting at the same time the prosperity of all the other members; their thirst for gain will not be satisfied, as at present, at the expense of their fellow-men, but will, on the contrary, conduce to their welfare. By this means individual selfishness will be neutralized, and made to subserve the good of the whole.

Under the present condition of things, the injury done to others by extortion or fraud, is individual gain; but in Association, where the interests of the Individual and those of the Mass are *identical*, no one can add to his own store without adding to that of the rest of the community. . . .

CITIES IN THE COMBINED ORDER

We have shown that Universal Association is contemplated by its advocates, and that the reform which will lead to it can be effected peacefully and gradually, without injury to any class or any interest in society. The universal establishment of this new Social Order renders it necessary that Cities should be provided for; the doctrine of Association would be incomplete and imperfect, if it did not provide for universal and collective arrangements in Society, as well as for the details and minute arrangements of a single Association. Cities are necessary parts of the social machine, and we will briefly glance at their construction and arrangement in the Combined Order, for they must differ materially and widely from Cities of the present social order.

The contrast between the Cities of the Combined Order and the Cities of existing society, will be as striking and as brilliant as the contrast between the comforts and splendours of an Association or combined household, and the inconveniences, monotony and dullness of the single or isolated household.

What is the general character of a City in civilized Society? and what will it be in the Combined Order? A brief answer to these questions may convey to the reader an idea of the difference between them.

A City at present is a heterogeneous mass of small and separate houses of all sizes, shapes, colors, styles and materials, which are crowded together without regard to architectural unity or design, convenience or elegance; it is cut up with irregular and narrow streets, dark lanes, confined courts, and cramped yards and alleys; it has its dirty and muddy streets, that annoy the inhabitants; its filthy gutters that fill the atmosphere with noxious exhalations which are injurious to health, and presents a scene of confusion, incoherence, waste and disorder.

A City of civilized Society is a vast and crowded receptacle of human beings not connected with each other in friendly union and orderly association, but huddled together in conflicting and antagonistic aggregation. It is, for the most part, a sink of poverty, and with its isolated dwellings, the hiding place of a thousand vices and crimes. All that our civilized Cities can boast of in regard to riches and splendor, intelligence, refinement and enjoyment, serves but to render the poverty, the ignorance, the degradation and suffering, which abound in them, more hideous and painfully disgusting.

The cities and capitals of Association must contrast most powerfully with those of civilized Society, and they will do so. A City in the Combined Order will be a Group of magnificent Associations, disposed with order and unity of design, surrounded by noble and extensive gardens and grounds, for the recreation and healthy occupation of the inhabitants, in which all the beauties of nature and the perfections of art will be combined and united to charm and delight.

For every twelve Associations there will be one Association which will be the Capital or head of the twelve, corresponding in some degree to the county town of a county. It will be the administrative centre of the Associated County, and at it will be held the periodical exhibitions of Industry, Art and Science, public celebrations, etc.

A District of country comprising several Associated Counties, or about one hundred and fifty Associations, will have a larger Capital, formed of a Group of Associations, as above described.

A State composed of several Associated Districts will have a larger Capital, formed of a Series of Associations, or of a number of single Associations arranged in Serial order. Nations and Continents will have, likewise, their Capitals, which will be embellished and adorned with all the resources of creative Art and Industry, and the magnificence of which can only be conceived when we consider the wealth and power of Nations in Universal Association, and the collective pride and interest which they will take in all grand unitary arrangements.

The science of Association teaches us the Unity of the Human Race, and that this unity requires universal unitary arrangements—political, social and religious—corresponding to their political, social and religious Unity, with grand central Metropolises for the regulation and government of the affairs relating to these Unities. Thus the Cities of the Combined Order will be great Centres—administrative, scientific, industrial, artistic and religious—each for the region over which it presides. There, the Legislative Bodies and great Councils of Industry, Art and Science, and the great annual industrial, artistic and scientific exhibitions will be held; and there also will be located the grand galleries of Art, the scientific collections, the libraries, universities, etc., upon a scale much more extensive and magnificent than those of single Associations.

The Cities in the Combined Order will be centres of collective Knowledge, which they will draw and collect in fragments from all parts of the world, and again communicate it to every Association. . . .

Association Discussed*
1847

Over a period of several months in 1847, these two men—Greeley, the Associationist and publisher of the New York *Tribune*, and Raymond, the conservative editor of the *Courier and Enquirer*—debated the merits of communitarianism in their respective newspapers. Later in the year the debate came out as a pamphlet under the title, *Association Discussed; or the Socialism of the Tribune Examined.*

[HENRY J. RAYMOND]
REPLY TO LETTER VI

In our last article we endeavored to show that the inherent vices and weaknesses of human nature would render impossible such a community of interest and of life as the Tribune advocates. The essential *selfishness* of man would be at war with the essential principle of Association, and would inevitably destroy it. While men continue vicious or imperfect, while they are governed or influenced by prejudice, passion, or self-seeking in any of its forms, they can not combine and carry forward such a community as that proposed. The Tribune, while professing to reply to this objection, actually concedes its full force and validity. Says the Editor of that paper:

I know that vicious persons *must have a new spirit breathed into them before* they can comprehend and act upon the vital principles of Social Unity. I know well that an Association of indolent or covetous persons *could not endure without a moral transformation of its members.*

Now it seems to us that this concession is fatal to the whole theory of Association. It certainly implies that individual Reform must *precede* Social Reform—that the latter must have its root in the former—that Association can not advance beyond the personal

* Pp. 28, 31–35, 37, 40–41.

reformation of the individuals who compose it. This point the Tribune concedes; and the same thing has been conceded by some of those who have hitherto been most zealous in support of Association. . . .

The position, then, is fully conceded that Men must become good—must have a "new spirit breathed into them:" must undergo a "moral transformation," *before* they can carry into effect the scheme of Association. This is essential as a preliminary step. How is it to be effected? The Tribune says, by Association! "I know also," says the Editor, "that its organism tends strongly to correct the faults inimical to its existence." This seems to us a gross absurdity. Association is thus expected to make its own indispensable conditions. It is to create its own creator—to produce its own cause—to effect that personal reform in which it must originate. The very statement of the case demonstrates its absurdity. . . .

[HORACE GREELEY]

LETTER VII

"Oh, moralists, who treat of happiness and self-respect in every sphere of life, go into the squalid depths of deepest ignorance, the uttermost abyss of Man's neglect, and say, *Can any hopeful plant spring up in air so foul that it extinguishes the Soul's bright torch as soon as kindled?*"—CHARLES DICKENS.

To the Editor of the Courier and Enquirer:

I intend in this article to discuss directly and sufficiently the doctrine of Circumstances, and their influence on Human Character and Destiny. It seems to be your chief difficulty in regard to "Association" that it requires good dispositions in its members, which dispositions it is obvious that a large portion of the Human Family now lack, and under existing circumstances are little likely to attain. Hence you argue, in the spirit of the Caliph who burned the Alexandrian Library, that, since the ignorant and squalid are now confessedly unfit for Association, they can only become so by an intrinsic melioration, which, if effected, would render Association unnecessary. Let us consider this:

Here is a community—say the people of Paterson, N. J., or of some Ward of this City—comprising every grade of fortune from boundless wealth to extreme indigence and emaciation. Some enjoy incomes of $50,000 per annum, with little labor or care on their

own part; others, by the most strenuous industry, can not earn
$200 per annum, yet from this must pay the rent, food, and fuel
of a family. Many, in the greatest need, can find no way to earn
a penny for weeks,—but are compelled to subsist at all events. And
is not this necessity calculated to degrade them in spirit and in
morals? Take two men of equal and medium qualities, and secure
to one ample, unfailing, remunerated employment, enlightened associates, daily opportunities to perfect himself in industrial, scientific,
and historical knowledge, with the moral certainty of an enduring
home and a generous subsistence, while you leave the other to
struggle with the wants, temptations, alternations of excessive labor
and involuntary idleness of a mere Laborer in this City at present,
and who can doubt that the former would naturally grow wiser
and better, increasing in self-respect and the respect of his associates, while the latter would steadily gravitate toward the grog-
shop and the Alms-House? Not that every individual circumstanced
like the former would become wise and good, nor that every hod-
carrier and street-sweeper of our City is doomed to end his days
intemperate and probably in the Alms-House, but that the *tendency*
in each case is to the result I have indicated.

Take another illustration: My religion teaches me, as I think
yours does you, that your son and mine are no better than the
children of equally tender years now growing up in the cellars of
Cross-street and the garrets of Republican-alley. Yet you know, as I
know, that the chance of these latter coming to what is called
"a bad end" is immensely the greater. The class of News-boys,
for example, is mainly recruited from the cellars and garrets tenanted
by our City's crowded wretchedness. They are by nature no better
and no worse than other boys just outgrowing infancy. And yet
few years pass before a large proportion of those who commence
as newsboys find themselves tenants of the House of Refuge, Black-
well's Island, &c., &c. How is this? These same boys, if early
trained to habits of industry and good conduct, would mainly have
been virtuous and useful members of Society. But a mere child of
ten or twelve years is driven forth by the intemperance or destitution of his parents—perhaps by the loss of them—to try to earn
a living by his own exertions; and almost the only business
upon which he can enter without preparation, without permission,
and without capital, is that of selling newspapers. A shilling will
start it, and the gains are in hand every evening. But this very

facility overstocks the calling, and renders its proceeds meager and precarious. Thus evening often falls upon the lad trudging wearily, hungrily home, his pockets empty, his papers unsold. He is morally certain of abuse, if not blows, should he thus seek the shelter of the miserable hovel which his parents inhabit. One desperate chance remains to him: he raises the cry, "Ere's the Hextra 'Erald, (Tribune or Sun), got the news of another great battle in Mexico —Santa Anna defeated, 5000 killed." At once his stock of papers is snapped up at double prices, and he turns the first corner and scuds home, with a full pocket and a light heart. He takes his oyster supper and a glass of grog with a chuckle at his own adroitness, and jots down in his mental note-book, that "Honesty is the best policy"—sometimes;—at others a little jocular roguery does better. To be sure, he has damaged his line of business, somewhat; but he has reaped all the benefit of that, while all but a thousandth part of the damage falls on others. Those who curse the trick and resolve never to believe a newsboy again will not identify him should they meet next day. So he has taken a degree in his education, and is ready for some more daring resort in his next fit of desperation or temptation. So with Hack-driving about our City, and scores of other callings which our existing Society creates and sustains after a fashion. Hundreds all around are making a livelihood in vocations which require no personal integrity on their part—many in ways which integrity would rather obstruct. The young man who deals out silks gracefully in a fashionable Broadway store, or mixes juleps dexterously in a genteel Broadway bar, may keep a mistress in the next street or spend his nights in the gambling-dens of Park-place; yet those by whom he lives know nothing of this; his current reputation is not affected by it. It is but a little while since a man intrusted with the responsible and lucrative business of collecting rents on a large City property was exposed and compelled to fly, after having for months, if not years, been engaged in decoying young women into his den under pretense of employing them as servants, and then accomplishing their ruin by violence when blandishments, threats, and drugs would not effect it. How many are now pursuing like nefarious courses can only be guessed, but all can see that our present Social arrangements afford the amplest facilities and impunity to such crimes. There is (or recently was) in the State Prison at Sing-Sing at least one poor servant girl who was sent there on a trumped-up charge of stealing, because she had been seduced by the son of her employer, and no other means occurred to the family of preventing an unpleasant expense and scandal. But I will not multiply examples. Briefly, it seems to me that if some malignant spirit had undertaken to contrive a Social framework which should subject the poor, the humble, the ignorant, to the greatest possible amount and variety of temptations—which should virtually constrain many and irresistibly draw far more to the ways of dissipation and sin—he could hardly, in the light of Christianity and such Civilization as we have, devise any thing more admirably adapted to his purpose than the Social System under which we now live.

What, then, do we propose and hope ultimately to accomplish? Granted that the mass of the destitute and squalid are incapable of rising by their own efforts to a level with the requirements of a just and beneficent Social Order—are unable even to appreciate such an Order, or to desire its establishment, what then? The good work must be done, nevertheless. I say let those who *are* capable of conceiving a true Society proceed at once to actualize it, as an example and encouragement to others. Let the Wealthy contribute of their wealth, the Wise of their wisdom, the Learned of their science, the Good of their piety and charity, to construct a Social Organization wherein no honest and industrious man can become a pauper or a serf, and no widow and orphans be driven out from home into a cold and cheerless world because the husband and father has been snatched from them by death. I know all men are not now capable of doing what is needed, but I know *some* men who are, and I am confident that these, by affording Example and Opportunity, could speedily work a vast change in others. Give but one hundred of the right men and women as the nucleus of a true Social Organism, and hundreds of inferior or indifferent qualities might be rapidly molded into conformity with them. I believe there are few of the young and plastic who might not be rendered agreeable and useful members of an Association under the genial influences of Affection, Opportunity, Instruction, and Hope. I see many now hurrying down to death-beds of drunkenness and pauperism whom I am sure might have been, would have been, retained in life, vigor, usefulness, and honor, had these influences surrounded them from childhood, and I trust that some of the thousands preparing to follow in the downward road will yet be arrested and preserved. Who ever heard of a drunken or begging Shaker?

When you persist in saying to me "That Reform must be effected by some other agency than that which Association offers—that agency is Christianity," you compel me to regret that I can not render myself intelligible to you. To my mind, Association is the palpable dictate of Christianity—the body whereof True Religion is the soul. I can not doubt that if Christ were here in New York to-day, and could gain access to the dwelling of our Astor, Lenox, Whitney, &c., He would say to them in terms as He has already done in substance, "Cease amassing wealth for yourselves or your descendants; cease building sumptuous palaces from which your brethren are expressly, and splendid churches whence they are virtually, shut out; cease isolating yourselves in heart and life from the masses who need to be benefited by your superior intelligence, wisdom, morality, refinement, if such you have; cease to make a gain of the wretched hovels in which Famine and Despair are now festering into Sin and Crime; employ your vast wealth in drawing forth from these dens of darkness and misery their crowded, shivering inmates, and placing them where they will have pure air to breathe, ample space to occupy, bread to eat, unfailing and fairly remunerated work to do, with all those refining influences of elevated Social Intercourse, judicious Counsel, ample Instruction, an enduring Home and a horizon of Hope, which you can so well appreciate and of which most of them know nothing." That, it seems very plain to me, is just what Christianity would have done, and which it is now urgently calling on the wise and wealthy to combine their efforts and their means to accomplish. . . .

[HENRY J. RAYMOND]
REPLY TO LETTER VII

In its reply to our last article, the Tribune professes to "discuss sufficiently the doctrine of Circumstances, and their influence on human character." By a strange oversight, however, it omits to state what that doctrine is. The omission is remarkable, because the question is important. If circumstances, or that arrangement of them which constitutes Society, be the actual *cause* of existing evils, then those evils may possibly be removed by changing that arrangement. But if evil has another and a far different origin, then it must clearly have another and a far different remedy: for the remedy in any case must not only modify the conditions, but remove the essential cause, of the evil it is designed to cure. We regret, therefore, that the Tribune does not tell us which of those opposite views it entertains.

We find in its article expressions which might warrant the inference, that the Tribune's "doctrine" regards circumstances as the *cause* of existing evil. But the only points distinctly stated are, that the ignorance, squalor, and general wretchedness of the degraded poor, subject them to temptations from which others are comparatively free: and that a change in their condition is very desirable, on moral as well as physical grounds. We can not understand why the Tribune should labor so hard to prove what we expressly conceded at the very outset of this discussion, unless its object be to excite odium, instead of answering argument. The existence of misery, and the necessity of relieving it, are not in controversy, for we have never doubted either. It is only upon the *remedy to be applied*, that the Tribune and ourselves are at variance. That paper insists that Association is the only agency by which the poor can be relieved: that the ignorant, the vicious, and the degraded, can not be reclaimed, unless the virtuous, the wise, and the rich establish with them a community of interests and of life; that to benefit a part, the whole must be changed; that to furnish some with good dwellings, all must abandon their houses and dwell together under a common roof; that the whole fabric of existing institutions, with all its habits of action and of thought, must be swept away, and a new Society take its place, in which all must be subject to common customs, a common education, common labor, and common modes of life, in all respects. This, its fundamental position, we deny. We deny the necessity, the wisdom, and the possibility of removing existing evil, by such a process. We would not thus destroy the good in order possibly to amend the bad. It is not the method of wisdom or benevolence: it finds no support in common sense or sober judgment. The Tribune promised to prove that it is not only the best, but the only means of relieving the poor; but thus far it has not even attempted to fulfill its promise. It has asserted and illustrated in every possible variety of forms the existence of evils, and the necessity of removing them, and has drawn fancy pictures of the state of things when that removal shall have been effected. But its proof that Association, and nothing but that, can accomplish it, is to come hereafter, if it come at all.

We, on the contrary, have sought to show, 1. That Association can never be established: 2. That if established, it could never endure: and 3. That if it were permanently established, it would *increase* tenfold the evils it is designed to cure. . . .

But, says the Tribune, Christianity commands the rich to relieve the poor; Association proposes to do that work; therefore "Association is the palpable *dictate* of Christianity;" and men if they be Christians, must be Associationists. Now here the premises are true, but they do not warrant the conclusion. The argument illustrates the Tribune's habitual assumption of the very point in dispute, namely, that Association is the only means by which the poor can be relieved. It assumes that no man can befriend the poor, unless he espouse Association. The best test of true benevolence is practice, not precept; let us look for what it *does*, not what it professes. And, bringing the matter to this standard, we have no hesitation in asserting, that the members of any one of our City Churches do more every year for the practical relief of poverty and suffering, than any Phalanx that ever existed. There are in our midst hundreds of female "sewing societies," each of which clothes more nakedness, and feeds more hunger, than any "Association" that was ever formed. There are individuals in every ward, poor, pious, humble men and women, who never dreamed of setting themselves up as professional philanthropists, who do more in visiting the sick, in seeking out and relieving the poor, in encouraging the despondent, and in meliorating the condition of the degraded and the destitute, than was ever done by any Associationist, from its first apostle down to the humblest of his deluded followers. And one of those three individuals, villified by name in the Tribune's article as the selfish, grasping despisers of the poor, has expended more money, and accomplished more actual good in aiding the poor, in providing for them food, clothing, education, and sound instruction, moral and religious, and all the blessings of which they stand in need, than has been effected by the advocates of Association in half a century, throughout the world. Hundreds of thousands of dollars have been expended by the Associationists, in propagating their *theories* of benevolence, and in making benevolent "experiments;" yet where is the practical good they have accomplished? Where are the starving whom they have fed, the naked they have clothed, the degraded they have raised, the vicious they have reclaimed, the poor whom, in any way, they have assisted and blessed? The Tribune sneers at practical Christianity as "filling wretched hovels with *Bibles* and *Tracts*," while bread, and clothing, and health are needed. Does the taunt come with good grace from a system which theorizes over starvation, but does not feed it; which scorns to give bread and clothing to the hungry and naked, except it can first have the privilege of reconstructing Society? And is not the taunt proved to be false, by the fact that all the relief which poverty gets comes from Christianity, either directly from its hand, or indirectly from the spirit of Charity which it has infused into every department of social life? All may not be done that should be done, for the poor, the wretched and the sinful; but of all that is done, how small is the share which the Social Reformers of the day contribute! . . .

[HORACE GREELEY]
LETTER VIII

To the Editor of the Courier and Enquirer:

As progress is my watchword and the appointed limit of this controversy approaches, I will endeavor to resist the strong temptation to follow you into an infinity of irrelevant discussions. It seems to me that the Doctrine of Circumstances—namely, That Circumstances of position, opportunity, encouragement, instruction, temptation, &c., exert a vast and often vital influence, whether for good or evil, over the formation and quality of the Human Character—has already been sufficiently set forth and illustrated. The deduction therefrom that we should systematically endeavor to secure to all, as nearly as may be, education and training under such circumstances as will tend to incline them to Industry, Temperance, Virtue, Self-Respect, instead of those which naturally tempt to Idleness, Dissipation, Vice and Debasement, seems too obvious to need more explicit assertion. I pass, then, to another branch of the general arrangement.

You say that I have not *attempted* to prove Association the best means of relieving the Poor—how truly the reader must judge. Most surely, if I have not *attempted* this, I have attempted nothing whatever. All my articles have had this single aim. True, I have not wished to assail nor undervalue other means or agencies of philanthropic effort; yet I deeply feel that other plans contemplate, mainly, a mitigation of the woes and degradations which are the *consequences* of extreme poverty, while Association proposes a way —in my judgment rational and feasible—of reaching the *causes* of these calamities, and absolutely *abolishing* Pauperism, Ignorance, and the resulting Vices. I need not, surely, recapitulate my statements of what Association is, and how it will do what it promises. You yourself seem to admit that the evils of Caste, Pauperism, constrained Idleness, Intemperance, &c., *have been* abolished by the Shakers, under an organization far less favorable (it seems to me) than that of Association. I know you say "the Shakers are virtuous, not because they belong to a Shaker establishment, but because they have within them virtuous principles;" but I ask you to consider the fact that these same Shakers are in the habit of taking gladly any such infants as they can get—foundlings, illegitimates, destitute orphans, &c.—the very material from which our Houses of Refuge, Penitentiaries, and Prisons, are mainly recruited, and training them up, with scarcely a failure, into these same industrious, moral, sober, virtuous adults. Does any one believe that the difference between the children trained about the Five Points and those educated by the Shakers, or under virtuous and comfort-giving auspices elsewhere, is intrinsic, and not superinduced by the force of circumstances? . . .

[HENRY J. RAYMOND]
REPLY TO LETTER VIII

We acknowledge, at the outset, the sincerity and success of the Tribune's "endeavor" to "resist the strong temptation" to follow the course of our last argument upon this subject. It is barely possible, to be sure, that the temptation was not so "strong" as the Editor would have his readers suppose, and that the struggle to resist it was, therefore, less severe than they might infer. But, at all events, the "endeavor" was successful. The temptation was resisted, and our entire argument remains untouched, except by the general plea that it was all irrelevant. Whether that plea be well founded or not, our readers can easily determine.

Association is urged by its advocates as a *substitute* for the Social System which now exists. It is presented as a plan for *"reaching the causes of social evil"*—for *"abolishing* pauperism, ignorance, and the resulting vices." It is intended, of course, for universal adoption —as a substitute for the present form of Society. Of course, therefore, its merits can be canvassed fully and fairly only by supposing it to have attained the universal dominion at which it aims. We may, it is true, discuss the principles on which it rests, and bring them to the test of established truth, without reference to the manner in which they are to be carried out. But if we seek to investigate the practical workings of the new system, it must be relieved from all the influences of the existing form. We must suppose Association to be universal. Suppose that all men were living, not as they now do, but as Association would have them: What would then be the tendency of things? What would then be the prevailing influences upon human character and human life? And what the results which, so far as reason can decide, those influences would produce? These are the questions involved in this discussion; and upon no other hypothesis can they find an answer.

This simple statement, it will be seen, sweeps away at once most of the Tribune's attempted arguments in defense of the system. It destroys, for example, the pertinence of the Tribune's references to the Shaker, Rapp, Moravian, and other communities which, it is assumed, have fully succeeded. The cases are not analogous. These little communities exist in the very heart of the old Society. They are surrounded on every side by its laws, its habits, and its atmosphere. They find in that Society markets for their produce; laws for the repression of crime; penalties for attempted fraud; a constant pressure which keeps them together; and a place into which they may expel all troublesome members. In Association, of course, when universally established, this could not be so. There could be no such thing as conditions of membership, or expulsion for misconduct. All classes, the wise and the stupid, the industrious and the lazy, the virtuous and the profligate, must then exist together; and must be entirely free from the laws, restraints, habits, and influences of the old Society. The Association could not avail itself of any of the aids or resources of the old form. It must exist alone, and furnish its own restraints, its own methods of education, of worship, and of promoting general order. And when all Society, moreover, had assumed that shape; when all the towns and cities in the land had been converted into phalanxes—each producing all the varieties of needed products—where would any of them find a market for their surplus? There would then be no world of "outside barbarians" to be supplied; but each would produce all it would need—and something more, as is affirmed. Here is a fatal difference between the two cases.

All these little communities, moreover, are under the complete control of some one or more persons. They are absolute monarchies on a small scale. They are held together, furthermore, by the bond of a common religious faith, which is different from that of the rest of the world. Their manner of life is a part of that religious faith; and their faith renders them passively subservient to the will of their leader. In Association there is to be no such head, and no such bond. There is to be no supreme power, clothed with authority, and with the means of enforcing it. While the new phalanxes exist in the bosom of the present Society; so long as they enjoy the defense and shelter of its laws and its influences, they may possibly hold together. But remove this support from them, make the system universal, and it would fall to pieces. At all events, the assumed success of the Shakers, Rappites, &c. (which, moreover, is not real), affords not even the shadow of a presumption to the contrary . . . .

The Harbinger
June 14, 1845

The following extract is from the first issue of *The Harbinger*, published by Brook Farm.

INTRODUCTORY NOTICE

In meeting our friends, for the first time, in the columns of the Harbinger, we wish to take them by the hand with cheerful greetings, to express the earnest hope that our intercourse may be as fruitful of good, as it will be frank and sincere, and that we to-day may commence a communion of spirit, which shall mutually aid us in our progress towards the truth and beauty, the possession of which is the ultimate destiny of man. We address ourselves to the aspiring and free minded youth of our country; to those whom long experience has taught the emptiness of past attainments and inspired with a better hope; to those who cherish a living faith in the advancement of humanity, whose inner life consists not in doubting, questioning, and denying, but in believing, who, resolute to cast off conventional errors and prejudices, are hungering and thirsting for positive truth; and who with reliance on the fulfilment of the prophetic voice in the heart of man, and on the Universal Providence of God, look forward to an order of society founded on the divine principles of justice and love, to a future age of happiness, harmony, and of great glory to be realized on earth.

We have attained, in our own minds, to firm and clear convictions, in regard to the problem of human destiny; we believe that principles are now in operation, which will produce as great a change on the face of society, as that which caused beauty and order to arise from the chaos of the primitive creation by the movings of the divine Spirit; and to impart these convictions and principles to the hearts of our readers, will be our leading purpose in the columns of this paper.

It will be, then, in the light of positive ideas, not of fanciful conceptions, that we shall criticise the current literature, the political movements, the social phenomena of the day; and without inquiring how far we may be in accordance with the prevailing standards of fashion or popular opinion, speak our minds on the subjects we shall discuss, with entire independence of outward authority.

Our faith in the high destiny of man is too profound to allow us to cherish the spirit of antagonism; we would not destroy but reconstruct; and if our readers expect to find in these pages, the fierce ebullitions of Jacobinical wrath, to be entertained with the virulence of invective against the evils which we condemn, or to be stimulated with the sallies of personal abuse, they will certainly be disappointed. Those who wish to indulge a taste for such condiments, must look elsewhere for its gratification. We trust that ruffian and reformer are not convertible terms;—if they be, we lay no claim to the title of the latter.

We mean to discuss all questions of public interest, with the utmost freedom, and with a single eye to the finding of the whole Truth, being well assured that the whole Truth and the highest Good, are connected in indissoluble union. But we have no desire wantonly to violate any cherished convictions, nor to maintain what is new simply because it is new.—It is our belief that there is much good, mingled with much error, in all the parties and sects both of the Church and of the State, and it is the duty of all persons who sincerely desire to aid in the progress of the human race, not to abandon themselves blindly to one particular doctrine, but to try all and to hold fast that which is good. The time has come for politicians and philanthropists to break the restraints of a barren, one-sided sectarianism, to assume some higher and broader ground, which will enable them to select the good of all partial creeds, to combine it in a consistent and glorious whole. Nor can this process degenerate into a meagre and barren Eclecticism, whenever we take our stand on the broad and universal principles, which the true science of human nature unfolds.

With a deep reverence for the Past, we shall strive so to use its transmitted treasures, as to lay in the Present, the foundation of a better Future. Our motto is, the elevation of the whole human race, in mind, morals, and manners, and the means, which in our view are alone adapted to the accomplishment of this end, are not violent outbreaks and revolutionary agitations, but orderly and progressive reform.

In Politics, it will be our object to present fair discussions of the measures of political parties, taking the principles of Justice to all men as our standard of judgment. By sympathy and conviction we are entirely democratic; our faith in democracy is hardly inferior to our faith in humanity; but by democracy we do not understand a slavish adherence to "regular nominations," nor that malignant mobocracy which would reduce to its own meanness all who aspire to nobler ends than itself, but that benevolent, exalting, and refining creed, which holds that the great object of government, should be to secure the blessings of Liberty, Intelligence, and Good Order, to the whole people. We believe in the Rights of Man,—best summed up in the right to a perfect development of his whole nature, physical, intellectual, and moral,—and shall oppose partial or class legislation, as inconsistent with the fundamental principles of Republican Institutions. Yet we shall take sides with no party, but proceed from time to time to remark upon all parties, with the frankness and independence which our position fully enables us to exercise. If our politicians take offence at what we shall say, the fault will be their own, and our only apology will be a little more severity.—Foreign politics, which are too much neglected by the journals of the country, will be regularly treated by us, in the form of well-digested reviews of the English, French, and German press.

In Literature, besides elaborate notices of new publications, with the aim to inform and improve the taste of the public, and not to gratify the cupidity of booksellers, it is our wish to keep a faithful record of literary intelligence, noticing the most important works that are issued in Europe and this country, and giving brief sketches of the matter of those most generally interesting to the American reader.

The Fine Arts too shall have due honor done them. Music, the Art most appreciable to the many, most associated with the hopes of Humanity, and most flourishing always where Humanity is most alive, we shall watch with almost jealous love; striving not only by criticism of all important musical performances, schools and publications, but also by historical and philosophical essays on the principles of the Art itself, and the creations of its master minds, to keep it true to the standard of pure taste, true to the holy end for which the passion of hearing harmonies was given to man. Painting, Sculpture, Architecture, the Drama, and all arts which seek the Good, by way of the Beautiful, will, we hope, be criticised in practice, and interpreted in theory from the same humanitary and universal point of view. For this end, we shall have correspondents in our principal cities, on whose taste and power of communication we can rely. Summaries of intelligence under this head from Europe too, from countries where Art has a home, will occasionally be offered to our readers. Musical criticism is a thing which has not hitherto existed in our country. Instead of the unmeaning praise, and petty partial censure with which all concerts are alike served up in our newspapers, we would humbly hope to contribute something, if only by our sincerity and impartiality, toward a sound and profitable criticism.

In Science, as far as the limits of a weekly newspaper permit, we shall preserve a record of the most important improvements and discoveries, considered with especial reference to their bearing on the great object of all our labors, the progressive well-being of man.

The interests of Social Reform, will be considered as paramount to all others, in whatever is admitted into the pages of the Harbinger. We shall suffer no attachment to literature, no taste for abstract discussion, no love of purely intellectual theories, to seduce us from our devotion to the cause of the oppressed, the down-trodden, the insulted and injured masses of our fellow men. Every pulsation of our being vibrates in sympathy with the wrongs of the toiling millions, and every wise effort for their speedy enfranchisement will find in us resolute and indomitable advocates. If any imagine from the literary tone of the preceding remarks, that we are indifferent to the radical movement for the benefit of the masses, which is the crowning glory of the nineteenth century, they will soon discover their egregious mistake. To that movement, consecrated by religious principle, sustained by an awful sense of justice, and cheered by the brightest hopes of future good, all our powers, talents, and attainments are devoted. We look for an audience among the refined and educated circles, to which the character of our paper will win its way; but we shall also be read by the swart and sweaty artizan; the laborer will find in us another champion; and many hearts, struggling with the secret hope which no weight of care and toil can entirely suppress, will pour on us their benedictions as we labor for the equal rights of All.

We engage in our enterprise, then, with faith in our cause, with friendship for our readers, with an exulting hope for Humanity, and with a deep conviction which long years of experience have confirmed, that every sincere endeavor for a universal end will not fail to receive a blessing from all that is greatest and holiest in the universe. In the words of the illustrious Swedenborg, which we have selected for the motto of the Harbinger, "all things, at the present day, stand provided and prepared, and await the light. The ship is in the harbor; the sails are swelling; the east wind blows; let us weigh anchor, and put forth to sea."

A. J. MACDONALD

Visit to the North American Phalanx
1851

Macdonald, the chronicler of American communitarianism, spent some time at the North American Phalanx, the most durable of the Fourierist colonies. His report was published in Noyes's *History of American Socialisms.**

It was dark when I arrived at the Phalanstery. Lights shone through the trees from the windows of several large buildings, the sight of which sent a cheering glow through me, and as I approached, I inwardly fancied that what I saw was part of an early dream. The glancing lights, the sounds of voices, and the notes of music, while all nature around was dark and still, had a strange effect, and I almost believed that this was a Community where people were really happy.

I entered and inquired for Mr. Bucklin, whose name had been given me. At the end of a long hall I found a small reading-room, with four or five strange-looking beings sitting around a table reading newspapers. They all appeared eccentric, not alone because they were unshaven and unshorn, but from the peculiar look of their eyes and form of their faces. Mr. Bucklin, a kind man, came to me, glancing as if he anticipated something important. I explained my business, and he sat down beside me; but though I attempted conversation, he had very little to say. He inquired if I wished for supper, and on my assenting, he left me for a few minutes and then returned, and very soon after he led me out to another building. We passed through a passage and up a short flight of steps into a very handsome room, capable, I understood, of accommodating two hundred persons at dinner. It had a small gallery or balcony at one end of it, and six windows on either side. It was furnished with two rows of tables and chairs, each table large enough for ten or twelve persons to dine at. There were three bright lamps suspended from the ceiling. At one end of the room the chairs and tables

* Pp. 473–481.

had been removed, and several ladies and gentlemen were dancing cotillions to the music of a violin, played by an amateur in the gallery. At the other end of the room there was a doorway leading to the kitchen, and near this my supper was laid, very nice and tidy. Mr. Bucklin introduced me to Mr. Holmes, a gentleman who had lived in the Skaneateles and Trumbull experiments; and Mr. Holmes introduced me to Mr. Williston, who gave me some of the details of the early days of the North American Phalanx, during which he sometimes lived in high style, and sometimes was almost starved. He told of the tricks which the young members played upon the old members, many of whom had left.

On looking at the dancers I perceived that several of the females were dressed in the new costume, which is no more than shortening the frock and wearing trowsers the same as men. There were three or four young women, and three or four children so dressed. I had not thought much of this dress before, but was now favorably impressed by it, when I contrasted it with the long dresses of some of the dancers. This style is decidedly superior, I think, for any kind of active employment. The dress seems exceedingly simple. The frocks were worn about the same length as the Highland *kilt*, ending a little above the knee; the trowsers were straight, and both were made of plain material. Afterward I saw some of the ladies in superior suits of this fashion, looking very elegant.

Mr. Holmes shewed me to my bed, which was in the top of another building. It was a spacious garret with four cots in it, one in each corner. There were two windows, one of which appeared to be always open, and at that window a young man was sleeping, although the weather was very wet. The mattress I had was excellent, and I slept well; but the accommodations were rather rude, there being no chairs or pegs to hang the clothes upon. The young men threw their clothes upon the floor. There was no carpet, but the floor seemed very clean.

It rained hard all night, and the morning continued wet and unpleasant. I rose about seven, and washed in a passage-way, leading from the sleeping-rooms, where I found water well supplied; passed rows of small sleeping-rooms, and went out for a stroll. The morning was too unpleasant for walking much, but I examined the houses, and found them to be large framed buildings, the largest of the two having been but recently built. It formed two sides of a square, and had a porch in front and on part of the back. It appeared as if the portion of it which was complete was but a wing of a more extensive design, intended to be carried out at some future time. The oldest building reminded me of one of the Rappite buildings in New Harmony, excepting that it was built of wood and theirs of brick. It formed a parallelogram, two stories high, with large garrets at the top. A hall ran nearly the whole length of the building, and terminated in a small room which is used as a library, and to which is joined the office. Apartments were ranged on either side of the hall up stairs. All the rooms appeared to be bed-rooms, and were in use. The new building was more commodious. There were well furnished sitting-rooms on either side of the principal entrance. The dining-hall, which I have before mentioned, was in the rear of this. Up stairs the rooms were ranged in a similar manner to the old building, and appeared to be very comfortable. I was informed that they were soon to be heated by steam. All these apartments were rented to the members at various prices, according to the relative superiority of each room.

As the bell at the end of the building rang a second time for breakfast, I followed some of the members into the room, and on entering took my seat at the table nearest the door. I afterward learned that this was the vegetarian table, and also that it was customary for each person always to occupy the same seat at his meals. The tables were well supplied with excellent, wholesome food, and I think the majority of the members took tea and coffee and ate meat. Young men and women waited upon the tables, and seemed active and agreeable. An easy freedom and a harmonious feeling seemed to prevail. . . .

[I] made the acquaintance of Mr. John Gray, a gentleman who had lived five years among the Shakers, and who was still a Shaker in appearance. Mr. Gray is an Englishman, as would readily be perceived by his peculiar speech; but with his English he had gotten a little mixture of the "down east," where he had lately been living. Mr. Gray was very fluent of speech, and what he said to me would almost fill a volume. He spoke chiefly of his Shaker experience, and of the time he had spent among the Socialists of England. He said it was his intention to visit other Communities in the United States, and gain all the experience he could among them, and then return to England and make it known. He was a dyer by trade (on which account he was much valued by the Shakers), and was very useful in taking care of swine. He spoke forcibly of the evils of celibacy among the Shakers, and of their strict regulations. He preferred living in the North American Phalanx, feeling more freedom, and knowing that he could go away when he pleased without difficulty. He thought the wages too low. Reckoning, for instance, that he had earned about 90 cts. per day for ten hours labor, he got in cash every two weeks three-fourths of it, the remaining fourth going to the Phalanx as capital. Out of these wages he had to pay $1.50 per week for board, and $12 a year rent, besides extras; but he had a very snug little room, and lived well. He thought single men and women could do better there than married ones; but either could do better, so far as making money was the object, in the outer world. He decidedly preferred the single family and isolated cottage arrangement. I made allowances for Mr. Gray's opinions, when I remembered that he had been living five years among the Shakers, and but four months at the North American, whose regulations about capital and interest he was not very clear upon. . . .

I might speculate on this strange mixture of minds, but prefer that the reader should take the facts and philosophize for himself. Here were persons who, for many years, had tried many schemes of social reorganization in various parts of the country, brought together not from a personal knowledge and attraction for each other, but through a common love of the social principles, which like a pleasant dream attracted them to this, the last surviving of that extensive series of experiments which commenced in this country about the year 1843.

I retired to my cot about ten o'clock, and passed a restless night. The weather was warm and wet, and continued so in the morning. Rose at five o'clock and took breakfast with Dr. Lazarus and the stage-driver, and at a quarter to six we left the Phalanx in their neat little stage.

During the journey to Keyport the Doctor seemed to be full of Association, and made frequent allusions to that state in which all things would be right, and man would hold his true position; thought it wrong to cut down trees, to clear land, to raise corn, to fatten pigs to eat, when, if the forest was left alone, we could live on the native deer, which would be much better food for man; he would have fruit-trees remain where they are found naturally; and he would have many other things done which the world would deem crazy nonsense.

THE ICARIANS

The History of the Colony or Republic of
Icaria in the United States of America*
1855

This is an extract from a translation by Thomas Treakle of Cabet's
Colonie icarienne aux Etats-unis d'Amerique (second edition), published in Paris in 1855. A year after the pamphlet appeared Cabet
was unceremoniously cast out of the colony he had founded.

PROVISIONAL ESTABLISHMENT AT NAUVOO

The colonists arrived on March 15th [1849] at Nauvoo.

They rented at once some dwelling houses, a farm and some
ground.

They purchased a number of buildings, grounds, horses, cattle, etc.
Shortly afterward, they bought the remains of the Mormon temple,
which had been burned two years before and now had only its four
walls standing, with an inclosure of 4 acres, for the purpose of
establishing there a School or an Academy.

They roughly organized each day, repairing the old houses and
making the most necessary furniture. They established individual
apartments, two schools—one for little girls and another for little
boys—two infirmaries and a pharmacy, a large kitchen and a dining
hall for common meals, a bakery, a butchery, a laundry and scullery.

The gardening and farming were organized at once while the
stables and the cattle were provided for. They soon purchased a
steam flour mill, with a distillery and a pig-sty, and later added a
saw-mill. Boats and fishing-nets were made which proved quite profitable, while the hunt furnished game for the infirmary.

The trades for men were organized—tailoring, shoe and sabot-mak-
ing, mattress-making, brick-laying, plastering, carpentering, joinery,

* *Iowa Journal of History and Politics*, April 1917 (Vol. 15), pp. 224–226, 233–239, 253–255, 285–286.

turning, wagon-making, coopering, blacksmithing, lock and gun-smithing, sheet iron working, stovesmithing, and tinning, watch-making, weaving, tanning, gardening, farming, wood-cutting, bak-ing, milling, cooking, etc.

Trades for the women were organized such as lace-making, dress-making, washing, ironing, cooking, etc.

A General Assembly was organized together with elections, either for Managers or for the Assembly Committees, for the Director of the workshops or for the Commissioners and officers.

Entertainments and merry makings were organized, as were also the rural recreations. Instrumental and vocal music classes, concerts and theaters, with courses and readings in common were established.

A store was established at St. Louis to sell the products of the shoe-makers, boot-makers, dressmakers, and lace-makers, of the mill-ers and of the distillery.

A coal mine was worked for fuel.

A printing and lithographic office was provided to print all home pamphlets and two newspapers, one in French and one in Ger-man.

There was a library, a small collection of physical and chemical apparatus, and a small assortment of hunting weapons.

All members of the Colony work and are distributed among the several shops for men and women.

Each trade or shop selects its managers.

Whenever the farmer calls for an unusual number all necessary help is taken from those shops or trades which can without incon-venience furnish it.

In the summer the work is suspended during the heat of the day.

There are no household servants, each woman having the care of her own household.

All enter and leave the workshops at the same time.

Breakfast, dinner and supper are eaten in common.

Women who are about to be confined or are nursing children may be authorized to work at their homes.

There is equality in meals as elsewhere.

The Managers are the servants of all their brothers.

After supper come the recreations, good times, meetings, courts, General Assembly, discussions.

On Sunday there is instruction in True Christianity, admission of new members, marriages, individual or common promenading with music and country-like meals, good times, a concert and the evening play.

The Colony has a *Constitution*, of 183 articles, deliberated upon during nine meetings and finally accepted unanimously. There was debated and voted upon also during many meetings a law in regard to the General Assembly and one regarding admission to, withdrawal and exclusion from Icarian membership.

The Colony has obtained from the Illinois Legislature an act which incorporates and recognizes the *Icarian Community*.

Twice, unanimously, Cabet has been elected President of the Community and was reëlected a third time in 1852 during his absence, and three times since. . . .

A GENERAL IDEA OF THE ICARIAN SYSTEM

DOCTRINE OR PRINCIPLE

NATURE.—GOD.—We, Icarian Communists, do not believe that the Universe was the effect of *chance*, and we do like to admit a *first cause* absolutely intelligent and provident, that is called a *Creator, Supreme Being, God, Nature, Providence*.

We believe it to be useless and dangerous to insist upon discovering the origin, form, and essence of this first Cause; *useless* because we are convinced that it is the one *mystery* and human intelligence has not the understanding, or the means, or the neccessary faculties to penetrate this mystery; *dangerous* because the examination of these questions leads to discussions which degenerate nearly always into disputes, divisions and even hatreds.

GOD, PERFECTION.—But we consider *God* as the *pre-eminent* and *all-powerful* One, as the *Infinite* and *Perfection* in all.

GOD, FATHER OF THE HUMAN RACE.—We like to consider God as the *Father* of the Human Race, as *love, goodness, justice, indulgence*; we imagine that he is the most perfect Father, the most just, the most tender; that this better Father has only love for his children and that he loves them all equally.

DESTINY OF HUMANITY; HAPPINESS.—We like to admit that God, the most perfect of Fathers, has willed *happiness* for his children on earth. We see that he has lavished all (air, warmth, light, water, earth, with its metals, fruits, and animals) to make us happy in satisfying all our needs (food, lodging, dress, protection, etc., etc.); and we believe that the *instinct, intelligence* and *reason* that he has given us, suffice with his other gifts, to assure the happiness of mankind.

EVIL, MISFORTUNE.—However, the history of all Peoples, in all times, shows us *evil* everywhere; the *wretchedness* of the mass by the side of the opulence of a small minority; *vices* and *crimes* born from opulence as from misery; ignorance and oppression; the exploitation of the Poor by the Rich; the desperation and insurrections of the Poor threatening continually the Rich and troubling their security; murders and criminal punishments; revolutions and reactions ceaselessly leading to new despair, new insurrections, and new calamities. In a word we see Man unfortunate nearly everywhere and always.

But we cannot believe that this must be the destiny of Humanity; we cannot believe that the *evil* must be without *remedy*; for Man is essentially sociable, intelligent and perfectible.

SOCIABILITY, GOOD NATURE.—Man is *sociable* and consequently attracted toward his like, sympathetic, compassionate, affectionate, naturally good.

INTELLIGENCE.—Man is eminently intelligent.

PERFECTIBILITY.—Man is evidently perfectible through experience and education.

But what is the *remedy* for the evil? and first, what is the cause?

CAUSE OF EVIL.—We believe that the cause is in a *bad social* and *political organization*, resulting from the ignorance, inexperience and error of Humankind from its beginning.

REMEDY.—We believe that the remedy must be in a *better social* and *political organization*.

THE BASIS OF A BETTER SOCIAL ORGANIZATION

We believe that this better social organization must have for its basis principles contrary to those which are the cause of evil; that is to say, *Brotherhood, Equality, Solidarity*; the suppression of poverty and individual property, in a word *Communism*. For us, the remedy is in the fraternal and politically equal association that we call the *Community*.

THE COMMUNITY.—The Community is a great association or a great universal society, partnership or company, organized and based upon the principle of human *Fraternity* with all its consequences, in which the associates consent to put in common all their goods, abilities and work, to produce and enjoy in common.

Society.—It is a true Society in which there are not any exploiters and exploited, but true associates, all brothers and equals.

It is an *organized* company which must show organization and order everywhere, with intelligence and reason as well.

Fraternity.—Fraternity is for us the essential, radical or fundamental principle, generator of all other principles, and which necessarily comprehends all in itself alone.

Fraternity is itself the consequence of the other principle stated at the beginning, that the Supreme Being or God is the Father of all men; from which it follows that all men are his children, that all are brothers, and that the Human Race forms only one family of which all the members should love one another and devote themselves mutually to their interest and common welfare, as we conceive that they should be the most perfect brothers.

For us, the consequences of Fraternity are Solidarity, Unity, Equality, Liberty, the suppression of individual property and money, the improvement of Education, the purification of marriage and the family and the organization of work.

The principle of *Fraternity* is a principle at once philosophical and religious, social and political.

In our eyes, it is the most advanced and fruitful idea; it is the principle of the Evangels and Christianity. In a way we believe we can say, from the present, that our Icarian Communism is the purest morality, the sweetest philosophy and the most sublime religion, since it is nothing else than *Christianity* in its primitive purity, such as Jesus Christ instituted. . . .

ICARIAN SOCIAL ORGANIZATION

In the Icarian system, the Colony, the State, or the Nation, forms a true Society.

This Society is perfectly free and voluntary, that is to say, it imposes itself on no one, and it does not force (can not force) any one to enter; it includes only those who, voluntarily, freely, in perfect knowledge of motive, consent to become a part; and it admits only those who understand well, and who adopt completely its principles and conditions, and who unite the necessary qualities.

This Society makes its own social contract or constitution and its laws.

It determines its own social and political organization, institutes its public functions and chooses its functionaries.

It takes all means of preventing wretchedness and poverty, ignorance or superstition, and of assuring well-being and abundance, Education, Equality, Order and Liberty.

Its organization has for its *fundamental* and *generative principle*, *Fraternity*.

And once for all, it can be said and repeated that it is the purest Morals, the sweetest Philosophy and most sublime Religion.

It is also a *Society* of *mutual help*, a *universal assurance*, a true family, the members of which call themselves brothers, engaging themselves to practice the principles of the Brotherhood.

There each works *for all*, and all work *for each*.

It has for secondary principles, Equality, Solidarity, Community and Unity, which are the necessary consequences of Fraternity.

It is a blending of Communism and individualism; the home, for example, is individual, each having a home for himself, wife and family; but the property, in place of being individual or personal, is social, undivided, and common or public or national.

Profoundly convinced by experience that one can have happiness only through *fraternal association* and *Equality*, the Icarians wished to form a *Society* founded on the basis of the most complete and perfect *Equality*. All must be *Associates, Citizens, Equals in rights and duties*, without any sort of privilege for any one; all must partake equally in the *expenses* of the association, each following his *necessity* and the *advantages* of the Society, and his own needs.

All must form only one family, of which all members are united by the ties of Brotherhood.

ICARIAN CONSTITUTION
PRELIMINARY CONSIDERATIONS

Nature has overwhelmed Man with kindness. She has poured out upon the earth, around Man, all the elements and productions necessary to teach him the use of these things. She has desired the happiness of Humanity above all things else. And still history shows us Man unhappy nearly everywhere and always.

Man is by nature sociable, consequently sympathetic, affectionate

and good. Yet history shows us, in every time and all countries, vice
and crime, oppression and tyranny, insurrections excited by despair,
and civil wars, proscriptions and massacres, anguish and torture.

But Man is highly *perfectible*; consequently human *progress*
is a natural law and evil can not be without remedy.

If evil had its origin in the vengeance of a jealous and pitiless
God who imposed eternal punishment upon the innocent posterity
of a sinful person, whose disobedience came through the temptation of an irresistible power, one must despair of a remedy and
resign himself to suffer. But this vengeance and punishment is re-
pugnant to all our ideas of justice, of kindness, of divine love and
perfection; consequently we must look elsewhere for the true cause
of evil.

This cause we find in a social *organization* resulting from inexperience, from ignorance and from the mistakes of Man in his
infancy. Hence, we may find the remedy in a *better social organization* founded on a superior principle.

Let us replace the olden times by the new, the reign of Satan or
of Evil, by the reign of God or of Good; spiritual Death by the
Resurrection, Regeneration and Life; Darkness by Light; Routine
and Prejudice by the Experience of the centuries; Error by Truth;
Ignorance by Knowledge and Learning; Injustice by Justice; Domination and Servitude by Enfranchisement and Liberty.

Let us substitute the welfare of all for the excessive opulence of
the privileged few who have nearly everything without working,
and who are running over with abundance while the masses who
work and produce have nearly nothing, lack the necessities, and
suffer from the enslavement of misery.

Let us substitute for a Religion overburdened with superstition,
intolerance and fanaticism, one that is reasonable and which
teaches men to love and help each other.

May we adopt a social organization in which the word *Society*
may not be a word of reproach and derision, but a truth and a
reality, and in which there is neither antagonism nor competition,
no exploitation of man by man, neither masters, servants, nor
hirelings, proletariat nor pauperism, idleness nor excessive labor.

Let us replace individual property, the source of all abuse, by
social property, common, undivided, which has none of the objections of the first and which is infinitely more productive for the
use of all.

Let us purify and perfect Marriage and the Family through the suppression of dowries, through the education of women as well as men, and through liberty in the choice of a spouse.

In a word, the old Society is based on individualism. Give us, as a basis for the new, Fraternity, Equality and Liberty, Communism or the Community. . . .

APPEAL TO ICARIANS OF EUROPE AND AMERICA AND TO PHILANTHROPISTS

Icarians of all countries, who are well acquainted with our Icarian system and our Icarian doctrine, who adopt them completely, who partake of our devotion to the cause of the People and of Humanity, who combine all the necessary qualities, who fill all the required conditions, and especially who consent freely and voluntarily to put all in common in order to bring about the triumph of our system of Fraternity and Community, Equality and Liberty, of Democracy and of the Republic, come, aid us to establish in the wilderness an Icarian Commune and afterward a State. Come, Brothers, and you will be welcome!

And you who can not come, but who have heroic spirits and generous hearts, you, friends of Progress and of Humanity, you Philosophers or Philanthropists of all classes, you sincere and zealous Christians who desire to contribute by your works to the realization of the true principles of Christianity, you philanthropic Societies, aid us with all your strength and all your means, in our great and difficult evangelical and humanitarian enterprise!

We have everything to create in the wilderness, our houses and our workshops, our agriculture and our industry; our sciences and our arts, our schools and our temples; we shall have need of land and of animals, of machines and of steamboats, etc. etc., that is to say, of money and of much money. Assist us by your knowledge and your advice, by your support, above all by your gifts or your loans.

There are many wealthy people who desire to make themselves useful without knowing how to satisfy their desires effectually. Let them promote the success of Icaria and the grateful Icarians will perpetuate their names as benefactors of Humanity.

The President of the Community.
CABET.

CHAPTER IV

THE GERMANS

While in Europe only a general revolution can form the means of uplifting the working people, in America the education of the masses will instill them with the degree of self-confidence that is indispensable for the effective and intelligent use of the ballot, and will eventually lead to the emancipation of the working people from the yoke of capital.

Constitution of the General German Workingmen's Union, October 1865

Whoever works for a living has the same interests that a wage-laborer has, and should assist the latter in his struggle for the rights of labor against the encroachments of capital.

Friedrich Sorge,
Socialism and the Worker, 1876

Let us not conceal the truth: the Socialist Labor Party is only a German colony, an adjunct of the German-speaking Social Democracy.

Party Secretary V. L. Rosenberg, March 1885

I did not advocate the use of force. But I denounced the capitalists for employing it for holding the laborers in subjection to them, and declared that such treatment would of necessity drive the workingmen to employ the same means in self defense.

Albert R. Parsons, Cook County Jail Cell, August 1887

The German party over there must be smashed up *as such,* it is the worst obstacle. The American workers are coming along already, but just like English workers they go their own way. One cannot drum the theory into them beforehand, but their own experiences

and their own blunders and the evil consequences of
them will soon bump their noses up against theory—
and then all right. Independent nations go their own
way, and of all of them the English and their offspring
are surely the most independent. Their insular, stiff-
necked obstinacy annoys one often enough, but it also
guarantees that once a thing gets started what begun
it will be carried out.

ENGELS to Herman Schlüter,
January 11, 1890

No honest man, if he is intelligent, and no intelligent
man, if he is honest, will consider that anything he
may have to give to the Socialist movement is a sacrifice. It is no sacrifice at all to invest our all,—time,
wealth, knowledge, and all else—so as to leave our
children the estate of the Socialist or Co-Operative
Commonwealth.

DANIEL DeLEON,
The People, January 26, 1898

The spectacular industrial development of the United States that
took place between the Civil War and the 1890s called forth no
socialist movement of consequence. Not that protests against the
massed power of the capitalists were lacking. Pitched battles between striking workers and the authorities and riots by the poor
and the unemployed broke out with insistent regularity. But these
upsurges of anger and violence, like the jacqueries of medieval
Europe, invariably petered out, or were suppressed, leaving behind hardly a trace of organized opposition to the system. Reformers and radicals criticized the excesses of the capitalists, but
not capitalism itself. It was in the name of free enterprise that they
opposed the monopolies and the plutocrats. Root and branch
criticism would have come from a socialist movement, had there
been one.

America's failure to produce such a movement was no mystery,
and men as disparate as Andrew Carnegie and Friedrich Engels
could agree on the reasons. The United States was the most advanced political democracy in the world. Americans took for granted
the quintessential freedoms that European socialists were still struggling to obtain: e.g., universal male suffrage, civil liberties, equal

protection of the laws, representative government. Americans assumed as a matter of course that any form of special privilege, any undue concentration of power, violated the laws of the land and would be resisted or struck down by the normal processes of majority rule. They were free of the inherited feudal rights and prerogatives under which Europeans groaned. Correspondingly absent from the lives of Americans—even from most of the newly arrived immigrants—was the one nutriment on which socialism elsewhere throve: class consciousness. Their response to the sudden rise of industrial capitalism, to the appearance all at once of men possessing incalculable property and power, was to affirm the pre-industrial values on which they had been bred—the values inculcated on farms, in small towns, among the inhabitants of homogeneous communities. And even after they had, by the turn of the century, come to terms with industrialism they continued to reject the notion of class as destructive of American ideals.

Between 1850 and 1890 almost all of the socialists in America were German immigrants, rarely numbering more than a few thousand at any one time—an infinitesimal fraction of the four million Germans who landed in the United States in that forty-year period. Yet, few as they were, the Germans gave socialism whatever life it had in this country. Generally it was a life lived in the penumbra of society. The German socialists were confined to their own neighborhoods in the cities, spoke their own language, published their own newspapers, organized their own parties, and carried on their own disputes—all quite remote from the concerns of native Americans. The German socialists were as isolated from America at large as the communitarians of the pre-Civil War days had been.

They constituted a sect, in the sense of a small, self-contained group that adheres to a narrow and exclusive ideology (or faith). But they were not a sect by choice; they did not seek to withdraw from society in order to transform it. In fact, they were categorically anti-sectarian. Whether they were Marxists, Lassalleans, or Anarcho-Communists (these differences will be explored later), the German socialists were uniformly opposed to "utopianism." The socialism they espoused was rooted in the reality of the times: in the industrial process, the travail of the working class, the imperatives of everyday life as the average person experienced them. They looked forward to the establishment of a cooperative commonwealth embracing the whole mode of production and distribution that had grown up under capitalism, regarding socialism as the highest stage of historical evolution, and the proletariat as the embodiment of civilization itself.

That they tended to be dogmatic, stiff-necked, and often incomprehensible to the masses they sought to reach is incontestable. All their attempts to link up with insurgent political groups and labor unions ended in failure, often with humiliating consequences. Nonetheless, the German socialists did exert, indirectly at least, some influence on the life of their times. Certainly American labor owed them much. The founders of the American Federation of Labor were closely associated with German socialism, and it was as Marxists that they discovered the formula under which workers were successfully organized; it was they who effected the transition from *class* consciousness to *trade union* consciousness. The ideas of the German socialists also found their way into the broader arena of public discourse, primarily through the work of such writers as Laurence Gronlund, Edward Bellamy, William Dean Howells, and through the native socialist movements that sprang up in the 1890s. By then, however, German socialism had ceased to be German and become another rivulet that fed into the inexhaustible American mainstream.

Among the million or so Germans who came to the United States in the 1850s, several thousand were political emigrés who had fled after the abortive 1848 revolutions. Most of them were liberal democrats who had dared to advocate constitutional, or republican, forms of government in the place of the despotisms that ruled the various states of their homeland. A tiny minority was socialist; that is, they had gone beyond political reform and demanded a re-distribution of wealth in favor of the workers and peasants who created it. The German socialists had been divided into numerous, highly contentious groups (as one can judge from Marx's early writings), and they brought these divisions with them to America. There were the friends of Marx who preached class conflict and proletariat revolution; the "Turners," members of the *Turnverein*, or German Gymnastic Union, who believed that socialism represented the unity of a healthy mind in a healthy body; the philosophers and pedagogues who established a Communist Club in New York as a discussion and education center; and the followers of Wilhelm Weitling who comprised the largest single group.

Weitling was an ex-tailor from Magdeburg whose writings on communism and activities as a revolutionist had made him notorious long before he emigrated. Immediately after settling in America he circulated a plan to promote cooperative production and exchange, the first step toward what he hoped would be complete communism. The plan won support from some German mechanics and artisans, and they formed a "General Working Men's League" to put it into effect. But the cooperative venture was short-lived, and Weitling withdrew into obscurity. In fact, by the end of the 1850s socialism had practically disappeared from the German-American community. Most of the socialists had gone over to the anti-slavery movement, either as Abolitionists or Republicans. (Some, including one of Marx's good friends, Joseph Weydemeyer, were to serve with distinction in the Civil War.) The Turners carried on as before, but they grew increasingly conservative and finally abandoned politics altogether.

Socialism came to life again in the late 1860s. Skilled workers, German-born and American, suffered from the installation of labor-saving machines during and after the war. For them, large-scale production meant unemployment or reduction in status to the level of factory hands. By 1869 over 200,000 men had confederated into a powerful and well led organization, the National Labor Union, which demanded a shorter work day, control over hiring and working conditions, and, most important, curtailed employment of cheap and unskilled labor. Many of the German workers in the union were also members of the London-based International Workingmen's Association, founded in 1864 by European, mainly British trade unionists who had come to realize that their problems were international in scope (e.g., the movement of labor from one country to another), and that unless they cooperated they would stand no chance against the free-wheeling capitalists.

In the United States the International was run entirely by German socialists. Its presiding officer, Friedrich A. Sorge, was, from his arrival in America in 1852 until his political retirement thirty years later, the single most influential socialist in the country. He was also the closest to Marx; his correspondence with Marx and Engels would fill a small volume. But he was no dogmatic apostle of Marxism. He hoped that the trade unions would provide the nuclei of a socialist political movement, and that German and

American workers would join together, draw on each other's experience, and so advance to a higher stage of solidarity.

For a while the International made headway. In 1870–71 a substantial number of sections (each of which contained at least twenty-five members) emerged in cities across the country. At one point the total membership reached 5000. Most of the sections were, of course, German. But there were also Irish sections, Bohemian, Scandinavian, French (exiled victims of the recently fallen Paris commune), and a smattering of American as well. The organization did not limit itself to any particular ideology; it threw out a wide net, and it caught some exotic fish. One section—Twelve of New York City—consisted of a heterogeneous gathering of American radicals and non-conformists led by two wild sisters, Victoria Woodhull and Tennessee Claflin. Through their magazine, *The Woodhull and Claflin Weekly*, they propagandized not so much for workers' rights as for female suffrage and sexual freedom (which they, at least, had no trouble exercising) and a host of other reforms. Soon Section One of New York, which was German, demanded the expulsion of Section Twelve on the grounds that it was misleading the public and discrediting the International with its "visionary ideas" and outrageous behavior. Local newspapers brought the dispute into the open (the sisters made excellent copy), giving the public something to laugh about. Section Twelve was expelled from the International in 1872. But it promptly held a convention of its own at which it changed its name to the Equal Rights Party and proceeded to nominate Victoria Woodhull and Frederick Douglass, the Negro leader, as presidential and vice-presidential candidates.

Having disposed of Section Twelve the American branch of the International, known as the North American Federation, looked forward to a period of further expansion. The prospects seemed favorable. The National Labor Union, having sponsored a series of losing strikes and wasted its substance on third party activities, was disintegrating, and some of its affiliates were expected to join the International. The prestige of the American branch received another boost when, in 1872, the headquarters of the organization was moved from London to New York. Marx, the International's chief strategist, decided on this course to prevent the Anarchists from taking it over, as they appeared about to do (they subsequently formed their own "Black International"), and Sorge was entrusted the task of preserving the organization until such time as it could be returned to its place of origin.

But it was fated for a different end. The Panic of 1873 and the depression that followed dealt it a death blow. Most of the sections dissolved, and what was left was torn apart by dissension. Socialists agonized over the question of what they should do during the crisis. American workers, oppressed by unemployment or wage reductions, were turning to the ballot box, or to more violent forms of action, such as protests, riots, and strikes, to redress their grievances. A majority of the International's members wanted to engage in politics, even if it meant collaborating with radical bourgeois groups. These were the devotees of the legendary Ferdinand Lassalle who had laid the intellectual foundation for the rise of the German Socialist Party. According to Lassalle, socialism ideally represented the fusion of the state and the proletariat. Through democratic political means—by voting in elections and putting up candidates— the proletariat should seek to appropriate the state. This formula was working in Germany, and the American Lassalleans had good reason to hope that it would in the United States too.

The other faction consisted of Sorge and those who shared his Marxist orientation. They answered the Lassalleans by re-affirming the exclusively working-class basis of socialism and the International. Accordingly, at its 1874 congress, the North American Federation of the International announced that it rejected "all cooperation and connection with the political parties formed by the possessing classes, whether they call themselves Republicans or Democrats or Independents or Liberals or Patrons of Industry or Patrons of Husbandry (Grangers) or Reformers or whatever name they may adopt. Consequently, no member of the Federation can belong any longer to such a party." The Lassalleans promptly left the International and established the Social Democratic Working Men's Party of North America whose objective was to take "possession of political power as a prerequisite for the solution of the labor question."

In Germany, meanwhile, the Lassalleans and the Marxists were moving toward a reconciliation. At the famous Gotha Congress of 1875 they finally hammered out a program acceptable to both factions and to the bulk of the trade union movement. The American socialists soon followed suit. On July 15, 1876, the International, reduced to a handful of sections, formally came to an end. That same week its leaders met with the Lassalleans and agreed to form a new organization, the Working Men's Party of the United States. Actually, the party platform reflected the defunct International's point of view rather than the Lassalleans'. The Lassalleans had done very poorly in the elections of 1874 and 1875 and had soured on politics. "We can only become strong," said the head of the Labor Party of Illinois (the Chicago Lassalleans), "when, instead of wasting our time and money at the ballot box we devote ourselves with all our energy to the demands of the trade unions and bring material advantages to the workers." This was what the Marxists had been saying all along.

As the depression deepened, labor's resentments exploded into violence. In July 1877 thousands of railroad workers rose up against their companies which had drastically cut their wages. The pattern everywhere was the same. A strike would be called; the company would bring in outside workers; in the ensuing conflict the militia, sometimes federal troops, would intervene to restore order. Pitched battles between workers and militiamen were frequent and bloody. In some instances (Pittsburgh, Reading, St. Louis) the workers routed the militia and temporarily took control of the railroads. Nothing like this kind of working-class rebelliousness was seen before (or since) in America.

Not surprisingly, the socialists abandoned their aversion to politics and ran in local elections throughout the country. The results were astonishing. In Chicago they polled 7000 votes, in Cincinnati 9000, in Buffalo 6000, in Milwaukee they elected several officials; elsewhere they cooperated with labor parties to good effect. Suddenly socialism had a future. Especially encouraging was the fact that not all the votes came from Germans. There were now eight English-language socialist newspapers (along with fourteen German). Confident that they were about to emulate the success of their colleagues in Germany, the socialists changed the name of their party in 1877 to the Socialist (or Socialistic) Labor Party, serving notice to bourgeois America that they would shortly be a political power of the first rank.

Their confidence proved to be misplaced. The fortunes of the Socialist Labor Party fell as rapidly as they had risen. In succeeding local elections the vote melted away; Party membership dropped sharply; and every English-language newspaper folded, as did all but three of the German. The socialists again found themselves a corporal's guard, a minor foreign sect. The reason for their decline was obvious enough. Prosperity had returned, and labor no longer supported sweeping social reforms. Workers focused their attention instead on economic improvement through such major trade unions as the Knights of Labor (which came into its own in the early 1880s) and the Federation of Organized Trades and Labor Unions (launched in 1881 and soon to become the American Federation of Labor). "The plundered toilers," the national chairman of the Socialist Labor Party commented sadly, "are rapidly being drawn back to the old paths, and are closing their ears to the appeal of reason. They are selling their birthright for a mess of pottage by rejecting the prospect of future emancipation in their greed for the trifling gains of the present."

The socialists were immensely disappointed. They had been led to believe that the capitalist system was on the verge of collapse, that the masses were in a revolutionary mood. But the capitalists emerged from the latest crisis more powerful, more buoyant than ever; the uprisings had been crushed and the workers were safely back in the fold. An increasing number of socialists came to feel that the Party's methods, based on its belief in rationality, the education of the masses, the peaceful acquisition of power, the permeation of trade unions, played into the hands of the capitalists. They insisted that the Party should arm its members and train them in techniques of self-defense. Many of them had begun doing just that by organizing their own "Educational and Defense Societies" (*Lehr und Wehr Vereine*). The Party promptly condemned these societies, maintaining that the ruling classes would like nothing more than to treat socialism as a police problem.

The proponents of direct action established their own Revolutionary Socialist Labor Party in 1881. A large contingent of German Anarcho-Communists, recent arrivals in the United States, augmented the ranks of the new party, furnishing it with an ideology and a program. As had been evident as far back as the 1860s, when Marx engaged in ferocious controversies with Michael Bakunin and the followers of Proudhon, the Anarcho-Communists differed from the orthodox Marxists in several important particulars. The Anarcho-Communists asserted that the state (i.e., all laws, all coercive institutions) must be abolished before men could freely and spontaneously seek their own means of self-fulfillment and create their own communities. Denouncing politics as a fraudulent compromise with the state, they condoned, though they did not necessarily advocate, acts of violence by the oppressed against the ruling classes, claiming that "propaganda by deed" educated the masses better than a thousand sermons or books. By 1883 the Anarcho-Communists and the other direct actionists had completely eclipsed the Socialist Labor Party in size and importance.

Certainly their leaders were far more interesting and colorful. Two of them stand out: Albert R. Parsons, an American, and Johann Most, a German. Parsons was born in Montgomery, Alabama, in 1848, and despite his youth managed to fight in the Confederate Army. Soon after the war he brought out a newspaper in Waco, Texas, affirming the rights of Negroes and justifying Republican Party rule in the South, which hardly endeared him to his neighbors. Worse yet, he married a dark-skinned Mexican (Lucy Gonzalez, who was later to distinguish herself in the Anarchist movement). When life in the South became untenable for him, Parsons moved to Chicago and joined the Social Democratic Labor Party. After running for office as a socialist, he became convinced that capitalism was nothing but theft and democracy nothing but a hoax, joined the Anarcho-Communists and was appointed editor of their English-language paper, *Alarm*.

To the Germans, Johann Most was a hero, or at least a legend, before he arrived in the United States. Back in the old country they remembered him as a fiery speaker, an inveterate troublemaker, a victim of "bourgeois justice." His detractors contended that his propensity for violence was psychological, that it was his way of making society pay for the tribulations of his youth. Born in Augsburg in 1846, he was brought up by a tyrannical stepmother. When an operation on his jaw left his face horribly disfigured and destroyed his hope to become an actor, he developed into an outstanding socialist orator. His speechmaking got him elected to the Reichstag; it also landed him in prison several times. By 1878 when he was thrown out of Germany under Bismarck's recently enacted anti-socialist laws he was well along on the road to Anarchism. In London he published a weekly, *Die Freiheit* (Freedom), which announced his conversion to the school of violence and propaganda by deed. His paper applauded the assassination of Czar Alexander II, and the British promptly jailed him. He came to the United States in December 1882 and immediately embarked on a triumphal tour. He reminded his German audiences that since

America under industrial capitalism was no different from the
despotisms of Europe, it was necessary to wipe out its religious
and political institutions by fire and sword, confiscate the wealth
stolen from the proletariat, and place the means of production in
the hands of the producers themselves. Most knew little about
America. He might have delivered the same speeches in Germany
or Austria or Russia.

Chicago was the unofficial headquarters of the Anarchist movement. There its most talented leaders were gathered, and it was
making impressive headway among the workers. Along with other
parts of the country Chicago was the scene of profound industrial
unrest between 1884–86, when workers struck time and again for
an eight-hour day. As active participants in these strikes, Anarchist
militants exhorted the men to go beyond bread-and-butter gains,
to take up arms, occupy the factories, and destroy the capitalist
class. In the spring of 1886 events moved toward a climax. On
May 1st a general strike was called for the Chicago area. Two days
later violence flared up at the McCormick Harvester plant, where
for months unionized workers had been replaced by strike-breakers
under the protection of Pinkerton men. During a speech given
by an Anarchist firebrand named August Spies, a fight broke out
between the old employees and the strikebreakers. The melee got
out of hand and the police arrived. They were met by bricks,
rocks and epithets from a nearby crowd, consisting largely of
women and children. The police fired into the crowd and killed
six people. This was what the Anarchists had been waiting for.

Later that same day they put out a flyer in German and English
that called upon the workers to arm themselves and "appear in
full force." On May 4, they appeared—about 3000 of them—at
Haymarket Square in Chicago to hear Spies, Parsons, and other
Anarchist speakers protest the killings. Present at the Square too
were the mayor, the police chief, and a large force of policemen.
The evening drew to a close and nothing had happened. The
speeches were surprisingly moderate—so moderate that the mayor
advised the chief to send home the reserves; he himself left.
Moreover, after Parsons spoke, heavy clouds gathered overhead,
and the crowd thinned to a few hundred. Then, for no explicable
reason, one of the police captains suddenly ordered the meeting
to end. As he did so, a bomb, thrown from an alley, landed in
the midst of the police detail. One policeman fell dead; others

were wounded. Heavy firing opened up on both sides. When the smoke cleared, eleven men had been killed—seven policemen and four civilians—and 110 had been wounded.

The country as a whole was mortified. The worst forebodings about the Anarchists had been confirmed. Violent speech had turned into violent deeds. Who had thrown the bomb was not (and never would be) established. But Chicagoans demanded Anarchist blood. The authorities—the police, the politicians, above all the courts—complied, and one of the most reprehensible trials in American history took place in Chicago between June 21 and August 20, 1886. Eight of the leading local Anarchists (including Parsons, who voluntarily surrendered out of solidarity with his comrades) were charged with complicity in the murder of a policeman. The prosecution did not attempt to link them with the throwing of the bomb. There was no evidence that they had had anything to do with it. Their crime, in presiding Judge Joseph Gary's words, was to have "generally by speech and print advised large classes of the people, not particular individuals . . . to commit murder . . . that in consequence of that advice . . . somebody not known did throw the bomb." The defendants, in other words, were accused of having made the killing possible by means of "speech and print."

Their conviction was a certainty—doubly so because the judge and the prosecutor, working closely together, saw to it that the right kind of jury was picked. Seven of the men were sentenced to die; one was given fifteen years. Of the seven two asked for mercy and received life imprisonment; one (a twenty-two-year-old) committed suicide. The remaining four (among them Spies and Parsons) were hanged on November 11, 1887, Anarchists to their last breath. Six years later the jailed men were pardoned by the reform governor of Illinois, John Peter Altgeld. In effect, Altgeld apologized to them, and to the memory of the dead, by denouncing the trial in all its aspects—from the behavior of Judge Gary to the testimony of the witnesses and the selection of the jury—as an unpardonable miscarriage of justice.

But by then the Anarchist movement in America was dead. The Haymarket affair had effectively discredited it even among its sympathizers, most of whom shied away from actual (as distinguished from rhetorical) violence. To be an Anarchist was to be a marked man. Furthermore, with the return of prosperity after 1887 and the temporary restoration of industrial peace, workers turned a deaf ear to appeals for direct action. Anarchism was thereafter confined to a few intellectuals and activists who hoped to spark a social revolution through daring, suicidal deeds of violence—e.g., Alexander Berkman's attempt on the life of industrialist Henry Frick, and Leon Czolgosz's assassination of President McKinley.

Meanwhile, the Socialist Labor Party proceeded on its Marxist, non-violent course. After descending to its nadir in the early 1880s, it began to pick up members. Then, in the very year of the Anarchist trial, it was offered a miraculous opportunity to enter— or rather to re-channel—the mainstream of American politics. In the mid-1880s, during the national campaign in behalf of the eight-hour day, local labor parties sprang up everywhere. New York City's United Labor Party was founded in 1886. The SLP was instrumental in organizing the new party and approved its mayoral candidate, the world-renowned political economist and reformer, Henry George, who had recently come to live in the city.

In accepting George, however, the socialists swallowed much that was unpalatable to them. His analysis of the system, set forth magnificently in his famous book, *Progress and Poverty* (which had been selling by the hundreds of thousands every year since its publication in 1879), they regarded as manifestly wrong-headed and, in its consequences, reactionary; this had been Marx's own view of it. George asked the right question: what accounted for pervasive poverty in the midst of so much wealth? It was his answer that disturbed the socialists. According to George, the root cause of the poverty could be traced to land monopoly. Originally the land belonged to all; now it belonged to fewer and fewer people, who did nothing but collect higher and higher rents (unearned increment) as the population increased. Men driven off the land therefore had no choice but to sell their labor; and small businessmen were ruined because they could not afford the rents, leaving the field of business enterprise to the great industrial concentrations. George's solution followed from this analysis. The government, he said, should expropriate the land by imposing a single tax on all unearned increment—the only tax that would be necessary to run the affairs of state. This was as far as George went in the direction of socialism. In fact, he was opposed to any form of collective or state restrictions on laissez-faire. He proposed the single tax in the name of maximum competition and free enterprise, and he looked forward to a period of social harmony and equal opportunity once rent-free land had been made available to all.

The socialists criticized the whole scheme as a Jeffersonian pipe dream, an eighteenth-century illusion, a pre-industrial romance. To the socialists the cause of the simultaneous rise of progress and poverty lay in the monopolization not of land—though this was evil and must be eradicated too—but of industry and the labor of the proletariat. To take the landlord's unearned increment would, accordingly, suit the capitalists fine and would, in the end, leave the problem entirely unresolved. Yet despite their reservations, the socialists enthusiastically supported George's candidacy and worked mightily to bring about his election.

George came remarkably close to winning. He received 68,000 votes to 90,000 for Democrat Abram S. Hewitt (the son-in-law of the late reformer, Peter Cooper) and 60,000 for Republican Theodore Roosevelt. Had the Catholic hierarchy not intervened against George (whom it regarded as a dangerous radical), he probably would have been elected. And had the Tammany machine not been in charge of collecting the ballots he certainly would have won. After his defeat it did not take long for the socialists and the single-taxers to fall out. George had come to feel that the socialists were an albatross around his neck, that the differences between his philosophy and theirs was irreconcilable, that the United Labor Party should be emphatically American and reformist. "The truth is," he said, "that state socialism, with its childish notions of making all capital the common property of the state . . . is an exotic, born of European conditions that cannot flourish on American soil." The socialists for their part were willing to maintain the uneasy marriage, for they assumed that the United Labor Party would continue to grow and eventually fall under their domination. But George held all the cards, and at the 1887 United Labor Party convention in Syracuse he had the socialists expelled on a pretext. The new platform explicitly repudiated socialism. That year George imprudently ran for a minor state office (Secretary of State) and did quite poorly. Soon his own single-tax camp was rent by schisms, and in 1888 the United Labor Party ran its last campaign.

The Socialist Labor Party was as minuscule as ever. But the ideas it stood for were not so remote, so alien, so forbidding as they once had been. By the end of the 1880s socialism was a well-known term, though few perhaps outside the circle of faithful understood its meaning. Americans now realized that the country was prone to the afflictions of industrial life, and that the growth of socialist parties in Europe might have more than passing relevance. The SLP reflected this change by attracting a new kind of membership. Its ranks were filled more and more by Russian Jews (hundreds of thousands of whom were now emigrating to America every year and settling in the urban ghettoes, especially New York's) and by native Americans, drawn mainly from the middle class. Heartened by these propitious signs, the SLP decided that it would go to the people itself and offer its own program to the electorate, openly and without compromise.

One of the men who entered the Party at this critical moment in its history was Daniel DeLeon. DeLeon is important not only because he was an interesting and original thinker in his own right, but because he shaped the ideology and strategy of American socialism precisely when it was poised for swift advance, when the country was more receptive to socialism than ever before. The 1890s was a decade of continuous turmoil, marked by the collapse of the economy, by the outbreak of war between labor and capital (the Homestead and Pullman strikes, Coeur D'Alene, Leadville, Tracy City, etc.), by agrarian uprisings in the South and West, and by a radical shift in party loyalties and coalitions.

Not much is known about DeLeon's early life. He was born in 1850 in Curaçao, Dutch West Indies, the son of a Dutch-Sephardic doctor. (For some reason he never acknowledged his authentic genealogy: he claimed that he descended from full-blooded Spanish grandees.) Educated in Europe, he emigrated to the United States in his early twenties, and after practicing law in Texas for a while was hired by Columbia University as a lecturer in international law. He first came to public notice in 1886, when he served as a featured speaker for Henry George. DeLeon was a rare bird; few academics at that time dared to espouse radical causes publicly. His exposure to socialism drove him leftward. Within three years he had become a member of the Socialist Labor Party. By then he had given up his position at Columbia (despite his large family) to devote his life to socialism.

Soon he headed the Party. He was a speaker and debater of commanding power. As editor of the Party's English language paper,

The People, he sent out weekly broadsides in which he laid down policy, instructed the readers in Marxism, flailed his enemies, and cast out the apostates. For DeLeon the truth was plain to see, and those who did not see it he regarded as ignorant, confused, or malevolent. He was an incorrigible polemicist—he crossed swords with every prominent man of the left in his time—and he spared no epithet, no detail of logic, in vanquishing his foe. A brilliant exponent of orthodox Marxism, he had the ability to frame his abstruse arguments in illuminating figures and images. He wrote in a folksy American idiom, modeling his style on such humorists as Petroleum V. Nasby and Mark Twain. As Party leader he certainly countenanced no opposition, either on matters of political tactics or ideology. He was "Pope" DeLeon, who defined infallible doctrines, pronounced anathemas, and handed down excommunications, always purifying the church militant over which he presided. It was also true, however, that he was a man of unusual personal integrity, who uncomplainingly suffered incredible personal hardships in behalf of his ideals.

DeLeon's originality lay in his attempt to give Marxism an American setting. He believed that revolutionary socialism would come first to America because industry was more fully developed here than anywhere else. There could be no escape, in his view, from the economic laws that Marx had laid bare. The economic crisis was bound to worsen and finally bring down the great trusts along with the whole superincumbent structure of laws and social relations. But at the proper moment capitalism would be banished not by violence, but by peaceful constitutional means—by the ballot, by majority rule. In its place would rise the cooperative commonwealth, the dream of all socialists. DeLeon had his own conception of what it would be like: a republic of syndicates. Political representation would correspond to the large-scale industries that capitalism had forged, not to meaningless geographic ones. This would be the ultimate stage in man's evolution from savagery to civilization, the stage in which each, though he depends on the labor of all, receives the full product of his labor because he owns the total means of production and distribution.

With customary vehemence DeLeon insisted that nothing less than the cooperative commonwealth as he envisaged it was acceptable. Wage increases, improved working conditions, social reforms of one kind or another—these were so many deceptions, and, as such, worse than the evils they purportedly combated. Only when capitalism was exposed in all its naked cruelty could it be defeated. DeLeon thus reserved his heaviest fusillades for the trade union leaders and the moderate socialists who favored "palliatives," who were willing to come to terms with the system. Actually, DeLeon was much more uncompromising than Marx himself ever was. Marx had repeatedly supported factory legislation and other remedial measures, as well as palliatives for trade unions. For that reason he had helped organize the First International.

Like the other revolutionary socialists of the time, DeLeon assumed that politics, or the struggle for domination by man over man, would disappear in the cooperative commonwealth. Until then, however, politics would have to be pursued as relentlessly as necessary. Accordingly, obedience to the Party was one's paramount duty; the Party was the vanguard of the working class. "In all revolutionary movements, as in the storming of fortresses," DeLeon wrote, "the thing depends on the head of the column— upon that minority that is so intense in its convictions, so soundly based in its principles, so determined in its actions, that it carries the masses with it, storms the breastworks and captures the fort."

Armed with DeLeon's insights, the Socialist Labor Party followed a twofold strategy in the 1890s. On the political field it solicited votes; on the economic it sought to bring the major labor unions under its control. The vote for SLP candidates sharply increased in the course of the decade. In 1892 it ran an old-line American, one Simon Wing, as its Presidential candidate and received some 21,000 votes in six states. By 1898 its national vote had risen to 82,000, and several of its local candidates had been elected to office. Comparisons were being made with the emergence of the Republican Party from similarly humble beginnings. But 1898 was the SLP's last good year. While its popularity had been growing, DeLeon had been putting down a series of devastating rebellions. The Jewish socialists of the Lower West Side were eliminated in 1897. Two years later the bulk of the Party's rank and file walked out. In 1900 the SLP vote was down to 33,000, and the Party's future was closed.

DeLeon's economic policy had been the main cause of these defections. The SLP tried variously to permeate ("bore-from-within") the American Federation and the Knights of Labor. As early as 1890 the nascent AFL, led by Samuel Gompers (perhaps

DeLeon's chief *bête noir*), rejected any kind of working relationship with the socialists; four years later the union decisively rejected the whole socialist program. The Knights of Labor, a dying organization, though it still claimed some 100,000 members, offered better possibilities, primarily because its largest district in New York City was an SLP enclave and was represented by none other than DeLeon himself. But the Knights threw out DeLeon, the SLP, and, indeed, the whole district. Chastened by these failures, DeLeon made a fateful decision. No longer would the Party try to deal in any way with the "labor lieutenants of capitalism." Instead, it would establish its own union, the Socialist Trade and Labor Alliance, a union dedicated, like the Party itself, to revolution and the realization of the cooperative commonwealth.

So far as the rest of organized labor was concerned DeLeon was guilty of *lèse majesté*. He was sanctioning "dual unionism"; he was seeking to wreck other unions in the hope of advancing his. The Socialist Trade and Labor Alliance was, Gompers said, "conceived in iniquity and brutal concubinage with labor's double enemy, greed and ignorance, fashioned into an embryonic phthisical dwarf, born in corruption and filth." At first the Alliance did take some members from other unions and at one point in the mid-1890s boasted a membership of 30,000. But whether this number was exaggerated or not, the STLA soon fell away to nothing, as the locals themselves refused to go along with the tactics of dual unionism and broke their ties with the Party. Meanwhile, the AFL, expanding relentlessly, enrolled almost a million members by the turn of the century.

Under DeLeon's severe tutelage The Socialist Labor Party offered America a transcendental measure of justice—one too high on the scale of values to count in the hurly burly of politics. Though it served as a vital training ground for men who later left its ranks to join other movements, it failed by its own standards. DeLeon conceived of the Party as an agent of revolution, not as a sect concerned with defining eternal truths. Yet it became such a sect. American socialism went its own way and passed the SLP by. It became a fossil on the political landscape.

American Confederation of the International Workingmen's Association Declaration of Principles and Platform 1872

The first congress of the American branch of the International was held in Philadelphia on July 9 and 10, 1872. Following are the highlights of its proceedings.

DECLARATION OF PRINCIPLES

That the emancipation of the working classes must be accomplished by the working classes themselves; that the struggle for the emancipation of the working classes means not a struggle for class privileges and monopolies, but for equal rights and duties and the abolition of all class rule.

That the economical subjection of the man of labor to the monopolizer of the means of labor—that is, the sources of life—lies at the bottom of servitude in all its forms, of all social misery, mental despotism and political dependence.

That the economical emancipation of the working classes is therefore the great end to which every political movement ought to be subordinate as a means.

That all efforts aiming at that great end have hitherto failed from the want of solidarity between the manifold divisions of labor in each country, and from the absence of a fraternal bond of union between the working classes of different countries.

That the emancipation of labor is neither a local nor a national, but a social problem, embracing all countries in which modern society exists, and depending for its solution on the concurrence—practical and theoretical—of the most advanced countries.

That the present revival of the working classes in the most industrious countries of Europe and America, while it raises a new hope, gives solemn warning against a relapse into the old errors, and calls for the immediate combination of still disconnected movements.

For these reasons, we do now in Congress assembled, declare

ourselves to be "The American Confederation of the International Workingmen's Association," and while proclaiming ourselves to be in harmony with the working people of the world, we reserve to ourselves the right to regulate this branch of the International Workingmen's association without dictation from the General Council at London, England, except so far as its decrees may be consistent with the orders of the General (or Universal) Congresses of the Association, in which we may be represented as from time to time they may be held; and we hereby proclaim the following

PLATFORM

First—The total abolition of all class rule and all class privileges.

Second—Complete political and social equality for all, without distinction of sex, creed, color or condition.

Third—Nationalization of the land and of all the instruments of production.

By which it is understood that the State shall, as speedily as possible, without harm to any one, assume possession of the lands and the labor-saving machinery which have been alienated from the people, and thus be able to accord employment to all who may need it.

Fourth—A reduction of the hours of labor, so as to allow more time for improvement and recreation.

Fifth—Education to be undertaken by the State; to be obligatory, gratuitous, secular, scientific and professional.

Sixth—The subject of religion to be ignored by the association; no religious creed or differences to be recognized.

Seventh—The abolition of standing armies, as being provocative to war, and hostility to war itself as being destructive to the best interests of mankind.

Eighth—Money to be issued by the government only, to be a legal tender and to bear no interest.

Ninth—The adoption of the principle of associative production, with a view to the complete supercession of the present system of capitalistic production.

Tenth—THE REFERENDUM.—Laws to be submitted to the people for their approval or rejection. . . .

FRIEDRICH A. SORGE
Socialism and the Worker*
1876

Socialism and the Worker was the only piece of writing that Sorge published in English. He wrote it a year before the establishment of the Socialist Labor Party.

Socialism has been attacked and incriminated at all times, but never with more animosity than recently. Socialists are reproached with every kind of wickedness; of the tendency to do away with property, marriage, family, to pollute everything that is sacred; they have even been accused of arson and murder. And why not? If we look at the originators of these incriminations we are not the least astonished, for they have to defend privileges and monopolies which in reality are in danger, if drawn to the broad daylight and handled by the Socialist. They act according to the old jesuitic stratagem: invent lies, pollute your enemy in every way you can; something will stick. But if we find those reproaches repeated and echoed even by working men whose interests are quite different we must wonder indeed.

If the workers, however, hate and attack Socialism it is not a clear perception of the wickedness of the aims of Socialism by which their judgment is guided, but by a dim and vague idea, and it is well known that spectres are awful things in the dark for people who believe in them.

But everybody who hates and persecutes other people for their purposes and pursuits should be convinced that he is right in doing so. For, if we hate and persecute persons whose purposes and pursuits are reasonable and right, we are wrong.

For this reason let us examine the real aims of the Socialists. I think I know them pretty well, and I promise to tell the truth and nothing but the truth about them.

When you have read this to the end you may persecute the Socialists with renewed hatred if you find they are bad; on the

* Pp. 3-4, 7-12, 14-16.

other hand, you will think favourably of them if you find their views good and right. For I am convinced that you, dear reader, whoever you are, have not a mind to love the bad and hate the good.

Foremost and above all it seems to be certain that the Socialists intend to divide all property. Everybody who owns anything must give up what he owns; this whole mass has to be divided equally among all the people, and each person may use his part just as he likes. After a while, when some have used up their allotted part and a new disproportion of property has arisen, a new division will be made; and so on. Especially the money and the soil are to be divided,—this is what some people say concerning Socialism.

Now, honestly, reader, have you ever seen or heard of a man of sound mind who really demanded such nonsense? No, you have not! Such a demand involves the highest degree of craziness. Just reflect, dear reader, to whose lot, for instance, should a railroad fall? Who should have the rails, or a locomotive, or a carriage? And since everybody would have a right to demand an equal share all these things would have to be broken and smashed up, and one would get a broken axletree, another the door of a carriage, or perhaps some bolts. Not even lunatics could recommend such a state of things.

A division of money or soil might possibly be thought of, but money and soil form only a small part of the wealth of a country. The ready money forms even a very small part. And if the soil should be divided all the new owners would be in need of houses, barns, stables, agricultural implements of all kinds. Such a distribution of the soil is, therefore, utterly impossible, and the Socialists know well enough that such a proceeding would benefit nobody. During the great French Revolution in 1789 something similar was tried; large estates were divided among poor country people to make them happy. What is the result? The French peasantry, generally, are so poor that thousands of them live in dwellings with only a door and no window at all, or with only one small window at the side of the door. And small farmers are not much better off in any country, except, perhaps, in the vicinity of large cities. . . .

Before we go on we must explain two conceptions:

I. What is Communism?

II. What is property?

About Communism many lies have been set afloat, especially by people whose interest it was to do so, viz., by those money-making idlers, so that most people cannot but connect with the word Communism the idea of rascality; Communist and scoundrel of the worst kind appear to them to be synonymous terms. Therefore it is not an easy matter to speak of Communism without running the risk of being condemned before one commences. Many people in such a case will not hear, will not see, will not judge. Their verdict is formed. All social prejudices are awakened and called forth by this expression. For that reason it is very difficult to come to a quiet understanding about it. But the reader, who has followed us so far, will follow us farther, not blindfolded, but using good common sense.

If we open our eyes and look around us, we find many beneficent and useful institutions established by many or by the whole people *in common*. In one place associations are formed, for instance, to save and shelter shipwrecked persons; at another place the *community* erect a school, or the State, the commonwealth, builds a harbour or a canal. In ordinary life everybody cares for himself, but in such cases as those just mentioned, people unite for advancing a *common, social* purpose. Experience teaches that in doing so they do admirably well; every one of them who will reflect a little must confess that his own welfare is greatly advanced by such institutions of *common* usefulness. What would people be without *common* roads, *common* schools, etc., that is, such as are built and instituted at the cost of the *community* for *common* use? We should be in a terrible situation if all at once the different insurance companies were to cease to exist, whose object is to transfer a calamity, by which a person might be struck heavily, or perhaps be ruined, from his shoulders to the shoulders of many. If I chose I could mention here a thousand other things, but the above named *common* institutions will be sufficient. Now all these institutions are nothing but *Communism*. For *Communism* is nothing but the principle of the *common interests* of society. In everyday life everybody looks out for his own interest, even at the cost of his fellow-men; here cold, ugly egoism is dominant. The large cotton mills have ruined thousands and thousands of weavers; but who cares for hundreds of honest, industrious, happy people who are ruined by one mill? Who cares how many honest shoemakers are deprived of a living by the large shoe manufacturers? What does the usurer care for the victims of his avarice? What do the speculating swindlers care for the fate of the shareholders after their hard-earned savings are gone? Nobody ever thought of caring for such things, and it is my firm belief that a business man in our days who should show any consideration for the welfare of his fellowmen in his transactions would be certain to become a laughing-stock. Egoism rules supreme. Everybody thinks of his own welfare, and does not care whether by doing so he destroys the welfare of others. "What business have I to care for others if I am comfortable?" In spite of the prevalence of Egoism, the *common* interest of mankind is irrepressibly gaining ground. More and more people unite to cultivate it, more and more associations are formed, the activity of the State and the community is extending its influence over more and more objects. Who would have thought in former times of all the different associations which are formed to-day to advance any number of *common* interests of every description? Who had an idea in former years, that whole countries would be cut in all directions by railroads, that telegraphs would communicate news to the remotest parts of the world in an instant? Who could have predicted the admirable development of our postal system? Who thought of waterworks or of gas? Who had an idea of the modern arrangement of the fire brigades? The root of all these is *Communism*. They represent the victory of *common* interest over hideous Egoism.

To turn institutions of *common* interest to the use of all is the tendency of the age, and however people may curse at Communism they are bound to obey its mandates. Everywhere *common* interests press their claims, and *Communism*, proudly elevating its head, marches on triumphantly with all conditions of human life in its train. . . .

What is property? "To be sure that which a person owns, possesses!" Well! But now tell me, are you certain that the Socialists are, or ever were, opposed to what Peter or Paul owns? Can you show me a sentence or passage from any of the writings or pamphlets of Socialists which justifies the supposition that they intend to attack the property of any person?

You cannot, because such an idea never entered the head of a Socialist. I should not wonder if you yourself have not thought sometimes that, considering the means and ways by which many amass their riches, it would be only just and right to take that ill-gotten wealth from their rascally owners. But it is a firm principle of Socialism, never to interfere with personal property in order to investigate its origin or to arrange it in a different way. Never and nowhere! And whoever asserts to the contrary either does not know the principles of Socialism or willingly and knowingly asserts an untruth. The Socialists deem an investigation into the origin of an acknowledged personal property an unnecessary trouble. They do not envy the Duke of Westminster or Lord Brassey their wealth. Although they perceive very well the constant changes with regard to property; although they investigate and are acquainted with the causes producing those changes; although they are well aware that fraud and meanness and violence in a great many instances are among those causes, they forbear to investigate how much these causes, how much others, have influenced the state of property of this or that single person. They consider the personal property an accomplished fact, and respect it; so much so that they consider stealing a crime. Every time Revolution was victorious in Paris bills were seen at the street corners threatening death to thieves. A remarkable fact is that Baron Rothschild fled suddenly from Paris as soon as these bills were posted. At Lyons during an insurrection in 1832 a man who had appropriated another man's property was shot by a labourer in command. During the reign of the Commune of 1871 Paris had no thieves, no prostitutes.

On the other hand, the right of the owner is not always respected in our time, but they are not Socialists who violate the sanctity of property in these cases, although it must be confessed that in many instances an abrogation of the right of a property-holder becomes necessary. Socialists cannot be reproached with ever having condemned houses or tracts of land for the purpose of building a street or opening a railroad. They certainly are not Socialists who seize and sell houses or lots at auction for unpaid taxes. Nor will you find Socialists who connive at those shamefully unjust appropriations of the property of others which however go on in a lawful form.

One thing, however, calls forth all the energy of the Socialists, and they will try with all their might to remedy it. I have stated already, they do not care whether a person owns hundreds of thousands or millions of pounds, whether that person makes use of his money one way or the other, whether he spends it wisely or foolishly. He may spend his own as he chooses. But—these sums of money are not used simply to be spent, but to bring interest, to increase, if possible, the wealth of the possessor. Does he himself want to work, to do something useful? Far from it. His money works for him, his money makes money, as the saying is; or in plain English, his money is the channel through which the earnings of other industrious people flow into his pockets. Socialists call all kinds of property in this respect "capital," this expression comprising all means for production. And because one class of the people possess, by their wealth, these means—that is, capital—another, and by far the largest class, have only their physical or mental strength and skill for labour. Hence capital becomes a means for enslaving workers, forcing them to give up the greater part of their produce to him who owns the capital. They themselves obtain hardly enough to support themselves and their families, while the capitalists enjoy life and get richer without working at all. This is the point: dead property deprives living work of its fruits. Now since work should, by rights, own what it produces as its sole and legitimate earning, dead property becomes the bitter enemy of working life.

Hence the struggle of labour against capital.

Returning to the question, "What is property?" the answer given above appears unsatisfactory. We must add another question: To whom justly belongs what the working part of the human race produces?

The answer to this question is of the greatest importance. Now it is capital which appropriates the greater part of it, leaving to the workers, who form by far the greater number, only so much of it that they may keep alive. They are treated like bees; they are robbed of the honey they make. This class is excluded from enjoying the blessings of civilisation; the greater part of their product is taken by capital.

What right has the owner of a beehive to rob the bees of the fruit of their industry and labour? They are his property, his is the might. What right has capital to rob the working class of the greater part of the fruit of their industry and labour? The wage-labourers, the mechanics, the farm hands, are they the property of the capitalist? Are they his slaves?

As things stand to-day, they are! Might is right, and by the title of such right the slaveowner considers the fruit of the work of his slaves his property; by this right, in former times, the feudal landowner made his serfs work for his employment and benefit. Slavery is injustice; serfdom is injustice; so the right which capital

claims to the work of the worker is injustice. I would not like to
be misunderstood here. As far as anything is the personal property
of a person he may enjoy it as he chooses; nobody has a right to
interfere. But as soon as he tries to use this property to enslave
other people, he steps over his domain and must be checked. For
I think it is acknowledged among civilised people that nobody has
a right of ownership over his fellowmen. Slavery has been abolished,
serfdom has been abolished, so the power which capital exercises
now will be abolished: its place will be occupied by the natural
and sacred right of the worker to the proceeds of his work. . . .

Some time ago the middle-class formed the firm and solid foundation of society and State. Machinery was invented and a change
occurred. Manufacturing, and even farming to a certain extent,
were conducted on a large scale; the middle-class people were
pressed down into a class of wage-labourers, and were employed
in large numbers by the manufacturers or employers. More and
more this middle-class cease to be property-holders; it is getting
more and more difficult for the mechanics and small farmers to
hold their ground; thus the middle-class is constantly decreasing,
the class of wage-labourers increasing, until there will be only two
classes of people—rich and poor. In this process the number of rich
people is diminishing, wealth becoming concentrated in the hands
of comparatively few persons who are getting enormously rich.

But this process must soon have its limit. There will be a time
when the large mass of the working-people will feel its consequences unbearable, and will abolish it. That will be the time when
Communism will enter into its rights. Labour will then be organised
according to a certain reasonable plan, and since, for that purpose,
the use of the existing capital—comprising soil, houses, railways,
shipping, manufactories, machines, &c.—will be necessary, those
comparatively few possessors of all the wealth of the nations will
have to be expropriated. Perhaps they then will consent themselves to such a measure, and give up everything necessary for
production of their own accord, honoured and praised for their
patriotism and humanity, and remunerated deservedly; perhaps they
will use their ample means to resist the common demand, and
will perish, overwhelmed by the newly-formed organisation of the
State. As I hinted before, in the new order of things all branches
of labour will be organised in a similar way to the arrangements
we see to-day in large factories, large estates, or institutions of the

Government. Unnecessary work will be avoided, and the reward for work done will be greater. Labour will not be wasted in making luxuries for the idle, but will be usefully employed in making the necessaries of life for other workers. It will be everybody's duty to work, hence everybody will have ample leisure for recreation and mental development. All will strive to ameliorate the conditions of the community they belong to; for, by doing so, everybody will improve his own private situation. . . .

The conception of "property of capital" will be transformed gradually into the conception of "property of work."

Nowhere, you will perceive, is abolition of property thought of by Socialists, and nobody, I trust, will object to the change just mentioned. The development of mankind to greater perfection never was and never will be arrested by the prevailing laws concerning property. For instance, it was not arrested, when humanity demanded abolition of slavery, by the pretended divine right of the slave owners. And if such rights and laws demand that humanity stop its progress, such demand is madness. Laws and rights concerning property are subjected to constant changes, when such changes are in the interest of progress. But even in our better institutions injustice is ruling, and the change just spoken of will abolish that injustice and lead mankind to a higher state of perfection. At the bottom of our institutions there is a remnant of slavery; as soon as capital shall cease to govern, wage-labour and the rest of slavery will be abolished.

Freedom and equality will then be no longer empty and cheap phrases, but will have a meaning; when all men are really free and equal, they will honour and advance one another. The working man will then no longer be deprived of the fruit of his work, his property, and everybody who will work will be able to spend a good deal more in food, clothing, lodging, recreation, pleasure and instruction than he can spend at present.

If the Socialists had nothing to offer to the suffering people but the consolation that Communism will bring help at some future time, when the condition of life, nearly unbearable now, will have become quite so, this consolation would be poor. Long enough a future state of bliss has been held out to suffering mankind, in which they would be rewarded for all the wants and sufferings and pains of this world, and now most people have lost confidence in such empty promises. They demand an amelioration: not words, not promises, but facts. They do not want to expect, with resignation, what may come after death: they demand a change of their unfortunate situation while living on earth.

The interests of all workers are the same! This is best shown by the fact that in many strikes working shopkeepers are in favour of the wage-labourers. Low wages are unfavourable to the farmer as well as to the mechanic, for when wages are low the struggle for economical independence is more difficult; large capital increases at the expense of small property. If the working people would only learn to comprehend the solidarity of their intersts!

As it is with the increase of wages, so it is with the decrease of working hours. Eight hours' work a day is judged sufficient by physicians. A person who has worked properly eight hours a day ought to have done his duty, and has a right to request some hours for recreation, for instruction, and for his family. Those who are the loudest in complaining of the laziness of the working men would soon make wry faces if they were compelled to work only six hours a day. This decreasing of the working hours will better the condition of the whole of the working class. Everybody can easily see that. Even in the country it could be done, although there such a shortening will meet with the greatest objections, but it will be done. What a great benefit will be achieved by this measure alone! Whole armies of paupers, tramps, &c., will find useful employment. They will disappear, and with them a great deal of mischief and crime.

Now if the wage-labourers of the cities and manufacturing places will be ready to lead the van in the struggle for the interest of labour, the rest of the whole working-class have no right to put themselves in the position of idle, indifferent, or even grudging and hostile spectators. On the contrary, it is the duty of the whole working-class to participate in this struggle, for this war is carried on in the interest of all workers, and the wage-labourers who have taken up the gauntlet are the Pioneers for the human race.

But in order to carry on this war successfully, the workers must be organised. Singly and isolated they are powerless; if all would unite for the same purpose, they would be a formidable power which nothing could resist. You may easily break many single matches, but you may try in vain to break a whole bundle of them tied together.

With regard to this, the Socialists have the gratification of seeing that their endeavours have not been fruitless. In Germany Socialism already forms a respectable power, which has puzzled even the great Bismarck. They have been able to elect twenty-four (now more than thirty) representatives into the German Parliament, who, by their untiring activity, by the speeches they have delivered, have opened the eyes of hundreds of thousands of people in Germany. And who would venture to pretend that those men strove for something that was bad, that they betrayed the interests of their constituents? But not only in Parliament, but in a great many municipal assemblies also we find members belonging to the working-class or representing its interests.

And all this has been accomplished in a few years. It is only twenty-four years since the labour party unfurled its banner there. And what has been tried and done during those twenty-two years to suppress the labour movement! It has been ridiculed, scorned, incriminated. Many of its prominent leaders have been put into prison. Many were deprived of their offices and situations, and customers. In spite of all this it grew and thrived. In France, Belgium, Holland, Denmark, Austria, Russia, Italy, Spain, and now in England—everywhere throughout the civilised world Socialism has taken root. Everywhere it has begun the struggle against capital, monopoly, and class rule, and its victory is assured. Concerning Socialism there might be said what was said in olden times about Christianity: If it is bad it will die of its own badness; if it is good it will conquer the world in spite of all persecutions!

And Socialism will conquer the world. Its principles will carry the whole human race to a higher state of perfection.

Reader, you may judge for yourself and decide either in favour of or against Socialism. If you think the aims and endeavours of the Socialists deserve your hatred, try to crush them; if, on the contrary, you are convinced that they are good, that the Socialists endeavour to promote the happiness and welfare of mankind, join them! And if you do not like to act publicly, help them secretly. Try to propagate their principles among your acquaintances, explaining them in your intercourse, destroying the falsehoods brought against them. Tell them that the Socialists form the true and only party of the working people. And if you are a capitalist yourself, reflect how much nobler it is to help to promote the welfare of the many than to serve only your own interest, ugly and hideous Egoism.

Manifesto of the International
Working People's Association*
1883

Anarchists throughout the nation gathered in Pittsburgh in late October 1883, and approved of the following definition of their social and political aims.

TO THE WORKINGMEN OF AMERICA.

Fellow-Workmen: The Declaration of Independence says:—

". . . But when a long train of abuses and usurpations, pursuing invariably the same object, evinces a design to reduce them (the people) under absolute Despotism, it is *their right*, it is *their duty* to throw off such government and provide new guards for their future security."

This thought of Thomas Jefferson was the justification for armed resistance by our forefathers, which gave birth to our Republic, and do not the necessities of our present time compel us to reassert their declaration?

Fellow-Workmen, we ask you to give us your attention for a few moments. We ask you candidly to read the following manifesto issued in your behalf, in the behalf of your wives and children, in behalf of humanity and progress.

Our present society is founded on the expoliation of the propertyless classes by the propertied. This expoliation is such that the propertied (capitalists) buy the working force body and soul of the propertyless, for the price of the mere costs of existence (wages), and take for themselves, *i.e.*, steal, the amount of new values (products) which exceeds this price, whereby wages are made to represent the necessities instead of the earnings of the wage-laborer.

As the non-possessing classes are forced by their poverty to offer for sale to the propertied their working forces, and as our

* Richard T. Ely, *The Labor Movement in America* (New York, 1886), pp. 358–363.

present production on a grand scale enforces technical development with immense rapidity, so that by the application of an
always decreasing number of human working forces, an always
increasing amount of products is created; so does the supply of
working forces increase constantly, while the demand therefor de-
creases. This is the reason why the workers compete more and
more intensely in selling themselves, causing their wages to sink,
or at least on the average, never raising them above the margin
necessary for keeping intact their working ability.

Whilst by this process the propertyless are entirely debarred from
entering the ranks of the propertied, even by the most strenuous
exertions, the propertied, by means of the ever-increasing plundering
of the working class, are becoming richer day by day, without in
any way being themselves productive.

If now and then one of the propertyless class become rich, it
is not by their own labor, but from opportunities which they
have to speculate upon, and absorb the labor-product of others.

With the accumulation of individual wealth, the greed and power
of the propertied grows. They use all the means for competing
among themselves for the robbery of the people. In this struggle,
generally, the less-propertied (middle class) are overcome, while
the great capitalists, par excellence, swell their wealth enormously,
concentrate entire branches of production, as well as trade and
intercommunication, into their hands, and develop into monopolists.
The increase of products, accompanied by simultaneous decrease
of the average income of the working mass of the people, leads
to so-called "business" and "commercial" crises, when the misery
of the wage-workers is forced to the extreme.

For illustration, the last census of the United States shows that
after deducting the cost of raw material, interest, rents, risks, etc.,
the propertied class have absorbed—*i.e.*, stolen—more than five-
eighths of all products, leaving scarcely three-eighths to the producers. The propertied class, being scarcely one-tenth of our population, and in spite of their luxury and extravagance, unable to
consume their enormous "profits," and the producers, unable to
consume more than they receive,—three-eighths,—so-called "over-pro-
ductions" must necessarily take place. The terrible results of panics
are well known.

The increasing eradication of working forces from the productive
process, annually increases the percentage of the propertyless popu-

lation, which becomes pauperized, and is driven to "crime," vaga-
bondage, prostitution, suicide, starvation, and general depravity. This
system is unjust, insane, and murderous. It is therefore necessary to
totally destroy it with and by all means, and with the greatest
energy on the part of every one who suffers by it, and who does
not want to be made culpable for its continued existence by his
inactivity.

Agitation for the purpose of organization; organization for the
purpose of rebellion. In these few words the ways are marked,
which the workers must take if they want to be rid of their chains,
as the economic condition is the same in all countries of so-called
"civilization," as the governments of all Monarchies and Republics
work hand in hand for the purpose of opposing all movements of
the thinking part of the workers, as finally the victory in the decisive
combat of the proletarians against their oppressors can only be
gained by the simultaneous struggle along the whole line of the
bourgeois (capitalistic) society, so therefore the international fraternity of peoples, as expressed in the International Working People's Association, presents itself a self-evident necessity.

True order should take its place. This can only be achieved when
all implements of labor—the soil and other premises of production,
in short, capital produced by labor—is changed into societary
property. Only by this presupposition is destroyed every possibility
of the future spoliation of man by man. Only by common, undivided capital can all be enabled to enjoy in their fulness the fruits
of the common toil. Only by the impossibility of accumulating
individual (private) capital can every one be compelled to work
who makes a demand to live.

This order of things allows production to regulate itself according
to the demand of the whole people, so that nobody need work
more than a few hours a day, and that all nevertheless can satisfy
their needs. Hereby time and opportunity are given for opening to
the people the way to the highest possible civilization; the privileges
of higher intelligence fall with the privileges of wealth and birth.
To the achievement of such a system the political organizations of
the capitalistic classes—be they monarchies or republics—form the
barriers. These political structures (States), which are completely
in the hands of the propertied, have no other purpose than the
upholding of the present order of expoliation.

All laws are directed against the working people. In so far as the opposite appears to be the case, they serve on one hand to blind the worker, while on the other hand they are simply evaded. Even the school serves only the purpose of furnishing the offspring of the wealthy with those qualities necessary to uphold their class domination. The children of the poor get scarcely a formal elementary training, and this, too, is mainly directed to such branches as tend to producing prejudices, arrogance, and servility; in short, want of sense. The Church finally seeks to make complete idiots out of the mass and to make them forego the paradise on earth by promising a fictitious heaven. The capitalistic press, on the other hand, takes care of the confusion of spirits in public life. All these institutions, far from aiding in the education of the masses, have for their object the keeping in ignorance of the people. They are all in the pay and under the direction of the capitalistic classes. The workers can therefore expect no help from any capitalistic party in their struggle against the existing system. They must achieve their liberation by their own efforts. As in former times a privileged class never surrendered its tyranny, neither can it be expected that the capitalists of this age will give up their rulership without being forced to do it.

If there ever could have been any question on this point, it should long ago have been dispelled by the brutalities which the bourgeoisie of all countries—in America as well as in Europe—constantly commits, as often as the proletariat anywhere energetically move to better their condition. It becomes, therefore, self-evident that the struggle of the proletariat with the bourgeoisie must have a violent revolutionary character.

We could show by scores of illustrations that all attempts in the past to reform this monstrous system by peaceable means, such as the ballot, have been futile, and all such efforts in the future must necessarily be so, for the following reasons:—

The political institutions of our time are the agencies of the propertied class; their mission is the upholding of the privileges of their masters; any reform in your own behalf would curtail these privileges. To this they will not and cannot consent, for it would be suicidal to themselves.

That they will not resign their privileges voluntarily we know; that they will not make any concessions to us we likewise know. Since we must then rely upon the kindness of our masters for whatever redress we have, and knowing that from them no good may be expected, there remains but one recourse—FORCE! Our forefathers have not only told us that against despots force is justifiable, because it is the only means, but they themselves have set the immemorial example.

By force our ancestors liberated themselves from political oppression, by force their children will have to liberate themselves from economic bondage. "It is, therefore, your right; it is your duty," says Jefferson; "to arms!"

What we would achieve is, therefore, plainly and simply,—

First, Destruction of the existing class rule, by all means, *i.e.,* by energetic, relentless, revolutionary, and international action.

Second, Establishment of a free society based upon co-operative organization of production.

Third, Free exchange of equivalent products by and between the productive organizations without commerce and profitmongery.

Fourth, Organization of education on a secular, scientific, and equal basis for both sexes.

Fifth, Equal rights for all without distinction to sex or race.

Sixth, Regulation of all public affairs by free contracts between the autonomous (independent) communes and associations, resting on a federalistic basis.

Whoever agrees with this ideal let him grasp our outstretched brother hands!

Proletarians of all countries, unite!

Fellow-Workmen, all we need for the achievement of this great end is ORGANIZATION and UNITY.

There exists now no great obstacle to that unity. The work of peaceful education and revolutionary conspiracy well can and ought to run in parallel lines.

The day has come for solidarity. Join our ranks! Let the drum beat defiantly the roll of battle, "Workmen of all lands, unite! You have nothing to lose but your chains; you have a world to win!"

Tremble, oppressors of the world! Not far beyond your purblind sight there dawns the scarlet and sable lights of the JUDGMENT DAY.

JOHANN MOST
*The Beast of Property**
1884

Following are extracts of a typical pamphlet by Most, written at a time when Anarcho-Communist agitation was at the height of its intensity.

"Among beasts of prey, man is certainly the worst." This expression, very commonly made nowadays, is only relatively true. Not man as such, but man in connection with wealth is a beast of prey. The richer a man, the greater his greed for more. We may call such a monster, the *beast of property*; it now rules the world, makes mankind miserable, and gains in cruelty and voracity with the progress of our so-called *civilization*. In the following pages we will define the character of this monster and recommend his extermination. Look about you! In every so-called *civilized* country about 95 of every 100 men are destitute and about five are money bags.

It is unnecessary to trace all the sneaking ways by which the latter have gained their possessions. The fact that they own ALL, while the others subsist, or rather vegetate, admits of no doubt, nor that these few have grown rich at the cost of the many. Either by direct brute force, by cunning, or by fraud, this horde has from time to time seized the soil with all its wealth. The laws of inheritance and entail and the changing of hands have lent a venerable color to this robbery, and consequently mystified and erased the true character of such actions. For this reason the *beast of property* is not yet recognized for what he is, but, on the contrary, is worshipped with holy awe.

And yet, all who do not belong to this class are its victims. Every offspring of a non-possessor (poor man) finds every nook and corner of the earth occupied at his entrance into the world. There is nothing which is *lordless*. Without labor nothing is produced;

* Unpaged.

and in order to labor not only ability and will are required, but room to work, tools, raw materials and means of subsistence. The poor man must, by the force of necessity, apply to those who possess those things in plenty. And behold! the rich give him permission to continue his existence. But in return for this he must divest himself of his skill and power. These powers his pretended superiors use for themselves. They place him under the yoke of labor—they force him to the utmost of his mental and physical abilities to produce new treasures, which, however, he is not entitled to own. . . .

To perpetuate this state of affairs is the only aim of the dominant classes. Though not always united among themselves—one seeking to gain advantage over the other by tricks of trade, cunning in speculation and diverse machinations of competition—yet in opposition to the proletariat they stand in one united hostile phalanx. Their political ideal is, therefore—in spite of all their liberal phrases—a most powerful, centralized and brutal government. If the poor man, who is momentarily unable to sell himself to an exploiter of labor, or is already flayed to complete helplessness by the *beast of property*, has recourse to begging—then the glutted bourgeois terms it vagrancy and calls for the police; he demands pillory and prison for the poor devil who refuses to starve between mountains of food. Should the unemployed apply a little of the much vaunted self help, that is, should he do in a small way what the rich do daily with impunity and on a grand scale, should he, in fact, steal in order to live—the bourgeoisie will heap burning coals of moral indignation upon his head and hand him over to the relentless state, in whose prisons he will be fleeced all the more effectively, i.e. cheaper.

When the workers combine in order to obtain better wages, shorter hours of labor, or similar advantages, the money bags immediately decry it as a *conspiracy* which must be prevented.

When the workers organize politically it is denounced as resistance to the divine order of things, which must be nullified by laws of exception or discrimination.

Should the people finally contemplate rebellion an unceasing howl of rage raised by the *gold tigers* will be heard throughout the world; they pant for massacres and their thirst for blood is insatiable. The life of the poor is valued as nothing by the rich. . . .

Women are cheaper than men: for this reason the capitalistic vampires seek their blood with insatiate rapacity. Besides, female labor procures them cheap mistresses.

Child flesh is the cheapest; what wonder, then, that the cannibals of modern society continually feast upon juvenile victims? What care they that the poor little ones are thereby bodily crippled and mentally ruined for life—that thousands of them, miserable and worn out at a tender age, sink into their graves? Stocks rise; that suffices.

As the bourgeoisie, by means of its capital, completely monopolizes all new inventions, every new machine, instead of shortening the hours of labor and enhancing the prosperity and happiness of ALL, causes, on the contrary, dismissal from employment for some, reduction of wages for others, and an increased and intensified state of misery for the entire proletariat. When increase of production is accompanied by an augmented pauperization of the masses, consumption must simultaneously decrease; stagnation and crisis must ensue. A superabundance of actual wealth in the hands of the few must create hunger, typhus and other epidemics among the many. The injustice—yea the idiocy—of this state of affairs is evident. The money bags, of course, merely shrug their shoulders. This they will continue to do until a rope, tightly tied around their necks, will end all further shrugging. . . .

In America the place of the monarchs is filled by monopolists. Should monopolism in the alleged *free* United States of America develop at the rate it has in the last quarter of a century, only daylight and air will remain free of monopolization. Five hundred million acres of land in the United States, about six times the area of Great Britain and Ireland, have been divided within a generation among the railroad companies and the great landlords of Europeo-aristocratic origin. Within a few decades Vanderbilt alone amassed $200,000,000; several dozen of his competitors in robbery bid fair to outdo him. San Francisco was settled hardly thirty years ago; yet today it harbors eighty-five millionaires! All the wealth of this great republic, its mines, its coal fields, its oil wells, etc., etc., has been taken from the people and are the property of a handful of daring adventurers and cunning schemers.

The sovereignty of the people falls prostrate into the dust before the influence of these money kings, railroad magnates, coal barons and factory lords. These fellows carry the whole United States in their pockets, and what is vaunted as untrammeled legislation and free ballot is a farce, a delusion and a snare.

If this be the condition of the green wood, what may we not expect of the decayed timber? If this young American republic, with its boundless territory and its almost inexhaustible natural resources, has been so fatally corrupted and ruined in such a short time by the capitalistic system—why be surprised at the results of long continued abuses of a similar nature in servile, rotten Europe?

Indeed it seems as though this young American republic had for the present but one historical mission, that of demonstrating beyond controversy, to the people on this side of the Atlantic as to those on the other, what an outrageous monster the *beast of property* really is. . . .

Let those who labor to live understand that this monster cannot be tamed nor be made harmless or useless to man; let them learn to know that there is but one means to safety: unrelenting, pitiless, thorough war of extermination! Gentle overtures are for nought. Scorn and derision will be the result if by petitions, elections, and the like silly attempts, the proletariat hopes to command the respect of its sworn enemies.

Some say general education will bring about a change; but this advice is, as a rule, an idle phrase. The education of the people will be possible only when the obstructions thereto have been removed. And that will not take place until the entire present system has been destroyed.

But let it not be understood that nothing could or should be done by education. Far from it. Whoever has recognized the villainy of the present conditions is duty bound to raise his voice to expose them and thereby open the eyes of the people. Only avoid reaching this result by super-scientific reflections. Let us leave this to those well meaning scientists, who in this manner tear the mask of humanity from the better class and disclose the hideous countenance of the beast of prey. The language of and to the proletariat must be clear and forcible. Whoever uses this kind of speech will be accused of inciting disturbance by the governing rabble; he will be utterly hated and persecuted. This shows that the only possible and practical enlightenment must be of an inciting nature. Then let us incite!

Let us show the people how it is swindled out of its labor power by country and city capitalists; how it is euchred out of its meagre wages . . . how priests of pulpit, press and party seek to destroy its intellect; how a brutal police is ever ready to maltreat and tyrannize it and a soldiery to spill its blood. Patience at last must forsake it! The people will rebel and crush its foes.

The revolution of the proletariat, the war of the poor against the rich, is the only way from oppression to deliverance.

But, some interpose, revolutions cannot be made. Certainly not, but they can be prepared for by directing the people's attention to the fact that such events are imminent, and calling upon them to be ready for all emergencies.

Capitalistic development, which, many theorists assert, must proceed to the total extinction of the middle class before the conditions favorable to a social revolution are at hand, this development has reached such a point of perfection that its further progress is almost impossible. . . .

Everything, therefore, is ripe for Communism; it is only necessary to remove its inveterate enemies, the capitalists and their abettors. During these crises the people will become sufficiently prepared for the struggle. Everything will then depend on the presence of a well-trained revolutionary nucleus at all points, a nucleus that is able to crystallize around itself the masses of the people, driven to rebellion by misery and want of work; a nucleus that can then apply the mighty forces so formed to the destruction of all existing hostile institutions.

Therefore organize and enlarge everywhere the socialistic revolutionary party before it is too late! The victory of the people over its tyrants and vampires will then be certain.

Instead of developing a program here, under the present conditions it is of far greater importance to sketch a plan of what the proletariat should do, immediately after the victorious battle, to maintain its supremacy.

The following should be done: In every local community where the people have gained a victory, revolutionary committees must be constituted. These execute the decrees of the revolutionary army, which, reinforced by the armed workingmen, now rule like a new conqueror of the world.

The former (present) system will be abolished in the most rapid and thorough manner when the bases of its support—the *beasts of property* and their horde of adherents—are annihilated. The case stands thus: If the people do not crush them, they will crush the people, drown the revolution in the blood of the noblest men, and rivet the chains of slavery more firmly than ever. The alternative is kill or be killed. Therefore massacres of the people's enemies must be instituted. All free communities will enter into an offensive and defensive alliance while combat continues. The revolutionary communes must incite rebellion in the adjacent districts. The war cannot terminate until the enemy (the *beast of property*) has been pursued to its last lurking place and totally destroyed.

In order to proceed thoroughly in the economic sense, all lands and so-called real estate, with everything on it, as well as all movable capital, will be declared the property of the prospective communes. Until the harmonious reorganization of society can be effected, the proclamation of the following principles and measures might suffice:

Every pending debt is liquidated. Objects of personal use which were pawned or mortgaged will be returned free. No rents will be paid. District committees on habitation, sitting permanently, will allot shelter to those who are homeless or who have inadequate or unhealthy quarters; after the Great Purification there will be no want of desirable homes.

Until everyone obtains suitable employment the Commune must guarantee the necessities of life to all. Committees on supplies will regulate the distribution of confiscated goods. Whatever is lacking —e.g., food—must be obtained by the proper agents. Taking such things from neighboring great estates by armed columns of foragers would be a most expeditious way of furnishing them.

The preparation of provisions will be done effectively by communal associations of workingmen, organized for that purpose.

The immediate organization of the workers according to their different branches of trade, and the placing of the factories, machines, raw materials, etc., etc. at their disposal for cooperative production—this will form the basis of the new society.

The Commune will—at least for the present—mediate and regulate consumption. It therefore enters into contracts with the individual workers' associations, grants periodic advances to them— e.g., drafts upon communal wares that have been collected and stored up—and thereby gives the death stroke to the old monetary system.

Good schools, kindergartens, and other institutions for education must be founded without delay. The education of adults, which will then be possible, must not be neglected or postponed. Truth and knowledge must be taught in all churches, where no priestly cant will be tolerated. All printing presses must be put into operation to produce books, papers and pamphlets of educational value by the millions; these are to be distributed everywhere, particularly in regions not yet liberated from thralldom.

All law books, court and police records, registers of mortgages, deeds, bonds, and all so-called valuable documents must be burned. . . .

And now let us take a look at the ideal we have in mind.

A free society consists of autonomous, i.e., independent Communes. A network of federations, the result of freely made social contracts, not of authoritarian government, unites them all. Common affairs are attended to through free deliberation and judgment by the interested Communes or associations. People of both sexes meet frequently in parks or suitable halls, not to make laws or to bind their own hands, but to decide from case to case on all matters touching public affairs, or on which individuals should carry out their resolves and hear their reports.

The exterior appearances of these Communes will be entirely different from those of the present cities and villages. Narrow streets have vanished; tenement prisons have been torn down; and spacious, well-fitted palaces, surrounded by gardens and parks, have been built in their places, giving accommodation to larger or smaller associations brought together by identical interests, increasing comfort to a degree which no individual or family arrangement could reach.

In the country the people will be more concentrated. One agricultural Commune, with city conveniences, will take the place of several villages. The uniting of farms hitherto separated, the general application and constant improvement of agricultural implements and chemical fertilizers, the growing perfection of the means of communication and transportation—for these reasons and others the process of concentration has been greatly simplified. The former contrast between city and country disappears, and the principle of equality gains one of its most important triumphs.

Private property exists no more. All wealth belongs to the Communes or the communal leagues. Everybody, whether able to work or not, can obtain from them such articles of necessity as he may desire. The sum total of necessities and comforts demanded regulates the quantity of production.

The time of labor for the individual is limited to a few hours a day, because all those able to work, regardless of sex, take part in production, because useless, injurious, or the like work will not be done, and because technical, chemical and other auxiliary means of production are highly developed and universally applied. By far the greater part of the day can be spent in the enjoyment of life. The highest gratification will be found in freely chosen intellectual employment. Some spend their leisure time in the service of their fellow men, and are busy working for the common weal. Others can be found in the libraries, where they apply themselves to literary pursuits, or to gathering material for educational lectures, or simply for private studies. Others again hasten to the lyceums and learn about science. Academies of painting, sculpture, music, etc., offer chances of education for those who follow the fine arts.

. . . Teaching will be done only in well-ventilated, lighted rooms, and, in fair weather, in the open air. And in order to secure the equal development of mind and body, merry play, gymnastics and work will alternate with the intense application of the mind.

Theatres and concert halls will offer free seats to all.

Forced or procured marriages will be unknown; mankind will return to the natural state, and love rules will be unconstrained.

Vice and crime will disappear along with their original causes: private property and general misery.

To a great extent diseases will disappear because bad lodging, murderous workshops, impure food and drink, overexertion, etc., etc., will cease to afflict men.

Man at last will enjoy life—THE "BEAST OF PROPERTY" IS NO MORE!!!

Speeches at the Chicago
Anarchist Trial
1886

The speeches delivered by the eight Anarchists at their trial were widely publicized. The excerpts below of three of them are from a book brought out the following year (by Lucy Parsons), *Anarchism, Its Philosophy and Scientific Basis.**

SPEECH BY AUGUST SPIES

. . . From their testimony one is forced to conclude that we had, in our speeches and publications, preached nothing else but destruction and dynamite. The court has this morning stated that there is no case in history like this. I have noticed, during this trial, that the gentlemen of the legal profession are not well versed in history. In all historical cases of this kind truth had to be perverted by the priests of the established power that was nearing its end.

What have we said in our speeches and publications?

We have interpreted to the people their conditions and relations in society. We have explained to them the different social phenomena and the social laws and circumstances under which they occur. We have, by way of scientific investigation, incontrovertibly proved and brought to their knowledge that the system of wages is the root of the present social iniquities—iniquities so monstrous that they cry to Heaven. We have further said that the wage system, as a specific form of social development, would, by the necessity of logic, have to make room for higher forms of civilization; that the wage system must prepare the way and furnish the foundation for a social system of co-operation—that is, *socialism*. That whether this or that theory, this or that scheme regarding future arrangements were accepted was not a matter of choice, but one of historical necessity, and that to us the tendency of progress seemed to be *anarchism*— that is, a free society without kings or classes—a society of sovereigns in which the liberty and economic equality of all would furnish

* Pp. 53–55, 57–58, 67–68, 82–96, 105–107.

an unshakable equilibrium as a foundation and condition of natural order.

It is not likely that the honorable Bonfield and Grinnell can conceive of a social order not held intact by the policeman's club and pistol, nor of a free society without prisons, gallows, and State's attorneys. In such a society they probably fail to find a place for themselves. And is this the reason why anarchism is such a "pernicious and damnable doctrine?"

Grinnell has intimated to us that anarchism was on trial. The theory of anarchism belongs to the realm of speculative philosophy. There was not a syllable said about anarchism at the Haymarket meeting. At that meeting the very popular theme of reducing the hours of toil was discussed. But, "anarchism is on trial" foams Mr. Grinnell. If that is the case, your honor, very well; you may sentence me, for I am an anarchist. I believe with Buckle, with Paine, Jefferson, Emerson, and Spencer, and many other great thinkers of this century, that the state of castes and classes—the state where one class dominates over and lives upon the labor of another class, and calls this *order*—yes; I believe that this barbaric form of social organization, with its legalized plunder and murder, is doomed to die, and make room for a free society, voluntary association, or universal brotherhood, if you like. You may pronounce the sentence upon me, honorable judge, but let the world know that in A.D. 1886, in the State of Illinois, eight men were sentenced to death because they believed in a better future; because they had not lost their faith in the ultimate victory of liberty and justice! . . .

We have preached dynamite. Yes, we have predicted from the lessons history teaches, that the ruling classes of to-day would no more listen to the voice of reason than their predecessors; that they would attempt by brute force to stay the wheel of progress. Is it a lie, or was it the truth we told? Are not already the large industries of this once free country conducted under the surveillance of the police, the detective, the military and the sheriffs—and is this return to militancy not developing from day to day? American sovereigns —think of it—working like the galley convicts under military guards! We have predicted this, and predict that soon these conditions will grow unbearable. What then? The mandate of the feudal lords of our time is slavery, starvation and death! This has been their programme for the past years. We have said to the toilers, that science had penetrated the mystery of nature—that from Jove's head once more has sprung a Minerva—dynamite! If this declaration is synonymous with murder, why not charge those with the crime to whom we owe the invention? To charge us with an attempt to overthrow the present system on or about May 4th by force, and then establish anarchy, is too absurd a statement, I think, even for a political office-holder to make. . . .

Grinnell has repeatedly stated that our country is an enlightened country (*sarcastically*). The verdict fully corroborates the assertion! This verdict against us is the anathema of the wealthy classes over their despoiled victims—the vast army of wage workers and farmers. If your honor would not have these people believe this; if you would not have them believe that we have once more arrived at the Spartan Senate, the Athenian Areopagus, the Venetian Council of Ten, etc., then sentence should not be pronounced. But, if you think that by hanging us, you can stamp out the labor movement—the movement from which the downtrodden millions, the millions who toil and live in want and misery—the wage slaves—expect salvation—if this is your opinion, then hang us! Here you will tread upon a spark, but there, and there; and behind you, and in front of you, and everywhere, flames will blaze up. It is a subterranean fire. You cannot put it out.

The ground is on fire upon which you stand. You can't understand it. You don't believe in magical arts, as your grandfathers did who burned witches at the stake, but you do believe in conspiracies; you believe that all these occurrences of late are the work of conspirators! You resemble the child that is looking for his picture behind the mirror. What you see, and what you try to grasp is nothing but the deceptive reflex of the stings of your bad conscience. You want to "stamp out the conspirators"—the "agitators"? Ah, stamp out every factory lord who has grown wealthy upon the unpaid labor for his employees. Stamp out every landlord who has amassed fortunes from the rent of over-burdened workingmen and farmers. Stamp out every machine that is revolutionizing industry and agriculture, that intensifies the production and ruins the producer, that increases the national wealth, while the creator of all these things stands amidst them, tantalized with hunger! Stamp out the railroads, the telegraph, the telephone, steam and yourselves—for everything breathes the revolutionary spirit.

You, gentlemen, are the revolutionists! You rebel against the effects of social conditions which have tossed you, by the fair hand of fortune, into a magnificent paradise. Without inquiring, you imagine that no one else has a right in that place. You insist that you are the chosen ones, the sole proprietors. The forces that tossed you into the paradise, the industrial forces, are still at work. They are growing more active and intense from day to day. Their tendency is to elevate all mankind to the same level, to have all humanity share in the paradise you now monopolize. You, in your blindness, think you can stop the tidal wave of civilization, and human emancipation by placing a few policemen, a few gatling guns, and some regiments of militia on the shore—you think you can frighten the rising waves back into the unfathomable depths, whence they have risen, by erecting a few gallows in the perspective. You, who oppose the natural course of things, *you* are the real revolutionists. *You* and *you* alone are the conspirators and destructionists! . . .

SPEECH BY MICHAEL SCHWAB

. . . We contend for communism and anarchy—why? If we had kept silent, stones would have cried out. Murder was committed day by day. Children were slain, women worked to death, men killed inch by inch, and these crimes are never punished by law. The great principle underlying the present system is unpaid labor. Those who amass fortunes, build palaces, and live in luxury, are doing that by virtue of unpaid labor. Being directly or indirectly the possessors of land and machinery, they dictate their terms to the workingman. He is compelled to sell his labor cheap, or to starve. The price paid him is always far below the real value. He acts under compulsion, and they call it a free contract. This infernal state of affairs keeps him poor and ignorant; an easy prey for exploitation.

I know what life has in store for the masses. I was one of them. I slept in their garrets, and lived in their cellars. I saw them work and die. I worked with girls in the same factory—prostitutes they were, because they could not earn enough wages for their living. I saw females sick from overwork, sick in body and mind on account of the lives they were forced to lead. I saw girls from ten to fourteen years of age working for a mere pittance. I heard how their morals were killed by the foul and vile language and the bad example of their ignorant fellow-workers, leading them to the same road of misery, and as an individual I could do nothing. I saw families starving and able-bodied men worked to death. That was in Europe. When I came to the United States, I found that there were classes of workingmen who were better paid than the European workmen, but I perceived that the state of things in a great number of industries was even worse, and that the so-called better paid skilled laborers were degrading rapidly into mere automatic parts of machinery. I found that the proletariat of the great industrial cities was in a condition that could not be worse. Thousands of laborers in the city of Chicago live in rooms without sufficient protection from the weather, without proper ventilation, where never a stream of sunlight flows in. There are hovels where two, three and four families live in one room. How these conditions influence the health and the morals of these unfortunate sufferers, it is needless to say. And how do they live? From the ash-barrels they gather half-rotten vegetables, in the butcher shops they buy for some cents offal of meat, and these precious morsels they carry home to prepare from them their meals. The dilapidated houses in which this class of laborers live need repairs very badly, but the greedy landlord waits in most cases till he is compelled by the city to have them done. Is it a wonder that diseases of all kinds kill men, women and children in such places by wholesale, especially children? Is this not horrible in a so-called civilized land where there is plenty of food and riches? Some years ago a committee of the Citizen's Association, or League, made an investigation of these matters, and I was one of the reporters that went with them. What these common laborers are to-day, the skilled laborers will be to-morrow. Improved machinery that ought to be a blessing for the workingman, under the existing condition turns for him to a curse. Machinery multiplies the army of unskilled laborers, makes the laborer more dependent upon the men who own the land and the machines. And that is the reason that socialism and communism got a foothold in this country. The outcry that socialism, communism and anarchism are the creed of foreigners, is a big mistake. There are more socialists of American birth in this country than foreigners, and that is much, if we consider that nearly half of all industrial workingmen are not native Americans. There are socialistic papers in a great many States edited by Americans for Americans. The capitalistic newspapers conceal that fact very carefully. . . .

SPEECH BY ALBERT R. PARSONS

In the effort of the prosecution to hold up our opinions to public execration they lost sight of the charge of murder. Disloyalty to their class, and their boasted civilization is in their eyes a far greater crime than murder.

Anarchy, in the language of Grinnell, is simply a compound of robbery, incendiarism and murder. This is the official statement of Mr. Grinnell, and against his definition of anarchy I would put that of Mr. Webster. I think that is pretty near as good authority as that gentleman's.

What is anarchy? What is the nature of the dreadful thing—this anarchy, for the holding of which this man says we ought to suffer death?

The closing hours of this trial, yes, for five days the representatives of a privileged, usurped power and of despotism sought to belie, misrepresent, and vilify the doctrine in which I believe. Now, sir, let me speak of that for a moment.

What is anarchism? What is it—what are its doctrines?

General Parsons—for which you are called upon to die.

Mr. Parsons—For which I am called upon to die. First and foremost it is my opinion, or the opinion of an anarchist, that government is despotism; government is an organization of oppression, and law, statute law is its agent. Anarchy is anti-government, anti-rulers, anti-dictators, anti-bosses and drivers. Anarchy is the negation of force; the elimination of all authority in social affairs; it is the denial of the right of domination of one man over another. It is the diffusion of rights, of power, of duties, equally and freely among all the people.

But anarchy, like many other words, is defined in Webster's dictionary as having two meanings. In one place it is defined to mean, "without rulers or governors." In another place it is defined to mean, "disorder and confusion." This latter meaning is what we call "capitalistic anarchy," such as is now witnessed in all portions of the world and especially in this court-room; the former, which means without rulers, is what we denominate communistic anarchy, which will be ushered in with the social revolution.

Socialism is a term which covers the whole range of human progress and advancement. Socialism is defined by Webster—I think I have a right to speak of this matter, because I am tried here as a socialist. I am condemned as a socialist, and it has been of socialism that Grinnell and these men had so much to say, and I think it right to speak before the country, and be heard in my own behalf, at least. If you are going to put me to death, then let the people know what it is for. Socialism is defined by Webster as "A theory of society which advocates a more precise, more orderly, and more harmonious arrangement of the social relations of mankind than has hitherto prevailed." Therefore everything in the line of progress, in civilization in fact, is socialistic. There are two distinct phases of socialism in the labor movement throughout the world to-day. One is known as anarchism, without political government or authority, the other is known as state socialism or paternalism, or governmental control of everything. The state socialist seeks to ameliorate and emancipate the wage laborers by means of law, by legislative enactments. The state socialists demand the right to choose their own rulers. Anarchists would have neither rulers nor law-makers of any kind. The anarchists seek the same ends by the abrogation of law, by the abolition of all government, leaving the people free to unite or disunite as fancy or interest may dictate; coercing no one, driving no party. . . .

Whoever prescribes a rule of action for another to obey is a tyrant, usurper, and an enemy of liberty. This is precisely what every statute does. Anarchy is the natural law, instead of the man-made statute, and gives men leaders in the place of drivers and bosses. All political law, statute and common, gets its right to operate from the statute; therefore all political law is statute law. A statute law is a written scheme by which cunning takes advantage of the unsuspecting, and provides the inducement to do so, and protects the one who does it. In other words, a statute is the science of rascality, or the law of usurpation. If a few sharks rob mankind of all the earth, turn them all out of house and home, make them ragged slaves and beggars, and freeze and starve them to death, still they are expected to obey the statute because it is sacred. This ridiculous nonsense that human laws are sacred, and that if they are not respected and continued we cannot prosper, is the stupidest and most criminal nightmare of the age. Statutes are the last and greatest curse of man, and when destroyed the world will be free. The statute book is a book of laws by which one class of people can safely trespass upon the rights of another. Every statute law is always used to oppose some natural law, or to sustain some other equally vicious statute. The statute is the great science of rascality by which alone the few trample upon and enslave the many. There are natural laws provided for every want of man. Natural laws are self-operating. They punish all who violate them, and reward all who obey them. They cannot be replaced, amended, dodged or bribed, and it costs neither time, money nor attention to apply them. It is time to stop legislating against them. We want to obey laws, not men, nor the tricks of men. Statutes are human tricks. The law—the statute law—is the coward's weapon, the tool of the thief, and more—the shield and buckler of every gigantic villainy, and frightful parent of all crimes. Every great robbery that was ever perpetrated upon a people has been by virtue of and in the name of law. By this tool of thieves the great mass of the people who inhabit our planet have been robbed of their equal right to the use of the soil and of all other natural opportunities. In the name of this monster (statute law) large sections of our race have been bought and sold as chattels; by it the vast majority of the human race are to-day held in the industrial bondage of wage-slavery, and in its name our fair earth has been times without number deluged in human blood. . . .

Anarchy, therefore, is liberty; is the negation of force, or compulsion, or violence. It is the precise reverse of that which those who hold and love power would have their oppressed victims believe it is.

Anarchists do not advocate or advise the use of force. Anarchists disclaim and protest against its use, and the use of force is justifiable only when employed to repel force. Who, then, are the aiders, abettors and users of force? Who are the real revolutionists? Are they not those who hold and exercise power over their fellows? They who use clubs and bayonets, prisons and scaffolds? The great class conflict now gathering throughout the world is created by our social system of industrial slavery. Capitalists could not if they would, and would not if they could, change it. This alone is to be the work of the proletariat, the disinherited, the wage-slave, the sufferer. Nor can the wage-class avoid this conflict. Neither religion nor politics can solve it or prevent it. It comes as a human, an imperative necessity. Anarchists do not make the social revolution; they prophesy its coming. Shall we then stone the prophets? Anarchists do not use or advise the use of force, but point out that force is ever employed to uphold despotism to despoil man's natural rights. Shall we therefore kill and destroy the anarchists? And capital shouts, "Yes, yes! exterminate them!" . . .

Anarchy has no schemes, no programmes, no systems to offer or to substitute for the existing order of things. Anarchy would strike from humanity every chain that binds it, and say to mankind: "Go forth! you are free! Have all; enjoy all!" Anarchism or anarchists neither advise, abet nor encourage the working people to the use of force or a resort to violence. We do not say to the wage-slaves: "You ought, you should use force." No. Why say this when we know they must—they will be driven to use it in self-defense, in self-preservation, against those who are degrading, enslaving and destroying them.

Already the millions of workers are unconsciously anarchists. Impelled by a cause, the effects of which they feel but do not wholly understand, they move unconsciously, irresistibly forward to the social revolution. Mental freedom, political equality, industrial liberty!

This is the natural order of things, the logic of events. Who so foolish as to quarrel with it, obstruct it, or attempt to stay its progress? It is the march of the inevitable; the triumph of progress.

ALEXANDER JONAS
Socialism and Anarchism*
1886

The official position of the Socialist Labor Party toward the Anarchists was articulated in this pamphlet, published shortly after the Haymarket affair. Jonas was editor for many years of the Party's German language paper, *The New Yorker Volkzeitung.*

In reading the newspapers, we find the two names mentioned above frequently put side by side. Nay, we find them also associated with the terms Communism and Nihilism, as though these four "isms" had the closest relation to each other. This is a mistake. *Socialism* and *Anarchism* are opposites which have nothing in common but their appurtenance to Social Science. Socialists and Anarchists as such are enemies. They pursue contrary aims, and the success of the former will destroy forever the fanatical hopes of the latter.

It is true that in theory both are thoroughly dissatisfied with the present state of human society and its politics, and that they severely criticize almost all the economical and political constitutions and laws, teachings and practices, as now understood. But they do so from very different points of view. The Anarchist worships at the shrine of Liberty. Liberty is his goddess, and his only deity, in theory at least. He rejects all laws imposed on him from without, and respects only such laws as he himself ordains. He wants no association but with men of his own turn of mind, no rule of the majority, no submission under any will but his own, no discipline. He imagines that human society may be reorganized in the following way: When persons enough are converted to his ideas, all present institutions are to be destroyed, State and church, property and laws, of course, foremost. Reorganization then may begin by the voluntary association of groups of such persons as are thoroughly in accord; these groups may form larger societies for certain special purposes of work or enjoyment; and these societies

* Pp. 1–2, 7–9.

may agree with other such for still more special aims, and so on till all mankind is voluntarily organized. And since men are changeable in their ideas, purposes and whims, each of the groups, societies and their connections may dissolve and differently reorganize themselves, as often as they see fit, without ever applying constraint upon one another. . . .

Socialism, on the other hand, is an antipode of Anarchism. It presupposes human society as a *growth* which develops itself from the simplest beginnings in oldest times through many changes into what it is. Society cannot be dissolved and reorganized. If it is to be renewed, it has to do it and does so gradually at all times. It obeys its own inborn laws, and the efforts of single men and sects cannot even give it any other direction but the one which is inherent and prepared. Scientific truth and discoveries may hasten or retard its development, but can little change it. This is the fundamental doctrine of that most modern form of Socialism which was originated by *Karl Marx*, which calls itself *Social Democracy*, and is so widely spread in Germany and many other countries of Europe, and bids fair to convert mankind. . . .

The evils engendered by private capitalism are so formidable and growing in so rapid a proportion, and the wisdom of "statesmen" and self-constituted rulers is so impotent, that society cannot continue in its old ruts much longer. The *anarchy* of society and politics will, within perhaps, the nineteenth century of our era, have exhausted its vitality and out of despair run into a new issue, akin to the Socialist proposition. And there is so much wisdom and scientific and artistic knowledge and experience still left in the world, though ousted from the right place, that, once directed in the proper channels, a complete renewal of society and constitutions may be brought about, without very violent and bloody convulsions. The conviction once impressed upon a majority of workers that private capitalism is doomed to abolition, together with wages, slavery, corruption and class dominion, a new form of social life and political practice may be inaugurated almost without severe throes of birth. What alone is needed in the meantime is enlightenment of the working masses (workers, both with mind and body) about the doom of private capitalism, a doom of its own make, which cannot be prevented.

From this short exposition it may be seen that Socialism is the most decided enemy to both the Anarchism of the capitalistic class, and the Anarchism of those revolutionists who have been rendered more or less crazy by the cruelties and revolting injustice of our present "law and order." In fact, this latter class of Anarchists hate us more than they hate the other class of Anarchists, *or anybody*. If they were paid by *Bismarck*, or *Czar Alexander III.*, or *Jay Gould* for destroying our organization, they could not more efficiently go about it than they really do. Their actions stultify their teachings, and *vice versa*. They conspire with the least enlightened and most pliant elements against us, the only apostles of a better future.

We do not in the least deny that we have little hope for an entirely peaceful renewal of society and politics, and that we may have to fight for the redemption of the working class from the threatening complete thraldom. But that war must be forced upon us—we try our best efforts to avoid it, and though this may be impossible in most of the European States, we must and do consider it possible in the United States, and wherever freedom of speech and of the press, the right to peacefully assemble and organize, and universal suffrage (inclusive of the suffrage of women) are not curtailed by existing laws. We are fully outspoken in our ideas and aims, all our working for redemption is above board, we shun secret organization for our purposes. Our platform of principles, which will be found at the conclusion of this treatise, means what it professes, no more, no less.

We, therefore, protest against being confounded and in any way identified with Anarchists of any type; we are the implacable enemies of all anarchism. And, if we are sometimes designated as *Communists*, we wish it to be understood that our Communism is different from all other Communism in that we demand nothing in common but capital—the great means of labor (land, buildings, machines, money) because all capital has been and is partly a gratuitous gift of Nature to all, partly being created by the labor of all mankind, and nothing can reasonably be private property but the full proceeds of one's own labor, as agreed upon by common compromise. Our Communism is not sectarian, but truly universal, and compatible with the highest degree of liberty which is at all attainable. The most correct term for our Communism would, perhaps, be *Collectivism*, as it is now called in France. As regards the term *Nihilism*, we have to state that, even in Russia, what was, half a century ago, stigmatized as Nihilism, is no longer in existence, but supplanted by either practical *Anarchism* of a propagandistic kind, or revolutionary conspiracy of all classes, as far as their reflection has begun.

Finally, as may be gathered from our platform, we are a propagandistic organization which goes hand in hand with the great labor movement that is now refermenting the society of the world; and we shall be revolutionists only when forced into being such by legislation and persecution withholding from us the means of a peaceable propaganda. We Socialists have come to stay; depend upon it.

Single Tax versus Socialism*
1887

On October 25, 1887 Henry George debated Serge Schevitch, one
of the best speakers in the Socialist Labor Party, before an audience
of 3000 who were jammed into Miner's Theater in New York.
The socialists sat in the left side of the aisle, the single taxers on the
right. The moderator was none other than Samuel Gompers, president of the American Federation of Labor. It may be noted,
parenthetically, that Schevitch, a onetime Russian revolutionary,
was married to the countess Helena von Rocowitza, the woman
over whom Ferdinand Lassalle had fought his duel and had lost his
life.

MR. SCHEVITCH'S ARGUMENT

Mr. Chairman, Ladies and Gentleman: In coming on this
platform tonight I come to you with all due consciousness of the
great task which I have undertaken, and of my unworthiness to
perform it. I ask your indulgence from the very beginning. I want
only to say that the words I will speak tonight will be that which I
consider to be the truth without any reference whatever to personal feeling.

The subject of discussion tonight is the scheme of Mr. George of
the single land tax, to substitute which for all other forms of taxation will, as he represents, solve the social and the labor problems
of our day. I propose to show that this single land tax system is not
only insufficient to solve those questions, but if considered alone,
if considered as a local panacea, independent of all other social reforms, it will be productive of results which will be more hurtful
to labor than beneficial.

I will in the second part of my remarks show how, on account of
this false basis on which the labor movement, so far as the united
labor party is concerned, has been placed, the whole political move-

* *The Standard*, October 29, 1887.

ment has been side-tracked, has been distorted, has been put on a platform on which no true labor movement can stand.

This is what I will attempt to show during my remarks.

Production, as it is organized now, is regulated by two vast instruments of labor: machinery, with all the powers of nature which now produce such tremendous wealth all over the civilized world, and the land, which produces the necessaries of life. Now let us see. If we nationalize one of these instruments of production, if we nationalize what Mr. George calls the natural opportunities given to man by nature—that is to say, the land—will this nationalization of the land by itself solve the problem? Mr. George does not advocate the nationalization of land. He does not want to disturb anybody in the title to property in land. All he wants is to confiscate the rent which the present proprietor of the land gets by a taxation equivalent to the whole rent. But let us study the question broadly. Let us assume that he does want to nationalize the land. What would be the consequence? The consequence would be that a certain lot of land which now belongs to a private citizen, Tom Jones, will belong to the community. The man who builds on that land will have to pay his rent, not to a private proprietor, but to the community. That rent will, perhaps in the long run, be a little less than the rent he pays now.

Now suppose a city in which there are ten factories. In each of these factories one hundred men are working for wages. The factories are supplied with all the necessary machinery. Three hundred men get two dollars a day under present circumstances. Now the system of nationalization of land is introduced. The man who owns the factory, the boss, will pay his rent not to the proprietor of the land, but to the community. Will his workingmen, in consequence of that simple fact, get higher wages? Why should they?

If tomorrow a new machine is made which renders half the men superfluous, the proprietor will throw out half his hands. Each of these factories will work with fifty men instead of with one hundred. The men thrown out will come to the proprietor and say, "We are ready to work for less wages; instead of two dollars give us a dollar and twenty-five cents." And other men, who have no families to support, will say, "Give us one dollar a day." The same process of competition between laborer and laborer, ground down by that terrible monster, the machine, will go on, whether the land belongs to the community or whether it belongs to Tom Jones. (Applause.)

But Mr. George will say: "This is not true. The competition between the laborers will be, if not entirely destroyed, at least greatly relieved by the fact that the land is free, that these men thrown out of employment by the machine may go out somewhere, in the uptown part of the city, take from the community for a very small rent a lot of land, construct their houses on it and live there in peace." How will they build a house on it? With their hands, with their nails, with their feet? (Applause and hisses.) Where is the money to purchase the instruments of labor? Where is that engine of production, capital? Does bare land give them anything except the land? Where are they to get the necessary machinery in order to bring materials so as to be able to subsist from the products of that land? I don't think that any answer can be given to these questions. (Laughter.) You may laugh, gentlemen, but it is nevertheless the truth. It is not the first truth that has been laughed at in the world. (Applause and hisses.) . . .

The single land tax would be a single tax. All other taxes would be abolished. The tremendous concentrations of capital would be entirely free of any taxes at all. It would mean absolutely free trade. American labor would have to compete with the combined force of capital all over the civilized world. (Applause.) If you introduce absolute free trade dozens of branches of industry would droop and die.

A voice: "Name them."

Thousands and thousands of workingmen would be thrown out of employment. A commercial crisis would be the consequence such as we have never seen yet in this country. The labor market would be over-crowded. What would we do with free land then! Sit on it or lie on it or be tramps upon it. (Applause and hisses.) Land without the instruments of labor to cultivate it is just as worthless as a boat without sails.

Mr. George takes the example of Robinson Crusoe and Friday. Suppose Robinson Crusoe said to Friday: "You are not only a free citizen of this island, but this land belongs to you just as well as to me. But there is a little hitch in the matter. I expect a vessel tomorrow to bring to me all the necessary engines to cultivate this land, and some workingmen, but you are free to do just as well as I." Where would poor Friday be then, without a penny in his pocket, without a single instrument to cultivate the land! (Laughter.) Would he not be the slave of Robinson Crusoe? . . .

The whole theory of the single tax is founded on the sophistry that the present robbery of labor centers in the one fact of private ownership of land, which is not true. If the means of production remained in private hands labor would be robbed just as it is now. The great land owners will immediately form a combine to resist the land tax. In a few years the condition of the laborer would be the same as it is now.

But what will not be the same as this—by that single land tax you will give to the government a tremendous power which it does not now possess. Mr. George likes to accuse the socialists of desiring a paternal government. I tell you Mr. George's scheme is a much more horrible paternal government than the socialists ever proposed. (Applause and cheers, mingled with hisses.) To the government will belong a vast amount of land. . . . Capitalists will have the same power over government officials that they now have. The government will fall into the hands of the monopolists of industry just as it does now into the hands of the monopolists of industry and land combined.

The single tax does not touch the labor question. That question centers in the robbery committed on labor by those who hold possession of the instruments of labor. And it is not the socialists who say so, it is the men of organized labor. (Applause.) Mr. George thinks that rent is the robbery committed on workingmen. He forgets that at the bottom of the robbery is the competition between labor and labor, and that competition will not be destroyed by any amount of single land tax.

The land tax scheme, whether it be wrong or right, is a utopian theory, born in one mind, uncorroborated by the actual state of facts. It is a theory of one man, and that theory has been forced upon the large labor movement while that movement was unprepared to understand or even to critically examine that idea. Mr. George may ask why did all the trades of New York as one man support him in that last campaign? "Where is the difference? I was the same man and my theory was the same." We can answer that. The great majority of the working population of this city supported Mr. George last year, not because of his land theory but notwithstanding his land theory (applause), as a sincere and honest man (tremendous applause)—because he had written in his book, *Progress and Poverty*, one of the most tremendous indictments against the present order of society that has ever been published. (Applause.) The critical part of his work is grand. Every man who is dissatisfied with the existing order will shake hands with Mr. George even now. The laboring population accepted him as a standard bearer, thinking he was broad minded enough to sink part of his petty theories in one vast, grand labor movement, which is not one sided, but which is many-sided and is as broad as the civilized world itself is broad. (Applause.) The man who can force one idea upon millions of people can be the originator of a sect, or if he is a politician, can be the originator of a political machine; but he will never be the originator of a great political party of labor. (Applause and hisses.) When Mr. George attempted to do so he smashed the party of united labor. (Hisses and applause.) As I told him on the Syracuse platform, under the ban of expulsion: "If you attempt to force this one idea upon the labor movement you will smash the party to pieces, and you have done it." (Cries of "No! no!" Hisses, applause and cries of "Order!" Mr. Gompers and Mr. George both rise and motion the audience to keep quiet.) . . .

HENRY GEORGE'S REPLY

Mr. Gompers then introduced Mr. George, who was received with intense enthusiasm. He said:

I am about to speak to you on the time limit, and therefore your applause will simply take away so much of my time. What Mr. George has founded and what he has not founded I do not propose here to discuss. We are here tonight for a more important object. We all agree that labor today does not get its fair earnings. I come to defend what I believe to be not merely the best but the only possible way to emancipate labor. I do not claim for this measure—the taking for the use of the community of the rental value of the land—that it would do everything. It is the beginning. After it is done all the other things will be made easier, and until we have done that we shall be rowing against the tide in all other reforms. (Applause and hisses.)

Now, the great difference between the opinions that I represent and the opinions that Mr. Schevitch represents may be seen in Lassalle's open letter to the workingmen of Germany. He accepted the law laid down by the orthodox political economists—the law that wages must always tend to the minimum which will enable the laborer to live and to reproduce. This he calls the iron law of wages. There I and those who think with me take issue. We do not believe that there is in nature any such thing as the iron law of wages. We hold that it is merely the law of wages where natural opportunities are monopolized.

This competition is a one-sided competition of men debarred of their natural opportunities for employment. The means of production, what do they consist of today? The answer will probably be land, machinery and various other things. There was in the beginning nothing but man and the earth. Human labor exerted upon the land brings out, produces, all other means of production. Therefore it is that land is more important than anything else. Given men and given land all other things can be produced. Give a man everything else and deprive him of land and it avails him nothing. (Applause and cheers.)

To recur to that illustration of Robinson Crusoe and Friday. Mr. Schevitch says that Robinson Crusoe having machinery and tools, Friday would have been perfectly helpless. Well, that I deny. Friday, without any machinery, could certainly have gone fishing. (Laughter and applause, cheers and hisses.) If the island had belonged to Robinson Crusoe he could not have done that. Friday could have done without machinery and tools, just as Robinson Crusoe did. Friday could have made him a hut out of the limbs of a tree. Friday could have lived and produced as a naked man, applying his labor to the natural opportunities offered by the island. If three or four others had come there, they could have lived and lived well. But the moment Robinson Crusoe owned the land, that moment he could say to Friday: "Unless you do so and so you walk off." (Laughter.) Friday would have been his absolute slave.

Wages in all branches of industry are not what they ought to be. That increase in productive power that comes from discovery and invention does not raise wages as it ought to do. But what is the reason of that? It is perfectly clear that wages in all occupations must tend to a general level. Now, the broadest of all occupations in the United States is—what? (A voice: "Farming.") Those occupations which apply directly to nature, which extract wealth from the soil. . . . The ordinary renting rate in the state of New York today is one-half the produce. The man who does the labor gets only one-half of what his labor produces. The rest goes to the owner of the farm. There, in that primary occupation, labor is divested of one-half its earnings. When, in that primary industry, labor is shorn of one-half of its earnings, what do you expect in those industries that rise above it? To put a tax on the value of land, removing all other taxes that now bear upon labor and to take for the use of the community the value that attaches to land by reason of the growth of the community, would have in the first place the operation that Mr. Schevitch concedes. It would make the holding of land on speculation unprofitable. That of itself would tend to destroy that competition which tends everywhere to press wages down. I don't mean to say that everyone would want to be a farmer. That is the one thing that all men could be. And enough could and would become farmers to relieve the glut in the labor market. (Applause.) . . .

Here is the principle of taxation. A tax which is levied upon the production of a thing that must constantly be produced by human labor will, by making supply more difficult, raise prices, and the man who pays the tax is thus able to push the tax upon the consumer. But a tax upon the value of land has no such effect. Land does not have to be constantly supplied in order to meet the demand. Its price is always a monopoly value, and a tax which falls upon land value does not fall upon all land, but only upon valuable land, and that in proportion to its value.

It is perfectly true that were we to raise our revenue in this way we could get along without the custom house and have absolute free trade. On the contrary, what labor wants is freedom, not protection. (Applause.) Absolute free trade in any sense worthy of the name means free production. Once make production free and labor can take care of itself. (Applause.)

In what consists the value of land? It is a premium, an advantage, which the use of any particular piece of land will give over what the same application of labor and capital can get from the poorest land in use. Therefore, if we take that premium for the use of the whole community we put all land upon a substantial plane of equality. We can abolish all other taxes and enormously simplify government. Opening opportunities for labor, we can get rid of that bitter competition that today everywhere tends to force wages down. Then we can go on, not to a paternal government that attempts to regulate everything, but to a government that controls businesses in their natural monopolies. (Applause.) Once put the social foundation on a firm and equal basis and then we can march forward in that as far as may be necessary. We do not hold that everything is done when this one single measure is carried out, but we do hold that a firm and true beginning is made. Men have lived and can live without the railroad and without the telegraph, but no man ever has lived or ever can live without the land. (Great applause.) . . .

MR. SCHEVITCH'S REJOINDER

"Mr. Schevitch now has his second inning," said Mr. Gompers, as Mr. George sat down.

Mr. Schevitch at once arose and was received with applause from the reds. "I would prefer," he said with a smile, "to get the applause from the other side of the house," pointing to the blues. The latter cheered him heartily, and he continued. . . .

Mr. George did not show that the competition of labor would be destroyed by the land tax system. He did not show, he simply made an assertion, that the natural opportunities would be open to labor. He said that laborers might go fishing, and he very graciously said that he did not expect a man to go naked in the city of New York. But that man would be naked practically, and the ideal of George's free land would be Shantytown. When I hear such things on a platform in New York City in the nineteenth century I begin to believe that Mr. George is a Rip Van Winkle of social economy. (Applause from the extreme left.) He actually has been born in antediluvian times and has all at once waked up in time for the Syracuse convention.

At this there was a storm of hisses from the right and cries of "Question! Question! Question!"

"It is the question," continued Mr. Schevitch amid hisses. "It is the question (hisses), and you can't choke me down."

The left broke out in applause, and the right went wild with yelling and hooting, amidst which there were cries of "Order! Order!" Mr. Gompers had to get up and speak for several minutes before he could quiet the trouble. Then Mr. Schevitch continued:

You surely do not expect me to compliment Mr. George. Mr. George seems utterly to forget that we are living in the grand century of machinery, in a great age of production on a large scale, where the mere laborer is absolutely the slave of those who possess the instruments of labor. This simple land tax does not free the laborer from competition with his fellow laborer. The laborer with his free land must have capital to construct his house, and capital to begin farming on a small scale even. And there will be a big man with a big boodle, who will come beside the laborer with his lot, and take not one but ten, twelve, twenty or two hundred lots and will crush down that free-born citizen on the lot by his side. (Applause from the reds.) . . .

HENRY GEORGE CONCLUDES THE DEBATE

Then Mr. George arose and said:

The object of the labor movement is the abolition of wage slavery. How do you propose to abolish it? That is the question. (Applause.) If any man has any better plan than that which I propose let him come and state it. Mr. Schevitch's plan, as I understand it, is that of forming a number of co-operative societies, embracing all the working classes, who are to be furnished with capital by the government.

(Cries of "No, no, no sir!" from the reds.)

Well, with machinery, then. That plan, I say, is utterly impossible. There attaches to it the same disadvantages that attach to all dreams of the elevation of the workingmen by the formation of co-operative societies. You must raise from the very foundation. You must make labor free. Now such catch-phrases as my picture of Shantytown as an ideal city can avail nothing with any thoughtful man. (Great Applause.) What I say is this: that even the poorest man, if he has free access to land, can make some use of it, and the condition of those Shantytown people, poor as it was, was very much better than that of many who are herded in tenement houses, liable to be turned out at the end of the week or month. (Applause.) . . .

Now, as to capital. When the farmer has to give up one-half of his produce for the privilege of applying his labor to the land; when through the other occupations the same law holds; when men have to pay to an individual for the use of what they call their country one-quarter, one-third, one-half the produce of their labor, is it any wonder that the working classes find it very hard to get capital! Capital is produced by labor exerted upon land. Here, in the fact that we make the land the private property of some of our number, is a constant drain of capital from those who produce it into the hands of those who are merely proprietors and monopolizers. "The destruction of the poor is their poverty." . . . Labor is the producer of all wealth (applause), but labor without land is helpless, and that is the reason why any attempt to bring about more healthy social conditions must begin with the land. (Applause.)

DANIEL DELEON
Reform or Revolution*
1896

This was the printed version of one of DeLeon's best known speeches. He presented it at Well's Memorial Hall, Boston, on January 26, 1896.

. . . I shall assume—it is a wise course for a speaker to adopt—that none in this audience knows what is "Reform" and what is "Revolution." Those who are posted will understand me all the better; those who are not will follow me all the easier.

We hear people talk about the "Reform Forces," about "Evolution" and about "Revolution" in ways that are highly mixed. Let us clear up our terms. Reform means a change of externals; Revolution—peaceful or bloody, and peacefulness or the bloodiness of it cuts no figure whatever in the essence of the question, means a change from within.

REFORM.

Take, for instance, a poodle. You can reform him in a lot of ways. You can shave his whole body and leave a tassel at the tip of his tail; you may bore a hole through each ear, and tie a blue bow on one and a red bow on the other; you may put a brass collar around his neck with your initials on, and a trim little blanket on his back; yet, throughout, a poodle he was and a poodle he remains. Each of these changes probably wrought a corresponding change in the poodle's life. When shorn of all his hair except a tassel at the tail's tip he was owned by a wag who probably cared only for the fun he could get out of his pet; when he appears gaily decked in bows, probably his young mistress' attachment is of tenderer sort; when later we see him in the fancier's outfit, the treatment he receives and the uses he is put to may be yet again, and probably are, different. Each of these

* Pp. 4–9, 16–23.

transformations or stages may mark a veritable epoch in the poodle's existence. And yet, essentially, a poodle he was, a poodle he is, and a poodle he will remain. That is REFORM. (Laughter.)

But when we look back myriads of years, or project ourselves into far-future physical cataclysms, and trace the development of animal life from the invertebrate to the vertebrate, from the lizard to the bird, from the quadruped and mammal till we come to the prototype of the poodle, and finally reach the poodle himself, and so forward—then do we find radical changes at each step, changes from within that alter the very essence of his being, and that put, or will put, upon him each time a stamp that alters the very system of his existence. That is REVOLUTION.

So with society. Whenever a change leaves the internal mechanism untouched, we have REFORM; whenever the internal mechanism is changed, we have REVOLUTION.

Of course, no internal change is possible without external manifestations. The internal changes denoted by the revolution or evolution of the lizard into the eagle go accompanied with external marks. So with society. And therein lies one of the pitfalls into which dilettanteism or "Reforms" invariably tumble. They have noticed that externals change with internals; and they rest satisfied with mere external changes, without looking behind the curtain. But of this more presently.

We Socialists are not Reformers; we are Revolutionists. We Socialists do not propose to change forms. We care nothing for forms. We want a change of the inside of the mechanism of society, let the form take care of itself. We see in England a crowned monarch; we see in Germany a sceptered emperor; we see in this country an uncrowned president, and we fail to see the essential difference between Germany, England or America. That being the case, we are skeptics as to forms. We are like grown children, in the sense that we like to look at the inside of things and find out what is there.

One more preliminary explanation. Socialism is lauded by some as an angelic movement, by others it is decried as a devilish scheme. Hence you find the Gomperses blowing hot and cold on the subject; and Harry Lloyd, with whose capers, to your sorrow, you are more familiar than I, pronouncing himself a Socialist in one place, and in another running Socialism down. Socialism is neither an aspiration of angels, nor a plot of devils. Socialism moves with its feet firmly planted on the ground, and its head not lost in the clouds; it takes Science by the hand, asks her to lead, and goes whithersoever she points. It does not take Science by the hand, saying: "I shall follow you if the end of the road please me." No! It takes her by the hand and says: "Whithersoever thou leadest, thither am I BOUND to go." The Socialists, consequently, move as intelligent men; we do not mutiny because, instead of having wings, we have arms, and cannot fly as we would wish.

What, then, with an eye single upon the difference between REFORM and REVOLUTION, does Socialism mean? To point out that, I shall take up two or three of what I may style the principal nerve centres of the movement.

GOVERNMENT—THE STATE.

One of these principal nerve centres is the question of "Government" or the question of "State." How many of you have not seen upon the shelves of our libraries books that treat upon the "History of the State"; upon the "Limitations of the State"; upon "What the State Should Do, and What it Should Not Do"; upon the "Legitimate Functions of the State," and so on into infinity? Nevertheless, there is not one among all of these, the products, as they all are, of the vulgar and superficial character of capitalist thought, that fathoms the question, or actually defines the "State." Not until we reach the great works of the American Morgan, of Marx and Engels, and of other Socialist philosophers, is the matter handled with the scientific lucidity that proceeds from facts, leads to sound conclusions, and breaks the way to practical work. Not until you know and understand the history of the "State" and of "Government" will you understand one of the cardinal principles upon which Socialist Organization rests, and will you be in a condition to organize successfully.

We are told that "Government" has always been as it is to-day, and always will be. This is the first fundamental error of what Karl Marx justly calls capitalistic vulgarity of thought.

When man started on his career, after having got beyond the state of the savage, he realized that co-operation was a necessity to him. He understood that together with others he could face his enemies in a better way than alone; he could hunt, fish, fight more successfully. Following the instructions of the great writer Morgan —the only great and original American writer upon this question— we look to the Indian communities, the Indian settlements, as a type of the social system that our ancestors, all of them, without exception, went through at some time.

The Indian lived in the community condition. The Indian lived under a system of common property. As Franklin described it, in a sketch of the history and alleged sacredness of private property, there was no such thing as private property among the Indians. They co-operated, worked together, and they had a Central Directing Authority among them. In the Indian communities we find that Central Directing Authority consisting of the "Sachems." It makes no difference how that Central Directing Authority was elected; there it was. But note this: its function was to direct the co-operative or collective efforts of the communities, and, in so doing, it shared actively in the productive work of the communities. Without its work, the work of the communities would not have been done.

When, in the further development of society, the tools of production grew and developed—grew and developed beyond the point reached by the Indian; when the art of smelting iron ore was discovered; when thereby that leading social cataclysm, wrapped in the mists of ages, yet discernible, took place that rent former communal society in twain along the line of sex, the males being able, the females unable, to wield the tool of production—then society was cast into a new mold; the former community, with its democratic equality of rights and duties, vanishes, and a new social system turns up, divided into two sections, the one able, the other unable, to work at production. The line that separated these two sections, being at first the line of sex, could, in the very nature of things, not yet be sharp or deep. Yet notwithstanding, in the very shaping of these two sections—one able, the other unable, to feed itself—we have the first premonition of the CLASSES, of class distinctions, of the division of society into the INDEPENDENT and the DEPENDENT, into MASTER and SLAVES, RULER and RULED.

Simultaneously with this revolution, we find the first changes in the nature of the Central Directing Authority, of that body whose original function was to share in, by directing, production. Just as soon as economic equality is destroyed, and the economic classes crop up in society, the functions of the Central Directing Authority gradually begin to change, until finally, when, after a long range of years, moving slowly at first, and then with the present hurricane velocity under capitalism proper, the tool has developed further, and further, and still further, and has reached its present fabulous perfection and magnitude; when, through its private ownership the tool has wrought a revolution within a revolution by dividing society, no longer along the line of sex, but strictly along the line of ownership or non-ownership of the land on and the tool with which to work; when the privately owned, mammoth tool of today has reduced more than fifty-two per cent of our population to the state of being utterly unable to feed without first selling themselves into wage-slavery, while it, at the same time, saps the ground from under about thirty-nine per cent of our people, the middle class, whose puny tools, small capital, render them certain victims of competition with the large capitalists, and makes them desperate; when the economic law that asserts itself under the system of private ownership of the tool has concentrated these private owners into about eight per cent of the nation's inhabitants, has thereby enabled this small capitalist class to live without toil, and to compel the majority, the class of the proletariat, to toil without living; when, finally, it has come to the pass in which our country now finds itself, that, as was stated in Congress, ninety-four per cent of the taxes are spent in "protecting property" —the property of the trivially small capitalist class—and not in protecting life; when, in short, the privately owned tool has wrought this work, and the classes—the idle rich and the working poor—are in full bloom—then the Central Directing Authority of old stands transformed; its pristine functions of aiding in, by directing, production have been supplanted by the functions of holding down the dependent, the slave, the ruled, i.e., the WORKING CLASS. Then, and not before, lo, the State, the modern State, the CAPITALIST STATE! Then, lo, the Government, the modern Government, the CAPITALIST GOVERNMENT—equipped mainly, if not solely, with the means of suppression, of oppression, of tyranny! (Applause.)

In sight of these manifestations of the modern State, the Anarchist —the rose-water and the dirty-water variety alike—shouts: "Away with all central directing authority; see what it does; it can only do mischief; it always did mischief!" But Socialism is not Anarchy. Socialism does not, like the chicken in the fable, just out of the shell, start with the knowledge of that day. Socialism rejects the premises and the conclusions of Anarchy upon the State and upon Government. What Socialism says is: "Away with the economic system that alters the beneficent functions of the Central Directing Authority from an aid to production into a means of oppression." And it proceeds to show that, when the instruments of production shall be owned, no longer by the minority, but shall be restored to the Commonwealth; that when, as the result of this, no longer the minority or any portion of the people shall be in poverty, and classes, class distinctions and class rule shall, as they necessarily must, have vanished, that then the Central Directing Authority will lose all its repressive functions, and is bound to reassume the functions it had in the old communities of our ancestors, become again a necessary aid, and assist in production. (Applause.)

The Socialist, in the brilliant simile of Karl Marx, sees that a lone fiddler in his room needs no director; he can rap himself to order, with his fiddle to his shoulder, and start his dancing tune, and stop whenever he likes. But just as soon as you have an orchestra, you must also have an orchestra director—a central directing authority. If you don't, you may have a Salvation Army powwow, you may have a Louisiana negro breakdown; you may have an orthodox Jewish synagogue, where every man sings in whatever key he likes, but you won't have harmony—impossible. (Applause.)

It needs this central directing authority of the orchestra master to rap all the players to order at a given moment; to point out when they shall begin; when to have these play louder, when to have those play softer; when to put in this instrument, when to silence that; to regulate the time of all and preserve the accord. The orchestra director is not an oppressor, or his baton an insignia of tyranny; he is not there to bully anybody; he is as necessary or important as any or all of the members of the orchestra.

Our system of production is in the nature of an orchestra. No one man, no one town, no one State, can be said any longer to be independent of the other; the whole people of the United States, every individual therein, is dependent and interdependent upon all the others. The nature of the machinery of production;

the subdivision of labor, which aids co-operation, and which co-operation fosters, and which is necessary to the plentifulness of production that civilization requires, compel a harmonious working together of all departments of labor, and thence compel the establishment of a Central Directing Authority, of an Orchestral Director, so to speak, of the orchestra of the Co-operative Commonwealth. (Loud applause.)

Such is the State or Government that the Socialist revolution carries in its womb. Today, production is left to Anarchy, and only Tyranny, the twin sister of Anarchy, is organized.

Socialism, accordingly, implies organization; organization implies directing authority; and the one and the other are strict reflections of the revolutions undergone by the tool of production. Reform, on the other hand, skims the surface, and with "Referendums" and similar devices limits itself to external tinkerings.

THE REFORMER—THE REVOLUTIONIST.

And now to come to, in a sense, the most important, surely the most delicate, of any of the various subdivisions of this address. We know that movements make men, but men make movements. Movements cannot exist unless they are carried on by men; in the last analysis it is the human hand and the human brain that serve as the instruments of revolutions. How shall the revolutionist be known? Which are the marks of the reformer? In New York a reformer cannot come within smelling distance of us but we can tell him. (Laughter.) We know him; we have experienced him; we know what mischief he can do; and he cannot get within our ranks if we can help it. He must organize an opposition organization, and thus fulfill the only good mission he has in the scheme of nature—pull out from among us whatever reformers may be hiding there.

But you may not yet be familiar with the cut of the reformer's jib. You may not know the external marks of the revolutionist. Let me mention them.

The modern revolutionist, i.e., the Socialist, must, in the first place, by reason of the sketch I presented to you, upon the development of the State, necessarily work in organization with all that that implies. In this you have the first characteristic that distinguishes the revolutionist from the reformer; the reformer spurns organization; his symbol is "Five Sore Fingers on a Hand" —far apart from one another.

The modern revolutionist knows full well that man is not superior to principle, that principle is superior to man, but he does not fly off the handle with this maxim, and thus turn the maxim into absurdity. He firmly couples that maxim with this other that no principle is superior to the movement or organization that puts it and upholds it in the field. The engineer knows that steam is a powerful thing, but he also knows that unless the steam is in the boiler, and unless there is a knowing hand at the throttle, the steam will either evaporate, or the boiler will burst. Hence, you will never hear an engineer say: "Steam is the thing," and then kick the locomotive off the track. Similarly, the revolutionist recognizes that the organization, that is propelled by correct principles, is as the boiler that must hold the steam, or the steam will amount to nothing. (Applause.) He knows that in the revolution demanded by our age, Organization must be the incarnation of Principle. Just the reverse of the reformer, who will ever be seen mocking at science, the revolutionist will not make a distinction between the Organization and the Principle. He will say: "The Principle and the Organization are one." (Applause.) . . .

FAKE MOVEMENTS.

Then, again, with this evil of miseducation, the working class of this country suffers from another. The charlatans, one after the other, set up movements that proceeded upon lines of ignorance; movements that were denials of scientific facts; movements that bred hopes in the hearts of the people; yet movements that had to collapse. A movement must be perfectly sound, and scientifically based or it cannot stand. A falsely based movement is like a lie, and a lie cannot survive. All these false movements came to grief, and what was the result?—disappointment, stagnation, diffidence, hopelessness in the masses.

K. OF L.

The Knights of Labor, meant by Uriah Stephens, as he himself admitted, to be reared upon the scientific principles of Socialism— principles found today in no central or national organization of labor outside of the Socialist Trade & Labor Alliance (loud applause)—sank into the mire. Uriah Stephens was swept aside; ignoramuses took hold of the organization; a million and a half men went into it, hoping for salvation; but, instead of salvation, there came from the veils of the K. of L. Local, District and General Assemblies the developed ignoramuses, that is to say, the Labor Fakirs, riding the workingman and selling him out to the exploiter. (Applause.) Disappointed, the masses fell off.

A. F. OF L.

Thereupon bubbled up another wondrous concern, another idiosyncrasy—the American Federation of Labor, appropriately called by its numerous English organizers the American Federation of Hell. (Laughter.) Ignoramuses again took hold and the lead. They failed to seek below the surface for the cause of the failure of the K. of L.; like genuine ignoramuses, they fluttered over the surface. They saw on the surface excessive concentration of power in the K. of L., and they swung to the other extreme—they built a tapeworm. (Laughter.) I call it a tapeworm, because a tapeworm is no organism; it is an aggregation of links with no cohesive powers worth mentioning. The fate of the K. of L. overtook the A. F. of L. Like causes brought on like results: false foundations brought on ruin and failure. Strike upon strike proved disastrous in all concentrated industries; wages and the standard of living of the working class at large went down; the unemployed multiplied; and again the ignorant leaders naturally and inevitably developed into approved Labor Fakirs: the workers found themselves shot, clubbed, indicted, imprisoned by the identical Presidents, Governors, Mayors, Judges, etc.—Republican and Democratic—whom their misleaders had corruptly induced them to support. Today there is no A. F. of L.—not even the tapeworm—any more. If you reckon it up, you will find that, if the 250,000 members which it claims paid dues regularly every quarter, it must have four times as large a fund as it reports. The fact is the dues are paid for the last quarter only; the fakirs see to this to the end that they may attend the annual rowdidow called the "A. F. of L. Convention" —and advertise themselves to the politicians. That's all there is left of it. It is a ship, never seaworthy, but now stranded and captured by a handful of pirates; a tapeworm pulled to pieces, contemned by the rank and file of the American proletariat. (Applause.) Its career only filled still fuller the workers' measure of disappointment, diffidence, helplessness.

The Henry George movement was another of these charlatan booms, that only helped still more to dispirit people in the end. The "Single Tax," with its half-antiquated, half-idiotic reasoning, took the field. Again great expectations were raised all over the country—for a while. Again a social-economic lie proved a broken reed to lean on. Down came Humpty Dumpty, and all the king's horses and all the king's men could not now put Humpty Dumpty together again. (Applause.) Thus the volume of popular disappointment and diffidence received a further contribution.

POPULISM.

Most recently there came along the People's Party movement. Oh, how fine it talked! It was going to emancipate the workers. Did it not say so in its preamble, however reactionary its platform? If bluff and blarney could save a movement, the People's Party would have been imperishable. But it went up like a rocket, and is now fast coming down a stick. (Laughter.) Is it not true? (Voices: Yes; yes.) In New York State it set itself up against us when we already had 14,000 votes, and had an official standing. It was going to teach us "dreamers" a lesson in "practical American politics." Well, its vote never reached ours, and last November when we rose to 21,000 votes, it dropped to barely 5,000, lost its official standing as a party in the State, and as far as New York and Brooklyn are concerned, we simply mopped the floor with it. (Laughter and applause.)

These false movements, and many more kindred circumstances that I could mention, have confused the judgment of our people, weakened the springs of their hope, and abashed their courage. Hence the existing popular apathy in the midst of popular misery; hence despondency despite unequalled opportunities for redress; hence the backwardness of the movement here when compared with that of Europe.

To return now to where I broke off. The Socialist Labor Party cannot, in our country, fulfill its mission—here less than anywhere else—without it takes a stand, the scientific soundness of whose position renders growth certain, failure impossible, and without its disciplinary firmness earns for it the unqualified confidence of the now eagerly onlooking masses both in its integrity of purpose and its capacity to enforce order. It is only thus that we can hope to rekindle the now low-burning spark of manhood and woman-hood in our American working class, and re-conjure up the Spirit of '76.

THE S. L. P. THE HEAD OF THE COLUMN.

We know full well that the race or class that is not virile enough to strike an intelligent blow for itself, is not fit for eman-cipation. If emancipated by others, it will need constant propping, or will collapse like a dishclout. While that is true, this other is true also: In all revolutionary movements, as in the storming of for-tresses, the thing depends upon the head of the column—upon that minority that is so intense in its convictions, so soundly based on its principles, so determined in its action, that it carries the masses with it, storms the breastworks and captures the fort. (Loud applause.) Such a head of the column must be our Socialist or-ganization to the whole column of the American proletariat. (Loud applause.)

Again our American history furnishes a striking illustration. When Pizarro landed on the western slope of the Andes, he had with him about 115 men. Beyond the mountains was an empire—the best organized empire of the aborigines that had been found in America. It had its departments; it had its classes; it was managed as one body, numbering hundreds of thousands to the Spaniards' hundred. That body the small army of determined men were to capture. What did Pizarro do? Did he say: "Let us wait till we get some more?" Or did he say: "Now, boys, I need every one of you 115 men?" No, he said to them: "Brave men of Spain, yonder lies an empire that is a delight to live in; full of gold; full of wealth; full of heathens that we ought to convert. They are as the sands of the sea, compared with us, and they are entrenched behind their mountain fastnesses. It needs the staunchest among you to undertake the conquest. If any, through the hardships of travel, feels unequal to the hardships of the enterprise, I shall not consider him a coward; let him stand back to protect our ships. Let only those stay with me who are determined to fight, and who are determined to conquer." About twenty men stood aside, about ninety-five remained; with ninety-five determined men he scaled those mountains, and conquered that empire. That empire of the Incas is today CAPITALISM, both in point of its own inherent weakness and the strength of its position. The army that is to conquer it is the army of the proletariat, the head of whose column must consist of the intrepid Socialist organization that has earned their love, their respect, their confidence. (Loud applause.)

What do we see today? At every recent election, the country puts me in mind of a jar of water—turn the jar and all the water comes out. One election, all the Democratic vote drops out and goes over to the Republicans; the next year all the Republican vote drops out and goes over to the Democrats. The workers are moving backward and forward; they are dissatisfied; they have lost confidence in the existing parties they know of, and they are seeking desperately for the party of their class. At such a season, it is the duty of us, revolutionists, to conduct ourselves in such manner as to cause our organization to be better and better known, its principles more and more clearly understood, its integrity and firmness more and more respected and trusted—then, when we shall have stood that ground well and grown steadily, the masses will in due time flock over to us. In the crash that is sure to come and is now just ahead of us, our steadfast Socialist organization will alone stand out intact above the ruins; there will then be a stampede to our party—but only upon revolutionary lines can it achieve this; upon lines of reform it can never be victorious. (Applause.)

CHAPTER V

THE NEW APOSTLES

No pampering, no poverty any longer, but the whole
country vibrating with the music of joyful labor.

LAURENCE GRONLUND,
Our Destiny, 1890

It is, of course, necessarily an economic reform, but
its most important aspect is that of a moral movement for uplifting, enlarging, and ennobling the individual life. . . .

EDWARD BELLAMY,
Letter to Thomas Wentworth Higginson, 1890

I wish that those who conceive that the abolition of
private capital and of energy expended for profit signify
complete regimenting of life and the abolition also of
all personal choice and all emulation, would read with
an open mind Bellamy's picture of a socialized society.

JOHN DEWEY,
"A great American Prophet," 1934

I should hardly like to trust pen and ink with all the
audacity of my social ideas; but after fifty years of
optimistic contact with "civilization" and its ability
to come out all right in the end, I now abhor it, and
feel that it is coming out all wrong in the end, unless
it bases itself anew on a real equality.

WILLIAM DEAN HOWELLS,
Letter to Henry James, 1888

To Laurence Gronlund, a member of the Socialist Labor Party
in good standing, it had become obvious by the late 1870s that
the socialist movement in America was on the wrong track. Not

that he found anything wrong with its Marxist, or German, orientation—as far as it went. The American economy was behaving just as Marx and his American followers (Gronlund among them) had predicted it would. But the American people were not behaving as predicted. Despite industrial violence, the depression, pervasive poverty and unemployment, and the rise of gigantic monopolies, the socialist movement continued to be the exclusive nesting ground of European, mostly German, immigrants. The failure of socialism, Gronlund concluded, lay with the socialists themselves. They were not bringing the truth to the American people in terms that meant anything to them. They were not presenting their principles to Americans in language that spoke to their experience. Gronlund then took the next step: he set about revising "German" socialism to fit the American mold.

Gronlund himself was a Dane who had emigrated to the United States in 1869, at the age of twenty-three. Practically nothing is known about his youth except that he came from a middle class family and held a master's degree from the University of Copenhagen. He studied law in Milwaukee, practiced it for a while in Chicago, and abandoned it in New York for socialism and freelance journalism. According to his own enigmatic account Pascal's *Pensées* converted him to socialism. Why Pascal of all people should have had this effect on him he never explained. Perhaps he received from Pascal the Christian inspiration that would one day dominate his socialist ideals. In any case, Gronlund mediated between the two worlds he sought to unite. He was simultaneously a member of the German socialist community and a journalist who wrote for English-language publications. He thus went much farther than his political confrères in gaining a perspective from which to survey the environment in which he lived and which he hoped to transform. In 1884 he brought out (at his own expense) the book that established his place in the history of American socialism: the *Cooperative Commonwealth*.

What the hierarchs of the Socialist Labor Party thought of the *Cooperative Commonwealth* is unknown. To orthodox Marxists of the time, it must have been outrageously heretical. Gronlund did follow Marx in assuming that industrial capitalism must, by the laws implicit in its development, destroy itself; as it must inexorably expand to live, so it must create its own antithesis: more and more "wage slaves" incapable of buying back the goods they

produced, and so it must undergo successive crises, each more
severe than the last, eventuating in its final collapse. But this was
as far as Gronlund was willing to go with Marx. The prospect of
class warfare, which Marx regarded as necessary and desirable,
filled him with dismay. He addressed himself to the middle class,
especially the professionals and the educated, hoping that they
would oversee the transition from the old order to the new. A
handful of such "reflective" men—several thousand perhaps—would,
he believed, be sufficient to redeem the country in its fateful hour.
"We then say," he wrote, "that the only thing that can save us and
our children from horrors, tenfold worse than those of the French
Revolution, that can save us from the infliction of such a scourge
as Napoleon, will be the activity of a minority, acting as the brains
of the Revolution."

To this minority would fall the responsibility of establishing the
cooperative commonwealth, nationalizing the means of production,
and eliminating competitive individualism as a way of life. Here
Gronlund diverged sharply from the Marxists of his party. Marx
conceived of the state as a coercive instrument, which the proletariat would capture and turn against their oppressors; once
capitalism was liquidated, the state would disappear. Gronlund, on
the contrary, valued the state as the highest possible good. It would,
in the cooperative commonwealth, at last come into its own as
the ultimate expression of human intelligence and morality. For
Gronlund, the *true* state—as distinguished from the factitious one
under capitalism—would be identical with the will of the people.
Their freedom, therefore, would consist in their obedience to it—
their obedience, really, to themselves. Gronlund was an idealist
of the Rousseauean or Hegelian school. "It is Society, organized
Society, the State," he declared, "that gives us all the rights we
have. To the State we owe our freedom."

Gronlund went even beyond Rousseau and Hegel in affirming
the mission of the state. They had maintained some degree of
differentiation, or tension, between the individual and the state,
which represented society as a whole. Rousseau, for example, distinguished between "the will of all"—the totality of self-interests
—and "the general will." Hegel distinguished between the "abstract
rights" of individuals and the ethical good of "civil society" as
embodied in the organs of the state. Gronlund, however, made no
such distinctions. He compared the cooperative commonwealth

to "a living Organism"—of which the individual person was presumably a mere cell—"differing from other organisms in no essential respect." This being so, the state that presided over the cooperative commonwealth would be justified in destroying refractory individuals (criminals, revolutionaries, etc.) just as the surgeon excises the diseased parts of an unhealthy body.

Gronlund did not say if he was prepared to go this far in defending his organic conception of society because he could not imagine that the cooperative commonwealth would ever experience opposition from its members. Since the causes of discontent— poverty, the desire for domination and wealth, the wide disparity of incomes, the oppression of women and children and workers— would be absent from human affairs, government as man had hitherto known it would be absent as well. Society would no longer be governed by politicians, creatures of avarice and duplicity; it would be administered by highly qualified public servants, a sort of meritocracy. "The whole people," Gronlund contended, "does not want, or need, any 'government' at all. It simply wants *administration—good* administration. That will be had by putting everyone in the position for which he is best fitted, and making everyone aware of the fact. That is what Democracy means; it means *Administration by the Competent.*" It would be well to keep in mind that Gronlund wrote the *Cooperative Commonwealth* at a time when American democracy had in fact degenerated into a great scramble for political plunder, when the chief responsibility of most public officials, both elected and appointed, was to line their pockets, reward their friends, and serve the privileged interests. Nevertheless the cooperative commonwealth conjures up a bureaucratic nightmare—all the more stark and terrifying because the twentieth century has made it real.

Gronlund was certain that public opinion, released from the coils of selfishness, would "rule these 'real rulers.'" In the cooperative commonwealth the people would have the power to vote officials out of office, recall them or their decisions, and through a free press subject them to unceasing criticism. But Gronlund was primarily concerned not with the limits but with the assertion of state power. The bureaucracy, after all, had an enormously important function: to free society from petty economic cares, thereby enabling men to attain spiritual transcendence and live in moral purity. The cooperative commonwealth, as Gronlund envisioned it, would be a community of saints; a community, that is, in which everyone would reach the highest stage of happiness: "rapture" and the "perfect blessedness" that comes from the unity of each and all. Socialism, in a word, was the City of God.

Gronlund really belonged to the American communitarian tradition. His main object was to define the material basis for the ethical transformation of man, and his cooperative commonwealth was his way of keeping faith with the Associationist ideal, an ideal he sought to vivify by rooting it in modern reality—forcing it to come to terms with an advanced industrial nation and reconciling it with "German Socialism."

The book proved prophetic in the years immediately following its publication. The rise of the anarchist movement and the thousands of strikes that took place in 1885 and 1886 presaged a new era of industrial violence. Against this background, the *Cooperative Commonwealth* gradually found its audience. It was read by precisely those "reflective" persons whom Gronlund had hoped to reach.

One of its readers was Edward Bellamy, then a little known writer of novels and short stories in his mid-thirties. Bellamy later claimed that no particular book converted him to socialism, that he arrived at his vision of the good society by his own route, through his own experiences and observations. From his early twenties on he had been a radical critic of capitalism. He had repeatedly called attention to the injustices inflicted by the new industrial plutocracy, to the sufferings of children and women condemned to live and die in factories. He did not have to travel far from his home town of Chicopee Falls, Massachusetts (Springfield and other industrial centers were nearby), to witness the brutalities of the system. "The toiling masses of the world," he said in a talk before the local Lyceum when he was only twenty-one, "are already fiercely questioning the right to exist of a society which is founded upon their subjection. The atmosphere is rife with revolution. Society in its present form will not long exist."

Mainly, however, he was a writer of romances, and as a rule, he kept his two worlds separate and distinct; his radical passion did not intrude upon his novels and stories. There was one exception: in 1879, the *Berkshire Courier* serialized his novel, *The Duke of Stockbridge*, which dealt sympathetically with Shays's Rebellion. Though not much of a novel, *The Duke of Stockbridge* gave ample proof of Bellamy's independence of mind and integrity. In defending the Shaysites as poor farmers who had fallen victim to bankers and speculators, he directly contradicted the generally held view of them as a mob of ignorant and avaricious men who had been put down by the disinterested forces of law and order. But few people outside the range of the *Berkshire Courier* knew about *The Duke of Stockbridge* until after Bellamy's death, when it was published as a book.

The critical events of 1886—the bloody strikes, the rancorous Henry George mayoralty campaign, the Haymarket affair—must have deeply troubled Bellamy. Late that year he sat down at his writing desk "with the definite purpose of trying to reason out a method of economic organization by which the republic might guarantee the livelihood and material welfare of its citizens on a basis of equality corresponding to and supplementing their political equality." He decided that this reasoning out should take the form not of an abstract treatise but of a "story." His "method of economic organization" would come to life in a society of the future, as seen "from the point of view of the representatives of the nineteenth century" (i.e. the reader). Despite his frail health and family reponsibilities, Bellamy in less than a year had completed his masterpiece, *Looking Backward*.

The plot fulfilled his intentions admirably. One day in 1887 Julian West, thirty years old and a typically smug member of Boston's idle rich, is hypnotized to sleep in the cellar vault of his house. (He has this done frequently, his inability to sleep being another indictment of the lives of the rich.) That night the house burns down, and his servant, who is to wake him, perishes in the flames. Miraculously, West sleeps on and on, until the year 2000. He is discovered and awakened by Dr. Leete who lives in the house that has been built above the vault. Through West's eyes we see a glorious new civilization, in which "the livelihood and material welfare" of the people are guaranteed "on a basis of equality." He stays with Dr. Leete's family, from whom he learns how happy the American people are. He also learns that Leete's daughter, Edith, is the grandaughter of his onetime fiancée; by then they have fallen in love. At the end of the book West wakes up back in 1887 and realizes that he has been dreaming. When he compares the attitude of his class and the social malaise of the times with what he has seen of the future, he is plunged into despair. But it turns out that this is the dream; that he is in fact living in the year 2000.

Looking Backward invites comparison with the classic utopias of the past, notably Plato's, More's and Campanella's; also with some of the science fiction being written by Bellamy's contemporaries: e.g. Alfred Denton Cridge's *Utopia; or the History of an Extinct Planet,* Henry F. Allen's *The Key of Industrial Cooperative Government,* and, especially, John Macnie's *The Diothas; or A Far Look Ahead.* In form, *The Diothas* closely resembles *Looking Backward.* Its hero also wakes up from a long sleep—77 centuries long. He also finds himself in a society of equals; only they have not been leveled down but up: they are all aristocrats. But they are aristocrats who seek no privilege, prize their common humanity, and willingly labor for the good of society. The hero, furthermore, falls in love with a girl who, he discovers, is his distant relation. Yet for all their formal resemblance *The Diothas* and *Looking Backward* were, in conception and purpose, very different books. Bellamy was not creating an imaginary society that was at once perfect and unrealizable. *Looking Backward* described a society (in general scheme if not in exact detail) that he believed was certain to come, that was gestating in the womb of the present.

The resemblance was rather with the *Cooperative Commonwealth. Looking Backward* was an ingenious elaboration of Gronlund's deliberately un-utopian work. Bellamy like Gronlund wanted to persuade the enlightened middle class that it must lead the way to a new order if the savageries of class war were to be averted. The middle class must send forth a generation of men able to provide a peaceful, rational, and just alternative to capitalism, now entering its final apocalyptic stage. Bellamy explicitly rejected the revolutionary alternative proposed by those he called "the Reds." Dr. Leete looks back on "the Reds" as a hindrance. They "so disquieted people as to deprive the best considered projects of social reform of a hearing." Though he damned capitalism and wished nothing so much as to see it extirpated, Bellamy always preached love, reason and tolerance.

He predicted in *Looking Backward* that the transition from the old order to the new would be accomplished in several steps. The majority of Americans would conclude that they could no longer put up with the disastrous cycles of boom and bust, the increasing waste and disorder and disparity of incomes and life conditions. A "Great Revival" would take place, a "melting and flowing forth of men's hearts toward one another, a rush of contrite, repentant tenderness," which would finally overwhelm the plutocrats, forcing them to surrender their control of industry to the state without a struggle. At that moment, the need for government, that is, for coercive laws and authorities, would disappear. Solidarity would be sanctified as society's supreme virtue, and national brotherhood would replace selfishness as its supreme ethic. America in the year 2000 would be a Brook Farm transmogrified into an industrial nation state, continental in size and inhabited by millions of people. Bellamy, again like Gronlund, had poured old wine into new bottles.

But he was prepared to outdo Gronlund in collectivizing the life of the individual. The new order would prescribe the same incomes for all, for surgeons and street cleaners. Everyone would have an allowance he could spend in any way he wished. One could even save and accumulate property, though property would be valueless since it could bring no material advantage to its owner. Production would be organized in accordance with the rigorously egalitarian method of distributing wealth. No one could shirk his duties or live off the toil of others. Everyone, therefore, except housewives, the incapacitated, and (curiously) artists, would, after graduation from college, serve in the industrial army of the nation for a maximum period of twenty-two years, the nature of the service to be determined by one's talents and desires. The officers of the army—a sort of Stakhanovite class—would be drawn from those who had distinguished themselves in their vocations. The general-in-chief would be nominated from among those who had risen from the lowest grade and had served the full twenty-two years, and he would be elected by veterans like himself—those who had retired from the army and were over forty-one. The highest ranking leaders of the industrial army would constitute the government of the future.

Bellamy's omnicompetent bureaucracy anticipated some of the dark utopias that have been put into practice in modern times. And it anticipated them, too, in threatening to visit terrible punishments on laggards and wrong-doers. Compassion in the new order would be as rare as alms-taking. "As for actual neglect of work, positively bad work, or other overt remissness on the part of men incapable of generous motives," Dr. Leete explains, "the discipline of the industrial army is far too strict to allow anything of the sort. A man able to perform his duty, and persistently refusing, is sentenced to solitary imprisonment on bread and water till he consents." Bellamy did not say what society would do to such a person if he refused to consent despite his punishment, if he regarded the authorities and not himself as being in the wrong. In fact, Bellamy acknowledged no circumstances under which the individual would be justified in witholding his labor, much less engaging in public protest or forming an opposition. "The organization of this utopia," Lewis Mumford has written, "is an organization for war; and the one rule that such a community would not tolerate is 'live and let live.' If this is the peace that 'industrial preparedness' ensures it is scarcely worth having."

Mumford's criticism of *Looking Backward* is the obvious one to make. But it misses the central point of Bellamy's nationalist program. The members of the industrial army honored their obligations as the visible manifestation of their spiritual solidarity. The external regimentation was necessary so that the household chores, as it were, could be cleared away as expeditiously as possible. The object was to get on with the important business of life: the redemption of souls. Having completed their chores (thanks to the numerous gadgets, scientific techniques, and methods of specializing labor—public kitchens, laundries, etc.—that Bellamy invented for them), men could devote their energies to their moral, cultural, and intellectual improvement. Surplus wealth would be spent "upon public works and pleasures in which all share, upon public halls and buildings, art galleries, bridges, statuary, means of transit . . . great musical and theatrical exhibitions, and in providing on a vast scale for the recreation of the people."

But the major theme of *Looking Backward* was the separation of spirit and flesh. The new order, by bringing an end to the competitive struggle and guaranteeing economic security, would cleanse the body of its vices and passions, rendering it neutral. The spirit —the selfless, rational, transcendental part of man—would then assume unchallenged preeminence. The ruthless collectivization of property would enable man to attain a true individuality, an individuality in which he could exercise his freedom without restraint (because it could not infringe on anyone else's), an individuality akin to the state of grace. *Looking Backward*, like the *Cooperative Commonwealth*, heralded the advent of the religion of humanity.

The literate middle class welcomed Bellamy's inspired message. By the end of 1888, its first year of publication, *Looking Backward* had become a runaway best seller, a status it maintained well into the 90s. It also generated a lively battle of the books. During the decade following its appearance over forty works were written attacking it, defending it, or expanding on it, many of them unashamedly using the same *mise en scène*, plot, and cast of characters. Competing with *Looking Backward* for the public's attention were such titles as *Looking Forward, Looking Beyond, Looking Within, Looking Further Backward, Young West,* and the like. The book provoked William Morris to write his great counter-utopia, *News from Nowhere,* a medieval idyll, where men were free to be artisans, craftsmen and non-conformists (like Morris himself), in a setting of green vales and purling streams.

While most readers of *Looking Backward* regarded it as a fantasy, there were many who felt, as Bellamy did, that it was "a forecast, in accordance with the principles of evolution, of the next stage in the industrial and social development of humanity, especially in this country." Determined to put Bellamy's ideals into immediate effect, they formed a Nationalist club in Boston in December 1888. Why they called themselves Nationalists instead of, say, socialists was indicated by Bellamy himself. "In the radicalness of the opinions I have expressed I may seem to outsocialize the socialists, yet the word socialist is one I could never well stomach. It smells to the average American of petroleum, suggests the red flag and all manner of sexual novelties, and an abusive tone about God and religion. . . . Whatever German and French reformers may choose to call themselves, socialist is not a good name for a party to succeed with in America."

Bellamy's analysis appeared to be right, for within two years over 150 Nationalist clubs, along with thousands of discussion groups and societies, had been established in twenty-one states. The movement had its own magazine, *The Nationalist,* which brought out its first number in May 1889. As a movement Nationalism was as inclusive and indiscriminate as the faith on which it rested. All men of good will were invited to join. The Nationalist creed eschewed any notion of class conflict or hatred of the rich, any gift between means and ends. "The ultimate triumph of Nationalism," Bellamy admonished his followers, "demands as its first condition that it be kept on the high moral ground it now occupies, and retains as its chief motive that pure and uncompromising enthusiasm of humanity which now animates it."

The composition of the burgeoning movement reflected its ideology—or rather lack of one. It attracted philanthropists, humanitarians, retired Army men, mugwumps, professionals, reform-minded women, clergymen of each of the major religions, even socialists. Daniel DeLeon was a Nationalist briefly, before moving into the Socialist Labor Party. Laurence Gronlund moved in the opposite direction. "The happiest effect of my book," Gronlund wrote in 1890, introducing a revised edition of the *Cooperative Commonwealth*, "is that it has led indirectly, and probably unconsciously, to Mr. Bellamy's 'Looking Backward.'" To be sure, Gronlund had reservations about some aspects of Bellamy's program, in particular its "love of militarism," fanatical equality of wages, and undemocratic method of electing officers. These criticisms did not, however, stop him from serving as a loyal yeoman in the Nationalist cause.

The most active of the Nationalists were the American disciples of Madame Blavatsky, the founder of modern Theosophy. Theosophists believed in a universalized and transcendentalized form of Christianity, and, on the temporal plane, in a system of social justice remarkably akin to Bellamy's. They tended, like Bellamy, to separate the spirit and the body, the one being immortal, the other transient. Among the Theosophists could be counted some of the leading Brahmins of the Boston area, and they dominated *The Nationalist* magazine and many of the clubs. Their influence largely explains the passionless character of the movement. The magazine, for example, barely condescended to notice the seething questions of the day. Its articles were primarily concerned with blandly praising the incipient religion of humanity and anticipating the arrival, at some indeterminate moment in the future, of the good society.

A segment of the Nationalist movement, however, grew dissatisfied with its aloofness—that is, with the influence of the Theosophists. Even Bellamy, who had a keen disdain for practical day-to-day affairs and problems, eventually published his own magazine, the *New Nation*, whose differences with *The Nationalist* were obvious from its first issue. The *New Nation* backed the recent agrarian uprisings in the South and West and urged concrete social (or socialistic) reforms: e.g., public ownership of utilities and the means of tansportation and communication, and relief for the destitute and unemployed. Populists and socialists for their part collaborated with the Nationalists wherever possible, and the great Populist platform drawn up at Omaha in 1892 owed much to the Nationalists' presence. But Bellamy lost the support of the Theosophists and others who were offended by his descent into the political maelstrom and thought that the movement had abandoned its commitment to pure idealism. *The Nationalist* magazine folded in April 1891; the number of Nationalist clubs rapidly dwindled; and in February 1894 the *New Nation* put out its final issue. By then the movement was practically defunct, and Bellamy had withdrawn to write the sequel to *Looking Backward.*

William Dean Howells, the leading American writer of the time, was one of those who sadly bore witness to the collapse of Nationalism. He was a friend of Bellamy's and had from the start given strong encouragement to the Nationalist cause, though he took no active part in it. Howells attended the opening session of the first Nationalist club, held in Boston on December 1, 1888, and during the next couple of years he regularly met with Bellamy, Gronlund, and young Hamlin Garland (then starting out on his literary career) in Boston's Church of the Carpenter, presided over by one of the founding ministers of the Christian Socialist movement.

Howells had been gravitating toward socialism for some time. Even as editor of the prestigious *Atlantic Monthly* in the 1870s, when he was a member in good standing of the Cambridge-Concord-Boston literary establishment and wrote genteel and pleasant drawing-room novels, he could not in his heart of hearts accommodate himself to the new industrial America. Having been born and raised in a village in Ohio where simple democracy was as much part of one's life as the forests and fields, he could recall the time when no impassable gulf separated man from man, class from class, when society was not divided into the urban proletariat and the poor farmers on the one hand and an immensely rich plutocracy on the other, when economics occupied a properly subordinate place in the affairs of men.

Howells slowly shook the dust of Boston from his feet and by 1885 had settled in New York City, where he witnessed first hand the afflictions of America. His novels of the late 1880s and early 1890s, in which economic conditions provided the themes, plots and personal conflicts, reflected the intensity of his concerns. The novels were tendentious; with few exceptions their leading characters were archetypes and strawmen. Howells did not conceal his sym-

pathy for such men as the good minister and selfless fighter for
justice (Peck, in *Annie Kilburn*); for the innocent criminal driven
to his peccant deed by the capitalist system (Northwick, in *The
Quality of Mercy*); for socialists, both revolutionary and meliorative
(Lindau, in *A Hazard of New Fortune*; Hughes, in *The World of
Chance*), for independent radicals and social workers (Basil March
and Conrad Dryfoos, respectively, in *A Hazard of New Fortune*), and
for the writer-artist prostituted by commercialism (Ray, in *The
World of Chance*). Nor did he leave any doubts about his attitude toward the rich, and especially toward their intellectual
yea-sayers. If there was a single moral theme in these novels it was
that everyone, whether advantaged or beaten, suffered from the
lawlessness of capitalism. "What I object to is this economic chance-
world in which we live and which we seem to have created," Basil
March asserts. "It ought to be law as inflexible in human affairs
as the order of night and day in the physical world, that if man will
work he shall have both rest and eat, and shall not be harassed with
any questions as to how his repose and provision shall come."

Howells' socialism derived in the first place from the Christian
personalism of Tolstoy, whose writings, which he discovered in
the mid-1880s, had a profound effect on him in art, ethics,
and religion. Tolstoy led him to appreciate the travails of common
men and imparted to him a sense of the significance of life, however
brutal and oppressive its burdens. Tolstoy also made him perceive
more clearly than before just how shallow and meretricious bourgeois
values were. "I believe he has helped me," Howells wrote, "so that
I can never again see life the way I saw it before I knew him."

Yet Howells was willing to accompany Tolstoy only so far. A
practical reformer, he rejected asceticism as the answer to the problem of social injustice. In one of his early economic novels he had
the minister surrender everything and go among the millhands, but
by the time he wrote *The World of Chance* (1893) he had concluded that the Tolstoyan way was irrelevant and, when carried to
an extreme, vicious. "In quitting the scene of the moral struggle,"
as Hughes puts it in *The World of Chance*, "Tolstoy begs the
question as completely as if he had gone into a monastery." And
speaking in his own voice Howells later added: "Solitude enfeebles
and palsies, and it is as comrades and brothers that men must save
the world from itself, rather than themselves from the world."

Christian personalism, then, must be buttressed by a social

ethic that treats all men "as comrades and brothers." Howells
found such an ethic in native soil that had been seeded by
Jefferson and Thoreau and the communitarians, and most recently
by his friends Gronlund and Bellamy. He demonstrated how much
he owed to all of them, especially to Gronlund and Bellamy, by
constructing his own cooperative commonwealth—the imaginary
land of Altruria, situated somewhere in the far south, near the
Antarctic.

A *Traveler from Altruria* is a brilliant piece of satire. Technically
a novel (although it lacks a plot and its characters are usually
nameless), it consists of a series of discussions between Mr. Homos,
the Altrurian visitor, and a representative group of middle and upper class Americans: a writer (the narrator), a banker, an industrialist, a minister, a lawyer, a professor of political economy (a
particularly pompous ass), and some ladies. Their justification of
prevailing social practices astonishes Mr. Homos, whose gently
ironic manner, however, never fails him. He learns the extent of
their hypocrisy, superficiality, ignorance, and parochialism. They
sum up the tragedy of the privileged class in America.

Mr. Homos is at last persuaded to deliver a public lecture on
Altruria. His lengthy description of it—the climax of the book—
makes his more open-minded listeners aware of how abominable
conditions are in America, the contrast being all the more painful
because Altruria's history is so much like their own. Altruria too
experienced epochs of primitive Christianity, feudalism, and commercial expansion culminating in a revolutionary movement dedicated to the ideals of liberty, equality, and fraternity. But in Altruria, as in the West, the rights of man came to mean the rights of
a new master class, the capitalists, and their retainers. Altruria
entered the age of machines, mass production, world markets.
"Money seemed to flow from the ground: vast fortunes 'rose like
an exhalation,' as your Milton says." And while the masses who
produced the fortunes toiled and groaned, the owners consolidated
their power. A period of "Accumulation" took place, corresponding, obviously, to the rise of the trusts in America after the Civil
War. Differences between the rich and the poor became grotesque;
the landscape was filled with factories and slums; what little beauty
remained in Altruria was set aside for the rich.

Then came the inevitable: a sort of divine retribution. The
whole immoral economy, which had been alternating between pe-

riods of glut and scarcity, went completely to smash. The people decided to bring an end to the Accumulation. There followed an era of "Evolution," when, thanks to the unions (which had been consolidating too) and the free ballot, the wealth of society slowly and peacefully passed into the hands of the state. This was possible, Mr. Homos explained, because the Accumulators underestimated the importance of suffrage, the one power that the people were permitted to retain from the days of the universal rights of man. Of course, it was only potential power, since the Accumulation had traditionally bought politicians and judges. But when the people finally rose up, they found the ballot available to them and they elected representatives who promptly legislated private industry into the public domain. The procedure was entirely legal. The Accumulation, having failed to realize what had happened, put up no resistance. It even welcomed its own expropriation as the necessary price of harmony and justice. The country was transformed "from a civility in which the people lived *upon* each other to one in which they lived *for* each other."

To Mr. Homos, Altruria is the Kingdom of Heaven on earth: its religion is the religion of equality, its wealth the patrimony of the whole society. The rights of individuals are no longer in question since rights, in the pre-Evolutionary sense of the term, do not exist. All men now submit to the same duties, and self-sacrifice is taken for granted. So far, Altruria is hardly distinguishable from the cooperative commonwealth envisioned by Gronlund and Bellamy. It significantly departs from them in assigning a subordinate place to industry, technology, and organization. Altruria has no industrial army, no vaulting bureaucratic superstructure, no huge urban agglomerates. Its people live in small communities and labor only enough to fulfill their simple, honest needs; the sole function of machines is to perform tasks too onerous and demeaning for men; arts and crafts flourish in response to the demand for products that are at once useful and beautiful.

Mr. Homos' central point is that Altruria has brought a new scale of values into the world. The economic problem is solved; the ethic of competition, egoism, and inequality has disappeared. The spiritual side of man is liberated and completely autonomous. In Altruria the "normal" person models his life on the philosopher, the saint, and the artist. The businessman is a museum piece. "We are still far from thinking our civilization perfect," Mr. Homos declares modestly, "but we are sure our civic ideals are perfect."

Howells allots Mr. Homos about thirty pages (one-sixth of the book) for his lecture. In that brief space Mr. Homos is able to present only the most cursory and tantalizing view of Altrurian institutions. He neglects to elaborate, for example, on how Altruria organizes its industry, educates its young, governs itself demo-cratically, treats its women as equals. The omission was deliberate. Howells had no intention of pursuing the subject more deeply than he did. Unlike Gronlund and Bellamy, he was not laying down an explicit program for the future. They assumed the cooperative commonwealth would soon be born. He regarded it as merely an exhilarating dream, an unrealizable hope—at most a standard of righteousness by which to judge the conduct of his contemporaries.

When *A Traveler from Altruria* was published in 1894 Gronlund, Bellamy, and Howells had already accomplished their mission. They had been the new apostles of socialism. They had shown how America's truer, or higher, nature could assert itself under modern conditions of life; how industrialism and state power could be made to subserve traditional communitarian ideals; how economic man—the paladin of the old order—could give way to ethical, re-ligious, and artistic man. It remained for others, at a later time, to discover the political concomitants of these moral values.

Gronlund, until his death in 1899, remained active in reform socialist circles. Bellamy barely managed to finish *Equality*, his sequel to *Looking Backward*, before he died in 1898. Though *Equality* offered little that was new and had a tendency to lose itself in trivia, it was, for those patient enough to read it, more interesting than *Looking Backward:* more informative, explicit, and better reasoned. But the Nationalist movement was gone, and *Equality* fell still-born from the press. Howells was the only one of the three to survive the nineteenth century and live to a ripe age. But long before he died in 1920 he had given up whatever con-nection he had had with radical causes. After 1894 he returned only once to the "economic" novel. In 1907 he brought out the sequel to *A Traveler from Altruria*, *Through the Eye of a Needle*, most of which had been written fifteen years before. Except for the bitterly ironic introduction, in which Howells told of the splendid progress America had made since Mr. Homos's visit, *Through the Eye of a Needle* lacked the bite and power of its predecessor. The title suggested where Howells stood on the subject of creating an ideal society: believing in the possibility of Altruria was like believing that a camel could go through the eye of a needle.

LAURENCE GRONLUND

The Cooperative Commonwealth*
1884

TO THE READER

A dialogue on "Political Optimism" in the *Nineteenth Century* for August, 1880, contains the following language:
"We see that political systems in all progressive societies tend toward socialistic democracy. We see everywhere that it *must* come to that. We all of us feel this conviction, or all of us, I suppose, who have reflected on the matter. We feel, too, that nothing we can do can avert or possibly long delay the consummation. Then, we *must* believe that the movement is being guided, or is guiding itself to happy issues."

This passage may serve as a key to the following pages.

They have been written that you may see that the social and political phenomena in all progressive countries, and particularly in our own country and Great Britain, are, in a perfectly natural manner, evolving a New Social Order, a Social Democratic Order, which we have called *The Cooperative Commonwealth*; in other words,—to speak pointedly,—that Socialism is no importation, but a *home-growth*, wherever found. They are written to give you good reasons for expecting that this New Social Order will be, indeed, a "happy issue" to the brain-worker as well as to the hand-worker, to woman as well as to man. They are written to give reasons for our convictions that it must come to that, here as elsewhere, within a comparatively short period, or to barbarism.

Barbarism!—Yes. Let not yourself be led astray by the remarkable increase everywhere of wealth on the whole,—possibly the undercurrent is, nevertheless, carrying us swiftly backwards. Suppose you had told a Roman citizen in the age of Augustus that his proud country *then* had entered on its decline—as every school-boy now knows it had—he would have thought you insane. Now, the many striking parallels between that period and the times in which

---

* Pp. 7–11, 75–79, 81–84, 98–99, 102–103, 220–224, 276–278.

we are living must have forced themselves on your attention, if you are of a reflective turn of mind, as we assume you are. You will have observed the same destructive forces to which history attributes the fall of pagan Rome busily at work under your very eyes. You see the same mad chase after wealth; you find everywhere the same deadening scepticism in regard to high ideals. You observe in all our centres of activity a corruption—I will not say as great as, but—promising in due time to rival that of the Roman Empire. Be careful not to be too scornful if we prophesy that in, say, twenty-five years from now,—if not the Cooperative Commonwealth should then, perchance, be realized—the demagogues of New York City will buy voters by free public feasts and theatricals, that you will hear the cry of *"panem et circenses"*—"give us bread and circuses," if you live then! Indeed, we have already read in the N. Y. Tribune: "Every one of our civil Justices has given a day's 'outing' to the wives and children of his district." Even now in many of the States wealth seems a pre-requisite to the attainment of Senatorial honors and millionaires and sons of millionaires are bidding for seats in the lower house of Congress.

But, for reasons hereafter set forth, we do not believe our race will return to barbarism. The Roman Empire was saved from that fate, finally, by being reanimated. Our age as fully needs reanimation as the period of the Caesars. We shall be reanimated: history will once more see Society reconstructed on a new basis.

Says Huxley: "The reconstruction of Society on a scientific basis is not only possible, but the only political object much worth striving for." True, emphatically true! Except so far as it is implied in this sentence that any individual or any nation can go to work and *arbitrarily* reconstruct Society on a scientific or any other basis.

Socialism—*modern* Socialism, *German* Socialism, which is fast becoming *the* Socialism the world over—holds that the impending reconstruction of Society will be brought about by the Logic of Events; teaches that *The Coming Revolution is strictly an Evolution*. Socialists of that school reason from no assumed first principle, like the French who start from "Social equality" or like Herbert Spencer, when in his *Social Statics* he lays it down as an axiom, that "every man has freedom to do all that he wills, provided he infringes not the like freedom of every other man"; but basing themselves on experience—not individual but universal experience—they can and do present clear-cut, definite solutions.

It is this German Socialism which is presented in the following pages, with this important modification that it has been digested by a mind. Anglo-Saxon in its dislike of all extravagances and in its freedom from any vindictive feeling against *persons* who are from circumstances what they are. In the first three chapters we present the Socialist critique of the phenomena of the era in which we are living; in the next three chapters we indicate the coming Social order which will, probably, develop itself out of the present system; in the three that follow we outline the political and legal machinery which very likely will be found necessary to the working of that new order; in chapters X, XI and XII, we point out the principal social effects which may be expected to follow from it, and in the last chapter we consider how the revolution—the change—is likely to be accomplished in our country and England.

We believe it is time that a work, containing all the leading tenets of Socialism in a concise, consecutive form should be presented in the English language—in the language of the two countries where the social, and specially the industrial conditions, are ripening quicker than anywhere else. Such a work, in fact, exists nowhere. Whenever any one now wishes to inform himself on the subject he has to wade through innumerable books and pamphlets, mostly German. That such a candid man as John S. Mill, who had a truly Socialist heart, did not become a Socialist we attribute to this fragmentary shape of Socialist thought, and that in a tongue unknown to him; for his "Chapters on Socialism," published after his death, show that he was familiar only with French speculations, of a time when Socialism was yet in its infancy. We can dismiss nearly all that thus far has been written in our language by Socialists on the subject with the remark that it is not exactly adapted to people of judgment and culture. We think that all Americans who simply want to be well-informed ought to make themselves acquainted with this new *philosophy*—and Socialism is nothing less than that—which is believed in by hundreds of thousands of our fellow-men with a fervor equalling the enthusiasm of the early Christians. We think they will make themselves acquainted with it, as soon as it is presented to them in readable English, and applied to American phenomena and American conditions by a writer possessing the American bias for the practical. Such Socialism, whether true or false, whether destined to be successful or unsuccessful, is a matter that concerns *you* personally.

But if the writer of this work did not hope to accomplish something beyond giving some, or even many, Americans more correct notions of the aims of Socialists than those they have, it would never have been written. We have a deeper purpose, far nearer our heart. Most reflective minds, if they do not go the whole length of the one who speaks in the dialogue with which we started, do admit that we are at the brink of an extraordinary change; that a crisis of *some sort* is impending, no matter if it is likely to burst out now or in ten or fifty years from now. We then say that the only thing that can save us and our children from horrors, ten-fold worse than those of the French Revolution, that can save us from the infliction of such a scourge as Napoleon, will be the activity of a minority, acting as the brains of the Revolution. For while there will be a revolution, it need not necessarily be one marked by blood. We hope it will not be such a one: a revolution by violence is to Society what a hurricane is to a ship struggling on the stormy ocean; it is only by herculean efforts that we shall succeed in avoiding the rocks and bring it into the secure haven, and even then we shall be but at the threshold of our task.

But, then, we must first have in our country this minority; a vigorous minority, even if but a small one; a minority of intelligent and energetic American men and women; a minority with sound convictions as to what the crisis means and how it may be made to redound to the welfare of the whole of Society and with the courage of their convictions. Such a minority will be indispensable to render the revolution a blessing, whether it comes peaceably or forcibly. Not that this minority is to *make* the coming Revolution —an individual, a clique, a majority even can as little make a revolution as the fly makes the carriage wheel roll; the Revolution makes itself or "grows itself";—but this minority is to prepare for it and, when the decisive moment has arrived, act on the masses, as the power acts on the lever. To reach and possibly win this minority —however small—this book has mainly been written.

We shall, for that purpose, address ourselves to the reflective minds of all classes, rich as well as poor, professional as well as working men—and, indeed, many, very many, literary men and women, very many lawyers, very many physicians and teachers are just as much in need of this Coming Revolution as most working men. But we shall assume, reader, that you are not one of those who are personally interested in the maintenance of the present Social Order, or rather *Social Anarchy*, for then it is hopeless to try to win you over. Very likely you will deem it a difficult feat to win you over, to turn you into a Socialist—All we ask of you is with us to view familiar facts of life from a standpoint, very different from the one you have hitherto been occupying, to look at them in other lights and shades, and then await the result. A man is never the same any more after he has once got a new impression. Much that we are going to say cannot but shock your preconceived ideas, but from St. Paul down many have been indignant at first hearing what afterwards became their most cherished convictions. We shall discard all common-places and phrases and throughout be mindful of Samuel Johnson's admonition: "Let us empty our minds of cant, gentlemen!" . . .

THE SPHERE OF THE STATE.

"It is only by being citizen of a well-ordered State, that the individual has got rights."—*Hegel*.

"Not State-action in itself, but State-action exercised by a hostile class it is that ought to be deprecated."—*Matthew Arnold*.

"Look to the State! From that you can expect the highest experience and skill, real and efficient control, a national aim and spirit."—*Frederic Harrison*.

We have concluded the Socialist critique of the present order of things. In a nutshell it is this: The Fleecings increase in our country and in all industrial countries at a very great rate. In order that Capital (the sum of these Fleecings) may be simply *maintained*, (mark that!) it must be constantly employed in production and a market must be found for the products which it enables Labor to create. Foreign markets will soon dry up; our autocrats, therefore, will be confined to their respective home-markets. But the masses at home are more and more becoming wage-workers from the operation of "Individualism"; wage-workers receive in wages only about half of what they produce; the masses, consequently, are becoming more and more unable to buy back the Values they create. Thus for lack of consumption, Capital will be more and more threatened with depreciation. The more Capital, the more "overproduction." The Wage-System and Private "Enterprise" *will*, indeed, involve capitalists and laborers in one common ruin.

This is the foundation for what may be called: "constructive"

Socialism. We are not under the delusion, that Nations can be *persuaded* by the grandeur, excellence and equity of our system. The Future is ours, because the present system will soon be *unbearable*; because, as we said, we might fold our arms and calmly wait to see the Established Order fall to pieces by its own weight. Our conception of Value, therefore, truly comprises the *whole* of Socialism.

When the culmination has been reached, the reins will drop from the impotent hands of our autocrats and will be taken up by an impersonal power, coeval with human nature: The STATE.

It is a pity that we must commence by guarding ourselves against the corrupt American use of the term "State"; but, writing mainly for our American countrymen, we cannot help ourselves.

The "State" of Pennsylvania and the other thirty-seven "States" are not, and never were, *States*. By State we mean with Webster "a whole people, united in one body politic." That is the meaning of *State* in all languages, English included—except the American language. Now, not one of our American "states" was ever for one moment a "whole people." They either were subjects to the crown of England, or parts of the Confederation, or of the Union. The Union then is *a State*, just as France and Spain are States, and it is emphatically so since the American people commenced to call themselves a Nation with a big N. This, however, by no means excludes local centres of authority, what we are wont to call "local self-government."

"The State" is a stumbling block to many very worthy persons. They apprehend—a fear very honorable in them—that State-supremacy would be prejudicial to Freedom. We hope to make it apparent, that State-action and individual Freedom, far from being antagonistic, are really complementary of each other.

The reason why "the State" is now-a-days such a bugbear to so many, is that this word has quite another meaning in the mouth of an individualist, wherever you find him, than when used by a Socialist. Indeed, the fundamental distinction between "Individualism" and Socialism must be sought in the opposition of these two conceptions.

Individualists, and foremost amongst them our autocrats, cherish this degrading notion of the State: that it is merely an organ of Society, synonymous with "Government"—with the political machinery of Society. We claim—to quote Webster once more—

that the State is "a whole people, united in one body politic," in other words, that

The State is the organized Society. . . .

We therefore insist, with even greater force than Spencer did, that the State is a living organism, differing from other organisms in no essential respect. This is not to be understood in a simply metaphorical sense; it is not that the State merely resembles an organism, but that it, including with the people the land and all that the land produces, literally is *an organism*, personal and territorial.

The "Government"—the punishing and restraining authority—may possibly be dispensed with at some future time. But the STATE—*never*. To dispense with the State would be to dissolve Society.

It follows that the relation of the State, the body politic, to us, its citizens, is *actually* that of a tree to its cells, and *not* that of a heap of sand to its grains, to which it is entirely indifferent how many other grains of sand are scattered and trodden under foot.

This is a conception of far-reaching consequence.

In the *first* place, it, together with the modern doctrine of *Evolution*, as applied to all organisms, deals a mortal blow to the theory of "man's natural rights," the theory of man's "inalienable right" to life, liberty, property, "happiness" &c., the theory of which mankind during the last century has heard and read so much; the theory that has been so assiduously preached to our dispossessed classes, and which has benefited them *so* little!

Natural rights! The highest "natural right" we can imagine is for the stronger to kill and eat the weaker, and for the weaker to be killed and eaten. One of the "natural rights," left "man" now, is to act the brute towards wife and children, and that "right" the State has already curtailed and will by-and-by give it the finishing stroke. Another "natural right," very highly prized by our autocrats, is the privilege they now possess of "saving" for themselves what other people produce. In brief, "natural rights" are the rights of the muscular, the cunning, the unscrupulous. . . .

It is Society, organized Society, the State that gives us all the rights we have. To the State we owe our freedom. To it we owe our living and property, for outside of organized Society man's needs far surpasses his means. The humble beggar owes much to the State, but the haughty millionaire far more, for outside of it they both would be worse off than the beggar now is. To it we owe all that we are and all that we have. To it we owe our civilization. It is by its help that we have reached such a condition as man individually never would have been able to attain. Progress is the struggle with Nature for mastery, is war with the misery and inabilities of our "natural" condition. The State is the organic union of us all to wage that war, to subdue Nature, to redress natural defects and inequalities. The State therefore, so far from being a burden to the "good," a "necessary evil," is man's greatest good.

This concept of the State as an organism thus consigns the "rights of man" to obscurity and puts *Duty* in the foreground.

In the *second* place, we now can ascertain the true sphere of the State. That is, we now can commence to build something solid.

We say *Sphere* on purpose; we do not ask what are the "rights," "duties" or "functions" of the State, for if it truly is an organism it is just as improper to speak of *its* rights, duties or functions towards its citizens as it is to speak of a man's rights, duties and functions in relation to his heart, his legs, or his head. The State has rights, duties and functions in relation to other organisms, but towards its own members it has only a sphere or activities.

The sphere of the State simply consists in caring for its own welfare, just as a man's sphere, as far as himself is concerned, consists in caring for his own well-being. If that be properly done, then his brain, his lungs and his stomach will have nothing to complain of.

So with the State. Its whole sphere is the making all special activities work together for one general end: its own welfare, or the *Public Good*. Observe that the Public Good, the General Welfare, implies far more than "the greatest good to the greatest number" on which our "practical" politicians of today base their trifling measures. Their motto broadly sanctions the sacrifice of minorities to majorities, while the "General Welfare" means the greatest good of every individual citizen.

To that end the State may do anything whatsoever which is shown to be expedient.

It may, as it always has done, limit the right of a person to dispose of himself in marriage as he pleases.

The State is, in the words of J. S. Mill, "fully entitled to abrogate or alter any particular right of property which it judges to stand in the way of the public good."

The State may tomorrow, if it judges it expedient, take all the capital of the country from its present owners, without any compensation whatsoever, and convert it into social Capital. . . .

We have observed that it is round the working-classes that the battle of progress has been waged; their condition has determined the stage of civilization, though history has given but scant account of them. During the two great periods that lie behind us: Slavery and Serfdom, they were in fact and in law subject to their lords who took the lion's share without disguise, as a matter of right. Based on that subjection, however, there was an intense feeling of *Unity* which pervaded the whole of Society; a Unity that made these systems so strong and so lasting, and without which Unity no social system can be enduring. But men rebelled against the subjection. Luther was fortunate enough to start that rebellion in the religious sphere, for it is always at the top that all radical changes commence.

Then was inaugurated the era in which we are living, which really is nothing but a *transition period* between the two great systems of the past and another great system of the future, *for it possesses no unity.* It corresponds exactly to the transition-period between Slavery and Serfdom, which Christianity was striving for mastery. It is an era of anarchy, of criticism, of negations, of opposition, of hypocrisy, as this was one. Instead of Slavery or Serfdom and *Subjection* we now have the wage-system and *contracts.* That is to say, while formerly the lords appropriated the results of labor openly, they now do it underhandedly. The wage-worker, if he will live, must *agree* to relinquish one-half of what he produces. There is, in fact, fully as much subjection now as formerly, but it has taken on a softer, a more hypocritic form. That is why the rebellion not only continues, but has reached down into the material sphere and is shaking the very foundation of Society. It will not cease before all slavish subjection is done away with.

Then this "Individualism," this re-action against unquestioned submission, will find its compensation in *another Unity.* Everybody will again feel a dread of living for himself only. We shall have *Corporate Responsibility, Equality, Freedom,* all three combined in INTER-DEPENDENCE, SOCIAL COOPERATION. It is with the Social organism as with a harmoniously developed man, who has three stages of growth: implicit obedience, then restless self-assertion, at last intelligent, loyal cooperation with what has a rightful claim to his allegiance.

This Inter-dependence will find its practical expression in THE COOPERATIVE COMMONWEALTH, which in the following chapter will be seen to be *now* expedient, *for the first time in human history*. . . .

[EXPEDIENCY OF THE COOPERATIVE COMMONWEALTH]

Extend in your mind Division of Labor and all the other factors that increase the productivity of Labor; apply them to *all* human pursuits as far as can be; imagine manufactures, transportation and commerce conducted on the grandest possible scale, and in the most effective manner; then add to Division of Labor its *complement:* CONCERT; introduce *adjustment* everywhere where now there is anarchy; add that *central regulative system* which Spencer says distinguishes all highly organized structures, and which supplies "each organ with blood in proportion to the work it does" and—behold the COOPERATIVE COMMONWEALTH!

The Cooperative Commonwealth, then, is that future Social Order—the natural heir of the present one—in which all important instruments of production have been taken under collective control; in which the citizens are consciously public functionaries, and in which their labors are rewarded according to results.

A definition is an argument.

It shows that our critics, when they style Socialism a Utopia, do not know about what they are talking. We can imagine a caterpillar, more knowing than its fellows, predicting to another that some day they both will be butterflies, and the other sneeringly replying: "What Utopian nonsense you are talking there!" Our censors are just as ignorant of the ground-work of Socialism. For our definition makes it evident that the Cooperative Commonwealth is not to be regarded as a product of personal conceit, but as *an historical product*, as a product in which our whole people are unconscious partakers. When the times are ripe for Social Cooperation, it will be just as expedient, as Feudalism was, or as Private Enterprise was, when each, respectively, made its appearance. It will prove its right to control by virtue of its own superior fitness.

Or is there anything Utopian in predicting that Division of Labor will go on increasing? Has not wholesale production already vindicated its right to be the ruling system, and is it Utopian to assert that Private Ownership of Capital, so far from being necessary to production in wholesale, will prove a greater and greater obstruction to its inevitable development? Is it Utopian to expect that all enterprises will become more and more centralized, until in the fulness of time they all end in *one* monopoly, that of Society? Are not, indeed, *Anti*-monopolists—as far as they believe that they can crush the big establishments or even prevent their growth—the real Utopists? . . .

[EDUCATION IN THE COOPERATIVE COMMONWEALTH]

We have seen that Social Cooperation demands first, and last, and at all time *Competence*. In order to get the greatest ability in every branch of affairs and in every post of duty: in order to sift out the most competent for the direction of affairs, and in order to make the citizens pass with ease from one employment to another, when required, all citizens will have to be trained all-sidedly and to the highest point. Monotonous toil now crushes out millions of potential luminaries of Society; if the true merits of mankind are to be brought out, it must be done by equalizing the opportunities for all.

And "minimum" education will not do at all. Simply to teach children to read and write is the same as to teach them the use of knife and fork without giving them a particle of meat; or as to furnish them the key to a larder, containing poisons as well as victuals, without telling them which is food, and which poisons. In fact, children are more likely to choose the poisons than the food: witness their voracious consumption of trashy novels and other vicious literature. The highest grade of education will be the best possible investment for the future Commonwealth.

Again, the Interdependent Commonwealth will take care that all children *do* get roast beef and plum pudding and that they, besides, have warm clothes to their backs, clean linen to their bodies, and comfortable shoes to their feet, and warmth and light at home, and these goodies will be provided before their education is thought of.

Again, the Interdependent Commonwealth will relieve children from the task of being bread-winners. The 182,000 children who according to the Census of 1880 were employed in manufactures in our country were not thus robbed of the bright days of childhood solely because employers could coin money out of them. The horrible fact is that their parents cannot make both ends meet without the labor of their children, and that in Massachusetts where a few weeks schooling yearly is required by law of children between 10 and 15, many parents feel themselves tempted to evade that law by false swearing in regard to the age of their children. It is an infamous system that bears such fruits. And yet there are political economists whose hearts are so seared and whose understanding is so obscured by being trained in that system that they glory in the fact that children can be utilized in augmenting the wealth of the country! These hundred thousands of children, as well as the urchins who gain their own precarious existence and partly that of their parents as newsboys, bootblacks, cash-boys, will have the most important period of their lives—that in which *character* is formed —saved to them, as soon as their parents are secured a decent living.

But that is by no means all. This that not only the children but that the parents also will have roast beef and plum pudding is of vast importance to the cause of education. For it will relieve the fathers and mothers of the body- and soul-devouring *care* which is the special curse of our age; it will give these fathers and mothers, to whom now even reflection is forbidden, LEISURE, and thus make them effective allies of the Commonwealth, because leisure is the incentive to all progress.

The bread-and-butter-question is therefore the fundamental question. We see here again how Socialism, by revolutionizing the economic relation of Society, will revolutionize all other relations.

Education, then, will be the second important branch of the activity of the New Commonwealth. Let us now consider what organ is likely to be intrusted with the function of education.

In the discourse above referred to our Episcopal Mentor also laid it down:

"God has instituted three coordinate authorities: the Family, the Church and the State. The Family is *imperium in imperio*—a dominion within the dominion;—the parent is exclusive master within that dominion."

Well, we can pretty safely assert to the contrary that the Coming

Commonwealth will not acknowledge the Church as a coordinate "authority."

There was a time when the two were coordinate authorities. At that time it was still doubtful which of them was destined to be the embodiment of the social organism. Out of that struggle the State has already virtually issued as the victor: the "Church" is in all civilized countries already virtually nothing but a voluntary association. "God" thus has already decided against the pretensions of the Church; and this, as we already noticed in the fifth chapter, is the most important step, perhaps, in the movement of the State toward Socialism.

And we can also be assured that the Church will not be made the organ of the State for education purposes.

There is one all-sufficient reason: *the Church is not competent.*

Circumstances for centuries gave education into the hands of the Church and she then perhaps performed that function as well as could be done. Let us grant that much. But we are not living in the Middle Ages. So far from being in our age an institution of enlightenment, the Church is now looked upon by all well-informed people as an institution to darken men's minds. We simply state facts. The men of science assume the falsity of all theological dogmas. The Church is incompetent, because she knows nothing worth knowing—we are again simply stating facts. The Church has still some influence, partly on account of our hypocrisy, and hypocrisy is prevailing as it is, just because this is a transition age; but the Coming Democracy will want to *know* and will wage an unrelenting war against all shams.

We, furthermore, maintain that neither will the *Family* be acknowledged a coordinate authority.

This, however, is a much more important assertion than the former, and is not quite as evident, though on reflection it will be found just as true. But we cannot fail in passing to remark that it is amusing to see the solicitude the Church has for the authority of the Family now, when her own importance is on the wane. When she had supreme power, she certainly did not consider the Family coordinate with herself.

The first evidence we shall adduce to show that the Coming Commonwealth will assert supremacy as against the Family is that which we everywhere throughout this book place at the head: the logic of events. *Just in the same proportions the State has ag-*

grandized itself, the Family has dwindled in importance. The State commenced to repudiate the "dominion" of the Family the moment it forbade parents to destroy their children; it absolutely rejected that "dominion" the moment it, the State, fixed the age of majority, when the child is entirely emancipated from parental control.

Why! the system where authority is vested in the Family, as distinguished from the State, is that patriarchal, barbaric, system from which we are more and more retreating. Proudhon is decidedly right when he says: "It is on the model of the Family that all feudal and antique societies have organized themselves, *and it is precisely against this old patriarchal constitution that modern democracy revolts and protests.*" It is yet sometimes said that "blood is thicker than water," but that is not often the case now; and this fact that the Individual has become almost independent of the Family is merely the preparatory step to the supremacy of the State.

Next, in the very nature of things, Family-Supremacy will be absolutely incompatible with an *Interdependent*, a solidaric, Commonwealth, for in such a State the first object of education must be to establish in the minds of the children an indissoluble association between their individual happiness and the good of all. To that end family exclusiveness must be broken down, first of all. A public spirit, *i.e.* the spirit of all being members of one social organism, must be substituted for family-spirit. Now please do not misunderstand the Socialist position in this respect! We do not make war on the *family*; on the contrary, our aim is to enable every healthy man and woman to form a family. But we *do* make war on family-*exclusiveness*—perhaps a better word than "selfishness"—on family-*prejudices* and family-*narrowness* and we are glad to be able to say that our common schools are doing very much to break down that spirit. . . .

When the Cooperative Commonwealth is achieved, there will be no room for any more revolutions. For revolutions are caused by the clashings of class-interests, and all class-distinctions are forever abolished the moment the lowest class is fully incorporated into Society.

But there will be plenty of room for progress, for further evolution. Even our Commonwealth, though it may take a long period to develop it, is but a step of the evolution. One Commonwealth after another may decay and disappear, but they will all contribute to the upbuilding of the *Organism* of *Humanity*.

With Organized Humanity will be evolved the Coming Religion, though we already noticed it in the preceding chapter, because people persist in mixing up morals and religion. But morals really relates to the social organism: *it makes the good citizen*. Religion relates to Humanity *and makes the saint*. The Coming Religion will make us feel that we are here for the sake of Humanity, with whose fate it may be found that we are personally far more concerned than is now supposed; it will make holiness consist in identifying ourselves with Humanity—the redeemed form of man —as the lover merges himself in the beloved. Individualism: the deception that we have been born into this world each for the sake of himself, or family, friend or kindred, *Selfness*, will be acknowledged to be the satanic element of our nature.

We therefore more than doubt, we deny Ward's proposition that individual happiness is the end of human life. If it is, the existences that were made miserable in order that mankind might be trained up to Social-Cooperation were failures; they are decidedly not failures, if, as *we* hold, the end of the individual existence is to further the evolution of Humanity, in whose fate it may be found, as we repeat, that we have a greater stake than is supposed. But happiness is a *fact*; as an *incident* of life and not an object of pursuit, it is a blessed fact. It is to man what the odor is to the rose.

That the New Commonwealth will very much diffuse and increase individual happiness there can be no doubt. It will make possible the harmonious exercise and development of all human faculties in everybody—that itself is happiness. It will, by banishing care and giving leisure, enable everyone to become familiar with all that is known about the universe and to explore its perpetual wonders and pore over its numberless riddles for himself—and that is more than happiness, it is *rapture*. Finally, it will be the grandest vehicle for serving Humanity and thereby generate the purest happiness, perfect *blessedness*.

But blessedness it is even *now* our privilege to obtain. We have the choice to live as Individualists and on our deathbed look back in despair on a dreary, hateful life of play-acting, or as Socialists fill our existences with those serious moods that make the grand tone of life, and in the hour of death stand on the mountain-top, as it were, and see with entranced eyes the rays of the Sun that soon will illumine the dark valleys below. I, for my part, deem it worth ten crucifixions to win for my memory a fraction of the adoring love which millions of the noblest men and women have felt for a Jesus.

CHAPTER I

A SHARP CROSS-EXAMINER

With many expressions of sympathy and interest Edith listened to the story of my dream. When, finally, I had made an end, she remained musing.

"What are you thinking about?" I said.

"I was thinking," she answered, "how it would have been if your dream had been true."

"True!" I exclaimed. "How could it have been true?"

"I mean," she said, "if it had all been a dream, as you supposed it was in your nightmare, and you had never really seen our Republic of the Golden Rule or me, but had only slept a night and dreamed the whole thing about us. And suppose you had gone forth just as you did in your dream, and had passed up and down telling men of the terrible folly and wickedness of their way of life and how much nobler and happier a way there was. Just think what good you might have done, how you might have helped people in those days when they needed help so much. It seems to me you must be almost sorry you came back to us."

"You look as if you were almost sorry yourself," I said, for her wistful expression seemed susceptible of that interpretation.

"Oh, no," she answered, smiling. "It was only on your own account. As for me, I have very good reasons for being glad that you came back."

"I should say so, indeed. Have you reflected that if I had dreamed it all you would have had no existence save as a figment in the brain of a sleeping man a hundred years ago?"

"I had not thought of that part of it," she said smiling and still half serious; "yet if I could have been more useful to humanity as a fiction than as a reality, I ought not to have minded the—the inconvenience."

* Pp. 1–13, 206–211, 245–249, 332–335, 349–354, 365–367, 378–381.

But I replied that I greatly feared no amount of opportunity to help mankind in general would have reconciled me to life anywhere or under any conditions after leaving her behind in a dream—a confession of shameless selfishness which she was pleased to pass over without special rebuke, in consideration, no doubt, of my unfortunate bringing up.

"Besides," I resumed, being willing a little further to vindicate myself, "it would not have done any good. I have just told you how in my nightmare last night, when I tried to tell my contemporaries and even my best friends about the nobler way men might live together, they derided me as a fool and madman. That is exactly what they would have done in reality had the dream been true and I had gone about preaching as in the case you supposed."

"Perhaps a few might at first have acted as you dreamed they did," she replied. "Perhaps they would not at once have liked the idea of economic equality, fearing that it might mean a leveling down for them, and not understanding that it would presently mean a leveling up of all together to a vastly higher plane of life and happiness, of material welfare and moral dignity than the most fortunate had ever enjoyed. But even if the rich had at first mistaken you for an enemy to their class, the poor, the great masses of the poor, the real nation, they surely from the first would have listened as for their lives, for to them your story would have meant glad tidings of great joy."

"I do not wonder that you think so," I answered, "but, though I am still learning the A B C of this new world, I knew my contemporaries, and I know that it would not have been as you fancy. The poor would have listened no better than the rich, for, though poor and rich in my day were at bitter odds in everything else, they were agreed in believing that there must always be rich and poor, and that a condition of material equality was impossible. It used to be commonly said, and it often seemed true, that the social reformer who tried to better the condition of the people found a more discouraging obstacle in the hopelessness of the masses he would raise than in the active resistance of the few, whose superiority was threatened. And indeed, Edith, to be fair to my own class, I am bound to say that with the best of the rich it was often as much this same hopelessness as deliberate selfishness that made them what we used to call conservative. So you see, it would have done no good even if I had gone to preaching as you fancied. The poor would have regarded my talk about the possibility of an equality of wealth as a fairy tale, not worth a laboring man's time to listen to. Of the rich, the baser sort would have mocked and the better sort would have sighed, but none would have given ear seriously."

But Edith smiled serenely.

"It seems very audacious for me to try to correct your impressions of your own contemporaries and of what they might be expected to think and do, but you see the peculiar circumstances give me a rather unfair advantage. Your knowledge of your times necessarily stops short with 1887, when you became oblivious of the course of events. I, on the other hand, having gone to school in the twentieth century, and been obliged, much against my will, to study nineteenth-century history, naturally know what happened after the date at which your knowledge ceased. I know, impossible as it may seem to you, that you had scarcely fallen into that long sleep before the American people began to be deeply and widely stirred with aspirations for an equal order such as we enjoy, and that very soon the political movement arose which, after various mutations, resulted early in the twentieth century in overthrowing the old system and setting up the present one."

This was indeed interesting information to me, but when I began to question Edith further, she sighed and shook her head.

"Having tried to show my superior knowledge, I must now confess my ignorance. All I know is the bare fact that the revolutionary movement began, as I said, very soon after you fell asleep. Father must tell you the rest. I might as well admit while I am about it, for you would soon find it out, that I know almost nothing either as to the Revolution or nineteenth-century matters generally. You have no idea how hard I have been trying to post myself on the subject so as to be able to talk intelligently with you, but I fear it is of no use. I could not understand it in school and can not seem to understand it any better now. More than ever this morning I am sure that I never shall. Since you have been telling me how the old world appeared to you in that dream, your talk has brought those days so terribly near that I can almost see them, and yet I can not say that they seem a bit more intelligible than before."

"Things were bad enough and black enough certainly," I said;

"but I don't see what there was particularly unintelligible about them. What is the difficulty?"

"The main difficulty comes from the complete lack of agreement between the pretensions of your contemporaries about the way their society was organized and the actual facts as given in the histories."

"For example?" I queried.

"I don't suppose there is much use in trying to explain my trouble," she said. "You will only think me stupid for my pains, but I'll try to make you see what I mean. You ought to be able to clear up the matter if anybody can. You have just been telling me about the shockingly unequal conditions of the people, the contrasts of waste and want, the pride and power of the rich, the abjectness and servitude of the poor, and all the rest of the dreadful story."

"Yes."

"It appears that these contrasts were almost as great as at any previous period of history."

"It is doubtful," I replied, "if there was ever a greater disparity between the conditions of different classes than you would find in a half hour's walk in Boston, New York, Chicago, or any other great city of America in the last quarter of the nineteenth century."

"And yet," said Edith, "it appears from all the books that meanwhile the Americans' great boast was that they differed from all other and former nations in that they were free and equal. One is constantly coming upon this phrase in the literature of the day. Now, you have made it clear that they were neither free nor equal in any ordinary sense of the word, but were divided as mankind had always been before into rich and poor, masters and servants. Won't you please tell me, then, what they meant by calling themselves free and equal?"

"It was meant, I suppose, that they were all equal before the law."

"That means in the courts. And were the rich and poor equal in the courts? Did they receive the same treatment?"

"I am bound to say," I replied, "that they were nowhere else more unequal. The law applied in terms to all alike, but not in fact. There was more difference in the position of the rich and the poor man before the law than in any other respect. The rich were practically above the law, the poor under its wheels."

"In what respect, then, were the rich and poor equal?"

"They were said to be equal in opportunities."

"Opportunities for what?"

"For bettering themselves, for getting rich, for getting ahead of others in the struggle for wealth."

"It seems to me that only meant, if it were true, not that all were equal, but that all had an equal chance to make themselves unequal. But was it true that all had equal opportunities for getting rich and bettering themselves?"

"It may have been so to some extent at one time when the country was new," I replied, "but it was no more so in my day. Capital had practically monopolized all economic opportunities by that time; there was no opening in business enterprise for those without large capital save by some extraordinary fortune."

"But surely," said Edith, "there must have been, in order to give at least a color to all this boasting about equality, some one respect in which the people were really equal?"

"Yes, there was. They were political equals. They all had one vote alike, and the majority was the supreme lawgiver."

"So the books say, but that only makes the actual condition of things more absolutely unaccountable."

"Why so?"

"Why, because if these people all had an equal voice in the government—these toiling, starving, freezing, wretched masses of the poor—why did they not without a moment's delay put an end to the inequalities from which they suffered?

"Very likely," she added, as I did not at once reply, "I am only showing how stupid I am by saying this. Doubtless I am over-looking some important fact, but did you not say that all the people, at least all the men, had a voice in the government?"

"Certainly; by the latter part of the nineteenth century manhood suffrage had become practically universal in America."

"That is to say, the people through their chosen agents made all the laws. Is that what you mean?"

"Certainly."

"But I remember you had Constitutions of the nation and of the States. Perhaps they prevented the people from doing quite what they wished."

"No; the Constitutions were only a little more fundamental sort of laws. The majority made and altered them at will. The people were the sole and supreme final power, and their will was absolute."

"If, then, the majority did not like any existing arrangement, or think it to their advantage, they could change it as radically as they wished?"

"Certainly; the popular majority could do anything if it was large and determined enough."

"And the majority, I understand, were the poor, not the rich— the ones who had the wrong side of the inequalities that prevailed?"

"Emphatically so; the rich were but a handful comparatively."

"Then there was nothing whatever to prevent the people at any time, if they just willed it, from making an end of their sufferings and organizing a system like ours which would guarantee their equality and prosperity?"

"Nothing whatever."

"Then once more I ask you to kindly tell me why, in the name of common sense, they didn't do it at once and be happy instead of making a spectacle of themselves so woeful that even a hundred years after it makes us cry?"

"Because," I replied, "they were taught and believed that the regulation of industry and commerce and the production and distribution of wealth was something wholly outside of the proper province of government."

"But, dear me, Julian, life itself and everything that meanwhile makes life worth living, from the satisfaction of the most primary physical needs to the gratification of the most refined tastes, all that belongs to the development of mind as well as body, depend first, last, and always on the manner in which the production and distribution of wealth is regulated. Surely that must have been as true in your day as ours."

"Of course."

"And yet you tell me, Julian, that the people, after having abolished the rule of kings and taken the supreme power of regulating their affairs into their own hands, deliberately consented to exclude from their jurisdiction the control of the most important, and indeed the only really important, class of their interests."

"Do not the histories say so?"

"They do say so, and that is precisely why I could never believe them. The thing seemed so incomprehensible I thought there must be some way of explaining it. But tell me, Julian, seeing the people did not think that they could trust themselves to regulate their own industry and the distribution of the product, to whom did they leave the responsibility?"

"To the capitalists."

"And did the people elect the capitalists?"

"Nobody elected them."

"By whom, then, were they appointed?"

"Nobody appointed them."

"What a singular system! Well, if nobody elected or appointed them, yet surely they must have been accountable to somebody for the manner in which they exercised powers on which the welfare and very existence of everybody depended."

"On the contrary, they were accountable to nobody and nothing but their own consciences."

"Their consciences! Ah, I see! You mean that they were so benevolent, so unselfish, so devoted to the public good, that people tolerated their usurpation out of gratitude. The people nowadays would not endure the irresponsible rule even of demigods, but probably it was different in your day."

"As an ex-capitalist myself, I should be pleased to confirm your surmise, but nothing could really be further from the fact. As to any benevolent interest in the conduct of industry and commerce, the capitalists expressly disavowed it. Their only object was to secure the greatest possible gain for themselves without any regard whatever to the welfare of the public."

"Dear me! Dear me! Why you make out these capitalists to have been even worse than the kings, for the kings at least professed to govern for the welfare of their people, as fathers acting for children, and the good ones did try to. But the capitalists, you say, did not even pretend to feel any responsibility for the welfare of their subjects?"

"None whatever."

"And, if I understand," pursued Edith, "this government of the capitalists was not only without moral sanction of any sort or plea of benevolent intentions, but was practically an economic failure—that is, it did not secure the prosperity of the people."

"What I saw in my dream last night," I replied, "and have tried to tell you this morning, gives but a faint suggestion of the misery of the world under capitalist rule."

Edith meditated in silence for some moments. Finally she said:

"Your contemporaries were not madmen nor fools; surely there is something you have not told me; there must be some explanation or at least color of excuse why the people not only abdicated the power of controling their most vital and important interests, but turned them over to a class which did not even pretend any interest in their welfare, and whose government completely failed to secure it."

"Oh, yes," I said, "there was an explanation, and a very fine-sounding one. It was in the name of individual liberty, industrial freedom, and individual initiative that the economic government of the country was surrendered to the capitalists."

"Do you mean that a form of government which seems to have been the most irresponsible and despotic possible was defended in the name of liberty?"

"Certainly; the liberty of economic initiative by the individual."

"But did you not just tell me that economic initiative and business opportunity in your day were practically monopolized by the capitalists themselves?"

"Certainly. It was admitted that there was no opening for any but capitalists in business, and it was rapidly becoming so that only the greatest of the capitalists themselves had any power of initiative."

"And yet you say that the reason given for abandoning industry to capitalist government was the promotion of industrial freedom and individual initiative among the people at large."

"Certainly. The people were taught that they would individually enjoy greater liberty and freedom of action in industrial matters under the dominion of the capitalists than if they collectively conducted the industrial system for their own benefit; that the capitalists would, moreover, look out for their welfare more wisely and kindly than they could possibly do it themselves, so that they would be able to provide for themselves more bountifully out of such portion of their product as the capitalists might be disposed to give them than they possibly could do if they became their own employers and divided the whole product among themselves."

"But that was mere mockery; it was adding insult to injury."

"It sounds so, doesn't it? But I assure you it was considered the soundest sort of political economy in my time. Those who questioned it were set down as dangerous visionaries."

"But I suppose the people's government, the government they

voted for, must have done something. There must have been some odds and ends of things which the capitalists left the political government to attend to."

"Oh, yes, indeed. It had its hands full keeping the peace among the people. That was the main part of the business of political governments in my day."

"Why did the peace require such a great amount of keeping? Why didn't it keep itself, as it does now?"

"On account of the inequality of conditions which prevailed. The strife for wealth and desperation of want kept in quenchless blaze a hell of greed and envy, fear, lust, hate, revenge, and every foul passion of the pit. To keep this general frenzy in some restraint, so that the entire social system should not resolve itself into a general massacre, required an army of soldiers, police, judges, and jailers, and endless law-making to settle the quarrels. Add to these elements of discord a horde of outcasts degraded and desperate, made enemies of society by their sufferings and requiring to be kept in check, and you will readily admit there was enough for the people's government to do."

"So far as I can see," said Edith, "the main business of the people's government was to struggle with the social chaos which resulted from its failure to take hold of the economic system and regulate it on a basis of justice."

"That is exactly so. You could not state the whole case more adequately if you wrote a book."

"Beyond protecting the capitalist system from its own effects, did the political government do absolutely nothing?"

"Oh, yes, it appointed postmasters and tidewaiters, maintained an army and navy, and picked quarrels with foreign countries."

"I should say that the right of the citizen to have a voice in a government limited to the range of functions you have mentioned would scarcely have seemed to him of much value."

"I believe the average price of votes in close elections in America in my time was about two dollars."

"Dear me, so much as that!" said Edith. "I don't know exactly what the value of money was in your day, but I should say the price was rather extortionate."

"I think you are right," I answered. "I used to give in to the talk about the pricelessness of the right of suffrage, and the denunciation of those whom any stress of poverty could induce to sell it for money, but from the point of view to which you have brought me this morning I am inclined to think that the fellows who sold their votes had a far clearer idea of the sham of our so-called popular government, as limited to the class of functions I have described, than any of the rest of us did, and that if they were wrong it was, as you suggest, in asking too high a price."

"But who paid for the votes?"

"You are a merciless cross-examiner," I said. "The classes which had an interest in controling the government—that is, the capitalists and the office-seekers—did the buying. The capitalists advanced the money necessary to procure the election of the office-seekers on the understanding that when elected the latter should do what the capitalists wanted. But I ought not to give you the impression that the bulk of the votes were bought outright. That would have been too open a confession of the sham of popular government as well as too expensive. The money contributed by the capitalists to procure the election of the office-seekers was mainly expended to influence the people by indirect means. Immense sums under the name of campaign funds were raised for this purpose and used in innumerable devices, such as fireworks, oratory, processions, brass bands, barbecues, and all sorts of devices, the object of which was to galvanize the people to a sufficient degree of interest in the election to go through the motion of voting. Nobody who has not actually witnessed a nineteenth-century American election could even begin to imagine the grotesqueness of the spectacle."

"It seems, then," said Edith, "that the capitalists not only carried on the economic government as their special province, but also practically managed the machinery of the political government as well."

"Oh, yes, the capitalists could not have got along at all without control of the political government. Congress, the Legislatures, and the city councils were quite necessary as instruments for putting through their schemes. Moreover, in order to protect themselves and their property against popular outbreaks, it was highly needful that they should have the police, the courts, and the soldiers devoted to their interests, and the President, Governors, and mayors at their beck."

"But I thought the President, the Governors, and Legislatures represented the people who voted for them."

"Bless your heart! no, why should they? It was to the capitalists and not to the people that they owed the opportunity of office-holding. The people who voted had little choice for whom they should vote. That question was determined by the political party organizations, which were beggars to the capitalists for pecuniary support. No man who was opposed to capitalist interests was permitted the opportunity as a candidate to appeal to the people. For a public official to support the people's interest as against that of the capitalists would be a sure way of sacrificing his career. You must remember, if you would understand how absolutely the capitalists controled the Government, that a President, Governor, or mayor, or member of the municipal, State, or national council, was only temporarily a servant of the people or dependent on their favour. His public position he held only from election to election, and rarely long. His permanent, lifelong, and all-controling interest, like that of us all, was his livelihood, and that was dependent, not on the applause of the people, but the favor and patronage of capital, and this he could not afford to imperil in the pursuit of the bubbles of popularity. These circumstances, even if there had been no instances of direct bribery, sufficiently explained why our politicians and officeholders with few exceptions were vassals and tools of the capitalists. The lawyers, who, on account of the complexities of our system, were almost the only class competent for public business, were especially and directly dependent upon the patronage of the great capitalistic interests for their living."

"But why did not the people elect officials and representatives of their own class, who would look out for the interests of the masses?"

"There was no assurance that they would be more faithful. Their very poverty would make them the more liable to money temptation; and the poor, you must remember, although so much more pitiable, were not morally any better than the rich. Then, too—and that was the most important reason why the masses of the people, who were poor, did not send men of their class to represent them—poverty as a rule implied ignorance, and therefore practical inability, even where the intention was good. As soon as the poor man developed intelligence he had every temptation to desert his class and seek the patronage of capital."

Edith remained silent and thoughtful for some moments.

"Really," she said, finally, "it seems that the reason I could not understand the so-called popular system of government in your day is that I was trying to find out what part the people had in it, and it appears that they had no part at all."

"You are getting on famously," I exclaimed. "Undoubtedly the confusion of terms in our political system is rather calculated to puzzle one at first, but if you only grasp firmly the vital point that the rule of the rich, the supremacy of capital and its interests, as against those of the people at large, was the central principle of our system, to which every other interest was made subservient, you will have the key that clears up every mystery." . . .

CHAPTER XXV

THE STRIKERS

Presently, as we were crossing Boston Common, absorbed in conversation, a shadow fell athwart the way, and looking up, I saw towering above us a sculptured group of heroic size.

"Who are these?" I exclaimed.

"You ought to know if any one," said the doctor. "They are contemporaries of yours who were making a good deal of disturbance in your day."

But, indeed, it had only been as an involuntary expression of surprise that I had questioned what the figures stood for.

Let me tell you, readers of the twentieth century, what I saw up there on the pedestal, and you will recognize the world-famous group. Shoulder to shoulder, as if rallied to resist assault, were three figures of men in the garb of the laboring class of my time. They were bareheaded, and their coarse-textured shirts, rolled above the elbow and open at the breast, showed the sinewy arms and chest. Before them, on the ground, lay a pair of shovels and a pickaxe. The central figure, with the right hand extended, palm outward, was pointing to the discarded tools. The arms of the other two were folded on their breasts. The faces were coarse and hard in outline and bristled with unkempt beards. Their expression was one of dogged defiance, and their gaze was fixed with such scowling intensity upon the void space before them that I involuntarily glanced behind me to see what they were looking at. There were two women also in the group, as coarse of dress and features as the men. One was kneeling before the figure on the right, holding up to him with one arm an emaciated, half-clad infant, while with the other she indicated the implements at his feet with an imploring gesture. The second of the women was plucking by the sleeve the man on the left as if to draw him back, while with the other hand she covered her eyes. But the men heeded the women not at all, or seemed, in their bitter wrath, to know that they were there.

"Why," I exclaimed, "these are strikers!"

"Yes," said the doctor, "this is The Strikers, Huntington's masterpiece, considered the greatest group of statuary in the city and one of the greatest in the country."

"Those people are alive!" I said.

"That is expert testimony," replied the doctor. "It is a pity Huntington died too soon to hear it. He would have been pleased."

Now, I, in common with the wealthy and cultured class generally, of my day, had always held strikers in contempt and abhorrence, as blundering, dangerous marplots, as ignorant of their own best interests as they were reckless of other people's, and generally as pestilent fellows, whose demonstrations, so long as they were not violent, could not unfortunately be repressed by force, but ought always to be condemned, and promptly put down with an iron hand the moment there was an excuse for police interference. There was more or less tolerance among the well-to-do, for social reformers, who, by book or voice, advocated even very radical economic changes so long as they observed the conventionalities of speech, but for the striker there were few apologists. Of course, the capitalists emptied on him the vials of their wrath and contempt, and even people who thought they sympathized with the working class shook their heads at the mention of strikes, regarding them as calculated rather to hinder than help the emancipation of labor. Bred as I was in these prejudices, it may not seem strange that I was taken aback at finding such unpromising subjects selected for the highest place in the city.

"There is no doubt as to the excellence of the artist's work," I said, "but what was there about the strikers that has made you pick them out of our generation as objects of veneration?"

"We see in them," replied the doctor, "the pioneers in the revolt against private capitalism which brought in the present civilization. We honor them as those who, like Winkelried, 'made way for liberty, and died.' We revere in them the protomartyrs of co-operative industry and economic equality."

"But I can assure you, doctor, that these fellows, at least in my day, had not the slightest idea of revolting against private capitalism as a system. They were very ignorant and quite incapable of grasping so large a conception. They had no notion of getting along without capitalists. All they imagined as possible or desirable was a little better treatment by their employers, a few cents more an hour, a few minutes less working time a day, or maybe merely the discharge of an unpopular foreman. The most they aimed at was some petty improvement in their condition, to attain which they did not hesitate to throw the whole industrial machine into disorder."

"All which we moderns know quite well," replied the doctor. "Look at those faces. Has the sculptor idealized them? Are they the faces of philosophers? Do they not bear out your statement that the strikers, like the workingmen generally, were, as a rule, ignorant, narrow-minded men, with no grasp of large questions, and incapable of so great an idea as the overthrow of an immemorial economic order? It is quite true that until some years after you fell asleep they did not realize that their quarrel was with private capitalism and not with individual capitalists. In this slowness of awakening to the full meaning of their revolt they were precisely on a par with the pioneers of all the great liberty revolutions. The minutemen at Concord and Lexington, in 1775, did not realize that they were pointing their guns at the monarchical idea. As little did the third estate of France, when it entered the Convention in 1789, realize that its road lay over the ruins of the throne. As little did the pioneers of English freedom, when they began to resist the will of Charles I, foresee that they would be compelled, before they got through, to take his head. In none of these instances, however, has posterity considered that the limited foresight of the pioneers as to the full consequences of their action lessened the world's debt to the crude initiative, without which the fuller triumph would never have come. The logic of the strike meant the overthrow of the irresponsible conduct of industry, whether the strikers knew it or not, and we can not rejoice in the consequences of that overthrow without honoring them in a way which very likely, as you intimate, would surprise them, could they know of it, as much as it does you. Let me try to give you the modern point of view as to the part played by their originals." We sat down upon one of the benches before the statue, and the doctor went on:

"My dear Julian, who was it, pray, that first roused the world of your day to the fact that there was an industrial question, and by their pathetic demonstrations of passive resistance to wrong for fifty years kept the public attention fixed on that question till it was settled? Was it your statesmen, perchance your economists, your scholars, or any other of your so-called wise men? No. It was just those despised, ridiculed, cursed, and hooted fellows up there on that pedestal who with their perpetual strikes would not let the world rest till their wrong, which was also the whole world's wrong, was righted. Once more had God chosen the foolish things of this world to confound the wise, the weak things to confound the mighty.

"In order to realize how powerfully these strikes operated to impress upon the people the intolerable wickedness and folly of private capitalism, you must remember that events are what teach men, that deeds have a far more potent educating influence than any amount of doctrine, and especially so in an age like yours, when the masses had almost no culture or ability to reason. There were not lacking in the revolutionary period many cultured men and women, who, with voice and pen, espoused the workers' cause, and showed them the way out; but their words might well have availed little but for the tremendous emphasis with which they were confirmed by the men up there, who starved to prove them true. Those rough-looking fellows, who probably could not have constructed a grammatical sentence, by their combined efforts, were demonstrating the necessity of a radically new industrial system by a more convincing argument than any rhetorician's skill could frame. When men take their lives in their hands to resist oppression, as those men did, other men are compelled to give heed to them. We have inscribed on the pedestal yonder, where you see the lettering, the words, which the action of the group above seems to voice:

" 'We can bear no more. It is better to starve than live on the terms you give us. Our lives, the lives of our wives and of our children, we set against your gains. If you put your foot upon our neck, we will bite your heel!'

"This was the cry," pursued the doctor, "of men made desperate by oppression, to whom existence through suffering had become of no value. It was the same cry that in varied form but in one sense has been the watchword of every revolution that has marked an advance of the race—'Give us liberty, or give us death!' and never did it ring out with a cause so adequate, or wake the world to an issue so mighty, as in the mouths of these first rebels against the folly and the tyranny of private capital.

"In your age, I know, Julian," the doctor went on in a gentler tone, "it was customary to associate valor with the clang of arms and the pomp and circumstance of war. But the echo of the fife and drum comes very faintly up to us, and moves us not at all. The soldier has had his day, and passed away forever with the ideal of manhood which he illustrated. But that group yonder stands for a type of self-devotion that appeals to us profoundly. Those men risked their lives when they flung down the tools of their trade, as truly as any soldiers going into battle, and took odds as desperate, and not only for themselves, but for their families, which no grateful country would care for in case of casualty to them. The soldier went forth cheered with music, and supported by the enthusiasm of the country, but these others were covered with ignominy and public contempt, and their failures and defeats were hailed with general acclamation. And yet they sought not the lives of others, but only that they might barely live; and though they had first thought of the welfare of themselves, and those nearest them, yet not the less were they fighting the fight of humanity and posterity in striking in the only way they could, and while yet no one else dared strike at all, against the economic system that had the world by the throat, and would never relax its grip by dint of soft words, or anything less than disabling blows. The clergy, the economists and the pedagogues, having left these ignorant men to seek as they might the solution of the social problem, while they themselves sat at ease and denied that there was any problem, were very voluble in their criticisms of the mistakes of the workingmen, as if it were possible to make any mistake in seeking a way out of the social chaos, which could be so fatuous or so criminal as the mistake of not trying to seek any. No doubt, Julian, I have put finer words in the mouths of those men up there than their originals might have even understood, but if the meaning was not in their words it was in their deeds. And it is for what they did, not for what they said, that we honor them as protomartyrs of the industrial republic of to-day, and bring our children, that they may kiss in gratitude the rough-shod feet of those who made the way for us."

My experiences since I waked up in this year 2000 might be said to have consisted of a succession of instantaneous mental readjustments of a revolutionary character, in which what had formerly seemed evil to me had become good, and what had seemed wisdom had become foolishness. Had this conversation about the strikers taken place anywhere else, the entirely new impression I had received of the part played by them in the great social revolution of which I shared the benefit would simply have been one more of these readjustments, and the process entirely a mental one. But the presence of this wondrous group, the lifelikeness of the figures growing on my gaze as I listened to the doctor's words, imparted a peculiar personal quality—if I may use the term—to the revulsion of feeling that I experienced. Moved by an irresistible impulse, I rose to my feet, and, removing my hat, saluted the grim forms whose living originals I had joined my contemporaries in reviling.

The doctor smiled gravely.

"Do you know, my boy," he said, "it is not often that the whirligig of Time brings round his revenges in quite so dramatic a way as this?" . . .

CHAPTER XXX

WHAT UNIVERSAL CULTURE MEANS

It was one of those Indian summer afternoons when it seems sinful waste of opportunity to spend a needless hour within. Being in no sort of hurry, the doctor and I chartered a motor-carriage for two at the next station, and set forth in the general direction of home, indulging ourselves in as many deviations from the route as pleased our fancy. Presently, as we rolled noiselessly over the smooth streets, leaf-strewn from the bordering colonnades of trees, I began to exclaim about the precocity of school children who at the age of thirteen or fourteen were able to handle themes usually reserved in my day for the college and university. This, however, the doctor made light of.

"Political economy," he said, "from the time the world adopted the plan of equal sharing of labor and its results, became a science so simple that any child who knows the proper way to divide an apple with his little brothers has mastered the secret of it. Of course, to point out the fallacies of a false political economy is a very simple matter also, when one has only to compare it with the true one.

"As to intellectual precocity in general," pursued the doctor, "I do not think it is particularly noticeable in our children as compared with those of your day. We certainly make no effort to develop it. A bright school child of twelve in the nineteenth century would probably not compare badly as to acquirements with the average twelve-year-old in our schools. It would be as you compared them ten years later that the difference in the educational systems would show its effect. At twenty-one or twenty-two the average youth would probably in your day have been little more advanced in education than at fourteen, having probably left school for the factory or farm at about that age or a couple of years later unless perhaps he happened to be one of the children of the rich minority. The corresponding child under our system would have continued his or her education without break, and at twenty-one have acquired what you used to call a college education."

"The extension of the educational machinery necessary to provide the higher education for all must have been enormous," I said. "Our primary-school system provided the rudiments for nearly all children, but not one in twenty went as far as the grammar school, not one in a hundred as far as the high school, and not one in a thousand ever saw a college. The great universities of my day—Harvard, Yale, and the rest—must have become small cities in order to receive the students flocking to them."

"They would need to be very large cities certainly," replied the doctor, "if it were a question of their undertaking the higher education of our youth, for every year we graduate not the thousands or tens of thousands that made up your annual grist of college graduates, but millions. For that very reason—that is, the numbers to be dealt with—we can have no centers of the higher education any more than you had of the primary education. Every community has its university just as formerly its common schools, and has in it more students from the vicinage than one of your great universities could collect with its drag net from the ends of the earth."

"But does not the reputation of particular teachers attract students to special universities?"

"That is a matter easily provided for," replied the doctor. "The perfection of our telephone and electroscope systems makes it possible to enjoy at any distance the instruction of any teacher. One of much popularity lectures to a million pupils in a whisper, if he happens to be hoarse, much easier than one of your professors could talk to a class of fifty when in good voice."

"Really, doctor," said I, "there is no fact about your civilization that seems to open so many vistas of possibility and solve beforehand so many possible difficulties in the arrangement and operation of your social system as this universality of culture. I am bound to say that nothing that is rational seems impossible in the way of social adjustments when once you assume the existence of that condition. My own contemporaries fully recognized in theory, as you know, the importance of popular education to secure good government in a democracy; but our system, which barely at best taught the masses to spell, was a farce indeed compared with the popular education of to-day."

"Necessarily so," replied the doctor. "The basis of education is economic, requiring as it does the maintenance of the pupil without economic return during the educational period. If the education is to amount to anything, that period must cover the years of childhood and adolescence to the age of at least twenty. That involves a very large expenditure, which not one parent in a thousand was able to support in your day. The state might have assumed it, of course, but that would have amounted to the rich supporting the children of the poor, and naturally they would not hear to that, at least beyond the primary grades of education. And even if there had been no money question, the rich, if they hoped to retain their power, would have been crazy to provide for the masses destined to do their dirty work—a culture which would have made them social rebels. For these two reasons your economic system was incompatible with any popular education worthy of the name. On the other hand, the first effect of economic equality was to provide equal educational advantages for all and the best the community could afford. One of the most interesting chapters in the history of the Revolution is that which tells how at once after the new order was established the young men and women under twenty-one years of age who had been working in fields or factories, perhaps since childhood, left their work and poured back into the schools and colleges as fast as room could be made for them, so that they might as far as possible repair their early loss. All alike recognized, now that education had been made economically possible for all, that it was the greatest boon the new order had brought. It recorded also in the books that not only the youth, but the men and women, and even the elderly who had been without educational advantages, devoted all the leisure left from their industrial duties to making up, so far as possible, for their lack of earlier advantages, that they might not be too much ashamed in the presence of a rising generation to be composed altogether of college graduates.

"In speaking of our educational system as it is at present," the doctor went on, "I should guard you against the possible mistake of supposing that the course which ends at twenty-one completes the educational curriculum of the average individual. On the contrary, it is only the required minimum of culture which society insists that all youth shall receive during their minority to make them barely fit for citizenship. We should consider it a very meager education indeed that ended there. As we look at it, the graduation from the schools at the attainment of majority means merely that the graduate has reached an age at which he can be presumed to be competent and has the right as an adult to carry on his further education without the guidance or compulsion of the state. To provide means for this end the nation maintains a vast system of what you would call elective post-graduate courses of study in every branch of science, and these are open freely to every one to the end of life to be pursued as long or as briefly, as constantly or as intermittently, as profoundly or superficially, as desired.

"The mind is really not fit for many most important branches of knowledge, the taste for them does not awake, and the intellect is not able to grasp them, until mature life, when a month of application will give a comprehension of a subject which years would have been wasted in trying to impart to a youth. It is our idea, so far as possible, to postpone the serious study of such branches to the post-graduate schools. Young people must get a smattering of things in general, but really theirs is not the time of life for ardent and effective study. If you would see enthusiastic students to whom the pursuit of knowledge is the greatest joy of life you must seek them among the middle-aged fathers and mothers in the post-graduate schools. . . .

"The two great points of the revolutionary programme—the principle of economic equality and a nationalized industrial system as its means and pledge—the American people were peculiarly adapted to understand and appreciate. The lawyers had made a Constitution of the United States, but the true American constitution—the one written on the people's hearts—had always remained the immortal Declaration with its assertion of the inalienable equality of all men. As to the nationalization of industry, while it involved a set of consequences which would completely transform society, the principle on which the proposition was based, and to which it appealed for justification, was not new to Americans in any sense, but, on the contrary, was merely a logical development of the idea of popular self-government on which the American system was founded. The application of this principle to the regulation of the economic administration was indeed a use of it which was historically new, but it was one so absolutely and obviously implied in the content of the idea that, as soon as it was proposed, it was impossible that any sincere democrat should not be astonished that so plain and common-sense a corollary of popular government had waited so long for recognition. The apostles of a collective administration of the economic system in the common interest had in Europe a twofold task: first, to teach the general doctrine of the absolute right of the people to govern, and then to show the economic application of that right. To Americans, however, it was only necessary to point out an obvious although hitherto overlooked application of a principle already fully accepted as an axiom.

"The acceptance of the new ideal did not imply merely a change in specific programmes, but a total facing about of the revolutionary movement. It had thus far been an attempt to resist the new economic conditions being imposed by the capitalists by bringing back the former economic conditions through the restoration of free competition as it had existed before the war. This was an effort of necessity hopeless, seeing that the economic changes which had taken place were merely the necessary evolution of any system of private capitalism, and could not be successfully resisted while the system was retained.

"'Face about!' was the new word of command. 'Fight forward, not backward! March with the course of economic evolution, not against it. The competitive system can never be restored, neither is it worthy of restoration, having been at best an immoral, wasteful, brutal scramble for existence. New issues demand new answers. It is in vain to pit the moribund system of competition against the young giant of private monopoly; it must rather be opposed by the greater giant of public monopoly. The consolidation of business in private interests must be met with greater consolidation in the public interest, the trust and the syndicate with the city, State, and nation, capitalism with nationalism. The capitalists have destroyed the competitive system. Do not try to restore it, but rather thank them for the work, if not the motive, and set about, not to rebuild the old village of hovels, but to rear on the cleared place the temple humanity so long has waited for.'

"By the light of the new teaching the people began to recognize that the strait place into which the republic had come was but the narrow and frowning portal of a future of universal welfare and happiness such as only the Hebrew prophets had colors strong enough to paint.

"By the new philosophy the issue which had arisen between the people and the plutocracy was seen not to be a strange and unaccountable or deplorable event, but a necessary phase in the evolution of a democratic society in passing from a lower to an incomparably higher plane, an issue therefore to be welcomed not shunned, to be forced not evaded, seeing that its outcome in the existing state of human enlightenment and world-wide democratic sentiment could not be doubtful. By the road by which every republic had toiled upward from the barren lowlands of early hardship and poverty, just at the point where the steepness of the hill had been overcome and a prospect opened of pleasant uplands of wealth and prosperity, a sphinx had ever stood, propounding the riddle, 'How shall a state combine the preservation of democratic equality with the increase of wealth?' Simple indeed had been the answer, for it was only needful that the people should so order their system of economy that wealth should be equally shared as it increased, in order that, however great the increase, it should in no way interfere with the equalities of the people; for the great justice of equality is the well of political life everlasting for peoples, whereof if a nation drink it may live forever. Nevertheless,

no republic before had been able to answer the riddle, and therefore their bones whitened the hilltop, and not one had ever
survived to enter on the pleasant land in view. But the time had
now come in the evolution of human intelligence when the riddle
so often asked and never answered was to be answered aright,
the sphinx made an end of, and the road freed forever for all
the nations.

"It was this note of perfect assurance, of confident and boundless
hope, which distinguished the new propaganda, and was the more
commanding and uplifting from its contrast with the blank pes-
simism on the one side of the capitalist party, and the petty aims,
class interests, short vision, and timid spirit of the reformers who had
hitherto opposed them. . . .

CHAPTER XXXVII

THE TRANSITION PERIOD

"It is pretty late," I said, "but I want very much to ask you
just a few more questions about the Revolution. All that I have
learned leaves me quite as puzzled as ever to imagine any set
of practical measures by which the substitution of public for
private capitalism could have been effected without a prodigious
shock. We had in our day engineers clever enough to move great
buildings from one site to another, keeping them meanwhile so
steady and upright as not to interfere with the dwellers in them,
or to cause an interruption of the domestic operations. A problem
something like this, but a millionfold greater and more complex,
must have been raised when it came to changing the entire basis
of production and distribution and revolutionizing the conditions
of everybody's employment and maintenance, and doing it, moreover, without meanwhile seriously interrupting the ongoing of the
various parts of the economic machinery on which the livelihood
of the people from day to day depended. I should be greatly
interested to have you tell me something about how this was done."

"Your question," replied the doctor, "reflects a feeling which
had no little influence during the revolutionary period to prolong
the toleration extended by the people to private capitalism despite
the mounting indignation against its enormities. A complete change
of economic systems seemed to them, as it does to you, such a
colossal and complicated undertaking that even many who ardently

desired the new order and fully believed in its feasibility when once established, shrank back from what they apprehended would be the vast confusion and difficulty of the transition process. Of course, the capitalists, and champions of things as· they were, made the most of this feeling, and apparently bothered the reformers not a little by calling on them to name the specific measures by which they would, if they had the power, proceed to substitute for the existing system a nationalized plan of industry managed in the equal interest of all.

"One school of revolutionists declined to formulate or suggest any definite programme whatever for the consummating or constructive stage of the Revolution. They said that the crisis would suggest the method for dealing with it, and it would be foolish and fanciful to discuss the emergency before it arose. But a good general makes plans which provide in advance for all the main eventualities of his campaign. His plans are, of course, subject to radical modifications or complete abandonment, according to circumstances, but a provisional plan he ought to have. The reply of this school of revolutionists was not, therefore, satisfactory, and, so long as no better one could be made, a timid and conservative community inclined to look askance at the revolutionary programme.

"Realizing the need of something more positive as a plan of campaign, various schools of reformers suggested more or less definite schemes. One there was which argued that the trades unions might develop strength enough to control the great trades, and put their own elected officers in place of the capitalists, thus organizing a sort of federation of trades unions. This, if practicable, would have brought in a system of group capitalism as divisive and antisocial, in the large sense, as private capitalism itself, and far more dangerous to civil order. This idea was later heard little of, as it became evident that the possible growth and functions of trade unionism were very limited.

"There was another school which held that the solution was to be found by the establishment of great numbers of voluntary colonies, organized on co-operative principles, which by their success would lead to the formation of more and yet more, and that, finally, when most of the population had joined such groups they would simply coalesce and form one. Many noble and enthusiastic souls devoted themselves to this line of effort, and the numerous colonies that were organized in the United States during the revolutionary period were a striking indication of the general turning of men's hearts toward a better social order. Otherwise such experiments led, and could lead, to nothing. Economically weak, held together by a sentimental motive, generally composed of eccentric though worthy persons, and surrounded by a hostile environment which had the whole use and advantage of the social and economic machinery, it was scarcely possible that such enterprises should come to anything practical unless under exceptional leadership or circumstances.

"There was another school still which held that the better order was to evolve gradually out of the old as the result of an indefinite series of humane legislation, consisting of factory acts, short-hour laws, pensions for the old, improved tenement houses, abolition of slums, and I don't know how many other poultices for particular evils resultant from the system of private capitalism. These good people argued that when at some indefinitely remote time all the evil consequences of capitalism had been abolished, it would be time enough and then comparatively easy to abolish capitalism itself—that is to say, after all the rotten fruit of the evil tree had been picked by hand, one at a time, off the branches, it would be time enough to cut down the tree. Of course, an obvious objection to this plan was that, so long as the tree remained standing, the evil fruit would be likely to grow as fast as it was plucked. The various reform measures, and many others urged by these reformers, were wholly humane and excellent, and only to be criticised when put forward as a sufficient method of overthrowing capitalism. They did not even tend toward such a result, but were quite as likely to help capitalism to obtain a longer lease of life by making it a little less abhorrent. There was really a time after the revolutionary movement had gained considerable headway when judicious leaders felt considerable apprehension lest it might be diverted from its real aim, and its force wasted in this programme of piecemeal reforms.

"But you have asked me what was the plan of operation by which the revolutionists, when they finally came into power, actually overthrew private capitalism. It was really as pretty an illustration of the military manoeuvre that used to be called flanking as the history of war contains. Now, a flanking operation is one by which an army, instead of attacking its antagonist directly in front, moves round one of his flanks in such a way that without striking a blow it forces the enemy to leave his position. That is just the strategy the revolutionists used in the final issue with capitalism.

"The capitalists had taken for granted that they were to be directly assaulted by wholesale forcible seizure and confiscation of their properties. Not a bit of it. Although in the end, of course, collective ownership was wholly substituted for the private ownership of capital, yet that was not done until after the whole system of private capitalism had brokn down and fallen to pieces, and not as a means of throwing it down. To recur to the military illustration, the revolutionary army did not directly attack the fortress of capitalism at all, but so manoeuvred as to make it untenable, and to compel its evacuation.

"Of course, you will understand that this policy was not suggested by any consideration for the rights of the capitalists. Long before this time the people had been educated to see in private capitalism the source and sum of all villainies, convicting mankind of deadly sin every day that it was tolerated. The policy of indirect attack pursued by the revolutionists was wholly dictated by the interest of the people at large, which demanded that serious derangements of the economic system should be, so far as possible, avoided during the transition from the old order to the new.

"And now, dropping figures of speech, let me tell you plainly what was done—that is, so far as I remember the story. I have made no special study of the period since my college days, and very likely when you come to read the histories you will find that I have made many mistakes as to the details of the process. I am just trying to give you a general idea of the main course of events, to the best of my remembrance. I have already explained that the first step in the programme of political action adopted by the opponents of private capitalism had been to induce the people to municipalize and nationalize various quasi-public services, such as waterworks, lighting plants, ferries, local railroads, the telegraph and telephone systems, the general railroad system, the coal mines and petroleum production, and the traffic in intoxicating liquors. These being a class of enterprises partly or wholly non-competitive and monopolistic in character, the assumption of public control over them did not directly attack the system of production and distribution in general, and even the timid and conservative viewed the step with little apprehension. This whole class of natural or legal monopolies might indeed have been taken under public management without logically involving an assault on the system of private capitalism as a whole. Not only was this so, but even if this entire class of businesses was made public and run at cost, the cheapening in the cost of living to the community thus effected would presently be swallowed up by reductions of wages and prices, resulting from the remorseless operation of the competitive profit system.

"It was therefore chiefly as a means to an ulterior end that the opponent of capitalism favored the public operation of these businesses. One part of that ulterior end was to prove to the people the superior simplicity, efficiency, and humanity of public over private management of economic undertakings. But the principal use which this partial process of nationalization served was to prepare a body of public employees sufficiently large to furnish a nucleus of consumers when the Government should undertake the establishment of a general system of production and distribution on a non-profit basis. The employees of the nationalized railroads alone numbered nearly a million, and with their dependent women and children represented some 4,000,000 people. The employees in the coal mines, iron mines, and other businesses taken charge of by the Government as subsidiary to the railroads, together with the telegraph and telephone workers, also in the public service, made some hundreds of thousands more persons with their dependents. Previous to these additions there had been in the regular civil service of the Government nearly 250,000 persons, and the army and navy made some 50,000 more. These groups with their dependents amounted probably to a million more persons, who, added to the railroad, mining, telegraph, and other employees, made an aggregate of something like 5,000,000 persons dependent on the national employment. Besides these were the various bodies of State and municipal employees in all grades, from the Governors of States down to the street-cleaners. . . .

"There is just one point about the transition stage that I want to go back to," I said. "In the actual case, as you have stated it, it seems that the capitalists held on to their capital and continued to conduct business as long as they could induce anybody to work for them or buy of them. I suppose that was human nature—capitalist human nature anyway; but it was also convenient for the Revolution, for this course gave time to get the new economic system perfected as a framework before the strain of providing for the whole people was thrown on it. But it was just possible, I suppose, that the capitalists might have taken a different course. For example, suppose, from the moment the popular majority gave control of the national Government to the revolutionists the capitalists had with one accord abandoned their functions and refused to do business of any kind. This, mind you, would have been before the Government had any time to organize even the beginnings of the new system. That would have made a more difficult problem to deal with, would it not?"

"I do not think that the problem would have been more difficult," replied the doctor, "though it would have called for more prompt and summary action. The Government would have had two things to do and to do at once: on the one hand, to take up and carry on the machinery of productive industry abandoned by the capitalists, and simultaneously to provide maintenance for the people pending the time when the new product should become available. I suppose that as to the matter of providing for the maintenance of the people the action taken would be like that usually followed by a government when by flood, famine, siege, or other sudden emergency the livelihood of a whole community has been endangered. No doubt the first step would have been to requisition for public use all stores of grain, clothing, shoes, and commodities in general throughout the country, excepting of course reasonable stocks in strictly private use. There was always in any civilized country a supply ahead of these necessities sufficient for several months or a year which would be many times more than would be needful to bridge over the gap between the stoppage of the wheels of production under private management and their getting into full motion under public administration. Orders on the public stores for food and clothing would have been issued to all citizens making application and enrolling themselves in the public industrial service. Meanwhile the Government would have immediately resumed the operation of the various production enterprises abandoned by the capitalists. Everybody previously employed in them would simply have kept on, and employment would have been as rapidly as possible provided for those who had formerly been without it. The new product, as fast as made, would be turned into the public stores and the process would, in fact, have been just the same as that I have described, save that it would have gone through in much quicker time. If it did not go quite so smoothly on account of the necessary haste, on the other hand it would have been done with sooner, and at most we can hardly imagine that the inconvenience and hardship to the people would have been greater than resulted from even a mild specimen of the business crises which your contemporaries thought necessary every seven years, and toward the last of the old order became perpetual.

"Your question, however," continued the doctor, "reminds me of another point which I had forgotten to mention—namely, the provisional methods of furnishing employment for the unemployed before the organization of the complete national system of industry. What your contemporaries were pleased to call 'the problem of the unemployed'—namely, the necessary effect of the profit system to create and perpetuate an unemployed class—had been increasing in magnitude from the beginning of the revolutionary period, and toward the close of the century the involuntary idlers were numbered by millions. While this state of things on the one hand furnished a powerful argument for the revolutionary propaganda by the object lesson it furnished of the incompetence of private capitalism to solve the problem of national maintenance, on the other hand, in proportion as employment became hard to get, the hold of the employers over the actual and would-be employees became strengthened. Those who had employment and feared to lose it, and those who had it not but hoped to get it, became, through fear and hope, very puppets in the hands of the employing class and cast their votes at their bidding. Election after election was carried in this way by the capitalists through their power to compel the workingman to vote the capitalist ticket against his own convictions, from the fear of losing or hope of obtaining an opportunity to work.

"This was the situation which made it necessary previous to the conquest of the General Government by the revolutionary party, in order that the workingmen should be made free to vote for their own deliverance, that at least a provisional system of employment should be established whereby the wage-earner might be insured a livelihood when unable to find a private employer. . . .

"The difficulty under the profit system had been to avoid producing too much; the difficulty under the equal sharing system was how to produce enough. The smallness of demand had before limited supply, but supply had now set to it an unlimited task. Under private capitalism demand had been a dwarf and lame at that, and yet this cripple had been pace-maker for the giant production. National co-operation had put wings on the dwarf and shod the cripple with Mercury's sandals. Henceforth the giant would need all his strength, all his thews of steel and sinews of brass even, to keep him in sight as he flitted on before.

"It would be difficult to give you an idea of the tremendous burst of industrial energy with which the rejuvenated nation on the morrow of the Revolution threw itself into the task of up-lifting the welfare of all classes to a level where the former rich man might find in sharing the common lot nothing to regret. Nothing like the Titanic achievement by which this result was effected had ever before been known in human history, and nothing like it seems likely ever to occur again. In the past there had not been work enough for the people. Millions, some rich, some poor, some willingly, some unwillingly, had always been idle, and not only that, but half the work that was done was wasted in com-petition or in producing luxuries to gratify the secondary wants of the few, while yet the primary wants of the mass remained un-satisfied. Idle machinery equal to the power of other millions of men, idle land, idle capital of every sort, mocked the need of the people. Now, all at once there were not hands enough in the country, wheels enough in the machinery, power enough in steam and electricity, hours enough in the day, days enough in the week, for the vast task of preparing the basis of a comfortable existence for all. For not until all were well-to-do, well housed, well clothed, well fed, might any be so under the new order of things.

"It is said that in the first full year after the new order was established the total product of the country was tripled, and in the second the first year's product was doubled, and every bit of it consumed.

"While, of course, the improvement in the material welfare of the nation was the most notable feature in the first years after the Revolution, simply because it was the place at which any improvement must begin, yet the ennobling and softening of manners and the growth of geniality in social intercourse are said to have been changes scarcely less notable. While the class differences inherited from the former order in point of habits, education, and culture must, of course, continue to mark and in a measure separate the members of the generation then on the stage, yet the certain knowledge that the basis of these differences had passed away forever, and that the children of all would mingle not only upon terms of economic equality, but of moral, intellectual, and social sympathy, and entire community of interest, seems to have had a strong anticipatory influence in bringing together in a sentiment of essential brotherhood those who were too far on in life to expect to see the full promise of the Revolution realized.

"One other matter is worth speaking of, and that is the effect almost at once of the universal and abounding material prosperity which the nation had entered on to make the people forget all about the importance they had so lately attached to petty differences in pay and wages and salary. In the old days of general poverty, when a sufficiency was so hard to come by, a difference in wages of fifty cents or a dollar had seemed so great to the artisan that it was hard for him to accept the idea of an economic equality in which such important distinctions should disappear. It was quite natural that it should be so. Men fight for crusts when they are starving, but they do not quarrel over bread at a banquet table. Somewhat so it befell when in the years after the Revolution material abundance and all the comforts of life came to be a matter of course for every one, and storing for the future was needless. Then it was that the hunger motive died out of human nature and covetousness as to material things, mocked to death by abundance, perished by atrophy, and the motives of the modern worker, the love of honor, the joy of beneficence, the delight of achievement, and the enthusiasm of humanity, became the impulses of the economic world. Labor was glorified, and the cringing wage-slave of the nineteenth century stood forth transfigured as the knight of humanity." . . .

EDWARD BELLAMY
"Looking Forward"*
1889

The first number of *The Nationalist* contained an article by Bellamy succinctly setting forth his philosophy.

It is an indication of the ripeness of the times for the National plan of industry that the predominating economic facts and tendencies of the epoch so lend themselves to its aims as to leave no question as to the practical policy of the movement. In order to realize in due time the Nationalist idea it is only necessary to take judicious advantage of the contemporary tendency toward the consolidation of capital and concentration of business control. The "Ship of State" is already being borne onward by a current which it is only needful to utilize in order to reach the desired haven. The progressive nationalization and municipalization of industries by substituting public control for the public advantage, in place of already highly centralized forms of corporate control for corporate advantage, is at once the logical and the inevitable policy of Nationalism.

In looking forward, however, to the future of the movement, and forecasting the work it may be able to accomplish, it is impossible not to recognize that more after all will depend upon its spirit than its method. Its method scarcely can be other than the one indicated, and this is so obviously the natural, and not an arbitrary method, as to give the best of ground for confidence that it is the right one. But an excellent method may be defeated by a bad spirit, while on the other hand, if the spirit be good and true, mistakes of method may be remedied, and will not prevent ultimate triumph. In offering some suggestions as to the spirit which should animate the Nationalist movement I do but describe what seems to me the characteristics of its present spirit and of the men and women engaged in it.

The first of these characteristics is unselfishness.

* *The Nationalist*, Vol. I, No. 1 (December, 1889).

The sentiment of human brotherhood which is the animating principle of Nationalism is a religion in itself, and to understand it in its full significance implies a sense of consecration on the part of those who devote themselves to it. Nationalism, is indeed, based also upon the soundest of economic laws; the principle of fraternal co-operation is as certainly the only true science of wealth-production, as it is the only moral basis for society; but the latter is so much more the important consideration that even if a brotherly relation with our fellowmen could only be attained by the sacrifice of wealth, not the less would the true Nationalist seek it. The ultimate triumph of Nationalism demands as its first condition that it be kept upon the high moral ground it now occupies, and retain as its chief motive that pure and uncompromising enthusiasm of humanity which now animates it.

The second of the characteristics essential to the spirit of Nationalism, if it is to succeed speedily, is a tolerant and charitable attitude toward the critical and the indifferent—toward our opponents.

There is the more need of dwelling on this point as there seems to be, curiously enough, something in the advocacy of reforms which tends to develop an intolerant and uncharitable spirit toward those who are not yet believers. And yet what could be more exquisitely absurd in itself than that spirit, on the part of a reformer, or more calculated to defeat his own supposed end. If it be true, as the tone of some reformers toward the rest of the world seems to indicate, that they are hopelessly better than the general mass of men, what expectation can they have of the success of their reform, since it can only succeed by converting these bad people? Until we call a man names, there is always a chance that we may convert him but, afterwards, none at all. And not only that, but we are not helping our case with the by-standers. It would seem plain that only reformers who have all the converts they need can afford to call their opponents names. There is especially one form of denunciation which Nationalists have thus far left to other sorts of social reformers, and it is hoped we may continue to. This is the denunciation of the wealthy in the supposed interests of the poor. Nothing could be more unjust and senseless. The rich could not, however disposed, abolish or greatly lessen poverty so long as the present industrial system remains. It is the system that is to be attacked and not individuals whose condition, whether of riches or poverty, merely illustrates its results. Of course, there are many rich men who have become so by vicious methods and these merit personal condemnation, but there are probably more to whose enterprise and leadership the community owes much of the little wealth and comfort it has. It is a very barbarous and wasteful sort of leadership, to be sure, and one for which we hope to substitute a mode of organizing industry infinitely more humane and efficient. But meanwhile let us not fall into the mistake of those who rant against capitalists in general, as if, pending the introduction of a better system, they were not,—no doubt selfishly, but yet in fact—performing a necessary function to keep the present system going.

It is the distinguishing quality of Nationalism and one on which its near success largely depends that it places the whole subject of industrial and social reform upon a broad National basis, viewing it not from the position or with the prejudices of any one group of men, but from the ground of a common citizenship, humanity and morality. Nationalism is not a class movement; it is a citizens' movement. It represents peculiarly neither men nor women, North nor South, black nor white, poor nor rich, educated nor ignorant, employers nor employed, but all equally; holding that all of us alike, whatever our label may be, are victims in body, mind or soul, in one way or another, of the present barbarous industrial and social arrangements, and that we are all equally interested, if not for our physical, yet for our moral advantage, if not for ourselves, yet for our children, in breaking the meshes which entangle us and struggling upward to a higher, nobler, happier plane of existence.

The third of the characteristics essential to the spirit of Nationalism—patriotism.

There are social reformers who believe, the less one's devotion to his own country and countrymen, the better he will love other countries and humanity at large, as if a man were usually found to be a better neighbor in proportion as he neglects his own family. This is a belief which Nationalists utterly repudiate. The very word Nationalism is an appeal to love of country. Patriotism, though so often misdirected, is the grandest and most potent form under which the enthusiasm of humanity has yet shown itself capable of moving great masses, and in its spirit is contained the promise and potency of the world-embracing love in which it shall some day merge. Social reforms must follow National lines and will succeed as they are able to adapt themselves to National conditions and sentiments and identify themselves with National traditions and aspirations. We as Americans do not, I am sure, love mankind any the less for the aspiration we cherish that, in the present world-wide movement for a better social order, America may maintain and justify that leadership of the nations which she assumed a century ago.

The fourth characteristic of the Nationalist movement which it must retain as a condition of success is its present spirit of conservatism as to methods, combined with uncompromising fidelity to ends.

Evolution, not revolution, orderly and progressive development, not precipitate and hazardous experiment, is our true policy. The intoxication of a mighty hope should not tempt us to forget that the success of the great reform to which we have set our hands depends not so much upon winning the applause of fellow-enthusiasts, welcome as this may be, as upon gaining and keeping the confidence of the law-abiding masses of the American people. To this end we have need to be careful that no party or policy of disorder or riot finds any countenance from us. It is my own belief that on account of its peculiar adaptation to present economic and social states and tendencies Nationalism is destined to move rapidly, but it is for this very reason that prudence and conservatism are called for on the part of those identified with it. Our mistakes alone can hinder our cause.

WILLIAM DEAN HOWELLS
A *Traveler from Altruria**
1894

"I could not give you a clear account of the present state of things in my country," the Altrurian began, "without first telling you something of our conditions before the time of our Evolution. It seems to be the law of all life that nothing can come to fruition without dying and seeming to make an end. It must be sown in corruption before it can be raised in incorruption. The truth itself must perish to our senses before it can live to our souls; the Son of Man must suffer upon the cross before we can know the Son of God.

"It was so with His message to the world, which we received in the old time as an ideal realized by the earliest Christians, who loved one another and who had all things common. The apostle cast away upon our heathen coasts won us with the story of this first Christian republic, and he established a commonwealth of peace and good-will among us in its likeness. That commonwealth perished, just as its prototype perished, or seemed to perish; and long ages of civic and economic warfare succeeded, when every man's hand was against his neighbor, and might was the rule that got itself called right. Religion ceased to be the hope of this world, and became the vague promise of the next. We descended into the valley of the shadow, and dwelt amid chaos for ages before we groped again into the light.

"The first glimmerings were few and indistinct, but men formed themselves about the luminous points here and there, and, when these broke and dispersed into lesser gleams, still men formed themselves about each of them. There arose a system of things better, indeed, than that darkness, but full of war and lust and greed, in which the weak rendered homage to the strong, and served them in the field and in the camp, and the strong in turn gave the weak protection against the other strong. It was a juggle in which the weak did not see that their safety was, after all, from

* Pp. 175–180, 183–186, 190–192, 203–205, 211–212.

themselves; but it was an image of peace, however false and fitful, and it endured for a time. It endured for a limited time, if we measure by the life of the race; it endured for an unlimited time if we measure by the lives of the men who were born and died while it endured.

"But that disorder, cruel and fierce and stupid, which endured because it sometimes masked itself as order, did at last pass away. Here and there one of the strong overpowered the rest; then the strong became fewer and fewer, and in their turn they all yielded to a supreme lord, and throughout the land there was one rule, as it was called then, or one misrule, as we should call it now. This rule, or this misrule, continued for ages more; and again, in the immortality of the race, men toiled and struggled, and died without the hope of better things.

"Then the time came when the long nightmare was burst with the vision of a future in which all men were the law, and not one man, or any less number of men than all.

"The poor dumb beast of humanity rose, and the throne tumbled, and the sceptre was broken, and the crown rolled away into that darkness of the past. We thought that heaven had descended to us, and that liberty, equality, and fraternity were ours. We could not see what should again alienate us from one another, or how one brother could again oppress another. With a free field and no favor we believed we should prosper on together, and there would be peace and plenty for all. We had the republic again after so many ages now, and the republic, as we knew it in our dim annals, was brotherhood and universal happiness. All but a very few, who prophesied evil of our lawless freedom, were wrapped in a delirium of hope. Men's minds and men's hands were suddenly released to an activity unheard of before. Invention followed invention; our rivers and seas became the warp of commerce where the steam-sped shuttles carried the woof of enterprise to and fro with tireless celerity; machines to save labor multiplied themselves as if they had been procreative forces, and wares of every sort were produced with incredible swiftness and cheapness. Money seemed to flow from the ground; vast fortunes 'rose like an exhalation,' as your Milton says.

"At first we did not know that they were the breath of the nethermost pits of hell, and that the love of money, which was becoming universal with us, was filling the earth with the hate of men. It was long before we came to realize that in the depths of our steamships were those who fed the fires with their lives, and that our mines from which we dug our wealth were the graves of those who had died to the free light and air, without finding the rest of death. We did not see that the machines for saving labor were monsters that devoured women and children, and wasted men at the bidding of the power which no man must touch.

"That is, we thought we must not touch it, for it called itself prosperity and wealth and the public good, and it said that it gave bread, and it impudently bade the toiling myriads consider what would become of them if it took away their means of wearing themselves out in its service. It demanded of the state absolute immunity and absolute impunity, the right to do its will wherever and however it would, without question from the people who were the final law. It had its way, and under its rule we became the richest people under the sun. The Accumulation, as we called this power, because we feared to call it by its true name, rewarded its own with gains of twenty, of a hundred, of a thousand per cent., and to satisfy its need, to produce the labor that operated its machines, there came into existence a hapless race of men who bred their kind for its service, and whose little ones were its prey almost from their cradles. Then the infamy became too great, and the law, the voice of the people, so long guiltily silent, was lifted in behalf of those who had no helper. The Accumulation came under control for the first time, and could no longer work its slaves twenty hours a day amid perils to life and limb from its machinery and in conditions that forbade them decency and morality. The time of a hundred and a thousand per cent. passed; but still the Accumulation demanded immunity and impunity, and, in spite of its conviction of the enormities it had practised, it declared itself the only means of civilization and progress. It began to give out that it was timid, though its history was full of the boldest frauds and crimes, and it threatened to withdraw itself if it were ruled or even crossed; and again it had its way, and we seemed to prosper more and more. The land was filled with cities where the rich flaunted their splendor in palaces, and the poor swarmed in squalid tenements. The country was drained of its life and force, to feed the centres of commerce and industry. The whole land was bound together with a network of iron roads that linked the factories and foundries to the fields and mines, and blasted the landscape with the enterprise that spoiled the lives of men.

"Then, all at once, when its work seemed perfect and its dominion sure, the Accumulation was stricken with consciousness of the lie always at its heart. It had hitherto cried out for a free field and no favor, for unrestricted competition; but, in truth, it had never prospered except as a monopoly. Whenever and wherever competition had play there had been nothing but disaster to the rival enterprises, till one rose over the rest. Then there was prosperity for that one.

"The Accumulation began to act upon its new consciousness. The iron roads united; the warring industries made peace, each kind under a single leadership. Monopoly, not competition, was seen to be the beneficent means of distributing the favors and blessings of the Accumulation to mankind. But, as before, there was alternately a glut and dearth of things, and it often happened that when starving men went ragged through the streets the storehouses were piled full of rotting harvests that the farmers toiled from dawn till dusk to grow, and the warehouses fed the moth with the stuffs that the operative had woven his life into at his loom. Then followed, with a blind and mad succession, a time of famine, when money could not buy the super-abundance that vanished, none knew how or why.

"The money itself vanished from time to time, and disappeared into the vaults of the Accumulation, for no better reason than that for which it poured itself out at other times. Our theory was that the people—that is to say, the government of the people—made the people's money, but, as a matter of fact, the Accumulation made it and controlled it and juggled with it; and now you saw it, and now you did not see it. The government made gold coins, but the people had nothing but the paper money that the Accumulation made. But whether there was scarcity or plenty, the failures went on with a continuous ruin that nothing could check, while our larger economic life proceeded in a series of violent shocks, which we called financial panics, followed by long periods of exhaustion and recuperation.

There was no law in our economy, but as the Accumulation had never cared for the nature of law, it did not trouble itself for its name in our order of things. It had always bought the law it needed for its own use, first through the voter at the polls in the more primitive days, and then, as civilization advanced, in the legislatures and the courts. But the corruption even of these methods was far surpassed when the era of consolidation came, and the necessity for statutes and verdicts and decisions became more stringent. . . .

"There had been, from the beginning, an almost ceaseless struggle between the Accumulation and the proletariate. The Accumulation always said that it was the best friend of the proletariate, and it denounced, through the press which it controlled, the proletarian leaders who taught that it was the enemy of the proletariate, and who stirred up strikes and tumults of all sorts, for higher wages and fewer hours. But the friend of the proletariate, whenever occasion served, treated the proletariate like a deadly enemy. In seasons of overproduction, as it was called, it locked the workmen out or laid them off, and left their families to starve, or ran light work and claimed the credit of public benefactors for running at all. It sought every chance to reduce wages; it had laws passed to forbid or cripple the workmen in their strikes; and the judges convicted them of conspiracy, and wrested the statutes to their hurt, in cases where there had been no thought of embarrassing them, even among the legislators. God forbid that you should ever come to such a pass in America; but, if you ever should, God grant that you may find your way out as simply as we did at last when freedom had perished in everything but name among us, and justice had become a mockery.

"The Accumulation had advanced so smoothly, so lightly, in all its steps to the supreme power, and had at last so thoroughly quelled the uprisings of the proletariate, that it forgot one thing: it forgot the despised and neglected suffrage. The ballot, because it had been so easy to annul its effect, had been left in the people's hands; and when, at last, the leaders of the proletariate ceased to counsel strikes, or any form of resistance to the Accumulation that could be tormented into the likeness of insurrection against the government, and began to urge them to attack it in the political way, the deluge that swept the Accumulation out of existence came trickling and creeping over the land. It appeared first in the country, a spring from the ground; then it gathered head in the villages; then it swelled to a torrent in the cities. I cannot stay to trace its course; but suddenly, one day, when the Accumulation's abuse of a certain power became too gross, it was voted out of that power. You will perhaps be interested to know that it was with the telegraphs that the rebellion against the Accumulation began, and the government was forced, by the overwhelming majority which the proletariate sent to our parliament, to assume a function which the Accumulation had impudently usurped. Then the transportation of smaller and more perishable wares—"

"Yes," a voice called—"express business. Go on!"

"Was legislated a function of the post-office," the Altrurian went on. "Then all transportation was taken into the hands of the political government, which had always been accused of great corruption in its administration, but which showed itself immaculately pure compared with the Accumulation. The common ownership of mines necessarily followed, with an allotment of lands to any one who wished to live by tilling the land; but not a foot of the land was remitted to private hands for the purposes of selfish pleasure or the exclusion of any other from the landscape. As all business had been gathered into the grasp of the Accumulation, and the manufacture of everything they used and the production of everything that they ate was in the control of the Accumulation, its transfer to the government was the work of a single clause in the statute.

"The Accumulation, which had treated the first menaces of resistance with contempt, awoke to its peril too late. When it turned to wrest the suffrage from the proletariate, at the first election where it attemped to make head against them, it was simply snowed under, as your picturesque phrase is. The Accumulation had no voters, except the few men at its head and the creatures devoted to it by interest and ignorance. It seemed, at one moment, as if it would offer an armed resistance to the popular will, but, happily, that moment of madness passed. Our Evolution was accomplished without a drop of blood-shed, and the first great political brotherhood, the commonwealth of Altruria, was founded.

"I wish that I had time to go into a study of some of the curious phases of the transformation from a civility in which the people lived *upon* each other to one in which they lived *for* each other. There is a famous passage in the inaugural message of our first Altrurian president which compares the new civic consciousness with that of a disembodied spirit released to the life beyond this and freed from all the selfish cares and greeds of the flesh. But perhaps I shall give a sufficiently clear notion of the triumph of the

change among us when I say that within half a decade after the fall
of the old plutocratic oligarchy one of the chief directors of the
Accumulation publicly expressed his gratitude to God that the Accumulation had passed away forever. You will realize the importance of such an expression in recalling the declarations some
of your slave-holders have made since the Civil War, that they
would not have slavery restored for any earthly consideration. . . .

"And so," the Altrurian continued, "when the labor of the community was emancipated from the bondage of the false to the free
service of the true, it was also, by an inevitable implication, dedicated to beauty and rescued from the old slavery to the ugly, the
stupid, and the trivial. The thing that was honest and useful became, by the operation of a natural law, a beautiful thing.

"Once we had not time enough to make things beautiful, we were
so overworked in making false and hideous things to sell; but now we
had all the time there was, and a glad emulation arose among the
trades and occupations to the end that everything done should
be done finely as well as done honestly. The artist, the man of
genius, who worked from the love of his work, became the normal
man, and in the measure of his ability and of his calling each
wrought in the spirit of the artist. We got back the pleasure of
doing a thing beautifully, which was God's primal blessing upon all
His working children, but which we had lost in the horrible days
of our need and greed. There is not a working-man within the
sound of my voice but has known this divine delight, and would
gladly know it always if he only had the time. Well, now we had
the time, the Evolution had given us the time, and in all Altruria
there was not a furrow driven or a swath mown, not a hammer
struck on house or on ship, not a stitch sewn or a stone laid, not a
line written or a sheet printed, not a temple raised or an engine
built, but it was done with an eye to beauty as well as to use.

"As soon as we were freed from the necessity of preying upon one
another, we found that *there was no hurry*. The good work would
wait to be well done; and one of the earliest effects of the Evolution
was the disuse of the swift trains which had traversed the continent,
night and day, that one man might overreach another, or make
haste to undersell his rival, or seize some advantage of him, or plot
some profit to his loss. Nine-tenths of the railroads, which in the old
times had ruinously competed, and then, in the hands of the Accumulation, had been united to impoverish and oppress the people,

fell into disuse. The commonwealth operated the few lines that were necessary for the collection of materials and the distribution of man-ufactures, and for pleasure travel and the affairs of state; but the roads that had been built to invest capital, or parallel other roads, or 'make work,' as it was called, or to develop resources, or boom localities, were suffered to fall into ruin; the rails were stripped from the landscape, which they had bound as with shackles, and the road-beds became highways for the use of kindly neighborhoods, or nature recovered them wholly and hid the memory of their former abuse in grass and flowers and wild vines. The ugly towns that they had forced into being, as Frankenstein was fashioned, from the materials of the charnel, and that had no life in or from the good of the community, soon tumbled into decay. The adminis-tration used parts of them in the construction of the villages in which the Altrurians now mostly live; but generally these towns were built of materials so fraudulent, in form so vile, that it was judged best to burn them. In this way their sites were at once purified and obliterated.

"We had, of course, a great many large cities under the old egoistic conditions, which increased and fattened upon the country, and fed their cancerous life with fresh infusions of its blood. We had several cities of half a million, and one of more than a million; we had a score of them with a population of a hundred thousand or more. We were very proud of them, and vaunted them as a proof of our unparalleled prosperity, though really they never were any-thing but congeries of millionaires and the wretched creatures who served them and supplied them. Of course, there was everywhere the appearance of enterprise and activity, but it meant final loss for the great mass of the business men, large and small, and final gain for the millionaires. These and their parasites dwelt together, the rich starving the poor and the poor plundering and mis-governing the rich; and it was the intolerable suffering in the cities that chiefly hastened the fall of the old Accumulation and the rise of the commonwealth." . . .

It is impossible to follow closely the course of the Altrurian's account of his country, which grew more and more incredible as he went on, and implied every insulting criticism of ours. Some one asked him about war in Altruria, and he said: "The very name of our country implies the absence of war. At the time of the Evolution our country bore to the rest of our continent the same relative proportion that your country bears to your continent. The egoistic nations to the north and the south of us entered into an offensive and defensive alliance to put down the new altruistic commonwealth, and declared war against us. Their forces were met at the frontier by our entire population in arms, and full of the martial spirit bred of the constant hostilities of the competitive and monopolistic epoch just ended. Negotiations began in the face of the imposing demonstration we made, and we were never afterward molested by our neighbors, who finally yielded to the spectacle of our civilization and united their political and social fate with ours. At present, our whole continent is Altrurian. For a long time we kept up a system of coast defences, but it is also a long time since we abandoned these; for it is a maxim with us that where every citizen's life is a pledge of the public safety, that country can never be in danger of foreign enemies.

"In this, as in all other things, we believe ourselves the true followers of Christ, whose doctrine we seek to make our life as He made it His. We have several forms of ritual, but no form of creed, and our religious differences may be said to be aesthetic and temperamental rather than theological and essential. We have no denominations, for we fear in this, as in other matters, to give names to things lest we should cling to the names instead of the things. We love the realities, and for this reason we look at the life of a man rather than his profession for proof that he is a religious man.

"I have been several times asked, during my sojourn among you, what are the sources of compassion, of sympathy, of humanity, of charity with us, if we have not only no want, or fear of want, but not even any economic inequality. I suppose this is because you are so constantly struck by the misery arising from economic inequality and want, or the fear of want, among yourselves, that you instinctively look in that direction. But have you ever seen sweeter compassion, tenderer sympathy, warmer humanity, heavenlier charity than that shown in the family where all are economically equal and no one can want while any other has to give? Altruria, I say again, is a family, and, as we are mortal, we are still subject to those nobler sorrows which God has appointed to men, and which are so different from the squalid accidents that they have made for themselves. Sickness and death call out the most angelic ministries of love; and those who wish to give themselves to others may do so without hinderance from those cares, and even those duties, resting upon men where each must look out first for himself and for his own. Oh, believe me, you can know nothing of the divine rapture of self-sacrifice while you must dread the sacrifice of another in it. You are not *free*, as we are, to do everything for others, for it is your *duty* to do rather for those of your own household! . . .

"The greatest distinction which any one can enjoy with us is to have found out some new and signal way of serving the community; and then it is not good form for him to seek recognition. The doing any fine thing is the purest pleasure it can give; applause flatters, but it hurts, too, and our benefactors, as we call them, have learned to shun it.

"We are still far from thinking our civilization perfect; but we are sure that our civic ideals are perfect. What we have already accomplished is to have given a whole continent perpetual peace; to have founded an economy in which there is no possibility of want; to have killed out political and social ambition; to have disused money and eliminated chance; to have realized the brotherhood of the race, and to have outlived the fear of death."

The Altrurian suddenly stopped with these words and sat down. He had spoken a long time, and with a fulness which my report gives little notion of; but, though most of his cultivated listeners were weary, and a good many ladies had left their seats and gone back to the hotel, not one of the natives, or the work-people of any sort, had stirred; now they remained a moment motionless and silent before they rose from all parts of the field and shouted: "Go on! Don't stop! Tell us all about it!"

I saw Reuben Camp climb the shoulders of a big fellow near where the Altrurian had stood; he waved the crowd to silence with out-spread arms. "He isn't going to say anything more; he's tired. But if any man don't think he's got his dollar's worth, let him walk up to the door and the ticket-agent will refund him his money."

The crowd laughed, and some one shouted: "Good for you, Reub!"

Camp continued: "But our friend here will shake the hand of any man, woman, or child that wants to speak to him; and you needn't wipe it on the grass first, either. He's a *man!* And I want to say that he's going to spend the next week with us, at my mother's house, and we shall be glad to have you call."

The crowd, the rustic and ruder part of it, cheered and cheered till the mountain echoes answered; then a railroader called for three times three, with a tiger, and got it. The guests of the hotel broke away and went toward the house over the long shadows of the meadow. . . .

CHAPTER VI

CHRISTIAN SOCIALISTS

Christianity without Socialism we believe to be a lie; Socialism without Christianity we consider a fatal mistake.

W. D. P. BLISS,
Dawn, 1891

If the state would be saved from the wrath of the rising social passion, it must believe in Christ as its Lord, and translate His sacrifice into its laws. Our institutions must become the organized expression of Christ's law of love, if the state is to obey the coming social conscience that is to command great moral revolutions in political thought and action. For society is the organized sacrifice of the people.

GEORGE HERRON,
The Christian State, 1895

We have accepted the law of love, the standard of Christ, the teaching of the same Spirit that led Christ and his disciples to have "all things in common." It is the sure way out of selfishness.

Circular on the Christian Commonwealth Colony, 1896

The religion of Jesus, depending as it did upon the experiences and intuitions of the unselfish enthusiasms, could not possibly be accepted or understood generally by a world which tolerated a social system based upon fratricidal struggle as the condition of existence. Prophets, messiahs, seers, and saints might indeed for themselves see God face to face, but it was impossible that there should be any apprehension of God as Christ saw him until social justice had brought in brotherly love.

EDWARD BELLAMY,
Equality, 1897

On February 18, 1889 a small group of clergymen, several of them active members of the Boston Nationalist Club, met at Boston's Tremont Temple to discuss whether they should form a separate Christian Socialist organization. They had no quarrel with Nationalism; they regarded Bellamy's proposed cooperative commonwealth as a return to the ideals of Christ and the Apostles. But they thought that as Christians they should be bound to no specific socialist doctrine or movement. A week later they launched the Society of Christian Socialists, the first such society ever created in the United States.

Shortly afterwards the Society issued a "Declaration of Principles" that was inclusive and general enough to appeal to all men of good will. It blamed the evils of American life—the concentration of wealth, ubiquitous poverty, moral debauchery, powerlessness of labor—on "economic individualism," and called for the establishment of a system of "social, political and industrial relations . . . based on the Fatherhood of God and the Brotherhood of Man, in the spirit and according to the teachings of Jesus Christ." Precisely what those relations should be the Declaration did not say. It affirmed only that the "aim of Socialism is embraced in the aim of Christianity," that "the teachings of Jesus Christ lead directly to some specific form or forms of Socialism, that, therefore, the Church has a definite duty upon this matter, and must, in simple obedience to Christ, apply itself to the realization of the social principle of Christianity." The Declaration, in short, was as mild and charitable as the Sermon on the Mount. Yet the members of the Society were taking a bold and provocative step. They knew better than anyone how conservative the Christian churches were, and by equating—worse, identifying—socialism and Christianity, they were advancing beyond dissent to the impermissible. They were inviting church officialdom to treat them as the Pharisees had treated Christ.

The emergence of Christian Socialism was the logical culmination of a leftward movement that had been gathering force in several Protestant denominations. Its trajectory can be traced in the career of the leader and chief organizer of the Christian Socialists, William Dwight Porter Bliss. Bliss was born in 1856 in Constantinople, Turkey, where his parents were missionaries, and came to the United States to complete his education at Amherst College and Hartford Theological Seminary. In 1882 he took up his duties as a minister of a Congregational church in Denver and enthusiastically preached the Social Gospel. The Social Gospel had arisen in the years following the Civil War when a number of clergymen began to realize that the churches' preoccupation with old, hard-bitten orthodoxies and literal interpretations of Scripture was increasingly irrelevant in an industrial and urban society. These clergymen maintained that man should be defined by his capacity for good as well as for sin, that God was concerned about man's temporal life as well as the incorporeal, and that, consequently, the churches should assume responsibility for man's ethical as well as for "spiritual" well-being.

The pioneers of the Social Gospel were far from progressive in their social philosophy, however. The main function of Christian ethics, as they conceived it, was to uphold the established order by, among other things, convincing the poor that they, too, had a vested interest in it and should quiescently submit to its dictates. "It is nothing that in great poverty single women or women having families are brought into conditions of unspeakable severity," Horace Bushnell, one of the first advocates of the Social Gospel, wrote in 1869, warning against legislation to reduce work hours for women: "we do not expect them to sink mournfully or moaningly under their lot, but to bravely bear, and dig, and climb till they are free. . . . There is no such possibility as a legally appointed rate of wages; market price is the only scale of earnings possible for women as for men." The ministers of the Social Gospel, then, were as committed as businessmen to the dogmas of classical economics and the morality of Malthus and Bentham. To their minds any attempts to succour the poor by government legislation only encouraged sloth and improvidence and penalized thrift and hard work. Property-owners, as another prominent Social Gospeler, Edward Beecher, put it, "are by no means desirous of making a division of their possessions for the benefit of the vagabonds and tramps, the drunkards and drones, the shiftless and criminal classes, who alone furnish permanent followers to ridiculous foreigners who have contrived to 'loaf' from Europe to America."

By the time William Bliss graduated from Hartford Theological Seminary, however, a more progressive reading of the Social Gospel had appeared. An increasing body of ministers were arguing that society owed something to individuals victimized by misfortune or by the rapacities of the rich, and that churches in particular should speak out in behalf of those condemned to toil for long hours at low pay. The most eloquent and influential representative of the progressive school was Washington Gladden who had witnessed the labor struggles of the 1870s and early 1880s from his Congregational pastorates in Springfield, Massachusetts, Columbus, Ohio, and elsewhere, and who took up the workers' cause when it was least popular to do so. The "wage system," he said, defying all the laws of political economy, "when it rests on competition as its sole basis, is anti-social and anti-Christian." In strong language he denied that labor—"the life of the nation"—was "a commodity to be bought in the cheapest market and sold in the dearest." Still, he was a moderate, not a radical. He assumed that the system, despite some serious flaws, was a just and good one. What it needed was an ample dose of compassion.

Progressivism also found its way into the centers of Christian learning. It became commonplace for the more prestigious seminaries—Union Theological, Princeton, Andover, Hartford—to offer courses on "Applied Christianity," "Christian Ethics," labor, industrialism, and social problems in general. More and more frequently colleges and seminaries heard lectures from such avant-garde Christian economists and sociologists as John R. Commons and Richard T. Ely, who, like Washington Gladden, contended that society was more than an aggregate of self-regarding individuals; it was in fact the source of individual rights and privileges and could, therefore, justifiably limit them as it saw fit. They also affirmed their sympathy with labor unions (labor being their special area of knowledge). Commons advised ministers to join unions in order to understand the workers' point of view. Ely referred to organized labor as "the strongest force outside the Christian Church making for the practical recognition of human brotherhood."

But the importance of progressivism within Protestantism as a whole should not be exaggerated. The largest denominations— Baptist, Methodist, Presbyterian, and Lutheran—were unimpressed by the Social Gospel and rejected progressivism. It was the Episcopal Church, the wealthiest of the Protestant churches and the most conservative in membership, that contained the greatest number of progressives. Episcopalianism embodied, as no other denomination did, the corporate, paternalistic, Anglo-Catholic traditions of the past. Furthermore, its independent-minded ministers, rectors, wardens, etc., could speak out freely since they were not directly answerable to the congregations over which they presided. The progressive Social Gospel penetrated the Episcopal Church so deeply that even its hierarchs came to recognize that (in the words of the General Convention of 1883) "the workers and the suffering classes" were "victims of social wrong, of unequal law, of intemperance in drink . . . and sometimes of merciless wealth." Several years later, the New York Episcopal clergy established an openly pro-labor group: the Church Association for the Advancement of the Interests of Labor (CAIL), which, virtually alone among Christian organizations, won the trust of the city's unions.

In 1886 Bliss gave up his Denver congregation and became an Episcopalian, not only because the Episcopal Church provided a more congenial home for radicals like himself, but also because it held out the best hope of achieving Christian unity, the ancient ecumenical ideal of "one body and one spirit." (Catholic unity he dismissed as coercive and authoritarian.) As an Episcopal minister in South Boston Bliss carried out the injunctions laid down by the CAIL group and sided with the workers of his parish against their employers (many of whom were Episcopalians). He served as a delegate to the 1887 Knights of Labor Convention and the next year turned down an offer by the Massachusetts Labor Party to be its candidate for lieutenant-governor. Meanwhile, he sedulously schooled himself in socialism, particularly in the writings of the English Christian Socialists, Charles Kingsley and Frederick Maurice; the Fabians (who had founded their first society in 1884); and assorted American radicals of a Christian bent, from Richard Ely and Henry George to Laurence Gronlund. The turning point in Bliss's career came in 1888 when he read *Looking Backward* and beheld the cooperative commonwealth.

Bliss was now no longer content with the half-way measures espoused by progressives and organizations like CAIL, though he continued to support them. He felt that what was needed was the total reconstruction of society; the minimal condition of equality and brotherhood was the nationalization of the means of production and distribution. And it was with this conviction that he and his confreres created the Society of Christian Socialists.

The members of the Society were expected to live like primitive Christians, according to a set of informal rules of conduct pre-scribed by Bliss. Their personal wants were to be simple and un-encumbered; they were to be at once infinitely demanding of themselves and infinitely charitable toward others; and they were to spend their spare time working for the cause of socialism, preaching, writing, educating, organizing, defending unions and the poor, struggling always for immediate political and economic reforms while keeping in mind the ultimate end: the cooperative commonwealth. Bliss himself exemplified the kind of life he recommended. In 1890 he founded a small Boston labor church, the Mission of the Carpenter, where social workers, emancipated women, union men, the poor, and distinguished outsiders such as Gronlund, Bellamy, and Howells gathered regularly for communal suppers of ham and pickles and for discussions long into the night.

Serving his church (itself a full-time job) was only one of Bliss's manifold activities; he was a man of prodigious energy. He edited the Christian Socialist journal, *Dawn*, traveled about extensively to speak before church and lay groups, helped found new organizations (among them, the American Fabian Society [whose paper, *American Fabian*, he also edited]), and wrote a farrago of articles on socialism and an occasional book as well.*

Thanks largely to Bliss's efforts and to the influence of *Dawn*, which was widely read if not widely bought, chapters of the Society of Christian Socialists sprang up in various parts of the country. Usually the Boston experience was repeated elsewhere: Christian Socialists and Bellamyites, being ideologically akin, tended to work closely together. Their objective was the same: to establish the cooperative commonwealth; so was their strategy: to permeate other groups, convince men to change their ways, or at least shift their political loyalties, and collaborate where possible with insurgent movements. The Society of Christian Socialists came out emphatically for the Populists, for the beleaguered strikers at Homestead and Pullman, for Coxey's Army, and for federal measures to alleviate the effects of the 1893 depression.

The Christian Socialists expected church conservatives to treat them like pariahs. They did not expect the antipathy of the progressives, to whom the word "socialism" summoned up images of partisanship, demagoguery, and class warfare. It did not matter that

---

* One of his books, *The Encyclopedia of Social Reform*, was a massive, 1500 page volume, containing popular yet scholarly accounts of the major social issues and prominent figures of the day. Though it was a cooperative effort, Bliss did most of the work on it himself. The *Encyclopedia* was a pioneer in its genre, a crude anticipation of the *Encyclopedia of the Social Sciences*, published some 40 years later.

the Christian Socialists were gradualist and peaceable to a fault. The fact that they called themselves socialists was enough to place them outside the pale of legitimacy, and the progressives continued to hope that Bliss and his brethren would return to the fold. This hope was largely borne out in the course of the 1890s. The polarization in American society, the development of what appeared to be a full-blown class conflict, confronted the Christian Socialists with an increasingly exigent choice: whether to accept class conflict with all its ugly implications, or to draw back and counsel patience and reconciliation. Most chose the latter course, and the movement, bereft of its former militancy, withered away. In 1896 Bliss ceased to edit *Dawn* (which promptly folded) and the *American Fabian* (which lasted until 1900), and gave up the Church of the Carpenter. Thereafter he was involved less in socialist and more in church affairs. He drew closer and closer to the progressives, and by the turn of the century he could no longer be distinguished from them.

One group of Christian Socialists, however, took an entirely different route: they revived the communitarian idea. Their spiritual leader, Ralph Albertson, a young Congregational minister from Springfield, Ohio, was convinced that Bliss and Bellamy were on the wrong track. Their error, he thought, lay in assuming that until true Christians inherited the state and the forces of capitalist production, they would have to go on living un-Christian lives. The Kingdom of Heaven, he concluded, must be established at once ("If not now, when?"). A community must be built where selfishness, competitiveness, and power would be replaced by Christ's love. The redemption of all must begin with the redemption of a few. Joining the head of a tiny Christian temperance colony and a contingent of subscribers, some of them affluent, Albertson late in 1896 planted the Christian Commonwealth Colony in an uninhabited plantation, half hillside, half swamp, several miles from Columbus, Georgia. There a "visible Kingdom of God on earth" was to be wrested by "purchase out of the hands of the selfish and given to the meek."

The Christian Commonwealth Colony encountered the same experiences that all of its communitarian predecessors had. Its 150 or so members had to struggle against a bitterly hostile environment; to create a viable division of labor and system of government; most of all, to avoid internal strains and conflicts. To compound their difficulties, they set exceedingly high standards for themselves. They resolved to live humbly and penuriously (though not ascetically) and to open the doors of the commonwealth to anyone who sought to enter, whatever his religion, however poor, wretched, aged, or diseased he was. Only one condition was asked—not required—of a newcomer, that he sign an oath promising to accept Christ's injunction that he love his neighbor, surrender his property (if he had any) to the community, yield himself up to "the cooperative life and labor of a local Christian Commonwealth," and work "for the production of goods for human happiness."

Remarkably, the Christian Commonwealth lasted four years. During that time it received wide attention and found support from reformers of all persuasions, including the mayors of Toledo and Cleveland; Jane Addams; Keir Hardie, the English socialist leader; and Henry Demarest Lloyd. Especially sympathetic to the colonists were the followers of Tolstoy, who agreed with their philosophy of self-renunciation. Tolstoy himself rejoiced "at the firmness of their views and beautiful expression of their thoughts." In the end it was overwhelming physical adversity that defeated them. When the crops began to fail in 1899, the colony entered a severe crisis; when a malaria epidemic struck later in the year its fate was sealed. And so in the spring of 1900 the Christian Commonwealth was dissolved, but not before its debts had been cleared and each family had received around eight dollars.

Some Christian Socialists, meanwhile, rejecting both progressivism and communitarianism, continued to move leftward and ended up in the Socialist Party. Certainly the outstanding person among this radical contingent was George Herron. It is a pity that no study has been written of Herron. Few men aroused the interest, the controversy, the degree of enmity and affection that he did in his time. Few did more than he to promote the cause of socialism. He was born in 1862 in Montezuma, Indiana, to pious Scotch parents. He was weaned on the Bible and the classics of Calvinist literature. At an early age he knew that his life would be a pilgrimage in search of the Kingdom of God. "I knew little of childhood play," he later recalled. "I could not dissociate a picket on a fence from the moral kingdom. God was my confidant. . . . The words and deeds of His servants were my recreation. Joseph and Elijah and Daniel, Cromwell and John Wesley and Charles Sumner were my imaginary playmates." Lacking much formal education he read

whatever he liked in sociology, philosophy, history, and belles-lettres
as well as theology. After attending Ripon Academy, Wisconsin,
and traveling abroad he entered the Congregational ministry. At
the age of twenty-one he married and became pastor of a church
in Lake City, Minnesota. As the years passed, his family grew
(there were five children) and he struck deep roots in his community. His career so far was typical of the career of thousands of
young Protestant ministers throughout the country.

Herron first came to the public's attention in 1890 when he
delivered a sermon, "The Message of Jesus to Men of Wealth,"
before a Congregational audience in Minneapolis. Though the
message was eloquent and passionate it was, on the whole, in-
offensive. Herron mostly wanted to remind the rich that they were
their brothers' keepers and their mission on earth was to raise
up the poor. The businessman in particular, he declared, had the
power "to be a savior of his fellow men." He went on to say—
and here he struck a potentially dangerous chord—that there would
some day be an accounting by the Christian commonwealth to
come.

Publication of "The Message of Jesus to Men of Wealth" caused
a stir in the West. Suddenly Herron stood out as a bright new
star in the Congregational firmament, and many churches offered
him their pulpits. He chose the First Congregational Church in
Burlington, Iowa, to which he moved late in 1891.

Among the members of the First Congregational Church was
Mrs. E. D. Rand, a wealthy widow, and her daughter, Carrie.
Before long, Herron was an intimate friend of the Rands and
was spending more time at their home than his own. Inevitably,
rumors circulated that he was having an affair with Carrie. Whether
this was true or not he and Carrie were, or were soon to be, in
love, and it was only a matter of time before his marriage broke
up. The Rands discovered a way out of the uncomfortable situation.
They all left Burlington in 1893, the year Mrs. Rand endowed a
chair of Applied Christianity for Herron at Iowa (later Grinnell)
College; Carrie at the same time became the college's dean of
women. Herron's new post gave him much greater freedom to
speak out in behalf of Christian Socialism. He was an enormously
popular teacher and sermonizer, and he spoke to large audiences
at the college and all over the country. He also brought out his

own journal, *The Kingdom,* an uncompromisingly radical exponent of the Social Gospel.

By the mid-1890s Herron was the best known advocate of Christian Socialism in America. And as his popularity increased so did his militancy. Against the background of depression and farmer-labor insurgency he called repeatedly for the nationalization of the trusts. Only then, he argued, would Christian morality prevail and the individuality of greed give way to the individuality of redemption through sacrifice exemplified by Christ. In the Christian commonwealth each person would be *authentically* himself by serving others. "The common ownership of the earth, with industrial democracy in production," Herron wrote in *The Kingdom,* "is the only ground upon which personal prosperity and liberty can be built, the only soil in which individuality may take root." But unlike the other Christian Socialists Herron did not easily forgive those who prevented the establishment of the Kingdom of Heaven. He directed his attacks less on the abstract ethics of capitalism and more on the capitalists themselves. He referred to the world of business as "unspeakably corrupt," the "chief danger to the nation," and the "greatest enemy of human life."

Accordingly, Herron enjoined Christians to recognize class exploitation as a fact and side with labor unequivocally against the "enemy of human life." Until "we all clearly see," he stated in language spoken by no other Christian Socialist,

> that what we call civilization is but the organized and legalized robbery of the common laborer, until we have a revolutionized comprehension of the fact that our churches and governments, our arts and literature, our education and philosophies, our morals and manners, are all more or less the expressions and deformities of this universal robbery, drawing their life and motives out of the vitals of the man who is down and underprivileged, out of his unpaid labor and exhausted life—until then, I say, our dreams and schemes of a common good or better society are but phillistine utopias, our social and industrial reforms but self-conceit.

The church was not exactly pleased by Herron's brand of Old Testament ferocity, his frontal assaults on the citadels of power. To plead with the rich to show mercy to the poor—as he had done in 1890—was one thing; to stir up the poor against the rich and proclaim the need for drastic action was quite another. Protestant officials closed their doors to him and anathematized his preachments.

Herron struck back at the churches, condemning them for allying with Mammon in a covenant of death. His indictment was sweeping and categorical.

> If I were to stand before any representative religious gathering in the land, and there preach actual obedience to the Sermon on the Mount, declaring that we must actually do what Jesus said, I would commit a religious scandal; I would henceforth be held in disrepute by the official religion that holds Jesus's name.

But, he went on, if

> the head of some great oil combination . . . though it had debauched our nation infinitely beyond the moral shocks of civil war, were to stand before any representative religious gathering with an endowment in his hand he would be greeted with an applause so vociferous as to partake of the morally idiotic.

Thanks to statements such as these most of the other Christian Socialists, chief among them W. D. P. Bliss, publicly dissociated themselves from Herron. His vehemence, in fact, helped drive them into the progressive camp.

By the end of the decade Herron's life had reached a crisis. His relations with Carrie Rand and his estrangement from his wife could no longer be concealed. His position at the college was untenable; he had become an embarrassment to the trustees. In 1899 he resigned under pressure, having concluded that academic freedom under capitalism was as much a farce as true Christianity. At the same time *The Kingdom* passed into other hands and ceased to be a forum for his ideas. In 1900 he openly proclaimed himself a member of the recently formed Social Democratic Party, led by Eugene V. Debs. Herron saw the Party as the unity of Christ and Marx, the fusion of moral right and economic necessity. In substance it stood for the Christian commonwealth; in form, for the workers' industrial state. "As American socialism goes on its way," he said in his speech opening the Party's Presidential campaign of 1900, "it will become a spiritual passion; not a cry for rights, but a call to elemental righteousness."

This commitment to a self-styled revolutionary party hardly endeared him to the church, and it can be safely assumed that his Congregational superiors were waiting for the right moment to declare him unfit for the ministry. That moment came in 1901, when his wife finally sued him for divorce, charging him with "cruelty culminating in desertion." The settlement they agreed on was generous. She received $60,000 for herself and their five children. It was Carrie Rand's entire fortune. (Mrs. Rand's was unaffected.) Two months after the divorce Herron and Carrie Rand were married by a Christian Socialist minister, who merely asked them if they took each other as husband and wife. Herron wanted it done that way to demonstrate that the most important personal decisions should be free of legalities and coercions. The ceremony (or absence of one) brought him into conflict with his superiors. The Council of Iowa Congregational Churches convened at once and removed him from the ministry, for having been "guilty of immoral and unChristian conduct." Herron accepted his martyrdom as though he had been fated for it. His sole concern was that he did not injure the socialist cause. As for him and his wife, they had already placed their lives "on the altar of human need."

Though Herron continued for some time to play a role in the emergent Socialist Party, his effectiveness was fatally impaired. He lacked an institutional base; he was merely another individual— gifted, eloquent, popular to be sure, but powerless. Moreover, he was not the sort of man who modestly gave himself to a cause. He was a leader whose ego demands were heightened by his peculiarly messianic sense of destiny. Several years after he lost his ministry he went to live in his mother-in-law's villa in Fiesole, outside Florence, Italy.* There he and his wife entertained intellectuals, artists, and statesmen from all over Europe, developing an acquaintanceship with them, as one scholar has put it, "probably

---

* It should be added that Mrs. Rand, before her death in 1905, set aside a trust fund in her will "to carry on and further the work to which I have devoted the later years of my life"—in other words, to advance the cause of socialism. The fund was used to establish the famous Rand School of Social Science of New York, which under a different name, exists down to the present. The Rand School accumulated an enormous library of social scientific and radical literature, and countless numbers of students and scholars have been served by it. Few socialist-inspired institutions have proved so durable.

unsurpassed by that of any other American." His new career set the stage for the final episode of his life: his service as an informal diplomat for President Wilson in the years immediately following World War I. By then his Christian Socialism was a faint echo of the distant past.

Declaration of Principles of the Christian Socialist Movement
1889

Following is the Declaration that launched the movement in Boston on April 15, 1889.

To exalt the principles that all rights and powers are the gifts of God, not for the receiver's use only, but for the benefit of all; to magnify the oneness of the human family, and to lift mankind to the highest plane of privilege, we band ourselves together under the name of Christian Socialists.

I. We hold that God is the source and guide of all human progress, and we believe that all social, political and industrial should be based on the Fatherhood of God and the Brotherhood of Man, in the spirit and according to the teachings of Jesus Christ.

II. We hold that the present commercial and industrial system is not thus based, but rests rather on economic individualism, the results of which are:

(1) That the natural resources of the earth and the mechanical inventions of man are made to accrue disproportionately to the advantage of the few instead of the many.

(2) That production is without general plan, and commercial and industrial crises are thereby precipitated.

(3) That the control of business is concentrating in the hands of a dangerous plutocracy, and the destinies of the masses of wage-earners are becoming increasingly dependent on the will and resources of a narrowing number of wage-payers.

(4) That large occasion is thus given for the moral evils of mammonism, recklessness, overcrowding, intemperance, prostitution, crime.

III. We hold that united Christianity must protest against a system so based, and productive of such results, and must demand a reconstructed social order, which, adopting some method of production and distribution that starts from organized society as a body and seeks to benefit society equitably in every one of its members, shall be based on the Christian principle that "We are members one of another."

IV. While recognizing the present dangerous tendency of business towards combination and trusts, we yet believe that economic circumstances which call them into being will necessarily result in the development of such a social order, which, with the equally necessary development of individual character, will be at once true Socialism and true Christianity.

V. Our objects, therefore, as Christian Socialists are:

(1) To show that the aim of Socialism is embraced in aim of Christianity.

(2) To awaken members of Christian Churches to the fact that the teachings of Jesus Christ lead directly to some specific former forms of Socialism; that, therefore, the Church has a definite duty upon this matter, and must, in simple obedience to Christ, apply itself to the realization of the Social principles of Christianity.

VI. We invite all who can subscribe to this declaration to active co-operation with us, and we urge the formation of similar fellowships in other places throughout the land.

W. D. P. BLISS
"What To Do Now"*
1890

In this article Bliss presented a typically shrewd and salient statement of the Christian Socialist position.

That something must be done, and done quickly, to right our social wrongs is patent to almost all; in what general direction we should move is clear, at least to Christian Socialists—yet exactly what steps we should essay, just what we should do now, is the question that presses for a reply. . . .

First, then, we say: We should hold firmly in view our exact objective point, and this, to Christian Socialists, is the realization of the Christian state. To this, we are to hold fast. We are not to exchange it for any Utopia in the clouds, any Oceanica within the west, any Boston of the year 2000, any Kaweah colony, any ideal paradise conceived of earth. Our aim is to be the realization of a divine state, a state which cannot be manufactured by human system. We are not, on the other hand, to relegate it beyond the clouds. "Thy Kingdom come; thy will be done on earth," was the sublime prayer of the master of Christian Socialists. On earth we are to realize heaven.

It is again to be a state, a kingdom, an organism; neither an anarchy nor mere collocation of individualities. It is to *live*, and its life is to be in every part; each is to live for all and all is to be for each; it is to be strictly an organism. This means that it is to be democratic, not paternal. Even God is not to rule over man; man is to be one with God; and God is to be realized in man. There is to be law, and love is to be its fulfiller; and the law itself is love. It is to be an earth-located spirit state, where there shall be the highest individuality for every member realized in the most highly developed social organism.

Second. This being our aim, we are to see to it that we do not waste our strength in wandering towards other goals, on the right

* *Dawn*, July–August, 1890.

hand or the left, no matter how alluringly they raise themselves before us. We are not to be captivated by any cure-alls of Individualism, such as The Single Tax, or Free Trade, as a panacea. We may believe in taxing land values and ultimately to the full; probably most Christian Socialists do, and certainly may believe in trade, free as the breezes upon the ocean, but we are not to forget that a mere individualism, which would let a man, after paying a full rental value for his portion of earth, feel thenceforth free to develop as he will, with no thought of his essential relation to his fellow-man, or holding the value of the raw material of the earth in common with other men, form combinations and monopolies of the strongest individualities, and take advantage in the true commercial method, of the weaker brother, is not the way to realize on earth the kingdom of self-sacrifice and love. Equally are we to shun the Charybdis, on the other hand, of a despotic Socialism, masked as Paternalism or as Aristocracy. We are not to be in haste to turn everything over to Uncle Sam, trusting to Uncle Sam to realize God's Kingdom in the United States. With every respect for Uncle Sam we still believe in the necessity of the development of the individual. We are to be eternally democratic. A true State is only possible in a true Society. This is as true as that a true Society cannot exist without a true State.

Third. Hence, without turning to the right hand or to the left, the path of Christian Socialism is to be a Via Media, and this is notoriously a straight and a narrow way, difficult for men to follow, because of the syren voices that call on either hand. The extreme individualist and narrow socialist, both will disown us. We are to comfort ourselves by faith that it is the strait gate and the narrow path that leads to enduring life. The socialist who sees no good in developing the individual is as narrow as the individualist, who sees no good in development of the State. The idea of the Christian Socialist being duplex, one in two, he is to work both to develop individual character, and to develop character in the State.

Fourth. The attention of the church, and to a less extent of the whole community, having been since the sixteenth century, mainly directed to the development and improvement of the individual, and to a very large extent being still mainly so directed, Christian Socialists are to make their main stand for the divine conception of the State, and the necessity of a true environment as one of the elements, though by no means the only element, in the development of perfect character. Hence we are in this sense, first and foremost, State Socialists.

Fifth. The State in America being Democratic, at least in theory, if not in fact—the majority of the people controlling the form and action of the State—our *immediate* objective point is to be the convincing of the majority of the people of this country of the truth of Christian Socialism. As soon as we have a majority in the country, we are not indeed to physically force our ideas upon the minority; that were the law of might and not of love. We are simply, without compulsion, ourselves to institute the forms of life, in which we believe, and if they be true, to expect the minority to gradually see this truth, and voluntarily to come to their acceptance. But now the one practical thing for Christian Socialists to do is to convince men of the truth of Christian Socialism. In other words, we are not to work to establish a Christian co-operative colony, no system of profit-sharing, no individualistic scheme, no *ignis fatuus* of associated charities and model houses and aristocratic patronage. We are to work for the development of the Christian *State,* and so for the conversion of people to our ideas.

But people desire the concrete, not the abstract. We are, therefore, to strive for those concrete forms that shall make most towards the development of the true State, and shall teach the people concretely the wisdom of State action. If we would teach as speedily as possible, we must work for some object lessons, that can be attained at no distant date. These are usually municipal activities rather than national activities. Hence municipalism is at present the most important form of Socialism. It, too, has the advantage of tending most to Democratic Socialism, and the development of local self-government. Above all, it can most speedily reach the most crying evils of our times, the evil, and unutterably evil, condition of our large cities. Hence Christian Socialists must work mainly for the development of a true municipal life. The exact forms that we should strive for are those that come nearest to what people are ready for. We must in this sense be opportunists. Municipal supplying of gas and electricity many are ready for now. This we may therefore strive for; the ownership, or at least, the control of, city railways; the immediate cessation of giving away or selling valuable street franchises to private monopolists; these we should strive for at once. Large use we should make, as examples, of the successful development on such lines of Glasgow and Bir-

mingham and Berlin in the old world, and a few less marked
examples in the new. Christian Socialists should teach by fact and
not by sentiment; by fact about city gas works, not by mere talk
about city brotherhood.

Sixth. Both of our great political parties being corrupt, Christian
Socialists should have a thought towards the development of a new
party. A new thought demands new voices; it is the belief of the
writer that to attempt to work through either of the old parties is
to work through bodies hopelessly dead in trespasses and sins. Yet a
new party cannot be manufactured. We must create a sentiment
that shall produce a party, not extemporize a party to grind out
true sentiment. Word upon word; precept upon precept; here a little
and there a little, must be our method. We shall work long and
quietly. . . .

The rich may even take up Nationalism and exploit it for their own
private purposes, turning everything over to the State, and seeing
that they themselves are the State.

To such paternalism, Christian Socialists most oppose fraternalism.
Development of the people must go hand in hand with development of State. Co-operation must be encouraged in all its forms,
to prepare people for the Co-operative Commonwealth.

Hence, the practical thing to do to-day is to educate. Hence,
classes, lectures, sermons, literature. To people who ask what we
are doing, we must answer, we are sowing seed.

This was the method of the Master. "Go ye into all the world
and preach the gospel to every creature." Thus He conquered
Rome; thus He is conquering the world. No system of co-operation
did He institute; no colony in Jerusalem or in Galilee; no patent
device for realizing heaven. Twelve men He chose; then seventy;
then a thousand; into them He poured the power of a new thought
and a new life, and sent them out to leaven the old thought and
the old life of the world. His method must be our method. Into
the old rock of selfishness make a little incision by the sacrifices of
your own life; into this put the dynamite of a new idea, fire it
with a torch lit from the altar of God and man, and the obstacles shall spring from the path of the coming of the Kingdom.
All power in heaven and in earth is given to self-sacrifice. At
sacrifice of self, of means, of position, declare for Christian Socialism; preach it to all; spread its literature; support its journals; so
shall ye preach the new old Gospel of the Fatherhood of God, the

Brotherhood of Man, the Holy Spirit of Sacrifice and Love. This is the practical thing now. It is not sentimental. It means the giving of dollars; it means the sacrifice of time. Most clergymen, and many laymen, say Christian Socialism is true, and then give it neither time nor money. Thus the Church earns and deserves its reputation for talk without action.

"The Christian Commonwealth"*
1898

Following is an explanation of the Commonwealth colony taken from the first number of *The Social Gospel*, its official publication.

The Christian Commonwealth was organized in January, 1897, by men and women who believe in the brotherhood life, of service, of self-outpouring, and who were therefore constrained to put their belief into practice. The leaders were writers and preachers and teachers and thoughtful mechanics and farmers. They came together from widely separated states, from Florida, Washington, Massachusetts, Nebraska, Ohio, California, etc., to organize "an educational and religious society whose purpose is to obey the teachings of Jesus Christ in all matters of life and labor and the use of property." They are a distinctly, distinguishably Christian people, not at all because of their professions, but because of their fraternal work and unity. They do not work for or verbally praise Christ one day, and strive each for himself six days, but make all their toil fraternal. They are seeking to serve instead of to gain; hence, so far as this is true, they manifest a spirit the opposite of the spirit of the business world, the world of buyers and sellers and private property seekers.

They preach repentance of selfishness, and apply to those who would join them a consecration test, an actual giving up test, which usually separates the all-centered from the self-centered. The Constitution in part says:

"The recognized unalterable organic law of the Christian Commonwealth shall be: Thou shalt love the Lord thy God with all thy heart, and thy neighbor as thyself."

"Membership in this body shall be open to all and never be denied to any who come to us in the spirit of love, unselfishness and true fellowship."

Deeds, not creeds, are required. Doctrinal differences do not debar from membership. No one set of intellectual opinions is

* *The Social Gospel*, February 1898, pp. 21–24.

called for. To love by serving is the substance of their religion. Work, being made the measure and manifestation of their love, is exalted into worship and fellowship, into a continuous sacrament which conveys the Divine life and love to one another, to each and all.

John Chipman of Tallahassee, Florida, furnished the cash to make the first payment on a plantation of 931½ acres, situated twelve miles east of the city of Columbus on the Central of Georgia railroad. Teams and tools and food supplies were brought by the families who came, and the fraternal system of industry was organized.

The work has been divided into Agricultural, Building, Lumbering, Orchard and Nursery, Gardening, Educational, Extension, Poultry, Dairying, Housekeeping, and other departments, a department superintendent being elected to be over each, and a general labor director over all the outdoor manual labor departments. Business meetings are held every Monday evening, or oftener if needed. Though hampered not a little by lack of sufficient capital, much has been accomplished. Hard work and very plain, frugal living, have helped the society to get along with little.

Considerable building has been done.

A post office and railroad station named Commonwealth have been secured on the Colony land. A sawmill has been put up and runs part of the time. A thirty-five acre orchard of the best peaches, plums, pears, apples, cherries, prunes, figs, apricots and quinces has been set out and cultivated.

Four thousand plum stocks and 3,500 peaches, bought or secured for the nursery, have been budded, and much more nursery and orchard stock is heeled in for spring setting.

Four or five acres of strawberries have been set out, and several hundred choice grape vines have secured a year's growth.

Four pastures, containing perhaps 300 acres, have been fenced.

A good deal of ditching, grubbing, and clearing up of fields has been done.

Nearly 500 bushels of sweet potatoes have been raised, also an unmeasured amount of corn, cow peas, peanuts, garden truck, melons, etc., a fair but not a full crop, because we lacked money to buy fertilizers.

Preachers, professors, and poets, have worked side by side with farmers and mechanics, shrinking from nothing in this hard pioneer year. There has been a constant temptation to overwork, rather than to shirk. And in the work there has been experienced a most delightful common fellowship, or brotherhood communion,—which must be "the communion of the saints."

The Social Gospel, which we have begun to publish, speaks for itself. It will be improved and enlarged as we get means to buy more type, etc. Our tasteful readers will excuse, for the time being, the imperfections of a $46 outfit, second-hand press and type.

We are in no respects a peculiar people, except that we really believe in brotherhood, and in a vicarious industrial Christianity. We are not being reduced to uniformity, but are as strong as ever in our individuality, in our God-made diversity of individual gifts and helpful differences. A Christian society will give utmost cultivation to and large labor room for all individual talents.

In what are known as "religious" matters we somehow do not divide. And why should we? There is freedom, but brotherhood in daily life seems to make brotherhood on Sunday entirely natural and easy. Sect divisions are forgotten and die. Love lifts us to a common ground that is above mere creeds, opinions, forms and sacramental signs. Perhaps this explains why in the New Jerusalem John saw no temple, no Methodist, or Baptist, or Presbyterian, or Episcopalian, or Greek, or Catholic, or other place of sectarian worship, all places and labors having become enlightened by God's Spirit and made worshipful.

We have a prayer and fellowship meeting every Thursday evening. On Sunday we have sermons, talks, Bible studies and select readings from the most helpful books, such as Herron's, Woolman's, Kelley's, and others. We do not drop into conventional ways in our meetings, but encourage each to communicate all he has of truth and love, the sisters as well as the brothers. The discussion after the sermon or selection is always interesting and helpful. Of course the sermons are brotherhood, Christ-life sermons, pointed, practical, instructive, inspiring.

In our Bible lessons we have been through the Sermon on the Mount and a series in the Old Testament. The political economy of the Hebrew theocracy; the law regarding usury; the fact and reasons for the year of jubilee; the rejection of God as king and of brotherhood equality, with consequent oppression and final national destruction; and the brave work of the prophets who by preaching brotherhood righteousness to one people spoke the truth for all people of all times;—these subjects have been in the line of our lessons.

We have a fuller intellectual life here than we could have as divided individuals or families. Our libraries are common or communized, giving each a much wider range of reading than he would be likely otherwise to cover.

We have had a Shakespeare class, an etymology class, and art and music classes, conducted by very able teachers. Our social life is also enriched by opportunities for frequent contact in larger or smaller groups, or as we work together. We often gather around our big open fireplaces in half circles and drop into all kinds of pleasant talk, exchange of witticisms and kindly discussions.

We have birthday celebrations, peanut parties and candy pulls, with innocent games, for the young people. And we have for them one of the best, if not the best, of schools to be found anywhere. Our young people have caught the inspiration of brotherhood and make us glad with their harmony, loyalty and faith.

We have had during this first year the disadvantage of crowding, having to live as whole families in single rooms, and nearly all under one roof, that of the old plantation house,—and this, with but few kinds of (not always most palatable) food, has called out occasional Israelitish complaints, and strained the faith of a few who lacked the larger vision. We have also learned that some need Christian correction and moral restraint, the individual conscience needing to be stirred up and educated by the more enlightened and by expressions of the general conscience.

Distinctly let it be understood that self-seekers cannot be happier here than elsewhere, probably not so much so. One must have faith to find unbroken joy in this life, because its beginnings, with small capital, are specially hard, and its contact close. Only the "good soldiers of Jesus Christ" can rejoice always in it.

In every pinch of economic trial the faith of the entirely devoted has held the victory. They were entirely sure that the brotherhood life they had entered upon is right, and nothing could shake their confidence that God would fulfill his promises and supply necessities. No such serenity could they have had, had they been in and a part of the selfish system of competition. They had sought "first the kingdom of God and his righteousness," the righteousness of brotherhood. And the promises of God have been fulfilled, graciously, wonderfully.

How We Organize.

The Christian Commonwealth is a movement of neighbor-love. It is a social obedience to the Law of Love. All who wish to be Christ's to a wrong, wronged and suffering humanity are invited to join us with their contribution of spirit and strength. Our membership consists of all persons who sign and keep the following covenant:

COVENANT.

I accept as the law of my life Christ's law, that I shall love my neighbor as myself. I will use, hold, or dispose of all my property, my labor and my income according to the dictates of love for the happiness of all who need. I will not withhold for any selfish ends aught that I have from the fullest service that love inspires. As quickly as I may be able I will withdraw myself from the selfish competitive strife and devote myself to the cooperative life and labor of a local Christian Commonwealth. As a member of this organization I will work according to my ability in labor together with God for the production of goods for human happiness.

Name ....

Address ....

Copies of this covenant are mailed free to all who request them, by Ralph Albertson, Commonwealth, Georgia. These covenants signed and returned to us constitute a simple bond of organic union between us. By being thus associated together we have strength of union, the distribution of literature, the increase of our numbers, the knowledge of those who are likeminded near us, and finally the organization with others which shall make the full life of love possible.

Did you ever think about the difference between the individual life of love and the social life of love? Of the one history has given us many beautiful instances, "whose music is the gladness of the world," but of the other there has been but very little, almost none. The individual life of love is a life of suffering and sacrifice leading to crucifixion. The social life of love, equally altruistic and unselfish, ministers with less suffering, pours out itself at less sacrifice, bears away sin at smaller cost and leads to the life of all. There is here no minimizing of the work of Christ. It was fundamentally essential to a social incarnation. But the social incarnation is the goal of Christ's work. He was "the first-born of many sons."

There is a man in a little New York village in whom dwells the Spirit of God. There is no purpose, no motive, no passion in his life but to be a Christ to his fellow villagers, but he stands alone. He lives in a neat house which he owns and which is a comfortable home for his family. Several of his "worthy" neighbors live in rented houses, are sometimes evicted for non-payment of rent, and some live in huts which are not comfortable shelter, to say nothing of the outside world out into which this Christian's heart goes with tenderest sympathies. "What shall I do?" he asks. Now we must advise him to follow the dictates of love, the example of Christ, and the instructions of Christ to those who asked him this question. If, still standing alone, he sells all that he has and gives to the poor he will have treasure in heaven and history will have another gem. But he will have been crucified, and the poor will have been but little benefited. Whereas, if he can join himself to others in a social life of love, by the organization of industry and mutualism of service he may pour out his all and not be utterly sacrificed, and he may give to the poor in such a way that the poor may be permanently housed, employed and blessed.

The Christian Commonwealth is organized to make this possible and to make it possible as rapidly as may be in the lives of the largest number.

Only one local community has as yet been organized, that being the one at Commonwealth, Ga., but there are members enough in the general organization, not living in this community, but in various states, to at once organize a new community when the obstacle of isolation can be overcome.

Very acceptable locations for the homes of new communities of the Christian Commonwealth are given us by members in Virginia, Tennessee, Colorado and Florida. Members who contemplate moving to a colony are requested to state their preference of locations. Those to whom transplanting would be too great an undertaking, or who for any good reasons consider it best to remain where they are, are urged to preach the gospel in season and out of season until they have gathered a band of converts about them with whom they can join hands, hearts and property in the uplifting redemptive work of our leader, Christ.

GEORGE HERRON
*The New Redemption**
1893

Like all of Herron's published work at this time, *The New Redemption* consisted of a number of sermons fusing modern socialism and primitive Christianity.

CHRIST AND THE SOCIAL REVOLUTION

What I have here to say treats of work, wages, and wealth; of the rights and duties of capital and labor. And I approach the social problem, not from the standpoint of the political economist, but of the Christian apostle; Christ did not save the world by a scientific study of the economic conditions of society. Nor shall I make use of statistics, the value of which is largely fictitious; it is a fallacy that figures cannot lie. My discourse will be chiefly concerned with principles. I wish to characterize some of the false principles which have bred social inequalities, and assert the true principles which can procure social justice.

The world is ruled by ideas. Every few centuries a great idea is born into the soul of man. Whether it becomes destructive or constructive depends upon what is done with it, and who has charge of the doing. Great ideas, arousing great moral passions, come to stay. Though we crucify them, they will not die: they thrive on persecutions, and are enthroned by crucifixions. They become man's weal or woe, his savior or destroyer, according to his acceptance or rejection of their rule. Two thousand years ago the master idea of the world was redemption. It was not confined to Judea. It was everywhere: among the Hindus, the rude Norse poets, the Greek philosophers, the Briton Druids, perhaps the American Aztecs. The peoples felt themselves to be under the victory and despotism of evil, helpless to save themselves, and waited for the redemption of a new, divine, and delivering power. Crude, sad, and

* Pp. 11–22, 28–30, 34–35, 173–175.

tragic efforts, both religious and political, were made to redeem the nations before a young Galilean carpenter, who was also the Son of God, so opened his life to the good that the whole power of God to help men swept into his soul. Nearly a thousand years ago God planted the idea of liberty in church and state, to become the seed of a new earth. The idea drew together a little band of German mystics. The burning of John Huss flashed the light of this idea over Europe. It kindled the mind of Luther, and made him the terror of God to the friends of darkness. It illumined the soul of Savonarola with the vision of Florence as a city of God. It tempered Cromwell, as God's rod of iron, to dash in pieces the divine right of kings, which had become the citadel of all that was false, vicious, and cruel in church and state. It guided the Pilgrims to the Plymouth Rock of the democracy and freedom that are in Christ.

A great idea is now leading the world's thought and lifting its hopes. Everywhere are the signs of universal change. The race is in an attitude of expectancy, straitened until its new baptism is accomplished. Every nerve of society is feeling the first agonies of a great trial that is to try all that dwell upon the earth and issue in a divine deliverance. We are in the beginnings of a revolution that will strain all existing religious and political institutions, and test the wisdom and heroism of the earth's purest and bravest souls; a revolution that will regenerate society with the judgments of infinite love. We must get ready for the change by making straight the way of the Lord Christ into the heart of the social strife, that he may purify it with the hope of justice; by giving him command of the revolution, that he may lead it into a larger redemption of the earth. God honors our generation by bringing upon it the sorrow and trial of seeking a road to social order; of finding a way to something like an equitable distribution of economic goods, a mutualism of the responsibilities and benefits of civilization. The idea of brotherhood, co-operation, unity, is both destroying and re-creating the world. The feeling that men were made to stand together, that the race rather than the individual is the unit, is widening and intensifying. The belief that sacrifice and not self-interest is the social foundation, that the Golden Rule is natural law, is everywhere gaining disciples and power. Men are beginning to see that the welfare of each is the responsibility of all, and the welfare of all the responsibility of each. Whether it be for good or ill, whether foolish or wise, the socialistic idea is leading the world. Whether the passion for oneness works the weal or woe of society depends entirely upon its reception or rejection by the Christian church.

It will not do to say the revolution is not coming, or pronounce it of the devil. Revolutions, even in their wildest forms, are the impulses of God moving in tides of fire through the life of man. To resist them is to be consumed, and to compel the remission of sins by the shedding of blood. To receive them as from God is to receive his kingdom almost without observation. The dangerous classes in every age and nation are they who, in the interest of religious or political parties, say that the wrong cannot be set right; that selfishness and injustice and inequality are natural virtues, essential to progress and the stability of civilization. They who say that man's conceptions of justice cannot be enlarged and purified are the ones who bring disaster and wrath upon the world. And they who seek to lift the works and institutions of men with visions of larger truth and assertions of wider justice are not destroyers, but builders; they make ready the way of the Lord into new redemptions of human life.

Nor dare we hope to avert the revolution by suffering what we have been mistaught to call the natural laws of trade to take their logical course. It is against the rule and validity of these laws the revolution directs itself. It is a fiction to characterize as law the principles that now govern economic production and distribution. In fact, we are and have been in a state of industrial anarchy; of social lawlessness. Selfishness is always social disintegration. Competition is not law, but anarchy. That competition is the life of industry is the most profane and foolish of social falsehoods. Cain was the author of the competitive theory. The cross of Jesus stands as its eternal denial. It is social imbecility. It is economic waste. It is the destruction of life. It is the deformity, brutality, and atheism of civilization. It will be as outrageous to the civilization of the future as cannibalism is to the civilization of the present. The speculation which competition makes a necessary element of production and distribution renders the life of man a game of chance. Modern monopolies are its natural fruits: the fruits which the strong and cunning reap through competition with the weaker, less cunning, or more conscientious. Speculative competition makes possible such social disruption and violence to human liberties, such absolute anarchism, as that of a recent coal combination, which arbitrarily reduced the wages of miners and increased the profits of coal millions of dollars, with neither more moral nor economic justification; here was anarchy of the worst type.

The social question is fast revolving itself into a question of whether or not capital can be brought into subjection to law. The social revolution is a search for law: for law that shall have power to procure justice and peace in place of the chance and strife that are everywhere the disorganization of society. The revolution comes not to destroy, but to organize society with a divine and deathless life. It means no evil to the institutions of state and religion, but would rebuild them upon eternal and righteous foundations, and secure them with the justice of love. It aims not to destroy wealth, but to save it by bringing it under the reign of law and consecrating it to the service of humanity. The demand for equality and unity is constructive at heart, even in its most unreasoning and destructive manifestations. The nihilisms and socialisms of our day are desperate yet real attempts to achieve the social ideal by a single bound; attempts to take the kingdom of justice by violence. With one stroke they would break the golden bowl of our modern industrial system, full of abominations. What Mr. John Rae says of the nihilists, in his conservative work on "Contemporary Socialism," may be said of even the most dangerous social revolutionists: "They are actuated by no love of destruction for its own sake; it is impossible to conceive any considerable body of human beings being so actuated. They would destroy, that others who come after them may build up. They sacrifice themselves for a cause, in whose triumph they shall not share; they work for a generation they shall not live to see."

The search for justice, even where it denies the authority of the personal Christ, is essentially a belief in the practicability of the principles which are the essence of Christ's gospel; a belief that brotherhood consists with nature, and that co-operation rather than competition is the natural law of material as well as moral progress; a belief that if mutualism could take the place of the chance and anarchy of speculation and greed, a thousand unknown forms of industry would spring up to add to the moral health and material wealth of man. For the hope of actualizing Christianity as the life of man the revolution is called in question by the religious Pharisees and the political Sadducees.

But before we try to guide the revolution, or attempt the solution of the social problem, we must take our stand upon the platform of duties, and not that of rights. The old passion for liberty, which has won for man so large triumphs in religion and politics, has done its work. It was a great work. But the selfishness that poisons every noble passion, when it rules rather than serves, has transformed the liberty of our fathers into the most intolerable despotism the world has ever suffered. And the social question is not so much a question of rights as of duties. If we are to find a way out of social confusion, if we are to achieve industrial freedom, we must cease to look at the mere rights of capital, or the rights of labor, and look in the direction of the duty of man to man. If we would work with God, if we would follow the Son of man as he leads the race into its purer liberties, we must move with the progress of the cross in the purchase of a new redemption through sacrifice. Society will learn obedience to the ideal of Jesus through the things which men suffer. The laborer will receive the fruits of his labor, and work and wages and wealth become accordant parts of a divine harmony of justice, through changing the social revolution from a passion for rights into a passion for duties.

Work is the first factor to be considered in the social problem. This is a world of work. God works and man works. Work is the manifestation of life. Work is communion with God. There is no righteous work that is not sacred and divine. All the work of man is a part of the creation of God, which is still going on. The work of the carpenter in building a house is as sacred as the work of God in building the earth. The men who do the world's work are the hands by which God works. The man who builds is one of God's builders. The man who plants the fields is God's artist-hand, and the field of green and the field of ripened grain are the glory of God painted upon the face of the earth. The industrial worker is a poet, a creator, an artist, a musician, because all work righteously done, to the best of one's ability, is a creation; it is a harmony. It is the music of God singing itself out through the life of man. And no man is true to his divine origin, no man is really a man, unless, to the extent of his ability, he works. The man who is able to work and works not is a pauper, whether rich or poor. Of all pauperism the most degraded and degrading, because utterly shameless and thriftless, is that aristocracy which idly luxuriates in money obtained through speculation, extortion, or inheritance. . . .

In the midst of great wealth, with the glory of its material enterprise, its blind luxury and mad speculation, its disregard for human life, for moral law, there is an increasing poverty and degradation; a deep and angry social discontent; a growing distrust in the reality of our liberties and the sincerity of our Christianity, proving that our competitive system does not belong to a divine order of things. It is unnatural that the strong should prosper at the expense of the weak; that the earning of one's daily bread should be an uncertain strife. It is a violation of nature that prosperity should come through the triumph of cunning over character, and the conflict of selfish interests. Our so-called industrial order is the disordering of nature. It is the disorganization of human life. There is enough in this world for all to have and enjoy in abundance, if there were a system by which there could be an equitable distribution of that abundance upon the principles of the divine economy.

The social problem is the call of the state to become Christian. The state can save itself only by believing in the Lord Jesus Christ as the supreme authority in law, politics, and society. The state is the social organ. To meet the strain that will be put upon it by the revolution, the state must be redeemed from the worship of property and from commercial theories of government. It can prove its right to be only by procuring a greater measure of social justice and giving a larger recognition to the sacredness of man. The state must have in it the mind that was in Jesus, who is the final political economist. The Sermon on the Mount is the science of society; it is a treatise on political economy; it is a system of justice. It consists of the natural laws which proceed from the heart of God, and operate in the creation and redemption of the world; in the evolution of man and the progressive development of society. It is the constitution of the divine and universal society which John in the Revelation calls a new earth. The establishment of its justice underneath the politics and social structures of man is the new Jerusalem which John saw coming down out of heaven from God. The business of the state is to adopt this social constitution of Jesus as the spirit and justice of the people, and bring every activity into subjection to its authority. . . .

An industrial democracy would be the social actualization of

Christianity. It is the logic of the Sermon on the Mount, which consists of the natural laws of industrial justice and social peace. The democracy that is in Jesus alone is sufficient to equalize social burdens and distribute social benefits. It is not merely spiritual law, but natural and economic law, that the strong shall bear the infirmities of the weak; that they who have the greatest powers and privileges shall bear commensurate responsibilities. Under our present industrial system the weak bear the burdens of the strong; they who have the largest privileges and powers bear the least responsibilities. Neither church nor state can escape destruction at the hands of an arrogant and irresponsible plutocracy, save by proceeding at once to bring the secular world under the reign of the moral law of Jesus. To unite capital and labor in a republic of duties, for the mutual consideration of each other's rights and the care of each other's interests, the state must join hands with the church in solving the social problem in the name of the Lord Jesus Christ, who is the head and the quality of man. Church and state must save themselves by the recognition of the fact that secularism is both atheism and anarchism. Now is the day of their salvation. . . .

THE UNITY OF LIFE

What else is the conflict between the employed and the employing classes, the combinations of the one in labor unions and the other in monopolies, but a stumbling of the world unawares into the brotherhood of Christ? What are our modern problems but the coming of Christ upon a vaster field of opportunity? What but a greater vision of Christ is lifting the eyes of the nations above commercial theories of government and materialistic notions of society? What but a preparation for new unfoldings of the truth as it is in Jesus can be the theological unrest that is shaking the bosom of the church universal? Who but Jesus, coming to kindle the fires of a long-quenched apostolic enthusiasm, is drawing together in holy places of ardent prayer, as if by divine accident, young men to each other personally unknown, and separated by leagues of land?

It seems to me that the morning of hope now breaking upon the horizon of human thought, troubling the sleep of a luxurious church, and calling a complacent pulpit to judgment, heralds a greater day of God than even his most inspired prophets foresee. Up and down the streams of human progress, new prophets are crying that the kingdom of heaven is at hand, and pointing to the Lamb of God that beareth away the sin of the world. The cross again is calling disciples who love not their lives unto death to climb a new Calvary with their master. The times in which we are living are greater and more prophetic than we know. We understand not yet, though we shall know hereafter, what the Christ of judgment is now doing as he walks among the churches. There are hours when I seem to see the ghostly faces of the glorified dead, who have cemented the structure of Christian history with the blood of their lives, peering out of the sad splendor of the martyr-ages, to wonder at our blindness to our opportunities, and stretch forth yearning hands to seize what we pass by, eager to suffer again for the grace that is being brought to us in the larger revelation of Jesus Christ.

May we follow the Son of man through the open door, always bearing his dying in our body, though he lead us in unknown ways that appal our faith, and kindle our souls with a flame that consumes our mortal life. Though, when we offer our lives most wholly and humbly, we sometimes wait long for the Lord's directing word, though our costliest good be often evil spoken of, this Christ of ours will never fail us; this is his world, redeemed with his own blood, and not the devil's world. If we abide in him, and he abide in us, we shall be forever unmovable, and bear the eternal fruit of righteousness, and the light that is in us shall shine on undimmed by time, not obscured by the ignorance of men or the slowness of their unbelief. And by and by, when Jesus comes in the fulness of his power, when the world becomes the dominion of his cross, when he shall come no more through the clouds that hide from us the face of our Father, we shall be manifested with him in the light unapproachable, and be filled with joy unspeakable, and pain shall not be any more, and the old things shall pass away, and the new earth rest in the peace of God.

"Why I Am a Socialist"*
1900

Herron delivered this moving speech before a gathering of the Social Democratic Party in Chicago on September 28, 1900. It was later reprinted in the Pocket Library of Socialism series.

. . . Three great lines are converging in the American Socialist outcome. We must name first the Socialist Labor people who brought from Europe to America what is sometimes called dogmatic socialism. These men have seemed to some of us to be sectarian and harsh, and to have carried class consciousness into class hatred. But is it to be wondered at that they have been bitter and dogmatic in their advocacy of socialism, and in their attacks upon the capitalistic order? Our early socialists were men who had themselves experienced the bitterness and devastation of life that comes to labor in the service of capitalism; they were men who spelled out their Karl Marx in the hideous misery of sweat-shops; men who pawned their threadbare coats to print their tracts. They were socialists when it took a fanatic and a hero to be a socialist; socialists when to be known as a socialist meant hunger or starvation for themselves and their families. They were men who made brave and pitiful self sacrifices for one another as comrades; men who, however fierce, practiced toward each other some of the ethics which we Christians are not even heroic enough to preach. These men do not make a Bible of their Marx, and they understand as well as any of us that the economic philosophy of fifty years ago will have to be recast in the mold of present American facts and ideals. What they now justly ask is, that socialism, under whatever name it appears, or by whatever party it is brought before the people, shall base itself upon the fundamental fact that those who live by selling their labor power to capital must become class-conscious of the fact that they are the rightful owners and real producers of the earth; and that this producing class must bravely and coherently set to

* Pp. 3-13, 28-31.

work to achieve its own liberty from the capitalistic and labor-consuming system of industry. I do not see how any socialist, or any nobly thoughtful man, can dispute this fundamental proposition, however fiercely it may have been advocated. Nor do I see how American Socialism can be established until American labor comes to such a consciousness of its manhood and worth as shall lift it into mighty response to the mightiest task to which mankind has ever summoned itself: the task of organizing out of the materials of nature and history a coherent and free society, in which every man shall equally inherit with every other man the resources and opportunities that open wholeness and gladness of life to the human soul.

Another converging line is that individualism which was the genius of our American political origins, and which was the meaning of eighteenth century political and social philosophy. The end which that individualism sought was right. Rousseau and Jefferson, and the French revolutionists, had a claim which shall be justly and fully acquitted in the court of American Socialism. Socialism does not come to destroy but to fulfill the ideals of liberty, fraternity and equality which made our century so big with promises in its beginnings, and so sad and skeptic with failure in its endings. The liberty which early American aspiration sought can be fulfilled only in the association which socialism offers; individualism can be fulfilled only in collectivism. I have often said from this platform that no man can be free, or ought to be free, until all men are free. The whole world is enslaved as long as there remains a single slave on the earth. Liberty is a social achievement, and must be achieved by men together; not in competition with each other. American democracy, which originally meant voluntary cooperation as the order of the State, will soon be lost, even as an ideal, unless it realizes itself in democracy and co-operation in production and distribution.

The third converging line is a new religious movement developing a much keener and more comprehensive spiritual consciousness in the common life. It is a movement so wide and deep that it is scarcely yet recognized and has nothing to do with the conventional religious experiences. It is so altogether outside of historic religious institutions, and has come upon the world so unawares, that it does not even know itself as religious or spiritual, but is nought else than the coming of the Son of Man to a consciousness of himself as a Son of God. It is upon the tides of this new spiritual movement that some of us have been borne into socialism, and we must be true to our inspiration, while fully recognizing the worth of other inspirations than our own.

Let me explain the point of view and advance from which this unobserved spiritual movement becomes one with economic socialism. We began our working life with the conviction that the individual soul is all that has any worth. The individual man, his wholeness and liberty, is the unrivaled concern of the universe and all that gives it any worth or meaning. Nature and economic things have a value just to the extent that they are the materials by which the human soul may freely express itself. All material things are intrinsically spiritual values; they are the coin of the spiritual realm. The goal of history, if the universe is sincere and has a meaning, is the liberty of each soul to at last become a divine law unto itself; the liberty of each man to individualize God and nature and truth for himself, and to live an original life of his own. If you examine closely enough just what it is that has made the centuries blood red with human struggle, you will find that it is just this struggle of the soul of man for emancipation from every form of coercion; this struggle of the individual life to freely and deliberately and unfearingly choose for itself what it should be, to richly and fully be what it should choose, and to actually lay up its treasures where its heart should be. It was upon the tides of a spiritual passion for this liberty that some of us were beaten against the hard fact that there is no liberty for the individual so long as some people own that upon which all people depend for bread. We have discovered that no spiritual freedom can achieve or maintain itself except it be realized in economic freedom. Private property in the natural resources upon which all men depend, and private property in that capital which all men create, is nothing less than private property and traffic in human souls; yea, it is the foundation of the ecclesiastical claim in God and the truth, which is no less vicious than the claim of the monopolist to private ownership of the earth. The liberty of the soul can be achieved only through the passing away of the capitalistic form of society, and the coming in of the free and co-operative state.

The soul cannot find its freedom in "a free field and a fair fight"; for the soul is not free so long as it is compelled to fight for anything; the individual is free only when he is liberated from fighting, that he may live for the common good in company with his brothers.

But there is still another factor in this spiritual movement towards socialism, and that is the ethical strain that has come to some of us who have faced the whole truth about our economic selves. We who are at once the receivers and victims of special privileges know that we are on the backs of our brothers. We know that our books, our clothes, our privileges are ours because we have dipped our hands into our brothers' blood. I am able to stand here tonight, and make my plea for socialism, because I have consumed the labor product which pays for all that I am able to be and all that I am able to give. I cannot believe that I can serve my comrades best by withdrawing from the problem, with the Tolstoyan, and setting up a private kingdom or heaven of my own; it would be an unspeakable relief to me to pay my world-debt so cheaply. But my place is in the thick of the social pain and travail, in the depth of the heat and chaos, even if I have to bear this ethical strain and shame to the end. The least that I can do to pay my debt to my brothers, the least that I can do to be decent, is to contribute the whole of my life to the emancipation of labor from that capitalistic order which makes the product of the millions the profit and luxury of the few.

I said when I began that the American Socialist movement had not yet been fully and coherently organized, and that these three ethical factors which I have named are converging in that movement. But whether you agree with me or not as to these converging lines, let me ask you to face clearly the fact that socialism in some form is coming, without any regard to what you or I want. Closely speaking, socialism can have but one meaning and issue. Loosely speaking, there might be many kinds of socialism. There can be a thoroughly democratic and spiritual socialism, and there might be an imperialistic or Bismarckian socialism, in which the State would own the people rather than the people be the State. If I might prophesy I would say that in twenty years from now there will be, as now, two great political parties in America; but both of them will be socialistic; one the party of Tory socialism, and the other the party of democratic socialism. But whatever the form under which collectivism comes, the next stage of the world will be a collective stage of production and distribution. We might just as well appoint a committee to sit down on the sun, to keep it from going on its way, as to attempt to obstruct the socialistic issue of the capitalist mode of production and distribution. We are nearing the end of an old stage of production and distribution, for competition and private industry no longer work, and they ought not to work. The present industrial system is approaching an economic world-crisis, which is also the world's spiritual crisis. . . .

In the truest sense, socialism is essentially conservative. It comes not to destroy, but to fulfill all the true ideals of order and liberty and property; it offers that equality which must be the foundation of brotherhood; that liberty which must be the vital breath of the love which the Lord Christ taught; it offers the economic basis for the realization of that fraternity which has been the dream of the ages. It comes with no attack upon property, but rather to save property from the attacks and ravages of a system that is the destruction of all that makes property sacred; for property is sacred only as it serves the highest uses of all men in common. It comes not to destroy private property; for capitalism has already destroyed the possibility of the bulk of mankind ever becoming property owners; but it comes to place within the reach of every man that private property upon which he may stand and live a free and original life of his own, and express his noblest ideals and being. It comes to make the strong bear the infirmities of the weak, until they, too, become strong; knowing well that if we do not actually become our brother's keepers, we shall be destroyed in our brother's destruction, as we ought to be. It comes to put all the temptations of life on the side of service and freedom and goodness, and to abolish the temptation to avarice and meanness and oppression.

I know that there is needed a vast spiritual preparation to prepare the way of political socialism; but that preparation will come. In its essence socialism is a religion; it stands for the harmonious relating of the whole life of man; it stands for a vast and collective fulfillment of the law of love. As the socialist movement grows, its religious forces will come forth from the furnace of consuming experience. No matter how materialistic its origin, when socialism brings men together in a great purpose it soon begins to develop fidelity and tolerance, and patience and good-will, and the noblest of human graces. As American Socialism goes on its way it will become a spiritual passion; not a cry for rights, but a call to elemental righteousness. It will make its appeal to the instinct of man for a divine public life, for communal heroism, and will show how the individual life can fulfill itself only by relating itself to the whole life of mankind. It will create a conscience that shall at last become cosmic and titanic, and able to grapple with all the problems the universe can bring forth. In place of the individual hero of the past, it will submit to you the ideal of a heroic common life; the ideal of a common citizenship that shall truly have its consciousness in heavenly things.

It seems to me that America stands in order to be the birthplace of just such an appeal, and the social ground for just such a realization. Emerson once said that America seemed like the last stand of Providence in behalf of the human race. If the sorrows and the struggles that have made the centuries blood red with effort are to have their fruition, it must be upon our American soil. Back there in the shadows, the oppressed peoples of history are waiting for some great word to be spoken that shall call them into resurrection and liberty. Egypt and Syria, Persia and Greece, Italy and peoples that we have forgotten, are waiting for the word from us that shall call them out into the sunlight and God-light. Peoples and nations unborn are stretching forth entreating hands to us from out of the future. If we should fail here in America, then six thousand years of history will have failed; for history has come to its limit on the shores of the Pacific; it has come back to its starting point. If we fail the heart of God will break again, and another cycle of history, with its weary procession of bleeding centuries, will have to begin. But we cannot fail, we dare not fail. Liberty and fraternity and equality are not tantalisms to hopeless human suffering, but ideals to be realized by human worth and effort. We must prove our worth and power to match these ideals. Potential within this meeting is the power which God might use for the freeing and the healing of the nations. Within this audience are the resources and weapons for conquering the world of love and liberty. The saving sword which the peoples now need is not the sword of Joshua or Cromwell, but the sword of an awakened and inspired and ennobled common life. And as the hand of God reaches out in the dark of our social chaos, it is our privilege to put within that hand the sword of comrade-love that shall liberate the world, and make every child indeed the heir of all the good of all the ages. I pray that the highest and most unselfish that lies in you and in me may respond to the highest and most unselfish inspirations of history, as we go forth to support this cause of socialism, and to support in its Presidential candidate one who has proven his fidelity to American labor, and who is in his rightful place as the leader of this first national campaign for social democracy.

CHAPTER VII

THE SOCIALIST PARTY OF AMERICA

> Let us be the party of the ideal, but let us also be
> the party of the actual.
>
> REV. FREDERICK O. MACCARTNEY,
> *Socialist Unity Convention,* 1901

> We are revolutionary not in the vulgar meaning of the
> word.
>
> VICTOR BERGER,
> *Social Democratic Herald,* 1906

> There is coming over the minds of the capitalist class
> of America a consciousness that the revolutionary tem-
> per is by no means the exclusive proprietary posses-
> sion of those whose forefathers came over and landed
> at Plymouth Rock, but that there is good fighting
> material among our alien proletariat.
>
> JOHN SPARGO,
> First National Congress of the Socialist Party, 1910

> The life of a Socialist propogandist is one continuous
> feast of speaking and writing.
>
> MORRIS HILLQUIT,
> *Loose Leaves from a Busy Life,* 1934

> Who shall be the John Brown of Wage-Slavery?
>
> EUGENE V. DEBS,
> *Appeal to Reason,* 1907

The Depression of 1893 was a chastening experience for American
socialists. Instead of bringing on the expected revolutionary crisis
in the capitalist system, it strangled the radical movements that

had come into being only a short time before. By the time the 1896 election took place the Nationalist and Christian Socialist crusades had died out and the Populists had thrown their support—in effect, capitulated—to the Democratic Party. The election itself was the crowning blow. It swept the arch-conservative Republican party into power at all levels of the government, reducing the Democrats to sectional malcontents. Among radicals, only the Socialist Labor Party, anchored as it was to distant and immutable goals, seemed unaffected by the melancholy turn of events.

But in the spring of 1897 an opportunity for a fresh start suddenly presented itself. On June 15th, the American Railway Union, at the behest of its leader, Eugene V. Debs, held a convention in Chicago to which a large number of outsiders had been invited. The convention was called not to take up union affairs—there was little to take up, the union having been decimated by the Pullman strike three years before—but to establish a new socialist organization, one inclusive enough to house the entire left in America: revolutionary socialists, communitarians, labor union leaders, and assorted radicals and reformers who felt that the old politics had betrayed them and America.

Debs's own life history demonstrated why so many found it necessary to resurrect a new faith from the shattered hopes of the past. Until recently he had been a loyal Democrat and militant trade unionist. While serving as secretary-treasurer of the Brotherhood of Locomotive Firemen in the 1880s he made his way up the ranks of the Indiana Democratic Party, first as city clerk in Terre Haute (where he had been born in 1855), then as a member of the state legislature. Debs was liked by everyone who knew him, and his splendid gifts as a speaker and organizer would have taken him far in politics. But its corruptions and compromises offended his high sense of integrity, and he chose to devote himself wholly to the cause of labor.

During his years with the Brotherhood of Locomotive Firemen he noticed that the profusion of labor organizations, each with its own jealously guarded interests, each concerned with its own status, worked to the advantage of the large corporations. He concluded that for the workers to meet the capitalists as equals they would have to form industry-wide unions under centralized leadership. Accordingly, in 1893 he agreed to head the newly established American Railway Union. Organized on the industry-wide lines that he had been advocating, the American Railway Union grew mightily in its first year. It defeated the great James J. Hill in a strike of the Great Northern and went on to enroll more members than all of the railroad brotherhoods combined. Then came the calamitous Pullman strike (called because the company had cut back wages) which brought down the union and resulted in Debs's imprisonment for six months.

In jail Debs reflected on the injustices to which he had borne witness. It was clear to him now that the assumptions of his youth were false, that the whole system was rigged in favor of the capitalists, that the courts and the rest of the government would use all the force at their disposal (as they had done during the Pullman and countless other strikes) to prevent the people from tampering with the privileges of the rich and asserting their equal rights. Though he read a great deal of socialist literature (he was particularly impressed by the writings of Bellamy and Gronlund), and though he was visited by a number of prominent socialists he was not converted to the faith. He was disillusioned with the system; but he was not yet prepared to abandon it. In fact, a year after his release, he was supporting William Jennings Bryan in the belief that perhaps Bryan and a victorious Democratic Party would begin to restore the government to the people.

It was Bryan's smashing defeat that drove Debs into the socialist camp. "The issue is Socialism versus Capitalism," he stated early in 1897, in a special message to the American Railway Union. "I am for Socialism because I am for humanity. We have been cursed with the reign of gold long enough. Money constitutes no proper basis of civilization. The time has come to regenerate society— we are on the eve of a universal change." Debs's conversion was one of the epochal events in American socialist history.

When the Railway Union met, Debs still had no definite idea of what kind of socialist he was. He seemed at first to be gravitating toward the large communitarian group that was at the convention. This group, calling itself the Brotherhood of the Co-Operative Commonwealth, had been thinking for some time about creating a socialist colony in the state of Washington. In its more extravagant moments the Brotherhood imagined that it would someday win over the entire state, ultimately the entire country. But Debs soon realized that the plan was chimerical, and he threw his support behind those socialists who wanted to launch a new political party.

In 1898 the colonizers and the politicals split apart. The colonizers went off to Washington and set up their short-lived community. The politicals formed the Social Democratic Party and immediately entered the lists in local, state, and federal elections. On the whole the Party did badly, or much worse than it had expected (winning only a few minor offices in Massachusetts). It was an inauspicious beginning.

Before long, however, the Party's prospects began to improve. With Debs as its main spokesman, its symbol, and its standard bearer in the 1900 Presidential election, the Social Democratic Party acquired some notoriety in the country. Debs was quite unlike the public's stereotype of the socialist; he was neither a foreigner, an intellectual, nor a fanatic. He was a humble, sweet-tempered Midwestern American who had emerged from the working class and spoke the plain language of his countrymen. That he wanted nothing for himself, certainly not power or wealth, was obvious to all. What he did want, as he made clear in the 1900 Presidential campaign (and in four subsequent ones), was an America worthy of its revolutionary heritage. Socialism, he maintained, was Americanism brought up to date; it was the fulfillment of ideals implicit in the Declaration of Independence. He beckoned Americans to accompany him on his pilgrim's quest for the cooperative commonwealth, the Zion in the wilderness.

Debs won the confidence of those old-line, mostly immigrant socialists who were dissatisfied with the Socialist Labor Party, now more inflexibly doctrinaire and authoritarian than ever. The Jewish group of New York City's Lower East Side, whom DeLeon had read out of his organization in 1897, joined Debs's party en masse. An even larger group of Socialist Laborites broke free of DeLeon two years later after challenging his policy of "dual unionism" (the creation of new unions to compete with existing ones). For a period these insurgents (known as "Kangaroos") retained the Socialist Labor Party label and put up their own Presidential candidate in 1900. But the Kangaroos at the last moment withdrew their candidate in favor of Debs. In the summer of 1901, at an historic convention in Indianapolis, the two parties—the dissident SLP and the Social Democrats—united to establish the Socialist Party of America.

The Socialist Party was an uneasy unity of opposites. Fundamentally, two factions or ideological tendencies—revolutionary and

moderate—contended for mastery. The revolutionists urged a declaration of outright and uncompromising war on the capitalists.
So far as they were concerned socialists had only one obligation:
to tell the workers the truth, however painful and discomfiting it
might be. And the truth was that they (the workers) and the
capitalists were locked in mortal combat, and that the government
and the labor unions were, all appearances to the contrary,
unequivocally on the side of the capitalists. It followed, therefore,
that any socialist who came to terms with the political system
(by voting, running candidates, etc.) or with the conservative
unions (by approving of such "palliatives" as higher pay and
better working conditions) was a traitor to the movement. The
Party should prepare the working class for the revolution that was
certain to come.

The moderates (or "constructivists," as they liked to call themselves) wished to make socialism relevant to the everyday needs
and problems of the people. The choice for socialists, they argued,
was simple: whether to become a movement or remain a sect;
whether to test socialist ideals in the marketplace or hold them
as inviolable abstractions. The moderates were more optimistic than
the revolutionaries. They were confident that capitalism would
evolve of its own accord into socialism. The change would come
peaceably, by degrees, not by a single apocalyptic leap. To ex-
acerbate class conflict would narrow the base of socialist support
and so delay the advent of the cooperative commonwealth.

The Socialist Party achieved unity by committing itself simultaneously to both positions. It affirmed its belief in an ethic of
ultimate ends, in its mission to transform America completely.
It also determined to struggle for immediate and piecemeal
victories, using the weapons forged by capitalism. The platform
agreed on at the 1901 Indianapolis convention called for the support
of unions "no matter how small or conservative," for the civil
rights of minorities, for the expropriation of monopolies, public
utilities, and the means of transportation and communication, for
welfare assistance to the aged, the infirm, and the unemployed,
for universal education to the age of 18, and for a host of political
reforms (initiative, referendum, recall, proportional representation)
designed to ensure democratic procedures. These proposals were
modest enough, and they might have been advanced by any
number of progressives at that time. But the platform kept coming

back to the Party's revolutionary ideal, emphasizing that reforms and improvements were insufficient, that the "exploitation of labor can be done away with entirely when society takes possession of all the means of production for the benefit of all the people."

When the Indianapolis convention ended the delegates must have wondered what the sound and the fury was about. For the Socialist Party of America was, after all, a very minuscule entity in 1901. Debs had received 95,000 votes the year before, and while that was more than any socialist candidate had ever received, it was less than one percent of the vote cast. But in little more than a decade after its founding, the Party's fortunes rose spectacularly. From 95,000 its vote increased to nearly 900,000. Party membership increased correspondingly: from less than 10,000 to well over 100,000. Even more impressive were the gains registered at local levels. In 1900 socialists held a few offices; in early 1912 they held over a thousand of them in various parts of the country, including one Congressman (Victor Berger of Milwaukee) and a plethora of state legislators, aldermen, mayors, and city commissioners. In 1900 hardly more than 30 socialist newpapers and magazines were printed; by 1912, according to Party estimates, the number had soared to 323, and some of them enjoyed quite large circulations: e.g., the *Appeal to Reason*, with an incredible 761,000, *The Jewish Daily Forward* and *National Rip-Saw*, each with about 150,000. Too numerous to mention were the weekly and monthly journals with respectable circulations of 20,000 readers or more.

Debs and the Party leaders were gratified but not surprised by the sudden upsurge of socialism in America. They saw themselves playing the same part that the abolitionists had played before the appearance of the Republican Party in 1854. Just as the abolitionists predicted the conflict between slavery and democracy, so now, in the first decade of the twentieth century, the socialists were predicting the inexorable conflict between capitalism and democracy. And just as one could trace the progress of the anti-slavery crusade from the tiny Liberty Party of 1840 to Lincoln's election in 1860, so the progress of the anti-capitalist crusade could already be discerned in the rapid growth of the Socialist Party. When, therefore, could the Party expect to take power? Its leaders were wary of speculating, but they believed it would be in the near future. Socialism was on the march everywhere. In Germany it was on the verge of securing an absolute majority in the Reichstag. In France,

Britain, Italy, Austria-Hungary, Belgium, the Netherlands, the Scandinavian countries, it was advancing irresistibly. "We are speeding toward it [the Presidency]," said Victor Berger, who was not ordinarily given to hyperbole, "with the accelerating velocity of a locomotive."

American socialists, however, did not measure the success of their movement solely, or even primarily, in quantitative terms. They were especially proud of the numerous writers and intellectuals in their ranks. Like the early Christians they valued words and ideas, the symbols of the future, and they wrote prodigiously. There were few prominent socialists, whatever their profession, who did not write as a matter of course. From such talented men as Morris Hillquit, William English Walling, John Spargo, W. J. Ghent, A. M. Simons, Louis Boudin, and (somewhat later) Louis Fraina, issued a great torrent of articles, pamphlets, and books, some of them quite original, dealing with the fundamental question of how to apply Marxism, or "scientific socialism", to American conditions. Their aim, in short, was to find in Marxist theory the justification for the particular policies they favored. There were as many interpretations of Marx in the Party as there were differences over policy, and one had to know the master's teachings fairly well to follow the subtle play of their dialectics and the levels of analysis in which they expressed their differences.*

American socialist writers distinguished themselves especially as journalists. They took keen advantage of the literary genre that had recently come into its own with the emergence of the mass-circulation muckraking magazines. The public at large was now receptive to the complaints (the deprivations of the working class, the lawlessness of the capitalists, the alliance between the trusts and the political machines) that the socialists and other radicals had been making for years. But there was an important difference between the socialist and the typically progressive muckraker. Upton Sinclair, John Reed, Gustavus Myers, Robert Hunter, Charles Edward Russell, and Walter Lippmann, the best known of the socialist journalists, went much deeper than even the most radical of the progressives (i.e., Lincoln Steffens and David Graham

---

* These men, it might be added, have been sorely neglected by historians of the era. In many ways, the writings of Hillquit, Walling, Spargo, et al., are astonishingly relevant today, and they may be profitably read by a generation that is rediscovering socialism.

Phillips) in seeking out the root causes of the evils they exposed. Socialists were not content to describe the malevolence of individual men and corporations; they went on to explain that the system was at fault, that the issue was the nature of capitalism, not the moral turpitude of its practitioners.

Among the "creative" intellectuals who belonged to or were closely associated with the Socialist Party were such famous contemporary novelists as Jack London, Ernest Poole, and Floyd Dell, such poets as Carl Sandburg and Louis Untermeyer, such essayists and literary critics as Randolph Bourne, Van Wyck Brooks, and Max Eastman, such artists as Stuart Davis, John Sloan, George Bellows, Boardman Robinson, and Art Young (to name only those who became famous). These writers and artists were united by a common detestation of bourgeois values. They were offended by the philistine style of life no less than by the capitalist mode of production. For them, avant-gardism and socialism stood for the same thing: liberation at once of the spirit and the body, image and act.

This desire for liberation called forth (in January 1911) what was unquestionably the most refreshing socialist publication of the period, *The Masses*. Many of the younger socialist poets, critics, journalists, and artists mentioned above appeared in *The Masses*, where they wrote or drew what they pleased (its cartoons by Sloan, Bellows, Davis, Art Young, Boardman Robinson, and others were magnificent as both caricature and commentary) on the theory that the revolution should be enjoyed, not undertaken as a duty. But its brilliance, irreverence and uninhibitedness created problems. *The Masses* brought to the surface tensions that had been building up between the older, more conventional, more puritanical socialists and the younger ones, who welcomed the revolutionary changes, in political ideas, attitudes toward sex, and artistic forms, that were beginning to shake the foundations of Western culture. *The Masses* "has found no trouble in mixing Socialism, Anarchism, Communism, Sinn Feinism, Cubism, Sexism, direct action and sabotage into a more or less harmonious mess," wrote W. J. Ghent, summing up the conservative view. "It is peculiarly the product of the restless metropolitan coteries who devote themselves to the cult of Something Else; who are ever seeking the bubble Novelty even at the door of Bedlam." The Ghents of the Party, however, need not have worried. *The Masses* found no imitators in its brief life.

Its intellectuals notwithstanding, the Socialist Party had by 1912 clearly established itself as an authentic American party. Organized like the major parties on federal lines, each state having wide autonomy, it was a loosely bound coalition of groups and interests, and individuals. Its main source of strength lay not with unskilled workers and the urban poor, but with those who had some propertied stake in society. The largest single bloc of socialists, in fact, consisted of small farmers who inhabited the region west of the Mississippi River. In percentage of socialist votes, the industrial states lagged far behind such emphatically non-proletarian centers as Oklahoma, Texas, Arkansas, Missouri, Nevada, Idaho, and Washington. Of all the states in the Union, sparsely populated Oklahoma (until recently a territory) gave the Party the most votes. The reason for this apparent anomaly was obvious enough. In the minds of many farmers, socialism was Populism in new dress. For them only the socialists could be trusted to carry on the sacred battle against the plutocrats and to protect their independence as homesteaders.

Its surprising rural strength presented the Party with a dilemma. It was, after all, the Party of the working class and the city, and it regarded small enterpreneurs, agricultural no less than industrial, as retrograde. In its 1908 convention the Party voted to socialize the land (along with other industries), even as it called on the farmers to vote for its candidates. But within two years, during which time it had become evident that farmers were beginning to vote socialist, the Party had changed its tune. The program it drafted in 1910 deliberately omitted the expropriation of farms. "Only to a very small extent is the land now, only to a very small extent is it likely to be for many years to come, a socially operated means of production. Even to declare in any dogmatic manner that all the land must eventually become social property is somewhat utopian; to demand that the ownership of all land shall be immediately socialized is to make ourselves ridiculous." The most orthodox Marxists in the Party did not quarrel with that statement.

The Socialist Party did command substantial support from workers, but they were mostly skilled workers and therefore they were mostly members of the conservative American Federation of Labor. As a result the Party (as we shall see in more detail in the next chapter) had to pursue an exceedingly cautious policy toward organized labor. On the one hand it opposed (just as DeLeon did) the

AFL and everything it represented: the exclusive concern for narrow economic gain, the shameless division of labor into aristocratic and plebeian subclasses, the official hostility to socialism. On the other hand, the Party was not going to make DeLeon's mistake and wage war on the AFL for the sake of industrial unionism and socialist ideals. Its policy was rather to bore from within the prevailing union structure and convince a majority of AFL members to join the socialist movement. In time, perhaps, Gompers and his "labor lieutenants of capitalism" would be overthrown and socialist leaders installed in their places. Socialists had good reason to think that this strategy would succeed. In 1912 a third of the AFL unions—a third of approximately 1,500,000 men—supported the socialist opposition to Gompers.

Ethnic groups formed the fourth important component of the Party (farmers, workers, and intellectuals being the others). To win over the ethnic groups it gave generous concessions. A foreign-language association could join the Party as an independent, self-governing body if it had five hundred or more members and furnished its own translator to the national office. Under the circumstances, large numbers of South Slavs, Italians, Hungarians, Bohemians, Jews, Germans, Poles, Slovaks, and Finns affiliated with the Party. By 1912 these foreign-language groups constituted nearly a sixth of the total Party membership, and their number was increasing rapidly. The socialists, then, carried the ideal of cultural pluralism very far—farther than any other institution carried it in America—but they were to pay a heavy price for their generosity.

Toward Negroes, the Party spoke with two voices. Those socialists who represented or were closely identified with organized labor, and who therefore answered to the rank and file, tended to be racists. In this respect they did not object to the AFL's Samuel Gompers, who was a notorious white supremacist. For example, Victor Berger, boss of the Milwaukee socialists and the leader of the state AFL, had no doubt that "the negroes and mulattoes constitute a lower race," and that "free contact with the whites has led to the further degradation of the negroes." But there were other socialists who resolutely championed the cause of Negro rights at a time when hardly anyone else was doing so. Charles Edward Russell and William English Walling, both prominent members of the Party, were founders of the National Association for the Advancement of Colored People. Debs unceasingly demanded equality for blacks. (He refused to speak before segregated audiences —an outrageously unconventional thing to do.) The Socialist Party, he insisted, would violate its "historic mission" and "deny its philosophy and repudiate its own teachings, if, on account of race consideration, it sought to exclude any human being from political and economic freedom." But Debs, and probably most socialists as well, reduced the Negro problem to a class problem. They assumed that equality would prevail in America the moment capitalism ceased to exist. Until that day they preferred to keep the race issue as far out of sight and hearing as possible.

Marching in the Party ranks along with the farmers, workers and ethnic groups were the sports, eccentrics, and non-conformists who congenitally have been drawn to American radical movements; also a smattering of millionaires and aristocrats (including some descended from pure Mayflower stock); also unreconstructed individualists (itinerant miners, lumberjacks, and agricultural workers) of the Rocky Mountain and Northwest regions; also a doughty contingent of Christian Socialists who continued to defy their superiors or their congregations; and, conspicuous above all the others, a band of exceptional women, among them Helen Keller, Margaret Sanger, "Mother" Jones, Kate O'Hare (publisher of the *National Rip-Saw*), and Rose Pastor Stokes (a Jewish immigrant who had married a Brahmin socialist), to name a few. These women belonged to the Party because they assumed that the oppression of women was inseparable from the oppression of the working class and the triumph of feminism would come only with the emancipation of society as a whole.

The Socialist Party, then, was a seething complex of diverse, often antipathetic, groups, persons, and political tendencies. How did it manage to cohere for as long as it did? Ideological parties are notoriously prone to factionalism. Usually they distintegrate the moment the issue that called them forth has ceased to be relevant. The main reason the Socialist Party stayed together, and indeed continued to grow, before World War I, was that the central issue on which it posited its existence—the irremediable wrong of industrial capitalism—retained its relevance. But there was another reason that was scarcely less important: the control that was exercised by a tight and efficient little machine. Theoretically, the Party was governed by an unwieldy National Committee consisting of some 30-odd delegates, one from each of the "organized" states (states with ten or more local chapters). Actually, decision-making power resided in a small segment of the Committee. This was the segment that represented the urban constituencies. The cities were able to command the Party councils, even though they delivered many fewer votes than the agricultural states beyond the Mississippi, first, because their members were concentrated and well-disciplined, whereas rural socialists were dispersed and ill-informed about intra-Party politics; and, second, because their leaders knew more clearly what they wanted and therefore what accommodations the Party should make with the system.

Milwaukee and New York were the two chief urban constituencies, and the men who spoke for them, namely Victor Berger and Morris Hillquit, were the men who dominated the National Committee. Their life histories, which were so similar in so many ways, help to explain their role as the yoke-fellows of American socialism. Berger was eighteen when he emigrated to the United States from Austria. While teaching German in Milwaukee he joined the Socialist Labor Party and so learned the fundamentals of Marxism. But he withdrew from the SLP when he realized that its program stood no chance of attracting support, even from German workers. Single-handedly Berger built up a powerful reform socialist machine in Milwaukee; it had its own newspaper (the *Social Democratic Herald*, later the *Milwaukee Leader*), it ran the city and state AFL unions (Berger himself was head of the local branch of the International Typographical Workers Union), and it held political offices and dispensed patronage. In time the Milwaukee Socialist Party eclipsed both major parties. It was backed not only by workers (mostly German, of course, but also Polish and native born), but by middle class reformers who admired it for its incorruptibility.

Hillquit (né Hillkowitz) arrived in New York in 1885 from Latvian Russia, where he had been born sixteen years before. Working his way through college and law school Hillquit became an active member of the Socialist Labor Party and helped organize the United Hebrew Trades on the Lower East Side where most working-class Jews in New York lived. It was he who led the "Kangaroos" out of the SLP. And it was he more than anyone who was responsible for the success of the 1901 unity convention. From then on Hillquit was the Socialist Party's Henry Clay, its Great Compromiser and Pacificator. Whenever a serious dispute arose he could be counted on to reconcile the contending factions or, on those rare occasions when reconciliation was impossible, to assert Party discipline. But there was more to Hillquit than a clever politician and committeeman. He was one of the best popularizers of socialism in the country. His debates with opponents, inside the Party and out, were famous. His books were always lucid; sometimes they were profound (see, for example, his *Socialism in Theory and Practice*). And he wrote a classic—A *History of Socialism in the United States*—which, though dated (the first edition was published in 1903), has not been surpassed. If the Party had an official spokesman it was Hillquit.

Their grounding in Marx enabled Berger and Hillquit to plot the Party's course in the years after the 1901 convention. From Marx they learned that revolution cannot be hurried, that the process of creating a socialist movement was arduous and slow, and that history would reveal when capitalism, paralyzed by its "contradictions," was about to fall. Socialists, it logically followed, must refrain from provoking—or being provoked into—violent class conflict. Berger and Hillquit had no doubt that their strategy of working in and through the liberal constitutional system, gathering the support of all groups, and fighting for reform, however transient and meliorist, accorded perfectly with the tenets of Marxism. They, too, regarded the industrial proletariat (including white-collar workers) as the chosen class—the class that would, through the Socialist Party, guide the nation in its period of transition from decadent capitalism to the cooperative commonwealth.

In practice, few socialists quarreled with the Berger-Hillquit strategy. Those who did, quarreled with it rhetorically and abstractly. Even "Big Bill" Haywood, the leader of the left-wing, pro-Syndicalist faction, for all his rotomontade in favor of class war and sabotage, played the game pretty much as the moderates did and acted responsibly in the strikes he conducted. And Debs, though he hated the AFL with rare ferocity, subscribed to the Party's policies without much cavil. He demonstrated his acceptance of the Berger-Hillquit leadership by sedulously keeping aloof from conflicts inside the Party. Questions of policy and organization he left to those who already determined them.

Immediately after 1912 the Party slipped in all the vital indexes of growth—votes, offices, membership, newspaper circulation—but the decline was not regarded as a dangerous portent. Nor was it.

The Party was as robust as ever. No serious losses had been sustained in its various constituencies. Its leadership and policies were intact. Socialists expected the Party's fortunes to rise again, carrying it beyond its prior peaks of achievement. Their optimism was undaunted. But that was because they did not foresee the seismic events of 1917—America's entry into the war and the Bolshevik Revolution—which shattered the Party beyond repair.

Socialist Party Platform of 1912*

The representatives of the Socialist party, in National Convention at Indianapolis, declare that the capitalist system has outgrown its historical function, and has become utterly incapable of meeting the problems now confronting society. We denounce this outgrown system as incompetent and corrupt and the source of unspeakable misery and suffering to the whole working class.

Under this system the industrial equipment of the nation has passed into the absolute control of plutocracy, which exacts an annual tribute of hundreds of millions of dollars from the producers. Unafraid of any organized resistance, it stretches out its greedy hands over the still undeveloped resources of the nation—the land, the mines, the forests and the waterpowers of every state in the Union.

In spite of the multiplication of labor-saving machines and improved methods in industry, which cheapen the cost of production, the share of the producers grows ever less, and the prices of all the necessities of life steadily increase. The boasted prosperity of this nation is for the owning class alone. To the rest it means only greater hardship and misery. The high cost of living is felt in every home. Millions of wage-workers have seen the purchasing power of their wages decrease until life has become a desperate battle for mere existence.

Multitudes of unemployed walk the streets of our cities or trudge from state to state awaiting the will of the masters to move the wheels of industry.

The farmers in every state are plundered by the increasing prices exacted for tools and machinery and by extortionate rents, freight rates and storage charges.

Capitalist concentration is mercilessly crushing the class of small business men and driving its members into the ranks of propertyless wage-workers. The overwhelming majority of the people of America are being forced under a yoke of bondage by this soulless industrial despotism.

* Socialist Campaign Book, 1912.

It is this capitalist system that is responsible for the increasing burden of armaments, the poverty, slums, child labor, most of the insanity, crime and prostitution, and much of the disease that afflicts mankind.

Under this system the working class is exposed to poisonous conditions, to frightful and needless perils to life and limb, is walled around with court decisions, injunctions and unjust laws, and is preyed upon incessantly for the benefit of the controlling oligarchy of wealth. Under it also, the children of the working class are doomed to ignorance, drudging toil and darkened lives.

In the face of these evils, so manifest that all thoughtful observers are appalled at them, the legislative representatives of the Republican and Democratic parties remain the faithful servants of the oppressors. Measures designed to secure to the wage earners of this nation as humane and just treatment as is already enjoyed by the wage earners of all other civilized nations have been smothered in committee without debate, and laws ostensibly designed to bring relief to the farmers and general consumers are juggled and transformed into instruments for the exaction of further tribute. The growing unrest under oppression has driven these two old parties to the enactment of a variety of regulative measures, none of which has limited in any appreciable degree the power of the plutocracy, and some of them have been perverted into means for increasing that power. Anti-trust laws, railroad restrictions and regulations, with the prosecutions, indictments and investigations based upon such legislation, have proved to be utterly futile and ridiculous.

Nor has this plutocracy been seriously restrained or even threatened by any Republican or Democratic executive. It has continued to grow in power and insolence alike under the administrations of Cleveland, McKinley, Roosevelt and Taft.

In addition to this legislative juggling and this executive connivance, the courts of America have sanctioned and strengthened the hold of this plutocracy as the Dred Scott and other decisions strengthened the slave-power before the civil war. They have been used as instruments for the oppression of the working class and for the suppression of free speech and free assembly.

We declare, therefore, that the longer sufferance of these conditions is impossible, and we propose to end them all. We declare them to be the product of the present system, in which industry is carried on for private greed, instead of for the welfare of society. We declare, furthermore, that for these evils there will be and can be no remedy and no substantial relief except through Socialism, under which industry will be carried on for the common good and every worker receive the full social value of the wealth he creates.

Society is divided into warring groups and classes, based upon material interests. Fundamentally, this struggle is a conflict between the two main classes, one of which, the capitalist class, owns the means of production, and the other, the working class, must use these means of production on terms dictated by the owners.

The capitalist class, though few in numbers, absolutely controls the government—legislative, executive and judicial. This class owns the machinery of gathering and disseminating news through its organized press. It subsidizes seats of learning—the colleges and schools—and even religious and moral agencies. It has also the added prestige which established customs give to any order of society, right or wrong.

The working class, which includes all those who are forced to work for a living, whether by hand or brain, in shop, mine or on the soil, vastly outnumbers the capitalist class. Lacking effective organization and class solidarity, this class is unable to enforce its will. Given such class solidarity and effective organization, the workers will have the power to make all laws and control all industry in their own interest.

All political parties are the expression of economic class interests. All other parties than the Socialist party represent one or another group of the ruling capitalist class. Their political conflicts reflect merely superficial rivalries between competing capitalist groups. However they result, these conflicts have no issue of real value to the workers. Whether the Democrats or Republicans win politically, it is the capitalist class that is victorious economically.

The Socialist party is the political expression of the economic interests of the workers. Its defeats have been their defeats and its victories their victories. It is a party founded on the science and laws of social development. It proposes that, since all social necessities today are socially produced, the means of their production and distribution shall be socially owned and democratically controlled.

In the face of the economic and political aggressions of the capitalist class the only reliance left the workers is that of their economic organizations and their political power. By the intelligent and class-conscious use of these, they may resist successfully the capitalist class, break the fetters of wage-slavery, and fit themselves for the future society, which is to displace the capitalist system. The Socialist party appreciates the full significance of class organization and urges the wage earners, the working farmers and all other useful workers everywhere to organize for economic and political action, and we pledge ourselves to support the toilers of the fields as well as those in the shops, factories and mines of the nation in their struggles for economic justice.

In the defeat or victory of the working class party in this new struggle for freedom lies the defeat or triumph of the common people of all economic groups, as well as the failure or the triumph of popular government. Thus the Socialist party is the party of the present day revolution, which marks the transition from economic individualism to Socialism, from wage-slavery to free co-operation, from capitalist oligarchy to industrial democracy.

WORKING PROGRAM.

As measures calculated to strengthen the working class in its fight for the realization of its ultimate aim, the co-operative commonwealth, and to increase its power of resistance against capitalist oppression, we advocate and pledge ourselves and our elected officers to the following program:

COLLECTIVE OWNERSHIP.

1. The collective ownership and democratic management of railroads, wire and wireless telegraphs and telephones, express services, steamboat lines and all other social means of transportation and communication and of all large-scale industries.

2. The immediate acquirement by the municipalities, the states or the federal government of all grain elevators, stock yards, storage warehouses, and other distributing agencies, in order to reduce the present extortionate cost of living.

3. The extension of the public domain to include mines, quarries, oil wells, forests and water power.

4. The further conservation and development of natural resources for the use and benefit of all the people:

(a) By scientific forestation and timber protection.

(b) By the reclamation of arid and swamp tracts.

(c) By the storage of flood waters and the utilization of water power.

(d) By the stoppage of the present extravagant waste of the soil and of the products of mines and oil wells.

(e) By the development of highway and waterway systems.

5. The collective ownership of land wherever practicable, and in cases where such ownership is impracticable, the appropriation by taxation of the annual rental value of all land held for speculation or exploitation.

6. The collective ownership and democratic management of the banking and currency system.

UNEMPLOYMENT.

The immediate government relief of the unemployed by the extension of all useful public works. All persons employed on such works to be engaged directly by the government under a workday of not more than eight hours and at not less than the prevailing union wages. The government also to establish employment bureaus; to lend money to states and municipalities without interest for the purpose of carrying on public works, and to take such other measures within its power as will lessen the widespread misery of the workers caused by the misrule of the capitalist class.

INDUSTRIAL DEMANDS.

The conservation of human resources, particularly of the lives and well-being of the workers and their families:

1. By shortening the workday in keeping with the increased productiveness of machinery.

2. By securing to every worker a rest period of not less than a day and a half in each week.

3. By securing a more effective inspection of workshops, factories and mines.

4. By forbidding the employment of children under sixteen years of age.

5. By the co-operative organization of the industries in the federal penitentiaries for the benefit of the convicts and their dependents.

6. By forbidding the interstate transportation of the products of child labor, of convict labor and of all uninspected factories and mines.

7. By abolishing the profit system in government work, and sub-

stituting either the direct hire of labor or the awarding of contracts to co-operative groups of workers.

8. By establishing minimum wage scales.

9. By abolishing official charity and substituting a non-contributory system of old-age pensions, a general system of insurance by the state of all its members against unemployment and invalidism and a system of compulsory insurance by employers of their workers, without cost to the latter, against industrial diseases, accidents and death.

POLITICAL DEMANDS.

1. The absolute freedom of press, speech and assemblage.

2. The adoption of a graduated income tax, the increase of the rates of the present corporation tax and the extension of inheritance taxes, graduated in proportion to the value of the estate and to nearness of kin—the proceeds of these taxes to be employed in the socialization of industry.

3. The abolition of the monopoly ownership of patents and the substitution of collective ownership, with direct rewards to inventors by premiums or royalties.

4. Unrestricted and equal suffrage for men and women.

5. The adoption of the initiative, referendum and recall and of proportional representation, nationally as well as locally.

6. The abolition of the Senate and of the veto power of the President.

7. The election of the President and the Vice-President by direct vote of the people.

8. The abolition of the power usurped by the Supreme Court of the United States to pass upon the constitutionality of the legislation enacted by Congress. National laws to be repealed only by act of Congress or by a referendum vote of the whole people.

9. The abolition of the present restrictions upon the amendment of the constitution, so that that instrument may be made amendable by a majority of the voters in the country.

10. The granting of the right of suffrage in the District of Columbia with representation in Congress and a democratic form of municipal government for purely local affairs.

11. The extension of democratic government to all United States territory.

12. The enactment of further measures for general education

and particularly for vocational education in useful pursuits. The Bureau of Education to be made a department.

13. The enactment of further measures for the conservation of health. The creation of an independent bureau of health, with such restrictions as will secure full liberty to all schools of practice.

14. The separation of the present Bureau of Labor from the Department of Commerce and Labor and its elevation to the rank of a department.

15. Abolition of all federal district courts and the United States Circuit Courts of Appeals. State courts to have jurisdiction in all cases arising between citizens of the several states and foreign corporations. The election of all judges for short terms.

16. The immediate curbing of the power of the courts to issue injunctions.

17. The free administration of the law.

18. The calling of a convention for the revision of the constitution of the United States.

Such measures of relief as we may be able to force from capitalism are but a preparation of the workers to seize the whole powers of government, in order that they may thereby lay hold of the whole system of socialized industry and thus come to their rightful inheritance.

Speech at Indianapolis*

1904

This speech, which kicked off Debs's presidential campaign of 1904, is a good specimen of his style and a cogent summary of his political position.

THE CLASS STRUGGLE.

We are entering tonight upon a momentous campaign. The struggle for political supremacy is not between political parties merely, as appears upon the surface, but at bottom it is a life and death struggle between two hostile economic classes, the one the capitalist, and the other the working class.

The capitalist class is represented by the Republican, Democratic, Populist and Prohibition parties, all of which stand for private ownership of the means of production, and the triumph of any one of which will mean continued wage-slavery to the working class.

As the Populist and Prohibition sections of the capitalist party represent minority elements which propose to reform the capitalist system without disturbing wage-slavery, a vain and impossible task, they will be omitted from this discussion with all the credit due the rank and file for their good intentions.

The Republican and Democratic parties, or, to be more exact, the Republican-Democratic Party, represent the capitalist class in the class struggle. They are the political wings of the capitalist system and such differences as arise between them relate to spoils and not to principles.

With either of these parties in power one thing is always certain and that is that the capitalist class is in the saddle and the working class under the saddle.

Under the administration of both these parties the means of production are private property, production is carried forward for capi-

---

* *Debs: His Life, Writings and Speeches* (Chicago, 1908), pp. 358–362, 371–373.

talist profit purely, markets are glutted and industry paralyzed, workingmen become tramps and criminals while injunctions, soldiers and riot guns are brought into action to preserve "law and order" in the chaotic carnival of capitalistic anarchy.

Deny it as may the cunning capitalists who are clear-sighted enough to perceive it, or ignore it as may the torpid workers who are too blind and unthinking to see it, the struggle in which we are engaged today is a class struggle, and as the toiling millions come to see and understand it and rally to the political standard of their class, they will drive all capitalist parties of whatever name into the same party, and the class struggle will then be so clearly revealed that the hosts of labor will find their true place in the conflict and strike the united and decisive blow that will destroy slavery and achieve their full and final emancipation.

In this struggle the workingmen and women and children are represented by the Socialist Party and it is my privilege to address you in the name of that revolutionary and uncompromising party of the working class.

ATTITUDE OF THE WORKERS.

What shall be the attitude of the workers of the United States in the present campaign? What part shall they take in it? What party and what principles shall they support by their ballots? And why?

These are questions the importance of which are not sufficiently recognized by workingmen or they would not be the prey of parasites and the service tools of scheming politicians who use them at election time to renew their masters' lease of power and perpetuate their own ignorance, poverty and shame.

In answering these questions I propose to be as frank and candid as plain-meaning words will allow, for I have but one object in this discussion and that object is not office, but the truth, and I shall state it as I see it, if I have to stand alone.

But I shall not stand alone, for the party that has my allegiance and may have my life, the Socialist Party, the party of the working class, the party of emancipation, is made up of men and women who know their rights and scorn to compromise with their oppressors; who want no votes that can be bought and no support under any false pretense whatsoever.

The Socialist Party stands squarely upon its proletarian principles and relies wholly upon the forces of industrial progress and the education of the working class.

The Socialist Party buys no votes and promises no office. Not a farthing is spent for whiskey or cigars. Every penny in the campaign fund is the voluntary offerings of workers and their sympathizers and every penny is used for education.

What other parties can say the same?

Ignorance alone stands in the way of Socialist success. The capitalist parties understand this and use their resources to prevent the workers from seeing the light.

Intellectual darkness is essential to industrial slavery.

Capitalist parties stand for Slavery and Night.

The Socialist Party is the herald of Freedom and Light.

Capitalist parties cunningly contrive to divide the workers upon dead issues.

The Socialist Party is uniting them upon the living issue:

Death to Wage Slavery!

When industrial slavery is as dead as the issues of the Siamese-twin capitalist parties the Socialist Party will have fulfilled its mission and enriched history.

And now to our questions:

First, all workingmen and women owe it to themselves, their class and their country to take an active and intelligent interest in political affairs.

THE BALLOT.

The ballot of united labor expresses the people's will and the people's will is the supreme law of a free nation.

The ballot means that labor is no longer dumb, that at last it has a voice, that it may be heard and if united shall be heeded.

Centuries of struggle and sacrifice were required to wrest this symbol of freedom from the mailed clutch of tyranny and place it in the hand of labor as the shield and lance of attack and defense.

The abuse and not the use of it is responsible for its evils.

The divided vote of labor is the abuse of the ballot and the penalty is slavery and death.

The united vote of those who toil and have not will vanquish those who have and toil not, and solve forever the problem of democracy.

THE HISTORIC STRUGGLE OF CLASSES.

Since the race was young there have been class struggles. In every state of society, ancient and modern, labor has been exploited, degraded and in subjection.

Civilization has done little for labor except to modify the forms of its exploitation.

Labor has always been the mudsill of the social fabric—is so now and will be until the class struggle ends in class extinction and free society.

Society has always been and is now built upon exploitation—the exploitation of a class—the working class, whether slaves, serfs or wage-laborers, and the exploited working class in subjection have always been, instinctively or consciously, in revolt against their oppressors.

Through all the centuries the enslaved toilers have moved slowly but surely toward their final freedom.

The call of the Socialist Party is to the exploited class, the workers in all useful trades and professions, all honest occupations, from the most menial service to the highest skill, to rally beneath their own standard and put an end to the last of the barbarous class struggles by conquering the capitalist government, taking possession of the means of production and making them the common property of all, abolishing wage-slavery and establishing the co-operative commonwealth.

The first step in this direction is to sever all relations with

CAPITALIST PARTIES.

They are precisely alike and I challenge their most discriminating partisans to tell them apart in relation to labor.

The Republican and Democratic parties are alike capitalist parties —differing only in being committed to different sets of capitalist interests—they have the same principles under varying colors, are equally corrupt and are one in their subservience to capital and their hostility to labor.

The ignorant workingman who supports either of these parties forges his own fetters and is the unconscious author of his own misery. He can and must be made to see and think and act with his fellows in supporting the party of his class and this work of education is the crowning virtue of the Socialist movement. . . .

In what has been said of other parties I have tried to show why they should not be supported by the common people, least of all by workingmen, and I think I have shown clearly enough that such workers as do support them are guilty, consciously or unconsciously, of treason to their class. They are voting into power the enemies of labor and are morally responsible for the crimes thus perpetrated upon their fellow-workers and sooner or later they will have to suffer the consequences of their miserable acts.

The Socialist Party is not, and does not pretend to be, a capitalist party. It does not ask, nor does it expect the votes of the capitalist class. Such capitalists as do support it do so seeing the approaching doom of the capitalist system and with a full understanding that the Socialist Party is not a capitalist party, nor a middle class party, but a revolutionary working class party, whose historic mission it is to conquer capitalism on the political battle-field, take control of government and through the public powers take possession of the means of wealth production, abolish wage-slavery and emancipate all workers and all humanity.

The people are as capable of achieving their industrial freedom as they were to secure their political liberty, and both are necessary to a free nation.

The capitalist system is no longer adapted to the needs of modern society. It is outgrown and fetters the forces of progress. Industrial and commercial competition are largely of the past. The handwriting blazes on the wall. Centralization and combination are the modern forces in industrial and commercial life. Competition is breaking down and co-operation is supplanting it.

The hand tools of early times are used no more. Mammoth machines have taken their places. A few thousand capitalists own them and many millions of workingmen use them.

All the wealth the vast army of labor produces above its subsistence is taken by the machine owning capitalists, who also own the land and the mills, the factories, railroads and mines, the forests and fields and all other means of production and transportation.

Hence wealth and poverty, millionaires and beggars, castles and caves, luxury and squalor, painted parasites on the boulevard and painted poverty among the red lights.

Hence strikes, boycotts, riots, murder, suicide, insanity, prostitution on a fearful and increasing scale.

The capitalist parties can do nothing. They are a part, an iniquitous part, of the foul and decaying system.

There is no remedy for the ravages of death.

Capitalism is dying and its extremities are already decomposing. The blotches upon the surface show that the blood no longer circulates. The time is near when the cadaver will have to be removed and the atmosphere purified.

In contrast with the Republican and Democratic conventions, where politicians were the puppets of plutocrats, the convention of the Socialist Party consisted of workingmen and women fresh from their labors, strong, clean, wholesome, self-reliant, ready to do and dare for the cause of labor, the cause of humanity.

Proud indeed am I to have been chosen by such a body of men and women to bear aloft the proletarian standard in this campaign, and heartily do I endorse the clear and cogent platform of the party which appeals with increasing force and eloquence to the whole working class of the country.

To my associate upon the national ticket I give my hand with all my heart. Ben Hanford typifies the working class and fitly represents the historic mission and revolutionary character of the Socialist Party.

CLOSING WORDS.

These are stirring days for living men. The day of crisis is drawing near and Socialists are exerting all their power to prepare the people for it.

The old order of society can survive but little longer. Socialism is next in order. The swelling minority sounds warning of the impending change. Soon that minority will be the majority and then will come the co-operative commonwealth.

Every workingman should rally to the standard of his class and hasten the full-orbed day of freedom.

Every progressive Democrat must find his way in our direction, and if he will but free himself from prejudice and study the principles of Socialism he will soon be a sturdy supporter of our party.

Every sympathizer with labor, every friend of justice, every lover of humanity should support the Socialist Party as the only party that is organized to abolish industrial slavery, the prolific source of the giant evils that afflict the people.

Who with a heart in his breast can look upon Colorado without keenly feeling the cruelties and crimes of capitalism! Repression will not help her. Brutality will only brutalize her. Private ownership and wage-slavery are the curse of Colorado. Only Socialism will save Colorado and the nation.

The overthrow of capitalism is the object of the Socialist Party. It will not fuse with any other party and it would rather die than compromise.

The Socialist Party comprehends the magnitude of its task and has the patience of preliminary defeat and the faith of ultimate victory.

The working class must be emancipated by the working class.

Woman must be given her true place in society by the working class.

Child labor must be abolished by the working class.

Society must be reconstructed by the working class.

The working class must be employed by the working class.

The fruits of labor must be enjoyed by the working class.

War, bloody war, must be ended by the working class.

These are the principles and objects of the Socialist Party and we fearlessly proclaim them to our fellowmen.

We know our cause is just and that it must prevail.

With faith and hope and courage we hold our heads erect and with dauntless spirit marshal the working class for the march from Capitalism to Socialism, from Slavery to Freedom, from Barbarism to Civilization.

WILLIAM JAMES GHENT
"The Next Step: A Benevolent Feudalism"*
1902

Ghent, born in Indiana in 1866, was a reform socialist and was
always identified with the right-wing of the Party (he served as
Victor Berger's secretary for a while). Ghent was an original thinker,
as this essay (later a book: *The Benevolent Feudalism*) amply
demonstrates.

The next distinct stage in the socio-economic evolution of America
may be something entirely different from any of the forms usually
predicted. Anarchist prophecies are, of course, futile; and the Tolstoyan Utopia of a return to primitive production, with its prodigal
waste of effort and consequent impoverishment of the race, allures
but few minds. The Kropotkinian dream of a communistic union of
shop industry and agriculture is of a like type; and well-nigh as
barren are the Neo-Jeffersonian visions of a general revival of small-
farm and small-shop production and the dominance of a middle-
class democracy. The orthodox economists, with their notions of a
slightly modified Individualism, wherein each unit secures the just
reward of his capacity and service, are but worshiping an image
which they have created out of their books and which has no real
counterpart in life; and finally, the Marxists, who predict the establishment of a co-operative commonwealth, are, to say the least,
too sanguine in foreshortening the time of its triumph. Whatever
the more distant future may bring to pass, there is but little evidence to prove that collectivism will be the next status of society.
Rather, that coming status, of which the contributing forces are now
energetically at work and of which the first phases are already
plainly observable, will be something in the nature of a Benevolent
Feudalism.

That the concentration of capital and the increase of individual
holdings of wealth will continue is almost unanimously conceded.
Forty years ago Marx laid down the formula of capitalist accumula-

* *The Independent*, April 3, 1902.

tion which has ever since been a fixed article of creed with the orthodox Socialists. "One capitalist always kills many" is its central maxim. . . .

The tendencies thus make, on the one hand, toward the centralization of vast power in the hands of a few men—the morganization of industry, as it were—and on the other, toward a vast increase in the number of those who compose the economically dependent classes. The latter number is already stupendous. The laborers and mechanics were long ago brought under the yoke through their divorcement from the land and the application of steam to factory operation. They are economically unfree except in so far as their organizations make possible a collective bargaining for wages and hours. The growth of commerce raised up an enormous class of clerks and helpers, perhaps the most dependent class in the community. The growth and partial diffusion of wealth in America has in fifty years largely altered the character of domestic service and increased the number of servants many fold. Railroad pools and farm-implement trusts have drawn a tightening cordon about the farmers. The professions, too, have felt the change. Behind many of our important newspapers are private commercial interests which dictate their general policy, if not, as is frequently the case, their particular attitude upon every public question; while the race for endowments made by the greater number of the churches and by all colleges except a few State-supported ones, compels a cautious regard on the part of synod and faculty for the wishes, the views and prejudices of men of great wealth. To this growing deference of preacher, teacher and editor is added that of two yet more important classes—the makers and the interpreters of law. The record of legislation and judicial interpretation regarding slavery previous to the Civil War has been paralleled in recent years by the record of legislatures and courts in matters relating to the lives and health of manual workers, especially in such cases as employers' liability and factory inspection. Thus, with a great addition to the number of subordinate classes, with a tremendous increase of their individual components, and with a corresponding growth of power in the hands of a few score magnates, there is needed little further to make up a socio-economic status that contains all the essentials of a renascent feudalism.

It is, at least in its beginning, less a personal than a class feudalism. History may repeat itself, as the adage runs; but not by identical forms and events. The great spirals of evolutionary progress carry us for a time back to the general direction of older journeyings, but not to the well-worn pathways themselves. The old feudalism exacted faithful service, industrial and martial, from the underling; protection and justice from the overlord. It is not likely that personal fidelity, as once known, can ever be restored: the long period of dislodgment from the land, the diffusion of learning, the exercise of the franchise, and the training in individual effort have left a seemingly unbridgeable chasm between the past and the present forms. But the personal fidelity, in the old sense, is improbable, group fidelity, founded upon the conscious dependence of a class, is already observable, and it grows apace. Out of the sense of class dependence arises the extreme deference which we yield, the rapt homage which we pay—not as individuals, but as units of a class—to the men of wealth. We do not know them personally, and we have no sense of personal attachment. But in most things we grant them priority. We send them or their legates to the Senate to make our laws; we permit them to name our administrators and our judiciary; we listen with eager attention to their utterances and we abide by their judgment. Not always, indeed; for some of us grumble at times and ask angrily where it will all end. We talk threateningly of instituting referendums to curb excessive power; of levying income taxes, or of compelling the Government to acquire the railroads and the telegraphs. We subscribe to newspapers and other publications which criticise the acts of the great corporations, and we hail as a new Gracchus the ardent reformer who occasionally comes forth for a season to do battle for the popular cause. But this revolt is, for the most part, sentimental; it is a mental attitude but rarely transmutable into terms of action. It is, moreover, sporadic and flickering, it dies out after a time, and we revert to our usual moods, concerning ourselves with our particular interests and letting the rest of the world wag as it will.

The new feudalism is thus characterized by a class dependence rather than by a personal dependence. But it differs in still other respects from the old. It is qualified and restricted, and by agencies hardly operative in medieval times. Democracy tends to restrain it, and ethics to moralize it. Tho it has its birth and nurture out of the "rough and unsocialized barbarians of wealth," in Mr. Henry D. Lloyd's phrase, its youth and maturity promise a modification of character. More and more it tends to become a *benevolent* feudalism. On the ethical side it is qualified by a growing and diffusive sense of responsibility and of kinship. The principle of the "trusteeship of great wealth" having found lodgment, like a seed, in the erstwhile barren soil of mammonism, has become a flourishing growth. The enormous benefactions for social purposes, which have been common of late years, and which in 1901 reached a total of $107,000,000, could come only from men and women who have been taught to feel an ethical duty to society. It is a duty, true enough, which is but dimly seen and imperfectly fulfilled. The greater part of these benefactions is directed to purposes which have but a slight or indirect bearing upon the relief of social distress, the restraint of injustice, or the mitigation of remediable hardships. The giving is even often economically false, and if carried to an extreme would prove disastrous to the community; for in many cases it is a transmutation of wealth from a status of active capital, wherein it makes possible a greater diffusion of comfort, to a status of comparative sterility. But, tho often mistaken as is the conception and futile the fulfilment of this duty, the fact that it is apprehended at all is one of far-reaching importance.

The limitation which democracy puts upon the new feudalism is also important. For democracy will endure, in spite of the new order. "Like death," said Disraeli, "it gives back nothing." Something of its substance it gives back, it must be confessed; for it permits the most serious encroachments upon its rights; but of its outer forms it yields nothing, and thus it retains the potentiality of exerting its will in whatever direction it may see fit. And this fact, tho now but feebly recognized by the feudal barons, will be better understood by them as time runs on, and they will bear in mind the limit of popular patience. It is an elastic limit, of a truth; for the mass of mankind, as both Hamlet and Thomas Jefferson observed, are more ready to endure known ills than to fly to others that they know not. It is a limit which, to be heeded, needs only to be carefully studied. Macaulay's famous dictum, that the privileged classes, when their rule is threatened, always bring about their own ruin by making further exactions, is likely, in this case, to prove untrue. A wiser forethought begins to prevail among the autocrats of to-day—a forethought destined to grow and expand and to prove of inestimable value when bequeathed to their successors. Our nobility will thus temper their exactions to an endurable limit; and they will distribute benefits to a degree that makes a tolerant, if not a satisfied people.

They may even make a working principle of Bentham's maxim, and after, of course, appropriating the first and choicest fruits of industry to themselves, may seek to promote the "greatest happiness of the greatest number." For therein will lie their greater security. . . .

Of the three under classes of the old feudalism—sub-tenants, cotters and villeins—the first two are already on the ground, and the last is in process of restoration. But the vast complexity of modern society specializes functions, and for the new feudalism still other classes are required. It is a difficult task properly to differentiate these classes. They shade off almost imperceptibly into one another; and the dynamic processes of modern industry often hurl, in one mighty convulsion, great bodies of individuals from a higher to a lower class, blurring or obscuring the lines of demarcation. Nevertheless, to take a figure from geology, these convulsions become less and less frequent as the substratum of industrial processes becomes more fixed and regular; the classes become more stable and show more distinct differences, and they will tend, under the new *régime*, to the formal institution of graded caste. At the bottom are the wastrels, at the top the barons; and the gradation, when the new *régime* shall have become fully developed, whole and perfect in its parts, will be about as follows:

I. The barons, graded on the basis of possessions.

II. The courtiers and court-agents.

III. The workers in pure and applied science, artists and physicians. The new feudalism, like most autocracies, will foster not only the arts, but also certain kinds of learning—particularly the kinds which are unlikely to disturb the minds of the multitude. A future Marsh or Cope or Le Conte will be liberally patronized and left free to discover what he will; and so, too, an Edison or a Marconi. Only they must not meddle with anything relating to social science. For obvious reasons, also, physicians will occupy a position of honor and comparative freedom under the new *régime*.

IV. The *entrepreneurs*, the managers of the great industries, transformed into a salaried class.

V. The foremen and superintendents. This class has heretofore been recruited largely from the skilled workers, but with the growth of technical education in schools and colleges and the development of fixed caste, it is likely to become entirely differentiated.

VI. The villeins of the cities and towns, more or less regularly employed, who do skilled work and are partially protected by organization.

VII. The villeins of the cities and towns who do unskilled work and are unprotected by organization. They will comprise the laborers, domestics and clerks.

VIII. The villeins of the manorial estates, of the great farms, the mines and the forests.

IX. The small-unit farmers (land owning), the petty tradesmen and manufacturers.

X. The sub-tenants on the manorial estates and great farms (corresponding to the class of "free tenants" in the old feudalism).

XI. The cotters, living in isolated places and on the margin of cultivation.

XII. The tramps, the occasionally employed, and unemployed—the wastrels of city and country.

This, then, is the table of socio-industrial rank leading down from the feudatory barons. It is a classification open, of course, to amendment. The minor shareholders, it may be suggested, are not provided for; and certain other omissions might be named. But it is not possible to anticipate every detail; and, as for the small shareholders, who now occupy a wide range, from comparative poverty to comparative affluence, it seems likely that the complete development of the new *régime* will practically eliminate them. Other critics, furthermore, will object to the basis of gradation. The basis employed is not relative wealth, a test which nine out of ten persons would unhesitatingly apply in social classification; it is not comparative earning capacity, economic freedom, nor intellectual ability. Rather, it is the relative degree of comfort—material, moral and intellectual—which each class contributes to the nobility. The wastrels contribute least, and they are the lowest. The foremen, superintendents and *entrepreneurs* contribute most of the purely material comfort, and their place is correspondingly high. But higher yet is the rank of the courtiers and court agents, the legates and nuncios. This class will include the editors of "respectable" and "safe" newspapers, the pastors of "conservative" and "wealthy" churches, the professors and teachers in endowed colleges and schools, lawyers generally, and most judges and politicians. During the transition period there will be a gradual elimination of the more unserviceable of these persons, with the result that in the end this class will be largely transformed. The individual security of place and livelihood of its members will then depend on the harmony of their utterances and acts with the wishes of the great nobles; and so long as they rightly fulfil their functions their recompense will be generous. They will be at once the assuagers of popular suspicion and discontent and the providers of moral and intellectual anodynes for the barons. Such of them, however, as have not the tact or fidelity to do or say what is expected of them will be promptly forced into class XI or XII, or, in extreme cases, banished from all classes, to become the wretched pariahs of society. . . .

A general view of the new society will present little of startling novelty. A person leaving this planet to-day and revisiting "the pale glimpses of the moon" when the new order is in full swing will from superficial observation see but few changes. *Alter et idem—*another, yet the same—he will say. Only by closer view will he mark the deepening and widening of channels along which the powerful currents of present tendencies are borne; only so will he note the effect of the more complete development of the mighty forces now at work.

So comprehensive and so exact will be the social and political control that it will be exercised in a constantly widening scope and over a growing multiplicity of details. The distribution of wages and dividends will be nicely balanced with a watchful regard for possible dissatisfaction. Old-age pensions to the more faithful employees, such as those granted by the Illinois Central, the Pennsylvania, the Colorado Fuel & Iron Company, the Metropolitan Traction Company, or the Lackawanna, will be generally distributed, for the hard work will be done only by the most vigorous, and a large class of destitute unemployed will be a needless menace to the *régime.* Peace will be the main desideratum, and its cultivation will be the most honored science of the age. A happy blending of generosity and firmness will characterize all dealings with open discontent; but the prevention of discontent will be the prior study, to which the intellect and the energies of the nobles and their legates will be ever bent. To that end the teachings of the schools and colleges, the sermons, the editorials, the stump orations, and even the plays at the theaters will be skilfully and persuasively molded; and the questioning heart of the poor, which perpetually seeks some answer to the painful riddle of the earth, will meet with a multitude of mollifying responses. These will be: From the churches, that discontent is the fruit of atheism, and that religion alone is a solace for earthly woe; from the colleges, that discontent is ignorant and irrational, since conditions have certainly bettered in the last one hundred years; from the newspapers, that discontent is anarchy: and from the stump orators that it is unpatriotic, since this nation is the greatest and most glorious that ever the sun shone upon. As of old, these reasons will for the time suffice; and against the possibility of recurrent questionings new apologetics will be skilfully formulated, to be put forth as occasion requires. On all sides will be observed a greater respect for power; and the former tendency toward rash and bitter criticism of the upper classes will decline.

The arts, too, will be modified. Literature will take on the hues and tones of the good-natured days of Charles II. Instead of poetry, however, the innocuous novel will flourish best; every flowery courtier will write romance, and the literary darling of the renascence will be an Edmund Waller of fiction. A lineal descendant of the famous Lely, who

> ". . . on animated canvas stole
> The sleepy eye that spoke the melting soul,"

will be the laureled chief of our painters; and sculpture, architecture and the lesser arts, under the spell of changed influences, will undergo a like transformation.

This, then, in the rough, is our Benevolent Feudalism to-be. It is not precisely a Utopia, not an "island valley of Avilion"; and yet it has its commendable, even its fascinating features. "The empire is peace," shouted the partisans of Louis Napoleon; and a like cry, with an equal ardency of enthusiasm, will be uttered by the supporters of the new *régime*. Peace and stability will be its defensive arguments, and peace and stability it will probably bring. But tranquil or unquiet, whatever it may be, its triumph is assured; and existent forces are carrying us toward it with an ever accelerating speed. One power alone might prevent it—the collective popular will that it shall not be. But of this there is no fear on the part of the barons, and but little expectation on the part of the underlings.

JACK LONDON
"What Life Means to Me"*
1906

London had been a socialist since 1895, when he read the *Communist Manifesto* and joined the Oakland branch of the Socialist Labor Party. A great admirer of Debs, he went over to the Socialist Party in 1901. For several years he was a very active member of the Party. He ran for mayor of Oakland twice and lectured and debated extensively for the Intercollegiate Socialist Society. London wrote "What Life Means to Me" for the Society, which originally published it as a pamphlet.

I was born in the working-class. Early I discovered enthusiasm, ambition, and ideals; and to satisfy these became the problem of my child-life. My environment was crude and rough and raw. I had no outlook, but an uplook rather. My place in society was at the bottom. Here life offered nothing but sordidness and wretchedness, both of the flesh and the spirit; for here flesh and spirit were alike starved and tormented.

Above me towered the colossal edifice of society, and to my mind the only way out was up. Into this edifice I early resolved to climb. Up above, men wore black clothes and boiled shirts, and women dressed in beautiful gowns. Also, there were good things to eat, and there was plenty to eat. This much for the flesh. Then there were the things of the spirit. Up above me, I knew, were unselfishnesses of the spirit, clean and noble thinking, keen intellectual living. I knew all this because I read "Seaside Library" novels, in which, with the exception of the villains and adventuresses, all men and women thought beautiful thoughts, spoke a beautiful tongue, and performed glorious deeds. In short, as I accepted the rising of the sun, I accepted that up above me was all that was fine and noble and gracious, all that gave decency and dignity to life, all that made life worth living and that remunerated one for his travail and misery.

* *Cosmopolitan*, March 1906.

But it is not particularly easy for one to climb up out of the working-class—especially if he is handicapped by the possession of ideals and illusions. I lived on a ranch in California, and I was hard put to find the ladder whereby to climb. I early inquired the rate of interest on invested money, and worried my child's brain into an understanding of the virtues and excellencies of that remarkable invention of man, compound interest. Further, I ascertained the current rates of wages for workers of all ages, and the cost of living. From all this data I concluded that if I began immediately and worked and saved until I was fifty years of age, I could then stop working and enter into participation in a fair portion of the delights and goodnesses that would then be open to me higher up in society. Of course, I resolutely determined not to marry, while I quite forgot to consider at all that great rock of disaster in the working-class world—sickness.

But the life that was in me demanded more than a meagre existence of scraping and scrimping. Also, at ten years of age, I became a newsboy on the streets of a city, and found myself with a changed uplook. All about me were still the same sordidness and wretchedness, and up above me was still the same paradise waiting to be gained; but the ladder whereby to climb was a different one. It was now the ladder of business. Why save my earnings and invest in government bonds, when, by buying two newspapers for five cents, with a turn of the wrist I could sell them for ten cents and double my capital? The business ladder was the ladder for me, and I had a vision of myself becoming a baldheaded and successful merchant prince.

Alas for visions! When I was sixteen I had already earned the title of "prince." But this title was given me by a gang of cut-throats and thieves, by whom I was called "The Prince of the Oyster Pirates." And at that time I had climbed the first rung of the business ladder. I was a capitalist. I owned a boat and a complete oyster-pirating outfit. I had begun to exploit my fellow-creatures. I had a crew of one man. As captain and owner I took two-thirds of the spoils, and gave the crew one-third, though the crew worked just as hard as I did and risked just as much his life and liberty.

This one rung was the height I climbed up the business ladder. One night I went on a raid amongst the Chinese fishermen. Ropes and nets were worth dollars and cents. It was robbery, I grant, but it was precisely the spirit of capitalism. The capitalist takes away the possessions of his fellow-creatures by means of a rebate, or of a betrayal of trust, or by the purchase of senators and supreme-court judges. I was merely crude. That was the only difference. I used a gun.

But my crew that night was one of those inefficients against whom the capitalist is wont to fulminate, because, forsooth, such inefficients increase expenses and reduce dividends. My crew did both. What of his carelessness he set fire to the big mainsail and totally destroyed it. There weren't any dividends that night, and the Chinese fishermen were richer by the nets and ropes we did not get. I was bankrupt, unable just then to pay sixty-five dollars for a new mainsail. I left my boat at anchor and went off on a bay-pirate boat on a raid up the Sacramento River. While away on this trip, another gang of bay pirates raided my boat. They stole everything, even the anchors; and later on, when I recovered the drifting hulk, I sold it for twenty dollars. I had slipped back the one rung I had climbed, and never again did I attempt the business ladder.

From then on I was mercilessly exploited by other capitalists. I had the muscle, and they made money out of it while I made but a very indifferent living out of it. I was a sailor before the mast, a longshoreman, a roustabout; I worked in canneries, and factories, and laundries; I mowed lawns, and cleaned carpets, and washed windows. And I never got the full product of my toil. I looked at the daughter of the cannery owner, in her carriage, and knew that it was my muscle, in part, that helped drag along that carriage on its rubber tires. I looked at the son of the factory owner, going to college, and knew that it was my muscle that helped, in part, to pay for the wine and good fellowship he enjoyed.

But I did not resent this. It was all in the game. They were the strong. Very well, I was strong. I would carve my way to a place amongst them and make money out of the muscles of other men. I was not afraid of work. I loved hard work. I would pitch in and work harder than ever and eventually become a pillar of society.

And just then, as luck would have it, I found an employer that was of the same mind. I was willing to work, and he was more than willing that I should work. I thought I was learning a trade. In reality, I had displaced two men. I thought he was making an electrician out of me; as a matter of fact, he was making fifty dollars per month out of me. The two men I had displaced had received forty dollars each per month; I was doing the work of both for thirty dollars per month.

This employer worked me nearly to death. A man may love oysters, but too many oysters will disincline him toward that particular diet. And so with me. Too much work sickened me. I did not wish ever to see work again. I fled from work. I became a tramp, begging my way from door to door, wandering over the United States and sweating bloody sweats in slums and prisons.

I had been born in the working-class, and I was now, at the age of eighteen, beneath the point at which I had started. I was down in the cellar of society, down in the subterranean depths of misery about which it is neither nice nor proper to speak. I was in the pit, the abyss, the human cesspool, the shambles and the charnel-house of our civilization. This is the part of the edifice of society that society chooses to ignore. Lack of space compels me here to ignore it, and I shall say only that the things I there saw gave me a terrible scare.

I was scared into thinking. I saw the naked simplicities of the complicated civilization in which I lived. Life was a matter of food and shelter. In order to get food and shelter men sold things. The merchant sold shoes, the politician sold his manhood, and the representative of the people, with exceptions, of course, sold his trust; while nearly all sold their honor. Women, too, whether on the street or in the holy bond of wedlock, were prone to sell their flesh. All things were commodities, all people bought and sold. The one commodity that labor had to sell was muscle. The honor of labor had no price in the market-place. Labor had muscle, and muscle alone, to sell.

But there was a difference, a vital difference. Shoes and trust and honor had a way of renewing themselves. They were imperishable stocks. Muscle, on the other hand, did not renew. As the shoe merchant sold shoes, he continued to replenish his stock. But there was no way of replenishing the laborer's stock of muscle. The more he sold of his muscle, the less of it remained to him. It was his one commodity, and each day his stock of it diminished. In the end, if he did not die before, he sold out and put up his shutters. He was a muscle bankrupt, and nothing remained to him but to go down into the cellar of society and perish miserably.

I learned, further, that brain was likewise a commodity. It, too, was different from muscle. A brain seller was only at his prime when he was fifty or sixty years old, and his wares were fetching higher prices than ever. But a laborer was worked out or broken down at forty-five or fifty. I had been in the cellar of society, and I did not like the place as a habitation. The pipes and drains were unsanitary, and the air was bad to breathe. If I could not live on the parlor floor of society, I could, at any rate, have a try at the attic. It was true, the diet there was slim, but the air at least was pure. So I resolved to sell no more muscle, and to become a vender of brains.

Then began a frantic pursuit of knowledge. I returned to California and opened the books. While thus equipping myself to become a brain merchant, it was inevitable that I should delve into sociology. There I found, in a certain class of books, scientifically formulated, the simple sociological concepts I had already worked out for myself. Other and greater minds, before I was born, had worked out all that I had thought and a vast deal more. I discovered that I was a socialist.

The socialists were revolutionists, inasmuch as they struggled to overthrow the society of the present, and out of the material to build the society of the future. I, too, was a socialist and a revolutionist. I joined the groups of working-class and intellectual revolutionists, and for the first time came into intellectual living. Here I found keen-flashing intellects and brilliant wits; for here I met strong and alert-brained, withal horny-handed, members of the working-class; unfrocked preachers too wide in their Christianity for any congregation of Mammon-worshippers; professors broken on the wheel of university subservience to the ruling class and flung out because they were quick with knowledge which they strove to apply to the affairs of mankind.

Here I found, also, warm faith in the human, glowing idealism, sweetnesses of unselfishness, renunciation, and martyrdom—all the splendid, stinging things of the spirit. Here life was clean, noble, and alive. Here life rehabilitated itself, became wonderful and glorious; and I was glad to be alive. I was in touch with great souls who exalted flesh and spirit over dollars and cents, and to whom the thin wail of the starved slum child meant more than all the pomp and circumstance of commercial expansion and world empire. All about me were nobleness of purpose and heroism of effort, and my days and nights were sunshine and starshine, all fire and dew, with before my eyes, ever burning and blazing, the Holy Grail, Christ's own Grail, the warm human, long-suffering and maltreated, but to be rescued and saved at the last.

And I, poor foolish I, deemed all this to be a mere foretaste of the delights of living I should find higher above me in society. I had lost many illusions since the day I read "Seaside Library" novels on the California ranch. I was destined to lose many of the illusions I still retained.

As a brain merchant I was a success. Society opened its portals to me. I entered right in on the parlor floor, and my disillusionment proceeded rapidly. I sat down to dinner with the masters of society, and with the wives and daughters of the masters of society. The women were gowned beautifully, I admit; but to my naïve surprise I discovered that they were of the same clay as all the rest of the women I had known down below in the cellar. "The colonel's lady and Judy O'Grady were sisters under their skins"—gowns.

It was not this, however, so much as their materialism, that shocked me. It is true, these beautifully gowned, beautiful women prattled sweet little ideals and dear little moralities; but in spite of their prattle the dominant key of the life they lived was materialistic. And they were so sentimentally selfish! They assisted in all kinds of sweet little charities, and informed one of the fact, while all the time the food they ate and the beautiful clothes they wore were bought out of dividends stained with the blood of child labor, and sweated labor, and of prostitution itself. When I mentioned such facts, expecting in my innocence that these sisters of Judy O'Grady would at once strip off their blood-dyed silks and jewels, they became excited and angry, and read me preachments about the lack of thrift, the drink, and the innate depravity that caused all the misery in society's cellar. When I mentioned that I couldn't quite see that it was the lack of thrift, the intemperance, and the depravity of a half-starved child of six that made it work twelve hours every night in a Southern cotton mill, these sisters of Judy O'Grady attacked my private life and called me an "agitator"—as though that, forsooth, settled the argument.

Nor did I fare better with the masters themselves. I had expected to find men who were clean, noble, and alive, whose ideals were clean, noble, and alive. I went about amongst the men who sat in the high places—the preachers, the politicians, the business men, the professors, and the editors. I ate meat with them, drank wine with them, automobiled with them, and studied them. It is true, I found many that were clean and noble; but with rare exceptions, they were not alive. I do verily believe I could count the exceptions on the fingers of my two hands. Where they were not alive with rottenness, quick with unclean life, they were merely the unburied dead—clean and noble, like well-preserved mummies, but not alive. In this connection I may especially mention the professors I met, the men who live up to that decadent university ideal, "the passionless pursuit of passionless intelligence."

I met men who invoked the name of the Prince of Peace in their diatribes against war, and who put rifles in the hands of Pinkertons with which to shoot down strikers in their own factories. I met men incoherent with indignation at the brutality of prize-fighting, and who, at the same time, were parties to the adulteration of food that killed each year more babies than even red-handed Herod had killed.

I talked in hotels and clubs and homes and Pullmans and steamer-chairs with captains of industry, and marvelled at how little travelled they were in the realm of intellect. On the other hand, I discovered that their intellect, in the business sense, was abnormally developed. Also, I discovered that their morality, where business was concerned, was nil.

This delicate, aristocratic-featured gentleman, was a dummy director and a tool of corporations that secretly robbed widows and orphans. This gentleman, who collected fine editions and was an especial patron of literature, paid blackmail to a heavy-jowled, black-browed boss of a municipal machine. This editor, who published patent medicine advertisements and did not dare print the truth in his paper about said patent medicines for fear of losing the advertising, called me a scoundrelly demagogue because I told him that his political economy was antiquated and that his biology was contemporaneous with Pliny.

This senator was the tool and the slave, the little puppet of a gross, uneducated machine boss; so was this governor and this supreme court judge; and all three rode on railroad passes. This man, talking soberly and earnestly about the beauties of idealism and the goodness of God, had just betrayed his comrades in a business deal. This man, a pillar of the church and heavy contributor to foreign missions, worked his shop girls ten hours a day on a starvation wage and thereby directly encouraged prostitution. This man, who endowed chairs in universities, perjured himself in courts of law over a matter of dollars and cents. And this railroad magnate broke his word as a gentleman and a Christian when he granted a secret rebate to one of two captains of industry locked together in a struggle to the death.

It was the same everywhere, crime and betrayal, betrayal and crime—men who were alive, but who were neither clean nor noble, men who were clean and noble but who were not alive. Then there was a great, hopeless mass, neither noble not alive, but merely clean. It did not sin positively nor deliberately; but it did sin passively and ignorantly by acquiescing in the current immorality and profiting by it. Had it been noble and alive it would not have been ignorant, and it would have refused to share in the profits of betrayal and crime.

I discovered that I did not like to live on the parlor floor of society. Intellectually I was bored. Morally and spiritually I was sickened. I remembered my intellectuals and idealists, my unfrocked preachers, broken professors, and clean-minded, class-conscious workingmen. I remembered my days and nights of sunshine and starshine, where life was all a wild sweet wonder, a spiritual paradise of unselfish adventure and ethical romance. And I saw before me, ever blazing and burning, the Holy Grail.

So I went back to the working-class, in which I had been born and where I belonged. I care no longer to climb. The imposing edifice of society above my head holds no delights for me. It is the foundation of the edifice that interests me. There I am content to labor, crowbar in hand, shoulder to shoulder with intellectuals, idealists, and class-conscious workingmen, getting a solid pry now and again and setting the whole edifice rocking. Some day, when we get a few more hands and crowbars to work, we'll topple it over, along with all its rotten life and unburied dead, its monstrous selfishness and sodden materialism. Then we'll cleanse the cellar and build a new habitation for mankind, in which there will be no parlor floor, in which all the rooms will be bright and airy, and where the air that is breathed will be clean, noble, and alive.

Such is my outlook. I look forward to a time when man shall progress upon something worthier and higher than his stomach, when there will be a finer incentive to impel men to action than the incentive of to-day, which is the incentive of the stomach. I retain my belief in the nobility and excellence of the human. I believe that spiritual sweetness and unselfishness will conquer the gross gluttony of to-day. And last of all, my faith is in the working-class. As some Frenchman has said, "The stairway of time is ever echoing with the wooden shoe going up, the polished boot descendings."

The Industrial Republic*
1907

Few who read *The Jungle*, which had vaulted Sinclair to world fame the year before, realized that he was a socialist, or, if they did, bothered to take it seriously. Now, with the publication of *The Industrial Republic*, he left no doubts.

It is my belief that the student of a generation from now will look back upon the last two centuries of human history and interpret them as the final stage of a long process whereby man was transformed from a solitary and predatory individual to a social and peaceable member of a single world community. He will see that men, pressed by the struggle for existence, had united themselves into groups under the discipline of laws and conventions; and that the last two centuries represented the period when these laws and conventions, having done their unifying work, and secured the survival of the group, were set aside and replaced by free and voluntary social effort.

The student will furthermore perceive that this evolutionary process had two manifestations, two waves, so to speak; the first political, and the second industrial; the first determined by man's struggle to protect his life, and the second by his struggle to amass wealth. The culmination of the first occurred successively in the English revolutions, the American and French revolutions, and the other various efforts after political freedom. After each of these achievements the historian notices a period of bitterness and disillusionment, a sense of failure, it being discovered that the expected did not occur, that Liberty, Equality and Fraternity did not become the rule of men's conduct. After that, however, succeeds a period of enlightenment, it having been realised that the work has only been half done, that man has been made only half free. The political sovereignty has been taken out of the possession of private individuals and made the property of the

* Pp. viii–xi, 215–219, 238–239, 242–247.

whole community, to be shared in by all upon equal terms; but the industrial sovereignty still remains the property of a few. A man can no longer be put in jail or taxed by a king, but he can be starved and exploited by a master; his body is now his own, but his labour is another's—and there is very little difference between the two. So immediately there begins a new movement, the end of which is a new revolution, and the establishment of THE INDUSTRIAL REPUBLIC.

What do I mean by an Industrial Republic? I mean an organisation for the production and distribution of wealth, whose members are established upon a basis of equality; who elect representatives to govern the organisation; and who receive the full value of what their labour produces. I mean an industrial government of the people, by the people, for the people; a community in which the means of production have been made the inalienable property of the State. My purpose in writing this book is to point out the forces which are now rapidly developing in America; and which, when they have attained to maturity, will usher in the Industrial Republic by a process as natural and as inevitable as that by which a chick breaks out of its shell or a child comes forth from the womb at the proper hour. I believe that the economic process is whirling us on with terrific momentum toward the crisis; and I look to see the most essential features of the great transformation accomplished in America within one year after the Presidential election of 1912.

If I had been a tactful person I should have kept that last statement until far on in my argument. For I find many people who are interested in the idea of an Industrial Republic, and some few who are willing to think of it as a possibility; but I find none who do not balk when I presume to set the day. Yet the setting of the day is a vital part of my conviction, and I should play the reader false if I failed to mention it in this preliminary statement of my argument. It is a conviction to which I have come with the diligent use of the best faculties I possess, and after a preparation of a sort that is certainly unusual, and possibly even quite unique. . . .

[THE INDUSTRIAL REPUBLIC]

One of the first objections that you will run up against, if ever you start out to agitate Socialism, is your lack of definiteness.

Give us your program, people will say—we want to know what sort of a world you expect to make, and how you are going to make it. And they will grow angry when they find that you have not a cut-and-dried scheme of society in your pocket—that you have stirred them up all to no purpose. And yet that is just what you have to go on doing. There used to be Utopian Socialists—Plato was the first of them and Bellamy was the last—who knew the coming world from its presidents to its chimney-sweeps; who could tell you the very colour of its postage-stamps. But nowadays all Socialists are scientific. They say that social changes are the product of the interaction of innumerable forces, and cannot be definitely foretold; they say that the new organism will be the result of the strivings of millions of men, acted upon by various motives, ideals, prejudices and fears. And so they call themselves no longer builders of systems, but preachers of righteousness; their answer to objectors is that I once heard given by Hanford, recent candidate for vice-president on the Socialist ticket, to a lawyer with whom he was debating: "Do you ask for a map of Heaven before you join the Church?"

This much we may say, however. The Industrial Republic will be an industrial government of the people, by the people, for the people. Exactly as political sovereignty is the property of the community, so will it be with industrial sovereignty—that is, capital. It will be administered by elected officials and its equal benefits will be the elemental right of every citizen. The officials may be our presidents and governors and legislatures, or they may be an entirely separate governing body, corresponding to our present directors and presidents of corporations. In countries where the revolution is one of violence they will probably be trade-union committees. The governing power may be chosen separately in each trade and industry, by those who work in it, just as the officials of a party are now chosen by those who vote in it; or they may be appointed, as our postmasters and colonial governors are appointed, by some central authority, perhaps by the President. All of these things are for the collective wisdom of the country to decide when the time comes; meanwhile it is only safe to say that there will be as little change as possible in the business methods of the country—and so little that the man who should come back and look at it from the outside, would not even know that any change had taken place. I have heard a distinguished Republican orator, poking fun at Socialism in a public address, picture women disputing in the public warehouses as to whether each had had her fair share of shoes and fish. In the Industrial Republic the workingman will go to the factory, will work under the direction of his superior officer, and will receive his wages at the end of the week in exactly the same way as to-day. He will spend his money exactly as he spends it to-day—he will go to a store, and if he gets a pair of shoes he will pay for them. The farmer will till his land exactly as he does to-day, and when he takes his grain to market he will be paid for it in money, and will put it in the bank and will draw a check upon it to pay for the suit of clothes he has ordered by express. The only difference in all these various operations will be that the factories will be public property, and the wages the full value of the product, with no deductions for dividends on stock; and that the street cars, the banks and the stores will be public utilities, managed exactly as our post-office is managed, charging what the service costs, and making no profits. In the year 1901 the U. S. Steel Corporation paid one hundred and twenty-five million dollars and employed one hundred and twenty-five thousand men; under Socialism the wages of each employee of the U. S. Steel Corporation would therefore be increased one thousand dollars a year, which is two or three hundred per cent. In the same way, the wages of an employee of the Standard Oil Company would be increased four thousand dollars, which is from eight to ten hundred per cent. The fare upon the government-owned street railroads in the City of Berlin is two and a half cents, which would mean that our workingman's car-fare bill would be cut by fifty per cent. The toll of the government-owned telephone of Sweden is three cents, which would mean that the workingman's telephone bill would be cut seventy per cent. The elimination of the speculator and the higher piracy of Wall Street would raise the price of the farmer's grain by fifty per cent; the elimination of the millers' trust and the railroad trust would lower the price of bread by an equal sum. The elimination of the tariff on wool, of the sweater and the jobber, the department store and the express trust, would probably lower the price of the farmer's suit of clothes sixty per cent; the elimination of the sweatshop and the slum might raise it to its original level, while decreasing the farmer's doctor's bills correspondingly. Of course I do not mean to say that the gains from the abolition of exploitation will be distributed in exactly the ratios outlined above. They will be distributed so as to equalise the rewards of labour. The point is that there will be a saving at every point—because at every point there is exploitation. . . .

I have outlined the economic and political conditions which I believe will prevail in the Industrial Republic; there remains to consider what influences these will exert upon the moral and intellectual life of men.

When people criticise the Socialist programme they always think about government censors and red tape, and limitations upon free endeavour; and so they say that Socialism would lead to a reign of tameness and mediocrity. They tell us that under the new régime we should all have to wear the same kind of coat and eat the same kind of pie. They argue that if all the means of production are owned by the Government there will be no way for you to get your own kind of pie; failing to perceive that government control of the means of production no more implies government control of the product, than government control of the post-office means government control of the contents of your letters. Said a good clergyman friend of mine: "What possible place, for instance, would there be for *me* in your Socialist society." And I answered, "There would be just exactly the same place for you that there is at present. How is it that you get your living and your freedom? You are maintained by an association of people who want the work you can do. Every clergyman in the country is maintained in that way—and so are thousands upon thousands of editors, authors, artists, actors—so are all our clubs, societies, restaurants, theatres and orchestras. The Government has absolutely nothing to do with them at present—and the Government need have absolutely nothing to do with them under Socialism. The people who want them subscribe and pay for them. Under our present system they pay the cost to private profit-seekers; under Socialism they would pay the State."

In the Industrial Republic a man will be able to order anything he wishes, from a flying machine to a seven-legged spider made of diamonds; and the only question that anyone will ever dream of asking him will be: "Have you got the money to pay for it?" There remains only to add that, the system of wealth-distribution being now one of justice, that question will mean: "Have you performed for society the equivalent of the labour-time of the article you desire society to furnish you?". . .

The one point to be made absolutely clear in this matter is that the Industrial Republic will be an organisation for the supplying of the *material necessities* of human life. With the moral and intellectual affairs of men it can have very little to do. What Socialism proposes to organise and systematise is industry, not thought. The difference between the products of industry and those of thought is a fundamental one. The former are strictly limited in quantity, and the latter are infinite. No man can have more than his fair share of the former without depriving his neighbour; but to a thought there is no such limit—a single poem or symphony may do for a million just as well as for one. With the former it is possible for one man to gain control and oppress others; but it is not possible to monopolise thought. And it is in consequence of this fact that laws and systems are necessary with the things of the body, which would be preposterous with the things of the mind. The bodily needs of men are pretty much all alike. Men need food, clothing, shelter, light, air, and heat; and they need these of pretty nearly the same quality and in pretty nearly the same quantity—so that they can be furnished methodically year in and year out, according to order. This is being done by our present industrial masters for profit; in the Industrial Republic it will be done by the State, for use.

Quite otherwise is it with things in which men are not alike—their religions and their arts and their sciences. The only conditions under which the State can with any justice or efficiency have to do with production in these fields, is after men have come to agreement—when opinion has given place to knowledge. For instance, we have in certain fields of science, methods which we can consider as agreed upon; it would be perfectly possible for the State to endow astronomical investigators, and seekers of the North Pole, and inventors of flying machines, and pioneers in all the technical arts. In the same way we come to agree, within certain limits, what is a worth-while play or book; in so far as we agree, we can have government theatres and publishing houses, government newspapers and magazines. If ever science should discover the rationale of the phenomenon of genius, so that we could analyse and judge it with precision, we should then have the whole problem solved.

You are a writer, perhaps; and you say that you would not relish the idea of bringing your book to a government official to be judged. Ask yourself, however, if some of your prejudice may not be due to your conception of a government official as the representative of a class, and of the interests of a class. In the Industrial Republic there will be no classes, and the officers of the coöperative publishing house will have no one to serve but the people. If they are not satisfactory to the people, the people can get rid of them— something the people cannot do anywhere in the world to-day. You think, perhaps, that you choose your own governors in this country—but you do not. What you do is to go to the polls and choose between two sets of candidates, both of whom have been selected by your economic rulers as being satisfactory to them.

While I do not profess to be certain, I imagine that an author who wanted his book published by the Government would have to pay the expenses of the publication. This would not be any hardship, for wages in the Industrial Republic could not be less than ten dollars for a day of six hours' work. With the rapid improvement in machinery and methods that would follow, they would probably soon be double that—and of course it would rest with the people who were doing the work to see that it was done in an attractive place, with plenty of fresh air and due safeguards against accidents. Under these conditions a man of refinement could go to a factory to work for pleasure and exercise, instead of pulling at ropes in a gymnasium, as he commonly does nowadays. And when a young author had earned the cost of making his book, he would have done all that he had to do. He would not have to enter into a race in vulgar advertising with exploiting private concerns; nor would the public form its ideas of his work from criticisms in reviews which were run to secure advertisements, and which gave their space to the books that were advertised the most. Neither would his critics be employed by a class, to maintain the interests of a class, and to keep down the aspirations of some other class. Also, the book-reading public would no longer consist—as our present society so largely consists—of idle and unfeeling rich, and ignorant, debased and hunger-driven poor.

And then, as I said, there is a second method—the method of the churches and clubs. Out in Chicago there was, four years ago, a man who thought there ought to be more Socialist books published than there were. He had no money; but he drew up a programme for a coöperative publishing house, to furnish Socialist literature at cost to those who wanted it. He got some ten thousand dollars in ten-dollar shares, and since then he has been turning out half a million pieces of Socialist literature every year. It seems to me a perfect illustration of what would happen in the new society, the second way in which books would be published. Such concerns— free associations, as they are termed in the Socialist vocabulary— would spring up literally by the thousands. They would cover every field that the liberated soul of man might be interested in, they would care for every type of thinker and artist, no matter how eccentric; they would offer encouragement to every man who showed the slightest sign of power in any field. The only reason we do not have many times as many of these associations as we have now, is simply that those people who really care about the higher things of life are almost invariably poor and helpless.

One of the curious things which I have observed about those who pick flaws in the suggestions of the Socialist, is how seldom it ever occurs to them to apply their own tests to the present system of things. How is it with art and literature production now—are all the conditions quite free from objection? Is the man of genius always encouraged and protected, and set free to develop his powers? . . .

MORRIS HILLQUIT
Socialism in Theory and Practice*
1909

No single book so effectively set forth the philosophy of the Socialist Party of America as this one.

Only half a century ago the labor movement was barely in its inception, weak in numbers, inefficient in organization and uncertain in its aims. To-day the workingmen are organized in legions of powerful trade unions, trained and drilled in the everyday battles for the advancement of their conditions of life. In a large number of countries they have created immense coöperative establishments successfully competing with the capitalist enterprises in the same industries. In all civilized countries of the world they have developed a socialist movement, so uniform in its aims and methods, so persistent in its struggles, so inspiring in its propaganda and so irresistible in its spread, that with perhaps the single exception of early Christianity the movement stands unparalleled in the annals of written history.

The trade unions fight the immediate and particular battles of the workers in the factories, mills, mines and shops, and educate their members to a sense of their economic rights. The coöperative labor enterprises train their members in the collective operation and democratic management of industries. The socialist parties emphasize the general and ultimate interests of the entire working class, and train their members in political action and in the administration of the affairs of government and state.

Marching over different routes, operating with different methods and conscious or unconscious of the effects of their own activity, all these forms of the labor movement make for one inevitable goal: the building up of a new and regenerated society.

And the workingmen are not alone in this movement. They receive large and ever larger accretions from all other classes—from the small business men displaced by the trust, the professionals

* Pp. 9–12, 14–17, 22–24, 29–35.

reduced to the state of "intellectual proletarians"; the farmers, exploited less directly but not less effectively by trustified capital, and even from the ranks of the capitalist class itself. The number of men of the "better classes" who embrace the cause of the people from motives of enlightened self-interest or from purely ethical motives grows as the evils of the decaying capitalist system become more apparent. These "desertions" from the ranks of the dominant classes into the camp of the subjugated class, are an infallible sign of the approaching collapse of the rule of the former.

The economic development which has thus furnished the conditions for a radical transformation of society and produced the forces to accomplish it, is also building up the basis of that transformation.

The great modern trust organizes industry on a national scale; it regulates the production and distribution of commodities, and brings all workers of the country under one administration. A trustified industry is in its essence a nationalized industry. It would be just as easy to-day for a governmental agency to run such an industry as it is for the individual trust magnates or their agents.

And it would be much more just. Our highly effective system of industry is the achievement of many generations, the heritage of all mankind; our marvelous tools of production and distribution are the fruit of the collective industry and intellect of the laboring population; they are operated collectively by the whole working class, and they are indispensable to the life of the entire nation. In equity and justice the capitalist has no better title to the modern social tools than the slaveholder had to his chattel slaves.

Socialism advocates the transfer of ownership in the social tools of production—the land, factories, machinery, railroads, mines, etc.—from the individual capitalists to the people, to be operated for the benefit of all.

This program has been denounced as confiscatory and revolutionary, but it is no more so than was the abolition of chattel slavery. It has been ridiculed as utopian and fantastic, but it is no more so than the demands of the eighteenth century capitalist for the abolition of the privileges of birth were to his contemporaries.

Our social progress is a movement towards perfect democracy. The successive stages of our civilization mark the disappearance of one class privilege after another. Why should mankind halt in reverence and awe before the privilege of wealth? When an heir to millions is born to-day, he has the same exceptional position in society and the same power over thousands of his fellow-men that the newborn duke or marquis had in times past; and the justice and logic of the situation are the same in both cases. A true democracy is one in which all babes are born alike, and all human beings enjoy the same rights and opportunities.

THE SYSTEM OF INDIVIDUALISM

Socialism and individualism are the two main contending principles underlying all modern social theories and movements. Both ideas are, comparatively speaking, new in the history of human thought, and the social philosophy based on individualism is the older of the two. . . .

The battles fought by the pre-Revolutionary bourgeoisie in the name of Individual Liberty have given to civilization a few great acquisitions. They have to a large extent emancipated man in the purely individual sphere of his life, and rendered into his own keeping his beliefs, views and tastes, his individual mind and soul. The freedom of press, speech, conscience and person are such acquisitions, and they are of everlasting benefit to mankind.

But the historical watchword had an altogether different fate in the field of politics and industry.

In the revolutionary period of the career of our ruling classes "Individual Liberty" in those fields stood principally for freedom from arbitrary political, industrial and social restraint, but with the fall of feudalism and the removal of feudal restraints, the phrase lost its original significance. The manufacturing and trading classes, as the struggling and subjected bourgeois of the seventeenth and eighteenth centuries, appealed to the sacred right of individual freedom as a means to deliver them from the oppression of the ruling classes of their time; but the possessing classes of the nineteenth and twentieth centuries, themselves in power and confronting a new dependent class, the class of wage workers, invoke the old god of their fathers only in order to strengthen their own rule. The "Individual Liberty" of the modern capitalist has come very largely to stand for the right to deal with his employees as he pleases, the unrestricted right to exploit men, women and children of the working class, and to be free from the interference of the state in his process of exploitation. An economic order based entirely on the principles of "laissez-faire," and a political organization of the type characterized by Huxley as "Administrative Nihilism" are the ideals of the modern priests of the god "Individual Liberty." In the hands of the capitalist individual liberty has degenerated into individual license, its philosophy is that of shortsighted egoism. The most consistent and logical representative of that philosophy is probably Max Stirner, whose work, "The Ego and His Own," has only recently, more than sixty years after its first appearance, been placed before the English-reading bourgeois to be acclaimed by them with unbounded delight. The views of that philosopher of individualism may be summed up in the following two brief quotations from the work mentioned:—

"Away then with every concern that is not altogether my concern! You think at least 'the good cause' must be my concern. What's good and what's bad! Why, I myself am my concern, and I am neither good nor bad. Neither has meaning for me.

"The divine is God's concern; the human man's. My concern is neither the divine nor the human, not the true, good, just, free, etc., but solely what is mine, and it is not a general one, but is unique, as I am unique.

"Nothing is more to me than myself."[1]

And again:—

"Every state is a despotism, be the despot one or (as one is likely to imagine about a republic), if all be the lords, *i.e.*, despotize one over the other."[2]

And in this extreme view of individual freedom the liberal capitalists find themselves entirely in accord with the radical anarchists. Both would rob society of all its social functions. Both base their philosophy on individual competition and the brutal struggle for existence rather than on the principle of human coöperation, both make an idol of individual liberty, both suffer from a morbid exaggeration of the Ego, and both sanction all means to attain the end of individual happiness.

The only difference between the conservative and patriotic capitalist and the violent anarchist is that the former represents the "individualism" of the rich, and the latter that of the poor.

The philosophy of individualism supplies a moral and pseudo-scientific sanction for the economic struggle between man and man, and appeals to the different classes of the population favorably or

[1] Max Stirner, "The Ego and His Own," New York, 1907, p. 6.
[2] *Ibid.*, p. 256.

unfavorably according to their chances and position in that struggle. The ruling classes with their overwhelming economic powers are best equipped for the uneven struggle of existence; they are bound to prevail in it and to reap all the advantages of the victory if not interfered with—they are, therefore, naturally inclined to individualism.

The dependent and non-possessing classes, on the other hand, are powerless in the individual struggle for existence under prevailing conditions. They stand in need of social protection against the abuses of the dominant class, and thus their strength lies in concerted action and coöperation. To the intelligent workingmen, individualism is as repellent as it is hostile to their interests—they naturally lean towards the opposite philosophy. Socialism is the manifestation of the working class revolt against the excessive individualism of the capitalists, just as individualism appeared originally as the expression of the revolt of the bourgeoisie against the excessive centralization of the ancient régime. . . .

The historical and uniform course of the evolution of the state and its overwhelming importance as a factor in human civilization have led the school of thinkers of which Auguste Comte, Saint-Simon and Hegel are the typical representatives, to the opposite extreme—the conception of the state as an organism. The "historical" or "organic" school sees in the abstract phenomenon of the state a concrete and independent being with a life, interests and natural history of its own. To these thinkers human society is a social organism very much like the biological organism. The social institutions are so many of its organs performing certain vital functions required for the life and well-being of the organism itself, while the individual members of society are but its cells. . . .

In short, the state is the end, the citizen is only the means. It is the old parable of the shrewd Mucius Scevola presenting itself before us in the fashionable garb of modern science.

And here again the two extremes meet. The extreme individualist deprecates all attempts on the part of the state to regulate the affairs of the citizens, on the plea that the state should not interfere with the liberty of the individual; the extreme sociocrat discountenances all attempts on the part of the citizens to model the state in their interest, on the ground that the individual *cannot* shape the life of the social organism. One bases his objections on the ground of expediency, the other on scientific necessity; but the practical results are the same in both cases—the separation of the state and the individual.

Although the ultra "organic" theory of the state has found some adherents among socialist writers, contemporary socialism has, on the whole, as little sympathy with the extreme sociocratic view as it has with that of the extreme individualist.

It is always dangerous to engraft a ready-made principle of any branch of scientific research on an entirely different branch, notwithstanding apparent analogies between the two, and the fallacy of that method is probably best illustrated by the introduction of purely biological laws into the domain of sociology. The social organization of men is a phenomenon vastly different from the biological organism. In the case of the latter it is the organism as such which is endowed with sensation, reflection and life—the individual cell has no conscious life of its own, and serves only to support the existence of the organism. In the case of the "social organism," on the other hand, it is the individual members of it who are endowed with conscious life, and it is the so-called organism that serves to support their individual existences.

The state is not the voluntary and arbitrary creation of man, but it is just as little a factor imposed on man by some power outside of him. The state is a product of logical historical development, but that only as an accompaniment of the logical historical development of man. The individual cannot dissociate himself from society, nor can society have any existence outside of the individuals composing it. The state represents the collective mind and attainments of all past generations, but also the collective intellect, will and powers of its present living, feeling and thinking members. The state has the power to regulate the conduct of its individual citizens, but its citizens have the power to determine the scope and nature of such regulations, and the higher mankind ascends in the scale of intellectual development, the more effective is its direction of the functions of the state. Man to-day is in a position to employ the state not merely for the good of the abstract "social organism as a whole," nor yet merely for the good of remote generations to come, but for his own present concrete good.

This is the view from which all socialist political activity proceeds, and this view is steadily gaining practical recognition in all spheres of society, as is eloquently attested by the ever greater extensions of the social functions of the modern state. . . .

THE INDIVIDUAL UNDER SOCIALISM

The commonest of all objections to the socialist ideal is that a state of socialism would endanger individual liberty. From such unimaginative novelists as Eugen Richter[3] and David M. Parry,[4] whose conceptions of the socialist commonwealth are those of the modern factory regulations extended to the scope of a national order, up to the thinker of the keenness of mind and universality of knowledge of Herbert Spencer who asserts that "all socialism implies slavery,"[5] all bourgeois philosophers seem to take it for granted that mankind is to-day enjoying a large measure of individual freedom and that socialism would greatly curtail if not entirely suppress it.

The socialists deny both assertions with equal emphasis.

Under our present system of economic dependence and struggles, individual liberty is but a fiction. The very small "leisure class," *i.e.*, the class of persons enjoying a workless and ample income and entirely removed from active participation in the industrial, professional, commercial and financial strife, no doubt enjoy considerable individual liberty, but for all other strata of modern society that liberty does not exist.

The workingmen, the largest class of the population, are anything but free: their work and their pleasures, their dress and their dwellings, their mode of life and their habits, are forced on them by their economic condition.

"Not as an exception, but universally," says Mr. H. D. Lloyd,[6] "labor is doing what it does not want to do, and not getting what it wants or needs. Laborers want to work eight hours a day; they must work ten, fourteen, eighteen. . . . They want to send their children to school; they must send them to the factory. They want their wives to keep house for them; but they too must throw some shuttle or guide some wheel. They must work when they are sick; they must stop work at another's will; they must work life out to keep life in. The people have to ask for work, and then do not get it. They have to take less than a fair share of the product; they have

---

[3] "Sozialdemokratische Zukunftsbilder."
[4] "The Scarlet Empire," Indianapolis, 1906.
[5] "The Coming Slavery."
[6] Quoted in Richard T. Ely's "Socialism and Social Reform," pp. 209, 210.

to risk life, limb or health—their own, their wives', their children's —for others' selfishness or whim."

Nor is the workingman alone deprived of individual liberty under present conditions. The toiling farmer burdened by mortgages and oppressed by the railroad companies, the professional man dependent on private and unregulated calls for his services, and the small business man struggling against odds to maintain his "independence," they are all tied to a routine of life and action not voluntarily chosen, but inexorably imposed on them by the economic exigencies of their business pursuits and callings.

And even the "powerful" and wealthy, the heads of the modern industrial structure, are anything but free: their wealth as live, active, investment-seeking capital, dominates them and suppresses their individual volition; they are the slaves of their wealth rather than its masters.

All these purely economic checks on individual liberty must of necessity be greatly palliated, if not entirely removed, in a socialist community, for the system of socialism implies primarily a state of greater economic security and industrial equality.

"But," it is asked, "assuming that socialism would remove some of the elements operating to-day against the full exercise of the freedom of the individual, would it not create new and more formidable restraints upon liberty? Under the present régime the individual has some say in the choice of his occupation and the mode of exercising his trade or calling; under socialism, on the other hand, the state would be the sole employer, and would determine for every citizen what, where and how he should work; would not the citizen thus become the slave of the state?"

This argument, so frequently urged against socialism, contains two fundamental errors: it assumes that a socialist state may be a power independent of and opposed to the body of individuals composing it, and that in a system of socialism, all industries must be concentrated in and controlled by the national government or "state."

The basic principle of every socialist community must be its democratic administration: the socialist state will assume such concrete form, powers and functions as the majority of citizens, unbiased by conflicting class interests, will freely choose to confer on it, and it is not at all reasonable to suppose that these citizens will deliberately encase themselves in an iron cage of rigid laws and rules of their own making.

Much more likely the men who will have the framing of the political and industrial system of a socialist commonwealth, will take ample care of their own individual freedom.

Nor is there any reason to suppose that under socialism "the state" would be the sole employer. Socialism implies the *collective* ownership of the social tools of production, and the *collective* management of industries based upon the use of social tools. Does that necessarily imply state ownership and management? By no means. Certain industries are even to-day organized on a national scale, and may be best managed or controlled as state functions; others come more appropriately within the scope of the municipal administration, others still may be most efficiently managed by voluntary coöperative associations with or without state control, while a variety of industries of an individual nature, such as the various arts and crafts, must of necessity remain purely individual pursuits. The phantom of the "despotic state" has taken such a strong hold of the minds of our social philosophers trained in the individualistic school of thought, that even writers like Professor Richard T. Ely, of whose candor and analytical powers there can be no doubt, and who is by no means unsympathetic to socialism, is not quite free from the fear of it. "Even," says Professor Ely, "if the functions of government should be reduced to the lowest forms compatible with socialism, those in whose hands were centered political and economic control would have tremendous power, however they might be selected or appointed. Nor can we forget the possibilities of combinations between different parties for certain purposes. It would, under socialism, be quite possible for two or three parties to act together as sometimes they do now. The frequent assertion that the Democratic and Republican parties have acted together in New York City to control the civil service, seems to be well founded; and it is quite conceivable that two or three parties might act together to promote the interests favorable to a few leaders, and to keep down, if not persecute, obnoxious persons."[7]

In voicing these apprehensions Professor Ely unconsciously transfers present conditions into an order of things in which the very causes of such conditions are altogether lacking. Political parties are the creatures and tools of class interests, and "the interests

[7] Richard T. Ely, "Socialism and Social Reform," pp. 212, 213.

favorable to a few leaders" which he mentions, are the economic interests of the class or group of men represented in politics by those leaders. Modern party politics is, as we shall attempt to show in a later chapter, a manifestation of the capitalist mode of production and of the economic struggle of the classes, and must disappear with the abolition of the present economic order.

Under socialism there can be no party politics, in the present sense, and whatever abuses may develop in the administration of the state or the industries, can be only casual, based on inexperience or error of judgment of the community or on personal incompetence, malice or ambition of the responsible officers, and in either case they can be more readily remedied than in a state in which such abuses have their roots in the very foundation of the industrial organization of society.

On a par with the assertion that socialism would be fatal to individual liberty is the kindred claim that socialism would destroy the individuality of man. The "dead level of intellectual equality and homogeneity" under socialism is a specter almost as terrifying to the good "individualist" as the phantom of socialist slavery. And it is fully as unreal. For if any industrial system tends to destroy the individuality of men, it is not the proposed system of socialism, but our present economic order. The aggregation of millions of workingmen in the modern industrial centers, employed under similar conditions, tied everlastingly to the same monotonous machine work, dwelling in the same uniform tenements and leading the same stereotyped bleak existence, tends to turn them into one undistinguishable, homogeneous mass, dressing, talking, looking and thinking substantially alike. The men of our active upper classes, all engaged in the same all-absorbing pursuit of wealth by the same methods and under the same conditions, and our leisure classes sorely tried by the rigid rules of conventional etiquette, and tied to a blasé life of uniform and tiring social functions, fashionable sports and prescribed recreations, develop a different but not less homogeneous nor more attractive type. This natural uniformity of type within the different social classes is accompanied by a sort of artificial uniformity produced by the present economic conditions operating in a more indirect manner. "One has only to look on whilst the sons of the *nouveaux riches* spend their money," remarks Mr. MacDonald, "or whilst the crowds which our industrial quarters have disgorged enjoy themselves, to appreciate the meaningless monotony of our pleasure. From our furniture, made by the thousand pieces by machine, to our religion, stereotyped in set formulae and pursued by clockwork methods, individuality is an exceptional characteristic."[8]

"Our standard of decency in expenditure," observes Professor Veblen, "as in other ends of emulation, is set by the usage of those next above us in reputability; until, in this way, especially in any community where class distinctions are somewhat vague, all canons of respectability and decency, and all standards of consumption, are traced back by insensible gradations to the usages and habits of thought of the highest social and pecuniary class—the wealthy leisure class."[9]

And Mr. Vail expresses the same idea when he says: "The tendency toward uniformity is due to the lack of equality in economic conditions. The inferior classes strive to imitate the superior classes in order to avoid an apparent social inferiority. The result is, society is continually run in the same groove. On the other hand, any system which would tend to decrease economic inequality would tend to kill imitation. Just in proportion as men become equal, they cease to gain by imitating each other. It is always among equals that we find true independence."[10]

[8] J. Ramsay MacDonald, "Socialism and Society," London, 1905, p. 7.
[9] Thorstein Veblen, "The Theory of the Leisure Class," New York, 1905, p. 104.
[10] Charles H. Vail, "Principles of Scientific Socialism," p. 227.

WILLIAM ENGLISH WALLING
*The Larger Aspect of Socialism**
1913

Walling, one of the "millionaire" socialists, was an interesting thinker, who sought to reconcile Marx with the tradition of American pragmatism as embodied in the writings of James and Dewey.

The tendency of the newer Socialist thought is not to struggle *against* the old, nor to turn the movement to the right or to the left, but to enable it to go *more rapidly* ahead—in the same revolutionary direction in which it originally started and, on the whole, has been traveling ever since. And in order to go more rapidly ahead the great need is not to patch up theories of 1850 for the purpose, but to employ such new principles and methods as most adequately express the present day movement and the present period generally. The older theories, as I have said, may be taken not only as having been satisfactory for the time in which they were formulated, but as still having, beyond doubt, a very considerable value to-day. But it is not necessary, in order to save what is of value, to try to adapt these older theories to present need, for whatever was vital and of lasting worth has long ago been embodied in the movement itself, at least wherever it has reached an advanced state, as for example in Germany. By basing our theory henceforth on the movement (where it is mature), instead of following the opposite method of trying to base the movement on a theory, we not only have the best possible form of Marxism and a policy in accord with modern thought, but we are gaining from the movement something which is vastly more important than all its theories, namely its actual experience—in which is incorporated not only a whole phase of modern civilization and a large part of the history of our generation but some of the deepest subconscious strivings, which are as yet not capable even of the most tentative formulation. If we study the Socialist press and periodicals, the tactics

* Pp. xvii–xx, 27–29.

of the leading Socialist Congresses and the writings of the most representative Socialist writers (when they are not dealing with theoretical questions), we not only gain a more profound insight into Socialism than by any other method, but we are laying the only possible authentic foundation for Socialist political and economic policy as well as Socialist culture and civilization.

Nearly all the difficulties of Socialism in the past have come from the efforts of this or that theorist or faction to narrow it to suit their purpose. But there is now an opposite and equally dangerous tendency, since the movement has begun to grow so rapidly, to make Socialism too broad. I have given many reasons why we should take the broader view of Socialism, but we cannot identify it with the universe or with all progress, for it would then have no definite meaning at all. We cannot agree with H. G. Wells, for example, that "scientific progress, medical organization, the advancement of educational method, artistic production and literature are all aspects of Socialism." This, to use a phrase employed by Wells himself in another connection (only a few lines below), is to do "sheer violence to language." And what is worse, it confuses Socialism with the stage of society which is preceding it, and against which Socialism is undoubtedly chiefly to be directed, namely "State Socialism." As we are now in a transition period between private or individualist capitalism and the so-called "State Socialism," much of the progress of the present must still be accredited to the first mentioned form of capitalism, while another part of present progress, and undoubtedly the larger part of the progress of the immediate future, will have to be accredited to "State Socialism," which is clearly what Wells means by Socialism in this passage.

Because of this confusion with collectivism or "State Socialism," many of the efforts to define Socialism, though of a purely practical character, and intended to be based on the movement, are as misleading as any dogma. The best known example is the statement that Socialism means democratic collectivism or industrial democracy, a formula that can easily be limited to the progressive reforms of individualist capitalism and of "State Socialism." The practical or political and economic problem of Socialism is neither how much of industry the government controls (the problem of collectivism), nor the form of government (the problem of democracy), nor even how much of industry a democratic form of government controls (the problem of democratic collectivism), but this—Does a class, or group of classes, control the government?

It is evident that collectivism, government ownership of monopolies, the appropriation of the land rent by the state, and the placing of labor on the level of maximum efficiency, are not Socialism.

"State Socialism" seeks merely to rearrange institutions; Socialism seeks to bring new social forces into a position of power, which is the same as to create new forces as far as practical results are concerned. One of the chief spokesmen of British "State Socialism" (J. R. MacDonald) says that "Socialism is not a *tour de force* of the creative intelligence." This holds true only of that "State Socialism," for which this writer speaks. Nor is genuine Socialism the product of the creative intelligence of a single person or of any limited number of persons, but it certainly is the product of *creative intelligence* of humanity. MacDonald expresses the "State Socialist" philosophy further when he says that society has not been and will not be "created by human voluntary agency." While Socialists would agree that humanity has been guided chiefly by involuntary forces in the past, the very essence of the great change that Socialism is to inaugurate is that the new society is to be consciously organized—nor can that great revolution in civilization and culture be prepared for except by voluntary effort. This is the meaning of Marx's well-known phrase, "With Socialism real history *begins*."

In the early stages of the political and economic movement Socialists were accused of being "destructive." They replied by proving that they not only favored and were ready and able to aid every constructive social movement, but had concrete plans for the complete reconstruction of society at every point, that is, for revolution. On its cultural side Socialism is more than constructive, it is *creative*. For it has sought, already with wonderful success, not merely to direct old forces into new channels, or to improve and accelerate good beginnings that have already been made, but to create new beginnings and new forces. And it has shown that in this creative function it is limited neither by abstract definitions, by political and economic programs, nor by historical precedents which we now call evolutionary "laws."

The work of the nineteenth century radicals, to abolish outworn institutions, though it may be viewed as a part of the process of construction, could scarcely satisfy the demand for a great *creative* social principle, as Spencer and Morley both acknowledged, nor can the solution of merely material problems, the providing of material means for civilization, the more systematic organization of industry and the more scientific exploitation of labor which is the kind of "construction" that capitalism has hitherto undertaken or proposes to undertake. The "State Socialism" of the immediate future promises to leave the present class culture intact. It remains for the Socialist movement to supply the principles and the forces required to create a new type of man and society. . . .

The most positive result of the pragmatic philosophy for Socialism, as far as its broader *generalizations* go (I discuss the *applications* of this philosophy throughout the remainder of the volume) lies in the fact that philosophy itself evolves and must continue to evolve; this means, of course, that both evolutionary and Socialist philosophy must evolve. And just as the former has already advanced from the vague shape which it held in the minds of Darwin and Spencer, so the latter has also advanced from the form it had with Marx and Engels, and these currents are coming together in the far more subtle and at the same time more practical pragmatism of such men as Dewey.

Not only do philosophies evolve, but the fact that they evolve must be made the basis of philosophy. "The thoroughly vital question for us all," says James, "is what is this world going to be—what is life going to make of itself?" And one of the most vital questions as to the future of the world and life is "What is philosophy going to be?" We can only hope to see ahead a few years, and even there our chief conclusions are negative, though none the less valuable for that. We can see, for example, that the philosophy of the future, like that which is forming to-day, is going to look ahead, and not backward, as a great deal of the philosophy of the past has done. To look ahead practically means for men to develop their power over their nature and themselves, and not to give their strength to abstract speculation. And this conclusion can seem negative only to those whose object is speculation and not life.

The most valuable part of every philosophy has always been that *intellectually negative* and destructive criticism of the previous philosophies which serves as an introduction to the new dogma at which the philosopher has aimed. For certain subconscious, involuntary, and unfelt assumptions that are too certain and matter-of-fact to be felt as being even worthy of expression underlie this criticism in large part and are at the bottom the most positive, social and lasting contributions of the philosophy. The so-called constructive ideas, on the other hand, have always been dogmatic, ultra-intellectual, unrelated to many important phases of life, largely individualistic, and *destructive* of the most vital impulses, of subconscious and semi-conscious strivings, and of new thought.

Pragmatism is the first philosophy that has rested satisfied with this criticism and has attempted no purely *intellectual* construction. It is only when considered from a purely intellectual standpoint that it is negative, however. For underlying this criticism is the assumption, become conscious, willed and felt at last, that the intellect is of no value whatever in itself but exists purely for the service of life.

Pragmatism therefore does not seek to show what the intellect in itself can accomplish for man, but what it can do to aid him in all his activities: natural science, sociology and psychology, education, literature and art.

Pragmatism, in a word, teaches that the purpose of philosophy is merely to supply methods of investigation and thought. In itself it is only a spirit drawn from the practical needs and activities of men; in its application it is a revolution in all the higher fields of human effort, the great social revolution, as it appears in the world of thought. . . .

CHAPTER VIII

SOCIALISM AND THE WORKERS

I want to tell you Socialists that I have studied your philosophy; read your works upon economics, and not the meanest of them. . . . I declare it to you, I am not only at variance with your doctrines, but with your philosophy. Economically you are unsound; socially you are wrong; industrially you are an impossibility.

SAMUEL GOMPERS,
American Federation of Labor Convention, 1903

The trade union and the Social-Democratic party are both a part of a labor movement, but they have different and separate functions. . . . Every thinking trade union man is bound to join the Social-Democratic party sooner or later.

VICTOR BERGER,
Social Democratic Herald, 1905

We are going down in the gutter to get at the mass of the workers and bring them up to a decent plane of living.

WILLIAM D. HAYWOOD,
First Convention of the Industrial Workers of the World, 1905

[The workers] are developing their industrial consciousness, their economic and political power; and when the revolution comes, they will be prepared to take possession and assume control of every industry. With the education they will have received in the Industrial Workers they will be drilled and disciplined, trained and fitted for Industrial Mastery and Social Freedom.

EUGENE V. DEBS,
Speech at Chicago, 1905

I am opposed to any tactics which involve stealth, secrecy, intrigue, and necessitate acts of industrial violence for their execution.

EUGENE V. DEBS,
International Socialist Review, 1912

How should socialism deal with organized labor? This was the central issue that confronted the Socialist Party in its halcyon years before World War I. The issue would not have bulked so large or been so divisive if it had not been for the fact that the only union of consequence at the time was the American Federation of Labor. The AFL's remarkable success—its growth since 1886, when it was founded, from several thousand to nearly 1,500,000 members—was, on the face of it, a devastating refutation of the socialist argument. For the socialists had been predicting that as capitalism entered its final phase, labor would become increasingly anti-capitalist, increasingly class-conscious, increasingly committed to the ideal of the cooperative commonwealth. Such was the pattern in England and the Continent; such would be the pattern in America.

But organized labor in America heedlessly went its own way. The AFL rejected any ideology other than "pure and simple" unionism. If it had an ultimate goal it was to secure the most pay and best working conditions possible for its members. It found nothing objectionable in capitalism as such. Officially, in fact, it applauded a system that allowed workers to organize their own autonomous unions. On the whole, its members, whose skills gave them some leverage in the "free" market, occupied a highly privileged stratum of the labor force. As such they felt little solidarity with—and they certainly had no intention of trying to organize— the proletariat: immigrants, Negroes, and unskilled labor in general.

The socialists feared that the leaders of the AFL, in particular its president, Samuel Gompers, were bent on driving the union even more deeply into the capitalist camp. Their fears were powerfully reinforced when, in 1901, Gompers joined Mark Hanna, August Belmont, George Perkins, and other high-ranking businessmen, as well as a host of public-spirited conservatives (e.g., Grover Cleveland and William Howard Taft), in establishing the National

Civic Federation. The stated purpose of the Federation was to mediate disputes between management and labor in the hope of preventing a polarization on both sides. The socialists denounced it as a conspiracy between the labor aristocracy and the capitalists to keep the other workers from organizing.

Yet, as we noted before, the leaders of the Socialist Party had to adopt a cautious, circumspect approach toward the AFL. Whatever they thought of Gompers they dared not repeat DeLeon's strategy of launching, or sanctioning, rival unions. They dared not do so for the compelling reason that the socialist movement was well entrenched in the AFL, controlling numerous international unions and city and state labor councils, and enjoying wide support from the rank and file. Just how wide was evident very early in the career of the Party. In 1902 the AFL convention barely turned down a socialist-sponsored resolution demanding that the union "advise" workers "to organize their economic and political power to secure for labor the full equivalent of its toil and the overthrow of the wage system and the establishment of an industrial cooperative democracy." The Socialist Party was confident that sooner or later a majority of the AFL would come over to its side. In the meantime it would respect the union's independence and avoid any challenge to its authority. This was the Party's fixed position.

The policy did not, however, go uncontested. A small group within the Party, led by Eugene Debs, opposed any kind of modus vivendi with the AFL. From his experiences as a union chief Debs had come to regard Gompers as the Judas Iscariot of the working class. "Between the pure and simple labor leaders and civic federationists, and the socialist agitators," Debs asserted in 1903, after the socialists had again been defeated at an AFL convention, "there is war, and the place to fight it out is not in an Alamo where they outnumber us a dozen to one, but out in the hearing of the working class." Debs was implying that the socialists should cease attempting to convert the AFL, that they should take their case directly to the great unorganized mass of workers. He was implying, in short, that socialists should back a rival union—if one appeared.

Soon one did appear. In January 1905 a band of dissident socialists met secretly in Chicago to discuss the creation of a revolutionary industrial union. They had decided to call the meeting because one significant union at least, the Western Federation of Miners, was prepared to challenge the AFL for the loyalty of the workers. The Western Federation of Miners was itself in the AFL at one time. That was back in the early 1890s, when the organizers of the Western Federation believed that labor and capital could live in peace. But the owners of the gold, silver, copper, and lead mines of the West refused to negotiate with the union, and the mountain fastnesses of Montana, Idaho, and Colorado shook with violence. In a series of armed engagements the miners (and sometimes their families) took on the company police, local posses, state militias, and occasionally federal troops as well. The battles of Coeur d'Alene, Cripple Creek, Leadville, and Tulleride, were among the bloodiest ever fought by American labor. They persuaded the Western Federation of Miners that the scales of justice were weighted in the capitalists' favor, and that the AFL, which rendered the union no assistance, was as perfidious, self-serving, and cowardly as its enemies. The leaders of the Western Federation declared themselves socialists and industrial unionists, and they vowed to break the AFL's hegemony over American labor. So they consented to answer the call of the radical socialists to meet in Chicago in January 1905.

Six months after this meeting, a full blown convention was held in Chicago. Revolutionists from all over the country descended on the city. Debs and his friends in the Socialist Party were there; so was DeLeon, representing his minuscule labor organization (the Socialist Trades and Labor Alliance); so were the delegates of other unions, all of them—with the single exception of the Western Federation of Miners—quite small; and so were a goodly number of intellectuals, Anarchists, and wayward radicals in general. Given its wildly heterogeneous composition the convention could easily have degenerated into pandemonium. But, despite the acrimoniousness and length of the debates, the convention accomplished what it had set out to do. It created a new labor organization, appropriately titled Industrial Workers of the World, and it adopted a constitution that was reasonable, even moderate, in tone and objective. This was due mostly to the influence exerted by the Western Federation of Miners, which was able to dominate the proceedings because it controlled more than a third of the convention votes—roughly the proportion of its membership to that of the whole body.

The famous preamble to the constitution plangently announced to the world what kind of union the IWW would be. "The working class and the employing class," it affirmed, "have nothing in common. There can be no peace so long as hunger and want are found among millions of working people, and the few, who make up the employing class, have all the good things of life." The traditional craft-oriented unions (the AFL), the preamble continued, could not "cope with the ever-growing power of the employing class," "the centering of management of industries into fewer and fewer hands." The aim of the IWW, accordingly, was to bring together *all* the workers in a single organization operating "on the political as well as on the industrial field," so that they can "take hold of that which they produce by their labor."

The structure of the IWW was a logical extension of this aim. The constitution specified that thirteen separate departments eventually would be established, each corresponding to an industry (transportation, mining, building, etc.), each having jurisdiction over its multifarious sub-divisions, down to the most highly specialized craft. The union as a whole would be governed by a president, a secretary-treasurer, and a five-man executive board. No longer would workers have to confront the dreadful alternatives imposed by the AFL; no longer, that is, would they have to struggle for privileges or engage in fratricidal war. Now, thanks to the emergent IWW, a dispute, however trivial, between any group of workers and their employers, would involve the entire industrial department, and if necessary the entire union. "An injury to one," would be "an injury to all."

The appearance of the Industrial Workers of the World embarrassed the leaders of the Socialist Party. If in their heart of hearts they wished it success because they believed in industrial unionism and labor class-consciousness, they could not say so openly. They certainly did not like DeLeon's association with it. His sole motive, in their view, was to bring it within the orbit of his political organization. Most of all they feared that the Socialist Party would suffer in a protracted conflict between rival unions. Gompers was bound to exploit the fact that Debs, the most prominent of the socialists, backed a union that wished to destroy the AFL. The Socialist Party thus emphatically dissociated itself from the IWW and stressed repeatedly that Debs spoke only for himself.

But as it turned out neither the Party nor the AFL need have

worried about the IWW. It proved to be too unstable an amalgam
to be an effective rival. Soon after its founding the IWW split
into two contending groups: the "conservatives," consisting of
most of the officials of the Western Federation of Miners, who
were essentially militant unionists seeking to improve the lot of
their men; and the "radicals," among them DeLeon, who favored
relentless class struggle whatever the immediate consequences and
however adverse the effects on labor. The radicals captured the
1906 convention, and DeLeon emerged as the IWW's chief ideo-
logue and tactician. But it was an organization suddenly void of
members and revenue, for the Western Federation, which had supplied both, promptly pulled out. Several years later, in an amazing
volte face, the Miners re-joined the AFL.

The IWW continued to seethe. By 1907 DeLeon found himself
cast in the role of a conservative. The radicals were now advocating
a species of Syndicalism similar to the one that had recently made
its appearance in some of the French labor unions. These Syndicalists maintained that each industrial department (or syndicate)
must be sovereign over the lives of all the workers belonging to it,
and that revolutionary unions must eschew politics, a meaningless
bourgeois ritual, in favor of "direct action" in the streets and
factories (the "general strike"). DeLeon condemned the radicals
in the IWW as "uncivilized," "slum proletarians" who were determined to commit suicide. In the 1908 Chicago convention the
Syndicalists, bolstered by an "overall brigade" and a contingent of
self-styled "bums" from the far West (they had come in via box
car) peremptorily threw DeLeon out of the IWW. Then they
expunged from the preamble the brief, innocuous reference to
political action.

Thereafter the IWW was an out-and-out Syndicalist organization,
even to the extent of espousing the doctrine of industrial sabotage.
It thus embarked on a lonely and dangerous course. Apart from
the logging and migratory camps of the West it had very few
friends; Debs had long since given up on it. But the diminutive
size of the IWW was no measure of the amount of attention it
received. IWW organizers created a stir wherever they showed up;
it was as though a gang of badmen were suddenly to come to town.
To make matters more tense, communities up and down the
West Coast passed ordinances prohibiting speeches and meetings
in the streets. These were promulgated expressly to keep union

organizers from talking to the men who worked in the nearby camps, who could not be appealed to except in the streets. The IWW resisted these ordinances. Its tactic was the same in every community, and in nearly every community proved successful. Provoking arrest, members of the IWW filled the jails, thereby taxing the community's resources to the breaking point. Soon the offending statute was repealed or modified. It was not the first time that an "extremist" group, for reasons of its own, had struck a blow for civil liberties.

Between 1909 and 1913, while waging its "free speech" campaign in the West, the IWW became embroiled in a series of spectacular labor conflicts elsewhere in the country. The strikers who allowed themselves to be led by the IWW did so because they faced insuperable difficulties—poverty, ethnic and racial discrimination, the ruthlessness of the employers, the brutality of the police and the courts, and the animosity of the American Federation of Labor —and only the IWW volunteered to defend them. It was no surprise that the IWW, bumptiously moving in where others had feared to tread, lost all but one of these strikes. The surprise was that the strikes took place at all; even more that they lasted as long as they did. As a result of its heroic defeats the IWW acquired a romantic aureole which continued to glow, particularly in the eyes of Eastern radical intellectuals, until it was extinguished during World War I.

The IWW, let it be noted, conducted its strikes as responsibly as any "pure and simple" union would have. The famous Lawrence (Massachusetts) strike—the only important strike it led to victory —was a case in point. Early in 1912 the IWW office in Chicago received a telegram from the representatives of the 25,000 or so employees of the American Woolen Company, asking it to take charge of the strike that had just broken out there. Some of the employees, about a tenth of the total, belonged to the United Textile Workers of the AFL. These were the more highly skilled native Americans who, over the years, had shown no concern for their unskilled co-workers, all of them recent immigrants from Poland, Italy, Lithuania, Belgium, and French Canada. The strike had been called because the American Woolen Company had just cut wages in response to a new state law reducing from 56 to 54 the maximum number of hours a week that women and minors could work. (The average weekly wage before the cut was $8.76—15 cents an hour.)

The IWW leaders displayed brilliant tactical ability throughout the strike. In the face of repeated police provocation, and despite their arrest on trumped-up charges, they kept violence down to a minimum. They saw to it that the ranks of the strikers held firm, that the discipline and solidarity were sustained. Just how difficult this was may be imagined. It was the middle of winter and there was no money available to tide over the 25,000 strikers and their families. Yet they were tided over, thanks to the ingenuity of the leaders. Help was procured from various ethnic organizations, from sympathetic labor unions (the AFL, however, opposed the strike and tried to break it), from the Socialist Party, and from liberal philanthropists. Also hundreds of the strikers' children were sent to homes in other cities.

The heavily publicized children's migration finally caused the authorities in Lawrence to do something quite stupid. On February 24, police and militiamen tried to prevent a group of children from boarding a train. A battle royal followed. The children and their parents were indiscriminately beaten, some of them badly, and thrown into jail. The ensuing court scene, the children and parents milling about waiting to be sentenced, was ludicrous. The charges against the victims were dismissed, and the children were permitted to leave town. Less than three weeks later the company, smarting from the public's criticism, capitulated to the demands of the strike committee. The wage increase established a pattern for the industry as a whole.

Though the Socialist Party supported the IWW-led strikes, it resolutely opposed the union's Syndicalist ideology. The issue was not an abstract one. The Party was becoming a formidable political force in America, and its hopes depended on the degree of trust it could expect to command from a skeptical public. The Party, in short, could not allow itself to be identified with the Syndicalist position—with disregard for laws and contracts, talk of sabotage, and direct action. In 1908, the year the Syndicalists definitely took over the IWW, the Socialist Party convention passed a constitutional amendment specifying that, "Any member of the party who opposes political action as a weapon of the working class to aid in its emancipation, shall be expelled from membership. . . ."

By 1912 the issue had come to a head. For the past two years

the Party's strength had grown appreciably, and it looked forward
to fresh advances in the coming Presidential election. It had, therefore, to be especially careful about its image of respectability. This
was all the more necessary since a pro-Syndicalist faction had
sprung up inside the Party itself. This faction gathered around an
outstanding socialist monthly, the *International Socialist Review*,
and particularly around the person of William D. Haywood. In
1911 he had been elected to the Party's Executive Committee by
an overwhelming vote of the rank and file. Far from being repulsed,
the enemy had penetrated the citadel of the movement.

Debs excepted, no socialist was more popular and more notorious
than "Big Bill" Haywood. Like Debs he started out as a worker.
He was a knockabout, itinerant laborer in the far West (he had
been born in Utah in 1869) until becoming a miner. Very early
in his life he learned that beneath the trappings of the law and
the courts, beneath the honeyed words and good intentions, lay
the violence that alone kept the workers in their place and gave
the rich their advantages. He accepted the class struggle as a fact
long before he knew anything about socialism. He was one of the
leaders of the Western Federation of Miners, and as such was one
of the prime movers in the formation of the IWW. He first came
to the public's notice in 1906, when he and two other union
officers were arrested and then illegally spirited across state lines
for their alleged complicity in the murder of a former Idaho
governor. The case of Moyer, Pettibone, and Haywood became
a national cause célèbre, with the forces of the left (including the
AFL this time) ranged on one side and those of the right on the
other. After a stay in jail (bail having been denied them), they
were acquitted in a spectacular trial, thanks to a virtuoso performance by defense attorney Clarence Darrow (the prosecutor for
Idaho was William Borah). By the completion of the trial Haywood
had broken with the miners' union in favor of the pro-Syndicalist
IWW. He went on to lead many of its strikes, notably the one
at Lawrence. He was a celebrity then, a hero of the West, a
survivor of *real* wars, not mere cerebral ones. Radical intellectuals
lionized him; he was a favorite at the Fifth Avenue salon of
Mabel Dodge Luhan, who was his mistress for a while. He cut
an awesome figure: he was a huge, bluff man, whose whole
manner and appearance (he had lost an eye and wore a patch
over it) bespoke his virile working-class origins and ideology.

Haywood left no doubt where he stood; he yielded not an

inch in his Syndicalist militancy. In January 1912, at Cooper Union, he held an extraordinary debate with Morris Hillquit on the question, "What Shall the Attitude of the Socialist Party Be toward the Economic Organization of the Workers?" To the audience that overflowed the hall, Haywood stoutly defended sabotage and direct action by labor, and ridiculed the ballot box among other formal democratic procedures. "I don't know of anything," he asserted, "that can be applied that will bring as much satisfaction to you, and as much anguish to the boss, as a little sabotage in the right place at the proper time. Find out what it means. It won't hurt you, and it will cripple the boss." From left to right, from Debs to Berger, party spokesmen condemned Haywood's justification of illegality as being both wrong and imprudent. And even though in his capacity as strike leader he conspicuously refrained from practicing what he preached—indeed, he repeatedly adjured the strikers to obey the law—the Party hierarchs determined to silence him or drive him from its councils at the earliest opportunity.

That opportunity arose at the Socialist Party convention of May 1912. The highpoint of the proceedings (Debs's nomination for the Presidency having been a foregone conclusion) was the debate over a constitutional amendment to strengthen the section prohibiting opposition to "political action." After bitter and protracted arguments the convention, as expected, passed the amendment by a vote of better than two to one. Now, under provisions of Article II, Section 6, the Party could expel any member "who opposes political action or advocates crime, sabotage, or other methods of violence as a weapon of the working class to aid in its emancipation." And "political action," the amendment went on to say, meant "participation in elections for public office and practical and administrative work along the lines of the Socialist Party platform." It was only a matter of time before Haywood would be punished.

Shortly after the national election, the New York State chapter of the Party charged Haywood with violating the constitution at a recent public meeting (he advocated crime, sabotage, etc.) and called upon the whole membership to dismiss him from the National Executive Committee. The Party leaders intended this to be a symbolic act; it would let the public know how democratic socialists felt about Syndicalism. The referendum took place early in 1913. With about a third of the members voting (approximately 35,000), Haywood was thrown off the Committee, again by a vote of more than two to one. The voting pattern revealed two interesting things about the Party: first, that Haywood received the bulk of his support from the Populist-oriented South and West; second, that the Eastern bloc, which opposed him, could always muster enough votes to carry out the policies of Berger and Hillquit. After his recall, Haywood left the Party altogether. By 1913, the Socialist Party, having purged itself of direct actionists, could present itself to organized labor and the electorate as a respectable political party, different from the bourgeois parties only in the ends it advocated, not the means.

The socialists, in other words, chose to alienate the extreme left rather than destroy their chances of converting the AFL rank and file and the public at large. As it turned out, however, they did neither. The left wing remained in the Party. This fact was borne out by the membership rolls, which, despite periodic fluctuations, were fairly constant between 1913 and 1917. But the Socialists failed to make much headway within the AFL. For one thing, there had emerged since 1909 a powerful anti-socialist movement in the union, the Catholic Militia of Christ; it had been founded to uphold the pillars of social order: church, family, and property. Just as important was the Wilson administration's effort to win the support of organized labor. No administration had ever gone as far as it went in befriending the unions, and Gompers reciprocated by tacitly sealing an alliance (which has endured down to the present) with the Democratic Party. Yet the effect of these moves was not so much to diminish the socialist appeal to labor as prevent it from growing more than it did. According to the best evidence available (see James Weinstein's illuminating study, *The Decline of Socialism in America, 1912–1925*), socialist "activity and strength" in the trade unions actually increased somewhat between 1912 and 1917. This was a remarkable feat when one considers the forces, progressive and conservative, arrayed against socialism at the time.

If socialism and the unions did eventually go their separate ways (though they were briefly re-united in the 1930s), it was not because of any failure in the Party's policy toward labor. It was because events supervened that proved too catastrophic for such a fragile movement to overcome.

Manifesto on Organizing the
Industrial Workers of the World*
1905

This is the statement put out by the delegates who met at Chicago in early January, 1905 to lay the groundwork for the IWW convention later in the year.

Social relations and groupings only reflect mechanical and industrial conditions. The *great facts* of present industry are the displacement of human skill by machines and the increase of capitalist power through concentration in the possession of the tools with which wealth is produced and distributed.

Because of these facts trade division among laborers and competition among capitalists are alike disappearing. Class divisions grow ever more fixed and class antagonisms more sharp. Trade lines have been swallowed up in a common servitude of all workers to the machines which they tend. New machines, ever replacing less productive ones, wipe out whole trades and plunge new bodies of workers into the evergrowing army of tradeless, hopeless unemployed. As human beings and human skill are displaced by mechanical progress, the capitalists need use the workers only during that brief period when muscles and nerves respond most intensely. The moment the laborer no longer yields the maximum of profits, he is thrown upon the scrap pile, to starve alongside the discarded machine. A *dead line* has been drawn, and an age limit established, to cross which, in this world of monopolized opportunities, means condemnation to industrial death.

The worker, wholly separated from the land and the tools, with his skill of craftsmanship rendered useless, is sunk in the uniform mass of wage slaves. He sees his power of resistance broken by craft divisions, perpetuated from outgrown industrial stages. His

* Report of the New York State Joint Legislative Committee Investigating Sedition (Lusk Committee), Vol. I, pp. 903–906.

wages constantly grow less as his hours grow longer and monopolized prices grow higher. Shifted hither and thither by the demands of profit-takers, the laborer's home no longer exists. In this hopeless condition he is forced to accept whatever humiliating conditions his master may impose. He is subjected to a physical and intellectual examination more searching than was the chattel slave when sold from the auction block. Laborers are no longer classified by differences in trade skill, but the employer assigns them according to the machines to which they are attached. These divisions, far from representing differences in skill or interests among the laborers, are imposed by the employers that workers may be pitted against one another and spurred to greater exertion in the shop, and that all resistance to capitalist tyranny may be weakened by artificial distinctions.

While encouraging these outgrown divisions among the workers the capitalists carefully adjust themselves to the new conditions. They wipe out all differences among themselves and present a united front in their war upon labor. Through employers' associations, they seek to crush, with brutal force, by the injunctions of the judiciary, and the use of military power, all efforts at resistance. Or when the other policy seems more profitable, they conceal their daggers beneath the Civic Federation and hoodwink and betray those whom they would rule and exploit. Both methods depend for success upon the blindness and internal dissensions of the working class. The employers' line of battle and methods of warfare correspond to the solidarity of the mechanical and industrial concentration, while laborers still form their fighting organizations on lines of long-gone trade divisions. The battles of the past emphasize this lesson. The *textile* workers of Lowell, Philadelphia, and Fall River; the *butchers* of Chicago, weakened by the disintegrating effects of trade divisions; the *machinists* on the Santa Fe, unsupported by their fellow-workers subject to the same masters; the long-struggling *miners* of Colorado, hampered by a lack of unity and solidarity upon the industrial battlefield, all bear witness to the helplessness and impotency of labor as at present organized.

This worn out and corrupt system offers no promise of improvement and adaptation. There is no silver lining to the clouds of darkness and despair settling down upon the world of labor.

This system offers only a perpetual struggle for slight relief within wage slavery. It is blind to the possibility of establishing an industrial democracy, wherein there shall be no wage slavery, but where the workers will own the tools which they operate, and the product of which they alone will enjoy.

It shatters the ranks of the workers into fragments, rendering them helpless and impotent on the industrial battlefield.

Separation of craft from craft renders industrial and financial solidarity impossible.

Union men scab upon union men; hatred of worker for worker is engendered, and the workers are delivered helpless and disintegrated into the hands of the capitalists.

Craft jealousy leads to the attempt to create trade monopolies.

Prohibitive initiation fees are established that force men to become scabs against their will. Men whom manliness or circumstances have driven from one trade are thereby fined when they seek to transfer membership to the union of a new craft.

Craft divisions foster political ignorance among the workers, thus dividing their class at the ballot box, as well as in the shop, mine and factory.

Craft unions may be and have been used to assist employers in the establishment of monopolies and the raising of prices. One set of workers are thus used to make harder the conditions of life of another body of laborers.

Craft divisions hinder the growth of class consciousness of the workers, foster the idea of harmony of interests between employing exploiter and employed slave. They permit the association of the misleaders of the workers with the capitalists in the Civic Federations, where plans are made for the perpetuation of capitalism, and the permanent enslavement of the workers through the wage system.

Previous efforts for the betterment of the working class have proven abortive because limited in scope and disconnected in action.

Universal economic evils afflicting the working class can be eradicated only by a universal working-class movement. Such a movement of the working class is impossible while separate craft and wage agreements are made favoring the employer against other crafts in the same industry, and while energies are wasted in fruitless jurisdiction struggles which serve only to further the personal aggrandizement of union officials.

A movement to fulfill these conditions must consist of one great industrial union embracing all industries—providing for craft autonomy locally, industrial autonomy internationally, and working-class unity generally.

It must be founded on the class struggle, and its general administration must be conducted in harmony with the recognition of the irrepressible conflict between the capitalist class and the working class.

It should be established as the economic organization of the working class, without affiliation with any political party.

All power should rest in a collective membership.

Local, national and general administration, including union labels, buttons, badges, transfer cards, initiation fees, and per capita tax should be uniform throughout.

All members must hold membership in the local, national or international union covering the industry in which they are employed, but transfers of membership between unions, local, national, or international, should be universal.

Workingmen bringing union cards from industrial unions in foreign countries should be freely admitted into the organization.

The general administration should issue a publication representing the entire union and its principles which should reach all members in every industry at regular intervals.

A *central defense fund*, to which all members contribute equally, should be established and maintained.

All workers, therefore, who agree with the principles herein set forth, will meet in convention at Chicago the 27th day of June, 1905, for the purpose of forming an economic organization of the working class along the lines marked out in this manifesto.

Representation in the convention shall be based upon the number of workers whom the delegate represents. No delegate, however, shall be given representation in the convention on the numerical basis of an organization unless he has credentials—bearing the seal of his union, local, national or international, and the signatures of the officers thereof—authorizing him to install his union as a working part of the proposed economic organization in the industrial department in which it logically belongs in the general plan of the organization. Lacking this authority, the delegate shall represent himself as an individual.

Adopted at Chicago, January 2, 3 and 4, 1905.

A. G. Swing,
A. M. Simons,
W. Shurtleff,
Frank M. McCabe,
John M. O'Neil,
Geo. Estes,
Wm. D. Haywood,
Mother Jones,
Ernest Untermann,
W. L. Hall,
Chas. H. Moyer,
Clarence Smith,
William Ernest Trautmann,
Jos. Schmidt,

John Guild,
Daniel McDonald,
Eugene V. Debs,
Thos. J. De Young,
Thos. J. Hagerty,
Fred. D. Henion,
W. J. Bradley,
Chas. O. Sherman,
M. E. White,
William J. Pinkerton,
Frank Kraffs,
J. E. Fitzgerald,
Frank Bohn.

"Revolutionary Unionism"*
1905

Debs delivered this speech in December, 1905, at Grand Central
Palace, New York, in the belief that the Industrial Workers of
the World would sweep everything before it, that the unskilled
and semi-skilled, amounting to nine-tenths of the labor force,
would join its ranks and overwhelm the AFL.

. . . The revolutionary movement of the working class will date
from the year 1905, from the organization of the INDUSTRIAL
WORKERS OF THE WORLD. (Prolonged applause.) Economic
solidarity is today the supreme need of the working class. The old
form of unionism has long since fulfilled its mission and outlived its
usefulness, and the hour has struck for a change.

The old unionism is organized upon the basis of the identity
of interests of the capitalist and working classes. It spends its time
and energy trying to conciliate these two essentially antagonistic
classes; and so this unionism has at its head a harmonizing board
called the Civic Federation. This federation consists of three parts;
a part representing the capitalist class; a part supposed to represent
the working class, and still another part that is said to represent the
"public." The capitalists are represented by that great union labor
champion, August Belmont. (Laughter and hisses.) The working
class by Samuel Gompers, the president of the American Federation
of Labor (hisses and cries, "sic him"), and the public, by Grover
Cleveland. (Laughter.)

Can you imagine a fox and goose peace congress? Just fancy
such a meeting, the goose lifting its wings in benediction, and the
fox whispering, "Let us prey."

The Civic Federation has been organized for the one purpose of
prolonging the age-long sleep of the working class. Their supreme

* Eugene V. Debs, *Life, Writings and Speeches* (Chicago, 1908), pp. 448–455,
464–466.

purpose is to keep you from waking up. (A voice: "They can't do it.")

The Industrial Workers has been organized for an opposite purpose, and its representatives come in your presence to tell you that there can be no peace between you, the working class, and the capitalist class who exploit you of what you produce; that as workers you have economic interests apart from and opposed to their interests, and that you must organize by and for yourselves; and that if you are intelligent enough to understand these interests you will sever your relations with the old unions in which you are divided and subdivided, and join the Industrial Workers, in which all are organized and united upon the basis of the class struggle. (Applause.)

The Industrial Workers is organized, not to conciliate, but to fight the capitalist class. We have no object in concealing any part of our mission; we would have it perfectly understood. We deny that there is anything in common between workingmen and capitalists. We insist that workingmen must organize to get rid of capitalists and make themselves the masters of the tools with which they work, freely employ themselves, secure to themselves all they produce, and enjoy to the full the fruit of their labors. (Applause.)

The old union movement is not only organized upon the basis of the identity of interests of the exploited and exploiting classes, but it divides instead of uniting the workers, and there are thousands of unions, more or less in conflict, used against one another; and so long as these countless unions occupy the field, there will be no substantial unity of the working class. (Applause.)

And here let me say that the most zealous supporter of the old union is the capitalist himself. August Belmont, president of the Civic Federation, takes special pride in declaring himself a "union man" (laughter); but he does not mean by that that he is an Industrial Worker; that is not the kind of a union he means. He means the impotent old union that Mr. Gompers and Mr. Mitchell lead, the kind that keeps the working class divided so that the capitalist system may be perpetuated indefinitely.

For thirty years I have been connected with the organized labor movement. I have long since been made to realize that the pure and simple union can do nothing for the working class; I have had some experience and know whereof I speak. The craft union seeks to establish its own petty supremacy. Craft division is fatal to class unity. To organize along craft lines means to divide the working class and make it the prey of the capitalist class. The working class can only be unionized efficiently along class lines; and so the Industrial Workers has been organized, not to isolate the crafts but to unite the whole working class. (Applause.)

The working class has had considerable experience during the past few years. In almost every conflict between labor and capital, labor has been defeated. Take the leading strikes in their order, and you will find that, without a single exception, the organized workers have been defeated, and thousands upon thousands of them have lost their jobs, and many of them have become "scabs." Is there not something wrong with a unionism in which the workers are always worsted? Let me review hurriedly some of this history of the past few years.

I have seen the conductors on the Chicago, Burlington & Quincy Railroad, organized in a craft union, take the place of the striking union locomotive engineers on the same system.

I have seen the employes of the Missouri, Kansas & Texas Railway, organized in their several craft unions, stand by the corporation as a unit, totally wiping out the union telegraphers, thirteen hundred of them losing their jobs.

I have seen these same craft unions, just a little while ago, on the Northern Pacific and Great Northern systems—I have seen them unite with the corporation to crush out the telegraphers' union, and defeat the strikers, their own co-unionists and fellow employes.

Just a few weeks ago, in the city of Chicago, the switchmen on the Grand Trunk went out on strike. All their fellow unionists remained at work and faithfully served the corporation until the switchmen were defeated, and now those union switchmen are scattered about looking for jobs.

The machinists were recently on strike in Chicago. They went out in a body under the direction of their craft union. Their fellow unionists all remained at work until the machinists were completely defeated, and now their organization in that city is on the verge of collapse.

There has been a ceaseless repetition of this form of scabbing of one craft union upon another until the working man, if his eyes are open, is bound to see that this kind of unionism is a curse and not a benefit to the working class.

The American Federation of Labor does not learn by experience. They recently held their annual convention, and they passed the same old stereotyped resolutions; they are going to petition Congress to restrict the power of the courts; that is to say, they are going to once more petition a capitalist Congress to restrict the power of capitalist courts. That is as if a flock of sheep were to petition a pack of wolves to extract their own fangs. They have passed these resolutions over and over again. They have been totally fruitless and will continue to be.

What good came to the working class from this convention? Put your finger upon a single thing they did that will be of any real benefit to the workers of the country!

You have had some experience here in New York. You have plenty of unionism here, such as it is, yet there is not a city in the country in which the workers are less organized than they are here. It was in March last that you had here an exhibition of pure and simple unionism. You saw about six thousand craft union men go out on strike, and you saw their fellow unionists remain at work loyally until all the strikers were defeated and sacrificed. Here you have an object lesson that is well calculated to set you thinking, and this is all I can hope to do by coming here, set you thinking, and for yourselves; for when you begin to think, you will soon begin to act for yourselves. You will then sever your relations with capitalist unions and capitalist parties (applause), and you will begin the real work of organizing your class, and that is what we of the Industrial Workers have engaged to do. We have a new mission. That mission is not merely the amelioration of the condition of the working class, but the complete emancipation of that class from slavery. (Applause.)

The Industrial Workers is going to do all for the working class that can be done in the capitalist system, but while it is engaged in doing that, its revolutionary eye will be fixed upon the goal; and there will be a great difference between a strike of revolutionary workers and a strike of ignorant trade unionists who but vaguely understand what they want and do not know how to get that. (Applause.)

The Industrial Workers is less than six months old, and already has a round hundred thousand of dues-paying members. (Applause.) This splendid achievement has no parallel in the annals of organized labor. From every direction come the applications for charters and for organizers, and when the delegates of this revolutionary economic organization meet in the city of Chicago, next year, it will be the greatest convention that ever met in the United States in the interest of the working class. (Applause.)

This organization has a world-wide mission; it makes its appeal directly to the working class. It asks no favors from capitalists.

No organization of working men has ever been so flagrantly misrepresented by the capitalist press as has been the Industrial Workers of the World; every delegate to the Chicago convention will bear testimony to this fact; and this is as it should be; the capitalist press is the mouthpiece of the capitalist class, and the very fact that the capitalist press is the organ, virtually, of the American Federation of Labor, is in itself sufficient to open the eyes of the working class.

If the American Federation of Labor were not in alliance with the capitalist class, the capitalist press would not pour its fulsome eulogy upon it.

This press has not one friendly word for the Industrial Workers, not one, and we do not expect it to have. These papers of the plutocrats know us and we know them (applause); between us there is no misunderstanding.

The workers of the country (the intelligent ones at least) readily see the difference between revolutionary and reactionary unionism, and that is why they are deserting the old and joining the new; that is why the Industrial Workers is building up so rapidly; that is why there is such a widespread demand for organizers and for literature and for all other means of building up this class-conscious economic organization. (Applause.)

As I have said, the Industrial Workers begin by declaring that there is nothing in common between capitalists and wage-workers.

The capitalists own the tools they do not use, and the workers use the tools they do not own.

The capitalists, who own the tools that the working class use, appropriate to themselves what the working class produce, and this accounts for the fact that a few capitalists become fabulously rich while the toiling millions remain in poverty, ignorance and dependence.

Let me make this point perfectly clear for the benefit of those who have not thought it out for themselves. Andrew Carnegie is a type of the capitalist class. He owns the tools with which steel is produced. These tools are used by many thousands of working men. Andrew Carnegie, who owns these tools, has absolutely nothing to do with the production of steel. He may be in Scotland, or where he will, the production of steel goes forward just the same. His mills at Pittsburgh, Duquesne and Homestead, where these tools are located, are thronged with thousands of toolless wage-workers, who work day and night, in winter's cold and summer's heat, who endure all the privations and make all the sacrifices of health and limb and life, producing thousands upon thousands of tons of steel, yet not having an interest, even the slightest, in the product. Carnegie, who owns the tools, appropriates the product, and the workers, in exchange for their labor power, receive a wage that serves to keep them in producing order; and the more industrious they are, and the more they produce, the worse they are off; for the sooner they have produced more than Carnegie can get rid of in the markets, the tool houses are shut down and the workers are locked out in the cold.

This is a beautiful arrangement—for Mr. Carnegie; he does not want a change, and so he is in favor of the Civic Federation, and a leading member of it; and he is doing what he can to induce you to think that this ideal relation ought to be maintained forever.

Now, what is true of steel production is true of every other department of industrial activity; you belong to the millions who have no tools, who cannot work without selling your labor power, and when you sell that, you have got to deliver it in person; you cannot send it to the mill, you have got to carry it there; you are inseparable from your labor power.

You have got to go to the mill at 7 in the morning and work until 6 in the evening, producing, not for yourself, but for the capitalist who owns the tools you made and use, and without which you are almost as helpless as if you had no arms.

This fundamental fact in modern industry you must recognize, and you must organize upon the basis of this fact; you must appeal to your class to join the union that is the true expression of your economic interests, and this union must be large enough to embrace you all, and such is the Industrial Workers of the World.

Every man and every woman who works for wages is eligible to membership.

Organized into various departments, when you join you become a member of the department that represents your craft, or occupation, whatever it may be; and when you have a grievance, your department has supervision of it; and if you fail to adjust it in that department, you are not limited to your craft alone for support, but, if necessary, all the workers in all other departments will unite solidly in your defense to the very last. (Applause.)

Take a plant in modern industry. The workers, under the old form of unionism, are parceled out to a score or more of unions. Craft division incites craft jealousy and so they are more or less in conflict with each other, and the employer constructively takes advantage of this fact, and that is why he favors pure and simple unionism.

It were better for the workers who wear craft fetters if they were not organized at all, for then they could and would spontaneously go out on strike together; but they cannot do this in craft unionism, for certain crafts bind themselves up in craft agreements, and after they have done this, they are at the mercy of the capitalist; and when their fellow-unionists call upon them for aid, they make the very convenient excuse that they cannot help them, that they must preserve the sanctity of the contract they have made with the employer. This so-called contract is regarded as of vastly more importance than the jobs, aye, the very lives of the workingmen themselves.

We do not intend that certain departments shall so attach themselves to the capitalist employers. We purpose that the workers shall all be organized, and if there is any agreement, it will embrace them all; and if there is any violation of the agreement, in the case of a single employee, it at once becomes the concern of all. (Applause.) That is unionism, industrial unionism, in which all of the workers, totally regardless of occupation, are united compactly within the one organization, so that at all times they can act together in the interests of all. It is upon this basis that the Industrial Workers of the World is organized. It is in this spirit and with this object in view that it makes its appeal to the working class.

Then, again, the revolutionary economic organization has a new and important function which has never once been thought of in the old union, for the simple reason that the old union intends that the wage system shall endure forever.

The Industrial Workers declares that the workers must make themselves the masters of the tools with which they work; and so a very important function of this new union is to teach the workers, or, rather, have them teach themselves the necessity of fitting themselves to take charge of the industries in which they are employed when they are wrested, as they will be, from their capitalist masters. (Applause.)

So when you join the Industrial Workers you feel the thrill of a new aspiration; you are no longer a blind, dumb wage-slave. You begin to understand your true and vital relation to your fellow-workers. In the Industrial Workers you are correlated to all other workers in the plant, and thus you develop the embryonic structure of the co-operative commonwealth. (Applause.) . . .

Don't hesitate because somebody else is falling back. Don't wait because somebody else is not yet ready. Act and act now and for yourself; and if you happen to be the only Industrial Workers in your shop, or in your immediate vicinity, you are simply monumental of the ignorance of your fellow-workers, and you have got to begin to educate them. For a little while they may point you out with the finger of contempt, but you can stand this; you can bear it with patience; if they persecute you, because you are true to yourself, your latent powers will be developed, you will become stronger than you now dream, and then you will do the deeds that live, and you will write your name where it will stay.

Never mind what others may say, or think, or do. Stand erect in the majesty of your own manhood.

Listen for just once to the throbbing of your own heart, and you will hear that it is beating quick-step marches to Camp Freedom.

Stand erect! Lift your bowed form from the earth! The dust has long enough borne the impress of your knees.

Stand up and see how long a shadow you cast in the sunlight! (Applause.) Hold up your head and avow your convictions, and then accept, as becomes a man, the consequences of your acts!

We need you and you need us. We have got to have the workers united, and you have got to help us in the work. And so we make our appeal to you tonight, and we know that you will not fail. You can arrive at no other conclusion: you are bound to join the Industrial Workers, and become a missionary in the field of industrial unionism. You will then feel the ecstasy of a new-born aspiration. You will do your very best. You will wear the badge of the Industrial Workers, and you will wear it with pride and joy.

The very contempt that it invites will be a compliment to you; in truth, a tribute to your manhood.

We will wrest what we can, step by step, from the capitalists, but with our eye fixed upon the goal; we will press forward, keeping step together with the inspiring music of the new emancipation; and when we have enough of this kind of organization . . . when we are lined up in battle array, and the capitalists try to lock us out, we will turn the tables on the gentlemen and lock them out. (Applause.)

We can run the mills without them but they cannot run them without us. (Applause.)

It is a very important thing to develop the economic power, to have a sound economic organization. This has been the inherent weakness in the labor movement of the United States. We need, and sorely need, a revolutionary economic organization. We must develop this kind of strength; it is the kind that we will have occasion to use in due time, and it is the kind that will not fail us when the crisis comes. So we shall organize and continue to organize the political field; and I am of those who believe that the day is near at hand when we shall have one great revolutionary economic organization, and one great revolutionary political party of the working class. (Cheers and prolonged applause.) Then will proceed with increased impetus the work of education and organization that will culminate in emancipation.

This great body will sweep into power and seize the reins of government; take possession of industry in the name of the working class, and it can be easily done. All that will be required will be to transfer the title deeds from the parasites to the producers; and then the working class, in control of industry, will operate it for the benefit of all. The work day will be reduced in proportion to the progress of invention. Every man will work, or at least have a chance to work, and get the full equivalent of what he produces. He will work, not as a slave, but as a free man, and he will express himself in his work and work with joy. Then the badge of labor will be the only badge of aristocracy. The industrial dungeon will become a temple of science. The working class will be free, and all humanity disenthralled.

The workers are the saviors of society (applause); the redeemers of the race; and when they have fulfilled their great historic mission, men and women can walk the highlands and enjoy the vision of a land without masters and without slaves, a land regenerated and resplendent in the triumph of Freedom and Civilization. (Long, continued applause.)

Double Edge of Labor's Sword*
1914

On May 22, 23, and 24, 1914, an illuminating confrontation took place between Hillquit and Gompers before the Industrial Relations Commission, presided over by Senator Walsh of Montana. They agreed to question and cross-examine each other on the relations between socialism and organized labor. The whole colloquy was published later in the year by the Socialist Party under the title, *Double Edge of Labor's Sword.*

MR. GOMPERS: Did the Socialist Party ever inaugurate a movement to supplant or to be in rivalry with the American Federation of Labor?

MR. HILLQUIT: The Socialist Party very emphatically did not. The Socialist Labor Party at one time conceived the notion of forming an organization of trades unions in opposition to the American Federation of Labor, and constituting a distinct Socialist economic organization. This act on the part of the Socialist Labor Party brought about a split within the Party, and the Socialist Party of to-day was organized largely on that issue and because it did not agree with that policy.

MR. GOMPERS: The Socialist Party which you now represent before the Commission is the successor of the Socialist Labor Party as it existed?

MR. HILLQUIT: It is the successor of that part of the Socialist Labor Party which rebelled against the labor policy just mentioned by you. Those who were opposed to the policy seceded and formed the new Socialist Party.

MR. GOMPERS: The Socialist Labor Party is still in existence?

MR. HILLQUIT: The Socialist Labor Party is still nominally in existence.

MR. GOMPERS: Do you think the members of the Socialist Labor

* Pp. 43–51, 64–69, 78–81, 118–132.

Party would agree with you in saying it is still nominally in existence?

MR. HILLQUIT: I don't know. They represent the same proportion in the Socialist movement as the I. W. W. represents in the American labor movement.

CHAIRMAN WALSH: In round numbers how many members are there in the United States of the Socialist Party?

MR. HILLQUIT: About 115,000 dues-paying members.

CHAIRMAN WALSH: And how many in the Socialist Labor Party, do you know?

MR. HILLQUIT: I estimate about 1,500.

CHAIRMAN WALSH: Where do you get that estimate?

MR. HILLQUIT: Pretty much from the Socialist Labor Party. The last time they gave out a statement of membership, it was between 2 and 3 thousand, and they have since fallen off as may be noticed by their referenda and other indications.

MR. GOMPERS: Who was the candidate of the Socialist Party for President of the United States in 1912?

MR. HILLQUIT: Mr. Eugene V. Debs.

MR. GOMPERS: Who was in 1908?

MR. HILLQUIT: Likewise.

MR. GOMPERS: And in 1902?

MR. HILLQUIT: 1902? There was no Presidential candidate in 1902, when you come to think of it.

MR. GOMPERS: 1904?

MR. HILLQUIT: It was Debs.

MR. GOMPERS: Is it unfair to assume that the candidate of your Party for the Presidency of the United States expresses the views of the Party? Is he the Party spokesman and standard bearer?

MR. HILLQUIT: It is entirely unfair to assume that, in view of the expressed position of the Party itself. In other words, Mr. Gompers, when the Socialist Party, in convention assembled, officially takes a stand on its relation to organized labor, no individual member of the Party, no matter what his position, can nullify or modify that stand.

MR. GOMPERS: Do you know that Mr. Eugene V. Debs was present at the First Annual Convention of the organization which formed the so-called Industrial Workers of the World?

MR. HILLQUIT: I do.

MR. GOMPERS: Have you read any of his speeches during that convention?

MR. HILLQUIT: I have read some.

MR. GOMPERS: Do you regard his expressions as being friendly or in favor of the trades union movement, the American Federation of Labor?

MR. HILLQUIT: As I understand his position, his attitude is not friendly toward the leaders of the American Federation of Labor. His attitude is more friendly toward the members of the American Federation of Labor. But these are his personal views to which he is entitled.

MR. GOMPERS: When Mr. Debs says: "The American Federation of Labor has numbers, but the capitalist class do not fear the American Federation of Labor. Quite the contrary." Do you regard that utterance as a friendly expression for the American Federation of Labor?

MR. HILLQUIT: I do not, nor do I regard it as an authorized utterance of the Socialist Party.

MR. GOMPERS: Speaking of the American Federation of Labor and of some Socialists, he says: "There are these who believe that this form of unionism can be changed from within. They are very greatly mistaken." Do you agree with Mr. Debs on that utterance?

MR. HILLQUIT: I do not agree. I think, on the contrary, the American Federation of Labor is being forced, and will be forced more and more to gradually change its form of organization, to adjust itself to the forms of modern industrial conditions.

MR. GOMPERS: I read this, and ask you for your opinion. Mr. Debs says in that speech: "There is but one way to effect this change, and that is for the workingman to sever his relation with the American Federation."

MR. HILLQUIT: I do not agree with that, nor does the Socialist Party agree with that. And, to make our position clear once for all, Mr. Gompers, I will say that it will be quite useless to quote Mr. Debs on his attitude to the American Federation of Labor. Mr. Debs took part in the organization of the Industrial Workers of the World. I think he has now lived to regret it, but whether he does or not, the fact is that he acted entirely on his own accord and on his own responsibility; that the Socialist Party at no time approved, directly or indirectly, of that stand, and at no time have endorsed the Industrial Workers of the World as against the

American Federation of Labor. And I will say further that the Socialist Party at no time made fundamental criticisms against the American Federation of Labor, although I am just as frank to add that the Socialist Party, or at least the majority of its members, do believe that the present leadership of the American Federation of Labor is somewhat archaic, somewhat antiquated, too conservative and not efficient enough for the objects and purposes of the American Federation of Labor. That is the general Socialist position.

Mr. Gompers: Of course as to the leadership, that must be determined. The leadership of the American Federation of Labor, I assume, must be determined by the membership of the organization, as it can best give expression to its preference.

Mr. Hillquit: Entirely so.

Mr. Gompers: Are you aware that the leadership to which you refer, has been elected and re-elected by practically unanimous vote for several years past?

Mr. Hillquit: We do not contest the election nor the legitimacy of office of the officials of the A. F. of L. We only wish they were a little more abreast of the time, and that they would keep pace with industrial developments.

Mr. Gompers: Reverting to Mr. Debs, he does not oppose the leadership only. In his speech——

Mr. Hillquit: If you will read all, you will find that his opposition is largely, if not exclusively, directed against the leadership as he sees it. And I reiterate once more that it is his individual stand.

Mr. Gompers: You have said that it is his individual stand, yet the speech to which I refer and in which he asks and urges the workmen to leave the American Federation of Labor, was made some time in June or July, 1908, and Mr. Debs was twice made the standard bearer of the Socialist Party as candidate for President of the United States since that time.

Mr. Hillquit: Yes, sir. He was. There was absolutely no reason why he should not be, in view of the fact that the Party itself had at the same time very explicitly declared its stand on organized labor, and it did not have to apprehend that any of its representatives might misrepresent its attitude.

Mr. Gompers: Do you know that Mr. Debs has, within these past weeks, issued a document in which he urges the secession of two of the largest organizations from the American Federation of

Labor, for the purpose of destroying the American Federation of Labor?

MR. HILLQUIT: I do. May I add, Mr. Gompers, that this likewise was wholly and fully done by his own initiative and on his own responsibility, and is in no way approved of or condoned by the Socialist Party. We allow liberty of expression and opinion within the Socialist Party, you know.

MR. GOMPERS: Do you regard that as the individual expression of opinion, when a man thrice the candidate of a political party, urges that a movement be inaugurated to dissolve the only general federation of organized workmen that ever existed for a period of time, such as the American Federation of Labor?

MR. HILLQUIT: I regard it purely as the individual expression of the man. The Socialist Party never places its program or views into the hands of an individual candidate. It speaks for itself in conventions.

MR. GOMPERS: And the candidate for the Presidency of your party does not express, then, the sentiments and the views of the Party itself, is that the inference to be drawn from your answer?

MR. HILLQUIT: You may draw this inference, that, whenever a candidate of the Socialist Party for the Presidency or otherwise, deviates from the declared principles of the Socialist Party, he does not speak for the Party, but speaks entirely on his responsibility.

Are you still quoting Mr. Debs?

MR. GOMPERS: Perhaps. Would you hold the same line of conduct to apply to, say, Mr. Taft, who was the candidate for President of the United States, nominated by the Republican Party?

MR. HILLQUIT: No, sir. The Republican Party has no declaration of general principles; no expressed attitude towards labor unions; no general social philosophy, and no social views of any kind. Its candidate for President therefore necessarily acts as the spokesman of his party. The Socialist Party is entirely different in this respect.

MR. GOMPERS: Would you say the candidate of the Prohibitionists, the candidate for President, if he were to make a declaration that was inconsistent with what his party would hold, would you regard that as simply his individual expression of opinion?

MR. HILLQUIT: If the candidate for President of the Prohibition Party were to take a drink, I would not say that the Prohibition Party was committed to the drink evil.

MR. GOMPERS: I prefer not to bring in the personal habits of any man. I don't know that that is illuminating or contributory to the discussion.

MR. HILLQUIT: I did not mean to be personal, Mr. Gompers.

MR. GOMPERS: The question as to the candidate for President of the Prohibition Party is nothing to me. I was speaking of personal declarations. Supposing I, as President of the American Federation of Labor, were to go upon the platform and give expression in a speech, or were to write an editorial in the American Federationist, urging the dissolution of the American Federation of Labor,——

MR. HILLQUIT: Of the Socialist Party, you mean, to apply your analogy.

MR. GOMPERS: Evidently you want to bandy words with me rather than to answer the question.

MR. HILLQUIT: Go ahead.

CHAIRMAN WALSH: Wait until the question is finished and then answer, if you can.

MR. GOMPERS: Supposing Mr. Gompers, President of the American Federation of Labor, were upon a public platform or in articles contributed to the Labor Press, to advocate the dissolution of the American Federation of Labor, would you regard that as a personal expression of my own?

MR. HILLQUIT: I would, decidedly. If you, as the President of the American Federation of Labor, were to advocate a dissolution of the American Federation of Labor, without such a resolution having been passed by the Federation, I certainly should not say that you voiced the sentiments of the organization.

Furthermore, with all due respect to you, your analogy does not apply, Mr. Gompers. Mr. Debs, a leading member of the Socialist Party, advocates certain changes in the American Federation of Labor. If you, as the President of the American Federation of Labor, were to advocate a change or dissolution in or of the Socialist Party, you would be in an analogous position, and I certainly would not regard that as an official expression of the American Federation of Labor. Furthermore, you, Mr. Gompers, have very often taken a stand hostile to the Socialist Party. I do not regard that as the official expression of the American Federation of Labor, for I know that the membership, or a very large portion of it, hold very different views on the subject. That does not come within your domain as President of the American Federation of Labor, although you, as an individual, are at liberty to hold such opinions, and the Federation does not in any way discipline you for holding them. There is your analogy.

MR. GOMPERS: Mr. Hillquit, these speeches which you have made a thousand and one times——

CHAIRMAN WALSH: I would not get into any arguments, Mr. Gompers, with the witness, but just question him. When you go on the witness stand, he is going to ask you questions, and I suppose you can make some when you come to go on there.

MR. GOMPERS: All right, Mr. Chairman. Now, of course, Mr. Hillquit, you understand that the articles or editorials which I have written and published in the American Federationist, all of them have been caused by the defensive attitude which the American Federation has been forced to take against the aggressiveness and hostility of the Socialist Labor Party and the Socialist Party?

MR. HILLQUIT: I don't think so at all, Mr. Gompers. If you ask me about my understanding of it, my understanding is that those articles have been caused by your fear of the increasing growth of Socialism in the ranks of the Federation. That is my understanding of it.

MR. GOMPERS: Well, of course, you would not attribute to me very great fear of anything, would you?

MR. HILLQUIT: Of anything?

MR. GOMPERS: Of anything.

MR. HILLQUIT: If you want my opinion, Mr. Gompers, I should say you are a very brave man, but you do hate to see the American Federation of Labor turning Socialistic.

MR. GOMPERS: The reason I do so is the result of conviction——

CHAIRMAN WALSH: Mr. Gompers, please do not get into an argument with the witness now. You can go on the witness stand and he will examine you and you will have the same latitude of stating your views. But just ask him questions, please.

MR. GOMPERS: Mr. Debs, in his speech, to which I have referred before, said: "I appeal to you to ally yourselves with the economic organization which embraces your entire class." He referred to the Industrial Workers of the World, organized in 1905. Will you give me your judgment as to the extent to which that organization embraces the entire working class?

MR. HILLQUIT: Of the world? Not very much, Mr. Gompers. It

was the fond hope of the organizers, which I never shared, that it would; but it does not.

MR. GOMPERS: He says further: "I would appeal to you to declare yourselves here and now, to be for once and forever true enough to yourselves to join the only industrial union that is absolutely true to you—the I. W. W." And the stenographer put "Loud Applause." Will you give your opinion of that statement?

MR. HILLQUIT: My opinion is the same that I have given you before. I think Mr. Debs was carried away by his enthusiasm, when he thought he could create an artificial organization to embrace all the workers joined in one great industrial union. I think his views of trade unionism are not sound. At any rate, they are not those of the Socialist Party and they are not mine; and you might just as well read 200 quotations from his speeches on that subject as five. . . .

MR. GOMPERS: The American Socialist Party has always declared, until quite recently, for the nationalization of all of the means of production and distribution, has it not?

MR. HILLQUIT: I don't think the word "all" occurs in any authoritative exposition of the principles of the Party.

MR. GOMPERS: But by the omission of the word "all," and without any qualification, nevertheless no other inference could be drawn from that declaration, could it?

MR. HILLQUIT: I would not say that was true.

MR. GOMPERS: Suppose I should say that this court room belonged to the State of New York or the city of New York, it would not be necessary for me to say that all the entire court room belonged——

MR. HILLQUIT: No, not in that connection, but I should think that the comparison is somewhat unfortunate. If I should say that Mr. Gompers can be heard by the people in the audience, it would not necessarily imply that he could be heard by all.

MR. GOMPERS: For instance, if you put it this way: "The Socialist Party demands the nationalization of the means of production and distribution." The absence of the word "all" there would not at all minimize the extent, would it?

MR. HILLQUIT: In my conception of it, Mr. Gompers, and I can give you only my understanding of it, I should say that the Socialist Party has always stood for the collective ownership of *social* tools of production and distribution.

MR. GOMPERS: As a matter of fact, isn't it so? We need not quibble——

Mr. Hillquit: (Interrupting): I am not quibbling.

Mr. Gompers: Isn't it so that it has been only within the past two or three years that the Socialist Party has made that distinction?

Mr. Hillquit: No, Mr. Gompers. You may have noticed it within the past two or three years, but the entire Socialist philosophy has always been based upon the conception that the tools of the work have become social in character and consequently Socialism always dealt with the social tool and never with the individual.

Mr. Gompers: I refer to the declaration excluding any private property.

Mr. Hillquit: There was no such exclusion at any time. Private property in articles of consumption has always been recognized and sanctioned by the Socialists; and as to the means of production, it is not my understanding—and I think I am more or less conversant with the literature on the subject—that it ever was intended to embrace within that category the individual tool or the individual industry.

Mr. Gompers: Take, for instance, the boot and shoe industry. There are shoemakers and bootmakers who are engaged in artistic shoemaking and make the whole shoe, using but few tools. If the boot and shoe industry became socialized, and owned and controlled collectively, would there be a separate arrangement for the artistic boot and shoemaker?

Mr. Hillquit: Now, Mr. Gompers, I don't see any reason in the world why the artistic boot and shoemaker should not continue to be an artistic boot and shoemaker under Socialism. I don't believe there would be any socialization of the individual shoe; at least, I should not wear it, if it were.

Mr. Gompers: The answer, of course, is quite germane.

Mr. Hillquit: To the question.

Mr. Gompers: Do you regard it as a fact that in the United States "the bourgeoisie has converted the position of the lawyer, the priest, the poet, the man of science into its paid wage laborers"?

Mr. Hillquit: Why, it is somewhat exaggerated, but substantially true. I can speak for the lawyers. (Laughter.)

Mr. Gompers: Do you believe that the statement, quoting again from Socialist authority: "Chattel slavery is dead, a greater slavery has grown up in its place. Wage slavery is so much greater than chattel slavery as the white people in this country are more numerous than the black people"?

MR. HILLQUIT: I think that is substantially correct.

MR. GOMPERS: Do you agree with the estimate that in the United States the number of men out of work are more than five million?

MR. HILLQUIT: At some time or another. I believe the census of 1900 gives the number of partially unemployed during the year at 6,000,0000.

MR. GOMPERS: Which authority?

MR. HILLQUIT: The 1900 census. The figure is based on the total of workers unemployed during all or part of the year.

MR. GOMPERS: Do you regard the Communist Manifesto of Marx and Engles as on the whole correct, as correct to-day as ever?

MR. HILLQUIT: That was published in 1848.

MR. GOMPERS: Do you regard the general principles laid down in that manifesto as on the whole as correct to-day as ever?

MR. HILLQUIT: The general principles, yes. The details, perhaps not.

MR. GOMPERS: Do you accept or repudiate the term, or the idea of communism?

MR. HILLQUIT: The term "Communist" as used in the Communist Manifesto signified something entirely different from what it signifies now. What the authors of the Communist Manifesto meant by the term "Communist" is what we mean to-day by the term "Socialist."

MR. GOMPERS: I should judge from the testimony you gave this morning that you do not accept the theory of cataclysm as a means to bring about the co-operative commonwealth?

MR. HILLQUIT: I do not believe in the cataclysm theory.

MR. GOMPERS: Your answers would indicate that the Socialist predictions of several years ago have scarcely been verified, including the inability of any government, either to destroy or regulate the corporate existence of capital, such as trusts?

MR. HILLQUIT: The question is, whether I admit that this prediction was wrong?

MR. GOMPERS: I simply want, if I can, to have you verify, or rather, re-state, by yes or no, or in such a way as you may care to whether there is to be in our society an evolutionary continuous improvement in the condition of the workers up to the point that may be regarded as a goal or a constant improvement?

MR. HILLQUIT: You asked two questions, there, Mr. Gompers. As to the ability of the Government to regulate or destroy business corporations or trusts, I still believe that the Government is quite incapable of doing so.

As to the process of gradual improvement, I believe in it. But whether such process of gradual improvement will eventually lead up to Socialism without violent, social or political disturbance, or civil war, I don't know.

MR. GOMPERS: Do you not see a departure from Marx' conception in the development of the joint stock company?

MR. HILLQUIT: Decidedly not. On the contrary a verification of his theory of concentration of capital.

MR. GOMPERS: Then you think that the growth and ownership of the joint stock company is a refutation of the theory of the development of the capitalist classes, or Marx' theory of the capitalist class?

MR. HILLQUIT: I don't think so. On the contrary I think, as I said, it is a verification of it.

MR. GOMPERS: Do you regard the population of the United States, as divided into a small master class and a vast servant class?

MR. HILLQUIT: No such conception was ever expressed by any authoritative Socialist author. What you read in the Communist Manifesto is an assertion that the population tends to develop into such two classes. That condition has by far not been reached in the United States.

MR. GOMPERS: Do you believe that the children of the working class are doomed to ignorance, drudgery, toil and darkened lives in the United States?

MR. HILLQUIT: Very largely, Mr. Gompers.

MR. GOMPERS: When you say that we have secured, or are securing, a material improvement in the general conditions of the working people, and the people generally, it does not conform to your latest answer. Which is true, your latest answer or your answer this morning?

MR. HILLQUIT: Both are absolutely true. We have improved conditions somewhat, but our achievements are as nothing compared with what is still to come. I presume that, as president of the American Federation of Labor, you know that we still have the evil of child labor with us in an abominably large extent.

MR. GOMPERS: I have been admonished that I must not argue with you, and I have no desire to do so. But I want to call your attention to the fact that you said just now that you agreed largely with this statement: "The children of the working class are doomed to ignorance, drudgery, toil and darkened lives." If you say that this is a fact, how does it conform with your statement this morning as to the general gradual improvement of the conditions of the working class, which, of course, includes the children?

MR. HILLQUIT: If you will read the document further, you will get your answer. The children of the working class are doomed to the lives described unless something very radical is done to relieve them from it. . . .

MR. GOMPERS: I take it that you are not in favor of what is generally known as State Socialism?

MR. HILLQUIT: I am not.

MR. GOMPERS: Not even as a step towards a democratic Socialism?

MR. HILLQUIT: If it were State Socialism, it would not be a step towards democratic Socialism.

MR. GOMPERS: Are not the present differences within the Socialist parties in the United States significant of fatal differences in the management of a revolutionary society?

MR. HILLQUIT: No, there are no fatal differences, Mr. Gompers. We have some differences of opinion within the Socialist Party, sometimes lively ones. I hope you have them in the American Federation of Labor. But we, nevertheless, manage to keep our organization and to work for a common purpose. I presume there will be strong differences of opinion, and some fights, even under Socialism. I should not want it to be otherwise.

MR. GOMPERS: I mean as to liberty. Under Socialism will there be liberty of individual action, and liberty in the choice of occupation and refusal to work?

MR. HILLQUIT: Plenty of it, Mr. Gompers.

MR. GOMPERS: I take it that you have no apprehension that under a democratic Socialist management, the administrators could or would attempt to exploit the workers under them, and one set of laborers would exploit another set; the lazy office-holders, the industrious artisans; the strong and bolder, the weaker and more modest ones, and the failures, the economically successful.

MR. HILLQUIT: I think it quite likely that there will be some abuses of that kind. Even under Socialism men will still remain human, no doubt. But, Mr. Gompers, we have every reason to believe that they will be small and insignificant as compared with present abuses, for the system will be based on a greater democracy and self-government, and will thus provide for proper means of remedy. Furthermore, there will be no great incentive to corruption such as we have in private gain under capitalism.

MR. GOMPERS: In the event that the Co-operative Commonwealth should be established, taking it for granted for the sake of the question, that it is possible, it would have for its present purpose the highest material and social and moral improvement of the condition of the workers attainable at that time, would it not?

MR. HILLQUIT: I think so.

MR. GOMPERS: And would there be any higher aim after that is established?

MR. HILLQUIT: Oh, there will be plenty more. There will be new aims coming every day.

MR. GOMPERS: Still more?

MR. HILLQUIT: Still further.

MR. GOMPERS: Still higher?

MR. HILLQUIT: Still higher.

MR. GOMPERS: Now, if that is so, isn't it a fact that it is not at all a goal, but simply a transitory ideal?

MR. HILLQUIT: Sure. It is our goal to-day. It is a transitory goal. There will be a movement toward a higher goal to-morrow.

MR. GOMPERS: In other words, you think even if that condition of affairs should be possible, it, like the conditions of to-day, is transitory and continually tending toward improvement?

MR. HILLQUIT: Yes.

MR. GOMPERS: And not a goal?

MR. HILLQUIT: Not an ultimate goal. There is no such thing as an ultimate social goal.

MR. GOMPERS: In the Socialist state, would you have each worker rewarded by the full product of his labor, or by an apportionment of the product according to his demands? In other words, would the rule be, to each according to his deeds, or to each according to his needs?

MR. HILLQUIT: I think neither, strictly speaking. I don't suppose his Socialist regime would at once radically change established standards of compensation. I think it would have to grow up and be built up on the existing basis. And I think it will largely be a system of salaries and wages, as nearly as possible, in proportion to the usefulness of the service—but they will be larger than they are to-day, because they will include the profits now paid to the idle capitalists.

Mr. Gompers: So, as a matter of fact, then, if the Co-operative Commonwealth is not a goal, is not an end, then why term it Socialism, and why not term it the ordinary, natural development of the human race to a higher and better state of society?

Mr. Hillquit: We may term it the ordinary and natural development of the human race to the point of Socialism. In other words, Mr. Gompers, we divide the history of mankind pretty arbitrarily into certain periods. We speak of the period of Slavery, the period of Feudalism, the period of Capitalism. Now we foresee the next step in development, and call it the period of Socialism. We cannot draw a line of demarcation where it starts or where it vanishes. It will certainly not be permanent. There will be something superior to it some time. In the meantime every stage of development is superior to the preceding stage; and by the same token as Capitalism is superior to Feudalism, Socialism is superior to Capitalism. That is all.

Mr. Gompers: You simply apply it as a term, and not an end?

Mr. Hillquit: Not an ultimate end in social development, no. . . .

[HILLQUIT NOW QUESTIONS GOMPERS]

Mr. Hillquit: Now, Mr. Gompers, to take up another subject, is it your conception or that of the Federation, that workers in the United States to-day receive the full product of their labor?

Mr. Gompers: I think, but I am not quite so sure, that I know what you have in mind.

Mr. Hillquit: Do you understand my question?

Mr. Gompers: I think I do. In the generally accepted sense of that term, they do not.

Mr. Hillquit: In any particular sense, yes?

Mr. Gompers: No.

Mr. Hillquit: Then the workers of this country do not receive the whole product of their labor? Can you hazard a guess as to what proportion of the product they do receive in the shape of wages?

Mr. Gompers: I am not a good guesser, and I doubt that there is any value in a guess.

Mr. Hillquit: You have no general idea, have you, on the subject?

Mr. Gompers: I have a most general idea, but I am not called upon to guess.

Mr. Hillquit: No. Will you please give us your most general idea?

Mr. Gompers: As to what proportion?

Mr. Hillquit: As to the approximate proportion of their product which the workers, as a whole, get.

Mr. Gompers: I will say that it is impossible for any one to definitely say what proportion the workers receive as a reward for their labor; but it is a fact that, due to the organized labor movement they have received, and are receiving, a larger share of the product of their labor than they ever did in the history of modern society.

Mr. Hillquit: Then one of the functions of organized labor is to increase the share of the workers in the product of their labor, is that correct?

Mr. Gompers: Yes, sir. Organized labor makes constantly increasing demand upon society for reward for the services which the workers render to society, and without which civilized life would be impossible.

Mr. Hillquit: And these demands for an increasing share of the product of labor continue as a gradual process all the time?

Mr. Gompers: I am not so sure as to gradual process. Sometimes it is not a gradual process, but it is all the time.

Mr. Hillquit: All the time?

Mr. Gompers: Yes, sir.

Mr. Hillquit: Then, Mr. Gompers, you assume that the organized labor movement has generally succeeded in forcing a certain increase of the portion of the workers' share in the general product, do you?

Mr. Gompers: Yes, sir.

Mr. Hillquit: And it demands more now?

Mr. Gompers: Yes, sir.

Mr. Hillquit: And if it should get, say, 5 per cent. more within the next year, will the organized labor movement rest contented with that, and stop?

Mr. Gompers: Not if I know anything about human nature.

Mr. Hillquit: Will the organized movement stop in its demands for an ever greater share in the product at any time before it receives the full product, and before complete social justice, as it sees it, is done?

Mr. Gompers: The working people are human beings—as all other people. They are prompted by the same desires and hopes of a better life, and they are not willing to wait until after they have shuffled off this mortal coil for the better life. They want it here and now. They want to make conditions better for their children so that they may meet the newer problems in their time. The working people are pressing forward, making their claims and presenting those claims with whatever power they have. Pressing forward to secure a larger, and constantly larger share of the products. They are working towards the highest and best ideals of social justice.

Mr. Hillquit: Now, "the highest and best ideals of social justice," as applied to distribution of wealth, wouldn't that be a system under which all the workers, manual, mental, directive and executive would together get the sum total of all the products of their toil?

Mr. Gompers: Really, a fish is caught by a tempting bait; a mouse or a rat is caught in a trap by a tempting bait. The intelligent, common-sense workmen prefer to deal with the problems of to-day, the problems with which they are bound to contend if they want to advance, rather than to deal with a picture and a dream which has never had, and I am sure never will have, any reality in the actual affairs of humanity, and which threaten, if they could be introduced, the worst system of circumscriptional effort and activity that has ever been invented by the human mind.

Mr. Hillquit: Mr. Gompers, I would like to get an answer. In your experience with the labor movement and its forward march towards ever greater improvement, and greater measure of social justice, can you locate a point at which the labor movement will stop and rest contented so long as the workers will receive less than the full product of their work?

Mr. Gompers: I say that the workers, as human beings, will never stop at any point in the effort to secure greater improvements in their conditions and a better life in all its phases. And wherever that may lead and whatever that may be in my time and at my age, I decline to permit my mind or my activities to be labeled by any particular ism.

Mr. Hillquit: I do not try to attach any ism to you, but the question I ask is whether the American Federation of Labor and its authorized spokesman have a general social philosophy, or work blindly from day to day.

Mr. GOMPERS: I think your question is——

Mr. HILLQUIT (Interrupting): Inconvenient?

Mr. GOMPERS: No. I will tell you what it is—it is a question prompted to you, and is an insult.

Mr. HILLQUIT: It is not a question prompted to me.

Mr. GOMPERS: It is an insult.

Mr. HILLQUIT: Why, Mr. Gompers?

Mr. GOMPERS: It insinuates that the men and the women in the American Federation of Labor movement are acting blindly day to day.

Mr. HILLQUIT: I have not insinuated——

Mr. GOMPERS (Interrupting): Your question implies it.

Mr. HILLQUIT: I am giving you an opportunity to deny.

Mr. GOMPERS: If a man should ask me whether I still beat my wife, any answer I could make would incriminate me. If I answered that I did not, the intimation would be that I had stopped. If I answered that I did, the inference would be that I was continuing to beat her.

Mr. HILLQUIT: But, Mr. Gompers, my question bears no analogy to that story——

Mr. GOMPERS (Interrupting): Your question is an insult, and a studied one.

Mr. HILLQUIT: Now, will you state whether you will or will not answer my question?

Mr. GOMPERS: Will you repeat the question?

Mr. HILLQUIT: My question was whether the American Federation of Labor, as represented by its spokesman, has a general social philosophy, or whether the organization is working blindly from day to day. Now, that is a plain question.

Mr. GOMPERS: Yes, it is a plain question—it is a plain insult.

CHAIRMAN WALSH: Do you refuse to answer it on the ground that it is insulting?

Mr. GOMPERS: Yes, sir.

CHAIRMAN WALSH: That is all, then.

Mr. HILLQUIT: Then inform me on this: In its practical work in the labor movement is the American Federation of Labor guided by a general social philosophy, or is it not?

Mr. GOMPERS: It is guided by the history of the past, drawing its lessons from history. It knows the conditions by which the working people are surrounded. It works along the line of least resistance and endeavors to accomplish the best results in improving the condition of the working people, men, women and children, to-day and to-morrow—and to-morrow's to-morrow and each day, making it a better day than the one that had gone before. The guiding principle, philosophy and aim of the labor movement is to secure a better life for all.

Mr. Hillquit: But in these efforts to improve conditions from day to day, you must have an underlying standard of what is better, don't you?

Mr. Gompers: No. You start out with a given program, and everything must conform to it; and if the facts do not conform to your theories, then your actions betray the state of mind "so much the worse for the facts."

Mr. Hillquit: Mr. Gompers, what I ask you is this: You say you try to make the conditions of the workers better every day. In order to determine whether the conditions are better or worse, you must have some standards by which you distinguish the bad from the good in the labor movement, must you not?

Mr. Gompers: Certainly. Does it require much discernment to know that a wage of $3.00 and a workday of 8 hours a day in sanitary workshops are all better than $2.50 and 12 hours a day under perilous conditions of labor? It does not require much conception of a social philosophy to understand that.

Mr. Hillquit: Then, Mr. Gompers, by parity of reasoning, $4.00 a day and 7 hours of work, and truly attractive working conditions are still better?

Mr. Gompers: Unquestionably.

Mr. Hillquit: Therefore——

Mr. Gompers (Interrupting): Just a moment. I have not stipulated $4.00 a day or $8.00 a day or any number of dollars a day or 8 hours a day or 7 hours a day or any number of hours a day. The aim is to secure the best conditions obtainable for the workers.

Mr. Hillquit: Yes; and when these conditions are obtained——

Mr. Gompers (Interrupting): Why, then we want better——

Mr. Hillquit (Continuing): You will still strive for better?

Mr. Gompers: Yes.

Mr. Hillquit: Now, my question is, will this effort on the part of organized labor ever stop before the workers receive the full reward for their labor?

MR. GOMPERS: It won't stop at all at any particular point, whether it be that towards which you have just stated, or anything else. The working people will never stop in their effort to obtain a better life for themselves, and for their wives and for their children and for humanity.

MR. HILLQUIT: Then the object of the organized workmen is to obtain complete social justice for themselves and for their wives and for their children?

MR. GOMPERS: It is the effort to obtain a better life every day.

MR. HILLQUIT: Every day, and always——

MR. GOMPERS (Interrupting): Every day. That does not limit it.

MR. HILLQUIT: Until such time——

MR. GOMPERS (Interrupting): Not until any time.

MR. HILLQUIT: In other words——

MR. GOMPERS (Interrupting): In other words, we go farther than you. (Laughter and applause in the audience.) You have an end; we have not.

MR. HILLQUIT: Then, Mr. Gompers, you want to go on record as saying that the American Federation of Labor goes farther in its endeavors than the Socialist Party. If the Socialist Party has for its present purpose the abolition of the system of profits and wages, and seeks to secure for the workers the full product of their labor, if this is the purposes which it seeks to obtain by gradual steps—then I understand you to say that the American Federation of Labor goes beyond that.

MR. GOMPERS: I have said this, and I say that no categorical answer, Yes, or No, can be given to that question. As just indicated, as to the abolition of private profits and wages—there are a number of employers who quite agree with you; they would reduce wages or take wages away entirely. The question of the co-operative commonwealth and the ownership of the means of production and distribution is implied by it. Now, let me say——

MR. HILLQUIT (Interrupting): It is not, Mr. Gompers.

MR. GOMPERS: Well, all right.

MR. HILLQUIT: I am not proposing any system. I want your aims and the limits of your aims.

MR. GOMPERS: By your question, you want to place me in the position of saying that I am for the system of society which some of you dreamers have conceived of, and then say that I go beyond it.

Mr. Hillquit: I do not, Mr. Gompers, you interrupted me——

Mr. Gompers (Interrupting): Well, you interrupted me, so we are even. And I say that the movement of the working people, whether under the American Federation, or not, will be simply following the human impulse for improvement in their condition, and wherever that may lead, they will go, without having a goal up to yours or surpassing yours. It will lead them constantly to greater material, physical, social and moral well-being.

Mr. Hillquit: Then, Mr. Gompers, you would not say that the difference between the program of the American Federation of Labor, and that of the Socialist Party is a quantitative one—that the Socialist Party wants more than the American Federation of Labor. You would not say that, would you?

Mr. Gompers: I don't know that it is necessary that I should make the comparison. It is not interesting at all, nor is it a contribution to the subject which the Commission desires to examine.

Mr. Hillquit: You decline to answer?

Mr. Gompers: The question is not germane to the subject under inquiry, and is not necessary.

Chairman Walsh: I would like to hear it answered if possible, Mr. Gompers. If it is not possible for any reason, very well.

Mr. Gompers: May I hear the question read?

(Question read.)

Mr. Gompers: Socialism is a proposition to place the working people of the country and of the world in a physical and material straight-jacket.

Mr. Hillquit: Pardon me, Mr. Gompers, I have not asked you your opinion about the effects of the co-operative commonwealth. I am speaking merely about the aim to abolish the wage system and the program to secure for the workers the full product of their labor; and I am asking you whether on these points we demand more than the American Federation has ultimately in view.

Mr. Gompers: I think you demand something to which the American labor movement declines to give its adherence.

Mr. Hillquit: Then do I understand you to say that the American labor movement would discountenance the abolition of the wage system and the return of the full reward of labor to the workers?

Mr. Gompers: Your question is an assumption, and is unwarranted, for as a matter of fact we decline to commit our labor movement to your species of speculative philosophy.

Mr. Hillquit: I have not introduced speculative philosophy, Mr. Gompers. If I cannot make myself clear, please tell me so.

Chairman Walsh: May I be permitted here to ask the stenographer to read that last question?

Mr. Hillquit: Certainly, Mr. Chairman.

(The question read as follows): I am speaking merely about the aim to abolish the wage system, and about the program to secure to the workers the full product of their labor, and I am asking in this respect whether we demand more than the American Federation of Labor has ultimately in view.

Chairman Walsh: That is with reference to getting the full product of labor alone?

Mr. Hillquit: Yes.

Chairman Walsh: Now, can you answer that directly, Mr. Gompers?

Mr. Gompers: No; that is impossible to answer by a Yes or No.

Chairman Walsh: Then let it stand there, because that implies that it is impossible to answer it.

Mr. Hillquit: Mr. Gompers, when you stated first that the workingmen of to-day do not get the full reward for their labor or the full product of their toil, will you tell me who gets the part which is withheld from the workers?

Mr. Gompers: Investment, superintendence, the agencies for the creation of wants among the people, and many others.

Mr. Hillquit: Well, then, in your opinion those are legitimate factors in industry entitled to reward?

Mr. Gompers: Many of them, yes; many of them are being eliminated.

Mr. Hillquit: Which ones are entitled and which ones are not entitled to reward?

Mr. Gompers: Superintendence, the creation of wants, administration, return for investment——

Mr. Hillquit: Return for investment? Does that include every kind of capital invested in industry, regardless of origin?

Mr. Gompers: No, sir.

Mr. Hillquit: Then what do you mean by return for investment?

Mr. Gompers: For honest investment. I don't mean watered stocks or inflated holdings, but honest investment.

Mr. Hillquit: Honest stock investment?

Mr. Gompers: Honest investment. I did not say "stock investment."

Mr. Hillquit: Well, I am talking about stock investment, Mr. Gompers. Do you consider dividends paid by corporations as distinguished from salaries paid for superintendence and so on—do you consider that a legitimate charge on the products of labor?

Mr. Gompers: That depends entirely as to the character of the services performed.

Mr. Hillquit: Now, I assume that no service is performed. So far as services are performed are concerned, we have classified those under the head of superintendence, management, initiation, and so on. Now, I am referring to the dividends on stock, which is paid to stockholders by virtue of stock ownership, and regardless of any activity on the part of the stockholder.

Mr. Gompers: I am speaking of honest investment, too, which you did not include.

Mr. Hillquit: Will you please answer that question with such qualifications as you may deem proper to make?

Mr. Gompers: I have already replied, and I now repeat, upon honest investment, yes.

Mr. Hillquit: Mr. Gompers, assume that I purchase to-day in the open market and pay the full price for, say, 100 shares of Steel Corporation stock. The next quarter year I get my dividends on it. Am I entitled to such dividends?

Mr. Gompers: Mr. Chairman, I suggest that if Mr. Hillquit is going to permit this investigation to degenerate into a question of high finance, why, we had better get a high financier here.

Chairman Walsh: I think that is a proper question and germane to this inquiry, but if you cannot answer it, you may say so.

Mr. Gompers: I wish respectfully, Mr. Chairman, to differ from that remark of the Chair——

Chairman Walsh: Then you don't care to answer?

Mr. Gompers: I decline to answer it on the ground that it is not material to the question, and purely a question of a financial character. It is not a question upon which proper interrogation can be made.

CHAIRMAN WALSH: I have ruled that it was, but we are not going to compel Mr. Gompers to reply to it.

MR. HILLQUIT: No, of course not.

CHAIRMAN WALSH: Go ahead.

MR. HILLQUIT: Will you please, define what you call honest investment as distinguished——

MR. GOMPERS (Interrupting): An honest man finds no difficulty in determining what is honest.

MR. HILLQUIT: Now, Mr. Gompers, that is really not an answer. You have made that statement, and I presume you mean something by it; I should like to know what you mean?

MR. GOMPERS: I mean honest, actual physical investment.

MR. HILLQUIT: Now, I am asking you, does the purchase of stock with real physical money, at the full price constitute such an honest investment?

MR. GOMPERS: First let me say in answer to that question, that with the manipulations of stocks and of the stock market, I am out of harmony. I am opposed to it, and have done and will do whatever I can to eliminate that speculation involved in the fundamentals of stock jobbery and stock sales.

MR. HILLQUIT: Mr. Gompers, you are familiar with industrial conditions as few men in this country. You know perfectly well that the most important industries in the United States are managed and operated by corporations, and you know that the income from such industries is distributed very largely in the form of dividends on stocks and interest on bonds, don't you?

MR. GOMPERS: Yes, sir.

MR. HILLQUIT: Now, I am asking you this question: As the President of the American Federation of Labor do you consider that the vast sum of money paid annually by industry in the shape of such dividends on stock and interest on bonds in the various industries are a legitimate and proper charge upon the product of labor, or do you not?

MR. GOMPERS: I do not.

MR. HILLQUIT: That is an answer. Then the stockholders or bondholders of modern corporations receive a workless income from the product of the workers who have produced it. Is that your opinion?

MR. GOMPERS: Unquestionably.

MR. HILLQUIT: And the efforts of the American labor movement to secure a larger share are directed against that class who gets such improper income?

MR. GOMPERS: Against all who——

MR. HILLQUIT: Against all who obtain a workless income which comes from the product of labor. Is that correct?

MR. GOMPERS: Well, all who illegitimately stand between the workers and the attainment of a better life.

MR. HILLQUIT: Which means, or does it not mean, those who derive an income without work by virtue of their control of the industry?

MR. GOMPERS: No.

MR. HILLQUIT: Whom do you except?

MR. GOMPERS: I except, as I have before called attention to, honest investment, honest enterprise.

MR. HILLQUIT: Have the efforts of the workers in the American Federation of Labor and in other labor organizations to obtain a larger share of the product, met a favorable reception from those who obtain what we may call the unearned part of the product?

MR. GOMPERS: If you mean the employers——

MR. HILLQUIT: Employers, stockholders, bondholders, the capitalist class generally.

MR. GOMPERS: As a matter of fact, there has been very much opposition to the efforts of the working people to secure improved conditions.

MR. HILLQUIT: And that opposition is based upon the desire of the beneficiaries of the present system of distribution to retain as much as possible of their present share or to increase it, is it not?

MR. GOMPERS: I suppose it is not difficult to determine that that is one of the reasons. But one additional reason is that there are employers who live in the 20th century and have the mentality of the 16th century in regard to their attitude toward working people. They still imagine that they are the masters of all that serve, and that any attempt on the part of the working people to secure improvement in their condition is a species of rebellion—a rebellious spirit which must be bounded down. But we find this, Mr. Hillquit, that after we have had some contests with employers of such a character, whether we have won the battle or lost it, if we but maintain our organization, there is less difficulty thereafter in reaching a joint agreement or a collective bargain involving improved conditions for the working people.

Mr. HILLQUIT: That is, if you retain your organization?

Mr. GOMPERS: Yes, sir.

Mr. HILLQUIT: And the stronger the organization, the more likelihood of securing such concessions, is that correct?

Mr. GOMPERS: Unquestionably.

Mr. HILLQUIT: Then it is not on account of the changed sentiment of the employer, that he is ready to yield, but on account of greater strength shown by the employees, is that correct?

Mr. GOMPERS: Not entirely.

Mr. HILLQUIT: No, why not?

Mr. GOMPERS: Not entirely, for, as a matter of fact, the employer changes his sentiment when he is convinced that the workingmen have demonstrated that they have the right to have a voice in determining the questions affecting the relations between themselves and their employers, as evidenced, if you please, by the late Mr. Baer, who, you may recall, once declared that he would not confer with the representative of the miners or anyone who stood for them; that he and his associates were the trustees of God in the administration of their property, and appointed to take care of the rights and interests of the working people. Well, he lived to revise his judgment, as many other employers live to revise their judgments, and have come to agreements with their workmen.

Mr. HILLQUIT: Now, Mr. Gompers, the employers as a class, being interested in retaining their share of the general product or increasing it, and the workers as you say, being determined to demand an ever greater and greater share of it, would you say that the economic interests between the two classes are harmonious or not?

Mr. GOMPERS: I say they are not, and as I am under affirmation before this Commission, I take this opportunity of saying that no man within the range of my acquaintance has ever been so thoroughly misrepresented on that question as I have. . . .

"Socialism, the Hope of the Working Class"*
1912

Following is a segment of a talk Haywood gave at Cooper Union in January 1912, before an audience of fellow Socialist Party members.

Comrades and fellow workers: I am indeed gratified with this splendid reception. In fact, I am always pleased with a New York audience, and I hope this will be no different from the many audiences that I have addressed in this city.

I am here tonight, as the chairman has stated, to speak on "Socialism, the Hope of the Working Class." (Applause.) And there are some differences between Socialists. If we are to judge socialism by the opinions that have recently been expressed in the present controversy going on in our Socialist papers, and if our judgment were based on those ingredients, I am sure that we would have a mental chop suey (laughter and applause), the mysticism of which would baffle the ingenuity of the brain of a Chinese mandarin. (Laughter.) But not all the things that you have read from the pens of our very learned brothers are socialism. Socialism is so plain, so clear, so simple that when a person becomes intellectual he doesn't understand socialism. (Applause.)

In speaking to you of socialism tonight I would urge that you do not turn your minds to the legislative halls at Albany or the halls of congress in Washington or the council chambers of the city hall in New York. I would prefer that you turn your minds inward and think of the machines where you are employed every day. I would like you to think of the relation that you hold to society, which occurs in three distinct phases: First, the individual relation, the relation to your home and family, the conditions that present themselves there; then the group relation, the industrial relation, without any regard to craft or trade divisions—not thinking that you

* *International Socialist Review*, February 1912.

are a particular craft man, but that you are working in some particular line of industry which is absolutely interdependent with all other industries; and then, having left your shop, your group or industrial relation, I would like your mind to turn home again, and you will not find that home isolated. It is a group of many homes. And there you assume another relation. There you become, not an individual of your family group, nor an individual of your social or industrial group, but you become a unit in the fabric of society. You become one then of the entire working class. And my definition of socialism here tonight will be clear enough indeed to the working class and also to the enemy of the working class; but to the go-between, to the opportunist, it will not be clear, and in all probability they would ask me to define my definition. I am not here to waste time on the "immediate demanders" or the step-at-a-time people whose every step is just a little shorter than the preceding step. (Laughter and applause.) I am here to speak to the working class, and the working class will understand what I mean when I say that under socialism you will need no passports or citizenship papers to take a part in the affairs in which you are directly interested. The working class will understand me when I say that socialism is an industrial democracy and that industrialism is a social democracy. (Applause.)

And in this democracy we know no divisions. There will be no divisions of race, creed, sex or color. Every person who is a factor in industrial activity will take a part in this industrial democracy. Under socialism we workers will not be subjects of any state or nation, but we will be citizens, free citizens in the industries in which we are employed. Therefore, I want you at all times while I am speaking to keep your mind closely riveted on your own personal interests. You don't have to go outside of your own shop, the place where you are doing productive work, to establish socialism. Socialism is not a thing remote, and it is not necessary for you to follow our brothers who are standing on the heights of Utopia beckoning you to come up and enjoy the elysian fields, where you will receive $4 a week after you become 60 years of age (laughter and applause), and where the conditions have arrived at such a perfect stage of security that no trust can do business if it holds more than 40 per cent monopoly of any particular line of industry. (Applause.) In this place that is being mapped out for you, you will find that it is very much more desirable to be exploited by three 33⅓ per cent trusts than it is to be exploited by one 100 per cent trust.

And now we will keep distinctly in mind the shop. I want to say at this point, and emphatically, that with the success of socialism practically all of the political offices now in existence will be put out of business. (Applause.) I want to say also, and with as much emphasis, that while a member of the Socialist party and believing firmly in political action, it is decidedly better in my opinion to be able to elect the superintendent in some branch of industry than to elect a congressman to the United States congress. (Applause.) More than that: under socialism we will have no congresses, such as exist today, nor legislatures, nor parliaments, nor councils of municipalities. Our councils will not be filled with aspiring lawyers and ministers (applause), but they will be the conventions of the working class, composed of men and women who will go there for purposes of education, to exchange ideas, and by their expert knowledge to improve the machinery so that we can use it for the advantage of the working class. We will then have made machinery the slave of the working class, rather than now when the working class is the slave of the man who owns the machinery.

Having established these facts, we will now begin to understand why the conditions are so much more violent in this stage of the world's history than at any previous period. There was never a time in all the history of the world but what the working class were dominated by tyrants. There never was a period so tyrannical as now. We have heard of the democracy of Athens and of that ancient civilization. All the beauties of that wonderful city of free men, with its marvelous sculptures of marble, rested upon the shoulders of the 300,000 slaves in the valley. There has never been a period in the world's history that the working class were free. They have been slaves, serfs, chattel slaves and today wage slaves. And more than that, they are being devoured today by the Frankenstein that they themselves created. The energy, genius and ambition of the working class have brought about this marvelous age of machinery and invention, until today a machine will do the work of ten, one hundred, aye, a thousand times as much work as a man could do 50 years ago. This then is what intensifies the struggle for existence on the part of the working class. The unemployed army is rapidly increasing, due largely to the fact that labor-saving machinery has been introduced in nearly all branches of industry. We find then that the very thing that should improve the conditions of the working class has contrived to make the condition of the working class deplorable indeed. . . .

And here tonight I am going to speak on the class struggle, and I am going to make it so plain that even a lawyer can understand it (laughter and applause). I am going to present the class struggle so clearly here tonight that even a preacher will know its meaning. (Applause.) And this, friends, is rather more difficult than you appreciate. The lawyer and the preacher have never fought with the under-dog. For the ages agone they have been the mouthpieces of the capitalist class. (Applause.) They are not entirely to blame. We Socialists recognize that it is largely the result of environment. You can't see the class struggle through the stained-glass windows of a cathedral. You can't see the class struggle through the spectacles of capitalist law, written by capitalist representatives in the interest of the capitalist class. To understand the class struggle you must go into the factory and you must ride on top of the boxcars or underneath the boxcars. You must go into the mills. You must look through the dirty windows of the working shop. You must go with me down into the bowels of the earth 1,000, 2,000, 3,000, 5,000 feet: there by the uncertain flicker of a safety lamp, there by the rays of a tallow candle you will understand something about the class struggle.

You must know that there are two classes in society. There are no half-way measures. Just two classes. On the one side the capitalist class. On the other side the working class. On the one side those who produce all and have little or none. On the other side those who produce none and have all. (Applause.) This struggle is between capitalism and socialism. Socialists are not responsible for it. We say that it exists. We know the conditions that have brought it about and we know the only remedy for it. We say that it will continue just so long as a favored few are given the special privilege of exploiting the many. This class struggle will continue just so long as one man eats bread in the sweat of another man's face. . . .

So you understand that we know the class struggle in the west. And realizing, having contended with all the bitter things that we have been called upon to drink to the dregs, do you blame me when I say that I *despise the law* (tremendous applause and shouts of "No!") and I am not a law-abiding citizen. (Applause.) And more than that, no Socialist can be a law-abiding citizen. (Applause.)

When we come together and are of a common mind, and the purpose of our minds is to overthrow the capitalist system, we become conspirators then against the United States government. And certainly it is our purpose to abolish this government (applause) and establish in its place an industrial democracy. (Applause.) Now, we haven't any hesitation in saying that that is our aim and purpose. Am I correct? (Tremendous applause.) Am I absolutely correct when I state this as being the position of the Socialist party not only of New York, but of the United States and of every nation of the world? (Applause.)

Well, then, it isn't only the men of the west who understand the class struggle. You understand it here just as well as we do there. . . .

I know that the hour is getting late, and I don't want to leave you without the constructive policy of this meeting. There are many ways to describe how the Socialists will get control of the industries. There are those who say that we will confiscate them. "Confiscate!" That's good. I like that word. It suggests stripping the capitalist, taking something away from him. But there has got to be a good deal of force to this thing of taking. You might have a majority of voters, but some of them might be crippled; they wouldn't be fighters. Remember that the capitalists have standing tonight their whole well-disciplined army of capitalism—bayonets, Maxim guns, long Toms, the navy, the army, the militia, the secret service, the detectives, the police are all there to protect the property of capital. I have got a better way, so I am temporarily going to pass up that confiscation idea.

Another one will say, "Well, competition. We could accomplish these things by competition." They look at the shop, it isn't a very big shop and they know that it was built by workers. "Well, why can't we build another shop and go into competition; build another railroad?" All these things can be done. But you can't build another Niagara Falls, can you, where the power is generated to run the shops? You can't build another coal bed, can you, nor another forest, nor other wheat fields? So we will have to pass up the idea of competition.

But another Socialist comes along with the idea of compensation, and that is the worst of the three C's. Really, we have already purchased these things, and haven't they been compensated enough? They have been riding on our backs all these years. (Applause.)

They have enjoyed life and luxury. Compensation means, then, that we are to take control of the industries and relieve them of the responsibilities and pay them interest-bearing bonds, gold bonds, and that these capitalists, whom we have always regarded as exploiters, will have no harder work than to hire some one to clip coupons for them; that we will have a bond-holding aristocracy in this country that will ride us harder than the aristocracy of any country in the world. No, I say, pass up this compensation.

Well, there is another fellow, the Christian Socialist. (Laughter.) He has an idea of "Conversion." And I want to say to you that a Christian Socialist is one who is drunk on religious fanaticism and is trying to sober up on economic truth (laughter and applause), and when he gets about half-sober he thinks that he can convert the capitalist to Christianity and that the capitalist will be willing to turn over all these things to the brotherhood of man. He overlooks the fact that the capitalist is a child of the devil, and that's a poor place for a Christian Socialist to proselyte. We will pass up the Christian Socialist with the "conversion."

Here is another man—they all follow in the line of C's. I use the C's so that you can—I was speaking down in Missouri where I had to show them—Confiscation, Compensation, Competition, Conversion. Now, the trade unionist believes in Coercion. I like that. I believe in the strike. I believe in the boycott. I believe in coercion. But I believe that it ought to be by two million men instead of by a handful of men. If they are going to play a game of coercion, let that game be strong so that the capitalist class will know that the trade unionists will mean every word they say. But they don't. Never did. Because they no sooner have the capitalists in a position where they recognize that this coercion means something, than some of their representatives will step in with a Compromise —there is another C—and then tie them up with a contract, and that contract for an indefinite period, one, two, or three years. And let me say to you that the trade unionist who becomes a party to a contract takes his organization out of the columns of fighting organizations; he removes it from the class struggle and he binds it up and makes it absolutely useless. For instance, let me give you a humble illustration. A labor organization is a fighting machine of the working class, or ought to be. If it is not, it isn't fulfilling its mission. You will all recognize this! (holding up a clenched fist.) As a fighting weapon it is composed of many members of several organizations, and they can all fight independently, work independently. They don't bother each other when they are at work, but if called upon for defense they settle down in a common fighting machine. Now suppose that I were foolish enough to tie one of them up with an agreement, a contract, running for a period of six months, what would become of it? It would rot off, wouldn't it; die off, decay? Not only that, but it would be useless to itself and all the others. I might better cut it off altogether. And so you might better not be organized at all than to be organized as you are now. (Applause.)

And now we come to the constructive program, the program which every Industrialist understands. Remember that there isn't an Industrialist but what is a Socialist, and knows why. There are many Socialists who are trade unionists, but they couldn't tell you why in a hundred years. They couldn't justify it in a hundred years, except that they have to be to hold their jobs. Then we have the constructive program of Socialism, which means that the working class can be organized in a constructive and a defensive organization at the same time. Let me show you what I mean. Now, I want to present it to you so clearly that you will take it home with you. Suppose that the United Mine Workers of America, organized as they are industrially—but let me say they are hampered with all the tools of trade unionism—suppose that they would join hands with the Western Federation of Miners and we would cut loose entirely from the capitalist class, recognizing them on the economic as well as the political field as our enemies, having absolutely nothing to do with them. We would start a program then of organization, having for its purpose the taking in of every man employed in the mining industry throughout the United States. This work having been accomplished, or nearly perfected, is there a man or woman in this hall who believes that with such an organization we could not protect our lives? Don't you believe that if we had a class-conscious organization of the miners we could compel the mine owners to properly ventilate the mine, to remove the coal dust, to equip them with safety appliances for the protection of life and limb and to furnish a sufficient amount of timber to work them?

Can we do this? You know that we could if we had this power behind us; this organization. We then could protect our lives. We would have the mines in better shape. We could produce more coal. But first having protected our lives we would think about our families and we would improve their conditions around the mines. We would see that there were better company houses for our families to live in; that the young men had first-class up-to-date apartment houses to dwell in; that the schools were first-class. Any reason why we couldn't? Not at all.

Having preserved our lives, improved the conditions of our homes, we would become better men physically and mentally. We can produce more coal. But—you garment workers have got all the power you need; don't need any more coal. We wouldn't produce coal just for fun, nor would we let each other ever deprive us of the luxuries and necessities of life. Not at all. How then could we reduce the output of coal? We would reduce the hours of labor. If we can produce enough coal in eight hours or six or four, you wouldn't want us to work any longer, would you?

Having preserved our lives, improved our home conditions, reduced our hours of labor, what does that suggest? Well, we would look around and see that the rest of the working class had kept pace with us, every one marching in rhythm, and we would say to you, "We will cut out the capitalist class now. We will lock them out. Every man that quits his job now is a scab. We want every man to work and we in turn will contribute for your labor everything that you need." This is the understanding that we would have. There would be no capitalist class in this game. There would be nothing but the working class. And this being an accomplished fact, we would say then that the Socialists despise covering up their aims and purposes. We would say that it is our purpose to overthrow the capitalist system by forcible means if necessary.

And I urge you workers tonight: determine upon this program. Workers of the world, unite! You have nothing to lose but your chains. You have a world to gain. (Tremendous applause and cheers.)

CHAPTER IX

WAR AND REVOLUTION

I am a Socialist, a labor unionist and a believer in
the Prince of Peace first, and an American second.

KATE O'HARE,
"*My Country*," April 1917

Better a hundred times to have two numerically small
Socialist organizations, each homogeneous and harmonious within itself, then to have one big party torn
by dissensions and squabbles, an impotent colossus on
feet of clay. The time for action is near. Let us clear
the decks.

MORRIS HILLQUIT,
"*Socialist Task and Outlook*," May 21, 1919

I did not leave a party of crooks to join a party of
lunatics.

LOUIS B. BOUDIN,
Communist Labor Party convention, September,
1919

The membership of the Communist Party as well as
the UCP [United Communist Party] is overwhelmingly
composed of foreign comrades who do not speak or
understand English.

The Communist, August 1, 1920

Now we can see and feel that we are not so near the
goal of the conquest of power, of the world revolution.
We formerly believed, in 1919, that it was only a
question of months, and now we say that it is perhaps
a question of years.

LEON TROTSKY,
Protocol of the Third International Congress, 1921

American socialists were staggered by the news that war had broken out in Europe. What they had feared most, what they had considered only a distant and terrifying possibility, now had come to pass. The shock and the grief was all the more profound because recent events had seemed to justify their optimism to an extravagant degree. The socialist parties of Western and Central Europe (not to mention their own) had been scoring rapid gains, and a number of them had even looked forward to taking power in the near future. Socialists in general had therefore assumed that the prevailing system of military alliances—the result of capitalist competition and mindless chauvinism—would be replaced by a socialist world order, a true universalism, arising from the solidarity of the working classes. But the socialist parties, it turned out, not only had failed to prevent the war from coming; they had warmly supported it when it came. Only a handful of important socialists, notably Karl Liebnecht and Rosa Luxemburg in Germany, Jean Jaurès in France, and Tom Mann in England (Lenin was then hardly known outside Russia and besides was in exile) had unequivocally opposed their governments and their parties. The fact was that patriotism had proved to be the triumphant ideology of the masses. Socialism had been the war's first casualty.

There was nothing the American Socialist Party could do but announce its strict neutrality toward the belligerents and pray that the war would draw to a speedy close. "We do not presume to pass judgment upon the conduct of our brother parties in Europe," the National Executive Committee stated shortly after hostilities began. "We realize that they are victims of the present vicious industrial, political and military system, and that they did the best they could do under the circumstances." A few Socialist Party members did declare their sympathy for the Allies and condemned Germany as the scourge of civilization. The war, said A. M. Simons, a prominent Socialist writer, was nothing less than "a conflict between progress and reaction." But, as usual, it was left to Hillquit to define the Party's position. "American Socialists," he wrote, "should not take sides with the Allies or against the Germans. The assertion that the forces of the allied armies are waging a war of democracy against militarism is a hollow catch-phrase devoid of true sense and substance. . . . From the true Socialist viewpoint the most satisfactory solution of the great sanguinary conflict of the nations lies in a draw, a cessation of hostilities from exhaustion, without determining anything."

American socialists had more than enough to worry about in their own back yard. In the spring of 1915 the Wilson administration began its campaign to persuade the American people to support the "preparedness" program then pending before Congress. Wilson launched the campaign (he himself went on a long speaking tour in its behalf) because he knew how much hostility there was in the country to creating a large army and navy. The socialists for their part overwhelmingly opposed preparedness. The depth of their feelings about it was reflected in the wording of an amendment to the Party constitution that was passed (by a vote of 11,000 to 780) in 1915. "Any member of the Socialist Party, elected to an office, who shall in any way vote to appropriate moneys for military or naval purposes, or war, shall be expelled from the Party." But unlike their European brethren American socialists were in no position to affect the course of events, and they watched helplessly as the country drew closer and closer to the vortex of the conflict. By February 1917 the last hope of avoiding it had gone, for Germany had resumed unrestricted submarine warfare.

Early in the year the Party called an emergency convention to take up the war question; it was to be held in St. Louis on April 8th. The men who chose that date proved clairvoyant: Congress declared war on April 7th. Realizing the gravity of the decision it would have to make, the convention as soon as it met formed a special committee to draft a report. It assigned fifteen of the Party's leading members to the committee, including Hillquit, Berger, Kate O'Hare, C. E. Ruthenberg (head of the Ohio branch), Louis B. Boudin, and John Spargo, thus assuring that all sections and ideological tendencies were represented. After several days of contentious deliberation the committee brought out one majority and two minority reports. They are worth examining at some length.

The majority report, delivered to the convention by Hillquit, recommended all-out opposition by the Party to the war. It was an indignant, sharply worded, and quite radical attack on the government, indicating how far left the Party hierarchy had shifted in recent months. Modern war, the majority report asserted, was intolerable, first of all, because it brought "wealth and power to the ruling classes, and suffering, death, and demoralization to the workers," and, second, because it produced a "sinister spirit of passion, unreason, race hatred, and false patriotism." The only legitimate conflict was class conflict. The report advised workers everywhere to resist their governments by any form of "mass action" (a phrase that was to haunt the Party) available to them.

The majority on the committee, in other words, rejected Wilson's definition of the war (now that the United States was in it) as a titanic struggle between two sovereign principles: liberal democracy and military despotism. In the words of the report: "It is cant and hypocrisy to say that the war is not directed against the German people, but against the Imperial Government of Germany. If we send an armed force to the battlefields of Europe, its cannon will mow down the masses of the German people and not the Imperial German Government." The report went on to accuse the "ruling class" and its servitors—the administration, Congress, the press—of using "trickery and treachery" to plunge the nation into a holocaust. "We brand the declaration of war by our government as a crime against the people of the United States and against the nations of the world."

Properly speaking, there was only one minority report; only one, that is, that urged socialists to support the war. The other (written by Boudin) agreed with the majority in all essentials and was for the most part written in the same language. *The* minority report bore only one signature—that of John Spargo. Over the years Spargo had been one of the superior writers on American socialism. In numerous books and essays he had lucidly explained how Marxism could be adapted to American conditions. Of late, however, he had been moving farther and farther to the right, toward Wilsonian progressivism. In his report he advised socialists to recognize the war as a *fait accompli* which they might turn to their advantage. Specifically, he urged them to work for a "program of democratic collectivism." Spargo set forth a new Socialist theory when he predicted the imminent collapse of capitalism because of its inability to meet military requirements. "The warring nations have had to give up the organization and operation of industry and primary economic functions for profit, and to adopt the socialist principle of production for use." No matter that the use in this case was destructive. For Spargo the important consideration was that the government, with Socialist support, might nationalize the means of production and distribution.

The vote of the convention floor corresponded to the vote within the committee. Only five delegates supported the Spargo report. A total of 171 backed the reports presented by Hillquit and Boudin. Later the Party membership as a whole ratified the "St. Louis Proclamation," as the majority report was called, by a vote of seven to one (approximately 21,000 to 3000). And so the Socialist Party of America became the third socialist party among the belligerent powers—the Italian and Bolshevik being the others —to defy the war policy of its government. Yet, however one might honor the courage of American socialists, the fact remained that they enjoyed a luxury not vouchsafed to European socialists. Lacking a mass constituency, and being by and large personally independent of politics, they could vote according to their consciences without fear of reprisal. There was no huge party apparatus at stake for which they had to assume responsibility. The conspicuous exceptions were men like Victor Berger, who headed a substantial movement in Milwaukee (largely a German one, to be sure), and James Maurer, leader of the Pennsylvania AFL—men whom their enemies on the left had always regarded as "opportunists" *par excellence*. The war issue threw the ideological spectrum into disarray. Traditional conservatives now found themselves in the Left Wing camp, in the company of Syndicalists and other revolutionaries.

The Party paid a heavy price for its decision. Its best known writers—Spargo, A. M. Simons, W. J. Ghent, William English Walling, Upton Sinclair, Gustavus Myers, Charles E. Russell, Robert Hunter—almost all of them, be it noted, native Americans—deserted it *en masse*. With one clean blow the war issue decapitated the Party, severing it of its most talented journalists. These apostates, moreover, tended to be ferociously vindictive toward their ex-comrades. Spargo, for example, publicly accused Hillquit—with whom he had once been very close—of "upholding the impudent claims of the guilty Hohenzollern dynasty." Myers (famous as the author of the *Hostory of Great American Fortunes*) asked Wilson to investigate subversive (meaning anti-war) Socialist literature. The government promptly hired Myers to do the investigating himself. Russell, who had recently run a valiant campaign as Socialist Party candidate for mayor of New York, thought his former friends "should be driven out of the country." J. G. Phelps Stokes, one of the millionaire socialists and husband of Rose Pastor, went farther: he recommended that they be "shot at once without an hour's delay."

Organized labor, too, defected from the Party. The AFL rank and file joined Gompers and the other leaders in championing the war. Like the middle class they were swept away by the rhetoric of patriotism. And President Wilson went out of his way to give unions a place in government-run agencies, thereby cementing the alliance between the administration and the AFL. Gompers, of course, seized on the opportunity to discredit the socialists. Hoping to root them out of his union once and for all, he helped establish, with government funds, an anti-socialist propaganda unit: the American Alliance for Labor and Democracy. No international union opposed the war. And by the time armistice was declared the socialists had been practically eliminated from the AFL. Certainly they were no longer a threat to the leadership.

The heaviest price was exacted by the government and the public at large. The country was enveloped in a deep psychosis of hatred and fear. Patriotic mobs employed "mass action" of their own, breaking up socialist meetings, hectoring and humiliating every socialist they could lay their hands on. To drive socialists from public life was the deliberate aim of the wartime state conspiracy laws, especially of the federal Espionage Act of 1917 (supplemented a year later), which gave government officials enormous powers to punish—with the help of jail sentences up to twenty years—anyone who dared criticize the war; it also gave them the absolute right to close the mails to anyone they deemed seditious.

The effect on the Party was catastrophic. Nearly every one of its newspapers and magazines was held up in the mails for longer or shorter periods, depending on the arbitrary (and usually ignorant) judgment of the Postmaster General. A number ceased publication as a direct consequence. Most of the Party leaders, from the highest echelons to the lowest, were indicted under the Espionage Act. Nearly all of them went to jail; when they did not it was because a superior court had thrown out the conviction on procedural grounds. The most famous case, of course, was Eugene Debs's. He received ten years for allegedly using "profane, scandalous and abusive language" in a speech at Canton, Ohio. He went to prison five months after the war had ended. And he stayed in prison until President Warren Harding, who held no grudges, pardoned him on Christmas day of 1921.

Socialists, it goes without saying, were not the only victims of the Espionage Act. Its wide maw swallowed up every species of dissenter. The Industrial Workers of the World were virtually annihilated. Its members, given no chance whatever, were convicted in a series of sensational mass trials. Big Bill Haywood, however, jumped bail and fled to Soviet Russia, where he spent the last ten years of his life. Countless pacifists also landed in federal penitentiaries. All told, some two thousand persons were tried and found guilty under the provisions of the Espionage Act.

Yet the news during the war years was not all bad for the socialists. They took heart from the results of the 1917 local elections. Large numbers of voters flocked behind the standard of the anti-war party (though its drum-beat was muffled) and elected, or came near to electing, hundreds of mayors, aldermen, councillors, and state legislators. It seemed like the salad days of 1911–12 all over again. And even where the Party had not done so well in the past—in the cities of the Northeast, for example—it did quite well now. Morris Hillquit ran for mayor of New York and threw a tremendous scare into the other parties, forcing them to set aside their partisan differences in order to defeat him. As it was, Hillquit drew 145,000 votes—three times the total for the Republican candidate. Meanwhile, ten socialists were elected to the New York Assembly and seven to the city's Board of Aldermen (the present-day City Council). These gains, repeated elsewhere in the country, were achieved in the teeth of continuous harassments and legal battles.

But the polls proved deceptive. The encouraging vote hardly compensated for the Party's monumental losses: the departure of so many of it intellectuals, and the alienation of most of its trade-union following. And even the vote gave an illusory index of its popularity. For what was at issue in the 1917 election was not socialist ideology but the socialist opposition to the war. Groups of people who were indifferent or unsympathetic to socialism (mainly Irishmen, Germans, and Scandinavians) voted for socialist candidates as a protest and would cease voting socialist the moment the war issue ceased to provoke them. True, the Party claimed that its membership rolls had been growing at an accelerating rate. But the membership statistics revealed that an alarming shift in the Party's center of gravity was taking place from the native born to the foreign born. In 1912, when its membership was 118,000 only 16,000—about 14 percent—had consisted of foreign-language affiliates. By 1917 these affiliates accounted for a third of the Party's 80,000 members. By 1919 they would account for more than half.

There were several reasons, apart from the war, why native Americans left the Party. In the first place, Wilsonian democracy appealed most to Western agrarian interests (they re-elected him in 1916), and a good many ex-Populists went over to the administration side. Secondly, socialism suffered whenever a grass roots reform movement arose in the West. The most successful of these movements was the Non-Partisan League, which had been founded (by socialists) in 1916. Its aim was to free the northern wheat farmers from the predatory middlemen (land speculators, bankers, terminal elevator owners) who controlled the state capitols. By 1918 the League had taken over North Dakota and made striking advances in South Dakota, Minnesota, Montana, and Idaho. In each of these states socialism fell by the wayside. Then there was the special case of Oklahoma, where socialism had always done best, where it seemed to have struck permanent roots. But in 1917, shortly after the United States entered the war, the Oklahoma Socialist Party led an abortive uprising, the Green Corn Rebellion, against the federal government, and was wiped out. It was as though it had never existed. And so, in every important respect, ethnically, geographically, occupationally, the Party was rapidly contracting. It was losing its amplitude and heterogeneity and becoming sectarian in composition and outlook, taking on the characteristics imputed to it by its enemies.

Nevertheless, the Socialist Party might have come back after the war. Nineteen-nineteen to 1921 were years of violent and protracted industrial conflicts involving millions of workers. Farmers were worse off than at any time since the great depression twenty-five years before. And the general disillusionment with the war and the administration, especially among youth, was profound. But American socialists poignantly learned that what history offers with one hand it may withdraw with the other. Their new opportunities in the immediate postwar years were more than offset by the effects of the Bolshevik Revolution. This mighty event, instead of heralding the advent of a new day for American socialism, sounded its knell.

The November 1917 uprising in Russia caught the American Socialist Party, as it caught the rest of the world (and the Russians as well), completely by surprise. Even more surprising was the ability of the new regime to survive one shattering vicissitude after another: the humiliating peace, foreign intervention, mass starvation, the onset of civil war. By the end of 1918 the Socialist Party was unstinting in its praise of the Bolshevik accomplishments. "Since the French Revolution established a new high mark of political liberty in the world," as one group of Party officials put it, "there has been no other advance in democratic progress and social justice comparable to the Russian Revolution." Hillquit remarked that Russia, once the "strongest resort of the darkest reaction, is today the vanguard of democracy and social progress. It is from top to bottom in the hands of the people, the working class, the peasants." Even Victor Berger, the extreme apostle of conservatism, offered the Bolsheviks his seal of approval. "All Socialists," he said, "are pro-Bolshevik today."

But American socialists were well-schooled in Marxism, and they regarded the Soviet regime as highly anomalous. Here was a self-styled proletariat government, rigorously Marxist in its principles, ruling over a country that was sunk in a pre-capitalist stage of development. Lenin and Trotsky, the two main architects of the Revolution sought to reconcile this stubborn fact with Marxist theory by maintaining that the Revolution was not meant to be self-sufficient, that least of all was it meant to be an end in itself. Its historic assignment was to inspire the working classes of the West to rise up in their turn and to bring about the *true* (i.e., post-capitalist) reign of socialism. Whatever socialists in the other Western countries thought of this logic, the leaders of American socialism at least were convinced that the working class in their own country was not about to revolt, the government was not about to disintegrate, and the contradictions in capitalism were not about to reveal themselves. They rejected the Bolshevik example as inapplicable to the American experience. While the party hierarchs expressed support for the regime, they saw no reason to acknowledge its authority. They had nothing to learn from it.

But the men who spoke for the Socialist Party of America did not necessarily speak for the rank and file. A growing proportion of Party members, in fact, belonged to the Left Wing faction. They believed that American socialism had everything to learn from the Bolsheviks. Once a small and submerged minority, they suddenly burgeoned into a force to be reckoned with, thanks to the prodigious rise of the foreign-language associations. In the year and a half following the Bolshevik Revolution, when Party membership increased from 80,000 to 105,000 (the second highest total in its history), their ratio increased from 35 percent to 53 percent. More ominous yet, the largest of these groups were Eastern Europeans (Russians, Ukrainians, Letts [Latvians], Lithuanians, Hungarians, Poles, and South Slavs), who backed the Bolsheviks as much for ethnic reasons—the Bolsheviks having promised independence to the various nationalities of the Czarist empire—as for ideological. They determined to re-shape America in the Soviet mold, and they joined the Socialist Party by the thousands in the hope of making it into a replica of Lenin's revolutionary vanguard party.

Other groups joined the Left Wing for reasons of their own. There were the young people, who contrasted the élan, heroism and confidence of the Bolsheviks with the ponderously didactic, legalistic character of the American Socialist Party. These newcomers to socialism, usually the children of recent immigrants (many of them Eastern European Jews), took the business of revolutionary politics very seriously; they brooked little levity and no compromise. Then there were the intellectuals, themselves quite young, notably John Reed, Max Eastman, Floyd Dell, Robert Minor, and others associated with *The Masses* or *Liberator*, who hailed the Revolution as the beginning of the epoch of total freedom in art, morals, and work. Finally, there were the Syndicalists, who found in the Soviets the fulfillment of their dream of autonomous industrial departments to be run by the workers themselves. It was as though the Russian Communists were following the formula laid down in the constitution of the Industrial Workers of the World.

These Left Wing groups, acting in concert, used the Russian Revolution as a springboard from which to mount their assault on the Socialist Party leadership. They accused Hillquit, Berger, and the other ancient argonauts of the Party of having deliberately misled the working class for decades into assuming that revolution was unnecessary, that the conservative unions would inevitably fall to socialism, that socialism would win an electoral majority, and that, in the meantime, bourgeois laws and proprieties must be obeyed. The Bolsheviks had pointed up the falsity of this strategy. They had demonstrated how a disciplined revolutionary cadre of several thousand at the most could seize the apocalyptic moment, wrest power from the capitalists and imperialists and reformers, and install a dictatorship of the proletariat. It was the masses who gave the Bolsheviks their constituency and who provided the source of their legitimate authority. The dictatorship of the proletariat was the product of "mass action" under the infallible guidance of the vanguard party. And the party was infallible because it embodied the whole of human history.

To emulate the Bolsheviks it was necessary for the Left Wing of the American Socialist Party to do two things: promote mass action and split with the moderates. One of the difficulties was defining the term mass action with any precision. Its most eloquent and persistent advocate was unquestionably Louis Fraina. Fraina, who had come to America from Italy as a child, was only twenty-three when the Bolsheviks took power, but he had already established his name as a revolutionist by his many articles and the Left Wing magazines he edited. More than any single person he was responsible for publicizing the writings of hitherto obscure revolutionists, chief among them Lenin and Trotsky. Like the rest of the Left Wing, Fraina looked to Central and Eastern Europe for justification and direction. "Mass action," he wrote in his book on the subject, which was published within a year of the Revolution, "is not a *form* of action as much as it is a *process* and *synthesis* of action. It is the unity of all forms of proletarian action, a means of throwing the proletariat, organized and unorganized, in a general struggle against Capitalism and the capitalist state. . . . Mass action is the instinctive action of the proletariat, gradually developing more conscious and organized forms and definite purposes. It is extra-parliamentary in method, and political in purpose and result. . . ."

But mass action by the American proletariat did not take place. While workers struck, often violently, immediately after the war, they did not do so for political reasons. There was nothing like "a general struggle against Capitalism and the capitalist state." Meanwhile, the Left Wingers would prepare themselves for the time when the proletariat would rise up. They would, that is, create a revolutionary cadre of their own, either by forming a separate Communist party or by driving the Old Guard from the Socialist Party. Both the Right and Left wings knew that the split was coming. If any doubts remained they were dispelled in January 1919, when Moscow sent out word that a meeting of the Third International would presently be convened. So far as the rival factions in the

Socialist Party were concerned, the only question left to be decided was how the break would come about and what form it would take.

The conflict over the body and soul of American socialism was acted out—the conclusion was foregone—between February and September 1919. Here we need present only the briefest summary of events. Early in February the New York section of the Left Wing issued a "Manifesto and Program" indicting the leaders of the Socialist Party for what was, in effect, treason to the working class and to history. After accusing them of being "social patriots" (supporters of the war) who had refused to unleash a "proletarian revolution," the Manifesto went on to demand Party approval of mass action, of attempts to overthrow the capitalist government, and of a system of Soviets under proletarian dictatorship. The Manifesto was a call to arms. The first objective was the Party. Then would come the state.

The election of the Party's fifteen-man National Executive Committee in the spring precipitated the break. That the Left Wing would carry the election was apparent, since the foreign-language associations held a majority of the votes. The Left Wing gave a hint of its power when it effortlessly captured some of the largest locals in the country. But this much was certain: the Old Guard was not going to yield control of the Party apparatus merely because an army of aliens had recently become members. "Veterans and pioneers of the movement," the National Executive Committee later said in self-exculpation, "who had served the Party in many ways for ten, twenty and thirty years suddenly found they had no rights within the party but to pay dues." The Old Guard thus "declared preventive war," as Theodore Draper has put it. Without concern for the niceties of due process, it simply excised the Left Wing from the Party: it suspended (which is to say, expelled) the seven offending foreign-language associations, deposed three state organizations, and cast out each of the Left Wing locals. Altogether some 35,000 members were lopped off the Party rolls.

The Left Wing was divided in its response. The larger group, consisting mainly of foreign-language associations, split off and established the Communist Party. The second group, made up of native-born radicals (John Reed, et al.) created their own Bolshevik-style party—the Communist Labor Party—which differed only slightly from the first. The difference turned essentially on how purely Marxist-Leninist the party should be. The Communist

Party held that it should be absolutely pure. It should therefore be as small and disciplined as possible, purged of opportunists and compromisers and dedicated to direct action on all fronts. The Communist Labor Party, though no less revolutionary in spirit and purpose, wanted to build a mass political base. Toward that ultimate end it was content to announce "only one demand: the establishment of the dictatorship of the proletariat." Each of the Communist parties denounced the other for being untrue to Marxism-Leninism; each claimed the privilege of representing the Third International in America.

The sundering of the socialist movement left a succession of humiliations, ironies, and minor tragedies in its wake. Instead of gravitating to the right after the departure of the Left Wing, the Socialist Party tried to steal some of the Communist thunder. In its 1919 convention, the Party came out for "constant, clear-cut and aggressive opposition to all parties of the possessing class," and for industrial unionism. The convention also voted to ask the Russian regime to admit the Socialist Party into the Third International. Moscow's answer, presented at the July 1920 congress of the Third International, was devastating. In its famous Twenty-One Points the congress declared that any group wishing to enter the Third International must submit to Communist Party rule and must repudiate such "notorious opportunists" as Hillquit, who was actually mentioned by name. The Twenty-One Points further stated that the only kind of party acceptable to the Third International was one built on solid Leninist foundations: "the communist party will only be in a position to do its duty if it is organized along extremely centralized lines, if it is controlled by iron discipline, and . . . is fully equipped with power, authority, and the most far-reaching faculties." The Third International flung down its gauntlet. It would wage mortal combat on the "Yellow" Second International, on all moderate and revisionist socialists, on any tendency to come to terms with Western liberal democracy.

The two Communist parties meanwhile had their wish: they went underground. For a little more than a year, between late 1919 and early 1921, federal and state agents, acting under the infinitely broad provisions of their respective sedition laws, terrorized American radicals. Some 10,000 of them were rounded up in their offices and homes at all hours of the night and kept incommunicado for long periods of time. Without a semblance of due process hundreds of them were deported. But the repression produced no revolutionary cadre. If anything it fragmented the Communist parties and rendered them impotent. Leaders were jailed or were involved in endless litigations; the most routine activities were conducted with laborious difficulty; membership dropped vertiginously. Without a sympathetic public, underground movements stand no chance. And the American public was, to say the least, unsympathetic to the Communist cause.

The Communist parties did surface again in 1921, but not before they fell victim to a profound irony. The persistent division within the ranks of the American left exasperated the directors of the Third International in Moscow, and they ordered the two feuding parties—Communist and Communist Labor—to unite at once. The International arrogated to itself the power to issue such an order. One of the Twenty-One Points specified that "All decisions of the Congresses of the Communist International, as well as the decisions of its executive committee, are binding upon all the parties belonging to the Communist International." Under Moscow's relentless prodding, the two American Communist parties did finally unite in May 1921, emerging later in the year as the Workers Party of America. But the Workers Party received one more order from Moscow. It was told that it must seek office like any other legitimate political party, and that it must work within, not against, the American Federation of Labor. The International insisted on this course because Lenin had come to realize that the working class in the West would not or could not, revolt, that the capitalists and the Social Democrats had effectively recovered their power. The proper strategy for Communists, he concluded, was to permeate the existing trade unions and seek political office by legal means. The era of conspiracy was over.

In other words, Lenin was instructing his revolutionary followers in America to pursue the same policy that the Socialist Party had been pursuing since its inception in 1901 and that the Left Wing had all along denounced as traitorous. He was telling the Communists that they must forswear (as a temporary tactic to be sure) the animosities of the past; they must speak softly on craft unionism and play the game of politics in the conventional manner. Some radicals found the change too cynical and self-serving. John Reed broke with the leaders of the Third International on the issue before his death in Russia in October 1920. Especially pathetic were the last years of Big Bill Haywood's life. As a political expatriate in Moscow he witnessed at first hand the betrayal, by the party of the revolutionary left, of all that he had fought for. The order to join the AFL was a repudiation of the IWW. When Haywood died in Moscow in 1928, he was a sick, lonely, and defeated man.

By 1922 the socialist movement in America had undergone an irreparable decline. The Socialist Party was only a shadow of its former self. Its membership, which had hovered around the 80,000 to 100,000 mark since 1910, was now down to a mere 13,000. Above all its prospects were gloomy. Its appeal historically had been to the non-revolutionary left, but this appeal was being pre-empted by the liberal left. Shortly after the break with the Communists, the Socialist Party did attempt to make common cause with liberal and labor groups, including the AFL. From this coalition sprang the Progressive Party of 1924, which ran Robert La-Follette as its Presidential candidate. But the coalition disintegrated even before the election took place. In the years that followed, the Party, now led by Norman Thomas, never attained the strength, prestige, or self-confidence it had had before World War I. Thomas, who ran for President six times, only once approached Debs's vote: in 1932, when he received nearly 900,000 votes. That number, however, was only two percent of the total, as against Debs's six percent in 1912. Thomas, moreover, received it in the most critical moment of the Great Depression, when the economy was paralyzed and it seemed that nothing short of revolution could get it moving. Never again would the opportunity for democratic socialism be so propitious. The Socialist Party steadily dwindled after that, and, by the end of World War II, had practically disappeared as a political entity.

The Communist (or, until 1928, the Workers') Party fared no better in the long run. From the time of its creation it suffered from three fatal disabilities: it favored revolution, it was subservient to the interests of the Soviet Union, and its strength rested primarily on immigrant groups. Americans regarded it as a foreign party—foreign in composition, ideology, and loyalty. So great were these disabilities that when the economy did collapse in 1919 the American Communists were no more able to gather up the pieces than the socialists. In the 1930s they managed to win over a number of intellectuals, and they were also instrumental in organizing some of the larger industrial unions (automobile, mining, steel, electric, etc.). During World War II the Communist Party acquired a measure of support precisely because of its identity with the Soviet Union. But the Party's influence was tenuous and superficial. The intellectuals abandoned the cause even before the war, and the unions ruthlessly eliminated whatever Communist officials had remained from the 1930s. The Communist Party suffered a succession of hard blows in the 1950s. First came the spy trials, the charges of subversion, the persecutions (reminiscent of World War I) by an inflamed public. Then came the Soviet admission that Stalin—the cynosure of world communism for 30 years—had been a tyrant all along. Finally came the Soviet suppression of the Hungarian uprising. Since the 1950s the Party has been a corporal's guard of aged, dull, and intimidated men.

We should add that the Communist movement in America was not exhausted in the Communist Party. In the late 1920s the Party split over the Trotskyite heresy. In successive steps since 1924 Trotsky had been anathematized by Stalin, purged of his power, and finally exiled from Russia because he continued to press for world revolution. In doing so he had opposed Stalin's doctrine of "socialism in one country." In practical terms, socialism in one country meant that the Third International, and therefore every Communist Party in the world, must devote itself to the preservation of the Russian regime and must, accordingly, obey Stalin implicitly in all matters of policy and dogma. The Trotskyites represented themselves as the true heirs of Marx and Lenin, the purifiers of the Bolshevik creed. But Trotskyism was an unstable, radically anti-nomian faith, and it broke into many pieces, each quite small, each concerned to develop its own theoretical structure. All Trotskyites, however, shared the same aversion to Stalin, who had turned the Revolution into an enormous bureaucratic despotism and a vehicle for his maniacal will to power. After World War II the great issues raised by the Bolshevik Revolution and the nature of the Soviet regime receded from view in the United States, as did most of the Trotskyites.

In the early part of the century socialism seemed on the way to becoming an important force in American life, and its leaders looked forward to its triumph in their lifetime. But the fall of socialism was precipitous. The break-up of the Socialist Party signalled the destruction of the Socialist movement as such. One cannot speak of a socialist movement at all today. There are, rather, a congeries of sects calling themselves socialist. There are old Trot-skyites, old pro-Russian Communists, old Social Democrats, and old Socialist Laborites who had been unswervingly faithful to the letter of Daniel DeLeon's teachings. There is also the New Left, which, as one writer recently observed, remains more a mood than a move-ment. It reflects the discontent with America felt by a growing host of middle class, college educated youth. But that discontent has not crystallized into an ideology or a coherent program. The openness and diffusion of the New Left, its refusal to be drawn into the problems that have traditionally concerned American radicals, is both its charm and its fatal limitation. Having denied the past it denies itself the future. Toward the New Left and toward all the existing Socialist sects the attitude of the American people remains what it has been since 1919: hostility tempered by ignorance and indifference.

St. Louis Manifesto
of the Socialist Party*
1917

Following is the majority report, advocating opposition to the war, adopted by the Party at its April 1917 convention.

The Socialist Party of the United States in the present grave crisis, solemnly reaffirm its allegiance to the principle of internationalism and working-class solidarity the world over, and proclaims its unalterable opposition to the war just declared by the Government of the United States.

Modern wars as a rule had been caused by the commercial and financial rivalry and intrigues of the capitalist interests in the different countries. Whether they have been frankly waged as wars of aggression or have been hypocritically represented as wars of "defense," they have always been made by the classes and fought by the masses. Wars bring wealth and power to the ruling classes, and suffering, death and demoralization to the workers.

They breed a sinister spirit of passion, unreason, race hatred and false patriotism. They obscure the struggles of the workers for life, liberty and social justice. They tend to sever the vital bonds of solidarity between them and their brothers in other countries, to destroy their organizations and to curtail their civic and political rights and liberties.

The Socialist Party of the United States is unalterably opposed to the system of exploitation and class rule which is upheld and strengthened by military power and sham national patriotism. We, therefore, call upon the workers of all countries to refuse support to their governments in their wars. The wars of the contending national groups of capitalists are not the concern of the workers. The only struggle which would justify the workers in taking up arms is the great struggle of the working class of the world to free itself from economic exploitation and political oppression, and we

* Report of the New York State Joint Legislative Committee Investigating Sedition (Lusk Committee), Vol. I, pp. 613–618.

particularly warn the workers against the snare and delusion of so-called defensive warfare. As against the false doctrine of national patriotism we uphold the ideal of international working-class solidarity. In support of capitalism, we will not willingly give a single life or a single dollar; in support of the struggle of the workers for freedom we pledge our all.

The mad orgy of death and destruction which is now convulsing unfortunate Europe was caused by the conflict of capitalist interests in the European countries.

In each of these countries, the workers were oppressed and exploited. They produced enormous wealth but the bulk of it was withheld from them by the owners of the industries. The workers were thus deprived of the means to repurchase the wealth which they themselves had created.

The capitalist class of each country was forced to look for foreign markets to dispose of the accumulated "surplus" wealth. The huge profits made by the capitalists could no longer be profitably reinvested in their own countries, hence, they were driven to look for foreign fields of investment. The geographical boundaries of each modern capitalist country thus became too narrow for the industrial and commercial operations of its capitalist class.

The efforts of the capitalists of all leading nations were, therefore, centered upon the domination of the world markets. Imperialism became the dominant note in the politics of Europe. The acquisition of colonial possessions and the extension of spheres of commercial and political influence became the object of diplomatic intrigues and the cause of constant clashes between nations.

The acute competition between the capitalist powers of the earth, their jealousies and distrusts of one another and the fear of the rising power of the working class forced each of them to arm to the teeth. This led to the mad rivalry of armament, which, years before the outbreak of the present war, had turned the leading countries of Europe into armed camps with standing armies of many millions, drilled and equipped for war in times of "peace."

Capitalism, imperialism and militarism had thus laid the foundation of an inevitable general conflict in Europe. The ghastly war in Europe was not caused by an accidental event, nor by the policy or institutions of any single nation. It was the logical outcome of the competitive capitalist system.

The 6,000,000 men of all countries and races who have been ruthlessly slain in the first thirty months of this war, the millions of others who have been crippled and maimed, the vast treasures of wealth that have been destroyed, the untold misery and sufferings of Europe, have not been sacrifices exacted in a struggle for principles or ideals, but wanton offerings upon the altar of private profit.

The forces of capitalism which have led to the war in Europe are even more hideously transparent in the war recently provoked by the ruling class of this country.

When Belgium was invaded, the government enjoined upon the people of this country the duty of remaining neutral, thus clearly demonstrating that the "dictates of humanity," and the fate of small nations and of democratic institutions were matters that did not concern it. But when our enormous war traffic was seriously threatened, our government calls upon us to rally to the "defense of democracy and civilization."

Our entrance into the European War was instigated by the predatory capitalists in the United States who boast of the enormous profit of $7,000,000,000 from the manufacture and sale of munitions and war supplies and from the exportation of American food stuffs and other necessaries. They are also deeply interested in the continuance of war and the success of the Allied arms through their huge loans to the governments of the Allied powers and through other commercial ties. It is the same interests which strive for imperialistic domination of the Western Hemisphere.

The war of the United States against Germany cannot be justified even on the plea that it is a war in defense of American rights or American "honor." Ruthless as the unrestricted submarine war policy of the German government was and is, it is not an invasion of the rights of the American people, as such, but only an interference with the opportunity of certain groups of American capitalists to coin cold profits out of the blood and sufferings of our fellow men in the warring countries of Europe.

It is not a war against the militarist regime of the Central Powers. Militarism can never be abolished by militarism.

It is not a war to advance the cause of democracy in Europe. Democracy can never be imposed upon any country by a foreign power by force of arms.

It is cant and hypocrisy to say that the war is not directed against the German people, but against the Imperial Government of Germany. If we send an armed force to the battlefields of Europe, its cannon will mow down the masses of the German people and not the Imperial German Government.

Our entrance into the European conflict at this time will serve only to multiply the horrors of the war, to increase the toll of death and destruction and to prolong the fiendish slaughter. It will bring death, suffering and destitution to the people of the United States and particularly to the working class. It will give the powers of reaction in this country the pretext for an attempt to throttle our rights and to crush our democratic institutions, and to fasten upon this country a permanent militarism.

The working class of the United States has no quarrel with the working class of Germany or of any other country. The people of the United States have no quarrel with the people of Germany or any other country. The American people did not want and do not want this war. They have not been consulted about the war and have had no part in declaring war. They have been plunged into this war by the trickery and treachery of the ruling class of the country through its representatives in the National Administration and National Congress, its demagogic agitators, its subsidized press, and other servile instruments of public expression.

We brand the declaration of war by our government as a crime against the people of the United States and against the nations of the world.

In all modern history there has been no war more unjustifiable than the war in which we are about to engage.

No greater dishonor has ever been forced upon a people than that which the capitalist class is forcing upon this nation against its will.

In harmony with these principles, the Socialist Party emphatically rejects the proposal that in time of war the workers should suspend their struggle for better conditions. On the contrary, the acute situation created by war calls for an even more vigorous prosecution of the class struggle, and we recommend to the workers and pledge ourselves to the following course of action:

1. Continuous, active, and public opposition to the war through demonstrations, mass petitions, and all other means within our power.

2. Unyielding opposition to all proposed legislation for mili-

tary or industrial conscription. Should such conscription be forced upon the people we pledge ourselves to continuous efforts for the repeal of such laws and to the support of all mass movements in opposition to conscription. We pledge ourselves to oppose with all our strength any attempt to raise money for payment of war expense by taxing the necessaries of life or issuing bonds which will put the burden upon future generations. We demand that the capitalist class, which is responsible for the war, pay its cost. Let those who kindled the fire, furnish the fuel.

3. Vigorous resistance to all reactionary measures, such as censorship of press and mails, restriction of the rights of free speech, assemblage, and organization, or compulsory arbitration and limitation of the right to strike.

4. Consistent propaganda against military training and militaristic teaching in the public schools.

5. Extension of the campaign of education among the workers to organize them into strong, class-conscious, and closely unified political and industrial organizations, to enable them by concerted and harmonious mass action to shorten this war and to establish lasting peace.

6. Widespread educational propaganda to enlighten the masses as to the true relation between capitalism and war, and to rouse and organize them for action, not only against present war evils, but for the prevention of future wars and for the destruction of the causes of war.

7. To protect the masses of the American people from the pressing danger of starvation which the war in Europe has brought upon them, and which the entry of the United States has already accentuated, we demand—

(a) the restriction of food exports so long as the present shortage continues, the fixing of maximum prices and whatever measures may be necessary to prevent the food speculators from holding back the supplies now in their hands;

(b) The socialization and democratic management of the great industries concerned with the production, transportation, storage, and the marketing of food and other necessaries of life;

(c) The socialization and democratic management of all land and other natural resources now held out of use for monopolistic or speculative profit.

These measures are presented as means of protecting the workers against the evil results of the present war. The danger of recurrence of war will exist as long as the capitalist system of industry remains in existence. The end of wars will come with the establishment of socialized industry and industrial democracy the world over. The Socialist Party calls upon all the workers to join it in its struggle to reach this goal, and thus bring into the world a new society in which peace, fraternity, and human brotherhood will be the dominant ideals.

EUGENE V. DEBS
Speech to the Court
1918

Debs knew that he would probably be jailed for the speech he
gave at Canton, Ohio, on June 16, 1918. "Justice" was swift.
He was tried on September 9th for violating the Espionage Act
and quickly found guilty. On September 14th, just before he was
sentenced, he addressed the court.

Your Honor, years ago I recognized my kinship with all living
beings, and I made up my mind that I was not one bit better than
the meanest on earth. I said then, and I say now, that while there
is a lower class, I am in it, while there is a criminal element I am of
it, and while there is a soul in prison, I am not free.

I listened to all that was said in this court in support and
justification of this prosecution, but my mind remains unchanged.
I look upon the Espionage Law as a despotic enactment in flagrant
conflict with democratic principles and with the spirit of free institutions. . . .

Your Honor, I have stated in this court that I am opposed to
the social system in which we live; that I believe in a fundamental
change—but if possible by peaceable and orderly means. . . .

Standing here this morning, I recall my boyhood. At fourteen
I went to work in a railroad shop; at sixteen I was firing a freight
engine on a railroad. I remember all the hardships and privations
of that earlier day, and from that time until now my heart has
been with the working class. I could have been in Congress long
ago. I have preferred to go to prison. . . .

I am thinking this morning of the men in the mills and factories; of the men in the mines and on the railroads. I am thinking
of the women who for a paltry wage are compelled to work out
their barren lives; of the little children who in this system are
robbed of their childhood and in their tender years are seized in
the remorseless grasp of Mammon and forced into the industrial
dungeons, there to feed the monster machines while they them-

selves are being starved and stunted, body and soul. I see them dwarfed and diseased and their little lives broken and blasted because in this high noon of our twentieth-century Christian civilization money is still so much more important than the flesh and blood of childhood. In very truth gold is god today and rules with pitiless sway in the affairs of men.

In this country—the most favored beneath the bending skies —we have vast areas of the richest and most fertile soil, material resources in inexhaustible abundance, the most marvelous productive machinery on earth, and millions of eager workers ready to apply their labor to that machinery to produce in abundance for every man, woman and child—and if there are still vast numbers of our people who are the victims of poverty and whose lives are an unceasing struggle all the way from youth to old age, until at last death comes to their rescue and stills their aching hearts and lulls these hapless victims to dreamless sleep, it is not the fault of the Almighty: it cannot be charged to nature, but it is due entirely to the outgrown social system in which we live that ought to be abolished not only in the interest of the toiling masses but in the higher interest of all humanity. . . .

I believe, Your Honor, in common with all Socialists, that this nation ought to own and control its own industries. I believe, as all Socialists do, that all things that are jointly needed and used ought to be jointly owned—that industry, the basis of our social life, instead of being the private property of the few and operated for their enrichment, ought to be the common property of all, democratically administered in the interest of all. . . .

I am opposing a social order in which it is possible for one man who does absolutely nothing that is useful, to amass a fortune of hundreds of millions of dollars, while millions of men and women who work all the days of their lives secure barely enough for a wretched existence.

This order of things cannot always endure. I have registered my protest against it. I recognize the feebleness of my effort, but, fortunately, I am not alone. There are multiplied thousands of others who, like myself, have come to realize that before we may truly enjoy the blessings of civilized life, we must reorganize society upon a mutual and co-operative basis; and to this end we have organized a great economic and political movement that spreads over the face of all the earth.

There are today upwards of sixty millions of Socialists, loyal, devoted adherents to this cause, regardless of nationality, race, creed, color or sex. They are all making common cause. They are spreading with tireless energy the propaganda of the new social order. They are waiting, watching and working hopefully through all the hours of the day and the night. They are still in a minority. But they have learned how to be patient and to bide their time. They feel—they know, indeed—that the time is coming, in spite of all opposition, all persecution, when this emancipating gospel will spread among all the peoples, and when this minority will become the triumphant majority and, sweeping into power, inaugurate the greatest social and economic change in history.

In that day we shall have the universal commonwealth—the harmonious co-operation of every nation with every other nation on earth. . . .

Your Honor, I ask no mercy and I plead for no immunity. I realize that finally the right must prevail. I never so clearly comprehended as now the great struggle between the powers of greed and exploitation on the one hand and upon the other the rising hosts of industrial freedom and social justice.

I can see the dawn of the better day for humanity. The people are awakening. In due time they will and must come to their own.

"When the mariner, sailing over tropic seas, looks for relief from his weary watch, he turns his eyes toward the southern cross, burning luridly above the tempest-vexed ocean. As the midnight approaches, the southern cross begins to bend, the whirling worlds change their places, and with starry finger-points the Almighty marks the passage of time upon the dial of the universe, and though no bell may beat the glad tidings, the lookout knows that the midnight is passing and that relief and rest are close at hand.

"Let the people everywhere take heart of hope, for the cross is bending, the midnight is passing, and joy cometh with the morning."

"He's true to God who's true to man; wherever wrong is done,
To the humblest and the weakest, 'neath the all-beholding sun.
That wrong is done to us, and they are slaves most base,
Whose love of right is for themselves and not for all the race."

I am now prepared to receive your sentence.

LOUIS C. FRAINA
Revolutionary Socialism*
1918

Fraina's book, published during the war, was the fullest and best argued defense of the Left Wing (later the Communist) position. What it owed to the Bolshevik Revolution is obvious from the text.

THE PROLETARIAN REVOLUTION

The theory of the gradual transformation of Capitalism into Socialism, of a peaceful "growing into" Socialism, depends upon two assumptions: the collectivism of State Capitalism is an approach to Socialism, that *will* gradually and of its own compulsion become transformed into Socialism; and State Capitalism, operating jointly with an enlightened and organized working class, will succeed in limiting and restraining the economic forces of Capitalism. Our analysis of actual facts and forces shows, however, that State Capitalism means Capitalism at the violent climax of its development, intensifying the subjection of the proletariat and the domination of the capitalist class. The economic forces of Capitalism have not been limited, they have burst forth in a violent upheaval, the most violent of the ages; and these forces will burst forth in new upheavals unless directed into the channel of Social Revolution. Nor have the organizations of the workers succeeded in restraining the tendencies of Capitalism: the imperialistic Capitalism of Germany, France and Great Britain, in which operate powerful Socialist and labor organizations, have precipitated the proletariat and the world into a catastrophe the agony and oppression of which are inconceivable. If all this means a limiting of the forces of Capitalism and a "growing into" Socialism, then may heaven have mercy upon the world and the proletariat!

This theory often appears in pseudo-Marxian garb; it is, in fact, a distortion and a repudiation of Marxism.

* Pp. 204–221.

Marxism conceives the Social Revolution as a dynamic process of proletarian struggles in a period when the forces of production in capitalist society come in conflict with the old relations of production, relations which develop into fetters upon the productive process. This conflict creates a social-revolutionary crisis, a revolutionary situation and a breach in the old order in which the proletariat breaks through for action and the conquest of power. All the developments of bourgeois society simply produce the objective conditions for the proletarian revolution out of which emerges Socialism; these developments alone never can and won't bring Socialism. The process consists of two phases: the objective development of Capitalism and the subjective development of the proletariat. Historically, these two phases of the process are one; actually, they are not necessarily a unity: Germany, with an intense development of Capitalism and an apparently mature proletariat, has not yet developed a proletarian revolution, in spite of the revolutionary activity of capitalistically inferior Russia.

The epoch of Imperialism, which means Capitalism at the climax of its development, meets the requirements of the Marxian analysis. All the violence, all the upheavals of Imperialism are symptoms of the revolt of Capitalism against the fetters placed upon the productive forces. The requirements of developing Capitalism are incompatible with the capitalist forms of production. The crisis is acute. Capitalism strives to break the fetters, annihilate the multiplying contradictions, through State Capitalism and Imperialism, only to strengthen the fetters and increase the contradictions, resulting in a mad, violent and destructive world war. The economic and social, the political and national bases of Capitalism are now fetters upon the forces of production: the fetters must be broken, they can be broken only by the Social Revolution; and Capitalism writhes in the agony of its struggles, a mad beast rending itself and the world.

Imperialism, accordingly, introduces a new epoch in Capitalism, the social-revolutionary epoch. Objectively, a revolutionary situation prevails; subjectively, the proletariat must prepare itself for the final revolutionary struggle against Capitalism.

It is the tragedy of Imperialism that it can produce maggots only. It cannot, except temporarily, dispose of the contradictions implied in a fettering of the forces of production. The imperialistic nation seeks to broaden the base of its economic activity through conquest and the development of new territory; but in accomplishing this, the base is correspondingly narrowed for other nations, and for the world. And even the imperialistically triumphant nation secures only momentary relief: the new territory is developed, and again there is a surplus of commodities and of capital, again the vicious circle of production of means of production for new commodity production; and again within the triumphant nation itself there is a crisis, supplemented by still more acute crises within the defeated nations. A new upheaval arises, new and more violent wars, new and more intense waste. War becomes the normal aspect of Imperialism.

There is no alternative for the proletariat: either war and again war, or the Social Revolution.

The world war has brought Capitalism to the verge of collapse. It has compelled the state to lay a dictatorial hand upon the process of production, and the nation to negate its own basis by striving to break through the limits of the nation. It has compelled industrial necessity to subordinate itself to the overwhelming fact of military necessity. The debts of the belligerent nations are colossal, and they will fetter the nations, constitute a crucial problem in the days to come. The war has weakened Capitalism while it has strengthened a fictitious domination of the capitalist class. Contradictions and antagonisms have been multiplied. War has become the normal occupation of Capitalism, and the transition to peace will shake Capitalism to its foundations, posing new and more acute problems for solution. Industry will have to adjust itself to a peace basis, and it will be a herculean task; the proletariat will have to adjust itself to the new conditions, new struggles and new problems, and the experiences of war are not calculated to make it submissive.

The proletariat will find upon the conclusion of peace that all its sacrifices have availed it naught, and that the old system of exploitation persists in intensified form. Capitalism will equally find that war has availed it naught: its old economic problems will not have been solved and new problems have been created. Will Capitalism answer with a feverish era of industrial expansion? But war debts will weigh upon the nation, and an era of expansion will simply hasten the new crisis and a new war. There is a point where Capitalism comes up against an impasse in the industrial process. The forces of production inexorably generate new contradictions and crises. Capitalism verges on collapse.

The fatalist uses these facts, and they *are* facts, as an argument for an inevitable collapse of Capitalism and an equally inevitable coming of Socialism. The argument is as futile as it is fatalistic. The world war, in which millions of workers have sacrificed and died in the cause of Imperialism, is a warning of an alternative. The fatalist attitude in practice allows Capitalism to dispose of things in its own brutal way. And instead of a coming of Socialism, the world may see the coming of a new barbarism, the "common ruin of the contending classes." If war becomes the normal state of society, if the proletariat as the modern revolutionary class has not the initiative and the energy to assume control of society, then instead of a new society we shall have a new era of rapine and conquest. Europe rending itself, Europe and America rending each other, and the two rending Asia, or Asia rending them all. A collapse of Capitalism, in one form or another, is inevitable; but the coming of Socialism is not equally inevitable. It may become a collapse of all civilization.

What determined the supremacy of the bourgeoisie was its possession of actual material power, of the ownership of capital. It was a propertied class, and property as a class prerogative imparts power and ultimate ascendancy. The proletariat is a non-propertied, an expropriated class; what will determine its supremacy is revolutionary energy and integrity, and these alone.

The development during the war of Socialist social-reformism into social-Imperialism is an acute expression of a danger that besets the proletariat. Is it imaginary, is it inconceivable, in view of the unbelievable events in Europe, that the proletariat, instead of an instrument of revolution, might become an instrument of imperialistic conquest and spoliation? Only an uncompromising adherence to the revolutionary task, only the conscious and definite emergence of revolutionary Socialism, may avert the catastrophe. The subjective factor of a revolutionary proletariat alone will convert the objective conditions of Capitalism into Socialism. The proletariat will act, but its action must be directed. It may be skewed awry by petty bourgeois Socialism, as was unsuccessfully attempted in Russia and as was successfully done in Austria and Germany. The shortcomings of the dominant Socialism might convert proletarian action into a weapon of proletarian suicide. The tactics of petty bourgeois Socialism may not completely destroy the revolution, but they may hamper it and prolong the period of agony of imperialistic Capitalism. . . .

The class character and independence of the revolution must be emphasized under any and all conditions; the proletariat must not be lured into compromises either with Capitalism or its own organizations, compromises that invade its class integrity and palsy its action. On with the struggle, in spite of all and everything! The epoch is an epoch of revolutionary, uncompromising struggle and this struggle alone shall prevail.

The process of proletarian struggles will, under the impact of antagonisms and a revolutionary situation, develop into the great and final struggle,—an intense, violent and uncompromising struggle against Capitalism. This struggle will not break out as a conscious, organized struggle for Socialism: it will break out under the impulse of a crisis, through mass action. Its character, of course, will initially vary in accord with prevailing conditions, although probably, at first, animated by petty or vague purposes. And its course will be determined by the sense of reality, consciousness of purpose and power of revolutionary Socialism, its capacity to propose and organize a revolutionary program around which the masses may rally for action and the conquest of power. Organizing and directing the revolution will become the supreme task of Socialism, a test equally of its uncompromising spirit and its sense of reality. The policy of revolutionary phrases is as disastrous as the policy of parliamentary rhetoric and dickering with the bourgeois state. Revolutions do not rally around dogmas, but programs; and the program of the proletarian revolution must be as practical and realistic as it is revolutionary and uncompromising. Reality and the revolution are one, united and made dynamic by the class character of the proposals and purposes of the proletariat in action.

The immediate objective of the proletarian revolution is the conquest of the power of the state; and this means the annihilation of the bourgeois state, its parliamentary system and bourgeois democracy, and the introduction of a new "state" comprised in the dictatorship of the proletariat. In his "Criticism of the Gotha Program" Marx projected this phase of the proletarian revolution:

"Between the capitalist and the communist systems of society lies the period of revolutionary transformation of the one into the other. This corresponds to a political transition period, whose state can be nothing else than the revolutionary dictatorship of the proletariat."

The alternative to this dictatorship of the proletariat is the bourgeois state, its democracy and parliamentary system. To compromise with this system is to yield up the revolutionary task and to allow Capitalism to dominate. The parliamentary bourgeois state must be destroyed not simply because it is the ultimate purpose of Socialism to do away with the state as constituted in bourgeois society, but because it is immediately necessary in the process of disposing of the old society and introducing the new. It is a tactical necessity. The dictatorship of the proletariat is a revolutionary recognition of the fact that the proletariat alone counts, and no other class has any "rights." The dictatorship of the proletariat places all power in the control of the proletariat, and weakens the bourgeoisie, makes them incapable of any concerted action against the Revolution. Organized in a dictatorship of the proletariat, the Revolution unhesitatingly and relentlessly pursues its task of reconstructing society on the basis of communist Socialism.

The parliamentary regime is the expression of bourgeois democracy,—each equally an instrument for the promotion of bourgeois class interests. Parliamentarism, presumably representing all classes, actually represents and promotes the requirements of the ruling class alone. Its trappings of army, police and judiciary are indispensable means of repression used against the proletariat, and the proletariat in action annihilates them all: in place of the army, the armed proletarian militia, until unnecessary; in place of the police, disciplinary measures of the masses themselves; in place of the judiciary, tribunals of workmen. The bureaucratic machinery of the state disappears. The division of functions in the parliamentary system into legislative and executive has for its direct purpose the indirect smothering of the opposition,—the legislature talks and represents the pretense of "democracy," while the executive acts autocratically. The parliamentary system is a fetter upon revolutionary class action in the epoch of the final struggle against Capitalism. The proletarian revolution annihilates the parliamentary system and its division of functions, legislative and executive being united in one body,—as in the Paris Commune and in the Russian Councils of Workers and Peasants.

The dictatorship of the proletariat, moreover, annihilates bourgeois democracy. All democracy is relative, is *class* democracy. As an historical category, democracy is a form of authority of one class over another: bourgeois democracy is the form of expression of the authority and tyranny of Capitalism. Authority is an instrument of class rule, historically: Socialism destroys authority. The democracy of Socialism, the self-government of the proletarian masses, discards the democracy of Capitalism—relative democracy is superseded by the individual and social autonomy of communist Socialism. The proletarian revolution does not allow the "ethical concepts" of bourgeois democracy to interfere in the course of events: it ruthlessly sweeps aside "democracy" in the process of revolutionary transformation. Capitalism hypocritically insists upon a government of *all the classes*; the Revolution frankly and fearlessly introduces the government of *one class, the proletariat*, through a proletarian dictatorship. The proletarian revolution is inexorable; it completely and ruthlessly annihilates the institutions and idealogy of the regime of communist Socialism.*

This problem of democracy is crucial in the proletarian revolution. Democracy becomes the last bulwark of defense of Capitalism, an instrument used by dominant Capitalism and the *petite bourgeoisie* in a last desperate defense of private property. Any compromise on the issue of democracy compromises the integrity of the Revolution, stultifies its purposes and palsies its action: it is an issue pregnant with the potentiality of fatal mistakes. And yet it is all simplicity itself: in the revolution, the proletariat may depend upon itself alone; it alone is necessary in the process of production; it alone is a revolutionary class, implacably arrayed against all other classes; it alone counts as a class in the reconstruction of society, and, ac-

---

* During the course of events in Russia, democracy was a fetter upon the development of the proletarian revolution; once this revolution was accomplished, democracy became a counter-revolutionary instrument used by the petty bourgeois Socialism of the Mensheviki and Social-Revolutionists of the Right through the Constituent Assembly. If the Soviet government had not dissolved the Constituent Assembly, it would have stultified itself and the Revolution. The Revolution, declared the decree of dissolution, created the Workers' and Soldiers' Council— the only organization able to direct the struggle of the exploited classes for *complete* political and economic liberation; this Council constituted a revolutionary government through the November Revolution, after perceiving the illusion of an understanding with the bourgeoisie and its deceptive parliamentary organization; the Constituent Assembly, being elected from the old election lists, was the expression of the old regime when authority belonged to the bourgeoisie, and necessarily became the authority of the bourgeois republic, setting itself against the revolution of November and the authority of the Councils; the old bourgeois parliamentarism has had its day and is incompatible with the tasks before Socialism, and that only such institutions as the Workmen's and Soldiers' Councils are able to overcome the opposition of the ruling classes and create a new Socialist state; "the central executive committee, therefore, orders the Constituent Assembly dissolved."

cordingly, the dictatorship of the proletariat refuses political "rights" and recognition to any section of the bourgeois class.

Through its dictatorship, the proletariat organizes itself as the ruling class, acquires social supremacy. The basis of the new "state" is not territorial, but industrial: its constituents are the organized producers. The other elements of the people function in this proletarian government in the measure that they are absorbed in the new industrial scheme of things, become useful producers. The process of transformation into communist Socialism is a process of the organized producers, and of these alone.

The dictatorship of the proletariat, naturally, will have many acute problems press upon it. Civil war, a revolutionary war, problems of general social reconstruction—all these are problems that will call forth all of the energy, clarity and capacity of the proletarian revolution. The central problem, of course, is the problem of economic reconstruction. The particular initial form that this reconstruction assumes will depend upon a number of factors, particularly the factor of the degree of industrial development. In the *Communist Manifesto*, Marx and Engels said: "The proletariat will use its political supremacy to wrest, by degrees, all capital from the bourgeoisie; to centralize all instruments of production in the hands of the state—that is, of the proletariat organized as the ruling class; and to increase the total of productive forces as rapidly as possible. Of course, in the beginning this cannot be effected except by means of despotic inroads on the rights of property and on the conditions of bourgeois production; by measures, therefore, which appear economically insufficient and untenable, but which in the course of the movement, outstrip themselves, necessitate further inroads upon the old social order and are unavoidable as a means of entirely revolutionizing the mode of production." The proletariat, in short, lays a dictatorial hand upon production. The control of industry is centralized in the administrative norms of the new proletarian state. . . .

The proletariat's dictatorial control of production develops, on the one hand, the forces of production; and, on the other, it develops the communist administration of the industrial process. At first the administration of control functions through general organizations, Councils of Workers. These organizations are gradually integrated, adapted to industrial divisions; and it is precisely at this point that industrial unionism, whether actual or potential, functions in the construction of the new society. Industry as a whole is divisible into constituent units,—the production of coal, of steel, of textiles, agriculture, transportation, etc. Each industry will constitute a department of the industrial state; the workers in each industry will organize in Local Councils and these unite into General Industrial Councils co-ordinated with other General Industrial Councils into a central administration of the whole productive process. Industrial unionism, organizing the producers industrially, becomes the vital basis of the new communist society, together with other administrative norms necessary to co-ordinate the non-industrial activity of society.

The industrial administration of communist Socialism institutes all the centralization necessary and compatible with autonomy, and all the autonomy necessary and compatible with centralization. The central administration is directive, and not repressive; it co-ordinates the whole industrial process as the General Industrial Council co-ordinates each phase of its particular industry; its functions are comprised in the statistical regulation and directive control of the forces of production.

The division of the product is ultimately determined on a communistic basis: from each according to his ability, to each according to his needs.

The dictatorship of the proletariat is temporary, its necessity ceasing as the task of destroying the old order and organizing the new is accomplished. The rapidity of this development depends upon the maturity of proletarian consciousness and class power, upon the relation of social forces within the nation and upon the general international situation. The development of the proletarian revolution lets loose violent antagonisms within the nation, and the vitality of these antagonisms will affect the rapidity of development; the proletarian revolution, moreover, lets loose equally violent international antagonisms. As the revolutionary proletariat reconstructs society, it may find itself compelled simultaneously to wage civil wars and revolutionary wars. It may even, temporarily, meet defeat: the process consists of a series of revolutionary struggles. But the proletarian revolution, acting through the dictatorship of the proletariat, actual or potential, partial or complete, adhering firmly to the class struggle and revolutionary Socialism, is determined in a course of action against which nothing but betrayals can prevail.

Manifesto of the Left Wing Section
of Greater New York*
1919

This announcement, sent out to all the locals in the country, officially launched the Left Wing assault on the citadel of the Socialist Party—the National Executive Committee. By now any chance of compromise between the two factions had disappeared.

Prior to August, 1914, the nations of the world lived on a volcano. Violent eruptions from time to time gave warning of the cataclysm to come, but the diplomats and statesmen managed to localize the outbreaks, and the masses, slightly aroused, sank back into their accustomed lethargy with doubts and misgivings, and the subterranean fires continued to smoulder.

Many trusted blindly—some in their statesmen, some in the cohesive power of Christianity, their common religion, and some in the growing strength of the international Socialist movement. Had not the German Social-Democracy exchanged dramatic telegrams with the French Socialist Party, each pledging itself not to fight in case their governments declared war on each other! A general strike of workers led by these determined Socialists would quickly bring the governments to their senses!

So the workers reasoned, until the thunder-clap of Sarejevo and Austria's ultimatum to Serbia. Then, suddenly, the storm broke. Mobilization everywhere. Everywhere declarations of war. In three or four days Europe was in arms.

The present structure of society—Capitalism—with its pretensions to democracy on the one hand, and its commercial rivalries, armament rings and standing armies on the other, all based on the exploitation of the working class and the division of the loot, was cast into the furnace of war. Two things only could issue forth: either international capitalist control, through a League of Nations,

* Report of the New York State Joint Legislative Committee Investigating Sedition (Lusk Committee), Vol. I, pp. 706–716.

or Social Revolution and the Dictatorship of the Proletariat. Both of these forces are to-day contending for world-power.

The Social Democracies of Europe, unable or unwilling to meet the crisis, were themselves hurled into the conflagration, to be tempered or consumed by it.

THE COLLAPSE OF THE SECOND INTERNATIONAL

Great demonstrations were held in every European country by Socialists protesting against their governments' declarations of war, and mobilizations for war. And we know that these demonstrations were rendered impotent by the complete surrender of the Socialist parliamentary leaders and the official Socialist press, with their "justifications" of "defensive wars" and the safeguarding of "democracy."

Why the sudden change of front? Why did the Socialist leaders in the parliaments of the belligerents vote the war credits? Why did not Moderate Socialism carry out the policy of the Basle Manifesto, namely: the converting of an imperialistic war into a civil war—into a proletarian revolution? Why did it either openly favor the war or adopt a policy of petty-bourgeois pacifism?

THE DEVELOPMENT OF MODERATE "SOCIALISM"

In the latter part of the nineteenth century, the Social-Democracies of Europe set out to "legislate Capitalism out of office." The class struggle was to be won in the capitalist legislatures. Step by step concessions were to be wrested from the state; the working class and the Socialist parties were to be strengthened by means of "constructive" reform and social legislation; each concession would act as a rung in the ladder of Social Revolution, upon which the workers could climb step by step, until finally, some bright sunny morning, the peoples would awaken to find the Cooperative Commonwealth functioning without disorder, confusion or hitch on the ruins of the capitalist state.

And what happened? When a few legislative seats had been secured, the thunderous denunciations of the Socialist legislators suddenly ceased. No more were the parliaments used as platforms from which the challenge of revolutionary Socialism was flung to all the corners of Europe. Another era had set in, the era of "constructive" social reform legislation. Dominant moderate Socialism accepted the bourgeois state as the basis of its action and strengthened that state. All power to shape the policies and tactics of the Socialist parties was entrusted to the parliamentary leaders. And these lost sight of Socialism's original purpose; their goal became "constructive reforms" and cabinet portfolios—the "co-operation of classes," the policy of openly or tacitly declaring that the coming of Socialism was a concern "of all the classes," instead of emphasizing the Marxian policy that the construction of the Socialist system is the task of the revolutionary proletariat alone. "Moderate Socialism" accepted the bourgeois state as the leaders, was now ready to share responsibility with the bourgeoisie in the control of the capitalist state, even to the extent of defending the bourgeoisie against the working class—as in the first Briand Ministry in France, when the official party press was opened to a defense of the shooting of striking railway-workers at the order of the Socialist-Bourgeois Coalition Cabinet.

"SAUSAGE SOCIALISM"

This situation was brought about by mixing the democratic cant of the eighteenth century with scientific Socialism. The result was what Rosa Luxemburg called "sausage Socialism." The "Moderates" emphasized petty-bourgeois social reformism in order to attract tradesmen, shop-keepers and members of the professions, and, of course, the latter flocked to the Socialist movement in great numbers, seeking relief from the constant grinding between corporate capital and awakening labor.

The Socialist organizations actively competed for votes, on the basis of social reforms, with the bourgeois-liberal political parties. And so they catered to the ignorance and prejudices of the workers, trading promises of immediate reforms for votes.

Dominant "moderate Socialism" forgot the teachings of the founders of scientific Socialism, forgot its function as a proletarian movement—"the most resolute and advanced section of the working class parties"—and permitted the bourgeois and self-seeking trade union elements to shape its policies and tactics. This was the condition in which the Social-Democracies of Europe found themselves at the outbreak of the war in 1914. Demoralized and confused by the cross-currents within their own parties, vacillating and compromising with the bourgeois state, they fell a prey to social-patriotism and nationalism.

But revolutionary Socialism was not destined to lie inert for long. In Germany, Karl Liebknecht, Franz Mehring, Rosa Luxemburg and Otto Ruhle organized the Spartacus Group. But their voices were drowned in the roar of cannon and the shrieks of the dying and the maimed.

Russia, however, was to be the first battle-ground where "moderate" and revolutionary Socialism should come to grips for the mastery of the state. The breakdown of the corrupt, bureaucratic Czarist regime opened the flood-gates of Revolution.

Three main contending parties attempted to ride into power on the revolutionary tide; the Cadets, the "moderate Socialists" (Mensheviki and Social Revolutionists), and the revolutionary Socialists—the Bolsheviki. The Cadets were first to be swept into power; but they tried to stem the still-rising flood with a few abstract political ideals, and were soon carried away. The soldiers, workers, and peasants could no longer be fooled by phrases. The Mensheviki and Social Revolutionaries succeeded the Cadets. And now came the crucial test: would they, in accord with Marxian teachings, make themselves the ruling class and sweep away the old conditions of production, and thus prepare the way for the Cooperative Commonwealth? Or would they tinker with the old machinery and try to foist it on the masses as something just as good?

They did the latter and proved for all time that "moderate Socialism" cannot be trusted.

"Moderate Socialism" was not prepared to seize the power for the workers during a revolution. "Moderate Socialism" had a rigid formula—"constructive social reform legislation within the capitalist state" and to that formula it clung. It believed that bourgeois democracy could be used as a means of constructing the Socialist system; therefore, it must wait until the people, through a Constituent Assembly, should vote Socialism into existence. And in the meantime, it held that there must be established a Government of Coalition with the enemy, the bourgeoisie. As if, with all the means of controlling public opinion in the hands of the bourgeoisie, a Constituent Assembly could or would ever vote the Socialists into power!

Revolutionary Socialists hold, with the founders of scientific Socialism, that there are two dominant classes in society—the bourgeoisie and the proletariat; that between these two classes a struggle must go on, until the working class, through the seizure of the instruments of production and distribution, the abolition of the capitalist state, and the establishment of the dictatorship of the proletariat, creates a Socialist system. Revolutionary Socialists do not believe that they can be voted into power. They struggle for the conquest of power by the revolutionary proletariat. Then comes the transition period from Capitalism to Socialism, of which Marx speaks in his "Critique of the Gotha program": when he says: "Between the capitalistic society and the communistic, lies the period of the revolutionary transformation of the one into the other. This corresponds to a political transition period, in which the state cannot be anything else but the dictatorship of the proletariat."

Marx and Engels clearly explain the function of the Socialist movement. It is the "moderate Socialists" through intellectual gymnastics, evasions, misquotations and the tearing of sentences and phrases from their context, who make Marx and Engels sponsors for their perverted version of Socialism.

PROBLEMS OF AMERICAN SOCIALISM

At the present moment, the Socialist Party of America is agitated by several cross-currents, some local in their character, and some a reflex of cleavages within the European Socialist movements. Many see in this internal dissension merely an unimportant difference of opinion, or at most, dissatisfaction with the control of the party, and the desire to replace those who have misused it with better men.

We, however, maintain that there is a fundamental distinction in views concerning party policies and tactics. And we believe that this difference is so vast that from our standpoint a radical change in party policies and tactics is necessary.

This essential task is being shirked by our party leaders and officials generally.

Already there is formidable industrial unrest, a seething ferment

of discontent, evidenced by inarticulate rumblings which presage
striking occurrences. The transformation of industry from a war to
a peace basis has thoroughly disorganized the economic structure.
Thousands upon thousands of workers are being thrown out of
work. Demobilized sailors and soldiers find themselves a drug
upon the labor market, unless they act as scabs and strikebreakers.
Skilled mechanics, fighting desperately to maintain their war-wage
and their industrial status, are forced to strike. Women, who during
the war have been welcomed into industries hitherto closed to
them, are struggling to keep their jobs. And to cap the climax,
the capitalists, through their Chambers of Commerce and their
Merchants and Manufacturers' Associations, have resolved to take
advantage of the situation to break down even the inadequate
organizations labor has built up through generations of painful
struggle.

The temper of the workers and soldiers, after the sacrifices they
have made in the war, is such that they will not endure the
reactionary labor conditions so openly advocated by the master
class. A series of labor struggles is bound to follow—indeed, is
beginning now. Shall the Socialist Party continue to feed the
workers with social reform legislation at this critical period?
Shall it approach the whole question from the standpoint of votes
and the election of representatives to the legislatures? Shall it
emphasize the consumers' point of view, when Socialist principles
teach that the worker is robbed at the point of production? Shall
it talk about the Cost of Living and Taxation when it should be
explaining how the worker is robbed at his job?

There are many signs of the awakening of labor. Strikes are
developing which verge on revolutionary action; the trade unions
are organizing a Labor Party, in an effort to conserve what they
have won and wrest new concessions from the master class. The
organization of the Labor Party is an immature expression of a
new spirit in the Labor movement; but a Labor Party is not the
instrument for the emancipation of the working class; its policy
would be in general what is now the official policy of the Socialist
Party—reforming Capitalism on the basis of the bourgeois state.
Laborism is as much a danger to the revolutionary proletariat
as "moderate" Socialism; neither is an instrument for the conquest
of power.

CAPITALIST IMPERIALISM

Imperialism is the final stage of Capitalism, in which the accumulated capital or surplus of a nation is too great to be reinvested in the home market. The increased productivity of the working class, due to improved machinery and efficiency methods, and the mere subsistence wage which permits the worker to buy back only a small portion of what he produces, causes an ever-increasing accumulation of commodities, which in turn become capital and must be invested in further production. When Capitalism has reached the stage in which it imports raw materials from undeveloped countries and exports them again in the shape of manufactured products, it has reached its highest development.

This process is universal. Foreign markets, spheres of influence and protectorates, under the intensive development of capitalist industry and finance in turn become highly developed. They, too, seek for markets. National capitalist control, to save itself from ruin, breaks its national bonds and emerges full-grown as a capitalist League of Nations, with international armies and navies to maintain its supremacy.

The United States no longer holds itself aloof, isolated and provincial. It is reaching out for new markets, new zones of influence, new protectorates.

The capitalist class of America is using organized labor for its imperialistic purposes. We may soon expect the capitalist class, in true Bismarckian fashion, to grant factory laws, old-age pensions, unemployment insurance, sick benefits, and the whole litter of bourgeois reforms, so that the workers may be kept fit to produce the greatest profits at the greatest speed.

DANGERS TO AMERICAN SOCIALISM

There is danger that the Socialist Party of America might make use of these purely bourgeois reforms to attract the workers' votes, by claiming that they are victories for Socialism, and that they have been won by Socialist political action; when, as a matter of fact, the object of these master class measures is to prevent the growing class-consciousness of the workers, and to divert them from their revolutionary aim. By agitating for these reforms, therefore, the Socialist Party would be playing into the hands of the American imperialists.

On the basis of the class struggle, then, the Socialist Party of America must re-organize itself, must prepare to come to grips with the master class during the difficult period of capitalist re-adjustment now going on. This it can do only by teaching the working class the truth about present-day conditions; it must preach revolutionary industrial unionism, and urge all the workers to organize into industrial unions, the only form of labor organization which can cope with the power of great modern aggregations of capital. It must carry on its political campaigns, not merely as a means of electing officials to political office, as in the past, but as a year-round educational campaign to arouse the workers to class-conscious economic and political action, and to keep alive the burning ideal of revolution in the hearts of the people.

POLITICAL ACTION

We assert with Marx that "the class struggle is essentially a political struggle," and we can only accept his own oft-repeated interpretation of that phrase. The class struggle, whether it manifest itself on the industrial field or in the direct struggle for governmental control, is essentially a struggle for the capture and destruction of the capitalist state. This is a political act. In this broader view of the term "political," Marx includes revolutionary industrial action. In other words, the objective of Socialist industrial action is "political," in the sense that it aims to undermine the bourgeois state, which "is nothing less than a machine for the oppression of one class by another and that no less so in a democratic republic than under a monarchy."

Political action is also and more generally used to refer to participation in election campaigns for the immediate purpose of winning legislative seats. In this sense, too, we urge the use of political action as a revolutionary weapon.

But both in the nature and the purpose of this form of political action, revolutionary Socialism and "moderate Socialism" are completely at odds.

Political action, revolutionary and emphasizing the implacable character of the class struggle, is a valuable means of propaganda. It must at all times struggle to arouse the revolutionary mass action of the proletariat—its use is both agitational and obstructive. It must on all issues wage war upon Capitalism and the state. Revolutionary Socialism uses the forum of parliament for agitation; but it does not intend to and cannot use the bourgeois state as a means of introducing Socialism: this bourgeois state must be destroyed by the mass action of the revolutionary proletariat. The proletarian dictatorship in the form of a Soviet state is the immediate objective of the class struggle.

Marx declared that "the working class cannot simply lay hold of the ready-made state machinery and wield it for its own purposes." This machinery must be destroyed. But "moderate Socialism" makes the state the centre of its action.

The attitude towards the state divides the Anarchist (anarcho-syndicalist), the "moderate Socialist" and the revolutionary Socialist. Eager to abolish the state (which is the ultimate purpose of revolutionary Socialism), the Anarchist and Anarcho-Syndicalist fail to realize that a state is necessary in the transition period from Capitalism to Socialism; the "moderate Socialist" purposes to use the bourgeois state with its fraudulent democracy, its illusory theory of "unity of all the classes," its standing army, police and bureaucracy oppressing and baffling the masses; the revolutionary Socialist maintains that the bourgeois state must be completely destroyed, and proposes the organization of a new state—the state of the organized producers—of the Federated Soviets—on the basis of which alone can Socialism be introduced.

Industrial Unionism, the organization of the proletariat in accordance with the integration of industry and for the overthrow of Capitalism, is a necessary phase of revolutionary Socialist agitation. Potentially, industrial unionism constructs the basis and develops the ideology of the industrial state of Socialism; but industrial unionism alone cannot perform the revolutionary act of seizure of the power of the state, since under the conditions of Capitalism it is impossible to organize the whole working class, or an overwhelming majority, into industrial unions.

It is the task of a revolutionary Socialist Party to direct the struggles of the proletariat and provide a program for the culminating crisis. Its propaganda must be so directed that when this crisis comes, the workers will be prepared to accept a program of the following character:

(a) *The organization of Workmen's Councils*; recognition of, and propaganda for, these mass organizations of the working class as instruments in the immediate struggle, as the form of expression of the class struggle, and as the instruments for the seizure of the power of the state and the basis of the new proletarian state of the organized producers and the dictatorship of the proletariat.

(b) *Workmen's control of industry*, to be exercised by the industrial organizations (industrial unions or Soviets) of the workers and the industrial vote, as against government ownership or state control of industry.

(c) *Repudiation of all national debts*—with provisions to safeguard small investors.

(d) *Expropriation of the banks*—a preliminary measure for the complete expropriation of capital.

(e) *Expropriation of the railways, and the large (trust) organizations of capital*—no compensation to be paid, as "buying-out" the capitalists would insure a continuance of the exploitation of the workers; provision, however, to be made during the transition period for the protection of small owners of stock.

(f) *The socialization of foreign trade*.

These are not the "immediate demands" comprised in the social reform planks now in the platform of our party; they are not a compromise with the capitalist state, but imply a revolutionary struggle against that state and against capitalism, the conquest of power by the proletariat through revolutionary mass action. They imply the new Soviet state of the organized producers, the dictatorship of the proletariat; they are preliminary revolutionary measures for the expropriation of capital and the introduction of communist Socialism.

PROGRAM

1. We stand for a uniform declaration of principles in all party platforms both local and national and the abolition of all social reform planks now contained in them.

2. The party must teach, propagate and agitate exclusively for the overthrow of Capitalism, and the establishment of Socialism through a Proletarian Dictatorship.

3. The Socialist candidates elected to office shall adhere strictly to the above provisions.

4. Realizing that a political party cannot reorganize and reconstruct the industrial organizations of the working class, and that that is the task of the economic organizations themselves, we demand that the party assist this process of reorganization by a propaganda for revolutionary industrial unionism as part of its general activities. We believe it is the mission of the Socialist movement to encourage and assist the proletariat to adopt newer and more effective forms of organization and to stir it into newer and more revolutionary modes of action.

5. We demand that the official party press be party owned and controlled.

6. We demand that officially recognized educational institutions be party owned and controlled.

7. We demand that the party discard its obsolete literature and publish new literature in keeping with the policies and tactics above-mentioned.

8. We demand that the National Executive Committee call an immediate emergency national convention for the purpose of formulating party policies and tactics to meet the present crisis.

9. We demand that the Socialist Party repudiate the Berne Congress or any other conference engineered by "moderate Socialists" and social patriots.

10. We demand that the Socialist Party shall elect delegates to the International Congress proposed by the Communist Party of Russia (Bolsheviki); that our party shall participate only in a new International with which are affiliated the Communist Party of Russia (Bolsheviki), the Communist Labor Party of Germany (Spartacus), and all other Left Wing parties and groups.

"Socialist Task and Outlook"*
1919

This article officially confirmed what everybody had known all along, namely that the leaders of the Socialist Party would not permit the organization to fall to the Left Wing, whatever the consequences.

It is safe to assert that at no time since the formation of the First International has the Socialist movement of the world been in a state of such physical disunion, moral ferment and intellectual confusion as it is today. The World War, so sudden in its outbreak, so titanic in its dimensions and so disastrous in its effects, had placed the Socialist movement in Europe before a situation, which it had not foreseen as a concrete reality and, for which it was entirely unprepared, and it reacted to it in a most unexpected and disheartening manner. Far from proving the formidable bulwark against war which their friends and enemies alike had believed them to be, the powerful cohorts of European Socialism on the whole supported their capitalist governments in the capitalist war, almost as enthusiastically and unreservedly as the most loyal Junker classes, and when, with the collapse of the war, the Socialist revolutions broke out in several countries, their forms of struggle were equally startling. The bourgeoisie, against whom the revolutions were directed, made little or no effective resistance, and the fight, repressive and sanguinary at times, was principally among those, who before the war called each other Comrades in the Socialist movement.

There is something radically wrong in a movement that could mature such sad paradoxes and that wrong must be discovered and eliminated, *if the international Socialist movement is to survive as an effective instrument of the working-class revolution.* What was wrong with the Second Socialist International, and how are its mistakes to be avoided in the future? This is the main question

* *New York Call*, May 21, 1919.

which agitates and divides the Socialist movement today, and upon the solution of which the future of our movement depends.

It may be somewhat premature to pass conclusive judgment upon the contending views and methods of contemporary Socialism or to attempt to formulate a complete revision of the Socialist program. Socialist history is still in the making, and history has recently shown an almost provoking disregard for preconceived theories and rigid formulae. But enough has happened since August 1, 1914, to justify several definite conclusions, both as to the wrongs and remedies of the situation.

Why did the Second International fail? Some of our neo-revolutionary ideologists conveniently account for it upon the theological theory of lapse from grace. The Socialists of the pre-war period had become too materialistic and "constructive," they paid too much attention to political office and reforms, they were corrupted by bourgeois parliamentarism—"they forgot the teachings of the founders of scientific Socialism" (how reminiscent of the familiar ecclesiastic complaint—"they abandoned the faith of their fathers!").

Marxian Socialists, accustomed to look to material causes for the explanation of political events and manifestations, can hardly accept this explanation, which after all only reiterates and describes, but does not explain, and furnishes no guide for correction. It asks sternly: What were the economic causes which deflected the Socialist movement of Europe from the path of revolutionary, proletarian internationalism? And the answer is as startling and paradoxical as the entire recent course of the Socialist movement. It was the economic organization of the European workers, and the pressure of their immediate economic interests (as understood by them) that broke the solidarity of the Socialist International.

It was not parliamentarism which was primarily responsible for the mischief. Excessive parliamentarism in the Socialist movement of Europe had undoubtedly contributed substantially to the disaster, negatively as well as positively, but on the whole the Socialists in Parliament expressed the sentiments of their constituents pretty faithfully.

The Social-Democratic Deputies of Italy, Russia, Serbia and Bulgaria knew how to use the Parliaments of their countries as revolutionary tribunals, and so did Liebknecht, Rueble and Ledebour in Germany.

The Parliaments of Germany and France were the scenes of Socialist betrayal. Its mainsprings lay much deeper.

The countries in which the Socialist movement failed most lamentably are precisely those in which the movement was most closely linked with organized labor, while the principles of international solidarity were upheld most rigorously in countries in which the economic labor movement was either very weak or quite detached from the Socialist movement. In the United States, where this detachment was more complete than in any other modern country, the American Federation of Labor, under the leadership of Samuel Gompers, outdid all jingoes in the orgy of profiteering, while the Socialist Party adopted the St. Louis platform. The bulk of the Social Democracy in Germany was made up of workers organized upon the same structure and looking to the same immediate ends as the American Federation of Labor. The German workers were more progressive than their American brethren. They acted politically within the Social Democratic Party. They had their own representatives in Parliament, and their social patriotic stand found parliamentary expression, just as the social patriotic spirit of the "non-political" American Federation of Labor vented itself in extra-parliamentary action. What is true of Germany applies also, though perhaps in varying degree, to Austria, Belgium, France and Great Britain. Conversely, in Russia, Italy and the Balkan countries, in all of which the element of organized labor was a negligible factor in the Socialist movement, the Socialists have on the whole successfully withstood the wave of nationalistic reaction, and when the first break came, it was Carl Liebknecht, Rosa Luxemburg and Franz Mehring in Germany, Fritz Adler in Austria, Lenin and Trotsky in Russia, and Jean Longuet in France, all intellectuals, that led the Socialist revolts in their countries.

What, then, is the inference to be drawn from these facts? Shall revolutionary Socialism hereafter disassociate itself from organized labor? By no means. A Socialist movement without the support of the workers is a sort of disembodied spirit; in fact, a spook. Socialism must remain the political and spiritual guide of the working class, but it must reorganize and re-educate the working class.

The fundamental weakness of the organized labor movement has been that it was a movement of a class within a class, a movement for the benefit of the better-situated strata of labor—

the skilled workers. As such semi-privileged class, the economic organizations of labor had attained large power in the leading countries of Europe and in the United States before the war. They enjoyed a sort of government recognition, and had accumulated considerable material wealth. They had certain "vested interests" in the capitalist regimes of their respective countries. In addition to this basic shortcoming, and largely because of it, the workers were organized along the narrow lines of separate trades and crafts. This form of organization naturally limits the efforts and activities of the workers to the petty struggles and interests of their own special trades. It creates a psychology of craft solidarity, rather than class solidarity, and deflects the workers' attention from the ultimate goal to immediate benefits.

In such conditions the parliamentary activities of labor's political representatives cannot but reflect the narrow economic policies of their constituents. The petty political reform measures of the pre-war Socialists correspond to the craft organization in the economic field, and the striving of the organized workers to preserve their economic position within the industrial system of their country and to protect it against the menace of enemy capitalists is the basis of the war-patriotism of their parliamentary representatives.

The first task of the post-war Socialist International must, therefore, be to organize and reorganize all grades and strata of labor on broad class lines, not only nationally, but internationally. Not as trade unions, nor even as mere industrial unions, but as one working-class union.

This first lesson to be drawn from the recent experiences and failures of the old International applies, of course, mainly, if not exclusively, to the countries still remaining under capitalist-class control. In the countries that have passed, or are passing, to a regime of Communist or Socialist government, the problem presents itself in a different and more advanced form. Shall the socialization of industries and national life be attempted by one master-stroke, or shall it be carried out gradually and slowly? Shall the working-class immediately assume the sole direction of the government as a working-class government, or shall it share governmental power and responsibilities with the capitalist class, at least "during the period of transition"?

While the question involved is primarily one of power, to be determined in each country according to the conditions existing at the critical moment, there can be no doubt about the stand which the Socialist International must take on it. In all cases in which the proletariat of a country in revolution has assumed the reins of government as a pure working-class government, determined upon the immediate socialization of the country, the true Socialists of all countries will support it. Whether we approve or disapprove of all the methods by which such proletarian government has gained or is exercising its power is beside the question. Each revolution develops its own methods, fashioning them from the elements of the inexorable necessities of the case.

The Socialists of the foreign countries are faced by an accomplished fact and by the simple alternative of supporting the revolution or counter-revolution. It is thus quite evident that no Socialist or Socialist Party that makes common cause with the ultra-reactionary elements of bourgeois and Czarist Russia in supporting foreign military intervention against the Soviet government, or in any other way actively opposes that government in the face of its life-and-death struggle with international capitalism and imperialism, has a legitimate place in the international Socialist movement. The same may, of course, be said of the Socialist attitude toward Hungary.

In countries like Germany, in which the struggle for mastery lies between two divisions of the Socialist movement, one class-conscious and the other opportunist, one radical and the other temporizing, the support of the Socialist International must, for the same reason, go to the former.

Such, it seems to me, must be the main outline of the guiding policy of the new International. Upon such or similar general program must the Third International be built. For the Third International of Socialism has not yet been created, nor have its foundations been laid, either at Berne or in Moscow.

The Berne conference proved hopelessly backward and totally sterile, although some elements in it showed a distinct understanding of the new order of things. The Communist Congress at Moscow made the mistake of attempting a sort of dictatorship of the proletariat in the Socialist International and was conspicuously inept and unhappy in the choice of certain allies and in the exclusion of others. It has not advanced the process of reorganization of the Socialist movement of the world.

The task of organizing the Third International is still before us. It must be accomplished on the basis of principles and conduct, not on that of personal likes and dislikes. It is the common task of all international Socialists.

The attitude of the Socialist Party of the United States toward International problems is thus clearly outlined. From the temper of its membership and from the official utterances of its administrative bodies, fragmentary as they necessarily had to be under extraordinary restriction, there can be no doubt about the party's advanced and militant position. How is that position to be translated into a domestic program?

The platform and the policies of the Socialist Party must be revised in keeping, not only with the development of Socialism abroad, but also with regard to the changes wrought by the war in the United States.

The United States emerges from the war the strongest capitalist country in the world, not only because of the superiority of its material and military resources, but also because the power of capitalism has been less shaken in the United States than in any of the advanced countries of Europe. Our "liberal" administration has turned to the lowest depths of reaction and repression without effective resistance or opposition on the part of any considerable section of the population. The "progressive" elements in politics and social reform have collapsed like a house of cards, and organized labor has so far remained inert and passive. The only voice of protest and the only vision of progress have come from the Socialist Party and a negligible group of industrial workers and radical individuals. But the Socialist Party is as yet an insignificant factor in the political and social life of America. The importance of American Socialism lies in the future, probably the immediate future. The futility of the war, the failure of "peace," the governmental persecution and repression, the stupid obscurantism of the press and the terrorism of countless private and public agencies are bound to cause a reaction of revolt, and a period of unemployment and intensified exploitation will arouse the American workers from the narcotics of their leaders' empty phrases. Then it will be that the workers of America will look for a new light and guidance, and then the Socialists of America will have their hearing and their opportunity. To prepare for that period, and to hasten its coming, is the present task of American Socialism, and that means primarily two things—propaganda and organization. Propaganda in international Socialism in the modern and advanced meaning of the term; propaganda of new class-line unionism, systematic propaganda through all methods available, including political campaigns and legislative forums, and organization of all effective organs of such propaganda. At no time was a comprehensive and harmonious plan of action along such lines so urgently imperative for the Socialist movement in America as it is just now.

All the more unfortunate is it that the energies of the Socialist Party should at this time be dissipated in acrimonious and fruitless controversies brought on by the self-styled "Left Wing" movement. I am one of the last men in the party to ignore or misunderstand the sound revolutionary impulse which animates the rank and file of this new movement, but the specific form and direction which it has assumed, its program and tactics, spell disaster to our movement. I am opposed to it, not because it is too radical, but because it is essentially reactionary and non-Socialistic; not because it will lead us too far, but because it will lead us nowhere. To prate about the "dictatorship of the proletariat" and of "workers' Soviets," in the United States at this time is to deflect the Socialist propaganda from its realistic basis, and to advocate "the abolition of *all* social reform planks" in the party platform means to abandon the concrete class-struggle as it presents itself from day to day.

The "Left Wing" movement, as I see it, is a purely emotional reflex of the situation in Russia. The cardinal vice of the movement is that it started as a "wing," i.e., as a schismatic and disintegrative movement. Proceeding on the arbitrary assumption that they were the "Left," the ingenuous leaders of the movement had to discover a "Right," and since the European classification would not be fully reproduced without a "Center," they were also bound to locate a center in the Socialist movement of America. What matters it to our imaginative "Left Wing" leaders that the Socialist Party of America as a whole has stood in the forefront of Socialist radicalism ever since the outbreak of the war, that many of its officers and "leaders" have exposed their lives and liberties to imminent peril in defense of the principles of international Socialism, they are "Right Wingers" and "Centrists" because the exigencies of the "Left Wing" requires it. The "Left Wing" movement is a sort of burlesque on the Russian revolution. Its leaders do not want to convert their Comrades in the party. They must "capture" and establish a sort of dictatorship of the proletariat (?) within the party. Hence the creation of their dual organization as a kind of "Soviet," and their refusal to co-operate with the aforesaid stage "Centrists" and "Right Wingers."

But the performance is too sad to be amusing. It seems perfectly clear that, so long as this movement persists in the party, the latter's activity will be wholly taken up by mutual quarrels and recriminations. Neither "wing" will have any time for the propaganda of Socialism. There is, as far as I can see, but one remedy. It would be futile to preach reconciliation and union where antagonism runs so high. Let the Comrades on both sides do the next best thing. Let them separate, honestly, freely, and without rancor. Let each side organize and work in its own way, and make such contribution to the Socialist movement in America as it can. Better a hundred times to have two numerically small Socialist organizations, each homogeneous and harmonious within itself, than to have one big party torn by dissensions and squabbles, an impotent colossus on feet of clay. The time for action is near. Let us clear the decks.

BIBLIOGRAPHY

Anyone interested in reading further on American Socialism is advised to consult Donald Drew Egbert and Stow Persons, editors, *Socialism and American Life* (2 vols., Princeton, 1952). Volume I is nothing less than a 510 page bibliography of the subject; it is exhaustive to a fault. One other book is indispensable, even though it was written more than sixty years ago: Morris Hillquit, *A History of Socialism in the United States* (2nd edition, New York, 1909). For the rest, I shall list those books that have proved helpful to me and that are reasonably accessible to the general reader.

The chapter by Stow Persons, "Christian Communitarianism in America," in Egbert and Persons, volume 1, cited above, is a probing analysis of the subject. Alice B. Tyler, *Freedom's Ferment* (Minneapolis, 1944), provides a warmly appreciative account of the religious sects. So does Franklin H. Littell in his "Prefatory Essay" to a recent reprint of Charles Nordhoff, *The Communistic Societies of the United States* (New York, 1965). Nordhoff's book, first published in 1874, is a series of his own eye-witness reports on some of the religious communities. For a detailed study of the Shakers, see Edward D. Andrews, *The People Called Shakers* (New York, 1953). The literature on John Humphrey Noyes and the Perfectionists is enormous, but only a few works seem reliable: Nordhoff, cited above, and R. A. Parker, *A Yankee Saint; John Humphrey Noyes and the Oneida Community* (New York, 1935).

A sound discussion of secular communitarianism may be found in T. D. Seymour Bassett's essay, "The Secular Utopian Socialists," in Egbert and Stow, cited above, volume 1. See also Alice Tyler, cited above, and, for descriptions of New Harmony and many of the Owenite and Fourierist settlements, John Humphrey Noyes, *History of American Socialisms* (Oneida, 1870). The definitive work on the Owenite movement in America—and a pleasure to read as well— is Arthur E. Bestor, *Backwoods Utopia* (Philadelphia, 1950). No single work deals with the Associationist movement as a whole, though there are many biographies of the famous individuals involved in it (e.g., Horace Greeley, George Ripley, Albert Brisbane, Theodore Parker, et al.). Noyes, cited above, devotes considerable space to Associationism. And Redelia Brisbane, *Albert Brisbane, A Mental Biography* (New York, 1893), traces its genesis, rise, and decline through her husband's life. On Cabet and Icaria, the only thorough study in English is Albert Shaw, *Icaria; A Chapter in the History of Communism* (New York, 1884).

Very little has been written on German Socialism in America. Hillquit, cited above, furnishes a fine, though all too brief, survey of the early period of the Socialist Labor Party. So, too, does Nathan Fine, *Labor and Farmer Parties in the United States, 1828–1928* (New York, 1928). An old book, Richard Ely, *The Labor Movement in America* (3rd edition, New York, 1890), is still useful in making one's way through the ideological thickets of the 1870s and 1880s. Volume two of John R. Commons, et al., *History of Labour in the United States* (4 vols., New York, 1919–1935), covers the relations between the Socialists and labor very thoroughly—thoroughness being the chief virtue of this thick and compendious work. Carl F. Wittke, *The Utopian Communist; A Biography of Wilhelm Weitling, Nineteenth-Century Reformer,* (Baton Rouge, 1950) gives us some idea of what the German Socialist community in New York was like in the 1850s. David Herreshoff, *American Disciples of Marx* (Detroit, 1967) has ample chapters on Weydemeyer, Sorge, and the American Branch of the International. There is no work on American Anarcho-Communism, and the pamphlets by or about such men as Parsons and Most are hard to find. (For anyone interested, however, see the bibliography in Egbert and Persons, cited above, volume 2, pages 167–168.) Nor is there (apart from doctoral dissertations) a full-length critical study of DeLeon, but he receives a great deal of attention in a book that concentrates on the years 1886–1901: Howard H. Quint, *The Forging of American Socialism* (Columbia, 1953).

Practically nothing has been written on Laurence Gronlund, and probably most students of American history have not even heard of him. The introduction by Stow Persons to a new edition of *The Cooperative Commonwealth* (Cambridge, 1965) sheds a bit of light on him. Most of Bellamy's papers perished in a fire many years ago, and so we are compelled to rely on Arthur E. Morgan, *Edward Bellamy* (New York, 1944), which presents an abundance of material, but is otherwise undistinguished. One would be better advised to read about Bellamy and Howells as apostles of Socialism in several first rate general literary studies: Walter Fuller Taylor, *The Economic Novel in America* (Chapel Hill, 1942), Daniel Aaron, *Men of Good Hope* (New York, 1951), and, of course, Vernon Louis Parrington, *The Beginnings of Critical Realism in America* (New York, 1930).

A number of books deal with Christian Socialism. The best of them is Henry F. May, *Protestant Churches and Industrial America* (New York, 1949). Two others worth consulting are: James Dombrowski, *The Early Days of Christian Socialism in America* (New York, 1936), and Charles H. Hopkins, *The Rise of the Social Gospel in American Protestantism 1865–1915* (New Haven, 1940). See also Quint, cited above, for the political aspects of the Christian Socialist crusade in the 1890s.

The last three chapters of this book, all of them on the Socialist Party of America, may be treated as a single unit in the bibliography. Quint, cited above, is important for the period just prior to the Party's birth. David Shannon, *The Socialist Party of America* (New York, 1955), is comprehensive—it carries the Party's history beyond World War II—but is too sketchy and peremptory for the task he assigns it. Much more detailed, within its limited scope, is Ira Kipnis, *The American Socialist Movement, 1897–1912* (New York, 1952). A useful corrective to Kipnis's thesis—that the Party sealed its own doom when it put down the left in 1911–12—is James Weinstein's penetrating study, *The Decline of Socialism in America 1912–1925* (New York, 1967). Certainly the most brilliant and influential piece of writing on modern American Socialism is Daniel Bell's essay, "Marxian Socialism in the United States," in Egbert and Persons, cited above, volume 1. Bell, too, maintains that the Socialist Party began its downward course in 1912, though he and Kipnis differ radically on the reasons for it. Bell's essay, it should be mentioned, conveys a tone of brusqueness and disdain, almost contempt, toward its subject. David Saposs, *Left Wing Unionism* (New York, 1926), though dated, is still valuable for an understanding of the relations between Socialism and labor before World War I. So is Fine, cited above, Commons, et al., cited above, volume 4, and a recent work, Marc Karsons, *American Labor Unions and Politics* (Carbondale, 1958). On the disintegration of the Socialist movement after 1917, Shannon, Bell, Fine, and Weinstein, all cited above, can be recommended. One book, however, towers above the rest for its profundity, scholarship, lucidity, and style: Theodore Draper, *The Roots of American Communism* (New York, 1957).

INDEX